Personal Adjustment and Growth

Personal Adjustment and Growth

A Life-Span Approach

Second Edition

Andrew I. Schwebel
Ohio State University

Harvey A. Barocas
CUNY—Baruch College

Walter Reichman
CUNY—Baruch College

Milton Schwebel
Rutgers University

Wm. C. Brown Publishers

Book Team

Editor *Michael Lange*
Production Editor *Kay J. Brimeyer*
Art Editor *Janice M. Roerig*
Photo Research Editor *Michelle Oberhoffer*
Permissions Editor *Mavis M. Oeth*
Visuals Processor *Andé Meyer*

 Wm. C. Brown Publishers

President *G. Franklin Lewis*
Vice President, Editor-in-Chief *George Wm. Bergquist*
Vice President, Director of Production *Beverly Kolz*
Vice President, National Sales Manager *Bob McLaughlin*
Director of Marketing *Thomas E. Doran*
Marketing Communications Manager *Edward Bartell*
Marketing Manager *Kathy Law Laube*
Production Editorial Manager *Colleen A. Yonda*
Production Editorial Manager *Julie A. Kennedy*
Publishing Services Manager *Karen J. Slaght*
Manager of Visuals and Design *Faye M. Schilling*

Cover image © Ken Rogers

Cover and interior design by Terri Webb Ellerbach

The credits section for this book begins on page 643, and is considered an extension of the copyright page.

*Dedicated to our wives,
children, parents, teachers,
colleagues, and students*

Brief Contents

Contents

P A R T

1

C H A P T E R

1

Perspectives on the Self

C H A P T E R

2

What Is the Healthy Personality?

Anxiety, Stress, and Depression

Coping and Defense

Psychological Disorders

Psychotherapy and Growth

Challenges in Infancy, Childhood, and Adolescence

CHAPTER 8

Friendship, Loneliness, and Love

CHAPTER 9

Sexuality

CHAPTER **10**

Marriage, Family, and Alternative Life-Styles

CHAPTER *11*

Work and Career Development

CHAPTER

12

Challenges and Rewards of Adulthood

CHAPTER

13

Death, Dying, and Bereavement

Preface

In recent years, the life-span developmental perspective has emerged as an exciting approach to the study of human behavior and has had a major impact in psychology. With its emphasis on continual change throughout the entire life cycle, this orientation provides an effective and comprehensive way of examining personal adjustment. It offers a conceptual framework for integrating a vast body of information on personal adjustment and a method for understanding our capacities for dealing with everyday challenges and events from birth to death.

This text was written from a life-span developmental viewpoint. It is designed to introduce students to what we refer to as a bio-psychosocial perspective, that is, one that stresses the importance not only of psychological aspects of adjustment but also of biological and social factors as well. Moreover, we realize that no single psychological perspective could do justice to the multidimensional complexities inherent in the concept of personal adjustment. Therefore, we have incorporated the major theoretical contributions and related research of behavioral, cognitive, humanistic, and psychoanalytic psychology. By drawing on these diverse sources we have provided the student with a broadly based overview of personal adjustment throughout the life cycle.

Personal Adjustment: A Life-Span Approach is divided into two broad sections. The first (Chapters 1 through 6) describes the life-span approach to adjustment and considers the ways in which growth and health can emerge from life's crises. The second section (Chapters 7 through 13) examines, in detail, the particular crises and adjustments that occur from infancy to old age.

Chapter 1 opens with a description of how the various schools of psychology define adjustment and introduces the life-cycle framework and the bio-psychosocial perspective. Chapter 2 defines the healthy personality as viewed from a number of diverse theoretical perspectives. It also emphasizes the importance of social factors that may impede psychological health. Chapter 3 explains what psychologists mean by anxiety, stress, and depression, while Chapter 4 discusses typical ways of coping with stress and crises and of defending against anxiety at various points in the life cycle. Chapter 5 focuses on the consequences of ineffective coping and on the psychological disorders that can result when adaptation fails. Chapter 6 considers how therapy can be useful in mastering life crises and dealing with psychological disorders. This chapter also describes the various types of therapy, examines the therapeutic relationship, and introduces methods of self-help.

In the second part of the book, Chapter 7 explores the process of growing up, focusing on the adjustment crises of infancy, childhood, and adolescence. Chapter 8 examines friendship and intimacy from childhood through old age. Chapter 9 reviews sex and sexuality throughout the life span. Chapter 10 deals with marriage, family, and alternative commitments. Chapter 11 explores work and career development; among the important issues covered here are choosing an occupation and adapting to the world of work. The material in this chapter should prove helpful to students in the process of formulating their career objectives. Chapter 12 deals with the challenges and transitions of middle age, in particular the opportunities for continued growth and development during the second half of life. The final chapter (13) deals with death, dying, and bereavement.

We have included a number of pedagogical features to help students understand the material and integrate what they have learned into their lives. Each chapter begins with a *chapter outline* that lists the major topics within the chapter. This is followed by a list of *focus statements* that offer a general explanation of the chapter outline. Important *terms* appear in boldface type when they are introduced in the text. Their definitions are provided in the margins. *Self-knowledge exercises* within each chapter are designed to help students apply concepts in the text to events and situations in their personal lives. Each chapter concludes with a *summary* and a list of annotated *suggested readings* for those students who wish to learn more about a specific topic.

Perhaps more than any other kind, a textbook in the psychology of personal adjustment is necessarily influenced by its authors' personal as well as professional experience, and we should be candid about this with our student readers at the outset. In the course of our own lives, we have encountered a variety of crises. These personal experiences, such as the development of new relationships, making career choices, the birth of children, illnesses, the death of loved ones, and success and failure of our own endeavors have influenced our approach to the subject and format of this book. So has our work in assisting students and clients with their adjustment problems. By combining our personal, clinical, and theoretical knowledge we believe we have written a comprehensive, usable book that will be of continuing value to students as they strive to understand and meet life's challenges.

We would like to express our gratitude to the following scholars and teachers in the personal adjustment field who reviewed the manuscript and helped in countless ways to strengthen the first edition:

John S. Baird, Jr., Bloomsburg State College
Kenneth S. Davidson, Wayne State University
Marie Dellas, Eastern Michigan University
Norman Gordon, Eastern Michigan University
Sandra L. Harris, Rutgers, The State University
Michael Hirt, Kent State University
James J. Johnson, Illinois State University

Michael D. Kahn, University of Hartford
Mary M. Kralj, University of Maryland
Donald Leivs, State University of New York–Buffalo
Stephen A. Lisman, State University of New York–Buffalo
David Locascio, Fairleigh Dickinson University, Madison
Gerald Mikosz, Moraine Valley Community College
John J. Mirich, Metropolitan State College
Sylvia O'Neill, Trenton State College
Robert J. Pellegrini, San Jose State University
Leon Rappoport, Kansas State University
William J. Ray, The Pennsylvania State University
Sarah C. Sitton, Southwest Texas State University
David G. Weight, Brigham Young University
Jeanne Zimmerman, Ph.D.

and the second edition:

Barbara Brackney, Eastern Michigan University
Jeanne Devany, Auburn University
William J. Dibiase, Delaware County Community College
Ronald G. Evans, Washburn University
Terry J. Knapp, University of Nevada–Las Vegas
Knud S. Larsen, Oregon State University
Fredric Medway, University of South Carolina
David L. Pancoast, Old Dominion University
John M. Reisman, De Paul University
John J. Schloss, University of Hartford
Donald M. Stanley, North Harris County College

In addition, we wish to thank our colleagues at The Ohio State University, Baruch College, and Rutgers University: Benjamin Balinsky, John Bauer, Angelo Dispenzieri, Susan Locke, Charles Maher, John Moreland, Samuel Osipow, and Donald R. Peterson for their support and encouragement. We also thank our graduate assistants and students who made important contributions during several stages of the project: John Craparo, Kerry Corthell, Lynn Gracin, Frank Guglilmo, Jan Judson, Kenny Levine, Sue Simmons, and most especially, Maureena Andrews Renner.

We are also indebted to our secretaries Jami Christopher, Millicent Hodge, and Patti Watson Overholster, who always managed to help us meet deadlines. Of course, any errors in fact or interpretation remain our responsibility.

On a more personal level, we would like to acknowledge, with much affection, the support, encouragement, and intellectual stimulation provided by our wives, Carol Schwebel, Carol Barocas, Marion Reichman, and Bernice Schwebel. We also wish to express gratitude to family members who read and commented on the book at several points in its preparation. Also a special note of thanks to our children, Davy, Sara, Briana, Solon, Howard, Judith, and Robert, who have enriched our lives and taught us much about developmental crises during the writing of this manuscript.

Andrew I. Schwebel
Harvey Barocas
Walter Reichman
Milton Schwebel

The Search for Personal Adjustment

Perspectives on the Self

1

- How individuals attempt to achieve personal adjustment by adapting to—and mastering—their environment over the life span
- The behaviorist view that all behavior is learned and that the specific reasons for people's behavior is found in the environment
- The classic psychoanalytic stance that unconscious emotions, conflicts, memories, and desires explain present behavior
- The view of more recent psychoanalysts that both internal and social pressures shape the human personality
- The existential-humanist approach that emphasizes the freedom and responsibility that individuals exercise over their own lives
- The cognitive approach that focuses on the ways in which people think, perceive, reason, and structure their views of the world
- The life span: a framework for studying personal adjustment

Nearly every student has at some time been asked to write an auto-biographical essay, or has kept a journal, that addresses the difficult question of "Who am I?" The answers they give will vary, depending on the point they have reached in their development. For example, those who are asked to describe themselves in high school, then later in college, usually find that the tone and content of the piece have changed greatly. In high school, for example, Jim wrote confidently:

> I think I know more about myself and my abilities as a result of the last few years. My grades have improved. And I have learned to compete without becoming upset when my performance is not as good as I expected. I am more easygoing at home too—maybe because I am at home less. My parents respect my need to work part-time, and they don't ask me so many questions about my money or my outside activities. I have an active social life and go out fairly often. Usually this stops short of a full relationship (and this doesn't bother me too much). I have plans to attend a college where I know I will be accepted. My area will be business and accounting. My father would like me to enter his firm, but he is not pressuring me.

As a senior, Jim described himself in this guidance course exercise as "pretty ordinary," outgoing, and increasingly able to handle responsibilities.

A year and a half later, when he decided to keep a journal, his entry on this subject was quite different. He wrote:

> I feel under pressure to make a decision about my future—and since I don't know what I want, this is difficult. My parents are pleased with my progress in school, and with my major and my tentative goals. But they do not realize how lonely I can be. I feel there should be something more to life—at least to my life. And yet I am hardly a unique person. I have ideas of doing something really meaningful. Even so, I end up spending my time in aimless reading.

Changes

Choose a time when you are unlikely to be interrupted by the telephone, visitors, and so forth. Take down the yearbook from your senior year of high school.

1. Look through the yearbook, and try to remember how you felt when you first received it. Which photos did you seek out first? What part of the yearbook did you rush to show a parent or sibling? What disappointments did you experience about the yearbook's coverage? *Re-create* your feelings as a high school senior.
2. Using the above reactions as a memory aid, *re-create* the person you were at the end of your senior year of high school. Is there much distance between that person and the person you are now?
3. If possible, note the ways in which you have changed. Begin by asking yourself which people or activities pictured in the yearbook were important to you as a senior—but seem less important now.   ▲

Everything seems complicated. Fortunately, I have a close friend whom I can talk to. She is very understanding; but we do not know if we want to become more than friends, so this is complicated too. My parents are busy preparing for my sister's wedding, so fortunately they have taken no note of my dilemma. Which is that, mainly, I have become a stranger to myself. . . .

Jim's experience is not uncommon. It is not, of course, the only way that a discontinuity between high school and college years may be experienced.

Excerpts from Linda's diary show important changes too. She wrote that she was bored, restless, and isolated in high school. But she really came alive in her early college years. "All at once," she noted, "I realized that I could study philosophy and art, and question ideas. And I could consider being something besides a teacher. For the first time I met people who were exciting and willing to take me seriously as an adult. . . ."

Both Jim and Linda found that the feelings and assumptions they had had about themselves in one period of life were not necessarily appropriate in the next. They spoke, in different ways, of trying to find themselves. And they realized that the self in question was in the process of emerging from daily experiences.

Personal Adjustment
The process of finding "one's place in the world" by effectively relating to and mastering the environment.

The attempt to find oneself is sometimes called **personal adjustment.** It involves two important processes. First, the individual attempts to *relate* effectively to the environment in which he or she lives—by developing skills, traits, and behaviors that will bring success, happiness, and other valued goals. Second, the individual attempts to *master* the environment—that is, to modify it for his or her own advantage. In young adulthood, for example, adjustment involves finding a job or a career commitment that will enable one to fit into the social environment—to produce results, be compensated accordingly, and possibly advance. Personal adjustment may also involve altering the environment, through work, research, political efforts, or other actions. In sum, personal adjustment involves responding effectively to the demands of the environment, recognizing opportunities in the environment, and knowing when and how to impose one's own terms.

Julia's experiences during her first weeks of living in the dorm illustrate both adjustment processes. An only child from a reserved family, she prepared for her first two quizzes in one of the dorm study rooms. Though she was bothered by the constant chatter, Julia remained in this location because "it's where *everybody* is." However, Julia soon discovered, this environment would not work for her. She failed both quizzes.

Two Fs led her to consider what would make her happy. Being honest with herself, she recognized twin goals: respectable grades and at least a few good friendships. Julia figured she could accomplish both by socializing before her dinner meal, then going straight to the library afterward. Following this plan, she earned high grades and built the circle of friends she sought. Julia had adjusted by learning how to relate effectively to the demands of her environment.

Second term, Julia ran for and was elected to the dorm council. Her first actions were to propose and help pass a rule designating one study room for quiet study while leaving the others available for music, talking, and light reading. Again, Julia had adjusted, this time by effectively altering an aspect of her environment so it better suited her needs (and those of her fellow students).

Sometimes the psychological concept of adjustment is likened to the biological concept of *adaptation*. In biology, an adaptation is a particular structure, physiological process, or behavior that enables an organism to better survive and reproduce in its environment. Sweating, for example, is an adaptation to hot, sunny weather—and so also is the long evolutionary process that provided people at the equator with darkened skins. Over these types of adaptations we, like other organisms, have little control. But human beings are uniquely able to plan and reason, and we have deliberately made changes in our environment to suit our needs. Air-conditioning units and the irrigation systems that serve large regions of the globe are also adaptations to hot, sunny weather. Man-made adaptations, like personal adjustment, involve both a response to and mastery over the environment.

Personal adjustment involves relating to and mastering the environment. People work at adjustment in all kinds of situations.

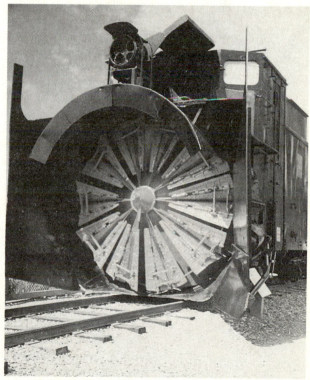

Psychology
The science that investigates behavior.

Mastery over the environment is one goal that people commonly have; mastery over oneself is another. As one student put it, "I want to change things. I also want to change *myself*." One of the ways in which people attempt to gain mastery and bring about change is through increased understanding of themselves. In this attempt, the study of psychology can be a powerful tool. **Psychology** is the science that investigates behavior, including thoughts, feelings, motivations, and interpersonal relationships. If you look in an unabridged dictionary, or a book describing the origin of words, you will discover that the term "psychology" comes from the Greek "psyche," meaning soul or mind, and from "logia," meaning a science or doctrine.

Psychologists address questions that are important to personal adjustment, such as: What makes us behave the way we do in a certain situation? What coping activities are effective in a crisis? What accounts for personal growth and change?

Many students enroll in a course on personal adjustment with the hope that they will learn something that will make a difference to them personally. Usually one thing they learn at the outset is that there is no one "psychology." There are different ways of viewing people and their problems and different ways of defining and treating psychological difficulties. Whether you are a scientist, a mental health practitioner, or a student, the view you accept makes a difference; it may come to influence the approach you take toward solving problems in life. (A behaviorist, as we will see, looks for different kinds of solutions than a humanist.) To you, the student, what is important, at least at first, is not to settle on any one interpretation but to realize that the assumptions one brings to a college course, or to adulthood, can be challenged and enriched by new information. As you master new material and explore alternative views of human behavior, you will have insights and new understandings of your own behavior and that of others.

In the following sections, we present four perspectives from modern psychology. Each—the behavioral, the psychoanalytic, the existential and humanist, and the cognitive—has **psychological theories** associated with them which:

Psychological Theory
A set of interrelated principles, based on observations and assumptions, that can be used to explain or predict behavior.

1. provide a common language to use in talking about behavior,
2. focus the thinking of scientists and practitioners on particular aspects of behavior,
3. help organize observations and thoughts into concepts and,
4. suggest how personal adjustment problems can be treated.

For example, if Billy is sent to the school counselor because he regularly misbehaves in class, the counselor's approach will vary with her orientation. If she is a behaviorist, she will focus on what environmental factors are rewarding Billy's socially unacceptable behavior. If she is cognitively-oriented, she will instead direct attention to Billy's thoughts about himself.

After the four perspectives are presented, we turn our attention to a discussion of the life cycle, which is a useful framework for organizing our understandings.

The Search for Personal Adjustment

THE BEHAVIORIST PERSPECTIVE

Jonathan came to college with more than the usual familiarity with psychological concepts. His father was a psychiatrist; his mother was a social worker in a city some twenty miles from where Jonathan's family lived. They encouraged Jonathan to be sensitive, to view each person with deep respect— for the circumstances that had shaped that person and for what, with help, he or she could become.

Not surprisingly, Jonathan developed into a sensitive person. However, as he made his way through high school, he did not seem to be especially happy. Almost as a matter of course his parents sent him to a clinical psychologist, who encouraged him to talk about his early life in some detail. Jonathan found this helpful, but occasionally he had the feeling that he was "making mountains out of molehills." His childhood, he felt, had been perfectly sound. The problem was *now*. He was terribly shy and unassuming in social situations. Although he had considerable understanding of people, he never knew what to say. All this might have been satisfactory—Jonathan had learned to appreciate many different personality styles—except that he had such a clear idea of the person he wanted to be: frank, direct, engaging, helpful to others. Maybe even a leader.

At college, Jonathan enrolled in a Personal Adjustment course, setting for himself one goal of learning more about shyness and what childhood factors might account for it. In class, he first encountered ideas that were exciting and promising to him:

> The professor spoke of therapists who concentrated on changing people's *behavior*. He described an approach to psychology that was primarily concerned with behavior, as it could be objectively measured and controlled. When Jonathan heard this (he would later say) it was "like the sun breaking through the clouds." He decided that he would stop worrying about his inner conflicts and how they had developed; instead he would work on changing his behavior. After all, he couldn't change his past, but he could eliminate the shy behaviors and disabling habits that now stood in his way. He could stop *behaving* like a shy person.
>
> Jonathan immediately enrolled in a five-session workshop at the college's counseling center. In this setting he learned and practiced more outgoing and assertive behaviors. After a time, Jonathan found that he could *do things* he had previously been unable to do. Instead of wondering why he was afraid to contact people on the telephone, he would pick up the telephone at the exact time he had planned to do so (in the past he had usually called people when he suspected they would be out). After he made the call he would note it in his assignment book, and if he made all his planned calls he would give himself some predetermined reward. Similarly, when he was with people, he found that he would stop worrying about his feelings, and everybody else's, if he concentrated on his actual behavior. So enthusiastic was Jonathan about his new approach that he did not for a moment hesitate to ask others for help. For example, he approached a socially successful junior whom he hardly knew and asked her to introduce him to her roommate. When one of his friends heard about this, he said, "That must have taken nerve, chutzpah, or *something*." Jonathan answered: "It only took doing."

Behaviorism
A psychological approach that
assumes all behavior is learned
and that personal change
results from the learning of
new behaviors.

Stimulus
Something, such as an event, a
situation, or a person, that
elicits a response from an
individual. The plural is
stimuli.

The approach that came to mean so much to Jonathan is called **behaviorism.** This psychological approach assumes that all behavior is learned, and that when people "change" it is because they have learned to respond to a **stimulus** with new behaviors. What makes them learn is the kind of feedback they get from their environment. The environment conditions under which learning takes place are not mysterious or subjective; they can be objectively identified not only for people but also for rats, dogs, chimpanzees, and other organisms. More important (at least for people like Jonathan), people can learn to behave in ways that are more satisfying to them.

Basic Assumptions of Behaviorism

The term "behaviorist" arose to describe a group of psychologists who, in the 1920s, wished to distinguish themselves from most other psychologists of their day. Whereas most psychologists were caught up with mental events, feelings, and states of mind, the behaviorist was interested only in behavior—what the organism actually did in its environment. The behaviorist asked the question: Under what conditions does behavior occur? Whereas most psychologists believed that "feelings" were the causes of behavior, the behaviorists hypothesized that the real causes were to be found in the environment. Moreover, they said, these causes could be specified with some objectivity.

The behaviorists dismissed much of introspective tradition and distrusted the individual's private account of his or her mental life. "The psyche is a metaphor . . . designed to remain in the depths. By contrast the environment is usually accessible" (Skinner, 1974). According to the behaviorist, a person's behavior over the life span depends on the whole history of rewards and punishments that the environment has furnished. And his behavior at the moment is under the control of the current setting.

Types of Conditioning

The first task of the behaviorist is to describe behavior in direct, objective terms. One distinction that has proved helpful is the distinction between respondent, or classical, and operant, or instrumental, conditioning.

Respondent, or Classical, Conditioning

We can see evidence of classical conditioning in nine-year-old Joy, who underwent injections to help alleviate her allergic reactions to pollen. Anticipating an end to her drippy nose and runny eyes, Joy cheerfully marched into the allergist's office for her first injection. However, it was painful and elicited substantial crying. Several "needles" later, as Joy called them, simply the sight of the allergist walking into the waiting room made Joy cry.

What had happened? Through classical conditioning, the sight of the initially neutral stimulus (the doctor), by itself, came to elicit in Joy an involuntary response (crying) originally elicited by the unconditioned stimulus (the painful injection). For Joy, the doctor has become a conditioned stimulus.

By definition, **respondent or classical conditioning** is a type of learning that comes about after a neutral stimulus is repeatedly paired with an **unconditioned stimulus**—one that elicits an involuntary response. As a result of the repeated pairing, the organism comes to respond to the formerly neutral stimulus as it did to the unconditioned stimulus: that is, with the same involuntary response.

Respondent or classical conditioning is sometimes called Pavlovian conditioning because it was first demonstrated by Ivan Pavlov (1849–1936), a Russian physiologist well known for his work on the physiology of digestion. Pavlov's St. Petersburg laboratory housed a large number of experimental dogs. In the course of his experiments on digestion, Pavlov discovered that his dogs began salivating at the mere sight or smell of food. In other words, certain stimuli associated with food brought about a specific physiological response. Subsequently Pavlov discovered something even more curious. If a bell were rung shortly before food (some meat powder) was placed on a dog's tongue, the bell alone would cause the dog to salivate, even in the absence of food.

Pavlov knew that the salivation is a usual (involuntary), **unconditioned response** to food in many organisms. Salivating at the sound of a bell, however, was not natural. The connection between the bell and the food had to be *learned,* or acquired, by the experimental animal. Through experimentation Pavlov made several further discoveries: (a) the more frequently the pairing was made, the stronger the salivary response became (until reaching its maximum), (b) the conditioning was strongest when the bell preceded the food by about one half a second, and (c) other stimuli, such as "a pull" on the animal's legs, could also induce salivation, if the stimuli were always paired with food.

Figure 1.1 illustrates how classical conditioning works. Note that before Pavlov began his experiment, the meat, the unconditioned stimulus (UCS), caused salivation, the unconditioned response (UCR), but the bell did not. After the bell and meat were paired a number of times, a link developed between the bell, which is called the **conditioned stimulus** (CS), and salivation, which is called the **conditioned response** (CR).

After the conditioning had taken place, suppose Pavlov sounded other bells. Would the dogs salivate? Through a process known as *generalization,* the dogs would respond by salivating when they heard bells similar to the original one.

Suppose after the conditioning Pavlov sounded the bell but repeatedly failed to deliver meat powder. What would happen? Through a process known as *extinction,* the association between the CS and CR would be weakened and, in time the dogs would no longer salivate when the bell sounded.

Pavlov's findings have had enormous implications for psychologists who work in the behaviorist tradition. These psychologists hypothesize that except for unconditioned responses, which are relatively few in number and perhaps unalterable biological functions, all behavior is learned. Classical conditioning, and the concepts of generalization and extinction help us understand (and treat) difficulties people experience in adjustment. For example, Betsy was stung by a bee at a family picnic. The next few weeks she told her parents,

Respondent, or Classical Conditioning
A type of learning in which an initially neutral stimulus, by itself, comes to elicit an involuntary response originally elicited by another stimulus it has been paired with.

Unconditioned Stimulus
A stimulus that produces an involuntary, unconditioned response. For example, a hot radiator, if touched, will cause a person to immediately withdraw his hand.

Unconditioned Response
A response that is a natural or unlearned reaction to a given stimulus.

Conditioned Stimulus
A stimulus that was originally neutral but that, through learning, has come to produce a given response.

Conditioned Response
A response to an originally neutral stimulus that has been produced through learning.

Ivan Pavlov, noted Russian physiologist, won a Nobel prize in medicine and physiology in 1904.

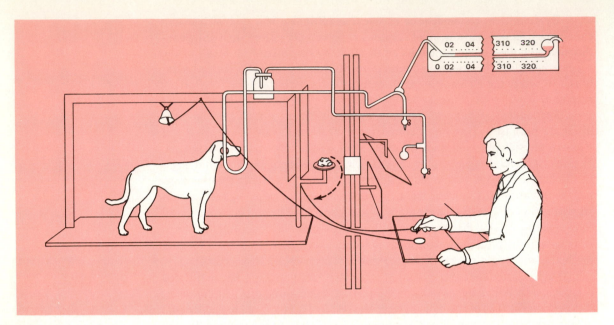

Figure 1.1a An artist's drawing of the type of apparatus Pavlov used for experiments in classical conditioning.

Figure 1.1b Diagram of classical conditioning procedure. At the start of conditioning, the UCS will evoke the UCR, but the CS does not have this capacity. During conditioning, the CS and UCS are paired so that the CS comes to elicit the response. The key learning ingredient is the association of the UCS and CS.

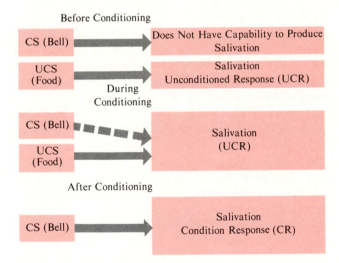

Before Conditioning

CS (Bell) → Does Not Have Capability to Produce Salivation

UCS (Food) → Salivation Unconditioned Response (UCR)

During Conditioning

CS (Bell) ⇢ | Salivation (UCR)
UCS (Food) →

After Conditioning

CS (Bell) → Salivation Condition Response (CR)

"I don't want picnics tomorrow or anymore." And her reaction to bees generalized. When she saw houseflies or mosquitos she would experience fear and run away from them.

Adults can be similarly affected. If a vehicle you have been driving has been stopped or had a "close call" with a police officer, you may experience a conditioned response when you see a patrol car in the rearview mirror. Because of generalization you may experience that same agonizing feeling in your stomach if you catch a glimpse in the rearview mirror of a taxicab, tow truck, or any vehicle with lights on its top.

Operant, or Instrumental, Conditioning

Pavlov worked with a simple physiological response. What, we might ask, of the many complicated behaviors that are characteristic of human life: learning to speak, for example, or assembling a machine?

B. F. Skinner (1904–), the well-known American behaviorist, has broadened the scope of behavioral explanation by showing that voluntary and perhaps complex behavior is also conditioned. In **operant, or instrumental, conditioning,** the behavior must first occur spontaneously. The caged rat, in its random exploration, pulls a lever; the infant in his or her babbling hits upon "da-da." If the behaviors of pulling a lever or uttering "da-da" are followed by the release of food or by a parent's smile, these behaviors will be more likely to reappear. In everyday terms, the lever pulling and verbalizing of the sound "da-da" have been rewarded. In behaviorist terms, they have been *positively reinforced.*

Voluntary behaviors that remove painful stimulus will also be strengthened or be made more likely to reappear through operant conditioning. For example, a rat that learns to jump a fence in order to escape an electric shock, or a person who puts on sunglasses to reduce glare, is reinforced for the action. Since he or she succeeds in subtracting a discomfort, this kind of reinforcement is called *negative reinforcement.*

As the following example illustrates, the behaviorist perspective suggests that behavior is controlled by its consequences. In other words, yesterday's reinforcements affect today's behavior. Ken's experiences when he went home for a weekend illustrate several of the many ways operant conditioning affects us in our daily lives. First of all, Ken left early and was *positively reinforced* for his behavior because he bought the last seat available on the bus. Friday night his mom had all his favorites on her menu. After dinner, Ken cleared the table and washed the dishes, *positively reinforcing* his mother for her efforts. She commented: "Terrific, now I'll cook clam chowder, beef bourguignonne, and double dark chocolate cake more often."

After cleaning the kitchen Ken planned to start his term paper but, as soon as he took out reference books, he felt anxious about the long task ahead. So, Ken packed the books away and his anxious feelings dissipated. Ken was *negatively reinforced* for postponing his studies; that is, he was rewarded by escaping anxiety and, as a result, his term-paper-postponing behavior was strengthened (it became more likely to recur).

Operant or Instrumental Conditioning
A type of learning in which an individual's response (or *operation* in the environment) is *instrumental* in achieving a reward. As a result of the reinforcement or reward, learning takes place and that response becomes more likely to occur in the same or similar situations.

B. F. Skinner, the famous behaviorist, further developed the ideas of Ivan Pavlov by demonstrating that many voluntary behaviors are conditioned.

In contrast to negative and positive reinforcement, which increase the probability that a behavior will recur, *punishment* decreases that probability. Punishment is defined as a painful or uncomfortable consequence that follows a particular behavior. For example, a rat receives punishment by being shocked after walking on a grid. A child receives punishment by "being grounded" after uttering a four-letter word. Punishment is one way an individual can teach another to not behave in a certain fashion. Another way is to not reinforce the undesired behavior. For example, consider Jim, a four year old who has recently been throwing nightly temper tantrums, frustrating his parents, Mr. and Mrs. Bilman.

The Bilmans explained to a psychologist, "every night Jim wakes up to go to the bathroom. If he discovers that either one of us are with the baby, he 'goes bananas.' He pounds the walls and floors and screams at the top of his lungs. One of us has to go into his room to calm him down."

The psychologist explained to the Bilmans that they were reinforcing Jim's behavior by giving him attention when he screamed, pounded, and yelled. He continued, "If you want to end Jim's tantrums you should praise him when he sees you with the baby and acts calmly. When he is having a tantrum you have a choice. You can punish Jim by scolding or spanking him, or you could ignore his tantrums and hence avoid reinforcing them."

The Bilmans decided to ignore Jim's tantrums. Although it took self-control, Jim's parents consistently held back when he "threw his fits." Much to their surprise, the tantrums soon became less frequent and eventually ceased. In behaviorist terms, the tantrums were *extinguished* because the Bilmans did not reinforce them.

Behaviors such as speaking, playing the flute, or performing piecework in a factory do not emerge full-blown, and so cannot be reinforced all at once. Behaviorists explain that these behaviors are developed in a step-by-step process that is called **shaping.**

Shaping
A method of producing a certain behavior whereby an organism is reinforced for responses that come closer and closer to the desired behavior.

Animal training supplies dramatic examples of shaping—dramatic because we are more likely to ask about an animal, "How did he learn to do that?" The behaviorists' explanation is that the animal performs a great variety of actions as it goes about its life in captivity. When one of these actions is rewarded by a trainer or experimenter, the animal performs it more often. As training progresses, actions that would seldom be performed in random activity can be shaped by the trainer, who rewards closer and closer approximations to the desired behavior. If the trainer wants a sea lion to walk through a hoop, for example, he will give it a fish for just turning in the direction of the hoop, then for touching the hoop with its flipper, then for passing through. He will build a *response chain* that results in the establishment of a certain behavior pattern.

Skinner believes that a great deal of human behavior develops as a result of shaping. Parents or a teacher select the responses they desire, and provide reinforcements as the child comes closer and closer. The singing teacher, for example, produces a tone and encourages the child as he more closely matches the desired tone—until finally the teacher's and child's tones are identical.

Social Learning

The **social learning** approaches further broaden the scope of behaviorists' explanations, taking into account how peoples' thoughts affect their responses to the environment. The studies of social learning theorists have shown that people learn new behavior not only by performing it themselves (and being reinforced) but also by observing others perform it (and being reinforced). A person from whom another learns in this indirect way is known as a **model.** Individuals do not have equal potency as models. We are most likely to "model" those with prestige or who appear similar to us.

Social learning theorists point out that modeling is important in everyday life and can be used as a therapeutic tool in clinical settings. Three major effects of modeling have been proposed (Bandura, 1969):

▸ An observational learning effect—observers acquire new behaviors by watching a model perform them. Tyrone, for example, the day before he left for college, learned how to iron shirts by watching his mother. Cal, who was attending the County School for the Developmentally Delayed, was taught social skills by watching models perform them.

▸ A disinhibitory or inhibitory effect—depending on the consequences of a behavior to a model, observers become more or less likely to perform that same behavior, one they already know but that is under personal or social constraint. Nancy, for example, after hearing Billi address the teacher by his first name and seeing him smile at her, decided to address the teacher similarly. Roger quit shoplifting CDs after hearing about a classmate who was caught and heavily fined in Mayor's Court.

▸ A response facilitation effect—observers become more likely to perform a behavior they have already learned and for which there are no personal or social constraints. Connie and Jack, for example, after seeing people line up to board an airplane, stood up themselves and joined the line. Chris and Pat, seeing others recognize the performer by lighting matches, pulled out their own Bics.

The social or observational learning we do ranges from simple imitation to mastering complex skills by observing models who are not present. For instance, we learn the route to an out-of-town restaurant by following a roommate's written directions or we gain new abilities by watching dance contestants or reading how-to books. And, sometimes, we learn how to behave in a situation from models presented on film.

In classical research investigations (Bandura, Ross, & Ross, 1961, 1963), groups of preschool children watched either "live" or filmed interactions between an adult model and a several-foot-tall inflatable, plastic clown. Some children saw the adult portray aggression toward the plastic clown while other groups saw the adult sit quietly next to it. After the children were exposed to the models, they were mildly frustrated and allowed access to the plastic clown.

Social Learning
The learning of a behavior by observing, or reading about, the performance of the behavior of others.

Model
A person whose behavior is observed by another and from whom the observer learns.

The top row of photographs show an adult woman acting aggressively toward a plastic clown. After observing the model and experiencing mild frustration, the children (second and third rows) also show aggresive behavior toward the plastic clown.

The results were clear; children imitated the model, tending to interact aggressively or in a more inhibited fashion, depending on the model they had seen. Further, it did not matter whether the children had seen live or filmed aggression. In both cases they were likely to kick, poke, or hit the clown with a toy hammer. Note the implications these classic studies have, even today, with regard to how television programs affect viewers.

Rewards are as important in social learning as they are in operant conditioning. When observers see a model rewarded for performing a particular action, they are much more likely to perform it themselves than if they do not see the model rewarded. Social learning theorists infer from this finding that learners have an *expectation* of a reward when they perform the modeled behavior. (Other behaviorists are reluctant to admit the existence of expectations because they are not observable anywhere in actual behaviors.)

Bandura (1986) argues the importance of another type of *expectation:* self-efficacy, or a person's belief that he or she is capable of performing a behavior successfully. A person who experiences an increase in self-efficacy will become more able to achieve his goals, behave assertively in formerly feared situations, and break addictive habits.

Finally, in contrast to strict behaviorists who maintain that the environment alone determines our behavior, social learning theorists believe in *reciprocal determinism.* This concept suggests a two-way street; the environment influences behavior, behavior influences the environment, and so on. Through this process and over time, individuals actively contribute to the molding of their environment (which, in turn, will affect their growth and adjustment in the future). Note how this idea and the two processes of adjustment discussed on page 6 run parallel.

In general, behaviorists believe, as is the case with any other behavior, the way in which a person adjusts to life crises is learned. For example, to a behaviorist, anxiety is not a subjective feeling that causes certain behaviors. Anxiety is a kind of behavior in itself. Its physiological aspects can be objectively observed and measured (as we will see in Chapter 3). The causes of anxiety can be found in an individual's personal learning history—or history of what consequences have been associated with his or her past behaviors. For example, a person who has been in an automobile accident may become measurably anxious when driving under conditions that resemble those that preceded the accident.

Patterns of adaptation are learned in exactly the same way. The ability of some people to persist in the face of misfortune is not a sign of some indefinable quality called "character" or "willpower." It is a result of the person having been exposed to a favorable reinforcement history, that is, to schedules of reinforcement that have generally rewarded persistence and successively greater efforts (Skinner, 1974).

The behaviorists have not been much interested in describing patterns over the life span. They propose no particular stages of development (other than those associated with physical maturation). When confronted with "stages-of-development" theories of other types of psychologists, the behaviorist holds to an emphasis on environment and the personal history of reinforcement. Skinner says that "if a child no longer behaves as he behaved a year before, it is not only because he has grown, but because he has had the time to acquire a much bigger [behavioral] repertoire, through exposure to new contingencies of reinforcement, and because the contingencies affecting children at different ages are different too" (Skinner, 1974).

Behaviorism holds out the possibility of unlimited personal development through changes in schedules of reinforcement and through control of the environment. Behaviorist research has contributed a great deal to our understanding of the way people of all ages adjust to their environments. For example, we will later discuss behavioral explanations of the way children learn aggression and sex-role behavior and of the way adults learn to handle physical stress.

PSYCHOANALYTIC PERSPECTIVES

Emalee came from a family of women—she liked to say, a family of *strong* women. Because of ongoing marital conflict, her father left when she was five years old. And though, after moving, he continued to visit his daughters regularly, the ongoing court battle between Emalee's parents finally took its toll. When a judge sharply cut her father's visitation, he stubbornly stopped coming by, illegally and defiantly ceased paying child support, and essentially disappeared.

Emalee's mother was strong-willed, hard-working, and scrupulously honest. She had worked her way up from an unskilled clerical job to a position as commercial artist in a catalog house. She had even managed to give her daughters some advantages: guitar and dance lessons when they were young, and half of their tuition when they were ready to enter the local community college.

Emalee considered herself practical rather than artistic. She longed for a career in business management, where she would be admired and earn a large salary. And most of all she longed to be popular. During her high school years, practically any boy who looked at her became the object of a crush. She suffered a great many romantic disappointments.

When Emalee entered community college, her main concern was to qualify herself for an entry-level management position in the "high-tech" plants being constructed in her hometown. One of her elective courses was Personal Adjustment, and as it happened, the course was organized into discussion groups for one period each week. In these discussion groups, students were encouraged to apply the lecture material to their own lives. Emalee was completely astounded by what she heard. So many of the students spoke freely of their resentment and hostility toward parents and siblings. They criticized their parents in no uncertain terms, blaming them in fact for many of their adjustment problems. Emalee was suddenly frightened. She had never in her life felt like criticizing her mother. She did not understand all the anger that she heard.

When it was her turn to speak, she said that her experiences had been quite different. She described her mother in the most positive terms, expressing deep appreciation for her strength, stability, and high standards. One member of the discussion group said in a kindly way, "Well, she must be a hard lady to live with if she's so perfect and expects the same from you." Another said, not so kindly, "I'll bet it kind of makes you want to pack your bags." The instructor intervened to bring more respectful attention to Emalee's experience. But Emalee hardly heard her.

After the class Emalee went to the office of her professor, a woman about the age of Emalee's mother. Emalee's voice shook as she fought back tears and said: "I'm angry but I don't know why. What I told the group was true, yet it upset me a lot when the others casually challenged me."

"I understand what you experienced," the instructor assuringly responded. "Sometimes we have feelings we aren't conscious of. There are things we are unable to remember because they are painful." She reminded Emalee that the Student Counseling Center was available to help students with any emotional problems, serious or not.

Emalee had no wish to begin counseling sessions or discuss her problems with others. But she began to spend a great deal of time reading about hidden conflicts and the effects of childhood experiences. In fact, she read practically everything that could be checked out of the library. As a result of study, insight, and hard intellectual effort, she came to some realizations. She harbored a deep resentment toward her mother—a resentment of which she had long been unaware. Irrational as it was, she blamed her mother for her father's having left home. It was almost as if her mother had deprived her of the one person she had loved. Of course Emalee realized that her father had many undesirable characteristics, but she had not understood this as a small child, which was when the hurt had occurred.

When Emalee began to discover these feelings, she decided she would enter therapy—she would be strong and push aside that initial hesitation most everybody feels when considering psychological help.

Since Emalee had come to utilize the *psychoanalytic,* or *psychodynamic,* way of seeing herself, and had already won new understanding and maturity with it, she sought a therapist with this orientation—one who would help her explore her early life experiences, with the goal of uncovering unconscious conflicts, memories, and desires.

Basic Ideas of Psychoanalytic Theory

Psychoanalytic theory, or *psychodynamic theory,* refers largely to the collected ideas of Sigmund Freud (1856–1939), the Viennese physician who is usually numbered among the most influential thinkers of this century. In the 40 years in which Freud wrote and practiced, he developed a rich and complicated theory of human development and adjustment, and psychoanalysis, the approach to treatment for which he is best known. Much of Freud's theoretical work grew out of his clinical practice with neurotic patients. He also drew on personal experience; he possessed a rare talent for systematic study of his own mental processes. His life, he said, was aimed at one goal only: to infer or to guess how man's psyche is constructed and what forces interplay with and counteract it.

Levels of Consciousness

As we know, human beings are not aware of many important physiological processes that take place within them; the first of Freud's great discoveries was that we are not aware of all the mental processes that take place either. There are thoughts, wishes, memories, and so forth that affect us significantly and of which we are not aware. Freud found evidence for this in dreams that expressed an internal conflict of which the person, on awakening, had no knowledge and in the many seemingly inexplicable actions of everyday life. Consider an unconscious spoken or written error—a "Freudian slip of the tongue." Freud said these slips revealed a wish or feeling about which the person was unaware at the time. Imagine a physician with a competing medical practice meeting Freud on the street and greeting him, "Good afternoon, Herr Dr. Fraud."

Freud's experience with patients suffering from inexplicable physical symptoms also pointed to the role of hidden processes. In some cases physical symptoms disappeared dramatically when a buried conflict was brought out through hypnosis or through a "talking cure." To the hidden or inaccessible part of the mind Freud gave the name "unconscious."

The discovery of the unconscious enabled Freud to describe mental life as operating at three levels: the conscious, preconscious, and unconscious. The **conscious** level of mental life consists of all that is within our awareness. According to Freud, the conscious mind contains relatively little, compared to

Psychoanalytic Theory
A way of viewing the human personality, developed by Sigmund Freud, that emphasizes unconscious processes, defenses against internal conflicts, and stages of psychosexual development in childhood.

Conscious
In psychoanalytic theory, that part of one's mind that is within one's awareness.

Sigmund Freud's groundbreaking work, begun in the late 19th century, radically changed the public's perception of the human personality. Freud offered a new theory of personality organization, largely based on the idea that unconscious forces motivate behavior, and developed psychoanalysis as a therapeutic method.

Unconscious
In psychoanalytic theory, the realm of those mental processes—including conflicts, desires, and memories—which are largely hidden from awareness.

what exists beneath. In the **preconscious** are all those thoughts, images, and memories that we can bring to consciousness with some effort. For example, the preconscious holds pleasant memories that can be evoked with the aid of a family scrapbook.

To use the analogy of an iceberg, the conscious and preconscious levels would be the small visible tip. Just as the bulk of the iceberg is underwater, Freud thought that the largest portion of the mind, by far, is the **unconscious,** the level containing those mental processes to which we do not have easy access. Included in the unconscious are past experiences we have "forgotten" because they are so painful, as well as desires of which we are unaware. Freud believed that the reason most of these experiences and desires remain in the unconscious is that our conscious mind stubbornly resists paying any attention to them at all. An important goal of Freud's therapeutic method (psychoanalysis) was to enable the patient to discover material in the unconscious, so as to deal with it effectively in daily life. During psychoanalysis, Freud helped patients gain access to their unconscious by interpreting dreams and slips of the tongue and by using free association. (To free associate, the patient said whatever came to mind, even if it seemed irrelevant or embarrassing.)

The Organization of the Personality

Although the levels of consciousness remained fundamental to psychoanalytic theory, Freud later expanded his view of mental life to include the dynamics of the total personality. According to Freud, personality results from an interaction between three processes: the id (Latin for *it*), the ego (Latin for *I*), and the superego (Latin for *higher I*). Freud did not see these processes as separate and identifiable entities. Nor did he attach much importance to the terminology (he often abandoned or changed it when addressing lay audiences). The main points are that each component has its own operating principles, and that all three interact to produce behavior.

Id
In psychoanalytic theory, the primitive part of the psyche that seeks immediate gratification and the fulfillment of needs that are often socially unacceptable.

The **id** is the primitive psyche that exists in infancy, before the ego and superego can be said to have developed. It is expressed in primitive, unsocialized behavior, in the screaming, clinging, and cooing of the infant, for example. The id is that part of us that cannot tolerate delay, discomfort, or deprivation. It operates according to the **pleasure principle,** seeking always to reduce the tension of unfulfilled needs, and looking for immediate gratification. The needs present in the id are often socially unacceptable ones, involving sexuality and aggression.

Pleasure Principle
In psychoanalytic theory, the id's tendency to reduce the tension of unfulfilled needs and seek immediate gratification.

Although the id is formless, timeless, and unorganized, it is the central structure of the personality and serves as a reservoir of energy throughout life.

Gradually, in early childhood, the "it" becomes "I"; the higher process of the ego begins to differentiate itself from id. In later life, primitive id impulses, as well as the memories of that time of life when the id was relatively dominant, are lost to us. That is, they exist only in the unconscious.

The **ego** is the conscious, rational part of the personality. It is the "I" or "me" with which we usually identify—the I who thinks, plans, expresses, and generally feels some obligation to bring order to life. The ego operates according to the **reality principle.** Instead of demanding, it plans for gratification, and if necessary, postpones it. Most of us recognize the difference between the "it" and "I" (the id and ego) processes in our own lives. We say "*It* came over me" to describe an inexplicably angry action over which we felt no control, but "*I* did it," to describe the usual actions of the conscious self.

Under ordinary circumstances, the ego controls or monitors the id. When the id experiences a tension, the ego comes up with an appropriate plan for reducing that tension. Cognitive or intellectual processes such as perceiving, problem-solving, thinking, and remembering are among the many ego functions that help us adjust to the demands of the real environment.

If humans were solitary creatures living in the wilderness, personality might consist only of an id to express bodily needs and an ego to mediate between those needs and the natural environment. But we are social animals, surrounded by others who have certain expectations of us, brought up in cultures that impose certain norms and values on us. These expectations, norms, and values must be taken into account if we are to survive. Freud believed that we *internalize* these social norms in childhood, creating another element of the personality—the **superego.**

It is the superego that strives for the ideal and exercises the restraints of conscience. It is the superego that can produce feelings of right-mindedness or pride—or feelings of shame and guilt. Because the superego acts to inhibit antisocial tendencies, it must often come into conflict with id needs: something like the voice of an inner parent who says "no" to sexual or aggressive behaviors. Sometimes the superego also inhibits the reality functions of the ego, in which case the person may be found to be overly moralistic, idealistic, deluded, or foolish, depending on the circumstances.

Defense Mechanisms

Psychologists who study personal adjustment usually focus on the ego, the personality process that integrates the personality and is responsible for the individual's adjustment to the environment. Serving a "management" function, the ego tries to allow gratification of the id to a degree, without violating the norms of the superego. It appears that when inner conflicts or outer reality become too painful for a person, the ego uses certain mechanisms to reduce anxiety and restore self-esteem. These **defense mechanisms** usually involve some distortion of reality. They operate on an unconscious level: that is, the individual does not choose a defense mechanism and is usually unaware of its role in his or her behavior.

Ego
In psychoanalytic theory, the conscious, rational part of the personality that plans, postpones gratification, and monitors the id.

Reality Principle
In psychoanalytic theory, the ego's tendency to behave rationally, planning for, and, if necessary, postponing gratification.

Superego
In psychoanalytic theory, the element of the personality— created through internalization of the values of others—that seeks to maintain proper or moral conduct.

Defense Mechanisms
Unconscious mental mechanisms, usually involving some distortion of reality, whose purpose it is to reduce anxiety, resolve inner conflicts, or restore self-esteem.

Repression
A defense mechanism whereby the ego prevents painful or disturbing material from reaching consciousness.

A defense mechanism to which Freud attached great importance—and which can serve as a prototype—is **repression.** In repression the ego prevents painful or disturbing material from reaching consciousness. In effect it relegates the material to the more primitive id. For example, a person may repress a traumatic memory or an unacceptable sexual desire. A certain amount of repression may be helpful. (If we were able to recall all the painful experiences in our lives during periods of depression, we might be overwhelmed.) However, the ego must expend energy to keep the repressed material from coming to consciousness. And sometimes this energy expenditure is so great as to damage the personality as a whole. For example, the ego's attempted repression of significant material may exhaust the person, leading to fatigue, an inability to work productively, sexual impotence, or psychosomatic disorders.

It is worth noting that the significance of defense mechanisms differs across the life span. For example, Freud found that repression of sexual interest during the so-called latency period (from about age 6 to age 11) was a normal part of development. The same repression in adulthood might represent maladjustment. Similarly, denial of reality is usually a costly way of coping with a problem. For a terminally ill patient, however, it might represent a satisfactory adaptation (Lazarus, 1981). We will see in Chapter 4 that some defense mechanisms are generally more successful than others. (That is, some offer more reliable and more mature ways of satisfying id energies.) However, every defense mechanism has the potential for being used in either a healthy or unhealthy way.

Stages of Psychosexual Development

A basic assumption of Freudian theory is that much of our adult personality is determined by what happens between birth and about the sixth birthday. During our early years we move through stages of development characterized by certain physical pleasures, and experience conflicts over their gratification. Each stage is associated with a zone of the body through which pleasure and conflict are expressed. For example, the first year or so of life is given to *oral* activities—first sucking, then biting. As infants, we derive pleasure from stimulation of the lips, from our connection with food. Freud theorized that those who had sufficient sucking and parental attention during the **oral stage** will become friendly, generous, and dependent while those who were not satisfied during the oral stage will be characteristically hostile toward, envious of, and overly competitive with others.

The second stage is the **anal stage,** which begins in the second year. During this stage our energies are directed toward those pleasures involving bowel control—alternately withholding and letting go. The anal stage is associated with the socializing process called toilet training, and, Freud suggested, the child's experiences during this stage can lead him or her to become a retentive or overly generous adult (as he or she was with bowel movements).

Oral Stage
In psychoanalytic theory, the first stage of psychosexual development, in which pleasure is derived primarily from oral activities.

Anal Stage
In psychoanalytic theory, the second stage of psychosexual development, in which pleasure involves bowel control.

Freud believed that the manner in which needs are gratified during the early stages affects later personality development and how individuals react under stress. In order to avoid being **fixated** at a psychosexual stage, an individual's needs must neither be overgratified nor undergratified at that stage. For example, Freud theorized that a person will be fixated if he or she is weaned too early (insufficient gratification) or too much emphasis is placed on feeding during the oral stage. At times of stress an individual fixated at the oral stage will overemphasize oral activities, such as eating, fingernail biting, kissing, smoking, and symbolic oral activities, like using the mouth to make biting comments or being gullible, "swallowing everything he hears."

Fixation in the anal stage can arise from difficult toilet training experiences and from harsh criticisms of "accidents." Fixation could cause the person, when stressed as an adult, to have problems with toilet habits. Fixation could also operate more symbolically, leading to an overly generous individual who gives away possessions or to a stingy and orderly person who saves everything and who keeps possessions perfectly neat and clean.

The third stage, the **phallic stage,** is reached at about the third year. It is marked by the discovery of masturbation; by competition, rivalry, and other identity strivings; and by sexual fantasies and feelings involving the parent of the opposite sex.

Fixation at the phallic stage occurs when the child has difficulty developing satisfactory and acceptable feelings toward his or her parents (see the discussion of Oedipus and Electra Complexes in Chapter 7). As a result of fixation, males handle stress by becoming bold, tough, and acting as if they need to continually prove their masculinity. Females fixated in this stage, in contrast, have unhealthy relationships with males, either being seductive or promiscuous on the one hand, or being castrating or harsh on the other hand.

In the fourth stage, **latency,** which begins at about age six, the sexual impulses are repressed or replaced by behaviors considered appropriate to the child's age. Finally, at adolescence, we attain mature sexual functioning. This **genital stage** prepares us for reproduction and for an adult relationship with society.

Freud described an orderly progression from oral to anal, phallic, latency, and genital stages. Today, however, the names of these developmental stages and the ways in which they are interpreted differ according to the orientation of the psychoanalyst. As we will see, later theorists in the Freudian tradition have tended to de-emphasize the biological or sexual nature of the conflicts in favor of social factors. However, in all interpretations a main point is that the experiences of early life do not disappear simply because we cannot remember them. And specific personality traits are often re-expressions of early experience.

Fixated
In psychoanalytic theory, arrested psychosexual development at a psychosexual stage that was caused by inappropriate gratification at that stage. When experiencing stress a person reverts to gaining the gratification associated with that stage.

Phallic Stage
In psychoanalytic theory, the stage of psychosexual development that is characterized by masturbation, curiosity about the genitals, and sexual feelings for the opposite-sex parent.

Latency Stage
In psychoanalytic theory, the stage of psychosexual development when sexual desires are repressed and other activities pursued.

Genital Stage
In psychoanalytic theory, the final stage of psychosexual development, when a person attains mature sexual functioning.

Psychosocial Interpretations of Freudian Theory

Freud died in 1939. Throughout his life his theories were controversial, and they remain so to this day. Besides being controversial, they have also been enormously stimulating. Numerous mental health specialists who grew up on Freudian theory (and were psychoanalyzed), proceeded to make original contributions to the study of human behavior. In time they found it necessary to take "a definite step beyond Freud—a step that is possible, though, only on the basis of Freud's discoveries" (Horney, 1937). In most cases this "step" brought the Freudian closer to social concerns, and to the growing disciplines of sociology and anthropology.

The **neo-Freudians,** as these theorists are called, questioned Freud's assumption that inner conflicts were basic to human nature. The source of conflict, especially in the disturbed patients they treated, could be found in *social conditions* and *social relationships.* The personality, they said, was not so strongly determined by early, biologically based experiences. It was the product of social interactions. It could, therefore, be modified by significant relationships in later life. Theorists of this orientation have included Karen Horney (1885–1952), Erich Fromm (1900–1980), Harry Stack Sullivan (1892–1949), and Erik Erikson (1902–).

Sullivan was perhaps the most original advocate of the importance of social interaction. He was also the first important American-born theorist in the psychoanalytic tradition (he was born on a farm in New York state). Sullivan's model of personality development was a complicated one. In summary, he believed that what we call personality is purely hypothetical; it really exists only insofar as it is manifested in interpersonal relationship. Sullivan recognized Freud's biologically based stages, but, like other neo-Freudians, he tended to recast them in social terms. Nursing an infant, for example, is seen as an interpersonal experience. Anxiety is not the result of inner conflict, but can be an experience communicated to the child by an anxious parent during early feeding. Sullivan emphasized communication problems and other difficulties in human relationships and did not feel that personality was set in early childhood. Indeed, Sullivan was unusually successful in treating severely disturbed adults. And he was one of the first neo-Freudians to describe developmental stages over the life span.

Perhaps closer to Freud than Sullivan were those theorists who sought to refocus the Freudian model on healthy ego development or **ego-psychology.** Instead of concentrating on the management of the id or the pressure of the unconscious, these *ego psychologists* emphasized the ego. That is, they described the ways in which healthy, ego-dominated people adjusted to their environment and culture. The most influential of this group is Erik Erikson.

Erik Erikson's most significant accomplishment to date is his description of the "wholeness of the human life cycle—a cycle that proceeds stage by stage, as well as generation by generation" (Erikson, 1976).

Erikson's first four stages are reinterpretations of Freud's psychosexual stages; that is, of the oral, anal, phallic, and latency stages. The last four stages deal with ego changes in adolescence and adulthood. (The concept of the adolescent "identity crisis" is perhaps Erikson's best-known contribution to

Neo-Freudian
A follower of Freudian theory as he or she modified it with his or her own contributions.

Ego-Psychology
An approach emphasizing the ego and how people cope rather than focusing, as Freud did, on the id and people's sexual and hostile impulses.

TABLE 1.1	*The Eight Crises Corresponding to Erikson's Eight Stages of Development and the Traits That Emerge if They Are Successfully or Unsuccessfully Resolved*

Stage Crisis Encountered (age period of stage)

1. Trust vs Mistrust (Birth–1)
    If the crisis is successfully resolved, hope emerges.
    If the crisis is unsuccessfully resolved, fear emerges.

2. Autonomy vs Shame and Doubt (1–3)
    If the crisis is successfully resolved, self-control and willpower emerge.
    If the crisis is unsuccessfully resolved, self-doubt emerges.

3. Initiative vs Guilt (4–5)
    If the crisis is successfully resolved, direction and purpose emerge.
    If the crisis is unsuccessfully resolved, feelings of unworthiness emerge.

4. Industry vs Inferiority (6–11)
    If the crisis is successfully resolved, competence emerges.
    If the crisis is unsuccessfully resolved, incompetence emerges.

5. Identity vs Role Confusion (12–20)
    If the crisis is successfully resolved, fidelity emerges.
    If the crisis is unsuccessfully resolved, uncertainty emerges.

6. Intimacy vs Isolation (20–24)
    If the crisis is successfully resolved, the capacity for love emerges.
    If the crisis is unsuccessfully resolved, promiscuity emerges.

7. Generativity vs Stagnation (25–64)
    If the crisis is successfully resolved, care emerges.
    If the crisis is unsuccessfully resolved, selfishness emerges.

8. Ego Integrity vs Despair (65–Death)
    If the crisis is successfully resolved, wisdom emerges.
    If the crisis is unsuccessfully resolved, feelings of despair and meaninglessness emerge.

Source: From B. R. Hergenhahn, *An Introduction to Theories of Personality*, 2e, © 1984, p. 114. Reprinted by permission of Prentice-Hall, Inc., Englewood Cliffs, New Jersey.

modern culture and is discussed in Chapter 7.) In Erikson's thinking, as in Freud's, conflicts are not simply resolved. Each is renewable as the next stage is reached, which means that later conflicts "open up" earlier ones. (In adolescence, for example, we reexperience the toddler's conflict between autonomy and shame—only now within an adolescent context. A person who did not develop self-control and willpower as a child, can develop it now as an adolescent.) Although no life escapes the crises, or the important turning points at each stage of human development, Table 1.1 shows that in successful circumstances the confrontations bring a favorable outcome and the *ego strength* to proceed to the developmental work of the next stage. A favorable life outcome is **ego integrity,** the sum of the ego strengths developed in the earlier stages.

Psychoanalytic theory, from Freud to Erikson, shows that a person's behavior throughout life is a response to internal and social pressures. The psychologists in this tradition emphasize that adult responses may be due to unresolved conflicts of childhood; in this sense they argue for the continuity of behavior. The psychoanalytic tradition has produced, in Erikson, the most widely accepted description of developmental stages over the life span.

Ego Integrity
Erik Erikson's concept of the favorable outcome achieved when one has successfully dealt with the crisis or conflicts that arose at different stages of one's life.

Herbert was to retire at the end of the spring semester. He had been teaching law at the university for 31 years, almost since he arrived in the United States. And he was 67 years old. Some people said he was in "failing health." Herbert said he was not failing but was merely "keeping pace." This was intended as a pun: last year as he had sat working late in his office, burglars had entered and held a gun to Herbert's head. He had had a stroke and was subsequently fitted for a pacemaker. Herbert still occasionally worked late in his office, but now he was careful to lock the door and take other precautions.

When Herbert reviewed his career as a teacher, he was profoundly satisfied. He had many students who were writing, working, and making contributions to the world. His own writings, though perhaps not famous, were often consulted. And he was respected in his field. Just last month he declined a judgeship, citing his age and his pacemaker (he had come to speak of it as a kind of third party, with veto powers).

Despite some limitations, Herbert remained active in a number of causes. For example, he continued to work with legal aid. This work involved innumerable frustrations and some real disagreements with colleagues. Herbert's wife and children said it drained his energy. He answered, in the professorial tones he hardly ever used with students, that it was necessary and fitting. "There are some things one does not forget," he said, "and one of them is what it feels like not to have your constitutional rights protected." "Besides," he would add, "the pacemaker is guaranteed for five more years."

Teaching, though, really was coming to an end. As Herbert prepared to meet with his last classes, he reflected on his career, thinking as always of the students. It was true that they were not as well prepared as in the past. Writing skills had fallen off slightly. Logical and mathematical abilities were not at a level that would have earned *him* a passing grade in his youth. But the interest! The interest in human beings was remarkable. His students today were so open to new ideas about themselves and others. And they were eager to make significant decisions about the kind of people they would become. Whatever the cost, they seemed fully committed to realizing their potential as human beings.

Herbert introduced his students to the discipline of law by asking them to pretend that they were leafing through their own biographies in the last days of their lives. "Pretend," he would say, "that you have just opened to the chapter dealing with the present. And by some miracle you have the power to decide what the next chapter will be. Imagine that it lies within your capacities to write afresh this crucial chapter of your life story. How will you shape the next hour, and the next day? Pretend it is still in your power to make corrections. What will you write?" Herbert finds that this exercise motivates students because it makes them realize the gravity of their being in the classroom at that very moment, among many other things.

Herbert's exercise, and his approach to life, may be characterized as *existential* or *humanist*. This approach emphasizes the freedom and responsibility that each individual exercises over his or her own life. And it celebrates the human striving to fulfill potential, at every stage in the life span.

Basic Ideas of Existential and Humanist Psychology

Existentialism is a philosophical movement that developed in France after World War II and quickly spread to Europe and the United States. It caught the imaginations of philosophers, writers, artists, and political thinkers. Its adherents included some of the most influential thinkers of the 20th century, among them the philosopher Martin Heidegger (1889–1976); the writers Albert Camus (1913–1960) and Jean-Paul Sartre (1905–1980); and the theologians Paul Tillich (1886–1965) and Martin Buber (1878–1965). Existentialism also affected the relatively young discipline of psychology. Especially important were the existentialist psychologists and philosophers who called themselves phenomenologists.

The phenomenologists were interested in perception and cognition, but, unlike other scientists, they did not investigate a person's relationship to objects and events in the external world. They investigated the act of perception itself; their concern was with immediate experience. For example, they described the *experience* of perceiving sights, sounds, and odors; of having feelings, thoughts, memories, and so forth. Their emphasis was on the moment of experiencing, on consciousness, on being, or existence itself—hence the term **existentialism.**

According to Viktor Frankl (1984, page 106), "The term 'existential' may be used in three ways: to refer to (1) *existence* itself, i.e., the specifically human mode of being; (2) the *meaning* of existence; and (3) the striving to find a concrete meaning in personal existence, that is to say, the *will* to meaning."

Existential psychologists are concerned with people's search for meaning, seeing that quest as the primary motivating force in humans. Each individual must conduct his or her own unique search, because only the individual can find self-satisfying answers. An important part of life's task is putting into perspective the reality of one's future death. According to the existential psychologist, the awareness of death is basic to human existence. It is death that gives meaning to individual existence, and significance to the life span. Frankl, a psychiatrist, summarizes the existential position:

> If we were immortal, we could legitimately postpone every action forever. It would be of no consequence whether or not we did a thing now; every act might just as well be done tomorrow or the day after or a year from now or ten years hence. But in the face of death as absolute finish to our future and boundary to our possibilities, we are under the imperative of utilizing our lifetimes to the utmost, not letting the singular opportunities—whose "finite" sum constitutes the whole of life—pass by unused (Frankl, 1955, p. 64).

Existentialism
A philosophy or approach to psychology that emphasizes immediate experience and the process of becoming.

Humanist psychologists are optimistic about the potential of people, reflecting an attitude long-prevalent in Americans. From the frontiers of the west to the frontiers of space, as Neil Armstrong put it, "One small step for man, one giant leap for mankind."

In other words, it is because we are aware of the temporal quality of life, and the impossibility of recovering lost moments, that we feel responsibility for making choices about what we will do now. Therefore, therapists in this tradition put emphasis on immediate experience, on the present, and how one feels here and now.

The idea of *choice* is also central to the existential position. As human beings we are responsible for our individual lives. We possess the awesome task of making choices that will result in our "utilizing our lifetimes to the utmost." How do we exercise this responsibility? Existential psychologists believe that the individual is always *becoming,* that healthy people chart a course of continuous growth. And they believe that human existence is characterized by a constant striving to utilize talents and achieve our potential as human beings. The striving is part of a search for purpose and significance in life. It is an attempt to endow our experiences with meaning, in spite of the inevitable anxiety and confusion that accompany much experience. We fail, according to existentialists, when we do not strive to become what we must be. And, if we do not exercise our responsibility over our lives, we become overwhelmed by feelings of alienation, meaninglessness, and despair.

American Interpretations

Humanist Psychology
An approach to psychology, based on existentialism, that emphasizes immediate experience, psychological health and growth, and the search for meaning.

Existential psychology, like existentialism in general, quickly became established in the United States. In the 1950s and 1960s it took on the American orientation we call **humanist psychology.**

On the one hand, humanist psychologists accept much of the philosophy of existentialism. For example, they emphasize the value of immediate experience, the striving for meaning in activities and in life, the awareness of

The Search for Personal Adjustment

death and, most important, the continual growth that is involved in realizing potential. On the other hand, they express some characteristically American values. They emphasize human freedom, the unlimited opportunities in life, and the possibility of self-actualizing growth, in much the same way we, as citizens, have expected the unlimited from America. Specifically, the humanist looks to each individual as we have looked to our nation from the earliest days of its history, respecting, yet taking for granted, the possibility of unencumbered growth. While earlier generations expected to win freedom, establish a new government, and tame the frontier, your parents *knew* Americans would conquer space and land on the moon. And, even today, you know that the rags-to-riches stories of Horatio Alger are still possible.

Humanists, as you can see, are optimistic, focusing on each individual's uniqueness and worth. They assume that all people have the potential to make the personally appropriate choices to solve whatever problems they encounter, and to enable them to become the people they are capable of becoming.

As therapists, humanists avoid the physician/authority role in order to enter the subjective world of the client as participating equals. They attend to the subjective reality of the person (what he experiences) in a holistic manner (as a psychological, cultural, and biological totality).

Compared to other psychologists, humanists accord little importance to the limits imposed by genetic endowment or by events of the past, assuming that an unhappy past can be overcome as present needs for growth are satisfied. Humanist psychology is sometimes referred to as *growth psychology,* and was associated with sensitivity training groups and the human potential movement that flowered in the relatively optimistic and affluent late 1960s and early 1970s.

Humanist psychologist Abraham Maslow believed that psychological health rather than illness should be emphasized. Maslow stressed the process of self-actualization—achieving one's potential and being open to all experiences.

Abraham Maslow: Self-Actualization

One of the best-known humanist psychologists was Abraham Maslow (1908–1970). It was Maslow who called humanist psychology the "third force" in American psychology (the first two being psychoanalysis and behaviorism). And it was he who first pointed out that the healthy person was more than simply an individual without disorders. The term Maslow used to define the truly healthy person was "self-actualizing." **Self-actualization** is the process by which a person becomes what he or she has the potential to be.

Self-actualizing people experience life vividly, with full concentration and total absorption (Maslow, 1971, p. 45). They are able to make choices, one after another, that lead toward personal growth—and they do so on the basis of their own needs and values, not for the sake of convention or to "keep up with the Joneses." They have a sense of destiny in their work and family life. And they are open to all experiences, even to moments in which they transcend the self in ecstasy or awe. As we will see in Chapter 2, Maslow identified many other characteristics of self-actualizing people, and he describes the kind of motivation that results in continuous growth.

Self-Actualization
The process by which one seeks to realize one's unique capacities.

Carl Rogers, a humanist, believed that people have a need for positive regard from others. With positive regard, in the form of love, caring, acceptance, and respect, people can form healthy self-concepts that accurately express their experiences as individuals.

Carl Rogers: The Self-Concept and Positive Regard

Carl Rogers (1902–1987), unlike Maslow, devoted much of his career to clinical practice with troubled people. On the basis of his experience, Rogers reached the optimistic conclusion that society's best hope is to let individuals express their innermost natures freely. Theorizing that human beings are guided by the master motive he called "the actualizing tendency," he expected people to seek experiences to develop the self—to enhance the quality of their lives in a creative, independent, and socially responsible manner.

As a therapist, Rogers was primarily interested in his clients' present experience, their mental life at the present moment. He recognized, of course, that past experience and developmental processes may influence the way a person experiences things now (mainly by leading him or her to expect certain outcomes from certain situations and actions). But Rogers was far less interested in what *influenced* present experience than in exactly what present experience *is*. For example, if a person was anxious about an upcoming interview, Rogers accepted this feeling and explored it with the client, instead of investigating the unresolved conflict that might lie behind it. Rogers' main concern was with the way in which the person perceived himself or herself in the world. He saw no need to propose the existence of an unconscious mind whose contents cannot be brought to the full awareness of the client.

Rogers believed everybody experiences the *need for positive regard*. This need is satisfied when others tell us, through love, warmth, caring, acceptance, or respect, that we are special. The task of earning positive regard begins when infants discover how they must behave in order to get it from their parents. Children, adolescents, and adults, too, must function in certain ways if they are to receive positive regard from those significant in their lives.

What, specifically, do individuals do to gain positive regard? Rogers thought most people came to forsake standards set by their own actualizing tendency, instead measuring the worth of their experiences by the standards of others. For example, a young son and daughter of traditional parents gives up the joy of playing with dolls and trucks, respectively, in order to gain their parents' positive regard. Earning positive regard in this manner causes what Rogers calls *incongruence:*

> (Incongruence) . . . is the basic estrangement in man. He has not been true to himself, to his own natural organismic valuing of experience, but for the sake of preserving the positive regard of others has now come to falsify some of the values he experiences and to perceive them only in terms based upon their value to others. Yet this has not been a conscious choice, but a natural— and tragic—development in infancy (Rogers, 1959, p. 226).

Problems in adjustment can arise when individuals face substantial incongruence, Rogerian theory suggests. These difficulties can be overcome by eliminating incongruence. Therapists can help clients toward this goal by giving them unconditional positive regard. This frees them to use their own values (because they will still get the therapist's positive regard), to remove false fronts and to be the people they really are.

Rogers found that most of the aspects of mental life are experienced as being outside the self. However, some are experienced as parts of the self or as pertaining to it, and these constitute what Rogers calls the **self-concept** (Rogers, 1959, pp. 184–256). The self-concept includes "what I am," "what I can do," and "what I should or would like to be." Like all other aspects of mental life, the parts of the self-concept are constantly changing, and can be brought to full awareness by focusing on what one is experiencing in the here and now.

The self-concept is a central part of Rogers' theory (which is sometimes called *self-theory*). A characteristic of the healthy person—and the goal of Rogers' therapy—is the development of a strong, stable, and positive self-concept. It is especially important that the self-concept remain open to change, and that it accurately reflect the experiences of the individual. Rogers notes that if the individual excludes certain experiences from his or her self-concept (because he or she has been told that such experiences are bad or unworthy), there is a lack of conformity between the world and the individual's experience of it, between what the person is and what he or she perceives the self to be. However, if the person totally accepts the self and its experience, he or she develops a self-concept that is realistic. Such a person is conscious of being his or her real self. And he or she is able to move toward the self-actualization that is the humanist ideal.

Self-Concept
As defined by Carl Rogers, the aspects of one's mental life that one experiences as part of oneself or as pertaining to oneself.

THE COGNITIVE PERSPECTIVE

At 37, Shirley was the oldest person in her Psychology of Adjustment class. In fact, she was older than the instructor. In her two other courses her age did not seem to matter. If anything, she felt a little humble as she tackled Biology and the Foundations of Political Thought. In Psychology of Adjustment, however, she felt her maturity was an asset. She knew a great deal about how people adjusted to life, and sometimes this made her impatient.

The problem was that Shirley considered herself a person of unusual common sense. It seemed to her that looking at things sensibly was the gist of being well-adjusted. Shirley did not see the need for examining repressed wishes, or teaching cats to lift levers in the laboratory. She knew these matters were important to psychologists, but, she said, "They are just beside the point to me."

What worked for Shirley was "common sense and positive thinking." For example, if something seemed difficult or overwhelming, Shirley took a deep breath and decided to call it a "challenge." If she was faced with a limitation she could not change, she set about changing her way of thinking about it. When she was hospitalized for a gallbladder operation two years ago, she pretended that it was happening to someone else and did crossword puzzles. When she felt the press of financial worries, she reminded herself of the mass poverty that affected whole populations in the Third World—a mental exercise that usually resulted in her feeling wealthy enough to send off a contribution. No matter the situation, Shirley was able to come up with a host of ideas for getting through it. "Not very scientific," she noted with a smile.

The instructor was neither annoyed nor amused at Shirley's attitude. She was thoughtful. She told Shirley that science does not always discover what is new or unexpected. Sometimes science helps us organize our experiences; it systematically investigates our most ordinary thinking; it validates what we already know. The instructor directed Shirley toward research that investigated the very coping strategies that she had informally described. When Shirley read through this material and saw some of "her ideas" in print, she said she felt a shock of intellectual pleasure unmatched in her educational career. "If I were a graduate student," Shirley shared with her instructor, "I would design studies that tested how well my coping strategies worked for others."

The professor, delighted with Shirley's enthusiasm, pressed her to be specific, as research projects must be. Shirley first outlined a plan to investigate patients hospitalized for gallbladder problems. The study would attempt to determine which thinking strategies were associated with lack of post-operative complications and early release. Then it occurred to Shirley that the Prepared Parenthood courses she had been hearing about offered another opportunity for research. She suggested a study to determine whether couples who were aware of the labor process and its complications fared better than those who were content to leave all details in the hands of the obstetricians. To her surprise, Shirley found that she had a strong interest in scientific thought and method. It took her some time before she could reconcile this with her reputation for motherly common sense. But she did not rule out the possibility of doing research at the graduate level.

The area of research to which Shirley was drawn is called **cognitive psychology.** Psychologists in this area study the ways people think, perceive, reason, and remember—in short, all the ways they organize their experiences of the world.

Contributions from Cognitive Psychology

Cognition can be defined as the act or process of knowing. Cognitive psychology is a relatively new science that is gathering experimental evidence about thinking and other activities that go on within the human mind. Research in cognitive psychology comes from an impressive number of disciplines, including computer science, linguistics, mathematics and logic, child development, and neurophysiology. The area of cognitive psychology is complex, and to date no single work, and no single psychologist, has been able to unify all that is going on (Hunt, 1982). Among the many topics now being studied are the acquisition of language, the mechanisms of memory, concept formation, and creativity. If we limit our attention here to personal adjustment, there are two major areas of cognitive psychology that are important.

The first is **cognitive development,** or the growth of what we usually call intelligence. The cognitive research of Jean Piaget (1896–1980), the Swiss biologist and genetic epistemologist (one who studies the development of knowledge in the individual), has shown that people do not simply perceive

Cognitive Psychology
A field of psychology that focuses on the ways in which people think, perceive, reason, and remember.

Cognitive Development
The growth of the intellect as a person progresses through different stages of life.

Goals

Many students enroll in a Personal Adjustment course with the idea of improving the quality of their lives in some way. In this chapter's case studies, we met students with different personal goals. Jonathan wanted to change some of the behaviors that were making him unhappy; Emalee discovered a need to better understand her past; Shirley consolidated her experiences and defined new academic goals in the field of psychology.

1. Following is an opportunity to define some of your goals as you begin your course in Personal Adjustment. Make notes in the blank spaces—or, if your goals are unclear, leave the spaces empty and return to the exercise later in the course.
   (a) Academic goals and career goals
   Include here goals related to degree requirements (or to career plans that you may have).

   (b) Immediate personal goals
   Include here any goals you may have for coping with specific problems, such as shyness, anxiety over course work, or an occasional unhappy mood.

   (c) Long-range personal development goals
   Include here your goals for developing strengths or solving problems over your life span (for example, improving personal relationships, gaining insight into the reasons behind your behavior, improving your self-concept).

2. We saw, in the case example of Herbert, that professors have a variety of goals in teaching their courses. Among Herbert's goals were making his students aware of the choices they exercised over their lives, and to help them find meaning in those choices.

   What do you think are your instructor's goals in teaching the course on Personal Adjustment? (If your instructor has said nothing specific about his or her goals, can you tell what they are from materials so far presented—for example, from a course outline, suggested readings, or an opening quiz, questionnaire, or exercise?) If possible, describe your instructor's goals and indicate how they relate to your goals just listed.
   ▲

Jean Piaget studied cognitive development at different age levels by closely observing children. He found that people do not simply perceive external realities before them; they construct reality from within, according to the mental structures they have developed. This photo was taken during Piaget's first visit to the United States.

external realities before them; they construct reality from within, according to the mental structures they have developed. And their version of reality varies with developmental level. Infants, for example, have no way of symbolically referring to an object that is not present. They have no words. Their understanding is limited to immediate sensory experiences.

If a favorite toy is removed from an infant's grasp and placed under a blanket in his full view, he will not reach to retrieve it, for he does not yet understand that objects exist when he does not see or hear them. The infant's eight-year-old sister understands this very well and can easily retrieve the object. If the toy was more deceptively hidden and she did not find it immediately, she will persist because she has developed intellectually to the point of knowing that "it has to be somewhere." The eight year old understands things differently from her younger sibling, and she has different problem-solving skills. By the same token, her 18-year-old sister has at her disposal a whole range of problem-solving skills that are beyond an eight year old. According to Piaget, she is likely to have attained the level of abstract thought. Whereas her eight-year-old sister's reasoning ability is limited to concrete, observable events and objects she can picture in her mind, the eighteen year old has reached the most developed level in logical thinking and can engage in abstract reasoning (Piaget, 1972). She can consider verbally stated hypotheses and can approach, for example, ethical problems in terms of higher principles or philosophical systems. When we discuss personal adjustment over the life span, we naturally observe that the stage of cognitive development helps determine the way in which a person will cope with his or her environment.

A second area of interest is the role that cognition plays in the way we, as adults, cope with threatening situations. Cognitive psychologists believe that cognitive processes play an important mediating (or go-between) role in determining our emotional reactions and behaviors. We see an event, or experience a pain, but how we feel about it and what we do depends largely on how we interpret it, cognitively. For example, if we believe that pain is a normal side effect of a medicine we have taken, the chances are that we will perceive it as being less disturbing, less intense, or less important than if we experience the very same pain but have no explanation for its cause (generalized from Nisbett & Schacter, 1966). Similarly, if we believe that we are in control of an unpleasant stimulus, such as an electric shock, it feels less painful and makes us less anxious than would be the case if it were administered in a seemingly arbitrary manner (Previn, 1963; LaPanto, Mooney, & Zenhausen, 1965).

As these examples suggest, our ability to cope with unpleasant or stressful events is influenced by our cognitions or beliefs about these events. Researchers in cognitive psychology have shown that beliefs about one's ability to control or escape unpleasant events are especially important. They have stressed the importance of **learned helplessness** in adjustment failures. Some people, it seems, learn that they are helpless to avoid unpleasant events; a history of seemingly unavoidable failure has resulted in learned helplessness. Life seems to be a matter of luck (always bad), and the most sensible response to any difficulty is, therefore, to "give up" or become depressed.

Learned Helplessness
A tendency to stop trying or become depressed as a result of a history of failure to bring about desired outcomes.

For example, in one laboratory experiment, students who had been given unsolvable problems (and therefore had a short history of failure) reacted to an unpleasant noise by giving up. They had learned to be helpless. But students who had earlier been given solvable problems did not feel helpless when subjected to the unpleasant noise. They quickly learned to avoid this laboratory punishment. So, in fact, did a third group of students who had been given no problems in the earlier part of the experiment (Hiroto & Seligman, 1975). Results of this and similar experiments suggest that the concept of learned helplessness explains many maladjustment reactions—including some cases of the most common adjustment to failure, depression, (Alloy & Abramson, 1980).

Current Trends

Today cognitive psychologists are investigating the many important ways in which the cognitive processes affect adjustment. For example, cognitive psychologists are designing research studies to answer questions like: How do thoughts affect feelings? What kinds of distorted thinking are found in people with particular kinds of disorders? How do our expectancies in a situation affect our response to what really happens? Do rewards and punishments (as described by the behaviorists) have much effect if the person believes that nothing he or she does makes a difference? What are the effects of perceived helplessness (or, alternately, hope) on the ability to cope with a threatening situation? When trouble is inevitable, what cognitive strategies enable a person to live successfully with the situation?

To give you a better sense of how cognitive approaches can be applied to treating adjustment problems, we have singled out the work of two people, Albert Ellis and Aaron Beck.

Albert Ellis: Rational-Emotive Therapy

A person's thoughts create his or her feelings. Ellis maintains that thoughts themselves determine emotions, and that what we think is what makes us feel good or bad, not the events we encounter or what others say or do to us. His Rational-Emotive Therapy (RET) is perhaps the best known cognitive treatment approach. It is based on the philosophy that people want to live life in a reasonably happy manner, on an observation that they encounter unhappiness often, and on the assumption that people's own irrational beliefs cause their discontent and upset (Ellis, 1962; Ellis & Bernard, 1985).

Common irrational beliefs are listed, along with explanations of why they cause distress:

▶ **"Everybody I meet must think I'm bright."** This belief is unrealistic and because it cannot be achieved, it leads to failure, anxiety, and so forth.

Decades ago Albert Ellis, a pioneer in the cognitive psychology area, proposed that people's thoughts determine their emotions, and not the events they encounter or what other individuals say or do to them. The area of cognitive psychology has begun to flourish in recent years.

▶ **"I need everything to go exactly as planned at the wedding."** This belief measures happiness in an all-or-nothing manner that leads to disappointment, anxiety, and so forth.

▶ **"It will be awful if nobody takes me to the St. Patrick's Day party."** By catastrophizing, or exaggerating the consequences, this belief leads a person to feel worse than necessary, to experience anxiety, and so forth.

To illustrate how irrational beliefs like these affect us, consider Erin, who worried about the St. Patrick's Day party. The night of the party she had nobody to accompany her and felt absolutely miserable. How did this misery come about? Ellis explains it in terms of an A-B-C sequence:

A—An Activating Event or Experience occurs that is unpleasant and stressful. Erin had no date.

B—The Belief System appraises A and defines it as a catastrophe. Erin engaged in self-talk/thought: "It's horrible. Not one person in this whole campus asked me—and it's the biggest event of the year. Everybody else has a date. I'm not popular. I'm not attractive. Nobody will ever ask me out. It's awful."

C—The Consequences are emotional reactions like anxiety, depressed feelings, anger, and other forms of emotional upset. These follow from Belief System thoughts (B) but appear to be produced by the Activating Event (A). Erin, sitting alone in her room, felt extremely distressed, a state she blamed on the fact that she had no date.

Following RET, Ellis would argue that changing Erin's beliefs would enable her to enjoy the social scene—and life—more fully. If Ellis encountered Erin in a psychotherapy session he would add a D to the A-B-C sequence, Disputing her irrational Beliefs (B), "The biggest event of the year? What about the Greek Ball you told me you attended?" "Nobody will ever ask you out?" "What are the odds of that?" Ellis would work to correct Erin's thinking and self-talk so she would no longer experience the negative Consequences (C).

Aaron Beck: Thinking Patterns and Depression

A person's thoughts can cause and maintain depression. Beck (1976) reasons this way: since thoughts determine emotions, consistently distorted thinking can produce psychological disorders. If a person's thinking leads her to view herself pessimistically, the world as frustrating and unrewarding, and the future as gloomy, depressed emotions can result.

Beck and his colleagues have observed that depressed individuals are prone to make these logical errors and distortions in thinking:

- **Arbitrary Inference.** The person draws a conclusion without adequate information. For example, Rick's boss momentarily forgot his name. Rick concluded, "The boss dislikes me and probably plans to fire me."

- **Dichotomous Reasoning.** The person thinks in absolutes or in all-or-none terms. For example, Sally tells herself, "If I get a B in any course this spring, I won't get a top job."

- **Overgeneralization.** The person draws a sweeping conclusion on the basis of little information. For example, after Jewel declined John's invitation to the dance, he decided, "I have no sex appeal. Nobody will ever want to marry me."

- **Magnification and Minimization.** The person inflates the importance of negative information and downplays positive information. For example, newlywed Beth thinks, "Christmas breakfast was a mess because I burned the bacon. The only reason everybody came back for dinner was because they had no place else to go."

THE FOUR PERSPECTIVES: A CONCLUDING STATEMENT

The four approaches to psychology that we have discussed—the behaviorist, psychoanalytic, existential-humanist, and cognitive approaches—contradict one another on many points. Behaviorists, for example, believe that reference to unmeasurable inner states is not helpful in understanding human behavior, while those who utilize Freud's psychoanalytic theory have developed entire explanations of the personality around the existence of unconscious processes that to date are not objectively measurable. Some theorists have combined aspects of the various perspectives, thinking this would enable them to better predict and explain behavior and to suggest more effective treatment strategies for personal adjustment problems. Donald Meichenbaum (1977), for example, has proposed a cognitive-behavioral approach while Arnold Lazarus (1976, 1985) has developed multimodal therapy, an eclectic approach that centers on seven areas: Behavior, affect, sensation, imagery, cognition, interpersonal relations, and drugs. These seven, which can be remembered by the acronym, BASIC ID, suggest important functions to be considered in understanding people and the causes and treatment of adjustment problems.

Our purpose in presenting these four perspectives on human behavior has not been to provide a forum for arguing their pros and cons. Still less do we intend to judge between them and try to determine if one is right and the others wrong. Our belief is that all four approaches have led to insights and findings that can be used to achieve personal understanding and growth. This book consists largely of these insights and findings, and ways in which people can apply them in everyday life.

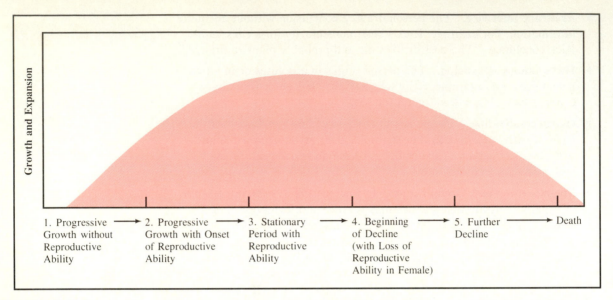

Figure 1.2 Buhler's stages of the life span.

The chart shows a curve of "Growth and Expansion" (vertical axis) over the following stages:

1. Progressive Growth without Reproductive Ability → 2. Progressive Growth with Onset of Reproductive Ability → 3. Stationary Period with Reproductive Ability → 4. Beginning of Decline (with Loss of Reproductive Ability in Female) → 5. Further Decline → Death

THE LIFE SPAN: A FRAMEWORK

Every so often, when things are perfect and our contentment is deep, we say: "If only things could stay this way." Perhaps we are newly in love . . . or on vacation watching the waves wash over the beach. Perhaps we are young parents watching toddlers play on the lawn . . . or grandparents having dinner before an open fire. We say, "If only things could stay this way. . . ."

The reason we say this—the reason that someone usually runs to get the camera—is that things will not stay the same. From the moment of birth, and even earlier, we are caught up in change. As a wise person once put it, "Change is unchanging in the course of human life." We must make continual adjustments to our changing selves, to changing others, and to an increasingly fast-paced environment. Not only that, we, ourselves, create change as we work, play, love, and live. Acknowledging the unchanging nature of change, it follows that personal adjustment is also an ongoing, lifelong task. Hence, to fully understand it, we must know something about how people *change over time* in their handling of life's challenges.

In other words, we cannot fully understand ourselves unless we back off for a moment and try to see our lives as a whole. For this reason, this book describes personal adjustment over the life span. It recognizes that the life span itself makes many types of adjustments necessary. "Young and old appear . . . to be the greatest opposites of which psychic life is capable," wrote Freud in his seventies. And yet, if we live, we must experience both—young and old—and the whole complicated sequence of changes in between.

Your Life Span

Charlotte Buhler, one of the first psychologists to describe the life span, focused on the biological foundations that underlie all life. As depicted in Figure 1.2, she saw the human lifetime as consisting of a period of growth or expansion, a stationary period, and a period of decline (Buhler, 1933). Buhler's work is important for historical reasons and we can also use it for personal learning.

On a separate sheet, draw a curve like the one in Figure 1.2. Number the stages 1 through 5, as is done in the figure.

1. Find your present place on the life span. Put a large dot on the curve and write down your age beside it. (For example, if you are 18, you will probably place your dot somewhere between Stage 2 and Stage 3.)
2. Try to estimate the ages at which you have entered (or will enter) the biological periods described by Buhler. Consider Stage 2, progressive growth with onset of reproductive ability. Buhler indicates that this begins in the teens and lasts until the person reaches physical maturity. Put a dot at the point at which you feel you entered Stage 2, along with approximate age. (If you are a female, remember that the onset of reproductive ability is usually about a year after the first menstrual period.) Place another dot and age at the point where you entered (or expect to enter) Stage 3, the stationary stage with reproductive ability.
3. Think about Stage 4, the beginning of biological decline. Mark the approximate age at which you expect to enter this period in your life. Buhler places this period anywhere from 45 or 50 to 60 or 70 years.
4. Look at your life span, as labeled on the curve. What feelings does it arouse in you?
5. Researchers in gerontology (the study of aging) often speak of the possibility of lengthening the human life span—for example, through new applications of preventive medicine and lifesaving medical technology. It is not clear, however, which periods of the life span would be increased. If we were more successfully able to treat the diseases of old age, we would add years to the ends of our lives. If we were able to interfere with the rate of aging, we might prolong the period of adult vigor. Circle the possibility that seems most desirable to you. To:
   a. Add 10 years to the end of your life span; enjoy a longer old age.
   b. Postpone old age; add 10 years to Stage 4, and enjoy a long, happy middle age.
   c. Add 10 years to Stage 3; prolong the period of adult vigor.
   d. Postpone the entry into adulthood; add 10 years to Stage 2 to allow for more extensive training and education.

Challenges over the Life Span

An overview of the changes individuals face in different areas over the life span is provided in Table 1.2 (Selim and the *Futurist* editors, 1979). As the table suggests by both its size and content, what constitutes personal adjustment is intimately related to our time of life. Not only the problems we confront but the way we confront them changes over time. The identity confusion of adolescence, the career crisis of mid-life, and the wisdom and detachment of old age are part of the many adjustments that occur at predictable stages of individual lives.

TABLE 1.2 *The Stages of Life: A Life-Cycle Calendar*

	Infancy and Early Childhood (0–5)	Late Childhood (5–12)	Adolescence (12–18)
Family	Mother is the center of universe. Child's behavior varies from complete devotion to unpredictability to outright rebellion. Dramatic changes in child's behavior can occur in only 6 months.	Still very dependent on mother, but goes to extremes of affection or dislike. Proud of father, family, and home. Generally good with siblings.	Family gradually becomes less important. . . . Sometimes adolescents feel the need to break away from family. Occasional embarrassment over parents or siblings.
Education and employment	Children are just entering school. Children show a wide range of skills and interest in letters and numbers.	Children most often like school, sometimes devoted to teacher. Increasingly comfortable with the three R's. Behavior varies from studiousness to boredom to explosive activity.	Adolescents vary in opinion of school and teacher. . . . Many students concerned about college. Beginning to get part-time jobs after school and full-time jobs in the summer.
Entertainment	Infant's first activity is simple sight—then interest in toys and objects, crawling, throwing, exploring, toddling, eventually leading to the crayons and puzzles of nursery school and kindergarten.	Swimming, roller skating, climbing, swinging, bicycling, simple ball games, jigsaw puzzles. Children this age collect anything and everything. Growing interest in organized sports and activities.	Some of the same activities as in childhood but more emphasis on organized sports. Growing interest in individual sports such as tennis and golf. Countless activities after school. Movies, parties, drug use.
Friends	Children make friends easily at about age 3 and grow more social, with occasional lapses, from then on. By age 5 many children are sure of themselves and at ease with almost everyone.	Considerable quarreling among friends, but some moments of good cooperation. Children this age begin to feel the importance of peer groups. Opinion of family members may be less valued than that of peers.	Friends become almost all-important. Prefer friends to family. Dating begins. Both sexes tend to socialize with large groups of friends. First sexual experience and increasing sexual activities.
Personal growth	Children speed through the developmental stages at a dizzying pace. Growth is marked by alternating stages of equilibrium and disequilibrium.	Children go through stages of introversion and extroversion. Steadily becoming more self-assured and independent.	Important physical and psychological changes. Puberty. Extended periods of self-analysis and withdrawal give adolescents a firmer grip on themselves.

Reprinted, with permission, from *The Futurist,* published by the World Future Society, 4916 Saint Elmo Avenue, Bethesda, Maryland 20814.

TABLE 1.2   *(continued)*

Young Adulthood (18–25)	Adulthood (25–40)	Middle Age (40–65)	Retirement Years (65 and Over)
Most people have left home. Many begin their own families.	Most people are married. . . . Many divorces occur in this stage. Single people often finally get married. Married couples may choose to have children before childbearing years end.	Family size may decrease as children leave home. Parents of middle-aged people are dying. Some middle-aged couples become grandparents.	Many will be grandparents. Many may find themselves alone due to the death of a spouse. Women, especially, may spend many years alone.
Many young adults are in college; some continue education after college. Most begin working. Many unemployed or underemployed. Career choices assume special importance for some.	Some adults go back to school. Many change jobs. Married women may reenter the work force. Increased emphasis on furthering career for breadwinners, who now have growing financial responsibilities.	Most workers are at the height of their careers. This is the stage of the most power and prestige at the workplace. For many, it brings the realization that their career can go no further. Some pick second careers.	Workers begin to retire. They may travel, resume education, develop new hobbies. For women who have stayed in the home, the job continues. Income will probably shrink.
Some organized athletics. Less recreation and more entertainment. Continued drug use, especially alcohol.	Spectator sports, travel, entertaining. Many start new hobbies such as pottery, painting, or photography.	Entertaining, travel, more expensive vacations. Hobbies may develop into second careers.	Increased opportunities to travel, entertain, spend time with relatives, concentrate on avocations, do volunteer work, etc., if money and health permit.
Friends and peer groups still very important. Single men and women searching for partners. Continuing emphasis on sexual activity.	Importance of friends declines as family size increases. Adults depend less on the opinions of peers to judge themselves.	As children leave home, friends may become somewhat more important. Sexual activity may decline.	Friends and peers are dying. There is more time to spend with those that remain. Old acquaintances are renewed.
The developmental pace slows and stages become less obvious. Psychologist Erik Erikson calls this the "intimacy vs. isolation" stage—a time for testing one's identity and growing further or hiding it and stagnating.	A stage of creation and production, often accompanied by dissatisfaction with past choices and an urge to change directions in order to build a new and more solid life.	A mid-life [adjustment] may come as individuals confront their own mortality and the consequences of choices already made.	The individual comes to accept his past, his life, and the approach of death, or grows bitter and despairing.

At each stage of the life span, individuals confront new social opportunities. At the age of five, for example, we leave our mother's side and learn to relate on a formal basis to teachers, peers, and the educational system. This major event is called "the first day of school" and most of us have memories and photos of it. Sometime in late adolescence we confront the crisis of leaving the protection of our parents' home, and typically we enter the larger world of advanced study, work, and parenthood. Events such as these are intimately related to the life cycle. We cannot understand them except in the context of the lifetime as a whole—which is why we attach a different significance to leaving home, for example, at 15 years than at 45.

Most of us are aware of the pattern of events that is expected to occur over a lifetime in our own culture. Traditionally, we have related to others on the basis of age and have had consistent ideas about the appropriate times for a person to graduate from high school, marry, retire, and so on (Neugarten et al., 1965). The lengthening of the life span in the last decades of the 20th century has encouraged us to reexamine some of these ideas. For example, it is now considered appropriate to graduate from high school in one's 50s if one hasn't done so earlier—or to become a first-time parent after 35. Still, our biological capabilities, as well as our social opportunities, as defined by others, change significantly over the life cycle.

Also important is the fact that individuals differ in the chronological ages at which they enter life's stages. For example, old age can be entered in the 60s or 70s or even, for those with great energy, in the 90s, depending on the health and attitude of the older person and the attitudes of others in his or her environment. The general structure of the life span, however, is invariable. Like all other complex organisms, we begin life with spectacularly rapid growth. We expand socially as well as biologically, becoming more complicated and more equal to the task of mastering our environment. During the extended period of time we call adulthood we continue to grow in many ways, but eventually there comes a point in time at which we only stand our ground.

And then, quickly or gradually, we decline. What remains are evidences of our life in the stream of history (Buhler, 1933).

The study of the pattern of psychological development over the lifetime is relatively new. With the field in its infancy, there are many areas in which theorists' ideas clash and researchers' conclusions disagree. Nevertheless, there is accord among experts in the belief that psychological developments are intimately related to biological development or maturation. And the connection between biology and psychology is especially obvious in the earliest stages of life.

Psychologists find, for example, that we cannot easily develop feelings of autonomy and self-reliance until we can walk alone and attend to our eating and toilet needs (Erikson, 1963). And we are not neurologically prepared to do this until sometime in the second year of life. Similarly, we cannot truly attend to ethical principles until we can reason logically, on the basis of abstract principles, and most of us are not neurologically prepared to do this until adolescence (Piaget, 1972). Knowledge of the later stages of life is sketchier.

Psychologists ask questions about the many ways in which psychological development arises out of increased maturation. And increasingly their concern has extended to the latter part of human life, about which we know relatively little.

In this book, we will follow the complex variety of events, confrontations, decisions, and emotions that occur in our individual lifetimes. We will be concerned with the whole person. That is, we will deal with the internal world of consciousness and the unconscious, the external world of society and the environment, and the biological endowment of human beings.

To achieve this goal, we will utilize the different perspectives presented in this introductory chapter. Most important, we will seek to develop a way of viewing our own lives systematically, and as a whole.

SUMMARY

1. *Personal adjustment* is the process by which a person attempts to respond effectively to his or her environment and to modify aspects of the environment to suit his or her own needs. Personal adjustment involves developing traits and behavior that bring happiness and other valued goals.

2. *Psychology* is the science that investigates behavior, including thoughts, feelings, motivations, and behavior in personal relationships. The findings of psychology help us answer important questions about personal adjustment.

3. Psychologists approach personal adjustment from different perspectives. Psychologists who adhere to the *behaviorist* perspective study only behavior that can be objectively described. They believe that all behavior is learned; what affects learning are the consequences of behavior. So, for instance, when people change, it is because new behaviors have been reinforced—that is, they derived a positive outcome from their behaviors and therefore repeat them.

4. The *psychoanalytic* perspective was originated by Sigmund Freud. Important to personal adjustment are Freud's explanations of the unconscious, of the parts and processes of the personality, and of the stages of psychosexual development. Some later Freudians (or *neo-Freudians*) reinterpreted Freud's biologically based stages in social terms; that is, they found the sources of many conflicts in social relations, as opposed to inherent, sexually based tensions. Neo-Freudian Erik Erikson built upon the Freudian stages but emphasized healthy ego development. Erikson extended Freudian theory to describe psychosocial development over the life span.

5. *Existential* or *humanist* psychology emphasizes being, experience, and existence itself. The existentialist-humanist psychologist believes that people are always *becoming* and that *choice* is crucial: we are responsible for the extent to which we utilize our potential and for the meaning with which we are able to endow our lives. American humanists, such as Carl Rogers and Abraham Maslow, have emphasized growth, a positive self-concept, and self-actualization.

6. *Cognitive psychology* studies the ways people think, perceive, reason, and otherwise structure their experience of the world. Research in cognitive development (notably the work of Jean Piaget) demonstrates that children do not simply perceive reality; they construct reality from within, and the way they do so varies predictably with developmental level. Cognitive psychologists demonstrate that the ways in which we interpret our experiences affect the ways in which we cope with events. For example, research on *learned helplessness* suggests that people whose experience has taught them to believe that they have no control over events tend to give up or become depressed.

7. Personal adjustment involves a person's responses to changes over the *life span*. The life span is an established sequence of biological stages that vary somewhat from individual to individual. At each stage individuals face new challenges and confront new opportunities. Psychologists find that what constitutes appropriate personal adjustment depends on one's stage of life.

SUGGESTED READINGS

Dyer, W. (1976). *Your erroneous zones*. New York: Avon Books; Dyer, W. (1978). *Pulling your own strings*. New York: Crowell. These two popular books offer self-help advice designed to assist people in dealing with obstacles in their personal adjustment.

Frankl, V. (1984). *Man's search for meaning* (3rd ed.). New York: Touchstone Books: Simon & Schuster. A hopeful, positive overview of Frankl's humanistic approach to life and to psychotherapy.

Hall, E. (1987). *Growing and changing: What the experts say*. New York: Random House. Hall's interviews with a number of noted psychologists provide a comprehensive, easy-to-read overview of development across the life span.

Nye, R. (1986). *Three psychologies: Perspectives from Freud, Skinner, and Rogers* (3rd ed.). Monterey, CA: Brooks/Cole. An excellent overview of the contributions of three leading theoreticians.

Rogers, C. (1981). *A way of being*. Boston: Houghton Mifflin. This volume illustrates how Roger's philosophy can be applied by individuals to promote personal growth.

Skinner, B. F. (1972). *Beyond freedom and dignity*. New York: Bantam. An application of the principles of behaviorism to modern society.

Thompson, C. (1950). *Psychoanalysis: Evolution and development*. New York: Grove Press. A comprehensive review of psychoanalytic theory and therapy.

What Is the Healthy Personality?

- Intuitive definitions of psychological health that many people arrive at

- The psychoanalytic conceptions of health, which emphasize devoting one's instinctual energies to love and work and developing ego strengths

- The humanists' focus on self-actualization and on the development of a positive and realistic self-concept

- Emphasis on problem-solving skills by the cognitive psychologists, and on foreseeing the consequences of one's actions by the behaviorists

- Situations—physical handicaps, poverty, homelessness, emotional deprivation, and so on—that can hamper the achievement of psychological health

Most young adults experience a certain amount of anxiety over the question of whether they are psychologically healthy. Sometimes, in order to answer that question, they find it necessary to reexamine their beliefs about psychological health. As Ted, a sophomore in college, put it, "I began to ask myself what kind of person it is worthwhile to be."

Ted is an example of a person who set out to discover the answers for himself. When he entered college he believed that psychological health was somewhat equivalent to popularity. According to his parents, a well-adjusted teenager was one who had numerous friendships. By this standard, Ted's outgoing younger sister was considered to be extremely well-adjusted. However, Ted appeared to be one of those people who kept to himself. If he did not come out of this, his parents feared, he would have "problems." They weren't overly worried—just concerned. And the fact that Ted had two serious, solitary friends like himself did little to console them. When Ted graduated from high school, his parents sighed appreciatively over his good grades. They helped him buy a stereo and a computer to take to college, with the unhappy thought that he would probably be spending much time in his room.

At college—a state school near his home—Ted found to his surprise that he was not the "maladjusted" type his parents had led him to believe. For one thing, he discovered it was easy to make friends the way his younger sister always had. There was little he needed to do to be included in the first round of social events; indeed, it was hard to avoid them. Ted decided to treat his awkwardness at the mixers and parties with a sense of humor. People liked him for his lack of pretension. In fact, they found him remarkably easygoing.

In the college environment, Ted developed new perspectives. A lively social life no longer seemed the test of psychological fitness. It was something he could choose to explore if he wished. At the same time Ted discovered that there was more to psychological health than being popular. Being able to sustain serious, nonsuperficial relationships with men and women, being able to cope with the pressures of exams, learning to handle alcohol, and dealing with unstructured time were equally important. Finally, Ted saw that, for him, becoming a psychologically healthy person meant being able to look critically at his goals and values, and possibly change them.

DEFINING PSYCHOLOGICAL HEALTH

Intuitive Definitions

Like Ted, most people have ideas about psychological health. And at different points in their life span they experience confusion over whether or not they are healthy. It is worthwhile to examine intuitive ideas of psychological health, since these are ideas we apply to ourselves when we ask, for example: "Am I experiencing normal difficulties, or am I seriously disturbed?" "Am I growing psychologically, or simply marking time?"

According to one definition—the definition that Ted's parents applied—the best evidences of psychological health are a pleasing personality and an ability to get along with others. We use this definition when we approve a person for having friendships of high quality and for being able to love, help, or sympathize with others. By the same token it is not uncommon for us to dismiss as unhealthy—often without much thought—people who do not date, or marry, or have children; people who live solitary lives; people who cannot get along with authority figures; and so forth.

Somewhat different is the view that psychological health is related to subjective feelings of happiness and optimism about the future. For example, another college sophomore said, "Being a psychologically healthy person, for me, would be feeling happy, generally . . . feeling good about myself and looking forward to things." The healthy person, according to this view, is one who is able to enjoy life. The capacity for enjoyment is said not to depend on the actual circumstances that the person encounters. To be psychologically healthy is to have a "talent for happiness," even when things are less than perfect.

Another common definition of mental health focuses on what the person is able to accomplish, on how he or she utilizes potential or talents. Students will often set psychological goals such as: "I want to be able to succeed at things that are important—including relationships." "I want to live up to my potential as a human being." "I think it's important to be the person you were meant to be, whatever that is." One student says simply, "I want to be a success." Important to people employing this definition are issues of fulfillment and control. The healthy person is expected to impose his or her own terms on life, and to experience life to the fullest.

Another definition that sometimes emerges has to do with maturity, stability, and self-knowledge. For example, students say: "Being a healthy person to me means being able to be on my own, and be responsible for my own life and relationships. It is the opposite of being immature." Or: "Being healthy means knowing yourself and understanding your past." These students view mental health as an achievement of the adult personality, that is, as a successful outcome of all formative experiences from childhood throughout adolescence.

Equally important are those definitions that at first seem to be less positive, in that they take account of life's difficulties. For example, a middle-aged mother of three who has returned to school said: "Being a healthy person means being able to adjust to things—no matter what life hands you—without breaking." According to her, the healthy person is one who is able to savor life—experience its joys and learn from its sorrows—without losing his or her psychological balance.

And finally there is the clinical definition, which many people arrive at intuitively. To be healthy, according to this definition, is to be free of psychological symptoms and unimpaired by emotional conflicts. Thus to one student being healthy would mean being free from anxiety attacks that occur before exams and interviews. To another it might mean overcoming obesity and feelings of inferiority. The clinical definition, as the term suggests, is based on a medical model of health—a model that identifies symptoms of "illness" and emphasizes the need for a healthy, well-functioning system.

Most of us utilize one or more of these intuitive definitions as we set personal goals. (Who, for example, has not initiated some project with the thought that it will result in the fuller realization of talent or potential? Who has not at some point wished to be free from symptoms of emotional suffering?) Still, intuitive definitions are not sufficient. Psychological health is an important goal—for individuals and for society—and attempts have been made to develop more scientific definitions.

Psychological Definitions

Before examining the conceptions that have emerged in modern psychology, we must note the problems that are involved in formulating a definition of psychological health that will have meaning to people in diverse circumstances.

The first and most important point is that terms like "psychological health" or "healthy personality" cannot be precisely or scientifically defined. While there are certain scientific elements involved in defining these concepts (for example, psychologists use personality assessment tests and other objective measures), our conception of psychological health is necessarily entangled with values. The term "health" is used to describe what we find good, virtuous, or desirable in human existence. Thus, if creativity is valued, the realization of creative potential becomes part of a definition of psychological health. If what is valued is an existence free from symptoms, this becomes a criterion. But there is considerable room for disagreement between people, families, groups, and cultures. As Lazarus has pointed out (1975, pp. 6–34), we should not use terms like "health" or "pathology" to disguise the fact that we are assigning values. We should only choose a definition of health that is based on the best scientific evidence about whether the characteristics described work to the best advantage of people in our culture.

In this chapter we will explain the major conceptions of psychological health that have been proposed by modern psychology. These conceptions are based on the best evidence we have, but they are neither strictly scientific nor universal. They naturally reflect Western and American values about what is good and bad, desirable and undesirable, in human existence. Thus most of the definitions emphasize autonomy, creativity, productivity, and competence in dealing with the environment. Fatalistic or conformist traits are not so often mentioned. We do not describe as healthy the person who submits to fate, poverty, or witches; or the person who feels compelled to do what a leader or neighbor does. Moreover, psychologists have not, until recently, emphasized the ability to retreat into the self, to meditate or monitor one's own physiological functions. Our definitions of health are directed at mastering the environment. They are biased in favor of the objective world. We value rational problem-solving abilities and realistic perceptions. And most of the traits that will be described operate to advance the fortunes of the individual.

There is nothing universal about our Western definitions of modern health. In some cultures, very different values are emphasized. For example, in contemporary China, conformity and contribution to the group are viewed as the ideal. Autonomy and insistence on individual modes of expression are seen as evidence of instability (Abel & Metraux, 1974). Similarly, among some Eskimo cultures the person who expresses himself spontaneously and individualistically is considered a show-off, a nonsurvivor (Coles, 1977). Definitions of psychological health are always value laden: they reflect cultural assumptions and cultural differences. People who develop such definitions support them with scientific evidence about what works best for individuals in their culture, and for the survival of the culture as a whole. The psychological definitions used in our culture, like all such definitions, must be understood in these terms.

PSYCHOANALYTIC CONCEPTIONS OF PSYCHOLOGICAL HEALTH

Freud: "To Love and To Work"

When Freud was asked what a healthy person should be able to do, he answered, "*Lieben und arbeiten*"—to love and to work. The answer has become famous for its brevity and precision. Psychologists of many traditions agree that the healthy person is in some sense productive, and that he is able to love somebody other than himself.

In his theoretical writings, Freud did not have a great deal to say about the way in which individuals developed these healthy capacities. Freud's interest lay in those conflicts that held people back: the conflicts that brought patients to his office with a history of failed relationships and blocked potential. Freud came to believe that many of these conflicts were also experienced by people who did not fit into the category of "patients." Human beings are *by nature* neurotic, or subject to inner conflicts, he said.

Many critics have felt that Freud's vision of man leaves little room for the healthy person. A common objection is that Freud dwelt too much on the darker and irrational forces in human life. Perhaps one reason for his doing so was that he believed that healthy people confronted life on the level of reality, without illusions. One could not be healthy if one did not acknowledge and

Many still agree with Sigmund
Freud's definition of
psychological health as an
ability "to love and to work,"
and also with his idea that
energy generated through inner
conflicts can be channeled into
playfulness, humor, and other
positive modes of expression.

deal with the primitive demands of the id, as well as the undisguised brutality
of other people. (Freud, it is worth noting, worked in Austria during World
War I and in his 80s was forced to relocate to England, as a result of Nazi
harassment.) The acknowledgement of basic pain, fantasy, and conflict was
necessary, Freud found, if one were both to savor and to tolerate life (Schur,
1972; Gay, 1988).

In the vocabulary of Freudian theory, psychological health implies ego
(reality) domination; harmony or integration between the three personality
components and the attainment of mature or genital sexuality. A famous line
that sums up Freud's psychoanalytic position is: "Where id is, let ego be."
Here Freud emphasized the importance of reality and rationality over impulses and instincts. Given the nature of civilization, health depends on the
ability of the id to tolerate frustration of at least some of its needs. Finally,
psychological health is immeasurably aided by the capacity for **sublimation,**
which Freud defined as the satisfaction of instinctual id goals in some socially
appropriate or valuable manner (for example, through work). According to
Freud, the healthy person is not untroubled. But he or she is able to effectively
control and release instinctual energies, thereby "recycling" some of the energy
generated by inner conflicts. As a result, he or she retains in the personality
an "animal vigor and *joie de vivre*" (Vaillant, 1977).

Erikson: Ego Strengths

Erik Erikson has described the healthy person in terms of **ego strengths** that
emerge at different stages in the life span, under favorable personal and cultural conditions. To Erikson, being healthy means having experienced a favorable outcome in the struggle between the healthy ("adaptive") and
unhealthy ("inhibiting") qualities of human existence. For example, being a
healthy person in young adulthood means that one has struggled with "intimacy versus isolation" and has achieved a dynamic balance in favor of intimacy. It means that one has developed (as a result of the struggle) the ego
strength that Erikson calls *love;* that one is ready to turn to the challenge of

Sublimation
In psychoanalytic theory, the
defense mechanism by which
instinctual (id) goals are
satisfied in some socially
appropriate or valuable
manner.

Ego Strengths
As defined by Erik Erikson, the
favorable outcomes that emerge
at different stages in the life
span when a person wins the
struggle between healthy and
unhealthy qualities of human
existence.

The Search for Personal Adjustment

TABLE 2.1   *Erikson: Ego Strengths of the Healthy Person*

Infancy	*Hope,* the enduring belief in the attainability of primal wishes in spite of the dark urges and rages that mark the beginning of existence.
Early Childhood	*Will,* the unbroken determination to exercise free choice as well as self-control, despite early experiences of shame and self-doubt caused by uncontrolled willfulness and despite rage over being controlled.
Play Age	*Purpose* (or purposefulness), the courage to playfully imagine and energetically pursue valued goals, uninhibited by the defeat of infantile fantasies, by the guilt they aroused, and by the punishment they elicited.
School Age	*Competence,* the free exercise of dexterity and intelligence in the completion of tasks, unimpaired by infantile inferiority.
Adolescence	*Fidelity,* the ability to sustain loyalties freely pledged, in spite of the inevitable contradictions and confusions of value systems.
Young Adulthood	*Love,* the mutuality of devotion forever subduing the antagonisms inherent in opposing forces (e.g., the hostilities caused by the oppositeness of male and female, the struggle between love and hate).
Maturity	*Care,* the widening concern for what has been generated by love, necessity, or accident; it overcomes the mixed feelings arising from obligations that cannot now be reversed.
Old Age	*Wisdom,* the detached and yet active concern with life in the face of death itself; wisdom maintains the integrity of experience, in spite of the decline of bodily and mental functions.

Adapted from *Childhood and Society,* Second Edition, by Erik H. Erikson, by permission of W. W. Norton & Company, Inc. Copyright 1950, © 1963 by W. W. Norton & Company, Inc. Copyright renewed 1978 by Erik H. Erikson and reprinted by permission of *Daedalus,* Journal of the American Academy of Arts and Science, "Adulthood," Spring 1976, Vol. 105, No. 2, Cambridge, Massachusetts.

caring for new generations. If a person falls short of psychological health at this stage, this is often because he or she has achieved an unfavorable balance in one of the earlier conflicts. For example, a child may emerge from the school years with predominating feelings of inferiority, and thus be unable to proceed in finding the adolescent identity that is the precondition for mature love.

Psychological health at any stage of life means a *favorable balance*—not a complete psychological victory—over the dark side of human existence. For example, Erikson sees "fidelity," the ego strength that emerges from the struggles of adolescence, as "the ability to sustain loyalties freely pledged *in spite of* the inevitable contradictions and confusions of value systems" (Erikson, 1976, italics added). The well-adjusted person is not spared the confusion. He or she develops the strength to deal with it in adolescence and throughout the life span. However, some critics have suggested that Erikson's stages reflect a middle class orientation and are not applicable across all classes in society. In addition, like Freudian theory, it is not supported by a strong foundation of empirical research (Hall & Lindzey, 1978). Yet this does not diminish the scope of Erikson's contributions in understanding the healthy personality.

In Table 2.1 we can see the ego strengths that emerge in the healthy person at different stages in the life span. It is important to note that what is psychologically healthy at one stage is not necessarily healthy at another.

Age-Appropriate Behaviors: Your View

What is psychologically healthy at one stage of life is not necessarily healthy at another. Below is an opportunity to see if you ordinarily take into account a person's age or life stage when you respond to his behavior. Read each description, try to imagine the person described at the ages listed, and write down your reaction. Do your responses differ, depending on the age of the people described?

1. Jennifer spends a good part of each morning talking to Ramona. She tells her everything that is planned for the day, being especially careful to explain anything that is out of the ordinary. Jennifer takes the time to describe interesting things in the environment to Ramona because she cannot see. Ramona can't be seen either. Ramona is an invisible playmate.

   Your Reaction

   Jennifer is 4 years old _____

   Jennifer is 24 years old _____

   Jennifer is 64 years old _____

2. Although she is not ill, Ellie is preoccupied with death. She has taken to making notes about who will have her things when she is gone. She is less interested than ever in going out, and prefers to spend her time listening to talk shows and reading the Bible and other books that she finds inspiring.

   Your Reaction

   Ellie is 15 years old _____

   Ellie is 45 years old _____

   Ellie is 85 years old _____

3. Phil is convinced that his unhappy social life is the result of his awful appearance. He spends hours contemplating his too-large ears, and reading books that tell him how to put on weight and develop his muscles. When he is with a group of people he is eager and happy—until he remembers the way that other people must see him. Then, unless people make a special effort to include him, he becomes quiet.

   Your Reaction

   Phil is 14 years old _____

   Phil is 24 years old _____

   Phil is 44 years old _____

Moreover, in order to treat adjustment difficulties, we must agree on what it means to be psychologically healthy at various stages of the life cycle, from infancy to old age. It is essential that we distinguish between behaviors that are considered age or stage appropriate and behaviors that may reflect problems in adjustment. Behaviors considered normal at one stage of development may be viewed as problematic at an earlier or later stage.

4. Willison is intensely devoted to the corporation. He works overtime every night and studies company documents over the weekend. He has decided that for now he cannot consider any time-consuming social engagements or relationships. His social life consists only of business lunches and drinks with colleagues after work. Willison reads everything published in his business area, and little else. His main hope (aside from rapid advancement) is that the corporation will try out some of his new ideas on physical distribution. If this happens, Willison is sure that his future will be "made."

Your Reaction

Willison is 26 years old _____

Willison is 56 years old _____

5. Bonnie feels that she would like to have a baby. She sees herself holding an infant who coos and smiles up at her. She imagines the child as a little girl whom she can dress in a pinafore and sandals. She thinks of taking her baby on a picnic, or to the new shopping mall in a foldable stroller. Later she will give her ballet lessons. Bonnie thinks that having a baby will make her happier. She imagines the baby as being very loving to her.

Your Reaction

Bonnie is 15 years old _____

Bonnie is 25 years old _____

Bonnie is 40 years old _____

6. Jane knows her own mind about most things and is seldom influenced by anyone else's opinion. She is especially well informed about her own strengths and limitations. While not exactly rejecting new experiences (she did *try* skiing), she tends to stick with familiar activities, and one or two good friends. Jane has neither the time nor the money to pursue a degree, so perhaps she will take a course in oil painting. It is an art she might take seriously, if she had a real talent. At any rate, she tells herself, a course might bring her in contact with some first-rate artists, which would be truly stimulating.

Your Reaction

Jane is 21 years old _____

Jane is 51 years old _____

For example, the identity crisis, with its favorable outcome of "fidelity," is associated with adolescence. A person who was involved in the seemingly endless psychological ponderings that we call "trying to find oneself" would not be regarded as unhealthy if this behavior occurred within this period of life. Those that understand adolescence would be understanding even if the person held four jobs in a year, traveled aimlessly with different companions, and experimented with alcohol. Such behavior might be part of a "moratorium" (during which the young person explored life options and decided what he or she would be faithful to). If the same behavior occurred in the person's late 30s, after 10 years of family and occupational commitment, it would have a different significance. Similarly, in an interesting study, investigators (Lieberman & Tobin, 1983) found that some attitudes and behaviors viewed as harmful during one's youth, may prove the most beneficial in old age. These authors found that people who are "a bit grumpy," obstinate, and who are willing to stick up, even fight, for their rights, tended to live longer. They did not suppress or swallow their feelings and remained feisty to a ripe old age.

As a middle-aged man, Erikson became the first psychoanalytic writer to describe the developmental crises of maturity and old age. His description of the last two psychological stages (in which we spend the greater part of our lives) presents ideas of what we might grow up to be.

Generativity
As defined by Erik Erikson, a caring and sense of responsibility for other people that arises in the healthy adult.

According to Erikson, concern for one's own identity broadens in adulthood to **generativity,** the care and responsibility for another person—and ultimately for the next generations and the society they will inherit. This acceptance of the responsibility for perpetuating what is constructive in one's life and culture, and for improving what is not, is characteristic of the healthy adult. Generativity is likely to lead to a favorable outcome in old age—which is, in effect, a favorable outcome of the entire life cycle.

In old age we face death and the fact of having lived, for better or worse, our one and only life cycle. If we have developed the ego strengths of the earlier stages, we will feel that we have dealt with life in the way that was best and necessary. We will be able to overcome (though not entirely vanquish) the despair that results from a short and uncertain future.

In old age, the healthy person looks back and realizes that something of himself will live on through his offspring and his accomplishments:

> Only in him who in some way has taken care of things and people and who has adapted himself to the triumphs and disappointments adherent to being, the originator of others or the generator of products and ideas—only in him may gradually ripen the fruit of these seven [earlier] stages—I know no better word for it than ego integrity (Erikson, 1963, p. 268).

HUMANIST CONCEPTIONS OF PSYCHOLOGICAL HEALTH

Maslow: The Self-Actualizing Person

Perhaps the most comprehensive model of the healthy adult personality was developed by Abraham Maslow in the 1960s. Maslow apparently suffered a lonely and unhappy childhood, only to find himself much strengthened by the events of young adulthood, in particular the birth of his child and his relationships with several outstanding teachers (Schultz, 1976). Increasingly, he became impatient with psychology's emphasis on illness and on the destructive aftermath of early experience. His interest drew him to the study of the healthy personality. He wrote that "it is reasonable to assume in practically every human being, and certainly in every newborn baby, that there is an active will toward health, an impulse toward growth, or toward the actualization of human potential" (Maslow, 1967).

Maslow became committed to the idea of self-actualization. He wanted to know what the prerequisites were for reaching this very desirable level of health. What did the individual need in order to achieve it, and under what circumstances did he or she succeed? As a result of his investigation, Maslow identified a **hierarchy of needs** that must be satisfied, one by one, if the individual is to come near attaining his or her full potential.

Hierarchy of Needs

Maslow's hierarchy begins at the most basic level of physiological need (the level at which the individual is motivated to find food and water) and builds toward the level of self-actualization (at which the individual can afford to pursue truth, justice, beauty, and other higher needs). Five levels of needs are identified. They are: (1) *physiological needs*—food, sleep, sex, sensory stimulation, and other requirements of the body and nervous system; (2) *safety needs*—removal of environmental threats, assurance of order and predictability in the environment; (3) *belongingness and love needs*—affection from others, membership in groups, friendship, love; (4) *esteem needs*—recognition and appreciation from others of what one can do, leading to confidence in one's own abilities and independence; and (5) *self-actualization needs*—being all one can be, realizing one's unique capacities.

The arrangement of needs in this hierarchical order (see Figure 2.1) reflects the fact that we cannot attend to our higher needs until our lower needs have been met. For example, a young man may be unable to perform confidently in his life's work (so as to meet esteem needs) because his social insecurities alienate him from colleagues and others (as a result of unmet love needs).

Maslow describes the first four levels of needs as **deprivation needs.** They stem from our *lack* of something, as the need for food stems from a lack of nutrients in the body, or the need for competence stems from a lack of mastery over the tasks of life. The self-actualization needs, on the other hand, are not caused by any lack. Rather, they arise in the effort to *be*—to actualize the potential that each person has for being and doing what no one else can be and do.

Self-Actualizing People

In the course of defining self-actualization, Maslow studied the lives and personalities of eminently successful people. (The living subjects, never revealed, probably included some of Maslow's teachers; and the historical subjects included people like Thomas Jefferson, Abraham Lincoln, Walt Whitman, Albert Einstein, and Eleanor Roosevelt.) It was with this unique sample that Maslow was able to document the importance of higher needs. His subjects, having

Hierarchy of Needs
Abraham Maslow's conception of five levels of needs, in which each succeeding need must be satisfied before an individual can go on to the next higher level.

Deprivation Needs
The lowest four levels of Abraham Maslow's hierarchy of needs, each of which is pursued because of some lack in a person's life.

Figure 2.1 Maslow's hierarchy of needs.

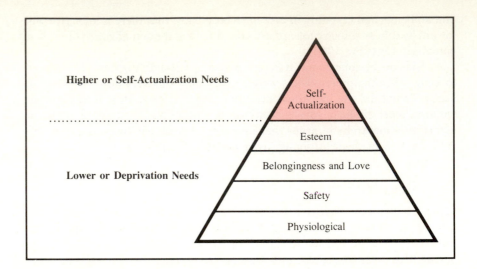

Margaret Mead, the eminent anthropologist, had many characteristics of "the self-actualized person," including creativity, independence, an ability to view reality without personal bias, and a deep concern over the threats facing humanity.

moved through the lower stages of human need, came to be motivated by the supreme need to satisfy their potential. Maslow estimated that only about 1 percent of the population ever reaches this level of functioning—the peak of the pyramid in Figure 2.1. Naturally he was interested in knowing what these people were really like.

The characteristics that Maslow identified give us a basic sketch of the self-actualizing adult, as compared to the rest of the human population (Maslow, 1954, 1970, 1987).

1. Self-actualizers have a superior perception of reality.
2. They show greater acceptance of self, of others, and of nature.
3. They are more spontaneous in their behavior.
4. They are problem-centered rather than self-centered. (That is, they can be interested in problems outside themselves and their own lives.)
5. They show greater detachment and desire for privacy.
6. They are more autonomous and independent than others.
7. They show greater freshness of appreciation of things and people; their emotional reactions tend to be rich rather than stereotyped.
8. There is a greater likelihood of their having had "peak experiences," mystical and sometimes religious experiences that involved profound bliss or self-transcendence.
9. They are able to identify more strongly with humankind; that is, they are capable of greater empathy and understanding.
10. They show a different pattern of interpersonal relationships. For example, they tend to have a few deep, intimate, and enduring relationships rather than many superficial ones.
11. They have a more democratic character structure. That is, they do not need to maintain postures of superiority toward others; they are able to respect and tolerate differences among people.

12. They show certain differences in value systems. For example, they can more clearly discriminate right from wrong and are less likely to compromise their standards out of self-interest or personal need.
13. They have a thoughtful or philosophical sense of humor, as opposed to a hostile sense of humor.
14. They show more "creativeness" than others. (To Maslow creativeness involves having access to one's full imaginative and inventive powers—not simply or necessarily engaging in some "creative" activity.)
15. They resist enculturation. That is, they tend not to be conformists; they stand their own ground when an issue is important.

From this summary, a general picture emerges—and most people in our culture will find it an attractive one. Fully healthy, self-actualizing people have an exceptional ability to see things as they really are. They are less prone than others to indulge in wishful thinking, to believe false claims of others, or to take self-serving attitudes seriously. And if self-actualizers are seldom deceived, neither are they likely to be disappointed by the realities they recognize. They accept themselves and others, neither fussing over nor ignoring faults.

Maslow found that self-actualizers are invariably devoted to their work, regarding it as a thing of importance for the world and a personal mission for themselves. They concentrate intensely on their work, often in solitude, and sometimes seem absentminded or detached from other matters as a result. Yet "work tends to be the same as play: vocation and avocation become the same thing. When duty is pleasant and pleasure is fulfillment of duty, then they lose their separateness and oppositeness" (Maslow, 1968, p. 207).

From this description one might think that the state of self-actualization, of being fully healthy, must be pure happiness. But Maslow and other humanists are quick to point out that it is not a finished stage at all. Rather, it is a constant *becoming,* a lifelong growth process. The self-actualizer has needs that he or she is working to fulfill. But these needs are meta-needs, or higher needs, such as the needs for truth and goodness; for justice, order, and meaningfulness in life (see Table 2.2). As the table shows, frustration of these meta-needs (for example, by the environment) may lead to a number of negative results and pose new challenges to the self-actualizing person. The nature of self-actualization needs is that they are never wholly satisfied; health lies in being free to work toward them.

Maslow also emphasizes that growth toward self-actualization is strenuous, frightening, disruptive, and demanding. "Each step forward," he writes, "is a step into the unfamiliar and is possibly dangerous" (Maslow, 1968, p. 204). We may have to leave some real satisfactions behind in order to grow, and in some cases growth may even mean separation from someone with whom we are quite comfortable. Yet, Maslow believes, we would all choose growth if we had the strength, the courage, and the supportive environment—for growth epitomizes human nature in full health.

TABLE 2.2   *Maslow: Meta-Needs That Motivate the Self-Actualizing Person*

The Need	Possible Results When the Need is Regularly Frustrated
Truth	Mistrust, cynicism, skepticism
Goodness	Hatred, repulsion, disgust, reliance only on self and for self
Beauty	Vulgarity, restlessness, loss of taste, bleakness
Unity, wholeness	Disintegration
Aliveness, sense of life as a continuing process	Deadness, "robotizing," feeling oneself to be totally determined by the past, loss of emotion and zest in life, feeling of emptiness
Justice	Anger, cynicism, mistrust, lawlessness, total selfishness
Simplicity	Sense of overcomplexity, confusion, bewilderment, loss of orientation
Richness, totality, comprehensiveness	Depression, uneasiness, loss of interest in the world
Playfulness	Grimness, depression, paranoid humorlessness, loss of zest in life, cheerlessness
Meaningfulness	Meaninglessness, despair, feeling that life is senseless

A critical appraisal of Maslow's theory reveals several problems, particularly its inspirational rather than scientific emphasis. Moreover, several theorists are not inclined to accept Maslow's basic premise of an active will toward health. In spite of these criticisms, Maslow's viewpoints are enormously attractive and popular with many psychologists (Hall & Lindzey, 1978).

Rogers: The Healthy Self-Concept

Rogers, like Maslow, describes a continuous process of growth or actualization. However, he emphasizes the self-concept—the way we come to regard ourselves and our experiences. When our self-concept is an accurate reflection of our experiences—when we are open, aware, and accepting of all feelings—then we are healthy (or "fully functioning"). There is a good fit, or congruence, between what we want to become and what we actually are.

According to Rogers, the self-concept emerges in infancy as the person begins to identify experiences that belong to "me," "I," or "myself." The self-concept develops as the baby befriends his toes, watches himself in the mirror, and finally pushes the mother away with words like "Me do."

If the infant is accepted exactly as he is—if he experiences what Rogers calls "unconditional positive regard" from parents—he develops into a person with feelings of self-worth. He or she is confident that all thoughts, feelings,

Personal Limitations, or "Nobody's Perfect"

Many psychologists have observed that the psychologically healthy person is able to accept himself (and others) in spite of his (or their) limitations. The healthy person neither ignores his or her faults nor becomes overwhelmed by them.

Suppose for a moment that you achieved your personal goals for psychological health. You would not have become a Perfect Person, would you? Chances are you would have some faults or limitations that you and others can accept.

1. List the faults or limitations that you would be willing to accept in yourself, under the most favorable conditions.
2. If possible, say why you believe these faults or limitations would not interfere with the attainment of psychological health. ▲

and behaviors belong to the self, and that they will be valued and respected by others. Sometimes, however, parents attach **conditions of worth:** that is, they value the child only insofar as he or she behaves in approved ways. For example, parents may refuse to recognize angry feelings, such as children sometimes harbor toward a younger sibling. Or they make it clear that they value the child because of his high grades. In such instances the child responds by trying to be the person that parents and others expect him to be. The child excludes some experiences from his self-concept because they seem unworthy: he denies to himself and others that certain feelings exist, and relates to life defensively. (The child who is valued chiefly for excelling may say "*I can't* play on the little league team because I'm not a star. If I make an error or strike out, I'm no good.") The result is the opposite of psychological health— a defensive, rigid, anxious response to at least some of life's opportunities.

Rogers believes that the *fully functioning* or healthy person is able to accept changes without feeling threatened. The self-concept, because it accurately reflects experiences and always has, is able to incorporate new and unexpected experiences. The person is able to grow. Moreover, he or she is secure enough to help other people grow. As a therapist, parent, or friend— or in some other role—the healthy person can promote the growth of others by helping them to achieve their potential in the context of a warm and caring relationship. Rogers observes that a large part of human health is "the ability to respect and like someone as a separate person, a willingness to let him possess his feelings his own way." The healthy person is able to give, because he has received unconditional positive regard.

Conditions of Worth
In Carl Rogers' terms, conditions that parents impose on the child whereby the child is valued only when he or she behaves in approved ways.

IDEAS FROM BEHAVIORISM

Behaviorists refuse to speculate about states of mind and characteristics of the personality. To the behaviorist it makes no sense to say that a person is angry—only that he or she engaged in a certain observable behavior, such as ripping up a term paper that received a "C" grade. Similarly, it is meaningless to say that a person is "psychologically healthy" or has highly valued characteristics. The behaviorist is more interested in whether or not a person's behavior represents a successful adaptation to his social and physical environment.

The question naturally arises: What is meant by a successful adaptation? In general behaviorists consider adaptive behaviors to be those that show an awareness of the consequences of one's actions, as these actions affect survival or the achievement of goals (Skinner, 1971). For example, the alcoholic student is probably not successful because his need for immediate escape or stimulation interferes with long-term physical health, as well as with other self-defined goals in work and relationships. The parent who administers harsh or inconsistent actions is also unsuccessful because the result of these actions (the behaviorist shows) will be more undesirable behavior from the child. In these examples, being successful would involve foreseeing the consequences of one's behaviors, and exercising self-control. Indeed, self-control is what much behaviorist therapy aims for. Programs in weight reduction, quitting smoking, and assertiveness training are structured to teach the person to identify and avoid behaviors that bring about negative consequences in his or her particular environment.

Researchers are finding that the sense of being in control and the desire to exercise self-control are crucial aspects of psychological health. In a recent study (Rudin, 1986), learned that increasing the sense of control among residents of nursing homes made them happier, increased their alertness, and significantly lowered their mortality. The increased control was brought about by simple changes, such as allowing the residents to plan their own meals and rearrange their furniture. This helped to undo the regimented existence of a nursing home, and fostered a feeling of self-control and autonomy.

Although behaviorists have specified ways in which individuals can adapt more successfully to specific physical and social environments, their theoretical interest is in controlling the environment itself. In a sense they are more interested in the healthy society than in the healthy person. The behaviorist seeks to determine which kinds of societies would enable us to attain our ideals of human development (Skinner, 1971). They ask: What kind of society would consistently produce (by rewarding) those behaviors that we agree are constructive, or valuable to survival? And which would eliminate (by, for instance, consistently punishing rather than inadvertently rewarding) the behaviors that lead to unwanted consequences, such as poverty, involuntary unemployment, waste of talent, pollution, escalating weaponry, and war? Skinner and other behaviorists have argued that the ultimate use of a science of behavior is to provide the knowledge needed for the design of a new society (Skinner, 1948, 1953).

The Search for Personal Adjustment

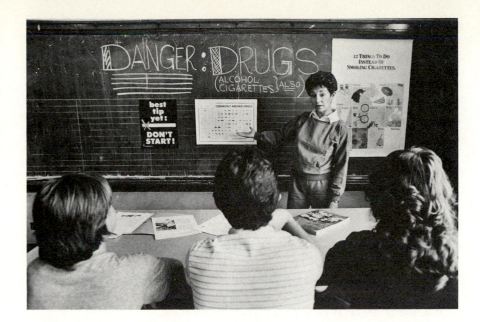

Many habit-control programs have a behaviorist orientation. Rather than investigate the causes of the problem, they teach people to change overt behavior.

IDEAS FROM COGNITIVE PSYCHOLOGY

A logical extension of behaviorism has been the emergence of cognitive psychology (Bandura, 1977; Mischel, 1973). To the cognitive psychologist, health depends, at least in part, on the way the individual interprets or evaluates events in the environment. Advocating a cognitive social learning approach, these investigators believe that an increased sense of self-efficacy serves to enhance our physical and psychological well-being. From the field of health psychology, several recent studies on hardiness, depression, stress, and susceptibility to illness all point in this direction (Bloom, 1988; Sagan, 1988).

The healthy person is one who interprets a threatening event in a way that enables him or her to maintain hope and use appropriate problem-solving skills. For example, before a stressful interview the healthy person seeks advice or rehearses possible questions with a friend. When faced with an operation, he or she learns all there is to know about outcomes (if this reduces worries) or leaves all details in the hands of a trusted doctor (if that works better).

When direct action is not possible—when little can be done to master the environment—the healthy person engages in cognitive strategies that, quite simply, make him or her feel better (Lazarus, 1966, 1979). For example, the person minimizes the danger, and reinterprets the situation as a challenge rather than a threat. Unable to change his situation, the healthy person changes his way of thinking about it, without significant distortion (Ellis, 1984).

In sum, the healthy or successful person is one who deals adequately with normal psychological stress, through active problem-solving or through cognitive strategies that allow him or her to live more comfortably with whatever threats are encountered. The unsuccessful or unhealthy person is one who feels helpless and is, in fact, unable to respond effectively to the demands of the environment (Meichenbaum, 1977; Beck, 1976).

POSITIVE MENTAL HEALTH: A SYNTHESIS

As we have seen, positive mental health is a quality of life that has been variously interpreted by psychologists (some of whom reject the concept of "health" altogether). And yet there emerges some rough consensus—some feeling for what a healthy person must be. The "superior perception of reality" discovered by Maslow is related to the domination of ego functions identified by the psychoanalysts. The college student's remark "She's together" may not mean the same thing as Erikson's "integrity," but it recognizes some of the same qualities in individuals. There appears to be a cluster of characteristics that most of us expect to find in a healthy person—and hope to find in ourselves.

Marie Jahoda has reviewed the varied conceptions of the psychologically healthy person—including many conceptions not treated here—and has given us a synthesis of important ideas (Jahoda, 1958):

1. Healthy people have positive attitudes toward themselves. They feel that in balance their "self" is good, capable, and strong. They have a sense of personal identity and know themselves.

2. They are characterized by continual growth, development, and self-actualization. Psychologists of many traditions emphasize the healthy person's need to realize his potential, to engage himself in life to the fullest extent permitted by his basic endowment.

3. Healthy people are "integrated"; they achieve a basic harmony, or coherence, of personality.

4. Healthy people are autonomous. They respect their own standards, make their own decisions, and act on them. (They decide which factors in the environment they wish to accept and reject.)

5. Healthy people perceive the world accurately, or in such a way as to permit efficient interaction with the environment. They are relatively free from need distortion (i.e., a distortion of their world view stemming from their own needs) and are able to differentiate between what fits their wishes and conceptions and what does not. In particular, they are able to perceive other people with sensitivity.

6. Healthy people achieve mastery over their environments. In specific areas of human functioning this amounts to: an ability to love; adequacy in work and play; adequacy in interpersonal relationships; and the ability to solve problems and adapt to change.

Jahoda, it should be noted, is reviewing the criteria for *adult* mental health. True, some qualities mentioned are potentially expressed at all stages of the life span. Self-confidence, for example, is certainly an attitude that is sensed in the happy toddler; maybe it characterizes healthy people at all stages of life. (Often, perhaps, it is somewhat less in evidence during adolescence and

old age.) But what about the ability to perceive other people and their needs accurately? Healthy toddlers are by no means able to do this. They see everything in relation to themselves. A three-year-old girl says, for example, that the rain falls because she and her parents want it to so that their lawn will grow.

A similar point might be made about autonomy. The infant begins to assert autonomy as he or she struggles from the parent's careful grasp and takes those first steps. However, autonomy in Jahoda's fullest sense—"the regulation of behavior from within, according to internal standards"—is not an option for children. The internalized standards of children are not yet developed enough to enable them to regulate their behavior in this way, and children are not able to make decisions about issues of value. Autonomy (as Erikson recognized) begins to be achieved in toddlerhood, but this limited autonomy is not what is expected of the healthy adult. It may be that real autonomy from other people's opinions and values is not achieved until middle adulthood.

Psychological Health: A Personal Application

If you should apply for a very desirable position in graduate school, business, or government, you may hear that grades or credentials are not enough. The university or employer is looking for people who are "well-rounded" or "well-adjusted"—in other words, psychologically healthy.

Assume for a moment that you are applying for such a position. Assume too that the person who processes your application and interviews you holds a view of psychological health that is consistent with Jahoda's synthesis. You have already demonstrated your positive self-concept by a well-groomed appearance, a confident manner, and a positive attitude toward past accomplishments. How will you convince the interviewer that you have other qualities associated with psychological health?

1. Below is an opportunity to describe yourself as a psychologically healthy person. With the interview situation in mind, provide one or two sentences to support each of the following propositions.

   a. You have a need to realize your full potential.
   b. You are independent (autonomous), a self-starter, and able to make your own decisions.
   c. You perceive people with sensitivity; you work well with people.
   d. You are able to solve problems and adapt to change.

2. Which of the above statements, if any, were difficult to support? On which point did you feel that you could be most convincing? ▲

In sum, Jahoda's synthesis gives us a good working description of psychological health in adulthood, the mature life stage toward which most people aspire. However, the qualities she describes are not always relevant to the healthy person in the earlier life stages.

OBSTACLES TO THE PURSUIT OF PSYCHOLOGICAL HEALTH

When people develop ideas about psychological health, they tend to look about to see how their ideas apply to others. Many students take a new look at their parents. They ask, Has my father been able to achieve spontaneity? Is he able to form intimate relationships? Has my mother fully developed her potential? Does she accept herself and others? And so forth. Sometimes the questions lead to new questions.

Paula, for example, always wondered why her father had never developed the creative side she occasionally glimpsed in him. He was quick in his appreciation of her own efforts in dramatics and was even surprisingly keen in his criticism. But he had never been involved in the theater and almost never chose to express his emotions, artistically or otherwise. Moreover, he seemed unable to play wholeheartedly with his many grandchildren.

When Paula asked him why he had never "learned to play" or developed his creative talents in some extracurricular way, he said he didn't know. But Paula's mother did. She said, "Your father was always too busy being poor, black, and out of work. In the years after the plant closed, there were nights when we didn't know if we'd have food for the table. *You* go on and be the playwright or actress or whatever it is. Lord willing."

As the youngest child in a large family, Paula had heard, and heard again, of the devastating poverty of her parents' early years. But she had never connected it with her father's shortcomings. She knew from her reading that some people can survive hardship and poverty and emerge as fully healthy and creative, even self-actualizing. Yet it would clearly be more difficult to do so—to become a dramatist, for example—if one were in desperate need of a job to feed one's family. And it would be especially difficult if one were systematically denied opportunities on grounds of race. Paula concluded that not everyone has the same chance to attain what his or her culture defines as psychological health.

In class discussions, students like Paula discover that there are many obstacles or handicaps to achieving positive psychological health. In some cases social obstacles interfere with the development of self-esteem, autonomy, or full expression of talent and potential. In other cases, the person's attempt to adapt to a stressful environment produces traits that society defines as unhealthy. For example, Paula had observed that some people who grew up in her parents' old neighborhood lacked self-esteem, were depressed, or were alcoholic. Unfavorable circumstances can make self-actualization and other psychological health goals more difficult to achieve, while at the same time increasing the risk of psychological impairment.

Following we will discuss three kinds of obstacles to psychological growth: physical handicap, poverty, and emotional deprivation and abuse.

Physical Disabilities

Nearly everyone can point to some physical trait which, to his or her mind, makes adjustment more difficult. In most cases the problem is minor and involves appearance only: a person may feel inferior, at different points in the life span, because he or she is too short or too tall, too large-boned or flat-chested, or otherwise not in conformity with the ideal physical type in society. Much less common, and generally more serious, are those disabilities which we refer to as "handicaps." Among these are birth defects of the face, such as harelip or a deformed nose or jaw; limb deformities, such as occur in cerebral palsy; and sensory disabilities, such as partial or complete blindness or deafness. Less visible conditions, such as diabetes and hemophilia, may also be experienced as handicaps.

Effects of a Handicap

Each physical disability or handicap presents special problems to the individual. Deafness, for example, handicaps the child in his efforts to establish communication and, subsequently, in social relationships. A deformed leg has the rather different effect of inhibiting the child's ability to explore his environment and participate fully in physical play. Although different handicaps have different effects on development, psychologists can make some generalizations about the adjustment problems of handicapped people.

Being born with a handicap means facing greater than average obstacles to psychological health. When a baby is discovered to be handicapped, the parents' expectations of a normal baby are suddenly altered. Many parents respond with love and a determination to solve the practical problems presented by the handicap. However, there is a greater than average risk that the response will be rejection, guilt, or denial of the problem. The experience can be a devastating blow to the parents' self-esteem and can lead to child neglect (Polansky, 1981). In other words, the child's initial relationship with his parents is atypical. During early childhood, parents of handicapped children are often overprotective, making it difficult for the child to become autonomous. Even if the child is encouraged in all activities, the nature of the handicap inevitably distorts, delays, or even makes impossible the acquisition of at least some new experiences (Pringle & Fides, 1970). This sometimes results in a slower acquisition of cognitive and social skills. Severe physical handicaps also interfere with the learning process. More often than is usual, the handicapped child is removed from school or home for hospitalization, surgery, and other stressful interventions.

As the child develops, new risks appear; new adjustments usually become necessary. A child with a deformed leg may come to be casually accepted and protected during the middle school years. At adolescence, however, he or she may feel suddenly isolated. Whereas many normal adolescents deeply fear that they are different and unacceptable, handicapped adolescents discover that, in the eyes of others at least, they *are* different. They possess an attribute that may place them in a less desirable social category (Goffman, 1963). In adolescence the handicap sometimes interferes with the development of relationships with the opposite sex, calling into question adult goals of marriage and family. And in some cases, the handicap restricts post-secondary education and career choices. Thus, the tasks of adolescence—difficult for most people—will usually be further complicated by the presence of a handicap.

Because the meaning of a handicap changes over the life span, it follows that a handicap acquired later in life will affect different aspects of development. A limb injury sustained in an automobile accident in mid-life will probably not affect the development of self-esteem or sexual identity so much as it will challenge the person's capacity for work, or his or her role in the family.

Physical disabilities complicate the developmental process. But love and encouragement greatly increase the coping abilities of the disabled child.

Outcomes

It is clear that handicaps provide challenges to personal growth at all points in the life span. The important question is: How do handicapped people cope? What enables the handicapped person to attain psychological health?

Research on the adjustment of one group of children yields conclusions that may be applicable to other people with handicaps (Pringle & Fides, 1970). Children involved in this Thalidomide study suffered from a variety of limb and sensory problems that were the result of their mothers having taken the tranquilizer Thalidomide during early pregnancy. The researchers found that the emotional adjustment and educational achievement of the children were related to two factors: the degree of the handicap and the environmental circumstances (for example, home background and parental attitudes). The less severe the handicap, and the more favorable the environmental conditions, the more likely the child was to realize his or her potential for growth and development.

Environment was slightly more important in affecting outcome. For example, one seven-year-old girl with very sensible, supportive parents is described as stable and well-adjusted, even though she has no arms and her hips are so dislocated that she cannot walk. She draws energetically with her feet, and manages well in an ordinary school. In this case, and in others, a severe physical disability was surmounted with the help of loving parents and cooperative school authorities.

On the other end of the scale is a boy whose disability was relatively slight compared to the other handicaps (his left arm ended in a stump at the wrist). Although this boy at first glance "looked for all the world like any other well-developed and well-cared for seven year old," the interviewers soon found him to be withdrawn, without expression, and unable to speak without his parents' approval. Psychological tests showed him to be vulnerable and "unsettled." In this case the parents had been unable to accept their child's defect; while repeatedly referring to him as normal, they prevented him from going to the school playground and in many other ways overprotected him. The parents said, when the child was out of earshot, that they "will never get over it." And the researchers concluded that a relatively minor defect could, in this family context, become a definite handicap.

The researchers found that when the emotional needs of Thalidomide children were met, the youngsters suffered less than might have been predicted on the basis of their disability. However, the nature and severity of a disability cannot be ignored. Nearly half of those in the most maladjusted group were profoundly deaf, and most multiple handicapped children with impaired hearing were to some degree emotionally disturbed. The most severely limb-deficient children, on the other hand, were remarkably well-adjusted. Among the handicapped, as among the nonhandicapped, the opportunity to achieve psychological health is not equally distributed.

Poverty

Our definitions of psychological health emphasize self-esteem, mastery of the environment, and realization of one's highest potentials. The person who is economically deprived is handicapped in attaining these goals. In our society it is difficult to maintain self-esteem if one is unable to find work or is dependent on public assistance. It is difficult to achieve mastery of the environment if one is poorly nourished and lives in a disorganized and crime-ridden neighborhood. As Maslow, for one, acknowledges, physical needs and safety needs must be satisfied before the person can be motivated to satisfy "higher needs" associated with positive psychological health.

Poverty creates restricted "paths to maturity," (Williams & Kornblum, 1985). For many individuals, there are several negative choices that tend to make poverty a life sentence: crime, prostitution, pregnancy and early parenthood, drugs, unemployment, and withdrawal into despair. Ross and Huber (1985) noted that the successful fulfillment of husbands' and wives' role obligations in the household affected psychological well-being. Ongoing economic hardship, that is the inability to adequately feed, clothe, and provide

shelter for the family, contributed to a failure in both breadwinner and homemaker obligations and increased the potential for depression in both spouses.

The ways in which extreme economic deprivation can affect psychological health have been described by Oscar Lewis, an anthropologist who studied families in the slums of Latin American countries and in the United States (Lewis, 1959, 1966). Lewis described a **culture of poverty** that develops among the very poor in countries where the dominant culture views the accumulation of wealth and property as a sign of personal worth. Unable to attain the goals set forth by the larger society, the marginal poor (those with little productive role in the society) react with feelings of helplessness, dependency, and inferiority.

Culture of Poverty
A cluster of traits, such as helplessness and inferiority, that often arise among the marginal poor in a society where wealth is highly valued.

Other characteristics that Lewis encountered were lack of impulse control, confusion of sexual identity, and an inability to delay gratification and plan for the future. These traits may be understood as a reaction of the poor to their marginal position in a capitalist society that strongly emphasizes social class and individual financial success (Lewis, 1966, p. xliv). People naturally lack autonomy when they lack money and a job; they fail to plan for the future when they cannot pay next week's rent, or be certain that their shacks or tenements will still be standing when the rent is due. But, however understandable these traits may be in the environment of poverty, they stand in opposition to our usual definitions of psychological health.

It is important to note that not all the characteristics that Lewis encountered in the urban slum were negative. For example, he observed that the very poor develop a capacity for living in the present and appreciating sensual experience that the middle-class, future-oriented person often does not have—and can recapture only with difficulty.

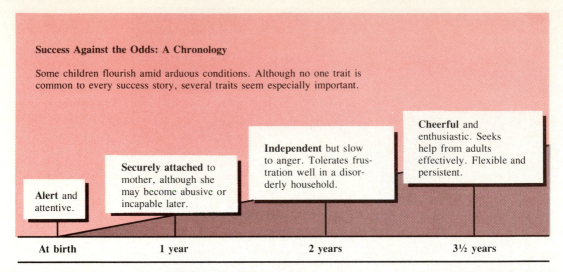

Success Against the Odds: A Chronology

Some children flourish amid arduous conditions. Although no one trait is common to every success story, several traits seem especially important.

Alert and attentive.

Securely attached to mother, although she may become abusive or incapable later.

Independent but slow to anger. Tolerates frustration well in a disorderly household.

Cheerful and enthusiastic. Seeks help from adults effectively. Flexible and persistent.

| At birth | 1 year | 2 years | 3½ years |

Figure 2.2 Success against the odds: A chronology.

Copyright © 1987 by The New York Times Company. Reprinted by permission.

As Lewis notes, there are many degrees of poverty. Perhaps only 20 percent of the poor in the United States were part of a true "culture of poverty" at the time of Lewis's writing. Yet many of the traits identified by Lewis are also understandable as responses to less severe poverty. For example, it appears that people who are economically deprived more often do see themselves as dependent on circumstances, as unable to affect their environment (Veroff, Douvan, & Kulka, 1981). And serious psychological illness appears to be more common at lower socioeconomic levels, as it is in all environments that submit people to greater than average stresses (Srole et al., 1962; Dohrenwend, 1973).

Throughout the United States we are currently witnessing a problem of increasing numbers of homeless people (Jones, 1986). Researchers and advocates for the homeless continue to be in conflict over both the extent and severity of the homelessness problem (Holden, 1986). America's homeless crisis began in 1963 when deinstitutionalization became social policy and hundreds of thousands of mental patients were released from large institutions (Jones, 1986). Unfortunately, adequate community resources have not been made available to provide the necessary follow-up care for these former patients, with many ending up on the streets.

A recent analysis of homelessness in America (Mowbray, 1985) suggests that many homeless people are neither derelicts nor deinstitutionalized mental patients, but simply poor people who cannot find affordable housing. Several common myths about the homeless were identified:

1. Homeless people come to shelters for free meals and would prefer to be out on the streets.
2. Homelessness in America is a new problem.
3. A solution is to simply provide more shelter beds.

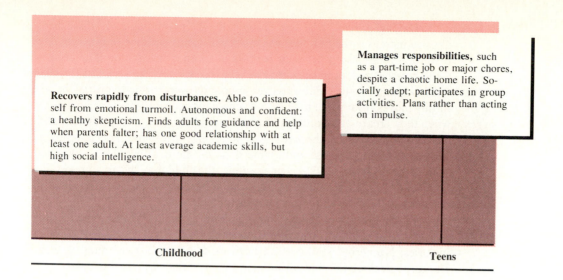

Recovers rapidly from disturbances. Able to distance self from emotional turmoil. Autonomous and confident: a healthy skepticism. Finds adults for guidance and help when parents falter; has one good relationship with at least one adult. At least average academic skills, but high social intelligence.

Manages responsibilities, such as a part-time job or major chores, despite a chaotic home life. Socially adept; participates in group activities. Plans rather than acting on impulse.

Childhood   Teens

In addition to the poor and those who, before deinstitutionalization would have been hospitalized, a new wave of homeless people has emerged; young children, mostly from minorities, and usually with their mothers. They constitute the fastest growing segment of the nation's homeless population. Several investigators believe that the problem of the homeless women and children is not simply the economics of poverty, but the breakdown of the family (Jones, 1986). Finding a solution to help ameliorate the miseries of all our homeless citizens will not be easy. From the standpoint of psychological health, what the homeless want most of all is their own home or a place to call their own.

High-Risk Environments

It has been shown that infant monkeys who are brought up without normal mothers and peers are severely handicapped in later life (Harlow & Harlow, 1969; Harlow, 1971). They do not display normal social behaviors. For example, they are unusually aggressive and are unable to engage in normal mating and parental behavior. Early and serious emotional deprivation leads to irreversible loss of social skills. In the past, psychologists observed similar losses in infants who were institutionalized under very unfavorable conditions. These deprived infants were seriously retarded in physical growth and in the acquisition of motor skills, language, and social responses (Spitz, 1945; Provence & Lipton, 1962).

Today there are fewer instances of infants being raised in situations of extreme social deprivation. Even institutionalized children are usually provided with caretakers and the stimulation of peers and toys. However, a number of early circumstances have been identified as representing serious risks to the child's emotional and social development. These circumstances create what is referred to as **high-risk environments** for psychological health.

High-Risk Environment
Harsh circumstances in a child's life, such as abuse or institutionalization, that increase the risk of psychological damage.

Having parents who are chronically ill, psychologically disturbed, or abusive increases the risk that the child will suffer emotional damage. A very disturbed relationship between parents is another risk factor. The child who is institutionalized, becomes a runaway, or is separated from parents, is thought to be at risk; so is the child who lives in poor or overcrowded housing, or whose family moves from place to place. Psychologists consider factors such as these when they create "risk profiles" for individual children in studies that seek to identify and measure the causes of emotional disorders. The psychological health of a child is most vulnerable if he or she is affected by a number of these factors (Rutter, 1978). For example, the child may live in a broken-down tenement, with an alcoholic mother and a sometimes absent father, and may periodically have to be placed in foster homes.

Psychologists have always been interested in identifying general risks to psychological health, as well as the particular sources of illness in their clients' histories. Numerous studies have been made of various risk factors. For instance, several studies have attempted to determine the possible risk to a child who has at least one parent who suffers from schizophrenia, a serious psychological illness. It appears that the chances are greater than average that the child will develop schizophrenia or other recurring difficulties (Mednick & Witkin-Lanoil, 1977). Other studies have found that a child who is abused and deprived of basic mothering is at risk for becoming a child-abusing parent (Spinetta & Rigler, 1972); that the child who experiences early or prolonged separation from a parent is at risk for depressive illness (Mahler et al., 1975); and so forth.

We cannot always say why such relationships exist any more than we can always say why a physical handicap exists. The relatively high frequency of schizophrenia in children of schizophrenics may be a result of a genetically inherited tendency, or inadequate parental care, or both. The point is that the children involved are handicapped in the pursuit of psychological health. They are at risk—that is, vulnerable to psychological illness.

The number of children from ages 5 to 13 wearing housekey necklaces (sometimes called latchkey kids) has been increasing steadily. Many single parents and two-career families feel that self-care is the only option available for their children before and after school, due to a lack of child-care facilities. Although some parents believe that this form of self-care fosters responsibility, several investigators (Robinson, Rowland, & Coleman, 1986) have questioned whether children are being pushed to grow up too soon. In an attempt to meet the needs of latchkey kids, several communities have instituted programs whereby school-age children can call in for assistance with homework as well as speak to a friendly ear. These are usually voluntary programs staffed by teachers, college students, and retirees.

A recent investigator of the poverty of affluence (Wachtel, 1983), suggests that youngsters coming out of well-to-do backgrounds may also be at risk due to problems of emotional deprivation and family neglect. Children of the rich, famous, and powerful are not immune to psychological problems.

Parental preoccupation with wealth, acquisition, and achievement can seriously impair a child's personality development, adversely affect their self-esteem, and serve as a further obstacle in the pursuit of psychological health (Miller, 1981).

Today, among psychologists and social policymakers, there is an increased concern with the factors that place children at risk, whether these are genetic or environmental in nature. This concern underlies many new "intervention" programs. As a society we increasingly seek to provide counseling for child-abusing parents (such as that offered by Parents Anonymous); we provide child-care courses and support groups for poor parents, single parents, and others under stress; we give economic assistance to parents who would otherwise not be able to raise their children at home. And sometimes we go so far as to remove children from extreme situations and place them in state-supervised foster care—so strong are our beliefs that an unfavorable early environment can severely harm and handicap a child.

In addition to the varied social and environmental factors, there are many psychological obstacles, that is, personal factors, that operate to block the development of the healthy person. Peoples' motivational limitations, avoidance of reasonable risks, procrastination, lying, inability to make decisions, social anxieties, lack of flexibility, inaccurate appraisals of threat, and poorly developed coping skills are some of the areas currently being investigated. Fortunately, many of these difficulties are overcome through personal growth and development and are amenable to change through therapy.

What We Don't Know

Carol [not her real name] is a nine-year-old girl who lives in desperately poor and crowded conditions. Her father is unemployed. Recently he was taken to court for beating her while drunk. Carol's mother cannot help her, for she herself suffers from chronic depression, a serious psychological illness. Carol herself must cope with a congenital dislocation of the hip that has resulted in a permanent limp.

It is not surprising that Carol was referred to a psychiatrist who was studying children at high risk for emotional problems. What is surprising is the psychiatrist's findings. "I was struck by her immediate friendliness," he wrote. "She settled down at the interview in a warm, comfortable, trustful way that utterly took me by surprise, since I was expecting almost the reverse. . . . She almost immediately put me at my ease and I soon found myself talking to her with much less guardedness than I usually use in a first interview" (Anthony & Koupernik, 1974). Carol, in other words, seemed not to have been overwhelmed by the many stresses in her environment.

After many years of seeking to explain the psychologically ill, researchers have begun to study the inexplicably healthy—people like Carol, who emerge from very unfavorable situations with a high degree of autonomy, achievement, and social competence (Anthony & Koupernik, 1974; Murphy & Moriarty, 1976). Psychologists are finding that some high-risk children see the environment as posing a challenge—an attitude that the cognitive psychologists in particular associate with psychological health. These people's extraordinary difficulties are surmounted through extraordinary confidence and cheer. Why this is so is something of a mystery. Anthony, a psychiatrist who works with children of severely disturbed parents, says: "We think, here's this awful home; here are these awful parents; here's this awful upbringing, and, we expect, here is this awful result. But instead here's a really remarkable child—contrary to one's predictions, to everything one might think possible" (quoted in Pines, 1979, p. 53).

Several books, "Vulnerable but Invincible" (Werner & Smith, 1983), "The Invulnerable Child," (Anthony & Cohler, 1987) have captured the excitement of psychologists exploring the baffling phenomenon of children's capacity to deal with adversity. These investigators found that "survivors, strivers, and thrivers" make up the unusual population of children who respond so unexpectedly to the onslaughts of calamity. Other studies are finding that traumatized, abused, or unloved children are not necessarily doomed to become psychologically crippled as adults (Thomas & Chess, 1984), and that the parents' early mistakes are not irrevocable. In their study, following 133 subjects from infancy to early adulthood, Thomas and Chess found that most of the troubled children in their sample grew into stability as they reached adulthood.

Another project showed that even a childhood of extreme deprivation was no obstacle to a satisfying adulthood (Long & Valliant, 1984). Reporting on a study following 456 inner-city children, whose extreme poverty and chaotic family lives placed them at risk, Long and Valliant found that by their mid-40s, their well-being was comparable to others who came out of a more favorable environment. Escape from poverty does not mitigate the significantly higher mortality and years of misery encountered by the disadvantaged. However, this wave of research has served to buttress psychology's new appreciation of the plasticity of human development.

Psychologists can no longer emphatically state that childhood trauma is a prime predictor of adult maladjustment. From the growing research evidence, it would appear that negative experiences in early life can be remedied by more favorable ones later. However, we cannot say that adverse experiences in childhood will lead to resilient, well-fortified adults. Some damaged children will indeed continue to experience problems into adulthood, but recent research studies support the view that childhood is characterized more by resilience than by lasting fragility (Rutter, 1984; Garmezy & Rutter, 1988).

Naturally, psychologists are seeking to identify the factors that seem to make some children invulnerable. Perhaps, they reason, it is encouragement from adults other than the parents, or an ability to detach themselves emotionally from the parents, or an ability to involve themselves in some creative activity or interest.

Several studies are currently under way to determine just what factors promote recovery and the development of competence in the midst of hardship and under conditions of extreme vulnerability (Garmezy, 1985). An individual's degree of vulnerability to stressors appears to be very much influenced by the development and current state of his or her intimate relationships (Bowlby, 1988). A recent study (Beardslee & Podorefsky, 1988) revealed that adolescents who were able to effectively cope with emotionally disturbed parents tended to be doers and problem solvers who valued strong intimate relationships and had high levels of self-understanding. These adolescents were very much aware of their parents' illness, but had an enhanced capacity for separating from them. They had an ability to establish a feeling of their own worth as individuals, together with the confidence and conviction that they could cope successfully with life's challenges.

"Protective processes" is the term that has been coined to describe those factors that help to counteract the hazardous effects of high-risk environments. Frequently, the availability of secure and supportive personal relationships can be a crucial factor (Rutter, 1987). These basic protective mechanisms, at significant turning points in the life cycle, enable individuals to negotiate risk situations while maintaining their self-esteem and self-efficacy. More research is needed to examine the complex relationship between risk factors, stressful life events, and protective mechanisms within the child and his environment.

At this point, however, we are far from understanding what makes one high-risk child turn out to be psychologically healthy, while another (perhaps a sibling in nearly identical circumstances) is either psychologically ill or has recurring, minor emotional difficulties. We do not know, either, why some children who grow up seemingly under the most favorable conditions do not develop the qualities we associate with psychological health. Are health and resilience a matter of nature or nurture?

People are born with unequal opportunities to achieve what is defined as psychological health in their society. But the outcomes are often surprising. Psychological health is a complicated outcome resulting from a person's characteristics and his or her environment. We can describe it and aspire to it without, by any means, being able to explain it for every individual.

SUMMARY

1. People hold many intuitive ideas about psychological health. For example, people tend to equate psychological health with being happy, having good relationships, living up to one's potential, being mature, or being able to handle stress. Many people arrive intuitively at the clinical definition that health means freedom from symptoms and emotional disturbances.

2. Definitions of psychological health—even those developed by psychologists and other social scientists—reflect the values of the society. For example, if one defines the healthy person as one who realizes his or her creative potential, this is because one values creativity. There are many different interpretations of what constitutes psychological health.

3. Freud, the originator of psychoanalytic theory, described psychological health as the ability to love and to work. It also requires the ability to confront life on the level of reality. Continuing in the psychoanalytic tradition, Erikson describes psychological health in terms of the *ego strengths* that emerge, under favorable conditions, at different stages of the life span. For example, psychological health in young adulthood means that one has struggled with "intimacy versus isolation," has achieved a dynamic balance in favor of intimacy, and has emerged with the ego strength called love. What is psychologically healthy at one stage of the life span is not necessarily so at another.

4. Humanist conceptions of psychological health emphasize growth and fulfillment of potential. Maslow defines the self-actualizing person as one who has satisfied lower-level or *deprivation* needs (for example, needs for food and safety) and has come to be motivated by the supreme need to satisfy his or her unique potential. Rogers describes the fully functioning or healthy person as one who has feelings of self-worth; the capacity to accept new experiences (including those that call for personal change); and the ability to accept and encourage growth in others.

5. Behaviorists do not describe a "healthy" person; instead, they speak of successful adaptation to the environment. Successful people are aware of and avoid behaviors that will bring them negative consequences. They can foresee the consequences of their behavior and exercise self-control. Because behaviorists believe that behavior is controlled by the environment, they are interested in designing a healthy environment that would enable us to attain our ideals of human development.

6. Cognitive psychology describes psychologically healthy people as those who interpret or evaluate events in the environment in ways that make them feel good (or hopeful) and that enable them to use appropriate problem-solving skills.

7. Although conceptions of psychological health differ, we can synthesize important ideas. Jahoda notes that most modern conceptions of psychological health include reference to the healthy person's positive self-concept, continuous growth, integration of the personality, realistic perception of the world (and other people), and mastery of the environment through love, work, and play.

8. Some people encounter significant obstacles to psychological health; these include physical handicaps, poverty, homelessness, and early experience in a *high-risk* (emotionally deprived or abusive) *environment*. Yet some of these people develop psychological health in the face of personal handicap or hardship. Researchers cannot say for certain what makes one "high-risk" child psychologically healthy, while another, raised in similar circumstances, develops psychological difficulties.

SUGGESTED READINGS

Deutsch, C. (1982). *Broken bottles, broken dreams: Understanding and helping children of alcoholics*. New York: Teachers College Press. Provides an excellent understanding of alcoholism and its impact on family members, and suggests methods of coping.

Elkind, D. (1982). *The hurried child*. Reading, MA: Addison-Wesley. Examines the psychological consequences of children being pushed to grow up too quickly.

Fromme, A. (1976). *The ability to love*. New York: Pocket Books. A practical guide to the psychology of love.

Harris, A. B. and Harris, T. A. (1985). *Staying OK*. New York: Avon Books. An exploration of the things that get in the way of feeling OK and methods for overcoming bad feelings.

Josselson, R. (1988). *Finding herself: Pathways to identify development in women*. New York: Aronson. A sensitive and insightful exploration of the paths that normal women follow in development of their identities.

Kaplan, L. (1984). *Adolescence: The farewell to childhood*. New York: Simon and Schuster. A fascinating examination of the adolescent struggle for autonomy and self-development.

Lasch, C. (1979). *The culture of narcissism*. New York: Norton. A critical analysis of contemporary cultural forces that give rise to the development of narcissistic characteristics.

May, R. (1969). *Love and will*. New York: Norton. An excellent humanistic examination of love, sex, and death.

Sheehy, G. (1986). *Spirit of survival*. New York: Bantam. Captures the resiliency of the human spirit to endure tragedies, overcome crises, and emerge strengthened.

Weiner, F. (1986). *No apologies*. New York: St. Martin's Press. A guide to living with a disability, written by the real authorities, their families and friends.

3

Anxiety, Stress, and Depression

- ▶ Anxiety, stress, and depression as normal life experiences
- ▶ New developments in the biological sciences that begin to explain the organic changes associated with anxiety, stress, and depression
- ▶ The varying psychological views about the causes, treatments, and prevention of anxiety, stress, and depression
- ▶ The importance of the meaning of an event or experience to an individual in determining whether it will arouse anxiety, be stressful, or precipitate depressed feelings
- ▶ Specific anxieties that arise at points in the life span
- ▶ How stress may result from anxieties, environmental pressures, and significant life events
- ▶ Depressions that commonly occur as a result of normal life crises

A lice is unable to eat before taking an exam. Usually she studies up until the last moment. Although she is well-prepared, during the exam her heart beats fast and her thoughts wander. Instead of thinking about the problems before her, she finds herself thinking about how much smarter the other students are, and whether it is likely that she will get through it—not just this course, but this school year. After an exam, Alice usually suffers from an upset stomach and has a need to talk at length with friends.

Unlike some students, Alice doesn't dread getting back her exams. She is almost indifferent. In most cases she can count on at least a "B." But even in courses in which she excels, her high grade on one exam does nothing to alleviate her worries about the next one. Alice suffers from test anxiety.

Test anxiety is common among students in our competitive educational system, and has even been called an "occupational hazard" of student life. The problem for students like Alice is that it assumes near panic proportions. Fortunately, such students can be helped with a combination of brief cognitive psychotherapy and study skills training (Dendato & Diener, 1986).

For many people other challenges, quite different from the academic test situation, arouse anxiety. For example, some people panic whenever they are asked to speak in public. Others are predictably and unbearably nervous about meeting new people at parties and formal social occasions. There are, too, people for whom anxiety is not associated with a given situation, but is more generalized. (The person may feel worthless, or frightened of the "powers that be.")

In any case, certain feelings tend to be experienced: the heart pounds; the pulse races; the palms become cold and sweaty; the stomach tightens, becomes jittery, or seems filled with an indigestible lump; there may be a need to urinate or defecate frequently, to breathe more deeply, to just "hold on." Taken together, the common symptoms of anxiety, which are shown in Table 3.1, make us painfully aware of this common human experience.

Some people experience anxiety when they must speak to a group. They may feel their stomach tighten and their palms become cold and sweaty.

Stress
The effects on an organism sustained as a result of pressures in the environment that are experienced as taxing and challenging.

We may also be aware of experiencing **stress**—by which we mean the physical and psychological wear and tear brought on by the strains of upsetting events in life, daily "hassles," and worry about being able to fulfill the challenges they present us with. And yet we do not altogether avoid situations that we find stressful. Most people sign up for new courses of study, and upon graduation they seek "challenging" jobs and new social roles as partners and parents. Being healthy includes knowing how to cope with stress—how indeed to move ahead despite the dangers posed by new life situations. At first, in a new situation, we may feel ourselves inadequate with respect to the environment and its demands. We experience anxiety. But life is not static, and if we are healthy we find that taking a step forward is more rewarding than accepting our present circumstances.

In this chapter we will discuss anxiety and stress, as well as one common outcome of stressful life events, depression. For the most part we discuss each of these separately, despite the fact that in life they are inextricably related. To illustrate this point, consider the case of a man just promoted to a position for which he believes he is ill equipped. He feels enormous stress about the heavy responsibility, anxious that he will fail, and depressed over the burden

TABLE 3.1 *Common Anxiety Symptoms and Self-Descriptions Indicative of High Anxiety*

Symptoms	Self-Descriptions
1. Nervousness, jittery	1. I am often bothered by the thumping of my heart.
2. Tension	2. Little annoyances get on my nerves and irritate me.
3. Feeling tired	3. I often become suddenly scared for no good reason.
4. Dizziness	4. I worry continuously and that gets me down.
5. Frequency of urination or defecation	5. I frequently get spells of complete exhaustion and fatigue.
6. Heart palpitations	6. It is always hard for me to make up my mind.
7. Feeling faint	7. I always seem to be dreading something.
8. Breathlessness	8. I feel nervous and high strung all the time.
9. Sweating	9. I often feel I can't overcome my difficulties.
10. Trembling	10. I feel constantly under strain.
11. Worry and apprehension	
12. Sleeplessness	
13. Difficulty in concentrating	
14. Vigilance	

From I. G. Sarason and B. R. Sarason, *Abnormal Psychology,* 4e © 1984, p. 134. Reprinted by permission of Prentice-Hall, Inc., Englewood Cliffs, New Jersey.

he carries, and the hopelessness of the situation. In his experience, the stress, anxiety, and depression are all one. It is useful to bear that in mind when reading this chapter.

Our discussion here is only a first step in understanding personal adjustment. What we need to know is how to defend ourselves against anxiety, stress, and depression, and how to cope with the real problems that life presents. These topics are discussed in Chapter 4.

ANXIETY

Anxiety is not a new human experience. Hippocrates, who lived about 2500 years ago, described a man who suffered from a height phobia and could not cross over bridges. Robert Burton, in a book published in 1621, told of one man who could not walk alone from his home out of fear he would die, some who could not be alone in a small room, and others who became overwrought if they were in a crowd of people in church or the village square. Besides being an ancient human affliction, anxiety is no respecter of status, education, or intelligence. Sigmund Freud himself, when he was in his thirties, had numerous symptoms of anxiety including fear of travel (Greist, Jefferson, & Marks, 1986).

From personal experience, most of us can describe the emotional state we call **anxiety.** In fact, one-third of all adults suffer from "nervous complaints," especially anxiety. We should point out that anxiety has been a major subject of study and that in the last 30 years more than 5000 articles and books have been published about it. Despite extensive research, experts are far from agreement about the nature of it.

Anxiety
A state of tension stemming from an undefinable, perceived threat to one's security or self-esteem.

Anxiety and Stress Defined and Compared

One problem in studying anxiety and stress is that the two terms are sometimes used interchangeably. Partly this reflects theoretical differences among psychologists. It is also due to the historical fact that the term "anxiety" was used almost exclusively during the first half of the century, even when the author was referring to the experience of stress. Leading students of stress, like Lazarus and Folkman (1984), acknowledge that there is considerable overlap between the meaning of the two. Nevertheless, there are important differences, and we want to highlight them, especially because an examination of those differences also shows how the two are related.

According to some theorists the term "anxiety" should be reserved for situations in which the source of danger is unclear to the individual. It would seem to have no discernible cause in the external environment. To the individual who experiences *anxiety,* it is a "pervasive feeling of dread, apprehension and impending disaster" (Goldenson, 1984, p. 53). In another vein it has been defined as "a diffuse, unpleasant uneasiness, apprehension, fearfulness, stemming from anticipated danger, the source of which is undefinable" (Rowe, 1983).

The meaning of anxiety is sharpened when it is contrasted with fear, which is a reaction to a clear, unmistakable danger in the here and now. We fear the dentist's drill or the surgeon's scalpel, but are anxious upon learning of the success of a sibling with whom we are competitive. A fear can be located in time and space—and perhaps avoided. But anxiety involves the essence of the personality. It is a threat to the individual's security and self-esteem. In ordinary language, one *has* a fear; but one *is* anxious (May, 1977, p. 207). Anxiety and fear have this in common: The body prepares to meet the threat. Muscles are tensed, breathing rate increases, and the heart beats faster.

The college environment generates anxiety in many, not only during stressful situations such as final exams, but as a general reaction to increased demands. Perseverance in meeting the new challenges, rather than a focus on one's sense of inadequacy, tends to lessen the anxiety.

In real life the distinction between anxiety and fear is far from clear, for one is often superimposed on the other. That is the case when a person fears falling from an exposed high place, and at the same time experiences anxiety due to an unconscious wish to jump from a height or to push another. A person may fear surgery and post-operative weakness; yet this fear may also include unrecognized anxieties derived from early experience—he or she may be anxious about becoming dependent on others, or about being abandoned.

According to Spielberger (1976), *anxiety* comes at the end of a sequence of events. That sequence begins with *stress,* which he defines as a situation objectively recognized as physically or psychologically dangerous. *Stress* has also been defined as a "state of physical or psychological strain which imposes demands for adjustment upon the individual" (Goldenson, 1984, p. 715). Stress may be internal in origin (for example, a need to be perfect in everything one does) or external (for example, five term papers due in one week). It can be temporary or persistent, in which case it may be overtaxing and may lead to a breakdown in the individual's functioning.

The sequence of stress, threat, and anxiety state involves a series of human activities. First is the *cognitive* in which the individual makes an appraisal of danger. If the individual perceives threat in the situation, then the cognitive activity is followed by *affective* and *psychological* activity. The person experiences the threat both psychologically and physically. Next this is followed by a *behavioral* act through which the individual responds or reacts, effectively or not.

Biological Basis

Faced with a potentially anxiety-provoking experience, such as a crucial examination or marriage, we have bodily sensations as well as thoughts and feelings about the event. If the event does arouse anxiety, it will set off physical manifestations of anxiety. The least controversial studies about anxiety are those that report the biological effects: the rapidly beating heart, deep breathing, trembling hands, and so forth. It is not surprising that these findings apply to fear as well.

Anxiety (like fear) is an alarm that tells us that something is wrong. There's danger afoot! The brain perceives a threat and immediately sends messages to the body through the nerve fibers, and by means of hormones, through the bloodstream. The brain's message-sending is facilitated through neurotransmitters, chemicals that help relay the message from cell to cell. One particular class of neurotransmitters is known as catecholamines. They are crucial in the physiology of fear and anxiety and receive considerable attention from researchers who develop drugs to counteract the effects of anxiety disorders (Mason, 1984).

With the alarm system set off, two nervous systems become instantly involved: The skeletal nervous system activates the muscles to prepare to fight, run, or just shake with fear, and the autonomic nervous system activates the adrenal glands which, in turn, release adrenalin. This hormone initiates other actions, one of the major ones being that of stimulating the heart (Goodwin, 1986). A rapid heartbeat assists the body's effort to direct blood away from digestive functions and toward the heart, lungs, and limbs so that the person can defend, attack, or escape the threatening situation. Heavier breathing delivers the additional oxygen needed during the emergency; the bowel and bladder may be emptied so that the person, unencumbered by digestive activities, will be prepared to run. Walter B. Cannon, the physiologist who first described these physical changes, noted that they are designed to prepare a person for *fight or flight* (1932/1967). However, in many instances of anxiety, because the cause of the feelings is unknown, the person is psychologically prepared to attack, defend, or flee without having a clear "enemy" or concrete danger.

More recent research has revealed some of the underlying physiological correlates of anxiety. We use the word "correlate" because it appears that the physical reactions follow the individual's mental awareness of danger and probably accompany the emotional reaction. A person "sees" danger (interprets some external or internal stimulus as threatening) and then "feels" it emotionally. After noticing or feeling his own reaction, a person might become even more anxious.

Human researchers are generally limited to non-laboratory, real-life methods of studying the psychological correlates of anxiety, such as measuring the amount of catecholamine in the blood or urine after the individual has experienced anxiety. (With animals, direct, intrusive methods in the laboratory such as electric shock, toxic chemical injection, or extreme temperature have provided valuable information.)

A general state of anxiety caused by an external danger produces physiological changes that prepare a person for "fight or flight." This photo was taken in Belfast in 1988 when grenades were thrown into a group of mourners during a funeral.

In one study of the effects of anxiety, samples of urine were collected from paratroop trainees prior to training. Later they were collected before and after mock jumps and actual jumps. Levels of epinephrine (a catecholamine) in the urine were highest on the first day of training jumps. While they dropped with increasing experience, they continued to be higher at each jump than the basal, pretraining levels. Training and experience reduced the level of anxiety, as indicated by the epinephrine, but did not eradicate it completely (Hamberger & Lohr, 1982).

In a different study the subjects were young physicians who had to undergo the anxiety of "Grand Rounds" in a hospital, which involves their presenting a lecture to an audience of all the physicians in their specialty. The epinephrine levels increased sharply before and at the start of the talk and then subsided during the course of the presentation. Norepinephrine (another catecholamine) increased gradually and remained high through the entire talk. Through assessments of hormonal levels and other biochemical functions, whether in connection with activities like driving a racing car, running, engaging in military action or experiencing a stressful life event like taking an important examination, researchers are providing us with new kinds of information about the physiological correlates of anxiety (Weiner, 1985).

Still another approach to examining the interplay of the physiological and other components of anxiety is to see the effects of chronic high anxiety. An influential study in this regard is the long-term follow-up of 200 Harvard freshmen. Among them, those who were troubled, uncertain, and *chronically anxious* in their late teens and early adulthood, were much more likely than the others, 35 years after the initial testing, to be chronically ill or dead (Vaillant, 1977).

Anxiety has been found to contribute to a variety of health problems. It is related to the onset of various processes that lead to heart disease, as we will see in the discussion of the Type A personality later in this chapter. Biological studies of anxiety have been important in adding to our understandings of other ailments. These include alcoholism, gastrointestinal disorders, skin ailments, and many other disorders that are frequently psychosomatic, that is, where mental and physical problems are tightly intertwined.

In the preceding paragraphs we have shown some of the destructive effects of anxiety. Unquestionably there is a large body of evidence for its negative consequences (Spielberger & Sarason, 1986). However, anxiety serves a positive function as well. We have already referred to anxiety as an alarm system. Also, research suggests that some degree of arousal (such as a moderate level of anxiety) tends to make a person function, learn, or perform better. Thus a certain degree of anxiety has a constructive effect (May, 1977). We often hear, for example, that stage fright is an asset to the actress ("It gets my adrenalin moving."). Similarly, a series of studies of sports parachutists showed that those who experience the physiological arousal associated with anxiety perform better than those who are not anxious (Fenz & Epstein, 1967). Freud's view, that anxiety is adaptive if the discomfort motivates people to learn new ways to approach life's challenges, is shared by contemporary experts on anxiety (Marks, 1986).

Much, of course, depends on past experience with the specific task to be performed. Research suggests that the effect of arousal is to strengthen those response tendencies that the individual *already* has in his repertoire (Spence, 1960). Thus stage fright enables the actress who knows her part to perform brilliantly, while hindering the actress for whom the right lines and movements have not yet become habit. It appears that the *level* of anxiety is also important. When anxiety is mild or moderate, the physiological arousal that accompanies it may help the individual deal with a threatening situation: we say it "keeps him on his toes." But when anxiety is at a high level, it tends to interfere with performance, especially when the task confronted is novel or complicated (Yerkes & Dodson, 1908).

Psychological Conflict and Anxiety

The human tendency is to avoid stimuli that are perceived to be aversive. High places, crowds, dances, competitive games—any of these, or others, that arouse anxiety level are given a wide berth. In some cases, though, avoidance is difficult because that which is to be avoided has some desirable features. The person experiences a conflict: he or she is motivated to avoid a painful stimulus and equally motivated to approach it for a perceived reward. The result may be indecision, confusion, and heightened anxiety.

The **approach-avoidance conflict,** as this predicament is called, has been dramatically demonstrated in the laboratory, in a classic experiment. Cats were taught to lift the lid of a box in order to obtain food (Masserman, 1964; Masserman & Siever, 1944). When this was accomplished—when the animals had

Approach-Avoidance Conflict
A predicament in which someone is motivated to avoid a painful stimulus and, at the same time, motivated to approach it for a perceived reward.

The Search for Personal Adjustment

Mild or moderate anxiety can improve performance by keeping people "on their toes" while they perform, play ball, or take a test.

learned to associate the lifting action with the desired reward—the experimenter introduced an aversive stimulus. Now when the cats raised the lid they received a blast of air in the face. The cats were presented with a conflict: whether to remain hungry and avoid the blast of air, or eat and suffer the discomfort. In this situation, the animals exhibited behaviors we associate with anxiety. They became irritable, distractible, and unable to cope with their environment.

The recognized limitations of animal research are worth noting at this point. Nevertheless, we face many situations which, though more complicated, resemble the approach-avoidance experiment. For example, one young man compared the blast of air in the face to the reaction he usually gets from a woman when he expresses his wish for sexual intercourse. He desires the sexual gratification that might follow, yet he fears the humiliation he received in the past when some women refused him. In other words, he wants to approach a sexual experience while at the same time avoid the possibility of rejection. In a conflict situation such as this, the person will experience anxiety until he can find an acceptable resolution.

Anxiety, Stress, and Depression

Figure 3.1 Although having two equally attractive options seems like it would be ideal, an approach-approach conflict can pose serious problems to humans, just as it did to the fabled mule who supposedly starved to death trying to choose which way to turn for his next meal.

Approach-Approach Conflict
A predicament in which someone is torn between two nearly equally attractive but incompatible choices.

Double Approach-Avoidance Conflict
A predicament in which someone is torn between two alternatives, each of which has desirable and undesirable features.

The **approach-approach conflict** arises when a person is faced with two very desirable but incompatible alternatives: Two equally attractive job offers, or marriage proposals from two equally desirable people. To the outside observer this situation seems to be the realization of a fantasy, but to the individual in the predicament, the process of choice-making can be physically and emotionally draining (see Figure 3.1). Continual preoccupation with the conflict in the form of worrying about making a serious mistake leads to disturbed digestion and sleep.

Slightly more complicated is the **double approach-avoidance conflict,** in which *each* alternative has both desirable and undesirable features. Consider the example of a 41-year-old woman who wants both a career and a child. If she leaves her job to have a baby, her career will suffer. If she stays with her job, she will become too old to conceive. The woman has two positive goals that she believes are mutually exclusive, and each also has drawbacks. She describes herself as "being in a bind." "Whatever I do, I lose," she says. More accurately, if the choices available are either career or baby, she should say, "Whatever I do, I win and I lose." Whatever she says, the conflict inevitably arouses anxiety, the extent of it depending on how prolonged the period before her decision, and on personality characteristics that relate to how she handles the choice process. If she spends countless hours deliberating about it, cutting in on relaxation, rest, and sleep, and affecting her powers of concentration, she could exhibit such behaviors as accident-proneness, and develop psychosomatic symptoms such as headaches.

The Search for Personal Adjustment

The double approach-avoidance conflict is a common one during the college years. It may manifest itself in the conflict between going to college and working part-time as opposed to full-time enrollment. The student thinks: "Part-time work really appeals to me because I won't have to be so dependent on my parents and also worry about spending money on a good time. But then it'll take me much longer to get my degree. With full-time college I can finish fast and get a decent, well-paying job, but look at the sacrifice—scrimping on every cent, and it's tough on my parents."

Two principles are worth following in coping with psychological conflicts that often arouse anxiety. The first is to use effective problem-solving methods: defining the problem clearly, obtaining as much information as possible (for example, about student loans, or about the number of credits one could take while working part-time), making a trial decision, living with it for a time, implementing it, and evaluating how well it works out with the possibility of reversing it at the first opportunity. The second is to act without delay, using only the time necessary to reach a soundly based resolution.

Psychoanalytic Interpretations

As a physician specializing in "nervous" diseases, Freud was initially much interested in the physiology of anxiety. In time, however, he turned his attention to the role of anxiety in personality development. Why, he wondered, did his "nervous" patients suffer so much more intensely from anxiety than others? He assumed that the answer to this question would "cast a flood of light on our whole mental life" (S. Freud, 1938/1969, p. 341). In other words, it might go far toward explaining normal anxiety as well.

Freud came to recognize three types of anxiety (Freud, 1926/1948). The first, **reality anxiety,** is a response to actual dangers that the person perceives in the environment (and is thus loosely equivalent to fear). It originates in the ego that Freud defined as the conscious, rational part of personality. In this category is the dread we experience when facing surgery or dental work—or when appearing in battle, before a grand jury, or in a dangerous neighborhood after dark. Reality anxiety is a reaction to "real-life" problems or crises.

A second type of anxiety Freud termed **neurotic anxiety** because it results from dread of our impulses (a fear that is extreme and irrational in neurotic patients). The experience of neurotic anxiety is by no means confined to the unhealthy person. All of us have reason to fear our impulses in those situations where we may well be punished for following them. Neurotic anxiety, Freud claimed, has its origins in the id, the primitive, unconscious part of personality that seeks immediate gratification of impulses. Its beginnings are in childhood, when we are routinely punished for losing control and acting impulsively. In childhood we fear punishment and shame. In adulthood, neurotic anxiety is more often a fear of the sexual or aggressive impulse itself.

The third type of anxiety, **moral anxiety,** is what we feel when we are "conscience-stricken." It is the guilt and shame we experience when violating, in thought or deed, some principle that we have incorporated into the superego. Like neurotic anxiety, moral anxiety is a response to temptations of a

Reality Anxiety
Sigmund Freud's term for what is commonly called "fear"—a response to actual dangers in the environment.

Neurotic Anxiety
Sigmund Freud's term for the dread one experiences of one's own impulses.

Moral Anxiety
Sigmund Freud's term for the guilt or shame one experiences when violating, or thinking about violating, a principle that one has incorporated into one's superego or conscience.

sexual or aggressive nature. It is derived from realistic fears that children have about punishment by a parent or other authority. In adulthood, however, moral anxiety is an intrapsychic (or inner) phenomenon. The person experiences anxiety as a result of having fallen short of his ideal, and not because anything threatening has appeared in the environment.

The three types of anxiety that Freud identified originate at different stages in the life span. But they all coexist in the adult, and in fact may be brought to the surface by a single situation. For example, a student might be anxious about participating in a violent demonstration because of the possibility of getting hurt or being expelled from school (reality anxiety). He might also be afraid of losing control and expressing certain hostile impulses toward authority (neurotic anxiety). Finally, he might feel guilty about the possible harm his actions will have on others (moral anxiety).

Behaviorist Interpretations

We have seen that certain anxieties appear in response to dangers perceived by the individual at predictable stages of the life span. Thus, separation anxiety is sometimes called "eight-month anxiety" and is assumed to be a universal phenomenon for infants of about this age. However, some anxieties we observe in people are clearly not universal. They center around purely individual experiences. Anxieties that appear in response to cats, thunderstorms, subway trains, sexual intercourse, and so forth fall into this category. In fact, a great many of our anxieties are learned from the circumstances of our individual lives.

According to the behaviorists, anxiety is a learned response. If an organism experiences something painful or unpleasant in a particular situation, it will react with anxious behaviors at some later time when it is confronted with stimuli that were present in the original situation. For example, an infant may come to associate the feeding situation with tension and discomfort; perhaps the infant suffered from colic during the first months of life, or perhaps the parent was nervous, clumsy, or arbitrary in maintaining the feeding schedule. In any case there is a greater than average chance that the infant will be a "poor eater" and he or she will suffer as an adult from ulcers and other digestive disturbances.

Generalization
In behaviorist terminology, a process through which a person learns to respond to stimuli that are similar to or associated with the original conditioned stimulus.

How We Generalize Fears   Behaviorists have shown that through the process of **generalization,** the person learns to fear stimuli that are simply *associated with* a fearful stimulus. Many common life problems are a result of this sort of generalization. For example, a child hates school because he or she has been humiliated by a bully in the schoolyard. The school is associated with the humiliating experience, and the unpleasant response to the humiliation is generalized to the school.

Another example is when a person learns to fear objects and situations that are *similar* to the original fear stimulus. A student is uncomfortable in the presence of a teacher because the teacher reminds her of an abusive parent. A similarity in speech or carriage between the teacher and the parent may be sufficient to cause this discomfort. Because the student often fails to see the

connection, he or she suffers the vague and inexplicable dread that is so characteristic of anxiety. In adult life we discover many examples of anxieties that appear to have no identifiable source but that in fact result from certain stimuli that once became associated with early pain and punishment.

The early behaviorists not only found evidence of generalization of learned fears but also developed methods to overcome them. Mary Cover Jones reported the case of a young boy, Peter, in 1924. For unknown reasons, Peter had developed severe anxiety reactions to animals as well as to a variety of furry objects such as fur coats and rugs, feathers and wool. Tests of his reactions to a whole range of animals and objects revealed his strongest fear-like response was to a rabbit. For that reason, a rabbit was used to counteract his conditioned fear, that is, to achieve counterconditioning. (Conditioned learning was discussed in Chapter 1.)

To help Peter overcome his anxiety reaction, Jones (1924) introduced a new approach. She decided to introduce the aversive stimulus (a rabbit) while Peter was engaged in a pleasurable distracting activity. While he was eating a favorite food she arranged to have a caged rabbit brought into the room at such a distance that it would not arouse a negative reaction more powerful than the positive one of eating appetizing food. With each passing day, while he was eating, the caged rabbit was brought closer without arousing noticeable anxiety. Finally, the rabbit was released, and in time Peter was able to have the animal on the table and in his lap, and he even spoke of it fondly. Further testing revealed that Jones' extinction method had generalized beyond the rabbit to the other fur-like objects (Bandura, 1969). In the normal course of his young life Peter had become conditioned to fear furry animals and related objects and, through the method of counterconditioning, that fear was extinguished.

Cognitive Interpretations

According to cognitive psychologists, anxiety is an emotion based on the **appraisal of threat**—an appraisal that involves symbolic, anticipatory, and uncertain elements (Lazarus & Averill, 1972). Appraisals of threat are *symbolic* because they are evoked by ideas, values, and cognitive systems rather than by concrete and immediate events. For example, a person may feel threatened by loss of self-esteem or by life's meaninglessness, both of which are very difficult to define in concrete terms. Appraisals of threat are *anticipatory* because they involve dangers that may appear in the future. Perhaps the person dreads being rejected, or that some unacceptable part of the self will be exposed in an upcoming situation. Finally, appraisals of threat involve an uncomfortable degree of *uncertainty,* both about the nature of the threat and about the way one might respond to it. The anxious individual becomes unable to interpret the environment in a manner that conforms to his or her usual ideas, and is consequently unable to prepare effectively for action.

Cognitive psychologists also note that anxiety may follow the **violation of expectancies** about something that is emotionally significant to the individual. For example, anxiety is experienced when a person is punished for behaviors for which he, on the basis of experience, expects to be rewarded. Behavioral studies with animals and humans have shown that an anxious state called "experimental neurosis" can be brought about when the subjects' expectancies are arbitrarily violated—and especially when subjects can do nothing to correct the situation.

In one of Pavlov's experiments, for example, dogs learned to make discriminations between a circle and an ellipse and were able to gain food by choosing the circle. The experimenter proceeded to increase the difficulty of the discrimination (by making ellipses more closely resemble circles) until the dogs were unable to make a choice that allowed them to predict whether or not the reward would be forthcoming. Unable to distinguish "correct" from "incorrect" behaviors, the dogs began to squeal, tear at their skin, and engage in other anxious behaviors (Pavlov, 1927). The child who is unable to avoid punishment because his parents are irrational, inconsistent, cruel, or simply at odds with one another may suffer anxiety for quite similar reasons. In a wide variety of experiences across the life span, violation of expectancies appears to be a factor in producing anxiety.

A related factor is **response unavailability** (Epstein, 1972), in which the individual is aroused but for some reason is unable to take action or otherwise express himself. The young adult who has made a career decision but is entirely lacking in the means of bringing it about suffers from response unavailability; so does the infant whose mother has disappeared, and who can

Appraisal of Threat
An evaluation of a situation by an individual—involving symbolic elements, anticipation of danger, and uncertainty—that cognitive psychologists propose as a basis for anxiety.

Violation of Expectancies
A situation where the results following one's behavior are different from what one had expected, with anxiety sometimes being a result.

Response Unavailability
A situation in which one is aroused but is unable to take action or otherwise express oneself.

do nothing whatsoever to bring her back. Sometimes people experience response unavailability because of how they have interpreted a situation and their ability to cope with it. Whatever the reason, being blocked from action can lead to feelings of helplessness, another reaction that is often associated with anxiety.

An important feature of the cognitive approach to anxiety is the emphasis it places on the individual's interpretation of danger (Beck, 1976). The identical challenge (e.g., having to speak before any audience) will arouse very different reactions, so that one person sees it as a great opportunity, which arouses mild anxiety, while another, who fears his/her weaknesses will be exposed, sees it as a potential calamity and consequently experiences a very high level of anxiety. Cognitive therapists direct the attention of the persons so overwrought with anxiety to the *meaning* they have given to the event. They help them alter the meaning and then revise their *appraisal of threat*.

Existential and Humanist Interpretations

According to existential and humanist psychologists, anxiety is an inevitable and potentially positive part of the human condition. It is inevitable because human beings are creatures who are aware of their own mortality. It can be positive because it is a necessary accompaniment of growth, freedom, and change. Nonetheless, anxiety is often a formidable threat. It threatens the self-concept (Rogers, 1951); it calls into question the core of essence of the personality (May, 1950/1977).

Existential philosophers and psychologists have made much of the importance of **death anxiety** to human consciousness. For example, the existentialists have written of the fear of nothingness and meaninglessness—the state of nonbeing of which death is the most perfect example. According to Ernest Becker, an American heir to the existentialist position:

> The basic insight of psychology for all time [is] that man is a union of opposites, of self-consciousness and of physical body. Man emerged from the instinctive thoughtless action of the lower animals and came to reflect on his condition. He was given a consciousness of his individuality and his part-divinity in creation, the beauty and uniqueness of his face and his name. At the same time he was given the consciousness of the terror of the world and of his own death and decay. This paradox is the really constant thing about man in all periods of history and society; it is thus the true "essence" of man (Becker, 1973, p. 69).

This development into self-consciousness carried the penalty of dread or anxiety. Becker continues:

> But the real focus of dread, . . . the final terror of self-consciousness is the knowledge of one's own death, which is the peculiar sentence on man alone in the animal kingdom. . . . Death is man's peculiar and greatest anxiety (Becker, 1973, p. 70).

Death Anxiety
The fear of death, and related fears of nothingness and meaningless, a concept particularly emphasized by existential psychologists.

To the existentialist—for whom man's very existence is the problem—threats of nonbeing are always present. And so is anxiety. Yet, it would be wrong to consider the position of the humanists to be dominated, or even strongly influenced, by death anxiety. On the contrary, Carl Rogers (1961) devoted most of his long career to understanding the meaning of "the good life" and ways to help individuals achieve that. Even a brief description of his definition of the good life reveals that it cannot be free of anxiety. "The good life is a *process,* not a state of being. It is a direction, not a destination. The direction . . . is selected by the total organism when there is psychological freedom to move in *any* direction." The characteristic qualities of this process, as Rogers saw this, are an increasing openness to experience, an increasing tendency to live fully, an increasing trust in his or her organism, and increasingly a more fully functioning individual. This kind of living entails the anxieties and fears associated with venturing forth into new horizons at the same time as it opens opportunities for immeasurable inner growth and deeper relationships with other people.

Anxiety and the Life Span

Freud (1936) observed that what is *really* dangerous to an individual depends on the person's level of development. For example, temporary absence of the mother is dangerous to an infant, but not (to the same degree) to an older child or adolescent. Both Freud and later cognitive researchers have shown that the *perception* of events in relation to the self also changes greatly as the individual matures. The temporary disappearance of mother in infancy is not only threatening in the physical sense, but also could be anxiety-producing because the infant has not developed certain mental abilities. The infant, for instance, does not understand that when mother is away she is somewhere else and will return, and that his safety is not threatened because he is in the hands of a competent mother substitute.

Both what is dangerous, and what is perceived as dangerous, vary with developmental level. What this means is that each stage of life is characterized by certain dangers, and therefore by certain anxieties. Psychologists have found it worthwhile to examine our early experiences, for the anxiety produced by the original danger situation sometimes persists, usually in a milder form after the danger is passed.

Separation Anxiety

Separation Anxiety
Anxiety, dating from the infant's fear of the mother's withdrawal, that is experienced when an individual feels threatened with the loss of someone he or she cares for.

In earliest infancy, when feelings of generalized uneasiness arise in the feeding situation, the infant is afraid of being "left empty" or simply "left" (Erikson, 1959, p. 6). As the infant develops and begins to be able to differentiate himself from the nurturing mother, the infantile fear develops into a more general anxiety called **separation anxiety.**

The Search for Personal Adjustment

An inevitable stage of psychological development is the young child's anxiety over being separated from the mother or other nurturing figure. Separation anxiety may recur in later years when there is threat of an important personal loss.

Separation anxiety is the great anxiety of early life. It develops as a result of the infant's attachment to the mother or other nurturer. Generally the closer the attachment, the earlier the separation anxiety appears. Thus, Ugandan infants, who are strapped to their mothers' backs and are almost never physically separated from them, show separation anxiety about two months earlier than American infants (Ainsworth, 1967). In our culture, separation anxiety appears at about eight months and peaks at about a year.

The year-old child shows unmistakable signs of distress when his mother unexpectedly leaves the room. In one experiment, children left to themselves cried, screamed, attempted to open the door, and in some cases resigned themselves to doleful rocking on the floor (Ainsworth & Bell, 1970). The mothers' absence in this experiment lasted only three minutes. In real life, if the mother remains absent for a significant period of time, the child may display all the signs of human bereavement. He is listless and sleepless, and may refuse food and comfort from others.

Earlier, psychologists believed that the child cried at mother's departure because he anticipated danger or pain in her absence. A cognitive approach to separation anxiety has thrown new light on it (Kagan, 1984). Let us consider a child a year old who by now is able to retrieve the past and hold it in memory. Studies show that such a child, playing contentedly in a strange room who discovers his mother has left, looks at the door where she was last seen and presumably engages in the following mental process.

1. Retrieves the schema (i.e., the mental representation) of his mother, compares that with the present situation, and tries to resolve the inconsistency.
2. Tries to generate a prediction about her return to resolve the painful uncertainty. If he is not successful he may cry. If he is successful, he may laugh, as children even of eight months do when they expect a novel event, like mother's sudden reappearance.

Maternal behavior has considerable bearing on how children react to anxiety. The children of mothers who provide attentive, loving care and who value self-reliance and control over anxiety, tend not to cry when their mothers leave the room (Kagan, 1984).

Cognitive theorists point out that the degree of separation anxiety depends somewhat on the infant's expectations. Even in the first year, most infants can easily tolerate the mother's absence in situations of which they have developed an appropriate understanding (Kagan, 1972). For example, an infant does not feel threatened when her mother leaves her alone for a nap, in part because the infant understands "nap" and in part because she can cause the mother to reappear by crying. However, when mother disappears unexpectedly and the infant cannot through any efforts bring her back again, separation anxiety is experienced. Violation of expectancy and unavailability of response are contributing factors.

By the age of three, most children can tolerate a half-day nursery school session (Fraiberg, 1977). They are able to understand that mother, when not here, is somewhere else. And they have had considerable experience with departures and returns. However, separation anxiety is never entirely overcome. It is experienced throughout life, whenever we are confronted with the threat of losing someone or something we have become attached to.

During the dating years, the end of an intimate relationship can bring panicky feelings of the sort first experienced in childhood. Old age, with its series of bereavements, also reawakens our earliest fears of being abandoned. Bettelheim has gone so far as to call separation anxiety "man's greatest fear": "There is no greater threat in life than that we will be deserted, left all alone," he writes, ". . . and the younger we are the more excruciating is our anxiety when we feel deserted, for the young child actually perishes when not adequately protected and taken care of. Therefore the ultimate consolation is that we will never be deserted" (Bettelheim, 1976, p. 145).

Reliable and consistent availability of adult caregiving, in sum, leaves the infant with no more than ordinary, non-pathological separation anxiety and leads to a sense of security and feelings of self-worthiness. From such care, children develop a sense of self-reliance, giving them the belief that "they can prevail even in the face of stress or adversity" (Sroufe, 1986, p. 844).

Monsters, Night Terrors, and Punishment Anxieties

During the preschool years, children learn from experience that when they throw the plate of cereal off the table, they are scolded and told they are "naughty." When they are touching or rubbing their genitals, their hand is removed, as the parent frowns. The psychoanalytic point of view suggests that preschool children experience anxiety because they are unsure of their ability to control these forbidden and punishable impulses.

Another source of children's anxiety is the child's need to feel that he or she is "good" (Kagan, 1984). Of course to be good means not violating the standards taught by the parents. It also means meeting their expectations. Even as early as the second year, if a child cannot perform in a way that the child feels is expected, perhaps to recognize a picture in a storybook, or to dance as another child does, he will show signs of anxiety. Kagan tells of a three-and-a-half-year-old girl who lost a balloon through the open window of the car. To the mother's surprise, when she offered to stop the car and search for the balloon, her daughter said it was not necessary because she had lost it through her own negligence. This little girl believed she had violated a standard and deserved the punishment of being deprived of the balloon. (The mother did retrieve it.)

The threat children perceive is often exaggerated or fanciful—and no wonder, when adults threaten to eat them up because they are so delicious, or have the "boogeyman" get them because they indulge in naughty behavior. According to psychoanalytic interpretation, the child's forbidden impulses (e.g., to hit a sibling) also become anxiety-provoking thoughts (to hurt a parent), and many of these are expressed in nightmares. Monsters appear ready to eat people up. Lions and tigers represent the adults who punish the small child for his or her hostile feelings. Suddenly, there is fear of the dark—the bedroom is "scary" due to the imagined presence of witches, robbers, and the like. Fantasies of punishment and revenge are also acted out in play. Usually the child "grows out of it" in the sense that he or she stops having scary dreams and jumping into the parents' bed in the middle of the night.

Moral Anxieties

In the early school years, the child develops a conscience as well as an ideal image of himself. He internalizes the parents' set of values, and in order to keep adhering to these values, he internalizes the parents' authority to punish as well. The "parent" that has been created within the child—a concept that Freud called the superego—threatens the child with severe punishment when values are violated. Instead of reacting with fantasies of feared punishment, as preschoolers do, older children experience guilt, shame, and disgust with themselves. Freud referred to these feelings as *moral anxiety;* we tend to say that the person is conscience-stricken or, in unhealthy cases, guilt-ridden.

In the beginning, the superego of the child is cruel and uncompromising. A child may overcontrol or constrict himself, while at the same time showing intolerance toward others (Erikson, 1959). He has not developed the capacity for abstract thought that would allow him to balance the rules of behavior against cases that are exceptional. At this stage conscience is all or nothing. Attention to the rule is far more literal than in the adult.

If, through interaction and mutual feedback, parents and child arrive at an understanding of what the child's responsibilities are, the child will gradually develop an appreciation for the rules and for social institutions that is compatible with his healthy functioning as an adult. However, if the parent exploits the child's developing conscience (for example, by overly strict punishment) or sets a hypocritical example, the child may grow up to be rigidly moralistic and incapable of enjoyment.

Moral anxiety, as Piaget explained it, leads to self-punishment. It also leads to expectations of punishment by others, including fears of mutilation. Psychoanalytic theory gives a central position to what is called **castration anxiety.** According to that theory, toward the end of the preschool period, at about age five, the child enters the stage of pregenital sexuality, or phallic stage. He or she discovers the genitals as a source of secret pleasure. At this stage, the romantic object in the child's fantasy life is the parent of the opposite sex, and toward that object he or she is newly aggressive and jealous. For example, about boys Erikson writes: "Infantile jealousy and rivalry, those often embittered and yet essentially futile attempts at demarcating privilege, now come to a climax in the final contest for a favored position with the mother; the usual failure leads to resignation, guilt, and anxiety" (Erikson, 1963, p. 256).

The small boy feels guilty about his romantic fantasies and fears that he will be punished by having his penis, the organ of masturbation, harmed or removed. The extent to which boys actually experience "castration anxiety" is open to question. However, childhood anxiety in girls and boys does arouse fears of being hurt, so that children who are exceedingly anxious about being hospitalized for a tonsillectomy may be responding not only to a realistic fear of surgery and to concern about being separated from parents but also by the expectation of being punished through some form of bodily mutilation. That is why, it is believed, some children are seen carefully examining their fingers and toes, to see if they "are all there."

In conclusion, the causes of fears and anxieties change over the years. One major source at the age of one is separation from parent or the appearance of a stranger; at three it could be darkness or animals; at six, supernatural beings (ghosts) or thunder and lightning; at eight, news reports on child kidnapping or nuclear war threat; at ten, school performance; and by the teens, sexuality and social performance (Greist, Jefferson, & Marks, 1986). These changes reflect both the individual's growing intellectual capabilities and mastery over self and the environment (hence, separation from parents and the appearance of strangers no longer hold the same threat), and also the new demands made by shifting roles.

Castration Anxiety
Literally, in psychoanalytic terms, a male's concern about harm to his penis; more generally, concern by either sex about any type of bodily mutilation.

In recent decades, we have been learning more about anxiety as part of everyday adult life. In the normal process of moving from one stage of life (for example, the teen years) to the next (the 20s) we go through a transition period that probably arouses some anxiety in most of us and considerable anxiety in others (Levinson et al., 1978). Each stage sets its own demands; for example, those in the 20s are usually establishing a career, and often entering marriage and having a family. Those in the 60s call for preparation for retirement and acceptance of a variety of social and physical changes.

Anxiety, Stress, and Depression

In sum, no period of life is free of anxiety. The situations that give rise to it may change (e.g., anxiety about performance and self-esteem in school and then in the workplace); the interpersonal situations may be different (e.g., going out on a first date and having a first child); the source of loss may change (e.g., the young child's feelings when mother leaves the house and the elderly person's feelings when the spouse dies). Beyond those differences is the fact of anxiety's appearance at every age (Kalish, 1982).

STRESS

Harold noticed that ever since he and his family moved abroad he has been assailed by a variety of physical and psychological symptoms. He frequently suffers from an upset stomach; he sometimes feels an overpowering need to cry or scream; and he is impulsive and excitable with his children. In part to calm his nerves, he has begun to drink and smoke a little more. Though he has been meaning to see a doctor, he felt he didn't have time to call for an appointment because his new responsibilities as International Sales Manager are overwhelming. As it happened, Harold had a minor accident while helping his wife install shelves in their new house. It was just as well that this finally forced him to seek medical help.

Harold has been suffering from stress as a result of having encountered too many demands in his new environment and he reacted in a typical manner, one that could lead to physical illness:

1. Besides experiencing alterations in bodily processes,
2. he engaged in coronary prone behavior, and showed
3. ignorance of symptoms requiring medical assistance (Holroyd & Lazarus, 1982).

The Nature of Stress

As indicated earlier, there is no general agreement on the meaning given to the term stress. A common complaint is that the term, borrowed from the physical sciences, is imprecise when applied to human behavior, and is often used interchangeably with anxiety. According to one of the major contributors to knowledge about stress, Richard Lazarus, there is a heavy overlap between the two, with anxiety being a product of stress. He defines stress as "a relationship between the person and the environment that is appraised by the person as taxing or exceeding his or her resources and endangering his or her well-being" (Lazarus & Folkman, 1984, p. 21).

Physiologist Hans Selye, a pioneer in the study of stress, gave the background to his discoveries. He acknowledged the important influence of Walter Cannon, the physiologist who gave the name "homeostasis" to the tendency of an organism to call on its own resources to maintain its balance, or its "staying power." Cannon's studies showed that when an organism perceives a threat in the environment, the body responds to the emergency through the physiological changes associated with the "fight-or-flight" response. The "fight-or-flight" response clearly is adaptive when we are confronted with a predatory animal, an armed enemy, a bush fire, or some other explicit danger. Such presumably were the sorts of dangers that confronted earliest human beings, and while those of today are different, the modern world is hardly free of dangers and emergencies (Cannon, 1932/1967).

The General Adaptation Syndrome

While still a medical student, Selye's interest was first drawn to what he called the "syndrome of just being sick": Diseases of different kinds exhibited similar symptoms such as weight loss, lethargy, and reduced muscular strength. Research over a 10-year period led to the discovery that any taxing demand on the organism, whether subfreezing temperature, infection, or nervous irritation, produced identical changes in the organs. Later writers have extended Selye's concept of stress to include a person's response to psychological threats: to noisy working conditions, changes in family structure, loss of job, or relocation—all those experiences that we describe as putting a person under stress. Whatever the **stressor,** certain overall bodily reactions followed. This observation led Selye (1936, 1986) to propose a three-step model he called the General Adaptation Syndrome (GAS).

Stressor
That which precipitates stress in an individual.

He observed, after repeated or long-term exposure to a stressor the individual enters the first, or *alarm stage*. Adrenalin is secreted and the heart and respiratory rates accelerate, enabling the muscles to receive more oxygen. The individual is alert and prepared for "*fight or flight.*" Other hormones are also released, enabling the body to get optimal use of its energy supplies. However, during the alarm stage the individual's resistance to other stressors is lower.

If the organism survives and the threat persists, the *stage of resistance* sets in. At this point the body tries to adjust to the stress, raising its resistance, but at the cost of a considerable expenditure of effort. Eventually, if the stressor persists and is not managed, then the individual enters the *stage of exhaustion*—the body, under constant stress, has worn itself out.

Diseases of Adaptation

When stress is prolonged or presents intolerable demands, body organs reacting to it may be damaged and a disease of adaptation may result. **Diseases of adaptation** (sometimes called "stress diseases") are not caused by a disease agent such as a germ or by stress alone. They are caused by the inadequacy of a person's *responses* to the disease agent or other stressors. Also many psychological difficulties seem to result from an individual's inability to cope with such threats to his safety and security.

Diseases of Adaptation
Adverse physiological reactions that result from a person's inadequate responses to disease agents or other stressors.

Selye and other researchers have pointed out that it is not only "bad" stress (or distress) that makes demands on the individual. "Good" stress (or eustress) also can occur, and makes its own demand for readjustment. Examples of good or pleasant stress include the demands presented by childbirth,

foreign travel, or athletic competition. In addition to good and bad stress, Selye has written of two more variations on the stress concept: overstress (hyperstress) and understress (hypostress) (Selye, 1980). Overstress results when stressful events pile up, and we exceed the limits of our adaptability. Understress exists when we are bored, unchallenged, or unstimulated. During the course of life most people experience all four variations of stress. They are portrayed in Figure 3.2.

Type A Behavior

The "fight-or-flight" response to threat appears to have evolved in humans as a way to cope with short-term emergencies. Today, however, some people sustain a high level of anxiety over long periods of time. Their bodily mechanisms do not return them to a "normal" or non-aroused state. They are "chronically mobilized in response to the demands of a changing environment" (Russek & Russek, 1981).

The behavior of the chronically mobilized person has been described at length by Friedman and Rosenman (1974), two cardiologists who became interested in the behavioral factors that increased a person's risk of developing heart disease. Friedman and Rosenman identified a pattern of chronic anxiety which they named **Type A behavior.** The patients displaying this behavior complex were unable to relax. The cardiologists recall that an upholsterer who came to do work in their offices asked them in some confusion why only the front edges of their chairs were so worn: the reason was that the anxious Type A patients were always literally on the edge of their seats.

Type A Behavior
A pattern of chronic anxiety and pressured behaviors that results in stress and an increased chance of illness and disease.

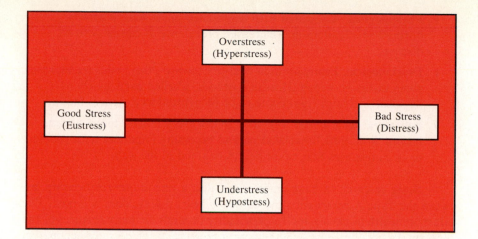

Figure 3.2. The four basic variations of stress.

Subsequently the cardiologists identified a number of characteristics that are typical of Type A patients. These patients appear to be engaged in a minute-by-minute struggle to get things done. They have an intense need to meet deadlines, and are impatient when events or coworkers move slowly. They kick elevators, curse at traffic, and eat and speak quickly, even when there is no apparent need to do so. They press themselves to do more than one thing at a time. And they are competitive even when they engage in potentially relaxing activities, such as golf, tennis, or casual conversation. Friedman and Rosenman, as well as other researchers, have shown that these behaviors eventually contribute to illness and disease. For example, the cardiologists found that the chronically mobilized Type A individual discharges excessive amounts of the "nerve hormones" norepinephrine and epinephrine, which contribute to high levels of cholesterol in the blood, ineffective clotting mechanisms, and other processes that can lead to coronary heart disease.

Type B individuals are more normal in the sense that they are less anxious and more relaxed. They show higher levels of self-esteem, are not so driven, and reveal less easily aroused hostility. And they do not have the same risk of heart disease. The contrast made between Type As and the rest of the population (Type Bs) should not give the impression of two distinct groups. There are some extreme Type As and Type Bs and in between a continuum, with many people probably possessing some characteristics of each. Furthermore, having Type A personality features does not, by any means, automatically lead to hypertension and coronary problems.

The Type A behavioral personality is multidimensional, and includes the following, each of which is illustrated by example:

▸ **Cognitive.** Self-worth is measured by accomplishments, so the individual must get ahead, no matter what the cost may be.

- **Physiological.** Associated with heightened physiological arousal during test situations and increased prevalence of coronary heart disease.

- **Psychological.** Easily aroused hostility toward others who are blamed when things go wrong. Hostile attitudes, labelled particularly as "cynical contempt," has come to be recognized as a critical factor.

- **Behavioral.** In a driven way, tries to use every minute to get ahead, leaving little time for relaxation and becoming impatient with people or circumstances that cause delays or stand in the way.

Some researchers have emphasized that a one-to-one relationship between the Type A personality and coronary heart disease does not exist. The effect on health of having such a personality depends on many features of the individual's life. These include the actual pressure of the person's occupation (quite apart from the pressure the person exerts on himself), the degree of social insecurity the individual experiences, and the routine traffic congestion to which the Type A person is exposed. Anyone with that kind of personality would be well served to avoid, insofar as possible, a highly pressured position and commuting during heavy traffic hours. These are not easily accomplished especially since such persons often do not define themselves as having the characteristics of the Type A. An observer, seeing their weekly work load as six or seven days with hardly a moment for relaxation, considers them to be making unrealistic demands on themselves. However, they may see themselves only as "ambitious."

There is reason to believe that the Type A personality has its roots in childhood. Besides such early temperamental attitudes that may predispose individuals to the development of that personality type (Thoresen, 1980), American society tends to reward children who exhibit the hard-driving, competitive Type A behavior (Steinberg, 1985). Whatever the origin, people with this kind of personality can now be treated. The use of behavior modification and prescription medicine (Beta blockade-therapy) can help the Type A individual control anxiety (Rosenman & Chesney, 1985).

People also can take active steps to help themselves. Besides the suggestions presented in the Self-Knowledge Exercise, the Type A individual can work toward:

- Eliminating self-destructive behaviors (e.g., making unrealistic demands on oneself).

- Adopting life-styles that favor good health (e.g., balanced combination of work and recreation).

- Becoming part of a social network and experiencing a sense of belonging (e.g., group of friends or college club) (Levi, 1983).

Type A Conversation

Do you possess a Type A behavior pattern? One way to help determine whether you do is to examine the ways you usually speak, listen, and behave in ordinary conversation. Listen to yourself, or use a tape recorder if you can do so without becoming self-conscious. See if you agree with the following statements (adapted from Friedman & Rosenman, 1974, pp. 82–85). If you do, you may be displaying the impatience, inability to relax, and competitiveness associated with Type A behavior.

Check the statements that are true.

_____ 1. I have a habit of speaking quickly.

_____ 2. I am a dramatic or emphatic speaker at all times. For example, I accentuate key words even when there is no special reason to do so.

_____ 3. I have a tendency to rush the last few words of my sentence.

_____ 4. I often finish other people's sentences for them. I find myself saying "Uh huh, uh huh," or "Yes, yes, yes" to hurry people along.

_____ 5. I always find it difficult to keep from bringing up whatever interests me. I feel uncomfortable waiting for the other person to finish.

_____ 6. I often pretend to listen, when I am actually thinking about something else.

_____ 7. I use certain characteristic gestures when speaking. For example, I clench my fist or jaw, or jerk the corners of my mouth backwards in a spasmodic way.

If you find that you display Type A behavior patterns in conversation, you can begin to change these behaviors through practice. For example, if you speak very quickly, practice speaking more slowly; listen to yourself on tape if possible. Become aware of other behaviors that you may be performing in a hurried manner—for example, eating and walking. Practice slowing your pace. If you find that you do not really listen to others, pay greater attention to the way you listen. Begin in friendly, nonpressured situations. As you listen, repeat briefly what others say; this will help you understand their points and also reduce your impatience (Suiin, 1976). To gain additional experience, seek out a person who has difficulty expressing himself, and listen calmly. For example, listen to a small child who is trying to explain something—without interrupting. ▲

How We Evaluate Stress

As we well know from observing people around us, what appears to be stressful, or a stressor, to one person is not necessarily stressful to another. A key factor in stress, as in anxiety, is the way in which a person evaluates or interprets events. And in stressful situations, what seems to be important is an *ongoing* process through which the person evaluates not only the initial threat or loss, but his ability to cope with it. He assesses his coping strategies with respect to their cost to him and their probability of success (Coyne & Lazarus, 1980). Is what has happened a catastrophe, or merely a challenge? Am I overwhelmed, or merely working to the best of my ability in a high-pressured environment?

Not surprisingly, research suggests that we experience more stress if we judge ourselves to be overwhelmed, without resources, and faring worse than we have in previous crises. A study of college students compared those seeking help from the counseling center with a matched group of other college students. The help-seekers had experienced a larger number of significant life events, and found more of them to be unexpected and undesirable than the non-help-seekers. Furthermore, the help-seekers experienced more pressure and felt less control over the events than the other group (Lubin & Rubio, 1985).

We may experience less stress if we can define a life situation as a *challenge* rather than a *threat*. Moreover, researchers expect that the person who feels challenged enjoys a better outcome, but the issue remains unsettled (Coyne & Lazarus, 1980).

Many stressors affect us because we are members of our society, and inhabitants of a particular social environment. These can be called **environmental stressors.** If we live or work in a large American city, for example, we probably are routinely subject to noise, litter, air pollution, and overcrowding (Glass & Singer, 1972). Our lives are an endless round of "hurried meals, hectic traffic, brusque and even hostile interpersonal exchanges" (p. 9), all of which we may fail to notice because we have become used to urban life, and accustomed to its inconveniences. Psychologists and the media are more attentive to these phenomena, and indeed much has been written about the stressful nature of modern society.

Among the conditions most often mentioned is overcrowding in urban centers. It is well known that laboratory animals exhibit physiological signs of stress, as well as decreased fertility, when housed in overcrowded quarters (Selye, 1956/1976). Crowding of human beings also produces stressful behaviors, ranging from "a fatigue of all social reactions" (Lorenz, 1963, p. 244) to irritability and aggression. However, crowding in and of itself may not be as significant as some of the accompanying trends: the weakening of community organization, the increased importance of social status and competition, and the increased levels of noise and other environmental pollutants.

Not only do the crowded bus, noisy traffic, and foul air of a typical urban center place demands on the individual, which may be characterized as a "continuous overload," but so does constant exposure to various media, resulting in an enormous increase in sensory input per time unit—especially visual and auditory input. This kind of "overload" represents a new and stressful demand in our environment. It is not confined to heavily urban areas but may be experienced anywhere a radio plays all day, to the accompaniment of one or more television sets. The glut of information, in the form of advertisements, magazines, and books, can be a source of stress to the print-oriented person, who sometimes reports a "depression" as the result of intellectual bombardment (Lapham, 1979).

A very different source of stress is isolation and loneliness. Students living in dormitories might consider whether the architectural design promotes or discourages social contact. Studies have shown that for some dormitories and housing projects the designs have been associated with social withdrawal and

Environmental Stressors
Factors in the environment that precipitate stress in an individual, such as noise, overcrowding, and competition on the job.

The Search for Personal Adjustment

perhaps even the encouragement of maladjustment (Fisher, Bell, & Baum, 1984). The breakdown of family bonds caused by mobility, the tendency of families to uproot themselves in response to job transfers and career changes—or in response to divorce—also causes loneliness and is a source of modern stress.

The association of stress with relocation, travel, and other aspects of urban living does not mean that these ingredients of modern life are necessarily "bad" for us, only that we must develop a means of adapting to them. To illustrate, frequent flyers learn to adjust to time zone differences by changing their sleep patterns in advance of trips. Urban dwellers learn to adjust to congested streets, subways, and offices by spending moments in city parks or in the country. And, good social support from family, friends, and others can help us manage these types of stressors (Fleming, Baum, Gisriel, & Gatchel, 1982; Holahan & Moos, 1985).

Other environmental pressures are a by-product of life in the nuclear age. In one study (Davidson & Baum, 1986), a sample of 52 adults who lived within a five-mile radius of the damaged Three Mile Island plant (TMI) in Pennsylvania was randomly selected almost five years after the nuclear accident. Despite the passage of time they were still exhibiting symptoms of stress.

Stress: Self-Observable Signs

There are many medical tests that can tell a person if he or she is under undue stress. Among these are the electroencephalogram, which measures the electrical activity of the brain; the galvanic skin resistance test, which detects variations in sweat secretion that occur under stress; and, of course, the blood pressure reading.

Hans Selye notes that there are also many signs that we can observe in ourselves when we are under unusual stress. The signs or symptoms are different for different individuals.

Below are statements that describe a person under stress (adapted from Selye, 1956/1976). Which, if any, describe you when you are under *unusual stress?*

_____ 1. Under stress, I am irritable and behave like a prima donna. I am impulsive and emotionally unstable.

_____ 2. Under stress, I am depressed, tired, lazy, and without joy in life.

_____ 3. Under stress, I experience feelings of unreality, weakness, or dizziness.

_____ 4. Under stress, I cannot concentrate on anything.

_____ 5. Under stress, I feel an overpowering urge to cry, or run and hide.

_____ 6. Under stress, I am tense and emotionally keyed up. I am so alert that I am easily startled (by loud noises, for example).

_____ 7. Under stress, I experience insomnia.

_____ 8. Under stress, I am unable to be still; I cannot relax; I move about aimlessly. ▲

Compared with a control group sample of 35 adults, comparable to the TMI sample in age, sex, education, and income, the TMI subjects showed higher levels of stress-related arousal. This was indicated by measures of hormones in the urine and of blood pressure. Psychological assessments also differentiated the two groups, showing the tendency of the TMI group to resort to avoidance of thoughts, feelings, and situations related to the accident, and especially to be subject to intrusive thoughts of the accident in the form of daydreams, dreams, and unwanted thoughts.

Even children and teenagers more than a hundred miles distance from the Three Mile Island accident, in written responses to questions about it, reported considerable concern. Weeks after the accident a higher percentage of the younger ones than the old, and of the girls than the boys gave answers that showed evidence of anxiety associated with nuclear power plants. These differences are explained in the following way: Children have less mastery over the environment than adolescents and therefore experience any threat more intensely. They are physically weaker in a world dominated by "big" people.

Living in a nuclear age, children and adults can experience anxiety about accidents at a power plant or the possibility of a nuclear war.

Intellectually they are not as advanced, and prior to about the age of 11 or 12, they are unable to engage in the logical thinking that helps them balance off safeguards and threats. For example, older teenagers can recognize, along with the risks, the precautions required by government to guard against accidents and also efforts by organized groups of citizens to reduce the number of nuclear plants. The differences between males and females is related to the difference in the socialization of the two sexes which still assigns the more commanding and controlling roles to males. Consequently, males tend to feel more secure and in control. It should be added that there is no "right" or "correct" amount of anxiety to show in response to the threat of a nuclear plant accident. However, extreme stress that immobilizes a person is both unhealthy and unhelpful in any circumstance, because it prevents the individual from seeking help or taking action. Similarly, unconcern and disregard for a potential threat is a maladaptive response because it means the person is ignoring a problem (Schwebel & Schwebel, 1981).

A related environmental source of stress in the nuclear age is the threat of war. Much research has been conducted, starting within a year after the atomic bombs were dropped on Hiroshima and Nagasaki in 1945. The last 10 years have been very productive in this regard, with some of the studies looking at the mental health effects of life in the nuclear age (Schwebel, 1986). Although the consequences of war-threat-related stress have not been conclusively established, close to 30 percent of high school seniors report that they worry about it often (Diamond & Bachman, 1986).

Unfortunately, many children in the world have to cope with more than the threat of war. They live their lives in the presence of armed conflict in one part of the world or another. Scientists have studied the effects on the children and the ways they and their families (if they still have intact families) try to adjust (Dodge & Raundalen, 1987; Kahnert, Pitt, & Taipale, 1983).

Stressful Life Events

Some stresses affect us because we live in a particular social environment. Others—such as death of a loved one or a job change—affect us individually, apart from our environment. Over the last 30 years, psychologists have devoted considerable research to identifying life events and scaling them according to their stressfulness, or "the magnitude of the adjustment they require." Researchers have attempted to discover which events seem to call forth our greatest coping efforts.

One scale, known as the Social Readjustment Rating Scale (SRRS), and the clinical instrument derived from it, the Schedule of Recent Events (SRE), developed by Holmes and Rahe (1967), have been widely used in research to find the relationship between life events on the one hand and stress, anxiety, depression, and physical illness on the other. The SRE, a self-administered questionnaire, contains 43 events. The researchers found significant agreement on the rating of life events. Serious losses, such as death of a spouse, divorce, and separation, were viewed as making the greatest demands on the individual and were more likely to result in general "wear and tear."

Holmes and Rahe, like Selye, assumed that it is the disruption of ongoing life patterns that produces stress and resulting impairment. The desirability or undesirability of the event was not considered in their experimental design. However, some researchers associate stress with undesirable events only. For example, stress has been defined as a state where the well-being or integrity of the individual is endangered—to the extent that he must devote all his energies to self-protection (Cofer & Appley, 1964, p. 463). According to this viewpoint, it is not change itself, but undesirable or threatening change, that is responsible for stress and its consequences. Indeed, Vinokur and Selzer (1975) have found that only undesirable events were significantly correlated with stress-related variables and that these events require the greatest adjustment.

Probably a more useful way to approach the problem of what kinds of experience constitute stress is by considering the person's own evaluation of it. A recent trend in research on stress avoids the direct linkage between the environment and health made both by Selye and by Holmes and Rahe. Instead, much more attention is paid to the psychosocial processes that intervene between the environment on the one hand, and the person's behavior and health on the other (Stokols, 1986). A seemingly positive life event like a promotion is a joy to one person, because she sees no threat in it and feels capable to cope with its demands. To another, it is the source of agonizing worries and sleepless nights so any ego satisfaction he might have immediately gotten is more than offset by stress. A life event is a source of stress to the extent that we perceive it as taxing or exceeding our resources to cope with it and as a threat to our well-being.

Recognizing the importance of the individual's perception of the desirability and impact of life events, Sarason, Johnson, and Siegel developed the Life Experience Survey (LES; 1978). This is a 60-item self-report measure divided in two sections, the first containing a list of 47 events plus three blank spaces for the individual to write in other events he or she might have experienced. The second section contains 10 events selected primarily for students. The subject indicates the following: whether the event was experienced in the last six or twelve months; whether the experience was positive or negative; how severe the impact was, with ratings of severity ranging from -3 to $+3$. The scoring is simple. The negative score is the total of all the minus ratings. The positive score is the total of all the plus items, and the total score is a sum of the negative and positive scores disregarding signs, that is -6 and $+9 = 15$. The LES is presented in the Self-Knowledge Exercise entitled, "Your Life Experience Survey."

Among the findings reported by those using the LES is that negative scores were related to a person's anxiety level so that, for example, the higher the negative score the more the person tends to show evidences of anxiety. Negative scores were also found to relate in a negative way to academic achievement: The tendency was the higher the scores, the lower the grade point average. A further study showed that college students who seek help from a university counseling center obtain higher negative scores on the LES than random groups of college students. In all, this is impressive evidence that people find negatively experienced life events stressful, and that anxiety, depression, poor academic performance, and recognized need for professional help are often associated with those events.

Further indication that the *same* life experience may lead to very *different* reactions may be found in material prepared as an aid in diagnosing mental health problems. Table 3.2 is a modified version of a table on psychosocial stressors in the most recent American Psychiatric Association's 1987 *Diagnostic and Statistical Manual of Mental Disorders*. Note that examples of adult stressors include new careers, and pregnancy and birth of a child, which are sources of pleasure to many people, and that child/adolescent stressors include vacation with the family and a new school year.

The examples given here suggest that particular events, such as the death of a close friend, have the potential of causing a particular level of stress in an individual. The degree of stress experienced depends upon many aspects of the individual that determine how he or she perceives and reacts to the event. Individual differences are very apparent, and such differences—lesser or greater reaction to the stressor—do not, themselves, indicate abnormality. On the face of it, we would expect a concentration camp experience to be much more severe (catastrophic, in fact) than the death of a close friend, and clinical observations confirm that difference. Nevertheless, some people survived the horrors of the camps reasonably well and some people are thoroughly broken up by the death of a friend.

TABLE 3.2 *Scale for Rating Severity of Psychosocial Stressors*

Term	Adult Examples	Child or Adolescent Examples
None	No apparent psychosocial stressor	No apparent psychosocial stressor
Minimal	Minor violation of the law; small bank loan	Vacation with family
Mild	Argument with neighbor; change in work hours	Change in schoolteacher; new school year; broke up with boyfriend or girlfriend
Moderate	New career; death of close friend; pregnancy; marriage	Chronic parental fighting; change to new school; illness of close relative; birth of sibling
Severe	Major illness in self or family; major financial loss; marital separation; birth of a child	Death of peer; divorce of parents; arrest; hospitalization; persistent and harsh parental discipline
Extreme	Death of close relative; divorce; victim of rape	Death of parent or sibling; repeated physical or sexual abuse
Catastrophic	Concentration camp experience; devastating natural disaster; suicide of spouse	Multiple family deaths; chronic life-threatening illness

Reprinted with permission from the *Diagnostic and Statistical Manual of Mental Disorders, Third Edition, revised.* Copyright 1987 American Psychiatric Association.

Other work in the general area of stress-related experience has taken a different direction. Instead of concentrating on life events, researchers have turned their attention to ordinary, run-of-the-mill daily "hassles." New careers, marriage, and the death of loved ones are not frequent occurrences, whereas being caught in a traffic jam, having it rain on weekends, or getting "called on the carpet," may occur much more often than we can tolerate. Here, too, the emphasis is on the individual's perception and experience of the occurrences that are stress-producing hassles for some people but not for others (Lazarus & DeLongis, 1983).

Stress and the Life Span

No age group can escape stress. We will briefly note its presence in children, college students, and elderly people.

In a study of almost 1000 first-to-fourth grade children, 22 percent had experienced at least one recent stressful life event (e.g., death or serious illness of a parent, sibling, or close relative; parents separated; family's severe economic difficulty) (Sterling, Cowen, Weissberg, Lotyczewski, & Boike, 1985). These children were rated by teachers as more maladjusted and less competent than matched peers who had not experienced crises during the same period. And children who had been confronted with multiple stressful events were rated as more maladjusted and less competent than those who had experienced a fewer number. The investigators regard the 22 percent finding as an underestimate and concluded that there was a need for interventions to help children cope with stressful events more effectively and with fewer destructive consequences.

Your Life Experience Survey

The Life Experience Survey (LES) was developed to help researchers assess the amount of stress in people's lives. You can use this slightly modified version of the LES to gain insight into your own life. Has it been a big year for personal changes? Do you regard the changes as positive or negative? As having had a weak or powerful impact on you? Or was the year one of those relatively uneventful ones that occur in every life?

1. Read the instructions carefully; then read each item in the Survey.
2. When you have completed the survey, add the minuses (3 points for a −3, 2 points for − 2, etc.) and the pluses separately and then total the two, disregarding signs. You will then have your total, plus and minus scores.
3. Make a rough comparison of your scores with those of other undergraduates. Since the negative and total scores are the most meaningful ones, we give you those.

   The average negative score for men was about 6. Two-thirds of the men had negative scores between about 0 and 12. The average total score was about 16, and two-thirds of the men had scores between 5 and 27.

   The average negative score for women was about 7. Two-thirds of the women had negative scores between 0 and 15. The average total score for women was about 17, and two-thirds of the women had scores between about 7 and 27.

4. Note that your scores say nothing about how you have been coping with the events in your life. If you have not developed appropriate coping mechanisms and have few outside supports, you may have experienced "extremely negative" events as very stressful. If you have developed successful coping mechanisms and can utilize many sources of support, even a major life crisis may seem to be manageable and maybe even a challenge, or a time of personal growth. Coping mechanisms and sources of support are discussed in Chapters 4 and 6.

The Life Experiences Survey

Listed below are a number of events which sometimes bring about change in the lives of those who experience them. *Please check those events which you have experienced in the recent past.*

For each item checked, *please indicate the extent to which you viewed the event as having either a positive or negative impact on your life* at the time the event occurred. That is, *indicate the type and extent of impact that the event had.* A rating of −3 would indicate an extremely negative impact. A rating of 0 suggests no impact either positive or negative. A rating of +3 would indicate an extremely positive impact.

Section 1	extremely negative	moderately negative	somewhat negative	no impact	slightly positive	moderately positive	extremely positive
1. Marriage	−3	−2	−1	0	+1	+2	+3
2. Detention in jail or comparable institution	−3	−2	−1	0	+1	+2	+3
3. Death of spouse	−3	−2	−1	0	+1	+2	+3
4. Major change in sleeping habits	−3	−2	−1	0	+1	+2	+3

	extremely negative	moderately negative	somewhat negative	no impact	slightly positive	moderately positive	extremely positive
5. Death of close family member:							
a. mother	−3	−2	−1	0	+1	+2	+3
b. father	−3	−2	−1	0	+1	+2	+3
c. brother	−3	−2	−1	0	+1	+2	+3
d. sister	−3	−2	−1	0	+1	+2	+3
e. grandmother	−3	−2	−1	0	+1	+2	+3
f. grandfather	−3	−2	−1	0	+1	+2	+3
g. other (specify) _____	−3	−2	−1	0	+1	+2	+3
6. Major change in eating habits	−3	−2	−1	0	+1	+2	+3
7. Foreclosure on mortgage or loan	−3	−2	−1	0	+1	+2	+3
8. Death of close friend	−3	−2	−1	0	+1	+2	+3
9. Outstanding personal achievement	−3	−2	−1	0	+1	+2	+3
10. Minor law violations (traffic tickets, disturbing the peace, etc.)	−3	−2	−1	0	+1	+2	+3
11. *Male*: Wife/girlfriend's pregnancy	−3	−2	−1	0	+1	+2	+3
12. *Female*: Pregnancy	−3	−2	−1	0	+1	+2	+3
13. Changed work situation (different work responsibility, major change in working conditions, working hours, etc.)	−3	−2	−1	0	+1	+2	+3
14. New job	−3	−2	−1	0	+1	+2	+3
15. Serious illness or injury of close family member:							
a. father	−3	−2	−1	0	+1	+2	+3
b. mother	−3	−2	−1	0	+1	+2	+3
c. sister	−3	−2	−1	0	+1	+2	+3
d. brother	−3	−2	−1	0	+1	+2	+3
e. grandfather	−3	−2	−1	0	+1	+2	+3
f. grandmother	−3	−2	−1	0	+1	+2	+3
g. spouse	−3	−2	−1	0	+1	+2	+3
h. other (specify)	−3	−2	−1	0	+1	+2	+3
16. Sexual difficulties	−3	−2	−1	0	+1	+2	+3
17. Trouble with employer (in danger of losing job, being suspended, demoted, etc.)	−3	−2	−1	0	+1	+2	+3
18. Trouble with in-laws	−3	−2	−1	0	+1	+2	+3
19. Major change in financial status	−3	−2	−1	0	+1	+2	+3
20. Major change in closeness of family members	−3	−2	−1	0	+1	+2	+3
21. Gaining a new family member (through birth, adoption, family member moving in, etc.)	−3	−2	−1	0	+1	+2	+3
22. Change in residence	−3	−2	−1	0	+1	+2	+3
23. Marital separation from mate (due to conflict)	−3	−2	−1	0	+1	+2	+3
24. Major change in church activities	−3	−2	−1	0	+1	+2	+3
25. Marital reconciliation with mate	−3	−2	−1	0	+1	+2	+3
26. Major change in number of arguments with spouse	−3	−2	−1	0	+1	+2	+3

	extremely negative	moderately negative	somewhat negative	no impact	slightly positive	moderately positive	extremely positive
27. *Married male*: Change in wife's work outside the home (beginning work, ceasing work, changing to a new job, etc.)	−3	−2	−1	0	+1	+2	+3
28. *Married female*: Change in husband's work (loss of job, beginning new job, retirement, etc.)	−3	−2	−1	0	+1	+2	+3
29. Major change in usual type and/or amount of recreation	−3	−2	−1	0	+1	+2	+3
30. Borrowing more than $10,000 (buying home, business, etc.)	−3	−2	−1	0	+1	+2	+3
31. Borrowing less than $10,000 (buying car, TV, getting school loan, etc.)	−3	−2	−1	0	+1	+2	+3
32. Being fired from job	−3	−2	−1	0	+1	+2	+3
33. *Male*: Wife/girlfriend having abortion	−3	−2	−1	0	+1	+2	+3
34. *Female*: Having abortion	−3	−2	−1	0	+1	+2	+3
35. Major personal illness or injury	−3	−2	−1	0	+1	+2	+3
36. Major change in social activities, e.g., parties, movies, visiting	−3	−2	−1	0	+1	+2	+3
37. Major change in living conditions of family (building new home, remodeling, deterioration of home, neighborhood, etc.)	−3	−2	−1	0	+1	+2	+3
38. Divorce	−3	−2	−1	0	+1	+2	+3
39. Serious injury or illness of close friend	−3	−2	−1	0	+1	+2	+3
40. Retirement from work	−3	−2	−1	0	+1	+2	+3
41. Son or daughter leaving home (due to marriage, college, etc.)	−3	−2	−1	0	+1	+2	+3
42. Ending of formal schooling	−3	−2	−1	0	+1	+2	+3
43. Separation from spouse (due to work, travel, etc.)	−3	−2	−1	0	+1	+2	+3
44. Engagement	−3	−2	−1	0	+1	+2	+3
45. Breaking up with boyfriend/girlfriend	−3	−2	−1	0	+1	+2	+3
46. Leaving home for the first time	−3	−2	−1	0	+1	+2	+3
47. Reconciliation with boyfriend/girlfriend	−3	−2	−1	0	+1	+2	+3

Other recent experiences (if any) which have had an impact on your life. List and rate.

	extremely negative	moderately negative	somewhat negative	no impact	slightly positive	moderately positive	extremely positive
48. _____	−3	−2	−1	0	+1	+2	+3
49. _____	−3	−2	−1	0	+1	+2	+3
50. _____	−3	−2	−1	0	+1	+2	+3

Section 2: Student Only

	extremely negative	moderately negative	somewhat negative	no impact	slightly positive	moderately positive	extremely positive
51. Beginning a new school experience at a higher academic level (college, graduate school, professional school, etc.)	−3	−2	−1	0	+1	+2	+3
52. Changing to a new school at same academic level	−3	−2	−1	0	+1	+2	+3
53. Academic probation	−3	−2	−1	0	+1	+2	+3
54. Being dismissed from dormitory or other residence	−3	−2	−1	0	+1	+2	+3
55. Failing an important exam	−3	−2	−1	0	+1	+2	+3
56. Changing a major	−3	−2	−1	0	+1	+2	+3
57. Failing a course	−3	−2	−1	0	+1	+2	+3
58. Dropping a course	−3	−2	−1	0	+1	+2	+3
59. Joining a fraternity/sorority	−3	−2	−1	0	+1	+2	+3
60. Financial problems concerning school (in danger of not having sufficient money to continue)	−3	−2	−1	0	+1	+2	+3

▲

College students, of course, are not immune to stress. On the Social Readjustment Rating Questionnaire, 25 percent of 159 students in a junior level psychology course reported death of a close family member during the prior year (De Meuse, 1985). Also, 7 percent reported death of a close friend, 14 percent personal injury or illness, and 3 percent, sex difficulties. The chief objective of the study was to find the relationship between classroom performance and stressful life events. The results were clear, although they did not apply to all students who experienced stress. Life stress was found to be inversely related to various indices of performance in the course; the probability was the more the stress the lower the grade. Next, De Meuse examined all the course grades earned by the students that term. Again the results suggested that the higher the level of stress, the greater the likelihood of lower grades. Fortunately, students can be helped. Stress management programs for college students have been found to be effective (Somerville, 1984).

With the elderly, results have varied with the sample studied. One group of retired, middle class, educated people reported stress from boredom and loneliness (Kennedy, 1985). For another sample of elderly in New York City (whose average age was 72.3, with 56 percent female and 93 percent white), stress items included family illness, mugging in the past year, and financial problems (Cohen, Teresi, & Holmes, 1985). This same study also showed the value of social networks to these subjects—133 single-room occupants of mid-Manhattan hotels. Such networks (e.g., with hotel staff, family members, and nonfamily contacts) "exert a direct effect on subsequent physical health" (p. 484). They actually reduced the *number* of subsequent physical symptoms in those with relatively low stress levels at the beginning of the one-year study. In addition, they served as a buffer to reduce the *effects* of stressful experiences in those who encountered high stress events. The authors concluded that social support systems are so powerful that interventions to reinforce them can be as significant as the implementation of medical treatment.

Finally, it should be noted that *attitudes* toward stressful life events vary with one's position in the life span. Schwebel et al. (1978) studied attitudes in an Ohio neighborhood where the socioeconomic and ethnic composition was changing, causing some social tension. Subjects assessed the seriousness of 125 problem areas, some social and others individual. The results were divided into two age groups, as shown in Table 3.3. Clearly there is some agreement, but events judged as problematic, or stressful, will depend on one's point in the life span as well as myriad other factors.

DEPRESSION

Jean's roommate tried to get her to go to class, but with no success. Jean just said, "What's the use?" and buried her head in a pillow. It began two days earlier when she suffered a double blow to her ego. At the end of her English class, when the first weekly paper was returned, she found a grade of C and the instructor's comment that it was "disappointing because your remarks in

TABLE 3.3   Rankings of Problem Areas by Two Age Groups

18- to 44-Year-Old Respondents	45-Year-Old and Older Respondents
1. Feeling safe walking at night	1. Feeling safe walking at night
2. Traffic	2. Poor health
3. Stray dogs	3. Being nervous and worried
4. Budgeting money for food	4. Adequacy of street lighting
5. Getting an adequate salary	5. Stray dogs
6. Drug abuse	6. Home's physical condition
7. Being nervous and worried	7. Traffic
8. Home's physical condition	8. Becoming a burden to family
9. Recreational facility availability	9. Budgeting money for food
10. Adequacy of street lighting	10. Basement or street flooding
11. Basement or street flooding	11.5 Neighborhood deterioration
12. Insufficient space in home	11.5 Adequacy of retirement income
13. Cost of maintaining a car	13. Drug abuse
14. Pests (rats, insects, etc.)	14. Fear of burglary
15. Lack of employment	15. Prospects for family's future

Adapted with permission from A. I. Schwebel, et al., "Developing a Community Concern Index" in *Journal of Community Development Society of America*, Spring 1978, 9(1), 80–89.

class led me to expect better quality." She felt devastated because this was her best subject and already she had disappointed the instructor and herself.

When she got back to her dorm she found a message from her friend Bill, "Something came up, can't make it for dinner, will call." In the evening, returning from the cafeteria, Jean saw him in the distance, walking with his arm around another woman. That night she couldn't keep her mind on her work and couldn't sleep.

The next day she just stayed in bed while her mind was occupied with thoughts about how she had ruined her reputation with her English professor, and how she must have lost out in competition for Bill.

When her roommate brought her a sandwich and coffee, Jean took a bite of the food and burst into tears. The world seemed like an awful place—almost too difficult to cope with. When her roommate reassured her that she was just "down in the dumps" and would soon feel better, Jean shook her head and began to weep. Her roommate was right: A week later Jean was beginning to come to life again and within two weeks she was almost her old self. She was no longer depressed. She had arranged an appointment with her English instructor who by this time had read and highly praised her second paper. As for Bill, whom she confronted and who gave her a lame excuse, she decided to forget him. Already she had met another man in one of her classes who invited her to a social. The mild depression that Jean had suffered was gone.

Normal and Clinical Types of Depression

Depression
A pattern of sad feelings, which range from a temporary "low" to a chronic psychological disorder.

For most if not all people, at least some time in life, a loss or defeat sets off feelings of **depression,** which are something akin to mourning and leaves us discouraged, sad, and apathetic. Our energy level is low, we show a lack of interest in our friends and surroundings, and become preoccupied with the precipitating events, such as those in Jean's case that gave her a sense of failure and loss. Feelings like these may appear at any time, from childhood to the end of life. Their normalcy are made dramatically apparent by an estimate made by Seligman that at any given time 25 to 30 percent of college undergraduates have symptoms of depression (Rosenhan & Seligman, 1984).

Earlier in this chapter we noted that anxiety and stress are normal human reactions and become abnormal or pathological only when they reach such proportions that they are disabling. The same applies to depression. It is difficult to go through life without feeling "blue" at some time or other. However, such mild depression must be distinguished from the mental illnesses that are known as the **affective disorders.** The similarities and differences between the normal and abnormal forms of depression seem to be well illustrated by the fact that depression is sometimes referred to as "the common cold of mental illness." While all people get colds from time to time in life, probably most people do not suffer from pneumonia. All people get depressed at some time in their life, but most people do not suffer from an affective disorder.

Affective Disorders
Psychological disorders involving disturbances of mood.

Unipolar Depression
A psychological disorder marked only by depression.

Bipolar Depression
A psychological disorder marked by alternate moods of elation and depression.

The affective disorders are presented in Chapter 5 along with other forms of psychopathology. Here we want to point out that psychopathological depression takes two forms: **unipolar depression,** in which the individual's symptoms are purely those of depression (e.g., hopelessness, shame, worthlessness), and **bipolar depression,** sometimes called manic-depression, in which the symptoms alternate between the depressive and the manic type of symptom (e.g., grossly inflated self-esteem, incessant talking, inappropriate elation). The symptoms of normal mild depression are similar to those of unipolar depression except that they are not so severe and long-lasting, and do not appear as frequently. Furthermore, a given individual with mild depression does not have as many symptoms as the patient with unipolar depression. A problem of differentiating between the two arises when the mild depression continues much beyond a month or two.

Theories to Explain the Causes of Depression

Many theories have been proposed to explain the origins of depression. We will present a few of the more prominent using the categories developed by Whybrow, Akiskal, and McKinney (1984). These theories are useful because they explain what leads people to be *predisposed* to depressive reactions. They are also useful in providing insight about experiences and events in everyday life that precipitate the "blues."

Attachment to other people is a basic human drive. Loss of a loved one, at any age, leads to the depressive symptoms of grief and mourning. John Bowlby (1982) has extensively studied the process of forming attachments and the consequences of separation and loss in primates. His findings and those of others suggest that disruption of the mother-infant bond leads first to what might be called an active protest stage, then despair, and finally withdrawal. The infant is depressed at separation and loss of mother. Loss at that age is devastating and, unless a new close bond is developed, can lead to serious lifetime consequences.

By contrast, loss at a later age is obviously more manageable. An interview study of 109 bereaved women who had been widowed showed that more than 50 percent were experiencing depressed moods, crying spells, and disturbed sleep. Their symptoms occurred mostly in the first few months after the husband's death. Although many of them had symptoms indistinguishable from seriously depressed people, the women themselves and their families recognized their reactions as normal bereavement, or reactive depression. The women as a group during this period showed no greater use of hospitals, physicians, or psychotropic (antidepressant) drugs than the general population (Clayton, Halikes, & Maurice 1971). They had experienced a loss, reacted to it with varying degrees of normal depressive symptoms, and came out of it satisfactorily.

The psychoanalytic term, "object loss," has been used to explain the cause of depression. It refers to separation from an "object" to which one has had a significant attachment. Such an object frequently is a loved one but may also be part of one's body such as a limb, or ideals that were central to a person's life and have been "lost" due to disillusioning experiences. A child's belief that a newborn sibling has become the parental favorite falls into this category of precipitators of depression. So, too, does the feeling of rejection when a friend or lover has chosen another person. Not only is loss of an "object" involved in the onset of depression but also, it is believed, the resultant loss of self-esteem. However, the extent to which self-esteem is affected depends on how the individual interprets the experience, a topic discussed next.

Negative Cognition

Aaron Beck's cognitive theory of depression is currently influential in explaining and treating this problem. According to Beck, disturbances in thinking are at the root of depression (Beck et al., 1979). Individuals are depressed because they process information in distorted ways. They distort because their thinking is dominated by what he calls a "cognitive triad," composed of a negative view of themselves, their experiences, and their future. The world is a hostile place that sets insurmountable obstacles before them. They, themselves, in contrast with others, are helpless in such a world and, as a result, feel hopeless and worthless. Consequently, when a loss occurs—a friend or

When a loss occurs,
individuals may process
information in a distorted way,
leading them to blame
themselves and view their
whole world negatively.

lover leaves them for another—their reaction, if they are predisposed to depression, is to blame themselves: "No wonder. I'm no good. Not attractive enough, and there's just nothing I can do about it."

Beck has said that it is not the cognitions or thoughts themselves that cause depression, but rather a deficiency in the cognitive apparatus (Beck & Emery, 1985). He explained the deficiency in this way: Ordinarily, opposing modes are at work to keep us in balance. For instance, a success may give us a feeling of elation. We enjoy that feeling for a while but then we "come back down to earth" again, if for no other reason than that life does not give us reason to be elated all the time and actually provides us with setbacks or just routine negative feedback to deflate us as often as we are elated. However, when something goes wrong and the opposing mode is not operating we remain elated all the time and end up in a manic state. The same applies to the experience of depression.

For instance, after we suffer a loss, as in the case of Jean who suffered a loss of self-esteem because of a low grade and rejection by her male friend, the opposite mode soon manifests itself and we take action, as Jean did in seeing her instructor and in seeking another male friend. From loss of attachment and self-esteem she moved to new attachment and regained self-esteem. One of the key points in Beck's cognitive theory is that how we *think* about an event, such as a loss of a lover, determines how we will react to it. Important as the event is, equally important is how we interpret it. People can learn to monitor their own reactions and avoid inappropriate interpretations like, "This is the end of the world," or "She turned me down, I just don't attract women."

Learned Helplessness

As we noted, Beck's theory gives helplessness a central position in depression. Martin Seligman (1975) carried this further by trying to explain the cause of feelings of helplessness. Harnessed dogs were first subjected to electric shock from which they could not escape. Later, when unharnessed, they failed to escape from the shock despite the fact that they were free to do so. Seligman applied his findings to human depression, claiming that the apathy, passivity, and resignation evident in depressives were the result of learned helplessness. Just like the dogs, he theorized, depressed people had had the unfortunate experience of being helpless to deal with a threatening experience. As a result, they learned to be helpless.

The theory of learned helplessness attracted much attention, but also criticism. When the approach was applied to humans, the results were inconsistent. Being in a situation in which they had no control did not by any means lead all people to be passive and depressed. The reason given is that unlike animals, the power of an event depends not only on the event itself but also on what it means to the individual (Lazarus & Folkman, 1984). One person rejected by a lover reacts with feelings of lowered self-esteem and depression; another person reacts with, "Good riddance. You're not worth my tears. I'll end up with someone a lot better." The concept of learned helplessness is useful if one bears in mind that events or experiences themselves do not cause the symptoms of depression. They must be combined with an individual's tendency to interpret the event as overpowering. That still leaves us with the question about what makes some people inclined to make very negative interpretations.

Noncontingent Reinforcement

Another theory, first proposed by Peter Lewinsohn (1981), postulates that depression arises as a result of adult failure to give adequate reinforcement to a child's healthy behavior. Humans interact with their environment from the beginning of life. Their behavior is repeated if it is appropriately reinforced. For example, when the child puts his arms around mother and gets a smile, a hug, or kiss, he will surely repeat this act. However, if the mother draws away, or expresses disapproval ("Get your dirty hands off my face"), and if the mother persists in giving such a response, or gives none at all, then the child will not touch her. If this reaction is characteristic of her relationship with the child, then it is likely that he will withdraw all the more in his relationship with her and will be ill equipped for close relationships with anyone. The mother's inappropriate reaction then lays the groundwork for depression in childhood, adolescence, or later in life.

Experiences of the kind just described make depression-prone people inadequately equipped with interpersonal skills. Hence, compared with others, they are not prepared to maximize satisfying relationships (and thus get positive reinforcement) and minimize negative ones (and avoid punishment).

Consistent with this theory, depressed people were found to have less involvement in social activities and less satisfaction from them (Dean, 1985). Put very simply, they were found to have less fun.

Such findings have led to two related types of treatment that are really two kinds of learning experiences. One is training to improve the person's interpersonal skills so that he can get more socially involved and more reward from such involvement. The other is a training program to encourage and assist people to schedule pleasant events in their lives and reduce the number of negative ones. A course for the elderly, which grew out of Lewinsohn's work on coping with depression by adults (1987), has been found to be effective in improving mood. Depression was considerably reduced and life skills improved. This training program, known as the Life Satisfaction Course, is regarded as effective for purposes of preventing depression (Breckenbridge, Zeiss, & Thompson, 1987).

Biological Explanations

Researchers have been searching for the biological underpinnings of depression. Although their interest is in clinical depression, rather than the types that most people experience, their findings may someday help in the treatment of "the blues." The work thus far has raised important hypotheses but are by no means conclusive.

The discovery of the biochemical influence has an interesting history. In the 1950s a drug called reserpine was used to treat cases of hypertension (high blood pressure). Reserpine was drawn from a plant called *Rauwolfia serpentina,* which had been used to treat mental illness in India for centuries (Winokur, 1981). In the 1960s it was noted that about 15 percent of those who had taken reserpine showed depression-type symptoms. One interpretation of this finding is that reserpine activates an already-present tendency toward depression. In other words, the 15 percent of those whom it affected in this way were probably predisposed to depression. The chemical effect of the reserpine was to deplete the individual of available biogenic amines. (Amines, derivatives of ammonia, are essential to well-being.) One explanation of the difference between depression and mania is that in the former too little amine is available and in the latter (mania), too much. It appears that lithium, a widely used drug in treatment of the affective disorders, helps achieve the proper balance of amines.

In real life, unlike laboratory and clinical study, all the forces—biological, psychological, sociological—work together. They are not separate. Loss of attachment to a loved one, the stresses of pregnancy and childbirth, and any of the other human experiences known to be related to depression have their physiological, psychological, and social effects very nearly at the same time. Those who propose theories that largely emphasize one over the other are aware of these interconnections.

The happy outcome of all the research and theorizing is the brighter outlook for the future. Not only have we seen breakthroughs in treatment, we are now seeing efforts at prevention. One example of that is an entire book devoted to *Depression Prevention* (Munoz, 1987).

Normal Life-Crisis Depression

Normal life-crisis feelings of depression sometimes develop in reaction to external events, such as death of a loved one, illness or injury, divorce, abortion or miscarriage, job loss, or academic failure. When the depression follows a bereavement, we tend to call it "grief" or "a grief reaction." It is important to note that a normal life-crisis depressed feeling can be precipitated by success as well as failure. For example, a writer may experience depression upon completing a major work; a student may feel depressed after graduation. They, too, have experienced a "loss" in the psychological sense, for they no longer have the goals and tasks to which they have been committed and the structured program that has organized their life for a year or more.

When we experience a normal life-crisis feeling of depression, we suffer from temporary loss of self-esteem. The illness, job loss, or other event that has occurred makes us feel powerless, humiliated, or bereft of love. For example, a man who has painfully ended a close relationship may have difficulty falling asleep at night or getting up in the morning. Perhaps he is uninterested in food or no longer takes pleasure in his hobbies. Even the colors in his environment appear dull. For most people, the depressed feeling usually subsides within a month.

Normal life-crisis feelings of depression occur more frequently among women partly because childbirth is a stressful experience. To give a fuller picture it should be said that stress connected with reproduction affects some women not only at childbirth but during the pregnancy and postpartum periods (time period immediately following childbirth) as well. Profound physiological, social, and psychological changes accompany all three periods (Hopkins, Marcus, & Campbell, 1984). Three different types of depressive reactions have been distinguished, with two of them falling within the normal life-crisis category. Before we examine those two, we can say that the most extreme form, known as postpartum psychosis, fortunately has a very low incidence, occurring in only about one in a thousand births. (Postpartum psychosis is like other cases of acute psychosis, involving delusions related to childbirth, including guilty thoughts about the baby and the husband.)

Normal Life-Crisis Feelings of Depression
Feeling blue or "down in the dumps," as a result of a normal reaction to stressful life events such as job loss, divorce, or even college graduation.

To turn now to the two other forms of depression associated with childbirth, the mildest and most common form, "maternity blues" affects an estimated 50 percent to 80 percent of all mothers. This very transient mood alteration lasts only about 24 to 48 hours. The next type, a mild to moderate postpartum depression, affects as many as 20 percent of mothers. Data on the duration of this condition are contradictory, some suggesting an average of six to eight weeks, while others show women reporting symptoms even a year after delivery. Although many studies have been conducted to assess the relationship of a host of variables to postpartum depression, that is, age, parity (number of previous childbirths), social class, pregnancy history, biological and psychological variables, various problems in the research prevent any firm conclusions. However, two lines of research appear to be promising.

First, increasing evidence shows a positive association between stressful life events during pregnancy (over and beyond that of childbirth itself) and the early postpartum period. One might think of this as the "last straw" phenomenon; that is, life events, such as serious illness of a parent, or marital discord, or financial hardships, or several of these together are capped off with the significant stressor that childbirth embodies. Second, social support, in the form of practical help as well as emotional closeness, may be highly important in preventing psychological problems. Significant among the sources of support is, as one would expect, a good confidential relationship with the husband or, especially for the single mother, with a relative or friend. Further research on this important disorder is important in the interest of the mother, the father, the mother-infant relationship, and the family as a whole. Also considering the high percentage of mothers in the work force today, their disablement for many weeks or months has its economic cost as well (Hopkins, Marcus, & Campbell, 1984).

In conclusion, social experience prior to the onset of depression of any kind seems to be inordinately important. According to cognitive theories of depression, certain thoughts or attitudes that arise from the individual's experience and history, and that are themselves depressing, precede the appearance of depressed moods. Bebbington (1985), drawing on three cognitive theories, has found those thoughts and attitudes to be of four related types. Each of them is presented here with a first-person statement indicating how a depressed person might express his or her experience of the attitude: low self-esteem ("I am incompetent"), self-blame ("I could have and should have prevented it"), helplessness/hopelessness ("I can't do anything about it now and nobody can"), and burden or imposition ("Why me? Why has this been put on *me*?").

Depression and the Life Span

Although many life crises are clearly related to stressful events, some appear to be the result of the normal maturation process. We are not confronted by a single dramatic event, such as a death or job loss; instead we experience the inevitable changes that take place as we grow up or grow older.

As we have already noted, young children show symptoms of depression when the caregiver fails to provide appropriate responses to the child's behavior, that is, when the adult is not loving and giving. Infants and young children who are given inadequate care and attention show such symptoms as weak crying, apathy, excessive sleep, and absence of smiles and alert responses.

Depression is found in school-age children, too. These may be a result of earlier and persistent deficiencies in parenting, may be combined now with the pressures of adjusting to school demands and of establishing relationships with peers. Family problems, especially between parents, may be unduly burdensome for a child who is temperamentally predisposed to a passive and withdrawing type of response to the environment.

Adolescence and young adulthood are periods that are characterized by special vulnerability to depression. As a result of significant physical and social changes, many adolescents experience a loss of security or a loss of self-confidence. In a sense they experience the loss of childhood itself. Adolescents sometimes become depressed over failure to achieve intimacy. Disappointment in love relationships, loss of childhood friendships, and disillusionment with parents often contribute to normal life-crisis feelings of depression. In later adolescence and young adulthood, the stresses involved in leaving home and establishing a life plan or vocation are also frequent causes of depression.

Among the symptoms that are common in depressed adolescents and young adults are loss of appetite; neglect of personal appearance; neglect of school work; withdrawal from social situations; physical complaints; and extreme uncommunicativeness (usually resulting in extreme loneliness). Sometimes a depressed person acts in an extremely hostile way, takes excessive risks, uses alcohol or drugs, or drives recklessly. This is called **masked depression** (Brody, 1979).

Middle age, sometimes called the "second adolescence," is also a period of heightened vulnerability to feelings of depression. In mid-life people begin to experience a loss of youth and physical vigor; they are confronted with a new awareness of mortality. At the same time they may experience the typical pattern of stressful life events that comes from having adolescent children, aging parents, accelerating financial responsibilities, and reduced opportunities to pursue the dreams of youth. The sources of normal mid-life crises are discussed in Chapter 12.

Masked Depression
A depression that is disguised by other behaviors in which a person engages in to avoid sad feelings.

Old age is also a period of increased vulnerability to normal life-crisis feelings of depression. The older person may experience repeated bereavement, difficulties in adjusting to retirement, and serious physical and social losses, such as neglect by children, losses in vision and hearing, and frequent hospitalization or institutionalization. Although it has usually been assumed that older people suffer more frequently from severe depressions than younger people, recent studies suggest that this may not be so (Woods & Britton, 1985). The sources of depression in old age are discussed in Chapters 12 and 13.

Depression is so prevalent that, as we have seen, it has been called the "common cold" of mental difficulties. What varies is its degree of severity, and how people respond to it. Some people, under the pressure of great stress or in the grip of a normal life-cycle depression, let their lives "fall apart" to a greater or lesser degree. But many continue to function relatively effectively, perhaps even to grow toward the larger goals they have set for themselves. Somehow they are able to maintain what one physiologist has called "the freedom and independence of (their) existence in the presence of profoundly disturbing conditions, either in the outer world or in (their) own organization" (Cannon, 1932/1967). How they do this is the subject we will explore in Chapter 4.

SUMMARY

1. *Anxiety* can be defined as an unpleasant state of physiological or psychological tension, stemming from a perceived threat to the individual's security or self-esteem. Many psychologists contrast anxiety, a response to a danger that is unclear, with fear, a response to a specific danger in the environment.

2. In studies of anxiety (and stress and depression as well) investigators usually concentrate on one aspect of the experience, that is, the cognitive, biological, or affective. However, in real life individuals experience the three inseparably: We *perceive* "danger" of some kind in the external world or in our own thoughts. Our *body reacts* to the situation. And we *feel* anxious (or stressed or depressed).

3. Anxiety is provoked by situations in which individuals experience conflicts in making choices. One such type is the *approach-avoidance conflict* in which an individual wishes to avoid a situation because of aversive consequences and also wishes to approach the situation for a perceived reward.

4. Freud recognized three types of coexisting anxieties: *realistic anxiety,* which is a response to real-life dangers; *neurotic anxiety,* which results from fear of our instincts; and *moral anxiety,* which is the guilt and shame we feel when we violate our superego or conscience.

5. According to behaviorists, anxiety is a learned response. If an organism experiences something painful or unpleasant in a particular situation, it will respond with anxious behaviors when it is again in that situation or if later confronted with a stimulus that was present in (or similar to) the original situation. Mysteriously apple pie becomes distasteful, but only because the person was eating it at a moment of great humiliation.

6. Cognitive interpretations of anxiety emphasize the individual's *appraisal of threat*. Threat appraisals are symbolic (evoked by ideas or values), they are anticipatory, and they involve an uncomfortable degree of uncertainty. Cognitive psychologists point out that anxiety results when there is *violation of expectations* and when people experience *response unavailability* (are helpless to do anything).

7. Existentialist or humanist psychologists regard anxiety as a necessary and potentially positive part of the human condition. *Death anxiety,* and the associated fear of nothingness or meaninglessness, is the human being's unique and greatest anxiety.

8. Psychologists have pointed out that each stage of life is characterized by different anxieties, all of which persist later on in milder forms. *Separation anxiety,* the great anxiety of infancy and childhood, involves fear of abandonment. Children next have anxieties about the body and its integrity, and then *moral anxieties,* which relate to the conscience. They want to feel that they are "good." Death anxiety emerges in late childhood and adolescence.

9. Adult *transition periods* often give rise to stress and anxiety. Graduation, starting a career, marriage, parenthood, retirement, are all points in life that offer challenge and opportunity, providing one can cope with change.

10. A key factor in stress is the way the individual evaluates or *interprets* events in the environment, not only the potential threat or loss, but his or her ability to cope with it.

11. As individuals living in a particular society, we are subjected to *environmental stressors,* among them noise, litter, and overcrowding. In this nuclear age, some children and teenagers show evidence of fear, anxiety, and stress in connection with nuclear plant accidents and the threat of nuclear war.

12. During our life spans we are subjected to *stressful life events* such as changes in family constellation, marital status, or economic situation. When an individual experiences many or significant stressful events, he or she becomes more vulnerable to physical and psychological illness.

13. When a person experiences prolonged stress, the response is often *depression.* The *normal life-crisis feelings of depression* are a temporary response to external events, such as bereavement or a job loss, or are a temporary response to losses that are inevitable in the course of growing older.

14. The type of depression that seems to be universal is the normal form that lasts a short period of time and is usually in reaction to a particular situation or a normal life-crisis. Individuals often overcome it on their own and with the support of family and friends. The more serious clinical types require professional help.

15. Various theories attempt to explain the *origins of depression:* Lack of opportunity to develop close attachment or loss of attachment to a loved one; the tendency to have negative cognition about oneself in relationship to other people and life in general; learned helplessness; failure to develop interpersonal skills; and biological explanations.

16. Like anxiety and stress, feelings of depression are evident during all periods of the *life span.* They may be precipitated by death of a loved one, illness or injury, divorce, abortion or miscarriage, job loss, academic failure, or even by success, such as graduation or a promotion.

SUGGESTED READINGS

Becker, C. (1987). *The invisible drama: Women and the anxiety of change.* New York: Macmillan. The author develops the theme that now that women have entered the workplace, anxiety is replacing depression as their number one problem. She explains why that is so, and reports on the process of coping with the new conditions.

Goodwin, D. W. (1986). *Anxiety.* New York: Oxford University Press. This colorfully written volume examines the meaning of anxiety, describes how antianxiety drugs were invented, and explains the chemistry of the brain and how it relates to anxiety. The various anxiety disorders are also discussed.

McCullough, C. J. & Mann, R. W. (1985). *Managing your anxiety: Regaining control when you feel stressed, helpless, and alone.* Los Angeles: Tarcher. This book, written as a self-care program, is useful both to those who wish to help themselves and those who would like to be aware of methods to prevent the ill effects of anxiety. It includes useful relaxation scripts.

Priest, R. (1983). *Anxiety and depression: A practical guide to recovery.* New York: Arco. Besides explaining anxiety and depression, this book shows what individuals can do about these human experiences and when they should seek the help of a specialist. The various drugs used in treatment of the two are introduced, with information on how they work and on their side-effects.

Whittlesey, M. (1983). *Stress.* Springhouse, PA.: Springhouse Corp. This slender volume produced by the American Family Health Institute gives a clear, concise, and well-illustrated profile of stress, stress diseases, and coping mechanisms.

Winokur, G. (1981). *Depression: The facts*. Oxford: Oxford University Press. This is a no-nonsense, straightforward discussion of the subject, including the role of family background, psychosocial influences, and biology. It also includes a chapter on suicide.

Zilbergeld, B. & Lazarus, A. A. (1987). *Mind power: Getting what you want through mental training*. Boston: Little, Brown. Designed to help people improve the quality of their lives, this book can be used to learn how to reduce stress and prevent anxiety.

Coping and Defense

- How the human mind maintains equilibrium just as physiological mechanisms keep the body stable

- Conscious coping mechanisms that people use to manage demands that they find taxing and to maintain their emotional balance

- Cognitive mechanisms that people use when their usual problem-solving abilities have failed them

- The usually unconscious defense mechanisms that offer a means, either successful or unsuccessful, of dealing with long-standing internal conflicts

- How individuals develop more mature coping and defense mechanisms during times of crisis and how they immunize themselves against stress

*K*arl Menninger, a distinguished psychiatrist who explored the extremes of human experience, also described in some detail the way we cope with the ordinary emergencies of life. Drawing on personal experience, Menninger (1963) tells what happened when he was involved in a minor automobile accident. At first, his concern was for the safety of his passengers (his wife and daughter). After that, a chain of psychological events began with a surge of aggressive feelings toward the other driver, which was followed by an exchange of insults and demands for names and addresses. After the other driver left the scene, Menninger found himself heatedly lecturing his wife on the recklessness of others, and repeating the culprit's license number over and over. After he aired fantasies of revenge, relief set in for a time. During the evening that followed, at his father-in-law's house, Menninger related the incident. Even while playing cards he remembered it vividly and observed himself to be shaken and uneasy.

By the next morning, the incident seemed somewhat amusing, but it was still on his mind. "I told several people about it as a joke on myself—how I had averted an accident by skillful driving only to be accused of almost causing one," he recalls. Gradually other matters claimed Menninger's attention, but a few evenings later the whole thing popped into his mind as he was lecturing students in a psychoanalytic seminar. It seemed the very thing to discuss and analyze.

Menninger eventually got over the incident. It lost its importance and vividness, and became "almost unreal." We relate it now, years later, because his recount of his experience illustrates the process of coping with emergencies. That includes the use of some effective methods of coping, such as releasing emotion, frequent verbal repetition, or "talking out" of the experience, and a good sprinkling of humor. These widely used mechanisms help us maintain what Menninger calls "the vital balance."

HOMEOSTASIS AND ADAPTIVE RESPONSES

Our bodies have a remarkable capacity to adapt to the most demanding of conditions. We can survive the rigors of subzero temperatures in the North Pole and the sweltering heat at the equator because of the ability of living things to maintain themselves in the face of threat and emergency. This special quality, which has long impressed biologists and philosophers, was first examined in detail by Walter B. Cannon, a Harvard physiologist who conducted much of his research during the 1920s and 1930s. Cannon demonstrated that humans and other complex mammals are endowed with **self-righting mechanisms** that automatically maintain stability, for example, in blood composition and body temperature. Such mechanisms account for the fact that human beings do not stop functioning when the outside temperature drops so low as to potentially freeze the materials of the tissues; nor do we find our blood diluted if we drink seven gallons of water in an afternoon. Certain mechanisms within the body automatically restore the healthy inner balance.

Homeostasis is the name that Cannon gave to the process of maintaining the constancy of the organism. The word is derived from the Greek *homeo* for "the same," and *stasis,* for "position" or "state." **Homeostasis** is roughly translatable as "steady state" or "staying power" (Selye, 1956/1976). It is sometimes defined as "adaptive stabilization" or "vital balance" (Menninger, 1963).

The body's attempt to maintain homeostasis is most dramatically observed in emergencies. As we have seen, the fight-or-flight reaction associated with arousal or anxiety involves numerous physiological changes that help us manage during a period of extreme physical exertion. But we cannot remain in this highly aroused state for very long. Equally important to our welfare are the self-righting mechanisms that return us to our normal state when the emergency is past. Antagonistic (that is, opposing) divisions of the nervous system act first to arouse us, then to quiet us down, as in accelerating and then slowing down the heartbeat. Any of us who have come close to a serious automobile accident but managed to avert it knows both of those bodily reactions: Our whole system is at top-alert, ready for action; then the emergency is over and we just seem to slump over, as if we had just carried a sack of potatoes up a steep hill.

Cannon described the homeostatic mechanisms of the organism with great precision. And he suggested that the principles of homeostasis might be applicable to other systems of organizations. There might, for example, be self-righting mechanisms in social systems (such as the economy). Other writers have applied homeostatic principles to psychological adjustment. Indeed, in our common language we often express our approval of a person by saying that she is "well-balanced," "well-adjusted," or "stable," or he "bounces back quickly." In sum, as Figure 4.1 suggests, both our minds and our bodies have a system to maintain our stability.

Self-Righting Mechanisms
Physiological mechanisms that automatically maintain the body's stability.

Homeostasis
The process by which the physiological constancy of an organism is maintained, a concept that is sometimes applied to a person's efforts to maintain psychological balance.

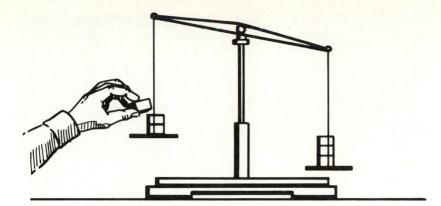

Figure 4.1 Homeostasis can be understood by analogy. Individuals are constantly striving to obtain balance, both physically and psychologically.

At the psychological level we work to maintain a "vital balance" in relation to our environment. Sometimes we fail. Sometimes our natural coping mechanisms get out of hand, and the self-righting mechanisms do not function to return us to a healthful, balanced state. We become overly aroused by a threat in the environment and the result is a decreased ability to respond and change, to adapt ourselves successfully to our environment.

Hans Selye, the researcher on stress discussed in Chapter 3, notes that it is sometimes difficult to tell the difference between an adaptive and a maladaptive response (Selye, 1956/1976, 1982). Suppose, for example, that you get a splinter in your finger: you then develop a boil or an abscess. This is a healthy, or adaptive, response because the boil provides a barricade that prevents spread of the microbes or poisons that may have been introduced with the splinter. But if the body overreacts to the small irritation of the splinter, a painful inflammation may occur; and it is this, not the splinter itself, that we complain about.

Selye concludes that many diseases result from the body's own excessive coping mechanisms, rather than from the threat or disease-producing agent itself. These diseases, as noted in Chapter 3, may be referred to as diseases of adaptation. With these diseases, an originally adaptive mechanism has gotten out of control. Hypertension and other cardiac malfunctions would fall into this category. An individual faced with an emergency is helped by rapid increase in heartbeat and blood pressure. But when these persist well beyond the emergency they turn from being helpful to harmful, from adaptive to maladaptive.

Like the concept of homeostasis, the concept of disease of adaptation is useful on the psychological level. Withdrawal or refusal to cope with the problems of everyday life is usually maladaptive. But so is excessive and inappropriate use of coping mechanisms. For example, we will see that eating, drinking, or shopping are means of relieving anxiety for some people; they help people regain emotional balance upset by the minor difficulties of life. But eating so much as to make oneself fat, or eating so that one becomes too drowsy to study would also be maladaptive.

Until recent years stress research has been based on psychological concepts that paralleled Selye's physiological theories. According to influential learning theorists (e.g., Dollard & Miller, 1950; Miller, 1980), stress represents a state of disequilibrium of the organism. They first studied animals and then applied their findings to humans. To survive, animals must learn to deal with tensions from physiological drives like hunger, thirst, and sex. The tensions arouse and disturb them and, in turn, lead them to use learned responses that have been successful in reducing the tensions, in obtaining food, drink, or a sex partner. Similarly, animals must learn to adapt to stressful aversive conditions, such as dealing with predators.

Lazarus and Folkman (1984) disagree with the animal/learning theorists (e.g., Miller, 1980), claiming that their focus is too narrow. Because humans must contend with thoughts, our experiences cannot be compared with animals. The guinea pig has no worries about an upcoming exam, no tensions about a deadline, and no stress over how well it will do in making an oral presentation in class. Cognitive functions like anticipating, imagining, and problem solving are centrally involved both in creating tension and stress and in developing methods to cope with them.

Lazarus and Folkman also disagree with the psychoanalytic model (Menninger, 1963) because it has led mostly to the study of coping traits or styles—characteristics of persons that lead them to respond in consistent ways. The Type A behavior pattern (highly competitive in work and play) is an example of a coping style. People, they argue, do not have a pathway of reacting to life. They vary in how they respond to stress-producing situations, depending on internal and external circumstances.

Instead, Lazarus and Folkman define coping as: ". . . constantly changing cognitive and behavioral efforts to manage specific external and/or internal demands that are appraised as taxing or exceeding the resources of the person (p. 141)." Several points should be noted about their definition. It makes coping a process-oriented rather than trait-oriented phenomenon, as shown in the words "constantly changing . . . specific . . . demands." How we cope varies from situation to situation. We do not have a single coping mechanism that comes into play no matter what the taxing situation happens to be, whether we feel overworked, embarrassed, depressed, or worried.

The next important point is that coping behavior occurs only when demands are appraised as "taxing or exceeding" the individual's resources; hence, coping is very different from automatized adaptive behavior, such as driving a car after one has mastered the skill, or unconsciously resorting to a defense mechanism. We *cope* when we recognize we are faced with taxing or over-taxing circumstances and decide to do something about it. Coping, in this definition, is equated with "efforts" that may or may not be successful. Even if we do not succeed in overcoming our worry about income, we coped if we carried out a plan. Finally, Lazarus and Folkman explain that the word "manage" in the definition is intended to show that coping is not equated with "mastery." As they put it, "Managing can include minimizing, avoiding, tolerating, and accepting the stressful conditions as well as attempts to master the environment (p. 142)."

They believe that there is much variability in the coping process, both across individuals and in the same person, from situation to situation. Consider a change in job or place of residence. The effects of a job change seem to depend on the stage of adulthood in which it occurs. Those between 36 and 55 find a job change more stressful and, presumably, are more hard pressed to cope with it than both younger and older members of the work force. Likewise, the effects of a residential move, which causes stress under any circumstances, seem to depend on who precipitates it. The degree of stress is greater when the move is involuntary, that is, when one is forced to change residence because of corporate reassignment. These results mean that the reaction to a job change or a residential move is not automatic and not dependent only on an individual's coping style. It is also influenced by contextual factors such as the age of the individual and the circumstances that compel relocation (McLanahan & Sorensen, 1984).

In the following sections we will examine everyday coping mechanisms, as well as the larger patterns of defense that are mobilized to protect our integrity and self-esteem. These coping and defense mechanisms are the self-righting mechanisms that we enlist to maintain our inner balance. But they are not always adaptive. On the psychological as well as the physical level, we find both adaptation *and* "disease of adaptation." Sometimes external events cause us to have problems with personal adjustment; sometimes it is our response itself that causes the problem.

How I Cope with Life's Pressures

This chapter is about how we cope with the demands of life, especially when we find them taxing. You may find it helpful before you read further to examine the following common sources of pressure in the lives of college students. Then rank order them for yourself, putting a "1" next to the most troublesome, a "2" next to the second most troublesome, etc.

_____ concentrating on my studies

_____ getting along with my family

_____ making friends

_____ sex fantasies

_____ anger at some people

_____ feeling lonely

_____ my health

_____ feeling depressed

_____ having enough money

_____ being able to earn suitable grades

Rank order the following methods according to how often you use them with the demands listed above. Which method do you use most often, which second most often, and so forth?

_____ I put it out of mind.

_____ I go out and have some fun.

_____ I ask someone to give me advice.

_____ I sit down and figure out what to do.

_____ I daydream about it.

_____ I joke about it.

_____ I cry to get it out of my system.

_____ I have a good workout to work it off.

_____ I eat or drink a lot.

_____ I sleep a lot.

Some Principles About Personal Coping

Here we wish to highlight some principles about personal coping that may make the material in the rest of the chapter more meaningful.

1. Demands on us are stressful only if we evaluate them as such. A heavy work load does not necessarily create stress. It does so only when we experience the demands as such. Responsibilities at college, at home, and on a job that some find burdensome and tension-producing are taken in stride by others.

COPING MECHANISMS OF EVERYDAY LIFE

Coping Mechanisms
Behaviors people use to reduce anxiety and to maintain emotional balance.

One person bursts into tears and "feels better." Another achieves the same result by talking on the telephone or working out with weights. Those observable behaviors that we use to reduce anxiety and maintain our emotional balance are called **coping mechanisms.** They come into play when we experience some departure from our normal state of being.

2. When pressures overtax us, we are faced with a problem; hence, a problem-solving approach is very much in order. That starts with careful appraisal of the situation to determine exactly what we are feeling and why we are feeling that way. One common cause of distress is the feeling of being overburdened. A college student put it this way: "I feel I'm in a rat race. Between school work and my job I have no time for myself. It gets me down. I'm discouraged and depressed." A good start in problem solving is to examine the situation objectively, putting down on paper all activities for about three days in a row, the time given to each one, and the feelings they evoke. You will find more details on problem solving in the section on Cognitive Coping Mechanisms later in this chapter.

3. There is no one best way of coping. Using the problem-solving method does not imply that we can eliminate the causes of our present overburdened state. It gives us information to help us choose solutions that are best for us in connection with the present situation. Usually a variety of options are open to us and many times no single one is the ideal.

4. Often we cannot change the external conditions that create stress. In some cases, we conclude that for a period of time we will be carrying a heavy work load. That does not leave us helpless. We can choose to do one or more of the following: Organize our lives so that the little free time we have is given to activities that counteract discouragement and depression. Organize our school work more systematically and do our assignments in less time, maybe with the help of a short study skills workshop. Modify our conception of the current overburden situation, rethinking it in some of the following ways: "The tough part will last only two years, with plenty of time for social life and fun during two holidays and the summer. . . . By being able to carry such a load I see that I have great strength and willpower and that makes me feel good about myself. . . . Think of the benefit I'll get from the hard work for the rest of my life."

5. Discussing the situation with another person can help us be objective. This can come before or after we have analyzed it ourselves, or at both points. A friend, roommate, or college counselor may be just the person to share our thoughts and feelings and test out our possible solutions.

6. Once having chosen the best possible solution we give it a fair trial. We see if it takes the emotional pressure, the discouragement, and depression, off of us. If not, we return to the job of reviewing our options and choosing another one.

7. Coping with the pressures of life can, in itself, be a valuable learning experience. We grow as we become aware of how we tend to confront problems. (Do we panic, try to flee from them, or seek workable solutions?) We learn the ways of coping that are best for us. We come to recognize and appreciate our own values and how to realize them. ▲

Coping mechanisms provide a means of expressing or discharging tension that has been building. (As does, for example, the infant's cry.) They may also contribute to the solution of the immediate problem (as when crying brings help and nourishment). Coping mechanisms may be compared to the homeostatic mechanisms that maintain our inner physiological constancy. Karl Menninger describes them as "normal regulating devices for the emergencies of everyday life" (Menninger, 1963, p. 149).

Sometimes coping mechanisms are conscious and deliberately chosen with considerable insight. A person may go for a long walk or join a dramatic group because he is aware, at some level, that this reduces overall anxiety. In other cases, the person is less aware of his coping strategies and tends to refer to them merely as "habits." Pacing the floor, smoking one cigarette after another, or coming down with a sore throat before a scheduled oral report are coping mechanisms that the individual may not define as such. Outside observers such as relatives and friends may regard some of our coping mechanisms as less than optimal, or even undesirable. We employ them nevertheless, presumably because they are the best that are accessible to us in our behavioral repertoire. If we are dissatisfied with them, we have the option to replace them with more desirable mechanisms, either through our own effort or with the assistance of a counselor or psychotherapist.

Touch, Rhythm, and Sound

An early way of coping with perceived danger is to bury one's head in the mother's breast or lap, seeking the reassurance of touch and rhythmic rocking. The frustrations of adult life sometimes bring forth a similar request: "hold me" and "just be close." Also important are the reassuring voice sounds of the familiar person (we say, "talk to me . . . it's just good to hear your voice"). Reassuring sounds may be sought in familiar music (religious music, oldies, "easy listening," etc.) and in recited prayer. Some people turn on the television because, regardless of the particular program, the sound of human voices has a tranquilizing effect.

Eating and Drinking

In infancy a major way of dealing with distress is to put a nipple or thumb in the mouth. As older children we are rewarded and bribed with sweets. And as adults we treat ourselves. Many people react to minor frustrations and emergencies by seeking the primary gratification of food and drink. We see this coping strategy in the person who finishes off a day's frustrations by devouring a bag of cookies, or by drinking a liquid that has soothing associations (hot milk, chicken soup, liquor, and so on). Such people attempt to restore their spirits, and perhaps re-create pleasurable feelings associated with the earliest feeding relationships.

Scientists have noted that the psychological value of eating is well recognized in our culture. Eating together is institutionalized in such comfortable rituals as the coffee break, the business lunch, the Passover meal, and the Thanksgiving dinner. In these instances, "what is absorbed by the stomach is probably less important for the total well-being of the individual than that which the process of eating together accomplishes psychologically" (Menninger, 1963, p. 135).

This individual uses jogging as a coping mechanism. After a difficult day, a three-mile run along this wooded path returns him (or her) to a healthy psychological state.

Eating and drinking do seem to reduce some of the physical symptoms associated with anxiety. A well-filled stomach increases the flow of blood to the gastrointestinal tract while decreasing the flow to the brain. This has a tranquilizing effect (and can sometimes make one drowsy). However, the use of food and drink can be counterproductive, particularly if the behavior is in response to an ongoing pattern of stress (e.g., continual marital conflict) rather than to a single brief event (e.g., taking the Scholastic Aptitude Test). When the body's defenses are mobilized, the stomach is not in a state to handle an increase in food. On the contrary, the more desirable approach is to reduce caloric intake and assure that the diet includes ample amounts of nutrients that are especially important at times of stress. These include vitamin C, B-complex vitamins, folic acid, and pantothenic acid (Shaffer, 1982).

Women are more subject to the use of food to alleviate stress because their still-persisting socially prescribed role has made them more susceptible to this response. As Zegman (1983) has explained, women who prepare meals and who view television food commercials are exposed to food cues far more than those who do not. Such cues are antecedents to eating in all of us and are particularly troublesome to those who have difficulty in resisting the cues and, as a consequence, become obese.

"Drinking your troubles away" is a phrase that expresses a commonly held view about the value of alcohol in dealing with stress. The problems of alcohol abuse are examined in Chapter 5. Here we wish to explore the way in which alcohol impacts upon "troubles." A recent study, which provides a working hypothesis rather than definitive conclusions, makes these suggestions: Following the onset of stress, alcohol does not have a direct effect on improving a person's feelings. Instead, it operates indirectly in the following fashion: Alcohol impairs the cognitive processes and, in that handicapped condition, an individual has only enough cognitive functioning capacity to devote to one activity. At this point, the combination of diminished cognitive capacity and an activity that distracts the person from thoughts about the cause of the stress leads to an improvement in mood. As the investigators say, "Cold sober, one can easily watch television and brood over a problem" (Steele, Southwick, & Pagano, 1986, p. 174). Intoxicated, a person is restricted to one activity, either engaging in a distracting activity, or dwelling on troubles ("crying in one's beer").

An experiment was carried out with university students. Stress was induced by means of a contrived I.Q. test made up only of difficult questions so that the subjects had immediate evidence of poor performance. Subjects were administered alcohol (vodka and tonic and lime juice) or a placebo (tonic and lime juice) and asked to engage in a distracting activity, making aesthetic judgments of art slides. The results supported the hypothesis; that is, neither alcohol nor the distracting activity alone led to a statistically significant reduction in stress in the subjects. The combined use of alcohol and distracting activity did yield a significant reduction (Steele, Southwick, & Pagano, 1986). Tentatively, then, it appears that alcohol itself does not diminish stress. The temporarily reduced cognitive capacity makes it easier for people to distract themselves and get the troubling thought out of their mind for a short time.

Distraction

Distraction, itself, has recently received attention as a coping mechanism in its own right, particularly in reference to pain. The subject of distraction is not new in psychological literature; however, for the most part, investigators were interested in its negative side. Many studies have been conducted on its widely known effect on concentration. Students know all too well the problems of carrying out assignments, especially those requiring reading, when they are distracted by other thoughts. They also know how distractions can impede their mental effectiveness and test-taking performance. Fortunately, some therapeutic methods, including cognitive restructuring and desensitization, both of which are described in Chapter 6, have been successful in overcoming such anxiety (Himle, Thyer, Papsdorf, & Caldwell, 1984).

It is also fortunate that the positive side of distraction—its use as a way of coping with pain—has been found effective. Common sense seems to say that putting our mind on something other than the dentist's drill or the pain following an injury incurred in a ball game will reduce our discomfort. McCaul and Malott (1984) found support for this in a study. Some subjects experienced "cold pressor" pain applied in a laboratory (coldness, pressure, and pin pricking to the point of distress), while other subjects suffered from real-life postoperative, chronic, or dental-work pain. The distractions used included pleasant imagery and a video game. The results showed that subjects who were instructed to distract themselves (e.g., by pleasant imagery) experienced less distress than those who were not instructed.

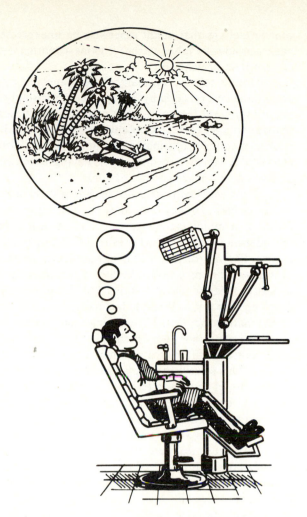

Figure 4.2 This patient is coping with the discomfort of dental care by picturing himself on a tropical island beach.

Two other findings seem consistent with common sense: (1) Distractions that require more attention will be more effective in reducing distress. Concentrating on a game of bridge or chess is more likely to displace the pain than focusing on a spot on the ceiling. (2) Distractions are more powerful with mild than with strong pain. They probably work well when the pain is due to dental drilling, an injection, or early childbirth labor.

Crying and Screaming

In infancy, crying is the most effective means of relieving fear and attracting the attention of parents. For many adults, crying or weeping continues to be an effective coping mechanism. The act of crying seems to provide relief from physical tension, for example, by softening or "melting" body rigidities associated with anxiety (Lowen, 1976). Crying provides a dramatic way of giving vent to feelings that might otherwise be unexpressed. And a good cry often has manipulative value, in that it gains attention, sympathy, and perhaps the desired item or behavior.

Deep emotions, especially those connected with the loss of a loved one, seem to be best released by crying. Not surprisingly, crying has been found to be an important feature of each of the three phases of grief: shock; despair, realization, and grief; and resolution (Weiner, 1985). If tears have been held back at first, the deep sobbing that finally comes with the profound realization of loss may signal a turning point; having found release, the person will be able to adopt a more positive outlook.

Differences between the sexes in the incidence of crying is very marked. When asked how many times they had cried during the prior year the average estimate of middle-aged men was 5.5 and of middle-aged women, about 29. In undergraduate students the estimates for men was about 6.5 and for women almost 48. In a further study, those undergraduates monitored their crying over a period of nine weeks, keeping a record of the following: each time they actually cried, or felt like crying but did not; what emotion they felt when they began to cry, or began to feel like crying but had no tears; one hour later, what emotion they felt. The ongoing monitoring showed that women cried or felt like crying more than men and that the subjects, men and women, felt better one hour afterward whether they had actually cried, or felt like it but did not. This second finding is especially striking because it says that people who are upset enough to feel like crying can get relief without going through the act of crying. They can decide to suppress it and still get the benefit of overcoming the emotions that set off that feeling (Kraemer & Hastrup, 1986).

Crying may also indicate a breakdown of inhibitions between loved ones, perhaps because tears are associated with vulnerability to strong emotion. In the popular 1970s novel and film *Love Story,* Eric Segal exploits our intuitive understanding of this phenomenon. To indicate the hero's reconciliation with his father, he has him say only, "I did what I had never done in his presence, much less in his arms. I cried."

Related to crying, but not nearly so common, is screaming. Screaming, produced under specified conditions, is basic to a number of therapeutic approaches, among them bioenergetics and primal therapy. At the very least, screaming has a cathartic (or purging) effect; it reduces muscular tension and releases the usual inhibitions that prevent dramatic self-expression. At its most effective, spontaneous screaming is said to release deeply repressed feelings of rage and fear. Screaming, like crying, is a coping mechanism that is most typical of early childhood, when language skills are relatively undeveloped. In adults, screaming often accompanies strong verbal expression, such as "ranting and raving" or cursing. The fact that screaming accompanies the release of tensions is reflected in a number of common expressions, such as "I'm so mad that I could scream," and "If you don't stop I'll scream."

Illness

Physical symptoms often appear when we are tense or anxious. The little boy who is afraid to go to school on the day of a test develops a headache or stomach pains that keeps him home, and perhaps he learns to respond to similar situations with the same symptoms. If so, he has added to his repertoire what psychosomatic researchers call a **beloved symptom.** This is a symptom that predictably appears in periods of difficulty, when the individual is indisposed to act. ("Indisposition" is an old-fashioned term for just such a minor illness.) Dunbar (1955) for example, writes of the "diplomatic cold" that allowed an English statesman to retire at difficult or embarrassing moments. Holmes and Masuda (1972) have identified what might be called the "mother-in-law cold": It tends to arrive when mothers-in-law, or "other disasters," visit. In such instances, the symptoms provide the person with a release from duties and generally bring sympathy.

Beloved Symptom
A symptom that predictably appears in difficult periods and which excuses the individual from duties.

The mechanisms of psychosomatic illness are complex. Here it is enough to note that some people cope with anxiety-producing situations by coming down with a characteristic (and not entirely unwelcome) symptom. In many cases the person recognizes the connection between the symptom and his or her situation. For example, a person will say things such as, "I'm sure that if I have to give a speech I'll come down with laryngitis." Or she will tell a marriage counselor, "My husband accuses me of being anxious about sex, because I say I have a headache when I'm not in the mood. Well, I *do* have a headache."

Because some of the illnesses-as-coping mechanisms are included in our store of humor, we can be trapped into looking lightly at them. That would be a mistake for they could be precursors to more serious illness. The psychosomatic symptoms—the stomachache that enables the child to avoid school, or the headache that allows a spouse to avoid sex—are the result of stress and are genuinely, organically experienced by the individual. When such organic symptoms of stress persist without intervention of some type, serious problems, such as ulcers, could eventually develop (Nuernberger, 1981).

There is a common belief that particular kinds of personalities are linked to a particular type of disease. Presumably "workaholics" are susceptible to heart disease, worriers to ulcers. To test this, two psychologists did a meta-analysis of 110 studies; that is, their subjects were prior studies, each of which had used a varying number of subjects. They concluded that the evidence thus far does not show that different diseases are linked with different personality types. However, the findings do give support to the concept that personality imbalances may predispose a person to all kinds of diseases. They point out that ". . . there is strong evidence of a reliable association between illness and chronic psychological distress" (Friedman & Booth-Kewley, 1987). Disturbance seems to affect the immune system and make one prone to illness.

Working It Off

A common way of coping with intense emotions is to indulge in direct physical exercise. Charles Dickens, for example, walked the streets of London when overexcited or frustrated in his life or work. Once, in a crisis, he walked 30 miles from his country home to London, at 5:00 in the morning, to work off the anger he felt at his in-laws. Walking enabled him to "do something," to move, and in this case, flee the scene of difficulties. Many other physical activities serve equally well to reduce tension. In muscular exertion, the "fight-or-flight" reaction is put to actual use. When the homeostatic mechanisms return the person to equilibrium, he or she feels less keyed up than before.

Working it off can involve sports, dancing, or shoveling the driveway, anything from engaging in a frenzy of housecleaning to hammering out a Beethoven piano sonata. As a coping strategy, working it off is most effective if it involves actions that in some way relate to the person's interests and goals (Menninger, 1963). For example, Dickens' walks provided him with visual settings for his novels. Least effective are activities that are aimless or reckless, such as canoeing unknown waters or driving the freeway as if it were a speedway.

Conscious Acting It Out

In the play *South Pacific,* the heroine announces: "I'm going to wash that man right out of my hair," and she proceeds to do so on stage with considerable energy. We expect that she feels better. Some people cope with strong emotions by engaging in actions of a symbolic and dramatic nature. Washing or cutting the hair, putting on new makeup, or making other symbolic alterations in oneself are among the possibilities. Many other examples can be drawn from experience: A person receives news of a lover's betrayal, then burns the letter and throws out all correspondence and gifts from the unfaithful one. A person who is angry pounds a pillow and curses the person, institution, or computer that is at fault. Actions such as rearranging the furniture, throwing possessions on the floor, or temporarily absenting oneself from home without explanation ("running away") serve to release tension and enable an individual to get over powerful feelings.

Psychoanalytic theory maintains that giving vent to hostility is the preferred response to the stress of frustration. Conscious acting out of strong emotion may be effective, especially if the feeling is not protracted and the acting out behavior is not frequent. To be effective it must also be met with tolerance by others.

Physical Habits

There are a great many physical ways in which we achieve temporary relief from tension. We cough nervously, fiddle with our hair, or pick at our nails, skin, or scalp. We also seek relief by emptying the bladder and bowel frequently, or by engaging in more frequent sexual activity. Sometimes we are aware of the relationship between the physical habit and tension. For example,

Acting out refers to an extreme or melodramatic behavior that others may regard as inappropriate. But psychologists find that actions that are symbolic or that harmlessly misdirect a strong emotion to another source can be constructive in relieving tension.

one young man says that "I masturbated a lot when I prepared for my examinations. . . . I did it all day long. If I didn't eat or smoke, I masturbated—and then I could go on studying" (Hessellund, 1977). In many other cases, the habit is not recognized as having any relation to a psychological state; only introspection enables us to make the association (Menninger, 1963).

Prayer

One way that people commonly cope with anxiety, unhappiness, and grief is by praying. In prayer, and perhaps in the recitation of words learned in earliest childhood, the person seeks spiritual solace and strength.

In a major study of mental health among Americans, it was found that prayer is a very important coping mechanism, particularly among middle-aged and older people. One reason that has been proposed for age differences in the use of prayer is that older people confront problems, such as aging and serious illness, that seem less likely to respond to the reassurance of others (Veroff, Douvan, & Kulka, 1981).

When young and old turn to prayer, sometimes they are seeking assistance they cannot obtain elsewhere. How people react to a situation that is stressful for them, such as a final exam or an illness, depends on their appraisal of how well they can manage it. If they feel that they lack the resources to handle it, they may seek help through prayer. For some people in some situations, prayer can be adaptive. Others must be alert to the fact that in using prayer they may be manifesting what for them is typically dependent behavior. People who give up easily in coping with life's problems, and are quick to hand over their problems to the power and authority of other people, or of prayer, might profit from also using more assertive coping mechanisms.

Play and Entertainment

Erikson describes the person at play as a person "on vacation from social and economic reality" (Erikson, 1963, p. 22), who is doing something that he has freely chosen, without fear or hope of serious consequences. A distressed person may play cards, play music, play chess, or join in a baseball game. It is not surprising that play affords relief from anxiety. Playful activities temporarily remove the mind from current troubles, and sometimes provide physical exercise. Further, playful activities may enable a person to express competitive or aggressive feelings while remaining relatively uninvolved.

Play also gives people the opportunity to learn about themselves in situations analogous to, but somewhat divorced from, everyday life. For example, Thomas Gallwey, in *The Inner Game of Tennis,* shows how the ability to be aware of and trust the body develops as a person learns the game (Gallwey, 1979). John Holt, an educator who plays the cello, tells how playing music as an adult enabled him to rediscover the baby's resilient delight in learning by becoming aware of mistakes and short-comings without being ashamed (Holt, 1978). The person who *plays,* who takes up tennis, or the cello, expects not only to take "a vacation from reality" but to return with an enhanced ability to cope. In play he or she learns something about the management of anxiety.

Closely related to play is entertainment, which involves our watching other "players." Traditionally, the theater and films have provided both diversion and an emotional release from personal suffering. In tragedy, according to Aristotle, we experience a purging of strong emotions (pity and terror) that leads to a renewed awareness of human greatness. In comedy we lose ourselves in laughter at our own frailties. Television viewing sometimes fulfills similar functions. Millions of people watch soap operas because, as one fan put it, "I care about the characters" and "It's escapism." In other words, television drama provides an opportunity for emotional release without any accompanying responsibility for the characters' lives. Other viewers describe television as simply a form of relaxation, something that helps then to "unwind" and escape for a time.

Daydreaming

In childhood, real difficulties can sometimes be neatly resolved in daydreams and fantasy play. Children can feel a degree of mastery in a world of towering and powerful adults and can also safely release their anger and aggression. Besides those advantages, the use of imagination helps children advance to higher levels of thinking as they work out problems in their mind. These "problems" may be how they are getting along with an imaginary playmate, or what activity the two of them will engage in. For adults, the daydream offers a safe mental space in which to discharge aggression or enjoy romance and accomplishment (Singer, 1976). It represents a reliable pleasure that can be turned on at will; for example, during a boring train ride or before going to sleep. Daydreaming seems to become more frequent during periods when we are under pressure of one sort or another. This is partly why we give ourselves over to daydreaming most readily during adolescence, the mid-life crisis, and pregnancy.

Shopping is an activity that should not always be taken at face value: many people embark on it to reduce feelings of anxiety, boredom, or inferiority. Advertisements play on this psychological tendency equating the products they offer with adventure, physical attractiveness, soothing experiences, and so on.

The relationship between daydreaming and mental health was recently studied in 48 undergraduates. After their mental health was assessed by use of a self-report instrument, the students kept a record of their daydreams over two weeks. In particular, they recorded how they felt both during the daydream and afterward. The findings showed that *during* the daydream the mentally healthy and the less healthy reacted the same: They felt good about enjoyable daydreams and had negative feelings about unpleasant daydreams. However, there was a clear difference between the two groups *after* the daydream. In contrast to the mentally healthy, the psychologically distressed subjects had negative feelings even after their pleasant daydreams. For instance, after a happy daydream in which the subject enjoyed great success, the reaction was, "I could never do that in real life. I'd just mess up." It seems that students in this study who felt inadequate and anxious about their performance used their daydreams as further evidence of their inadequacy. (Gold, Gold, Milner, & Robertson, 1986/87).

Shopping

It is a premise of most advertising that buying things will make us feel better. For many people, this seems to be true. Going on a shopping spree, or purchasing something expensive and unnecessary, is an everyday way of reducing anxiety, particularly those anxieties that accompany personal failure or boredom. Sometimes acquiring things is in itself consoling (it is symbolically

Vacations

Have you ever had the feeling that if a vacation had not come up just when it did, you might not have been able to cope? If so, perhaps you allowed yourself to become overwhelmed because you knew that you would have the "safety valve" of a vacation. Many people organize their work or otherwise pace themselves around their vacations.

1. Write down your vacation schedule for the school year. If you hold a job, note vacations from work too.
2. Review your vacation schedule. How many days will you be off from school? If you are working, how many days are you entitled to be off from work? Will you take more time than you are entitled to (perhaps by taking some days without pay)? Less time? Or exactly what you are entitled to? What is the longest period that you expect to go without a single day of vacation?
3. Have you ever taken a vacation that made you feel substantially better, either physically or psychologically? If so, *re-experience* the vacation, and describe it.
4. Evaluate your answer to number 3. Which of the following comes closest to describing what you seem to need or want in a vacation?
   _____ escape from everyday routine
   _____ escape from pressures and responsibilities
   _____ rest and relaxation
   _____ time for self-exploration and renewal
   _____ the stimulation of new experiences and places
   _____ the opportunity to visit and reestablish ties with people or places that represent past chapters of your life
   _____ other
5. Do you fantasize about possible vacations with some regularity? If so, *review* your favorite fantasy, and describe, if you can, how it qualifies as a "coping mechanism of everyday life." ▲

equivalent to eating a bag of cookies). Often the new object directly contributes to self-esteem or "gives one a lift." Thus, Erica Jong's heroine, in *Fear of Flying,* wittily compares the purchase of a pair of shoes to an hour's worth of psychotherapy, and determines that the cost and benefits are about the same (Jong, 1974). In shopping we obtain not only products, but reassurances regarding our attractiveness, power, usefulness, and ability to provide for ourselves.

Vacation, Travel, and Retreat

Some people literally escape their problems by taking the next airplane or bus out. The change of environment gives them time to rebuild their energies and more calmly consider their problems. It also makes them feel in control (able, at any rate, to remove themselves). For financial reasons, of course, vacation and travel are coping mechanisms that are not equally available to all.

Periodic withdrawal from life's difficulties is recognized as beneficial by institutions that give leaves of absence and sabbaticals and by a variety of

companies and government offices that organize "retreats" for their employees. The desired result is improved morale and performance. Getting away together—removing oneself from dull or troubled surroundings—is also thought to improve marital relationships. Marriage "encounter sessions" spanning a weekend are used by some couples as a means of coping with recurring tensions.

Talking It Out

Perhaps the most common way of coping with a problem is talking it out. Most people find that discussing frustrations and problems with a sympathetic person results in a reduction of anxiety. We speak of being able to unburden ourselves, "get it off our chest," or "let off steam." Sometimes, in stating a problem to another, we come to a new awareness of our options. Sometimes we succeed in clearly defining what was before a rather formless difficulty, and we can then think of ways to handle it. Sometimes we hope to obtain a reliable new perspective, some practical advice, or perhaps reassurance that others have faced and overcome the same problem (Thoits, 1986). Many kinds of relief seem to become available in the act of communication.

Psychoanalysis was originally called the "talking cure," and most psychotherapies that were developed from its model achieve benefits from simply giving the patient an opportunity to talk with someone who will listen. The importance of this coping method is recognized by clergymen, physicians, hotline workers, and others who in one way or another assist people during periods of crisis. For example, victims of assault or the recently bereaved are encouraged to talk it out as soon as possible after the event. The counselor accepts the expression of anger or guilt as a first step in the healing process (Whitlock,

1978). Psychoanalysts note that some people who suffer a traumatic event are compelled to describe it repeatedly, because doing so seems to make them feel better. And physicians find that encouraging a patient to talk about his condition, whether it is a terminal illness or an emotionally based complaint, results in a reduction of anxiety (and sometimes of symptoms).

In society as a whole we have seen a trend toward "talking out" problems that were once concealed; among them death, cancer, old age, child abuse, and incest. A "speak out" on incest, or a talk show on death, is thought to benefit speakers and listeners, whether or not it produces new data and solutions. The assumption is that speaking out reduces fear.

Talking it out often brings social support which, in turn, can buffer the effects of stress. The question now being addressed is what components of social support actually do the buffering. A tentative answer suggests that "talking" contributes to the buffering effect. In one study of 382 college women, four components were found to contribute to the buffering effect (Martin & Burks, 1985). The four all involve talking to some extent, and the last two to a very great extent.

▶ **Tangible support:** "Whom could you count on to help you out in a crisis situation by doing things when you may need it, such as helping with school work or transportation, lending you things, or even loaning money?"

▶ **Social availability:** "Whom could you call upon to engage in some social or athletic activity like going to dinner, movies, parties, sporting events, playing tennis, and so on?"

▶ **Information/guidance:** "Whom could you count on to provide guidance, advice, or information that would help you cope with a problem?"

▶ **Emotional support:** "Whom would you feel free to talk to about a troubling problem and count on to listen uncritically to your innermost feelings, to give you their full attention?" "Who will comfort you when you need it?" (Martin & Burks, 1985, pp. 452–453).

Relaxation Techniques

A textbook on behavioral psychology notes that "the common remedy of 'relaxing' or 'hanging loose' when feeling anxious has been the subject of much serious study. In fact, systematic training in muscle relaxation is now one of the most pervasive and useful tools of the behavior therapist" (Redd, Porterfield, & Anderson, 1979). One of the appeals of relaxation techniques is their relative simplicity, namely, to apply the principles of tension control for the purpose of preventing and reducing stress and tension problems. To state it in different terms, the purpose is to help people avoid being "uptight" and, failing that, to help them "unwind." Tension can be understood as the contraction (or tightness) of the skeletal muscles; relaxation, on the other hand, as the elongation (or loosening) of those muscles (McGuigan, 1984).

Relaxation techniques are used by therapists in various traditions. Especially well known is the "progressive relaxation" method of Edmund Jacobson (1938, 1978), the pioneer in this field. The client practices relaxing different muscle groups, systematically, one after another as illustrated, until he learns what complete relaxation of each muscle group *feels* like. Gradually, and with practice, he learns to achieve complete body relaxation. Many people who are not familiar with Jacobson's method engage in similar relaxation techniques. For example, when under stress they concentrate on a certain muscle group that they know from experience will become tense. A person who becomes anxious in a crowded room or at a party may consciously attempt to relax the muscles in his forehead or neck, because experience has shown that this results in general relief of anxiety.

The procedures used in progressive relaxation frequently follow this pattern (Pargman, 1986): The therapist or instructor begins by having the subjects seated comfortably, neckties and tight-fitting garments loosened. They are asked to close their eyes and concentrate on their breathing, the aim being to reach the stage of deep rhythmic breathing. Then the subjects are instructed to tense their hands as follows:

> Clench the hand—hold it—hold it—feel the tension—feel the tightness. And relax. Let the muscular tightness escape. Now let the hand relax. Notice the difference in how your hand feels now and how it felt a moment ago when it was firmly clenched (Pargman, 1986, p. 183).

The same method is used with the facial, neck, shoulder, foot, and leg muscles, always having the subjects note the difference in their experience of tension and relaxation. With practice, the subjects can eliminate the tensing stage, and upon command from the instructor or from themselves, they can relax the muscles.

Through this process, participants become conscious of what it feels like to have a very tight muscle and a thoroughly relaxed one. Many people are simply not aware of their body states, especially those who are tense much of the time. Either they never were conscious of them or have forgotten. The change process requires that they know the difference between the two before they can replace tension with relaxation.

Many other methods of conscious relaxation have been devised. A person may learn to achieve relaxation on cue—that is, upon thinking of a specific word or image. A common method is to focus on breathing and think the word "calm" (Paul, 1966). Other techniques include thinking of a peaceful setting (such as a favorite beach or forest) or a comforting emotional situation (such as being held in the arms of a loved one). One writer, experimenting with a biofeedback mechanism that allowed her to "hear" the tension of the muscles in her forehead, found that she could achieve complete relaxation by imagining herself as a small infant, lying on the table, kicking and laughing, with her smiling mother leaning over her (Scarf, 1981). The ways in which people learn relaxation, and the imagery that helps them achieve it, are increasingly of interest to psychologists.

In closing this section we want to point out that the results of studies that evaluate active coping are indeed promising. They demonstrate that people can reduce debilitating anxiety through active methods of coping: by learning to recognize their own symptoms of anxiety, relating them to the events that precipitated the feelings, and taking action to meet the challenges of the situation. In other words, by learning to cope actively with sources of stress, people tend to increase their sense of control over aversive events and reduce the painful consequences (Hamberger & Lohr, 1984).

COGNITIVE COPING MECHANISMS

Experience suggests that some of life's emergencies can be overcome cognitively, or as we sometimes say, with mental effort. One kind of mental effort is problem solving, which has been studied by psychologists in a variety of contexts. In this section we are interested in the coping mechanisms that people use when their usual problem-solving skills prove insufficient, and they are experiencing emotional distress. Two cognitive coping mechanisms that may be effective in these circumstances are reconceptualizing the problem and defensive reappraisal of the threat.

Reconceptualizing the Problem

Often a person experiences emotional discomfort because she believes that a certain problem in her life is insoluble. Her negative thoughts or cognitions are: "Everything has been tried, nothing can be done." A way of coping is **reconceptualizing the problem** as one that *is* solvable. The person forces herself to consider interpretations or solutions other than those that have contributed to her negative view. This reconceptualizing activity may also be characterized as the "search for alternative solutions" (Beck, 1979).

In reconceptualizing a problem, the person may herself arrive at solutions that were outside her original conception. In most cases, however, she must seek out people who can help her by providing a different viewpoint or better information.

For example, a student who fears that he has failed a calculus exam may at first conclude that he is a "failure," is "no good at math," cannot pass calculus, and must abandon his premedical studies. The problem may well seem insoluble. But if the student arranges to meet with his instructor, he may gain new information or interpretations that enable him to reconceptualize the problem. For example, the instructor might point out that the student's high school mathematics preparation was simply inadequate in several topics, and that there is a review book or remedial course that might help. Or he may say that nearly everyone did poorly on the exam (in which case the problem may lie in the construction or timing of the exam itself). Finally, the instructor may offer the student a way of objectively testing his evaluation of himself as a failure in math; for example, by taking an aptitude test.

Reconceptualizing the Problem
A cognitive coping mechanism where one takes a new view of a problem one had previously considered insoluble.

The likely result is that the student will abandon his all-or-nothing view of his mathematical abilities and find out that, rather than being absolutely "no good at math," he is weak in a specific area. Any one of these reconceptualizations will reduce stress and help the student resolve his problem.

Defensive Reappraisal

Appraisal and reappraisal of stressful situations are important in determining how individuals choose to cope. In this connection, an investigation (Lazarus & Folkman, 1984) of how 100 middle-aged men and women appraised over 1,000 stressful encounters during the period of a year is illuminating. Monthly, they reported the stressful episodes they faced, how they appraised each one (i.e., whether they could do something to change the situation or whether they had to accept it or get used to it), and just what they did to cope with each one. The appraisal made by these people tended to predict how they would cope. In particular, the appraisal predicted whether they would resort to a problem-focused coping mechanism, which they did when they felt they could do something about the stressful situation, or to an emotion-focused coping mechanism, which they did when they felt they could do nothing to change the situation.

Even in those situations in which undesired outcomes seem inevitable, and in which it appears that the best we can do is to resign ourselves to them (Levi, 1981), something can be done that people have found helpful: using a cognitive mechanism called defensive reappraisal. **Defensive reappraisal** is the reevaluation of a threat or danger in the environment, in the absence of any new or objective information. It is an act of saying and believing that things

Defensive Reappraisal
Cognitive coping mechanism by which a person reevaluates a threatening situation in a manner that distorts reality to some degree.

are not as bad as they appear to be. Technically speaking, the individual distorts reality in order to reduce his level of anxiety or alleviate other psychological stress. The process is not a simple one. Convincing ourselves of something seemingly contradictory to the evidence requires constant appraisal and reappraisal, a ransacking of the mind and a scanning of the environment for anything that might support a more positive view.

Defensive reappraisal seems to be an effective response in some situations where facing reality head-on would not lead to effective action. One life situation of this nature is serious or terminal illness. In one study psychologists measured the physiological stress reactions of parents whose children were suffering from a terminal illness (Wolff et al., 1964). They found that those parents who were able to deny the fatal nature of the child's disease exhibited less stress than those who were not so defended. In other words, denial of the seriousness of the problem in the absence of any supporting evidence (a defensive reappraisal) may have enabled these parents to cope more effectively.

Similarly it has been observed that surviving heart attack victims cope better (and are less likely to have subsequent attacks) if they deny the gravity of their medical condition. Denial has been observed to promote adaptation in coronary care units (Strain, 1978). And in recovery, deniers report fewer emotionally related symptoms and are better able to resume work and sexual activity (Lazarus & Folkman, 1984).

Of course the effectiveness of this kind of defensive reappraisal is limited to situations where another response, such as direct action, is not preferable. If a person is having a heart attack and must summon an ambulance, denial is not adaptive. Nor is it an appropriate response for a previous heart attack victim to be careless about taking medication because of denial that he ever suffered such an attack. From an adaptive point of view, he can only deny the seriousness of his condition, for here there is room for ambiguity, self-delusion—and hope.

Defensive reappraisal takes many familiar forms. We utilize this method, for example, when we minimize or make light of a troubling situation, when we assume that certain things cannot be a threat to *us,* or when we choose to "pay no attention" to a threat. Related responses that help us feel better about stressful situations, whether or not we logically have reason to, include distancing (pretending that the event is not happening to us), deliberately thinking of something else, or finding the silver lining in the dark cloud confronting us.

Other Cognitive Techniques

Reconceptualizing the problem and defensive reappraisal are cognitive coping methods that have been extensively studied. There are others, however. Through the use of **cognitive rehearsal** people prepare for an unavoidable upcoming event that gives them "butterflies." Instead of putting it out of their mind, they go over it time and again until the event has lost some of its dread. Besides reducing negative feelings, rehearsal has the additional value of making individuals better prepared to play their part in the event. (See the Self-Knowledge Exercise on cognitive rehearsal.) A second method, known as **role-**

Cognitive Rehearsal
Going over in one's mind an upcoming and stress-producing event or activity and, thereby making it less anxiety-provoking.

The Search for Personal Adjustment

Cognitive Rehearsal

Cognitive rehearsal is a technique used by cognitive therapists. It involves asking the client to imagine each successive step of a task that he would like to complete but has so far been unable to undertake. The mental "rehearsal" forces the client to pay attention to details, to anticipate minor problems and their solutions, and to imagine himself as having succeeded in the task.

The technique of cognitive rehearsal is often used, less rigorously, by individuals in everyday coping situations. Below is an opportunity to apply it in your own life.

1. Think of a task that you would like to complete but that you have put off because it is difficult or anxiety-producing. Common examples are going for an important interview, making an unpleasant telephone call, or driving an unfamiliar route at night.
2. Imagine each successive step in the sequence you would follow in completing the task. For example, if you are going for an interview, the first step may be to give your name to the receptionist. Attend to all details: Imagine what might go wrong at each point, and visualize how you would cope with each difficulty.
3. If possible, engage in an actual rehearsal of your behavior. For example, if you are going for an interview, ask a friend to listen to your summary of past experience and your reasons for wanting the job. Better yet, have your friend role-play the interview with you. This could be done several times, with your friend playing the role of a warm interviewer and also of one who is as difficult as you fear the interviewer might be.
4. What effect, if any, do you think this exercise will have on your ability to complete the task? ▲

play, is, in fact, a form of rehearsal, except that the thoughts are acted out with the cooperation of another person(s). The trepidation some people may feel about an oral examination or appearing before a selection committee can be minimized as a result of practicing the feared event with others in a role-play.

Using **imaging,** or somatic (body) imaging, a person, usually with the guidance of a therapist, attempts to reduce stress-related symptoms including anxiety or certain types of pain, by visualizing a state of relaxation or another desirable state. As discussed earlier, visualizing oneself in a state of deep calm can help a person relax in the face of difficulties. Indeed, a variety of imagery-based techniques have been used by cognitive and behavioral therapists in the treatment of anxiety problems (Kazdin & Smith, 1979), and some have been adapted for self-help use (Lazarus, 1984).

Children's use of these cognitive techniques and others changes with age and their level of development. The change is illustrated in a study by Brown, O'Keefe, Sanders, and Baker (1986) that examines the use of positive self-talk, a coping strategy involving cognitive rehearsal. In one part of the study they asked subjects to imagine facing a troubling personal experience. They were to write down the thoughts that would be going through their heads, and the things they would tell themselves as the encounter unfolded. The results indicated that positive self-talk doubled from the ages of 8–9, when about 43 percent of the children used it, to 16–18, when 86 percent used it.

Role-Play
The procedure of adopting a role (as in a drama) and acting out an upcoming event with another person.

Imaging
A cognitive technique, aimed at reducing stress-related symptoms, in which a person visualizes a desirable state.

DEFENSE MECHANISMS

Defense Mechanisms
Usually unconscious patterns of adjusting used by everybody to protect themselves from anxiety, guilt, and other aversive feelings.

Coping mechanisms help us maintain our balance in the face of everyday emergencies and frustrations. We choose them to help us deal with demands from the outside world, that we find excessive. **Defense mechanisms,** by contrast, come into play to help us deal with the conflicts of our inner world. These conflicts arise when people have unacceptable impulses (an impulse to hurt a parent that, of course, conflicts with the beliefs that children should love and respect their parents). To cope with such conflicts an individual, in most instances, unconsciously develops use of a mechanism that will "defend" him against aversive emotions such as guilt (for having such hurtful desire) and anxiety (expecting punishment). The individual might "displace" (transfer) to another person the anger felt toward the parent. That way the individual is relieved of the anger, of the guilt about wanting to hurt the parent, and of the anxiety about being punished for harboring such an impulse toward his parent. However, there may well be a price for displacing anger on an innocent person. The innocent recipient of unjustified anger, and persons who witness it, may not long tolerate the behavior of the individual who expressed anger for no apparent reason.

Unlike the coping mechanisms of everyday life, defense mechanisms operate at an unconscious level. Unlike coping mechanisms, defense mechanisms are automatic and unplanned in the sense that we do not choose them and are usually unaware of their precise effects on our behavior.

Defense mechanisms in the personality, as in the physical body, may be either successful or unsuccessful. Sometimes a defense mechanism protects the person against underlying anxiety; sometimes it is excessive and out of proportion, rather like the inflamed tissue that we find so difficult to distinguish from the infection it was meant to fight. Whatever the outcome, defense mechanisms are a form of self-deception, and it may be argued that virtually all self-deception is risky.

Intellectualization
A defense mechanism whereby a person overuses intellectual concepts and words to avoid emotional experience.

To understand how defense mechanisms function, we will consider one with which college students tend to have experienced: **intellectualization.** Technically, intellectualization is the overuse of intellectual concepts and words to avoid emotional experience. The person who intellectualizes has a great many ideas about threatening matters, but he cannot really be said to possess the feelings that normally accompany them.

Alan offers a perfect example. At 18, one of his chief delights is to discuss philosophic ideas on love, politics, and death. But he thinks very little about his daily life. His lofty views on love in no way prevent him from being childish and callous with women. He wittily criticizes the middle-class marriage for its imperfections and hypocrisies. But he cannot move past the most obvious clichés in his own relationships. Similarly, whenever the opportunity arises, he belittles the "typical, costly American funeral," as he calls it, and claims nobody in his family would ever have one.

Perhaps most striking is the way Alan handles sex. He talks about it and reads books, including marriage manuals and intellectual histories translated from the French. When he is attracted to a woman, he tends to involve her in long discussions about the philosophic implications of sexual freedom and commitment. What Alan does is to intellectualize, or connect his feelings with abstract theories, with the result that he seldom experiences his feelings at all.

Intellectualization of the sort that Alan engages in is not necessarily maladaptive in adolescence. In fact, some psychoanalytic writers approve of it. They feel that people do need to get a grip on sexuality and other powerful needs by connecting them with ideas that can be easily dealt with at the conscious level (Freud, 1936/1966). Eventually, however, we expect the person to be able to experience sexual feeling, and to turn his intellectual abilities to solid actions and achievements. As a defense mechanism, intellectualism is successful when it enables the ego to become stronger, to mature to the point at which further defense becomes unnecessary. The defense mechanism is unsuccessful if it persists beyond the stage at which it is developmentally appropriate, when, for example, a 27-year-old man writes, "I'm still trying to determine why I have not yet engaged in sexual relations for I have no objection to it" (Vaillant, 1977, p. 132).

Intellectualization, like other defense mechanisms can become an obstacle to personal growth. That is, the defense of intellectualization is developmentally appropriate in adolescence, and becomes less useful as a person matures. However, it would not be accurate to say that the mature, healthy adult abandons this technique. He retains it in his repertoire, much as the modern army retains its foot soldier. Defenses that have been successful in the past are activated whenever the ego is too weak to consciously handle anxiety. What this means is that people resort to defense mechanisms in times of crisis.

Vaillant points out that the ego utilizes defense mechanisms not only to resolve developmental crises (such as emerging sexuality), but to master a variety of life conflicts. Defense mechanisms may be used for the following purposes (adapted from Vaillant, 1977, p. 10):

1. To contain emotions during sudden life crises (e.g., after a death)
2. To obtain time out to master changes in self-image (e.g., after major surgery or an unexpected promotion)
3. To handle unresolvable conflicts regarding people, either living or dead, whom one cannot bear to be without (e.g., an unfaithful spouse or runaway child; a dead parent)
4. To survive major conflicts with conscience (e.g., killing in wartime; putting a parent in a nursing home)

TABLE 4.1 *Defense Mechanisms*

Defenses of Childhood	Illustration
Denial: Behaving as if obvious facts were not so.	Person with pre-heart attack symptoms ignores them, insisting "It can't happen to me."
Repression: Excluding from consciousness forbidden and/or other unpleasant thoughts.	A seemingly forgotten experience of guilt for not helping a friend who was later killed in an accident.
Projection: Attributing one's own unacceptable traits, impulses, or thoughts to another person or object.	The disobedient child says the teddy bear was "very naughty." An adult with strong but unacceptable sex desires complains that "teenagers are oversexed."
Reaction Formation: Adopting behaviors and attitudes that are opposite to one's own unacceptable impulses.	The child who is overly affectionate to a newborn sibling may be reacting to feelings of envy and hostility. The adult who refuses help from friends may be reacting to longings to be dependent.
Regression: Returning to the attitudes and behaviors of an earlier state when life seemed more secure, and one could be cared for by parental figures.	The 35-year-old woman begins to dress like a girl and becomes preoccupied with her doll collection as she withdraws from adult society.
Displacement: Redirecting strong feelings from one person to another who is a more acceptable and less threatening target.	A father, very angry at the boss who treats him very harshly, redirects his anger to his wife and children.
Fantasy Formation: Replacing the real world with a safer, private, imaginary one.	Unlike the normal fantasy of everyday life, a woman creates a set of imaginary people who give her a safer and more controlled environment than the one from which she withdraws.
Defenses of Later Childhood and Adolescence *Identification*: Internalizing characteristics of another person or group.	The boy feels strong by behaving like the home run hero. The woman feels strengthened or weakened by the performance of her favored ball club.

From G. Vaillant, "Mechanisms Illustrated in a Single Case" in *Empirical Studies of Ego Mechanisms of Defense.* Copyright © 1986 American Psychiatric Association, Washington, D.C.

In the following section, we will describe some of the most common defense mechanisms, as they normally emerge over the life span, and as they are successfully and unsuccessfully employed in crises.

We subdivided them into three groupings: defenses of childhood; later childhood and adolescence; and maturity. These groupings indicate the period of life with which the mechanisms are identified, generally because they make their first appearance at that time. Once adopted, a defense mechanism may persist into adulthood and all through life. As we would expect, the mechanisms of childhood are less sophisticated than the later ones. They are simple, show much distortion of reality, and for the most part are handicapping to the individual who employs them. By contrast, the defenses of the next two groupings, especially those of maturity, are often constructive in their effects.

TABLE 4.1   *Continued*

Defenses of Childhood	Illustration
Compensation: Seeking to excel in order to overcome feelings of inferiority.	The younger daughter who feels her sister has won out in the "looks department" struggles to become "the brainy one."
Rationalization: Using a more socially acceptable justification for behavior or outcome than is really the case.	The college student who comes in second in a race insists "If I'd trained more I could've won, but it wasn't worth it."
Acting Out: Indulging in actions that express unconscious impulses without awareness of the underlying conflict.	The teenager expresses his hostility toward his parents by delinquent behavior; the woman deals with her conflicts about real intimacy by breaking off relationships before they become too emotionally close.

Defenses of Maturity

Sublimation: Redirecting ones interests and desires to those defined by the individual as more socially valued.	The young teenager redirects sexual interests and energies into sports. The parent whose child was killed by a drunken driver redirects her grief and outrage into energy to build an organization dedicated to combating drunken driving.
Humor: Using wit to make a painful experience more tolerable and even enjoyable.	Novelist Ernest Hemingway and actor Gary Cooper, both suffering from terminal diseases, and both horsemen, joked with each other as to who would "get back to the barn first."
Suppression: Consciously putting aside unacceptable or unproductive thoughts and impulses.	The college student is infuriated by acts of unfair treatment but decides to suppress them temporarily in order to be able to study for exams.

Defenses of Childhood

Denial

As children we are sometimes confronted with disturbing situations that we can neither escape nor explain. A primitive mechanism, **denial** of reality, is brought to our defense. Small boys, confused or disturbed by the sight of female genitals, often respond by denying that people without penises exist. Children deny that they are angry, that they were ever babies, and so forth. A classic example of childhood denial can be found in William Wordsworth's poem "We Are Seven." A small girl insists that there are seven children in her family, though it becomes clear that her brothers and sisters are dead or departed, and she must play alone. Denial is the ability to function on a conscious level as if the facts were not what they are. It is not a deliberate process, and is thus distinguished from lying.

Denial
A defense mechanism in which a child or adult functions as if obvious facts were not so.

In childhood, denial is a necessary defense because the child does not have more effective ways of dealing with troublesome situations. In adulthood, overreliance on denial suggests that mature problem-solving methods have not been learned, and that the individual is to some extent maladapted. Familiar examples are alcoholics who refuse to admit that they drink much, and obese people who do not see that their own habits contribute to obesity ("it's glands," they say, contradicting all evidence).

For the healthy adult, denial is utilized in emergencies. It is a common first reaction to terminal illness and bereavement. The person says "Not me" or "There is some mistake," and for a time behaves as if he or she had not learned the facts. It is expected that the person will eventually move beyond the stage of denial and employ more mature coping and defense mechanisms. However, the advantages of doing so are not the same for everyone. Denial enables people to live through an unbearable ordeal and, as we said earlier, some cognitive research on coping mechanisms indicates that in certain situations denial effectively reduces stress.

Habitual denial of life's problems can be self-defeating. For one thing, denial often prevents our seeking help or taking precautions for our safety. Neglecting to buckle seat belts because "It can't happen to me," or neglecting to let one's conscience be aroused because "It can't happen in our country," are clearly maladaptive reactions because they leave people more vulnerable to events.

There is some suggestion that denial, the most primitive effort toward adaptation, is involved in the early break with reality that leads to serious psychological illness. Suppose, for example, that to survive a young girl must deny the fact that her mother abuses her. But if denial is to be complete, the child must also deny the validity of any negative thoughts or feelings that she has in response to her mother's behavior. She must deny the real meaning of what is happening—and in denying her experience, she is ultimately denying herself. Schizophrenia, or another serious psychological illness is a possible result.

Repression

Repression is the process by which forbidden or anxiety-laden thoughts, feelings, and memories are excluded from consciousness. In psychoanalytic terms, the ego dissociates itself from the forbidden material by banishing it to the unconscious, where it is seemingly forgotten. However, in the unconscious, "nothing can be brought to an end; nothing is past or forgotten" (Freud, 1936, p. 518). The repressed material continues to exert pressure on the personality. We find evidence of its emergence in dreams, fantasies, slips of the tongue, accidents, and physical symptoms.

In the classic psychoanalytic example, the individual represses memories of early sexual feelings and experiences (in which the parent is usually an object). In so doing, he or she avoids being aroused by unacceptable feelings and is spared the conscious guilt that these feelings would cause in the older self. Yet the person pays a price, in not having access to whole areas of childhood experience. In maintaining repression, he or she expends psychic energies that might be put to more creative or pleasurable uses.

Repression was the first defense mechanism investigated by Freud. So basic is this defense to psychoanalytic theory that for many years Freud alternately spoke of "defense" and "repression" as rough equivalents. Today repression is considered to be one of several defense mechanisms that protect the person from the demands of sexuality and other threatening instincts. Many writers identify it as the most commonly used defense. Anna Freud notes that it may well be the most dangerous, for when the person is cut off from whole areas of emotional or instinctual life, integrity of personality is destroyed. The person is not whole. In psychoanalysis a major goal is to bring repressed material to consciousness, and liberate the person from past conflicts. In ordinary life, repression lifts when the person discovers that the repressed material is not quite so dangerous to him. The middle-aged person may suddenly remember, with all good humor, the childhood masturbation or sibling jealousy that he repressed during his youth. Feelings of personal security and increased understanding of human nature have made the memories less threatening.

Unfortunately, many adults never discover that fears of their childhood are without real basis. Life reinforces their early perceptions of danger, and they continue to rely on repression to a significant degree. When we describe a person as "repressed," we generally mean that he is rigid, unspontaneous, and unable to move toward meeting the challenges of life. The person cannot make progress because when conflicts are repressed, they remain unchanged.

This does not mean that repression is always an unsuccessful defense. In limited ways we regularly repress painful or embarrassing material, without incurring great discomfort. For example, we forget something hurtful someone said to us because we want to remain friendly. (Perhaps we also forget to send a birthday card!) We forget to mail an application because unconsciously we do not want to work the weekend hours the job requires. In these examples, repression is a way of coping with everyday problems, not a means of cutting ourselves off from whole areas of our past.

Projection

In **projection** we attribute our own traits, impulses, or behavior to some other person or group in the environment. Naturally it is the socially unacceptable behavior that is projected. The nursery school child comes home bursting with the need to tell his mother that Johnny and Jason were naughty and would not share. He is wide-eyed and serious; the tale is an attempt to come to terms with his own behavior of being "naughty" and not sharing. Children project their impulses onto objects and animals too. There is nothing strange in this. "It is normal for the undeveloped ego to get rid of impulses and wishes by handing them over in full measure to others" (A. Freud, 1936/1966, p. 123).

In adulthood, projection is less useful. Occasionally most of us discover shortcomings in others that are, in fact, our own unacknowledged traits. Similarly, we may blame the system or some minority group or the elite for our difficulties. However, when the tendency to project unacceptable feelings becomes a predominating feature, a distortion of the personality occurs. The person habitually complains, is oversensitive, and is touchy about his or her own importance. Unwarranted suspicions may arise, making close relationships difficult. And the inability to judge other people's motives often leads to poor work adjustment. Vaillant found that of all the Harvard college sophomores followed in a longitudinal study, those who utilized projection to a significant degree had the worst career adjustments. On the other hand, none of the men whose relationships were above average had made significant use of this mechanism (Vaillant, 1977).

When projection becomes intense and habitual, when distortions persist, uncorrected by the continuous reality-testing of everyday life, the individual can become psychologically ill. In the most severe cases, the person may come to believe that others are watching him, controlling his mind, or sending him messages.

Reaction Formation

Reaction formation is the adoption of behaviors and attitudes that are diametrically opposed to one's unacceptable desires. The classic example is the "puritanical" behavior of the young man whose sexual impulses are unacceptable to himself or his culture. Such a person may show an exaggerated interest in the strengthening of antipornography laws. And he may apply unduly rigorous standards to his own behavior. Just as familiar, though less striking, is the person who behaves in an oversolicitous or submissive manner as a reaction against underlying hostility. Dickens' Uriah Heep insisted that he was humble, yet took a stance of servility because, in fact, he wanted power. The unacceptable desire is transformed into its opposite. In some cases the resulting behavior might easily be mistaken for a constructive change in personality, were it not for the fact that the reaction is so exaggerated (A. Freud, 1936/1966).

Reaction formations are a normal part of child development. Just as children show the capacity to reverse the facts in denial, so are they able to behave in ways that represent the exact reversal of their impulses. A common example is that of the little girl who is overly affectionate toward the new baby (Lidz, 1976). Through hugs, kisses, and other "good girl" behaviors she succeeds in concealing from her conscious mind the difficult hostility she harbors. Also typical is the exaggeratedly independent behaviors of the child who is terribly afraid of being on his own.

Reaction formation, like repression, is an important means of protecting the ego against overwhelming and unacceptable demands. However, as a permanent fixture of the personality, reaction formation can be maladaptive. It is an all-or-nothing response that leaves the person little leeway in a crisis. It tends to result in exaggerated or rigid behavior that is threatened by the slightest lapse. If the reaction breaks down, it is because the original, unacknowledged impulse has become more forceful than the reaction and perhaps more forceful than is normal. For example, we read about the "puritanical" person who breaks down into promiscuity or lewd behavior or the "good" husband who becomes violent toward his wife and children.

Regression

Regression means "going back," in this case going back to a stage of development in which one felt more secure. Generally, security is associated with the benevolent dependency of being cared for and having one's gratifications assured. Lidz notes that regression is a major adaptive strategy of childhood. Over and over again the child falls back to regain security after overreaching for greater independence (Lidz, 1976). Typically the child also regresses when an event interrupts the usual supply of parental attention. When a sibling arrives, or the family changes residences, the preschool child may temporarily lose control of bowel or bladder functions and be unusually clinging.

Regression occurs naturally as we approach sleep, and in dreams. Anyone who has lived with a small child can observe regression practically at 24-hour intervals (Sullivan, 1953). When the child is tired, there is a collapse of behavior patterns that have not been thoroughly established in the personality. The "big boy" is gone and the thumb returns to the mouth. Adults too have a tendency to "act like children" when they are fatigued. And regression seems to be an unavoidable part of being ill and having to be cared for by others.

Regression is not uncommon as a response to severe injury or trauma. Joyce Carol Oates, in *Them* (a novel based on a case history of one of Oates' students), describes the regression of a young girl who has been beaten by her

Regression
A defense mechanism where one returns, in some fashion, to a stage of development in which one felt more secure.

stepfather. The girl spends 13 restless months in bed. She grows fat, and her face has "a puffed shiny look to it." She is hungry, her mouth waters. "Food is something to fill up her body and keep it heavy and peaceful." She is aware only of voices and the jiggling of the bed (Oates, 1969, pp. 211, 293–294). This is, of course, regression to infancy.

Regression to early childhood as a result of trauma has been well described by Bruno Bettelheim, who was imprisoned in a concentration camp during World War II. Bettelheim noted that prisoners lived like children in the immediate present. They told tales, made improbable boasts, and were not ashamed to be found out. They were unable to form durable friendships, but fought childishly and made up. Like toddlers, they regarded defecation as one of the most important daily events (Bettelheim, 1943). In this case, being in the position of a helpless child seems to have brought about regression. (That is, having to ask permission to visit the bathroom, and being unable to avoid soiling oneself.) Bettelheim's observations are applicable to many less extreme situations in which a person finds himself "reduced to a child."

Under ordinary circumstances, overuse of regression in adulthood contributes to emotional disturbance. For example, a person who regresses to the narcissistic (or self-loving) position of early childhood is unable to achieve intimacy with others and is unwilling to accept the obligations that are part of caring for the next generation. Moreover, overreliance on regression is characteristic of many disturbed people.

Displacement

In **displacement** the person redirects strong feelings from one person or object to another that seems more acceptable and less threatening. Especially common is displacement of negative feelings, such as hostility and aggression. The young man who feels anger toward his father will express that feeling to some other object or symbol of authority. He may deliberately provoke a teacher or defy a college regulation.

Fantasy Formation

In normal, healthy development, small children often seek comfort and solve problems through **fantasy formation.** When they are powerless to control others, they create imaginary playmates or animals who obey them. When they are threatened by guilt, they conjure up monsters. As children develop, creative fantasy is a way of preparing for reality and relieving pain. If used in appropriate ways and in appropriate situations, fantasy formation, as we have already seen in connection with daydreaming, can be a constructive form of coping all through life.

Fantasy ceases to be an adaptive coping mechanism when it replaces the real world. Under those circumstances individuals retreat from relationships

The Search for Personal Adjustment

of all kinds in order to avoid feelings they cannot handle. They defend themselves against the internal conflicts experienced when they interact with people in the real world by creating one of their own. This kind of fantasy, which causes a serious psychological disturbance, is worlds apart from the normal fantasy of everyday life.

Defenses of Later Childhood and Adolescence

Identification

The process of **identification** involves the internalization of characteristics of another person, and it is a complicated, lifelong psychological process that is basic to personality development. As noted in Chapter 1, the superego develops through identification with parents and their values. Gender identity involves identification with the parent of the same sex.

In later childhood a defense mechanism emerges that relies primarily on identification. The school-age boy or girl identifies with a hero (for example, a movie star or rock singer). He or she becomes motivated to find out every last fact about this hero, and may imitate aspects of the person's style and appearance. This identification is a temporary way of gaining security and postponing the confrontation with individual identity. For a time, the young person is absorbed in, and patterned upon, someone else.

In adulthood, people tend to identify with organizations, athletic teams, and political leaders. Such identification can bolster the individual's feelings of self-worth and protect him or her from anxieties. However, it also makes the person vulnerable. If a football team loses badly, an overidentified member of the team may suffer a depression that partially reflects a loss of self-esteem. When John Lennon was shot, some people who had strongly identified with him suffered feelings of disillusionment for their own hopes and dreams.

A different kind of identification that may emerge under unfavorable conditions in late childhood or adolescence is identification with the aggressor. Older children, who are able to think for themselves and clearly differentiate themselves from others, must nevertheless submit to authorities. In harsh situations they may defend themselves from anxiety by identifying with the aggressor, by unconsciously adopting characteristics or behaviors of the person they most fear. Adults who are subjected to intolerable authorities sometimes defend themselves by identifying with authority— another phenomenon first noted by Bettelheim in the concentration camp situation (Bettelheim, 1943).

Compensation

As we grow able to compare ourselves with others, most of us experience anxiety in connection with real or perceived inferiorities. **Compensation** is a defense mechanism that enables us to defend against these feelings.

Identification
A defense mechanism applied when a person internalizes characteristics of another person, or sometimes of a group.

Compensation
A defense mechanism directed at preserving self-esteem, in which one may overachieve in an area where one was judged weak or excel in a different area.

Compensation may involve attempts to achieve in an area where one is originally disadvantaged or inferior. A legendary example is Theodore Roosevelt, a physically weak child who developed an exercise program, and a life philosophy, for the achievement of superior strength. Another form of compensation involves making up for an original weakness by developing skills in a different or opposite direction. Robert Louis Stevenson, also a weak child, wrote adventure tales that not only removed him imaginatively from the sick bed, but utilized a nonphysical skill. In a similar manner, an individual may compensate for the shortcomings of his environment. Someone who is denied entry into society because of his background may respond by amassing and displaying wealth, possibly engaging in corrupt activities to do so. A person denied entry into the mainstream of a profession may compensate by charting an original course. Freud, the founder of psychoanalysis, faced limited opportunity for advancement in academic medicine. And Haydn, founder of the classical style in music, explained that he was so cut off from the world that he was "forced to become original."

Compensation is ordinarily seen in the relationship between family members. If an older daughter is said to be beautiful, the younger, not-so-well-endowed, may compensate by becoming the family "intellect." Such a strategy can be adaptive if it helps develop a person's real capacities without unnecessarily limiting his or her self-concept. For example, becoming an intellectual may be a good solution for the younger sister, if she can actually succeed as a student and if she does not cross off the possibility of becoming attractive or socially desirable.

In some cases, a person compensates for weaknesses of the family as a whole. The child of uneducated parents may be especially well motivated to attend college and equip himself or herself with the manners of the dominant culture. The student who comes from a troubled family (and who is aware of personal problems) not infrequently decides to become a psychology major and then a psychologist. An interesting variation on this is Walt Whitman, chief celebrant of "the religion of healthy-mindedness": He emerged from a family in which four siblings suffered from mental illness, feeblemindedness, or alcoholism (Kaplan, 1979). There are many examples of children born to wealthy families who felt they have to compensate by "making it on their own," identifying with the poor, or embracing philanthropy.

Rationalization

Similar to intellectualization is **rationalization,** a defense mechanism that becomes useful as the adolescent develops the capability for logical reasoning. Rationalization involves developing a socially acceptable justification for some action or for an existing state of affairs. It is equivalent to "seeing the silver lining" or concluding that the out-of-reach grapes must be sour. In college, common examples of rationalization heard after the posting of finals grades are: "The test was unfair"; "The instructor graded me harder than the others"; "I only wanted to pass the course, anyway."

The Search for Personal Adjustment

Many times there is an element of truth in rationalization. But insofar as rationalization protects us from recognizing the real reason for our behavior, it may be maladaptive. A form of self-deception like other defense mechanisms, rationalization can be especially dangerous to society when it is used (as it often is) to relieve someone from feeling guilt over a wrongful action performed.

Acting Out

When people indulge in actions that express unconscious impulses, and when such actions prevent them from becoming aware of their impulses, we say they are **acting out.** For example, fast driving or experimenting with drugs may enable young people to avoid conscious anxiety about death, or acts of juvenile delinquency may hide unconscious hostility toward parents.

Acting out is usually a temporary measure employed during a developmental crisis. Like the temper tantrum, acting out tends to disappear as we acquire more mature ways of dealing with our needs.

In adulthood, acting out is usually a maladaptive way of defending ourselves from the anxieties associated with long-standing conflicts. An example is the middle-aged person who gets a divorce and runs off with a new partner, often in an impossibly romantic way, rather than experience old anxieties about sexuality or love.

Acting Out
A defense mechanism whereby a person takes direct action that expresses unconscious impulses without awareness of the underlying conflicts that led to the action.

Defenses of Maturity

Sublimation

Sublimation involves the redirection of aggressive or sexual desires toward a socially valued activity, as defined by the individual. In Chapter 2, we saw that the capacity for sublimation is a characteristic of the healthy person. An example is the young man whose hostility toward a parent finds productive outlet in legal struggles for the disadvantaged, or the child whose sexual curiosity is later channeled into the goals of scientific research. Striking examples of sublimation are found in the lives of those who have contributed toward society's highest goals. Freud identified a classic case in Leonardo da Vinci, whose paintings of madonnas expressed, he thought, a longing for the mother from whom he had been separated in childhood (Freud, 1910/1947). A sensitive journalist offers a more recent example in Pope John Paul II, relating his rebirth in the Mother Church to a longing for the mother who died when he was a child—and noting that one of the Pope's religious poems is entitled "Mother" (Szulc, 1979).

As these examples suggest, the term sublimation is used to refer to successful or adaptive responses. "Sublimation" actually means adaptive uses of the defense mechanism, displacement, discussed earlier. In the more general process of displacement, the person redirects his feeling from one object to a more acceptable or obtainable substitute. The rationale is that if he is blocked from discharging tension by one route, he will seek another that is as similar to the forbidden path as it can be.

Sublimation
A defense mechanism whereby a person channels unacceptable aggressive or sexual desires into activities he or she socially values.

The mature adaptive response that we call sublimation is usually the result of a series of displacements. Suppose, for example, that a young girl is unable to gain exclusive possession of the father she unconsciously desires. According to the principle of displacement, she seeks substitute objects. The first "crush" may be a music teacher, or an older boy in the neighborhood. As these objects prove unattainable (and there seems to be no real alternative), the young girl may turn to fantasy, selecting a hero from a television show or movie as her imagined partner. As she enters adolescence and young adulthood, she will dispense with these unsatisfactory objects and perhaps form an attachment to an older mentor, an academic or professional sponsor who has some of the traits of the father ideal. Finally she finds, and may marry, a man who resembles the father-ideal in many ways. A series of displacements has occurred.

At every point in this series of displacements, blocked energy—energy that cannot be discharged on the original love object (Freud's term)—is distributed over life activities. The adolescent who fixes upon romantic fictional characters may also develop an interest in reading or writing literature. The unfavorable comparison between the romantic heroes and the boys in her class at school may lead her to direct her energies to intellectual activities of continuing value. Similarly, at a later stage, the relationship to a mentor influences career choice and development. The blocked energy may be compared to a dammed-up river (Hall, 1954). It overflows into interests, hobbies, personal habits and traits, values, attitudes, sentiments, and attachments.

Sublimation is not a defense displayed in crisis, to protect the temporarily weak ego. It is a lifelong defense against our realization that we cannot have what we most want (or, put another way, that the needs of society are opposed to the fulfillment of our instincts). As our desires are displaced from one object to another slightly less desirable one, some satisfaction is lost: the substitute object is never so satisfying as the original would seem to have been. The individual gives up a complete primitive satisfaction in favor of a broader and more diversified investment in society. The trade is not perfect. It cannot be. That is the reality that sublimation defends against.

Humor

Freud wrote that humor can be regarded as the highest of the defensive processes (Freud, 1905/1960). The humanist psychologists list the faculty of nonhostile humor as a distinguishing characteristic of the healthy personality (Maslow, 1968). And we commonly call healthy any person who can laugh at himself. The person who is humorless, or derives his pleasure from hostile humor at the expense of others, is usually perceived as less healthy.

Humor is an efficient defense because it allows the individual to confront painful material directly and consciously, with minimal suffering; indeed, with some pleasurable effect on his listeners. For example, the great-grandfather who accepts his old age and is able to be humorous about it is facing an undeniable fact of life. He may make casual reference to the time when he'll be

Humor
The defense mechanism of joking and wit, which makes possible the conscious and enjoyable expression of painful material.

The Search for Personal Adjustment

"pushing up the daisies." He may, like baseball's Casey Stengel, make some statement like: "Most people my age are dead." In such cases, the person confronts a difficult truth in a pleasurable and essentially honest manner.

The adaptive value of humor is readily felt when people describe their life difficulties. In answer to a question on marital adjustment, one man, with warmth on his face and love in his voice, quipped that he had never considered divorce—only murder (Vaillant, 1977). The response, in addition to being funny, recognized an essential truth about the marital relationship, the intensity of anger and conflict, and suggested that this had been honestly dealt with.

In a chapter on the functions of humor as a defense mechanism, Ziv (1984) explains the defense purposes of three types of humor: black (which suggests the color of mourning), self-disparaging, and sexual. In each, something that is very frightening is turned into the ludicrous; the ensuing laughter reduces the fearfulness and allows the individual to return to the sensitive subject again and again. Just as the child seeks out and uses frightening fairy tales to master anxiety, adults use humor for the same purpose. For example, black humor protects us against anxieties associated with death, and other greatly feared events. It is well illustrated by Woody Allen's classic remark, "I'm not afraid of death. I just don't want to be there when it happens." What we seek is freedom from crippling anxieties and what we admire is mastery over the worst of them. Black humor (sometimes called gallows or sick humor) gives us opportunity to achieve such mastery, as in the following anecdote from Ziv (p. 53).

Standing in front of the firing squad, the prisoner is asked by the officer in charge if he wants to smoke a last cigarette.

"No, thanks," he answers. "I've been trying to give it up."

Self-disparaging humor is a defense against attack or criticism by others. By laughing at one's own weaknesses others are deterred from doing that. He uses the weapon before they can use it against him. Ziv tells of a 260-pound "delightful comedienne" who says in one of her routines: "I don't want to add to the comments about my body structure, but there are those who say that if I was in India I would be holy" (p. 62). Audiences appreciate the courage of a person who can laugh at herself and probably lose any desire they might have had to laugh at her shape. The individual, having induced the audience to join her in laughter at herself, has reduced her own anxiety and gained mastery over the situation.

Sexual humor is a defense against the enormous anxiety that this highly pleasurable activity can create. The role of anxiety in sexual dysfunction is discussed in Chapter 9. Here we want only to show that sexual humor allows people to approach sexual topics that are both unavoidable (in that they show up in conversation and the news if not in one's own thoughts), and also anxiety-provoking. For example, about bisexuality Woody Allen's humor is again illustrative: "I'm a heterosexual, but there are advantages in bisexuality. It doubles your chances for a date on Saturday night" (Ziv, p. 69).

Crisis Jokes

Humor is a defense mechanism that can be utilized by a community that is confronting significant stress. During the Three Mile Island nuclear power plant reactor crisis of 1979, a professor of sociology and anthropology collected examples of crisis jokes that circulated on his campus just 23 miles from the Pennsylvania reactor site (Kassovic, 1980). Among the examples: "Do you know the five-day forecast for Harrisburg?" "Two days." And: "What melts on the ground and not in your mouth?" "Hershey, Pennsylvania." When the situation grew more serious, and the governor of Pennsylvania ordered a partial evacuation, the joking seemed to stop.

1. What crisis jokes, if any, have ever circulated in your community? If possible, collect a few examples.
2. Do you ever find yourself making jokes about a real problem that is facing your community or group? Can you say why you do this? What kind of joke, in your experience, is most successful?
3. Is there a point in a crisis past which joking is no longer effective as a defense mechanism? If so, how would you characterize that point?

Humor is a defense that serves us well because life is full of absurdities, incongruities, and challenges to our rational senses. And so, indeed, are people. ▲

Suppression and Forbearance

Suppression
The defense mechanism of deliberately putting aside unacceptable or inappropriate thoughts or impulses.

Suppression involves temporarily putting aside, or forgetting, unacceptable or unproductive thoughts and impulses. The person decides to endure for a time, to forgo gratification. He or she puts the conflict that is being experienced out of consciousness and carries on as usual. (The conflict recedes into the hazy area of the preconscious, from which it can be brought up at some time more favorable to action.) In ordinary language this mechanism is described as "biting the bullet," "gritting one's teeth and bearing it," or "taking it with a stiff upper lip." Like Scarlett O'Hara in "Gone with the Wind," we tell ourselves that we will think about it tomorrow, and we generally do.

Of the major defense mechanisms, suppression is the only one that has been recognized as being volitional. If the defense mechanisms are thought of as being on a continuum, then repression would be at one end as being the most unconscious, and suppression at the other end as the most conscious. Individuals protect themselves from undesirable feelings and thoughts (maybe about an experience perceived as humiliating) and bodily sensations (maybe anger and tension) by eliminating them or reducing their prevalence or strength.

Defense Mechanisms

Imagine that you were at a get-together at a friend's house last Saturday, and that, during the course of the evening, you listened in on many conversations. Below are statements taken from four conversations, each containing one defense mechanism. On the line following the statement, write the name of the mechanism.

Marge said that she had an exam in biology during the past week, on the topic of genetics. She didn't understand it. "Anyway," she said, "what am I ever going to do with genetics. It's just not important to me. Instead of wasting my time studying I went out on a date and had a good time."

_____ .

Lisa said to Jim, "You have strong arms. I really go for that in a guy." Jim's cheeks turned red. He started a long monologue about how human limbs evolved, how they were different from those of the primates, how important they are to the human species, etc., etc., until finally Lisa yawned, got up, and left.

_____ .

Mike and Joe were involved in a conversation, while Karen who came to the party with Joe, sat by and only rarely had anything to say. Suddenly Mike sharply criticized Joe. It was clear that Joe was enraged but was controlling it, probably because he seemed afraid of Mike. With his face red with anger Joe turned to Karen and, out of the blue, yelled at her "for not ever speaking up."

_____ .

Larry heard the loud voices of people arguing in front of the house and said it reminded him of his early years. "I got into trouble for starting fights in every grade. Then when I got a little older I went out for boxing and wrestling and I haven't had any trouble since then."

_____ . ▲

Despite its importance in everyday life and in psychoanalytic psychotherapy, the topic of suppression, compared with the unconscious mechanisms like projection and repression, has been "relatively neglected in the psychoanalytic literature" (Werman, 1985, p. 405).

When suppression becomes the usual way of surmounting difficulties, we speak of **forbearance** or stoicism. This is the attitude that allows a person to accept life on the terms offered, at least for a time. Forbearance is seen, for example, in the husband who remains in a stormy or unsatisfying marriage,

Forbearance
The pattern of behavior that results when one adopts the defense mechanism of suppression (putting aside unacceptable impulses) as one's usual way of dealing with difficulties and conflicts.

Coping and Defense   171

and recognizes his difficulties rather than using a denial defense. For some reason, which he can usually articulate, sticking it out seems the best solution. He relegates the conflict to his preconscious, and postpones gratification to some other time, some other place.

In an age of spontaneity and unembarrassed self-assertion, it is fashionable to disparage suppression. However, if we are intellectually honest we cannot rule out the possibility that the best adjustment to some bad situations, for some people, is simply to forbear. Vaillant, in his longitudinal study of Harvard sophomores, found that suppression (or stoicism) was the defensive style most closely associated with successful adaptation (Vaillant, 1977). Those who used this defense had less use for immature defenses such as denial, projection, and reaction formation.

Defense Mechanisms Illustrated in a Single Case Vaillant (1986), using a case study approach, has provided us with a helpful set of illustrations of most of the defense mechanisms described above. He introduces the patient as follows:

> A woman, married at age 30, had one miscarriage and then tried for seven years to have children. Then, following a cervical biopsy that showed early cancer, at age 38 she underwent a total hysterectomy. She had always felt inadequate compared to her younger sister, who already had four children and had been the one in the family who won praise as "being good with kids." The woman's husband desperately wanted children. Below are a number of possible responses to her surgery [Only those defense mechanisms described in this chapter are included.]:
>
> 1. She started ordering the nurses to move her upstairs to the maternity ward. She wandered about the hospital looking for *her* baby. She experienced no postoperative pain. [Denial]
> 2. She found herself unable to remember the name of the operation, except that it was for "a little nubbin in my tum-tum." She "forgot" her first follow-up visit to the physician. On coming home she broke into tears when she broke an inexpensive, amphora-shaped flower vase; she had no idea why. [Repression]
> 3. Following a slight postoperative wound infection, she wrote long, angry letters to the papers blaming the hospital for unsanitary conditions. Blaming her doctor for not doing a Pap smear earlier, she threatened to institute malpractice proceedings. [Projection]
> 4. She renewed her old college interest in planned parenthood and passionately argued with her younger friends to limit their families. She suddenly "remembered" that she had always been afraid of the pain of childbirth and remarked to her husband how lucky she was to be spared the burden. [Reaction formation]
> 5. She asked the nurse not to permit visitors because they made her "sad." She threw out all her flowers and instead read and reread a copy of *Parents* magazine and *The Family of Man*. She would go down the corridor to the newborn nursery daydreaming about what she would call each child if it were hers, and once a floor nurse had to ask her not to whistle lullabies so loudly. [Fantasy]

6. She became very interested in growing tulips and daffodils in her hospital window. Although she never asked the doctor questions about her own health, she worried about a funny mold on the bulbs she was growing. Knowing his hobby was gardening, she repeatedly asked her surgeon's advice about the growth on her bulbs. [Displacement]

7. Shortly after leaving the hospital she was unfaithful to her husband with four different men in a month, twice picking up men in cocktail lounges and once seducing an 18-year-old delivery boy. Prior to that time she had had no sexual interest in any man but her husband. [Acting out]

8. She got great pleasure from "get well" cards from her sister's children, agreed to teach a Sunday School class of preschoolers, and had a poem published in her hometown weekly on the bittersweet joys of the maiden aunt. [Sublimation]

9. She laughed so hard tears came to her eyes and her ribs ached when she read the *Playboy* definition of a hysterectomy, "throwing out the baby carriage but keeping the playpen." She explained her private mirth to a startled and curious nurse with, "The whole thing is just so damned ironic." [Humor] (Vaillant, 1986, pp. 117–120.)

CRISIS OUTCOMES

Each person learns through trial and error, direct teaching, and imitation a repertoire of coping and defense mechanisms (Baldwin, 1979).

Through coping and defense mechanisms, individuals strive to maintain a vital balance, a physical and psychological state that enables them to function at their best. We have called this state homeostasis or equilibrium. Most of us are familiar with the feeling of actively trying to maintain our equilibrium. We say "if we can just get settled," or "if things would just fall back in place." At the same time we realize that things can never be the way they were. Changes occur in the outside world, in our workplace, among our friends, in our family, and in ourselves. There is no way to escape them.

At many points in life we face life events that result in personal change. These include maturational life events such as graduation or the birth of a first child, which escalate to the level of crises when individuals are unable to cope with the changes that are entailed. We also experience situational or traumatic crises such as miscarriage or business failure. It is in the period of crisis that the coping and defense mechanisms are mobilized and tested. The individual may react with immature, non-reality-based mechanisms, or with adaptive mechanisms appropriate to his or her level of development. The way of responding depends on earlier experience.

In many cases, the person learns that coping and defense mechanisms that worked in the past are inappropriate. A man who has used denial, projection, and reaction formation, for example, learns with the help of a psychotherapist, that these do not serve him during a crisis of serious illness. The pain cannot be denied, and blaming others only alienates him from the sources of comfort. His exaggeratedly independent behavior is now entirely out of place: nothing can defend him against the deep and realistic need for dependency. It is important to note that even a happier sort of event can precipitate a crisis for which the individual's usual means of coping are inadequate. For example, the birth of a first child challenges a 25-year-old woman who has used regression and the accompanying dependency to protect herself from anxiety. To have a psychologically healthy home, she must become independent and able to nurture the child herself. In such a case, the person alone, or with the help of others, can develop more mature defenses so that she will emerge from the crisis with a more stable personality and a better ability to deal with the future.

Caplan, an authority on preventive psychiatry, has said that crises represent turning points toward or away from mental disorder (Caplan, 1964). The person who can mobilize mature and efficient coping and defense mechanisms establishes a new equilibrium—one that offers greater stability for the future. The person who relies on regressive, ineffective coping mechanisms may develop symptoms of psychological illness. If the defense becomes greatly exaggerated, the individual may suffer from a disease of adaptation in which his efforts to right himself result in further psychological distress.

Recent knowledge about development over the entire life span has highlighted the importance of the transition periods during adulthood. These periods include "early adult transition" from about ages 17 to 22 and the "age 30 transition" from about 28 to 33 (Levinson, Darrow, Klein, Levinson, & McKee, 1978). These critical years may lead, on the one hand, to renewed growth and very positive advances in the person's development or, on the other hand, to personal crisis. A crisis suggests that the individual did not resolve some conflict during an earlier life stage; for example, a 20 year old may be having difficulty at college or a job because of her strong dependency needs, or another may have difficulty in establishing relationships because of his anxiety about closeness and intimacy. If the conflict is resolved, the possibility is open for continued growth of the person in the next stage of life. If it is not resolved, the individual is likely to resort to ineffective coping and defense mechanisms, and the mental health outlook is less favorable. That is why specialists in mental health are giving considerable attention to the transition phases in the life span (Golan, 1983, 1986).

In the next chapter we will examine some of the forms that psychological distress may take in individual lives. Before that, however, we wish to introduce the positive concept of immunization against stress and some related ideas that have come from recent thinking and research in psychology.

IMMUNIZATION AGAINST STRESS

AIDS (Acquired Immune Deficiency Syndrome) has made us painfully aware of the importance of the immune system. From a biological point of view, the immune system is responsible for the integrity of the organism; that is, it protects the organism from foreign substances such as bacteria and viruses. The physiological process whereby that occurs is well understood (Stein & Schleifer,

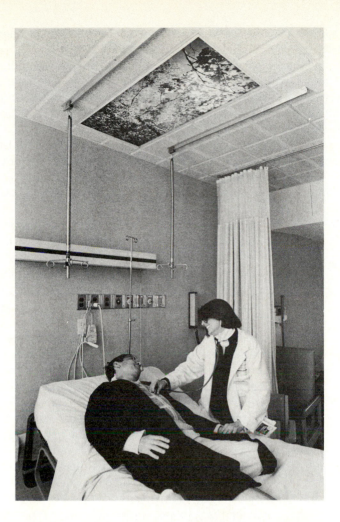

Psychosocial factors can affect the course of immune system disorders. Support, love, and a relaxing environment can be very helpful.

1985). What is not well understood is the complex relationship between the psychological experience of stress and the biological processes involved in safeguarding the organism. However, Stein and Schleifer conclude: "Considerable evidence demonstrating a relationship between stress and immune function is accumulating" (p. 111), and suggesting that in a person under stress, the immune system's effectiveness may be modulated, thus leading to the development of a range of illnesses.

Now, from the psychological point of view, come the following questions: Does the organism have an immune system to protect its integrity against the onslaughts of stress? If so, can that immune system be strengthened, especially in those in whom it is weak and in those who expect to confront potentially traumatic experiences? The evidence so far gives us the following answers: Yes, yes, and yes.

The recently developing field of psychoimmunology has led to new lines of research. It has also led to the concept that psychosocial variables may be involved in the etiology of all illnesses, not just a few like hypertension or peptic ulcers (Lazarus & Folkman, 1984). For example, psychosocial factors have been found to affect outbreaks of herpes symptoms as a result of changes in the functioning of the immune system. Stress, by itself, did not directly cause herpes symptoms; but those who were depressed had fewer of the lymphocytes (white blood cells) in their immune system necessary to fight infections *and* had more herpes outbreaks (Kemeny, Cohen, & Zegans, quoted in Stark, 1985).

Besides making such important connections, research in psychoimmunology has directed its attention to strengthening immunity to stress. Coping skill training procedures proposed by Meichenbaum (1977) can be used for immunization purposes. His system consists of three phases:

1. in the educational phase individuals are provided with a conceptual framework to help them understand the nature of their responses to stress;
2. in the rehearsal phase they are taught various coping techniques;
3. in the application phase, under conditions of stress, they practice use of the newly acquired coping techniques.

His system was tested by investigators interested in immunizing people against learned helplessness, which was discussed in Chapter 1. After one group of introductory psychology student subjects was given the innoculation—the coping skills training—they and a nonimmunized comparison group underwent the learned helplessness experiment. This consisted of two parts: first, some of both groups were confronted with three insoluble ("helpless") problems, then they were asked to solve anagrams. The results showed that the students who had been immunized by means of coping skill training needed fewer trials to reach the criterion of solving three consecutive anagrams in less than 15 seconds each (Altmaier & Happ, 1985). Presumably, the innoculation immunized the subjects against learned helplessness and some of the effects of stress, enabling them to solve these problems more effectively.

The use of stress inoculation also has been found effective with other problems faced on campus. In one study, speech-anxious undergraduates were "inoculated" by means of experiences designed to give them feelings of success. After their training they showed confidence levels related to speech that were superior to those of the controls (Altmaier, Leary, Halpern, & Sellers, 1985).

Finally, a study (Holahan & Moos, 1986) on stress resistance, assessed each subject's personality, coping mechanisms, and available family support in order to predict their physical and psychological adjustment a year later. The results indicated that the qualities that protect individuals from negative psychological consequences of stress are: self-confidence, an easy-going disposition, the tendency not to use avoidance as a means of coping with problems, and the availability of family support. Prevention-oriented stress inoculation programs could help people develop these qualities and resources.

SUMMARY

1. People are endowed with self-righting mechanisms that automatically maintain stability at the physiological level. The process of maintaining stability is called *homeostasis*.

2. On the psychological level, there are self-righting mechanisms that help us maintain our emotional stability and adjust to the environment. We refer to these as *coping* and *defense mechanisms*. Sometimes the mechanisms are used in a way that is excessive or inappropriate. A disease of adaptation, or problem resulting from the mechanisms themselves, may occur.

3. The *coping mechanisms* of everyday life offer a means of managing demands on us that we find taxing and they sometimes help us solve an immediate problem. Among the most common of these mechanisms are eating and drinking, crying and screaming, talking it out, working it off, and daydreaming. Coping mechanisms are usually conscious and deliberately chosen.

4. Cognitive coping mechanisms that enable people to cope with situations in which their usual problem-solving skills are ineffective include *reconceptualizing the problem* and *defensive reappraisal*.

5. *Defense mechanisms* are the larger adjustment patterns that we utilize in our attempt to resolve long-standing emotional conflicts. If effective, these mechanisms defend us against threats to our integrity and self-esteem. They are usually unconscious: that is, we do not deliberately choose them and are usually unaware of our reliance on them.

6. A defense mechanism may be said to be successful when it enables the person to master a developmental crisis or a variety of other life conflicts, such as keeping emotions within bearable limits after the death of a loved one or handling a difficult moral dilemma. A defense mechanism may be said to be unsuccessful when it persists beyond the stage at which it is developmentally appropriate or when it is overutilized.

7. The defense mechanisms normally emerge and become important during specific developmental periods, after which (except in the case of the mature defense mechanisms) they become less important. Defense mechanisms that normally emerge in early childhood include *denial, repression, projection, reaction formation, regression, displacement,* and *fantasy formation*.

8. Defense mechanisms most common in late childhood and adolescence are *identification, compensation, rationalization,* and *acting out*.

9. Defenses of maturity include *sublimation, humor, suppression* and *forbearance*.

10. In periods of crisis, our coping and defense mechanisms are mobilized. Sometimes a person finds that coping and defense mechanisms that worked in the past are now inappropriate. Under favorable conditions, the person uses more effective or mature defenses, and achieves an improved equilibrium.

11. The state of the biological immune system is of enormous importance in defending us against disease. Now, it appears, the psychological experience of stress can affect the immune system's ability to protect us from illness. Research is suggesting new ways we can strengthen ourselves in order to deal more effectively with expected stressors.

SUGGESTED READINGS

de Bono, E. (1984). *The art and science of success.* Boston: Little, Brown and Co. Famous for his work on teaching people to think creatively, de Bono interviewed successful people and, in this book, describes how the reader can be more effective in his or her environment.

Faraday, A. (1972). *Dream power.* New York: Berkeley Books. Advice concerning the creative use of dreams in problem solving.

Frank, J. D. (1982). *Sanity and survival: Psychological aspects of war and peace.* New York: Vintage Books. An analysis of and insights into the psychosocial forces that contribute to international crises, war, and peace.

Harvey, J. with Katz, C. (1985). *If I'm so successful, why do I feel like a fake?* New York: St. Martin's Press. This popular volume describes how to deal with a feeling many people cope with when they experience success; that is, a sense that they deceived others into overestimating their strengths or abilities.

Kirsta, A. (1987). *The book of stress survival: Identifying and reducing the stress in your life.* New York: Simon and Schuster. A very practical and well-illustrated book on "stress proofing" one's life-style, dealing with high-stress situations, and approaching relaxation through muscular activity, breathing, nutrition, time management, and visual imagery, among others.

Lazarus, A. A. (1984). *In the mind's eye: The power of imagery for personal enrichment.* New York: Guilford. Points the way to harnessing the human capacity for fantasy and imagination so that they may be used to counter phobic reactions and improve performance.

Murphy, L. B., & Moriarty, A. E. (1978). *Vulnerability, coping and growth: From infancy to adolescence.* New Haven, CT: Yale University Press. An investigation of how children cope and deal with problems, anxieties, and stressful life events.

Shaffer, M. (1982). *Life after stress.* New York: Plenum. Written for use by the lay person who wishes to learn about the nature of stress, and the methods to prevent, resist, and cope with it.

Sheehy, G. (1981). *Pathfinders.* New York: William Morrow. An examination of the mechanisms that enable individuals to cope with and overcome life crises.

Youngs, B. (1985). *Stress in children.* New York: Arbor House. This book discusses the causes of stress in children and techniques that can be used to teach children to cope.

Psychological Disorders

- ▸ How the concept of "psychological illness" is culturally defined
- ▸ The value of and problems with applying diagnostic labels to psychological disorders
- ▸ Psychological disorders that represent departures from normal development in childhood and adolescence
- ▸ Adult psychological disorders that may involve excessive anxiety, unexplainable and distressing physical symptoms, or a loss of memory or sense of identity
- ▸ Schizophrenia, which involves severe disturbances in thoughts and emotions, and the mood disorders, characterized by extreme mood states
- ▸ Personality disorders—primarily antisocial and narcissistic—and disorders in which there is abuse of alcohol, opiates, or other substances

*A*t 24, Charlotte was a flight attendant with 200 hours of professional flight time to her credit. She was described as popular, outgoing and independent, and pretty (she had been a runner-up in her state's beauty pageant as a teenager). She had lived by herself in New York City as a young adult. Life seemed not only normal but happy until one afternoon, flying toward an Atlanta airfield in a private plane, Charlotte was seized by an uncontrollable fear that made her throw herself down on the floor of the plane and threaten to jump if she were not let out immediately. The surprised pilot landed safely in a cotton patch.

In the years that followed this incident, Charlotte suffered intermittently from panic attacks. Sometimes they occurred in the supermarket, sometimes at a social gathering of family and close friends. Eventually there was nowhere Charlotte felt really safe. Doing even the simplest things became impossible. And worst of all was the shame that came from having these unreasonable fears. "I couldn't have friends over," she recalls, "I couldn't go to their houses. Whenever I tried to leave my parents' house I was terrified and so ashamed of having these feelings for no apparent reason that I didn't tell anyone about them. How can anyone understand your terror of a supermarket or restaurant if you don't understand it yourself?"

Charlotte had panic-free periods, one lasting as long as two years. She spent some time as a voluntary patient in a psychiatric hospital, consulted a number of therapists, and married a psychiatrist whom she met on a blind date. Especially during her "normal" periods, life seemed to offer all the possibilities for happiness. But the panics returned.

Finally, after many years, Charlotte's problem was diagnosed and treated for what it was: a psychological disorder called agoraphobia.

Agoraphobia is the fear of being in an open space or public place (such as a store), from which the person perceives escape as being difficult or help unavailable. Charlotte found a group of people who suffered from the same disorder, people who understood. Through a combination of desensitization and relaxation, under therapeutic guidance, Charlotte slowly began to experience some improvement. Today her agoraphobia is under control, to the extent that she can be involved in helping other people who suffer from the disorder.

Charlotte's case sounds as if it might have come from a psychologist's file, or a discussion at hospital rounds. To many people (including Charlotte and her fellow sufferers) the problem seems bizarre and unusual. In actuality, Charlotte's case was described at length in a large-circulation women's magazine (Barrett, 1980). The editors of the magazine knew that the article would be of interest because the problem is a common one. It affects perhaps two million American women. That sounds like a large number, especially when we consider all the individual suffering that is involved.

It is perhaps still more surprising to hear that at any one time between 20 and 32 million Americans suffer from psychological distress of such severity that they are in need of mental health care (President's Commission on Mental Health, 1978; Myers et al., 1984). Myers' group surveyed 10,000 people in Connecticut, Maryland, and Missouri. They found nearly 20 percent of adults questioned were suffering from disorders that ranged in severity from mild anxiety to schizophrenia. Each of the following affected between 6–8 percent of those surveyed: anxiety disorders, drug abuse or dependence, and mood disorders (depression or its opposite, mania). About 1 percent had schizophrenia. These are conservative estimates of the number of people affected by mental illness. And they do not include people who could benefit from assistance because they are extremely unhappy or suffering from severe emotional stress. Further, they do not take into account the adjustment problems faced by another 30–40 million Americans who are affected because of the relationships they have with people having psychological disorders (Horowitz, 1984). In sum, psychological disorders are not uncommon. They are part of our lives, and the lives of many of the people we know.

WAYS OF LOOKING AT PSYCHOLOGICAL ILLNESS

The disorders we will describe, as well as those not discussed here, have several things in common. They involve patterns of behavior, thought, or feeling that are significant to psychologists and other clinicians as departures from what is normal or desirable. They are associated with pain and distress in the individual, or with some impairment in functioning, usually in work or social relationships. Before describing specific disorders, we want to emphasize that the concept of psychological illness—being "ill," suffering from one or more disorders—is one that is related to culture and value judgments, and open to varying interpretations.

Some individuals could benefit from the assistance of a mental health professional—not because of a disorder—but rather because they are persistently and extremely unhappy.

Cultural Definitions

Whether or not we care to listen, our culture tells us what is within the boundaries of normal behavior and what is not. Psychologists, physicians, teachers, and other accredited members of society identify psychological problems and devise treatments. And ordinary people in the social environment play a large part in making an individual feel "sick" or "OK" (Neff & Husaini, 1985).

Most of us realize that definitions of psychological illness vary from culture to culture. Anthropological findings of the 19th and 20th centuries have shown that there is great variety in the kinds of behavior that human cultures tolerate. Karen Horney, a neo-Freudian psychiatrist, applied these findings to our understanding of psychological illness, noting that what was considered unhealthy (or "neurotic," in her terminology) differed significantly from culture to culture. She also found that different patterns of illness developed in countries as similar as the United States and England (Horney, 1937).

Consider, for example, a person who converses by the hour with his or her dead grandfather, or who reacts with dread to the possibility of being in the presence of a menstruating woman. Today, in the United States, these people would be thought to suffer from some sort of disorder (probably schizophrenia and phobic disorder, respectively). However, in certain native American (Indian) tribes that were studied in the 1930s such behaviors were "absolutely normal" (Horney, 1937). By the same token, we would feel very uneasy with a child who regularly reported on his or her classmates and made

Cultural Definitions

We say that "mental illness" is culturally defined. And to support this point we provide examples of behaviors that seem "sick" to us but are acceptable and normal in another culture. The tribesman who hallucinates or converses with his dead ancestors; the primitive who fears menstruating women—these examples come easily to us. But what about common behaviors in our own culture that might look positively disturbed to people of another culture? What about our excessive fear of cancer (a fear far out of proportion to the frequency with which the disease occurs)? Or our dread of wrinkles and other natural signs of aging? And what about those little ticking things we carry with us, looking at them all the time?

1. Assume for the moment that you are a visitor from a different culture. List some behaviors that are normally engaged in by people in U.S. society but which would be seen as "sick" or "mentally disturbed" in your kind of culture.
2. Compare your list with those of others in your class or group. Are there any common themes?　　　　　　　　　　　　　　　　　　　▲

public confessions of personal faults. We would probably refer such a child to the school psychologist. Yet this is the usual behavior in Soviet schools. One teacher proudly said, "We get the pupils to judge their own behavior and not just in class. The other day one of my boys raised his hand to admit that he had not paid his bus fare" (Whitney, 1978). Naturally, there are behaviors common in our culture that might be viewed as evidence of psychological disorder by members of other cultures.

The ideas of what constitute psychological illness differ not only from one culture to another, but within the same culture over the course of time. For example, you may have discovered that your parents (or grandparents) held different ideas about what constituted normal sexual behavior than you do. Today a mature woman who is overwhelmed by feelings of guilt and unworthiness over a loving premarital encounter would be considered by many people to have a problem. She might be seen by a therapist. In the 1920s or 1930s, the same feelings would probably have been accepted as normal for a "fallen woman" (a term then in use). We have seen even more explicit changes in our view of homosexuality. Ten to fifteen years ago the person with a homosexual orientation was, by clinical definition, psychologically disturbed and in need of treatment. Today, homosexual orientation is not by itself an indication of psychological disorder. A disorder is present only in cases where homosexuality is clearly unwanted by, alienating, or stressful to the individual.

Society's views about mental health are constantly changing. This recently-closed hospital building first opened in 1870, following a ceremony led by Governor Rutherford B. Hayes. Over its 100+ years of operation the hospital has operated under 9 different names. Each name, whether the Ohio Insane Asylum, the Ohio Lunatic Asylum, or the Central Ohio Psychiatric Hospital, reflects a change in society's thinking about mental illness, its treatment, and the mentally ill.

As we can see from such examples, our ideas about psychological illness are greatly shaped by the conditions under which we live. So are our clinical definitions.

In this regard, scientists have asked whether traditional sex-role biases have affected clinical definitions of disorders. Depression and certain types of personality disorders, for example, are diagnosed more frequently in women (Kaplan, 1983; Nolen-Hoeksema, 1987). Is this because of sexism, because of differences in how men and women learn to behave under stress, or because of biological differences between men and women? Much work will be necessary to answer these questions. However, as Kaplan (1983) explains, women are trained to behave in ways that are much like the symptoms of certain personality disorders. Specifically, to a greater or lesser extent, females are taught to have great concern with their physical appearance, to seek approval or reassurance from others, to lean heavily on others' advice in making important decisions, to be easily hurt by disapproval or criticism, and to be immobilized when a close relationship ends. Kaplan (1983) points out that some symptoms of personality disorders are exactly these but performed in excess. Therefore, a woman following the dictates of a traditional sex role to the fullest could run the risk of being mislabeled as disordered.

As a Part of Life

Concepts of psychological illness are not only culturally influenced and changing over the years; they are also controversial at any given time. Scientists involved in writing the most recent version of the American Psychiatric Association manual of disorders (DSM-III-R) debated whether to include

Premenstrual Syndrome (PMS). First described in a 1931 psychiatric journal as a premenstrual disturbance stemming from faulty ovarian functioning (Frank, 1931), its causes, whether biological, social or both, are still unclear. In the DSM-III-R it is listed as Late Luteal Phase Dysphoric Disorder in an appendix of categories suggested as needing further study.

There is no clear line between psychological health and psychological illness, no fixed boundary between one diagnosable disorder and another. We can seldom pinpoint the exact moment at which we become ill or well again. (Is a person healthy during the active, symptom-free time when a malignant lesion is developing, or during the time that an allergy is dormant?) We are seldom completely well, or for that matter completely ill. And yet, when we map out our lives we know without hesitation that there were periods of predominating health and predominating illness. We say, for example, "Spring and summer are bad for me, with my allergies." Or: "These last winters have been healthy ones for the children."

During the course of our lifetimes, we cross the boundary between psychological health and illness many times (A. Freud, 1969). When adjustment is challenged and our vital balance is disturbed, some symptoms of psychological disorder are a likely consequence. If we are unable to right ourselves, a pattern of disorder or a period of illness may follow. It may be brief or lengthy; it may be confined to one "difficult" period or recur at times over the life span; it may even become chronic. In any case, it is a part of our lives.

To think of disease or disorder as something abnormal and external, which *causes* us to break down or fall ill, seems to have a great appeal to us (Engel, 1962). However, many psychologists feel that life is a series of active adjustments within the environment, and that health and disease are both natural phases of life. Disease or disorder is not something that happens *to* the person. It corresponds to his failures in growth and development; it occurs when he is unable to function effectively, in fulfilling his needs, and in responding to the demands of the environment.

As a Failure of Adjustment

In some cases psychological disorders appear to result from a person's extreme or inappropriate attempts to adjust to his or her situation. For example, we saw that drinking and fantasy formation are among the ways we often cope with psychological emergencies. Denial and displacement are among the long-standing defenses of the personality (Chapter 4). However, if used excessively or inappropriately, these usual coping methods can result in symptoms of psychological disorder, or even in prolonged illness. Excessive drinking often leads to alcoholism. Displacement of all one's fears onto phobic objects leads, of course, to phobic disorders. In fact, many insights can be gained by viewing psychological disorders as failed attempts at adjustment. They may be likened to "diseases of adaptation," in which a response originally intended to defend the person from a problem becomes the problem itself.

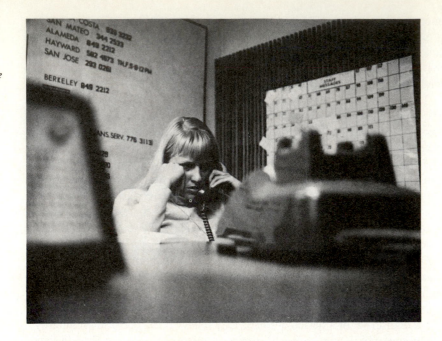

This view of psychological illness is attractive to students of personal adjustment, for it enables them to develop a unified concept of psychological health and illness.

Although many disorders are associated on more than a casual basis with such events as separation from a parent in childhood, or sudden loss of a loved person or a valued role and although the illness may be seen as the person's way of responding to the event we must recognize that such explanations are controversial and incomplete. They do not explain similar instances of illness in which no such event is discovered. They do not explain why some people who experience these events develop different symptoms or no symptoms at all. And they do not recognize that, for example, alcoholism or schizophrenia is also "explained," so to speak, by biological or neurological vulnerability. Having made these points, it makes sense to again note that viewing psychological illness as a disease of adaptation, or as an understandable response to personal crisis, can help us to understand and treat some individuals. With this thought in mind, we turn attention to the use of diagnostic labels to categorize psychological disorders.

A WORD ABOUT DIAGNOSTIC LABELS

Each person's psychological illness is unique (Menninger, 1963). It consists of a combination of symptoms, and fits a description of no single disorder exactly. The disorders described in the following pages are no more than generalizations, or ideal types. Some people have been ill in precisely the ways the definitions suggest, but many others have symptoms that overlap or even contradict the definitions.

What Ideas Do You Have about Mental Illness?

Perhaps you have thought about the broad topic of psychological disorder; perhaps not. In any case, the more familiar term " mental illness" will have been brought to your attention. Undoubtedly your response to this term will involve certain attitudes, understandings, and experiences. The questions below offer an opportunity to discover what ideas you bring to this chapter on psychological disorders but not, of course, what you will get out of it.

1. From what sources have you derived your information about mental illness? (If your main source of information has been the media, specify which books, films, dramas, and so forth have influenced you.)
2. Have you ever bought a book about mental illness, or about a mentally ill person? If so, name the book, and tell (if you can) why you were motivated to buy it.
3. Have you ever known a person who suffered a "nervous breakdown" or some other serious psychological crisis? If so, describe what you understood to have happened to this person.
4. Have you ever learned, to your surprise, that a person you knew and felt was perfectly normal had consulted a psychotherapist or counselor because of a problem? If so, describe the person.
5. Have you ever visited a person who was hospitalized for a "mental illness"? If a friend were hospitalized in a psychiatric facility, how would you feel about visiting him or her?
6. Have you ever consulted a psychotherapist or counselor, or felt a need to do so?
7. You are now reading a chapter on psychological disorders. As you begin the chapter, is there any one disorder that you find yourself looking out for or reading toward? If so, name the disorder and say, if you can, why it interests you.
8. After reading this chapter, note whether, during significant crises in your life, you have ever reacted with any of the psychological disorders described. ▲

In fact, the **diagnostic labels** that psychologists use are a matter of convention. They change as our understanding of disorders changes. In 1980, the American Psychiatric Association published a third edition (since 1952) of its *Diagnostic and Statistical Manual of Mental Disorders* (abbreviated as *DSM-III*), which was revised again in 1987. The revised volume, called DSM-III-R, is the source of much of the information in this chapter. In each edition new disorders appear, and old ones are removed. For example, in reading this chapter you may notice that the term "neurotic" is no longer used as a diagnostic category. People who suffer from neurotic disorders, as described in earlier editions, have not disappeared from the clinical landscape. Psychologists have simply come to a different understanding about their condition.

Diagnostic Labels
Terms, which change over time, that psychologists use in referring to individuals' symptoms and making diagnoses.

For purposes of diagnosis, psychologists now find it more useful to describe these disorders in terms of symptoms (as, for example, "anxiety disorders" or "mood disorders"). There have been many such changes in the history of diagnosis. In the words of the DSM-III-R: ". . . each of the mental disorders is conceptualized as a clinically significant behavioral or psychological syndrome or pattern that occurs in a person and that is associated with present distress (a painful symptom) or disability (impairment in one or more important areas of functioning) or with a significantly increased risk of suffering. . . . In addition, this syndrome or pattern must not be merely an expectable response to a particular event, for example, the death of a loved one. . . . There is no assumption that each mental disorder is a discrete entity with sharp boundaries (discontinuity) between it and other mental disorders, or between it and no mental disorder (page xxii)."

Although diagnostic labels are necessarily imperfect and changeable, they are also useful. They provide a common language in which psychologists and other mental health professionals can communicate about clients, conduct research, and educate students. They also make it possible for psychotherapists to know how other therapists have treated clients similar to (in the same diagnostic category as) their clients.

While the application of diagnostic labels to abnormal or deviant behavior holds promise to advance scientific understandings and treatment techniques, their use is not without controversy. Consider some criticisms that have been raised.

First, the idea that deviant behavior should be labeled as ill has been challenged. Szasz (1961) wrote in "The Myth of Mental Illness": ". . . in modern medicine new diseases were *discovered,* in modern psychiatry they were *invented.* **Paresis** was *proved* to be a disease: **hysteria** was *declared* to be one" (p. 12). Szasz asks why, when people deviate from social and moral codes, their problems are considered medical. Once the cause is assumed to be medical rather than being due to a lack of information or skills, treatment instead of training is prescribed (Schwebel, Kaswan, Sills, & Hackel, 1976; Moreland, Schwebel, Beck, & Wells, 1982; Hersen, Eisler, & Miller, 1988). Further, professionals, rather than the individual, his support group, or a teacher, must assume major responsibility for remedying the problem.

Second, critics ask, What is achieved by applying labels? and, At what cost? These questions suggest several important considerations. They point out that labels can lead us to believe we have a more superior understanding of a problem than we might have. To illustrate, one author interviewed a teenager and his parents. All three agreed Bill's academic difficulties were due to his "laziness." In the role of psychotherapist, the author asked, "What do you mean by lazy?" They explained, "Bill doesn't study or finish his homework," thus completing a circular definition. The family was helped when they dispensed with the label and considered why the problematic behavior developed, what maintained it, and what steps the three of them were willing to take to improve matters.

Paresis
A disorder involving partial paralysis of muscles.

Hysteria
A disorder thought to involve the conversion of unconscious conflicts into physical symptoms to protect an individual against anxiety. Freud believed a person anxious about sexual impulses might experience paralysis of the hands; paralyzed hands cannot masturbate.

Labels lead us to assume psychological disorders, like medical diseases, can be reliably differentiated and that the most appropriate treatment will follow from the diagnosis. While considerable progress has been made in differential diagnosis, that is, specifying characteristics of particular disorders, much work lies ahead. Similarly, there has been advancement in developing treatments and matching them with diagnoses since, several decades ago, it was argued that the psychiatric labels applied had little impact on the nature of the treatment delivered (Ash, 1949; Schmidt & Fonda, 1956). Again, however, much work lies ahead.

Another concern about labels is that they stigmatize the patient (Goffman, 1963; Scheff, 1975). Once people are labeled substance abusers or schizophrenics, others may react differently to them. Senator Thomas Eagleton's case only a few decades ago illustrates this. After being nominated by the Democratic Party to run for vice president, news was released that earlier in his life he had been mentally ill. Although he had long since recovered and served in the U. S. Senate, Eagleton had to leave the ticket for fear that the American public would not accept him. It was an unhappy moment in history for mental health. Since then, more people with psychiatric disorders are being treated in the community, on an outpatient basis (Teplin, 1984), and some of the stigma associated with mental illness has been reduced.

Finally, there is concern that once a diagnostic label is applied, the behavior of the individual and the behavior of others toward that individual can change to bring about a self-fulfilling prophecy. A person called "slow" by parents and teachers may come to act slow in reaction to how he is being treated by them. Similarly, once a person is labeled as "mentally ill," others may react to him or her in entirely new ways. While some research demonstrating the operations of the self-fulfilling prophecy has been criticized, the work of Farina et al. (1971), Goldenberg (1974), and Rosenhan (1973) show the enduring power of a label in shaping social interactions.

Having raised concerns about possible unintended consequences of psychodiagnostic labels, it is appropriate to again underline the value they have in the field of adjustment. Practitioners and researchers who hold a variety of theoretical perspectives will share in the use of DSM-III-R diagnostic labels until that volume is replaced during the 1990s by DSM-IV. In this chapter we, too, benefit from the DSM-III-R and the recent research that has been generated in response to it and its predecessor, DSM-III.

DISORDERS OF INFANCY, CHILDHOOD, AND ADOLESCENCE

Many psychological disturbances of adulthood may be traced to (or otherwise associated with) adjustment failures in childhood. The disturbed adult will often be discovered to have experienced a childhood trauma or psychological injury, or to have suffered to an unusual degree from physical illnesses, eating or sleeping difficulties, parental separations, and so forth. In most cases the childhood problem was not diagnosed as a psychological disorder but was thought to be a normal (if disruptive) stage in development. And so it may have been. In fact, it is more difficult in childhood than in other life stages to distinguish between psychological disorder and the disturbances that normally accompany transitions or crises of development. Why this is so is obvious: Growth in childhood and adolescence is more rapid and more turbulent than it is in maturity. Therefore, disruptions that are likely to be disregarded in the child may be viewed as "disturbed" in the adult.

Some psychological disorders, however, are readily diagnosed in infancy, childhood, and adolescence. They represent distinct departures from normal development and they affect over 11 percent of youngsters at any point in time (Gould, Wunsch-Hitzig, & Dohrenwend, 1981).

The DSM-III-R describes several dozen disorders of infancy, childhood, and adolescence. In this section we have selected for description several disorders that have come to public attention, either because of their prevalence in the population, the attention they get from the media, or because of the significant challenge they present to our understanding. A major class of disorders, mental retardation, is excluded here. It should be noted, however, that psychologists sometimes find it difficult to distinguish between the mentally retarded and the psychologically disturbed, for both show inabilities to develop normal skills and relationships.

Autistic Disorder

Autistic Disorder
A childhood psychological disorder characterized by lack of communication, unresponsiveness to affection, and poor and distorted language development.

The symptoms of **autistic disorder,** also known as infantile autism or Kanner's syndrome, typically appear before three years of age. The child seems unreachable and unresponsive, so much so that the parents seek medical help, frequently wondering whether their youngster is deaf or blind.

Autism is rare, affecting four to five children in 10,000 (Schopler & Dalldorf, 1980) on a world-wide basis. However, since first described some 50 years ago by Leo Kanner M. D., the disorder has attracted much sympathetic interest, probably because of its severe symptoms and the elusiveness of identifying its cause and effective treatment. Once thought an early manifestation of childhood schizophrenia, research suggests that this is not the case (Beitchman, 1985). Interestingly, while American scientists believe it is caused by organic factors, their European counterparts seem more divided, stressing both social and biological explanations (Sanua, 1987).

Children with autism lag developmentally in reciprocal social behaviors like waving "bye-bye," imitating simple behavior (shaking a rattle), and cuddling (but may instead stiffen their bodies when being held). Because they are not aware of the feelings or even the existence of others, they cannot play simple games or make friends. Instead they engage in solitary activities, shunning interactions with others, even at times of illness or distress when most peers would seek hugs from mother.

Both verbal and nonverbal communication is impaired. A child may greet people with a fixed stare, instead of a smile, and use other gestures and facial expressions in markedly abnormal ways. There may be no speech, speech that develops slowly and has unusual qualities (abnormal pitch, rate, rhythm, or volume), or speech used only for voicing lengthy monologues. Those children who do converse may display symptoms like reversing the pronouns "you" and "I," introducing irrelevant topics (talking about baseball during a discussion of dinner plans), and displaying an inability to name common objects (swings, seesaw, or sandbox).

Finally, children with an autistic disorder often become attached to odd objects or rituals. They tend to be fascinated by machine-like, repetitive motions. A father describes his toddler, diagnosed as autistic, by noting that "His idea of play was flexing and unflexing his hands before his eyes, picking at infinitesimal shreds of lint on the floor, bounding up and down on sofas and couches and beds, or endlessly rocking. He *seldom interacted with anybody*" (Greenfeld, 1977, italics added).

Autistic children obtain very low intelligence scores, in part, no doubt, because they cannot easily be tested for verbal skills. However, many autistic children appear to have excellent memories. The media has brought attention to unusual autistic individuals who have talents like the ability to multiply large numbers in their heads or play musical pieces after hearing them only once. More often, autistic individuals are able to recite jingles or recall telephone numbers and birth dates after long periods. Sometimes such mechanical speech makes up the whole of their communication (Applebaum, 1979).

Autistic disorders are three to four times more common in males than females and found more often in children whose siblings have the disorder. While most with autism grow up impaired and unable to live independently, some have overcome their difficulties and completed college and graduate training.

Functional Enuresis

This disorder is characterized by repeated incidences of involuntary or intentional urination in clothes during the day, or in bed at night. Of course, this diagnosis is made only in children physically and psychologically mature enough to expect continence and only after physical causes (e.g., diabetes or urinary tract infection) are excluded. By definition, this disorder cannot begin before age five. At that age, 7 percent of boys and 3 percent of girls are affected. At age 18, 1 percent of males still suffer from the disorder.

Most individuals have what is called nocturnal functional enuresis, and void during the night, perhaps during dreams about urination. When children have had a year-long period of continence, and then develop this problem, it is called secondary functional enuresis. This may develop, for instance, in a firstborn child after the arrival of a baby sibling.

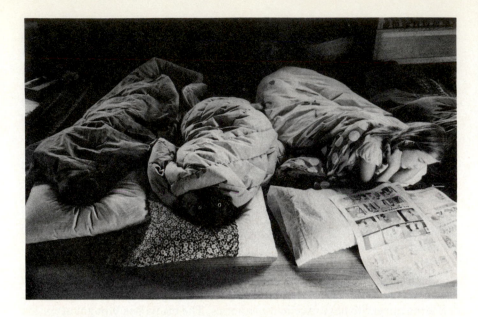

The problems caused by functional enuresis are well-illustrated in the case of seventh-grader Matt. When his brother and sister and some of the neighborhood children got mad at him (and when no adults were around) they teased Matt by calling him "Pee-Wee." Besides enduring verbal taunting, Matt has been deprived of many social opportunities. For instance, he has never had a sleep-over with his peers and he "failed" at his only attempt at overnight camp. Matt has been trying to overcome his problem. For years he has exercised remarkable self-discipline and has had no drinks after supper—even on hot summer days.

Before Matt began treatment, his self-esteem was low, he had few friends, and faced periodic outbursts of anger from his parents who themselves had become very frustrated. With guidance from a psychologist and help from a book on bedwetting control (Azrin & Besalel, 1979), Matt overcame the problem.

Attention-Deficit Hyperactive Disorder

Attention-Deficit Hyperactive Disorder
A childhood psychological disorder characterized by an inability to sit still, a short attention span, work oversights, and resistance to control.

Hyperactivity is the older, more widely used name (and outstanding feature) of what is now called an **attention-deficit hyperactive disorder** (ADHD). Young children with this disorder cannot sit still or are always on the run. They move and fidget. Their attention spans are short. Even when they are motivated, their work is characterized by oversights and hasty omissions. They are often impulsive, obstinate, prone to temper tantrums, and otherwise resist control (Clark, 1980).

The problem often appears in toddlerhood, when the child continually fails to carry out the parent's instructions, but it is not labeled or treated until the child enters school and does not adjust to classroom behavior norms. He tests his teacher's patience because of his difficulty listening to lessons and carrying out independent work. Further, his inattentiveness and impulsiveness means messy papers, careless errors, and classroom interruptions. Fellow students frequently reject their peers who, because of ADHD and the associated lack of self-control, often disobey classroom and playground rules, speaking without being recognized, cutting into line, and otherwise failing to conform to expectations. Although antisocial behavior has been associated with ADHD, quality parenting and a supportive, healthy environment reduce the chances of such behavior, even in severe cases (Atkins, 1985).

The disorder tends to persist over the childhood years, although the signs of its presence change. For example, older youngsters and adolescents outgrow the "motor-running, gross overactivity" symptom that had characterized their earlier behavior and, instead, display a restlessness and a tendency to fidget. In about a third of the cases, restlessness, impulsiveness, and a limited attention span continue into adulthood, affecting the individual's ability to perform sustained work and to maintain social relations.

Found in 3 percent of all children, boys are at least three times more likely than girls to have ADHD. An example of how children who are diagnosed as having ADHD behave in the classroom is provided in one student teacher's diary (Schwebel, Schwebel, Schwebel, & Schwebel, 1979, p. 168–170):

> 1/11 George is testing me to see how far he can push me. I don't quite know how to handle (him).
> 1/20 George started about three little battles in the classroom. After I settled the third one down, George hit Raymond. . . .
> 1/23 I had problems with George today. He was disturbing the class, running about the room, talking and constantly out of his seat. . . .
> (Over the next several weeks George continued to misbehave and produce poor quality work. He was unable to sit alone in class and do math and other seatwork and he had difficulty completing a committee project in geography. During this period the student teacher continued her struggle with one of the greatest challenges in the elementary school: how to meet the needs of a child with ADHD as well as those of his classmates.)
> 3/3 George . . . didn't want me to do my unit and he insisted on running all over the room and talking until the kids couldn't possibly remember anything I said because every sentence was broken by my having to correct George. Finally, I just told him to get into the coatroom until we were finished.

Children with ADHD are typically treated with psychotherapy and academic tutoring and often with medication. There has been a good deal of controversy regarding the need for and the value of medication in treatment programs (Gadow, 1985).

Specific Developmental Disorders (Learning Disabilities)

Specific Developmental Disorders (Learning Disabilities)
Any of a number of disorders, such as difficulty in reading or arithmetic, which persist although the child has had adequate educational opportunities and shows no other signs of retardation.

Dyslexia
A learning disability characterized by faulty reading, with omissions, distortions, and insertions of words.

Learning disabilities, referred to by psychologists as **specific developmental disorders,** are diagnosed in some children who experience a persistent and baffling difficulty in reading, arithmetic, comprehension of spoken language, language articulation, or motor skills. Although no evidence of neurological or physical disorders can be found, and the children have had adequate educational opportunities, they perform in these areas significantly below their general intellectual capacities, which in some cases may be exceptional. Usually children with learning disabilities show no other symptoms of disturbance or retardation. Accordingly, they are treated within educational systems rather than in mental health facilities. Often the disorders persist in modified form into adulthood.

One of the more common disorders is **dyslexia,** which appears as faulty reading, with omissions, distortions, and insertions of words. Comprehension is reduced and reading is slow. Often associated with dyslexia are difficulties in discriminating among sounds and in putting words in proper order in sentences.

Some experts studying learning disabilities suggest that at one point during fetal life, the left and right sides of the brain develop at different rates in people who will become dyslexic. Such growth enables them to excel in "right brain" activities like art, music, and spatial perception (athletics, mechanics, photography, architecture), but causes difficulties in "left brain" skills, like reading (Baker, 1984). Others place greater emphasis on social factors (Coles, 1987).

Dyslexia is common, affecting from 2 percent to 8 percent of school-age children and at least twice as many boys as girls. Although typically diagnosed in the early elementary school grades, this is not always the case. Some bright youngsters, like high-school sophomore Heather, learn to compensate for the handicap and may not have it diagnosed until much later. However, late diagnosis is often a source of serious discomfort to the sufferer, who may hide the difficulty and come to consider herself as stupid or inferior. Once the problem is identified and treated, steps can be taken to help the individual manage more effectively. Heather came with her parents to a psychologist because of her grades and family friction. It was only then that dyslexia was diagnosed. Heather first explained matters to her psychologist as follows:

> Mom and dad brought me here because I'm always fighting with them.
> They think I don't study hard. But I put in the hours . . . I'm just slow in reading assignments and the next day I can't remember what I read.
> Every night mom sneaks into my room to check whether I'm studying. It makes me mad that they don't believe how hard I try.
> I get my report card next week. They'll kill me. I'm getting at least one D and probably a D— or an F. I'll be grounded again.
> Dad's already mad at me for losing my job at Ted's Diner. I lied and told him I was laid off because business was slow. Really, I messed up giving change so often that Ted fired me. Dad thinks I don't have the ambition to find another job, but I'm afraid I'll be canned again. If I don't have a job this summer, it's early curfew and no cheerleading practice.

Once dyslexia was diagnosed, Heather received permission to tape record class lectures, mom and dad hired a tutor and, with the help of psychotherapy, peace and trust returned to the daughter-parent relationship. Three years after the diagnosis, Heather brought home a college grade card filled with the A's she had earned during her first term in a special program for people with learning disabilities.

Though dyslexia may affect people in adulthood, if they feel comfortable with themselves and understand their handicap, they can adjust to and overcome whatever difficulties it presents.

The developmental arithmetic disorder is a second example of a learning disability. It is less common than dyslexia and has been studied less (Svein & Sherlock, 1979). Dyscalculia, as it is sometimes called, is typically identified in the elementary school grades when children have trouble doing the required arithmetic. Their difficulty could stem from their inability to attend to the task, copy problems accurately, read the numbers accurately, or follow the correct sequence of mathematical steps.

A third example of a learning disability is the developmental coordination disorder. Affecting as many as 6 percent of children in the 5–11 age bracket, its symptoms are problems with clumsiness, which interfere with day-to-day activities. These may be seen in younger children as difficulties in dressing themselves and tying their shoes. At older ages the children may encounter problems in areas like penmanship, ballplaying, and solving puzzles.

Eating Disorders

Many children are "problem eaters" at one stage or another. However, some children and adolescents experience gross disturbances in eating behavior. In addition to obesity, which is not associated with any distinct psychological syndrome, there are several other eating disorders of a serious nature. Among them are bulimia (characterized by abnormal eating binges); rumination disorder of infancy (a potentially fatal disturbance characterized by repeated vomiting in the absence of nausea); anorexia nervosa (a refusal to eat, resulting in extreme or even fatal weight loss); and, pica (repeated eating of nonnutritive substances such as paint, string, cloth, or leaves).

Anorexia nervosa, occurring primarily in females (over 90 percent) and mostly during adolescence, has received the most attention of these disorders. It affects from about ¼–1 percent of teenage girls, generally "model" children who are attractive and eager to please. Preoccupied with body image, these children develop a distorted fear of obesity. Psychoanalytic theorists also presume a fear of sexuality: Weight loss prevents the development of breasts, as well as the onset or regularity of menstruation. In adults there is usually a decreased interest in sexual activity. Anorexic children often come from rigid, overprotective families and some family therapists believe anorexic children use their eating habits as a means to gain attention from and control over other family members.

Because people with anorexia nervosa feel fat and fear obesity, even when underweight, they may engage in exhausting exercise as well as dangerously restricting their intake of food even though their appetites, at the outset of the disorder, are normal. Prolonged dieting, with or without excessive exercise, can produce such severe weight loss that hospitalization and intravenous feeding become necessary. Research suggests that anorexia nervosa causes death in 5–18 percent of its cases, placing this psychological disorder among the few that can cause death (DSM-III-R, 1987). Unfavorable outcomes are more likely in cases with extreme weight loss, delays before treatment is sought, and severe problems in child-parent relationships (Morgan, Purgold, & Welborne, 1983).

Typical thoughts of an adolescent with anorexia are described by Wenar:

> Gaining or losing weight, sickness or health are not viewed in terms of bodily pleasures and pains but in terms of pleasing or displeasing parents. Eating, in particular, has nothing to do with personal enjoyment but has everything to do with parental preferences and values . . . parental evaluations are so prepotent that the adolescent literally cannot see herself realistically. One patient had difficulty discriminating between two photographs of herself even though there was a seventy-pound difference in her weight. Another said she could see how emaciated her body was when looking in a mirror, but when she looked away she reverted to her belief that she was larger (1982, p. 179).

Anorexia Nervosa
A psychological disorder in which a person develops a distorted fear of obesity and may cease eating to the point of starvation.

The eating disorder of anorexia nervosa has received increasing public attention in the past two decades. Those with anorexia nervosa are primarily adolescent girls who refuse to eat because they see themselves as obese, despite evidence that their weight is below normal. Karen Carpenter was a victim of this disorder.

Bulimia nervosa is characterized by binge eating, in which the individual consumes large amounts of food, often high in calories, over a limited period of time. After binges, during which the eating is out of control, the individual frequently experiences abdominal pain and may engage in self-induced vomiting. Persistent concern over weight may lead to the use of laxatives, fasting, and vigorous exercise. Found much more often in women than in men, this disorder typically begins in adolescence or young adulthood and is rarely, but can be, life-threatening.

Childhood Disorders That Are Not Age-Related

Autism and anorexia nervosa are examples of disorders of childhood and adolescence. They appear to develop in response to developmental crises experienced by the growing child. And they arise during specific periods of heightened vulnerability.

Some disorders suffered by children are not so directly linked to age. For example, major depression, a disorder common in adults, may be diagnosed in children of all ages. The manifestations of depression vary with age and circumstances, but many of the essential features are similar over the life span. The seriously depressed elementary schoolchild, like the depressed adult, shows lack of interest in friends and activities, sees the self as worthless or hopeless, and complains of a variety of bodily and emotional hurts. Their feelings are gloomy (Kaslow & Wamboldt, 1985) and, by elementary school age, they are capable of thinking in ways like depressed adults (Cole & Kaslow, 1988) that maintain depression and lower self-esteem (Seligman et al., 1984).

Major depression is one of a number of affective (mood) disorders that are experienced both by children and adults. Anxiety disorders, substance (drug) abuse, and schizophrenic disorders are other adult disorders that may be diagnosed in children. These are discussed in the next section.

MAJOR DISORDERS OF ADULTHOOD

Most psychological disorders become evident in adulthood, many in early adulthood. The diagnostic categories described here include anxiety disorders, somatoform disorders, dissociative disorders, schizophrenia, mood disorders, personality disorders, and substance use disorders. Among the important categories that we have omitted are organic mental disorders (which arise from abnormal brain function) and psychosexual disorders. Examples of the latter will be described in Chapter 9.

Anxiety Disorders

Anxiety, we have seen, is a generalized, unpleasant state of physiological and psychological tension that is experienced when we feel threatened or endangered. The physical symptoms of anxiety may include rapid heartbeat, shortness of breath, dizziness, diarrhea, or upset stomach. Psychological manifestations include apprehension and feelings of "nameless dread."

Everybody experiences anxiety from time to time. For some people, however, anxiety is so pronounced, so frequent, or so debilitating that an **anxiety disorder** may be said to exist. Characterized by symptoms of anxiety and avoidance behavior, these are the most common mental health disorders in our society (American Psychiatric Association, 1987). In some (such as phobic and panic disorders), the individual is very much aware of his or her anxiety. In others (such as obsessive-compulsive disorders), anxiety is not experienced directly. Instead the individual engages in bizarre or debilitating behaviors that appear to keep him or her from directly confronting dreaded thoughts, objects, or impulses.

Phobic Disorders

Phobos, the Greek god of fear, is remembered in the name **phobic disorders.** With these disorders, a person experiences fear when near a particular object, situation, or individual or in the midst of a particular experience. Nothing is physically wrong with the sufferer and, except for his involuntary fear that he recognizes as excessive, he functions normally. Traditionally, Greek prefixes have been used to identify the different phobias. Table 5.1 lists several disorders you may have heard about through the media. For instance, triskaidekaphobia is often mentioned in Friday the 13th human interest stories.

A good sense of what a person with a phobic disorder experiences is provided by a college professor's description of the discomfort he experiences as he physically approaches the phobic object (in his case a train). Note how his fear grows as he nears it.

> Let me assume that I am walking down University Drive by the Lake. I am a normal man for the first quarter of a mile; for the next hundred yards I am in a mild state of dread, controllable and controlled; for the next twenty yards in an acute state of dread, yet controlled; for the next ten, in an anguish of terror that hasn't reached the crisis of explosion; and in a half dozen steps more I am in as fierce a panic of isolation from help and home and of immediate death as a man overboard in mid-Atlantic or on a window ledge far up in a skyscraper with flames lapping his shoulders (Leonard, 1927, pp. 321–322).

In some cases the fear spreads to objects associated with the one initially feared. For example, a phobia involving trains could become generalized to streetcars, train stations, or traffic.

The DSM-III-R list three types of phobias: Agoraphobia, which is discussed elsewhere in this chapter, and simple and social phobias, which are discussed next.

Simple Phobias.   Simple phobias are characterized by a phobic reaction to a specific, clear-cut object or situation (see Table 5.1). The cause of simple phobias (and the other phobic disorders) is unclear. Psychoanalytically oriented theorists believe they stem from a failure in a person's defense mechanisms, whereas behaviorists think they are learned avoidance responses. Still

Anxiety Disorders
Psychological disorders in which anxiety has become very pronounced, frequent, or debilitating.

Phobic Disorders
Psychological disorders in which a person experiences excessive fear when faced with a certain object or situation.

TABLE 5.1	*Some Simple Phobias*
Claustrophobia	Fear of closed places
Nyctophobia	Fear of darkness
Ochlophobia	Fear of crowds
Zoophobia	Fear of animals
Acrophobia	Fear of heights
Mysophobia	Fear of germs
Taphophobia	Fear of being buried alive
Hodophobia	Fear of travel
Haphephobia	Fear of being touched
Ophidiophobia	Fear of snakes
Aerophobia	Fear of flying
Amaxophobia	Fear of driving or of vehicles
Gephyrophobia	Fear of bridges
Triskaidekaphobia	Fear of the number 13

others conclude that humans are born biologically prepared to learn to fear situations or objects that threaten survival (McNally, 1987). They reason that although such a "pre-wired" learning mechanism has survival value for individuals, sometimes it leads them to acquire an irrational fear of a particular situation or specific object that, in turn, interferes with the routine of their lives. Such a fear, which is accompanied by a compelling wish to avoid the situation or object, produces what we call a simple or specific phobia.

Common phobic objects are animals (dogs, snakes, rats, and insects), flying, heights, and closed areas. People try to avoid phobic stimulus/stimuli but if it/they are encountered, anxiety (perhaps in the form of panicky feelings) sweating, and strained breathing may be experienced. Simple phobia is diagnosed more frequently in females than in males.

Different types of simple phobias are more likely to develop at particular points during the lifetime: animal phobias tend to appear during childhood, blood-injury phobias during adolescence and young adulthood, and phobias of air flights, driving, heights, and closed spaces come most often in middle-age. Simple phobias developed during childhood are typically overcome without treatment. This is not the case with those first appearing in adulthood.

Social Phobias. A social phobia is the fear of and compulsion to avoid particular situations in which one might be criticized by other people. Individuals are usually afraid of one or more specific experiences: speaking in public, blushing when called on in class, writing in front of others, using public restrooms while others are present, and so forth. Although individuals are aware that their fear is irrational, they try to avoid the social phobic situation. Sometimes, however, they must force themselves to endure it, such as when they are required to speak in class or when they must use a public restroom. While facing the phobic situation, individuals experience signs of intense anxiety, such as nervousness, sweating, and feelings of panic. Added to their concern about public speaking, for example, which may center on worrying about making foolish comments or not knowing the correct answer, is a fear of being humiliated if others detect trembling hands, a shaky voice, or other signs of panic. These worries, in turn, could hamper performance and lead to a failure that individuals could then use to "confirm" their original apprehension.

Social phobia is more common in men than in women. It often develops during the latter years of childhood or the earlier stages of adolescence, when individuals become especially self-conscious.

As John R. discovered, social phobias typically interfere with people's social activities or work life. John R. called one of the authors who had been his undergraduate advisor:

> After I graduated I moved to Houston and took a great job at an oil company. In less than a year I was promoted. The problem was that my new post required giving presentations to groups of 20–50 people. The day after my promotion I beelined it to a psychologist. I was surprised. Without going into my whole life story, he helped me and now I can comfortably give three or four talks a week.
>
> The psychotherapist assisted John R. by providing direct advice and guidance, approaches found to be effective with those having social phobias (Persson & Nordlund, 1985).

Panic Disorders

In **panic disorders,** panic attacks (also called "anxiety attacks") occur unpredictably, and not invariably in the presence of a particular stimulus (as with phobias). The attacks are characterized by feelings of severe apprehension, even terror. Physical symptoms include palpitations, dizziness, and choking. Psychological manifestations include feelings of being "unreal" or losing control, and fears of "going crazy" or of dying. Attacks usually last minutes, though they can continue for hours, and may be limited to a single brief period of life, or may recur, perhaps chronically, over the life span.

As might be expected, a complication of panic disorders is fear of new anxiety attacks. This fear, in turn, leads some to restrict their activities, perhaps to the point of becoming mostly or completely housebound. Such individuals are said to experience a panic disorder with agoraphobia. Agoraphobia is the fear of being in an open space or public place, from which the person perceives escape as being difficult or help unavailable. (The *agora* in Greek towns is the marketplace.)

Panic Disorders
Psychological disorders in which anxiety attacks occur unpredictably.

Twice as many women as men are treated for panic disorder with agoraphobia in contrast to the equal number of men and women who are treated for panic disorders without agoraphobia, a much less limiting problem vocationally and socially.

Laurie's case illustrates panic disorder with agoraphobia. A few weeks after her June honeymoon and the day after her 26th birthday, Laurie and her husband Jim took a cruise on her in-laws' new boat. Not long after the dock disappeared beyond the horizon, Laurie felt nausea. She later explained to a therapist:

> Suddenly I felt trapped. My heart skipped beats, I felt chilled and my body trembled. I thought I was having a heart attack. Jim asked what was wrong. I couldn't tell him the truth . . . not in front of everybody. So I bit my tongue and claimed to need a bathroom badly. That was less embarrassing than telling him that for seemingly no reason I was overcome by panic and a sense of impending doom. But I had to get off that boat.
>
> After a stop on shore, I couldn't get back on the boat. But that was only the start. The next day we went to a restaurant with friends. I was afraid "it" would come again, so I sat on the outside of the booth. After dinner I just couldn't walk the mall as planned. Me . . . a person born to shop.
>
> Over several months we adjusted. Jim did our shopping and I did most of our driving. That way I could stop the instant I felt anxious. But it all came to a head when I had to fly to a convention with Jim. I was deathly afraid. I did force myself to go to the airport, but I couldn't handle the airplane. Jim had to go alone and I decided to seek help.

With assistance from a cognitively-oriented psychotherapist who helped her learn to monitor her thoughts, and excellent support from her husband and family, Laurie recovered. Though she still harbors a distant fear that "it" will strike again, she returned to her "old self," as she put it, and her full schedule of activities.

Obsessive-Compulsive Disorders

Obsessions are persistent thoughts or images that seem to invade a person's mind. They often involve violence, like repetitive worries that a loved one might be killed in an automobile crash, or doubt, such as whether the front door was left unlocked. While obsessions are not produced voluntarily, people may intentionally try to manage them by actively thinking about other matters or by engaging in distracting activities.

Compulsions are acts intentionally performed in response to obsessions. For example, an individual washes his hands several times an hour so as to avoid being contaminated by germs on door knobs or circulating in the air. The hand-washing is always done in a particular fashion, as if certain rules must be followed in order to prevent the unwanted event—the contamination—from occurring. Except for young children and a minority of adults, those affected by compulsions generally recognize their behavior as excessive.

They also recognize when it is unrealistically connected to presumed goals, such as when a person carefully walks between the cracks in the sidewalk so as to prevent tragedies from befalling her family members. People often resist their compulsive acts, but eventually tensions build that can only be released by indulging the compulsion once more.

Compulsive acts differ from excesses in drinking or sex, for example, because they yield no pleasure. In fact, individuals who suffer from **obsessive-compulsive disorders** are likely to be overly conscientious, inhibited, and unable to enjoy themselves. In some cases the obsession or compulsion is so distressing that it interferes with the individual's functioning. For example, a parent may be disturbed by persistent thoughts of harming his or her own children; a worker may be slowed by the compulsion to check and recheck a procedure.

People with this disorder may experience distress because obsessions and compulsions are time-consuming and disruptive to their day-to-day routines. In more serious cases, for example, one patient spent more than an hour brushing her teeth after each meal while another spent 8–10 hours a day at a sink trying to wash "beauty marks" off the skin on his ankles (Insel, 1985).

Obsessive-Compulsive Disorders
Psychological disorders in which a person is preoccupied with persistent unwanted thoughts and performs stereotyped, largely irrational acts.

Posttraumatic Stress Disorders

Posttraumatic stress disorders sometimes occur after a person experiences a trauma (or psychological injury) that in its suddenness and seriousness far exceeds the ordinary life stresses for which he is prepared. Examples of traumas include natural disasters such as volcanic eruptions and tornadoes that devastate one's town and kill scores of neighbors. Man-made or technological accidents can also precipitate the disorder. The uncertainties surrounding the contamination of the environment near Love Canal (Niagara Falls, New York), Three Mile Island (Pennsylvania), and Chernobyl (Soviet Union), undoubtedly resulted in extreme psychological stress in some families. Posttraumatic stress disorder may also develop in response to instances of violent crimes, such as rape or torture, or in the aftermath of military combat (Barocas & Barocas, 1980).

Posttraumatic Stress Disorders
Psychological disorders linked to specific traumas or injuries, with common symptoms being nightmares about the trauma, difficulty in sleeping, and a sense of numbness.

People suffering from posttraumatic stress disorder reexperience the trauma in painful conscious recollection and in nightmares. They may have trouble sleeping. Some undergo an "emotional anesthesia": they become numb, estranged from others, unable to experience pleasure from the activities they formerly enjoyed. Some have impaired concentration and memory. They avoid experiences that might cause them to relive their pain. Sometimes this avoidance results in a drastic change-of-life pattern. For example, an entertainer who was raped in a hotel corridor may find herself unable to continue "on the road" or to perform before a live audience.

Symptoms of posttraumatic stress disorder typically develop soon after the event or injury, but can surface months or years after the trauma (Horowitz, 1986). Posttraumatic stress disorder strikes children as well as adults. Although youngsters may be unable or unwilling to discuss the trauma directly, play therapy often helps them deal with what they have encountered and with the recurring fears, worries, and nightmares they suffer.

A natural disaster, such as a tornado, sometimes produces a posttraumatic stress disorder in the person affected, with possible symptoms ranging from emotional numbness to recurring nightmares. The prognosis is best if the stress reactions are treated soon after the original trauma. This Columbian man lost his family in a mud slide avalanche.

This disorder was recognized as far back as during the Civil War when the term "shell shocked" was used to label soldiers suffering from anxiety symptoms thought to have been produced by repeatedly experiencing rounds of artillery fire (Ettedgui & Bridges, 1985). These soldiers reactions to minor annoyances sometimes led them to be aggressive, even to the point of losing control and physically harming themselves or others. Over a century later, a Viet Nam veteran offered this explanation of how posttraumatic stress disorder affected him:

> My marriage is falling apart. We just don't talk any more. . . . She's tried to tell me she cares for me, but I get real uncomfortable talking about things like that, and I get up and leave. Sometimes I get real angry over the smallest thing. I used to hit her when this would happen, but lately I just punch out a hole in the wall, or leave and go for a long drive. . . .
> I really don't have any friends. . . . The world is pretty much dog eat dog, and no one seems to care much for anyone else. . . . Sometimes I get so angry with the way things are being run, I think about placing a few blocks of C-4 (a military explosive) under some of the sons-of-bitches. A couple of times a year I get into fights at bars. I usually pick the biggest guy. I don't know why. I usually get creamed. . . .
> (When I get depressed I drink heavily and sometimes think about suicide.) . . . I've sat with it (a gun) loaded, once I even had the barrel in my mouth and the hammer pulled back. I couldn't do it. I see Smitty back in Nam with his brains smeared all over the bunker. Hell, I fought too hard to make it back to the world (the U.S.); I can't waste it now. How come I survived and he didn't?

. . . Night is the hardest for me. I think of so many of my Nam experiences at night. Sometimes my wife awakens me with a wild look in her eye. I'm all sweaty and tense. Sometimes I grab for her neck before I realize where I am. Sometimes I remember the dream; sometimes it's Nam, other times it's just people after me, and I can't run anymore (Goodwin, 1980, pp. 1–2).

Somatoform Disorders

Some people persistently suffer from physical symptoms that have no discernible physical cause but are generated by psychological factors. These symptoms stem from a set of disorders called the **somatoform disorders** (from the Greek word for body, *soma*). People with these disorders do not intentionally produce the symptoms and the symptoms are not like what we typically call "psychosomatic" (where physical causes can be detected in a medical examination).

Somatoform Disorders Psychological disorders in which a person persistently suffers from physical symptoms that have no discernible physical cause.

Conversion Disorder

In a **conversion disorder,** a temporary loss of or alteration in physical functioning appears to be caused by a psychological conflict (as opposed to a physical factor). According to some clinician practitioners, free-floating anxiety is "converted" into a local physical problem. Classic examples are blindness, seizures, and paralysis. In some instances it is thought that an individual keeps a conflict from awareness by symbolically preventing a response to it: The person who must suppress rage, for example, may experience a paralysis of the arm. The person who watches a traumatic event may become temporarily blind (as may the person who does not feel able to see a feared event or situation). An individual also benefits if the disorder helps him or her to avoid unwanted activities or gain wanted social support from others. To illustrate, a soldier who becomes unable to walk or stand cannot return to the front, and an elderly parent who loses his ability to talk after moving to a nursing home will earn much attention from his children and others. Conversion symptoms typically appear suddenly and following substantial stress. They also disappear suddenly. Although conversion disorders are infrequently diagnosed today, they were common a few generations ago.

Conversion Disorder Psychological disorders in which there is a temporary loss of, or alteration in, physical functioning that is apparently psychologically based.

Somatoform Pain Disorder

Much more common is **somatoform pain disorder,** involving pain experienced in the absence of physical causes or of greater intensity than one would expect. Although relatively little is known about this disorder, it is encountered with some frequency in medical practice. Affecting twice as many women as men, it typically impairs people to the point that they leave their jobs and become invalids. While this disorder can strike at any age, it most frequently develops in the 30–49 age bracket.

Somatoform Pain Disorder Pain experienced in the absence of physical causes or of greater severity than expected, given the physical symptoms.

Psychological causes are sometimes evident. The person may first experience pain after a psychologically difficult event (being fired from a job) or when avoiding unwanted activities (preparing the house for an in-laws' long-term stay). Dismissing the idea that psychological factors are involved, the person typically makes frequent use of medical services, often switching from physician to one specialist after another. Research data indicates the levels of distress, anxiety, and depression in those suffering from this disorder parallels the levels in patients with known physical causes for their pain (Trief, Elliott, Stein, & Frederickson, 1987). Pain-relieving drugs and minor tranquilizers are common treatments for the pain, but they do not address underlying psychological problems.

Hypochondriasis

Hypochondriasis
A psychological disorder in which the person is unreasonably preoccupied with bodily functions and is convinced, without medical evidence, that he has physical ailments.

A psychological disorder well known to physicians and other health professionals is **hypochondriasis.** The person who suffers from this disorder is unreasonably preoccupied with bodily functions, and absolutely convinced, in the absence of supporting evidence, that he will or has contracted a serious disease. He takes bodily signs (sweating, coughing, the rate at which sores heal) and sensations (in the heartbeat, digestion, and so forth) as indicators of illness, even though physicians assure him that his conclusions or fears are unwarranted. While hypochondriasis can develop at any age, it most commonly begins during a person's 20s.

As the disorder develops, the individual may experience increasing friction with his physician and often decides, "I am not being taken care of." This leads to doctor-shopping and the problems created when a person receives uncoordinated medical treatment. For instance, such people use great amounts of medicine and have frequent medical tests. In some cases they succeed in subjecting themselves to unnecessary surgery or other dangerous procedures. Many clinicians believe that the patients (unconsciously) use the disorder to gain attention and sympathy and at the same time avoid underlying depression and anxiety. Because they do not consciously choose their form of behavior, people with hypochondriasis are not mere malingerers or fakes. And their prognosis is poor: they only hesitantly accept treatment from psychologists or psychiatrists because they are offended at the suggestion that their fears are unrealistic. Further, preoccupation with their health often damages their support groups, straining friendships and affecting job performance.

Dissociative Disorders

Dissociative Disorders
Psychological disorders in which there is a loss of memory or alteration in identity.

Suddenly or over a period of time, once or chronically, persons affected by **dissociative disorders** experience a loss or change in their memory or in their identity. Each becomes dissociated from his usual self and may forget important facts about himself and even adopt a new identity. Among the dissociative disorders are amnesia, fugue, and multiple personality.

The Search for Personal Adjustment

Psychogenic Amnesia and Psychogenic Fugue

Psychogenic amnesia involves an inability to recall information about oneself, in the absence of an explanatory physical condition such as brain damage. It usually appears suddenly, soon after an individual encounters a significant psychosocial stress, one which could range from confronting a life-or-death situation to coping with a personally unacceptable behavior, such as having an extramarital affair.

In all four forms of this disorder various types of information are forgotten. Most common is localized amnesia in which the "lost" information generally concerns the events following a trauma. For example, a woman might forget what happened to her in the hours or days following a tornado in which her child was killed. The guilt she might feel in not having died with him could help produce the amnesia. With selective amnesia only some events during a time period are forgotten. For instance, the woman might remember running with her child in her arms to the hospital, but nothing else. More infrequently are cases of generalized and continuous amnesia. In these, respectively, the sufferer loses memories of his or her entire life, or memories subsequent to a specific time or event up through the present. During the period of amnesia the person may wander about seemingly confused and without purpose.

Recovery is typically abrupt, and recurrences are unusual. The disorder itself is rare. It is most likely to appear during periods of war and natural disaster, when many people experience abrupt breaks with the reality of their past lives.

Similar to amnesia is **psychogenic fugue,** in which a person suddenly flees his or her surroundings, forgets the past, and adopts a new identity. Although a history of significant alcohol use may make an individual more susceptible, an episode is usually triggered by a harsh psychosocial stress like being in a military battle, a victim of or witness to a disaster, or betrayed by a loved one. Mostly the fugue is brief, lasting a few hours or days during which the person would seem to others to be acting normally. Sometimes, however, the fugue lasts considerably longer, with the person adopting a new name and involving herself in a new community so effectively that there is no evidence of a mental disorder. With her new friends and business associates she may be "Ms. Personality," whereas previously she was shy and retiring. When the fugue ends, the person returns to the previous self and situation, with no recollection of what has taken place. As with psychogenic amnesia, recovery is rapid, recurrences infrequent, and the disorder rare.

Multiple Personality

Multiple personality is a dissociative disorder in which an individual possesses more than one distinct personality, only one of which is dominant at any given time. While some alternate personalities may not be fully developed, in classic cases there are two or more fully developed personalities, each with its own first name, self-image, and set of memories. The personalities may be of different races, have different IQs, respond differently to medication, and require different strengths in eyeglasses.

Psychogenic Amnesia
A psychological disorder in which the person is unable to recall information about himself.

Psychogenic Fugue
A psychological disorder in which the person flees usual surroundings, forgets the past, and adopts a new identity.

Multiple Personality Disorder
A psychological disorder in which an individual possesses more than one distinct personality.

The personalities of Billy Milligan express themselves quite differently, as illustrated by these two pictures.

From The Minds of Billy Milligan *by Daniel Keyes. Copyright © 1981 by Daniel Keyes and William S. Milligan. Reprinted by permission of Random House, Inc.*

Christine's note to Attorney Judy Stevenson

The talent of a person with a multiple personality disorder can vary as the personality in control changes. Both of these works of art were drawn by the same man.

The Search for Personal Adjustment

The personalities can have very different patterns of behavior. A quiet office worker may alternate with a dashing playboy. A controlled, seemingly mature woman may alternate with adolescent personalities of both sexes. The transition from one personality to another is usually triggered by stress, and mostly takes place within seconds or minutes.

Multiple personality disorder is generally chronic. Although much publicized in popular books and movies, it is not very prevalent. Found many times more frequently in women than in men, one continent-wide study of 100 patients found that 97 percent had encountered significant trauma in their childhood (Putnam, Guroff, Silberman, Barban, & Post, 1986). Sexual abuse was experienced by 83 percent, physical abuse by 75 percent, and 45 percent had witnessed a violent death, usually of a family member. The more trauma a child had experienced, the more alternate personalities he or she was likely to develop.

The 100 subjects had a median of nine personalities (Putnam et al., 1986). Most (85 percent) had at least one that was a child; some (30 percent) had at least one that was chronologically older than the patient; and more than half had at least one personality of the opposite gender. Further, considerably more than half of the patients had at least one personality that was unaware of any others and at least one that was aware of all the other personalities.

Schizophrenia

One percent or nearly 3 million Americans have or will develop **schizophrenia,** one of the most common yet most serious mental health disorders (Nietzel & Bernstein, 1987). Approximately half of the hospital beds occupied on any given day are filled by patients with schizophrenia (President's Commission on Mental Health, 1978), placing it first among all physical and psychological disorders in hospital bed usage.

Schizophrenia
A disorder characterized by a deterioration in functioning and usually by a disturbed sense of self and severe disturbances in thought and feelings.

Hal, a 24-year-old man with schizophrenia, told one of the authors how he left the hospital grounds every night with friends through a secret passageway, which he called the "hydraulic escape chamber" (actually the water valve in the shower). Hal then described exactly what had happened the night before when he "left the city" with others from the ward. His description of what people said, and the thinking that underlied his report, is not comprehensible, although Hal believed he was explaining the events most clearly:

Hal:	Burn the engines.
Burn:	Channel 0 test 4.
Fem:	Head to Target.
Punk:	Pail to horse.
CC:	City of Science, hyper-space mikes assigned.
Sky:	Skyhawk to tomcatt. Communications to associate coordinater completed. Marry me Barb.
Barb:	Hal, play B-52.
Kelly:	Prisoners Military Enlistment terms. Category A. Must we be pressed?
Warden:	No.

Guard:	Yes, Sir.
Perky:	No shield?
Shogun:	Always? Jane is the Emerald Queen.
Perky:	I saw the FLAGS WIPED OUT where she lives in a cell in Buckingham Palace.
Illovatar:	You asked for it so we gave it to ya no corregiadoke. I'm an owl.
King:	In the US they sometimes are.
Lincoln:	Hey we're up here!
Booth:	Man what the hell are we into?
Lincoln:	I don't know but we better find a home somewhere Windy.
Hal:	Everything has got a hydraulic system. Man we better get ourselves home. Cut back on your stick until the radio is about half warped and half witty.

Schizophrenia involves a disturbed sense of self and, by definition, a deterioration in functioning that has lasted six months at work and at home, in personal care, and in social relationships. The illness typically begins before age 45, most often during adolescence or early adulthood. Although no single symptom is invariably present, nearly all patients show disturbances in thought, in feelings, in perception, in self-view, in motivation, and in relating to the social and physical environment.

Thinking is typically self-centered, chaotic, and fragmented. The sufferers are not able to communicate effectively with others; they make sense only according to their own very private rules of logic. Often it appears that they do not draw general conclusions from concrete details, and do not sort out the relevant and irrelevant features of a situation. One patient interpreted the saying "A stitch in time saves nine" to mean, "I should sew nine buttons on my shirt." Another, having heard that she was a "blue baby" (born in need of blood transfusion), believed as an adult that she had been "born dead." Patients also usually show a blunting or inappropriateness of affect (emotion). Voice and face are expressionless; laughing at disease or death is common. The individual complains of no longer having feelings, of not being himself. Often other people are viewed in the same light. The afflicted person may recoil from others who are seen as "having rubber faces" or "wearing masks." A friendly touch may be interpreted as a blow.

Patients' problems in perception center around hallucinations, particularly auditory ones in which a person "hears voices." Hal, "when he travels on the space ship" hears the voices of these characters. The "voices" may say hostile and insulting things, sometimes commenting on a person's behavior, "bad bad bad," and sometimes commanding a person to harm or mutilate himself. Tactile hallucinations (tingling and burning) and somatic hallucinations (perceptions that the heart is rotting or that spiders are crawling inside the stomach) also occur.

People with schizophrenia experience difficulty in interpersonal relations and increasingly retreat from others and involvement with the world about them. Difficulties in socializing can occur because of what Kurt Schneider (1887–1967) described as first-rank symptoms of schizophrenia. Specifically, a patient may believe his thoughts are audible to others ("thought broadcasting"); that his thoughts are not his own but they have been implanted by

"Mummy its dark in here."
Although the artwork of
people with schizophrenia may
seem chaotic, there is usually
a distinct inner logic: the art
expresses fear, conflicts, or
perceptions of the world that
are unrealistic but consistent.

others ("thought insertion"); that his feelings are under the control of another, even a dead person; that another person is imposing bodily sensation on him; and that the voices he hears (auditory hallucinations) are verbalizing his thoughts.

The DSM-III-R has identified four types of schizophrenia, each dominated by a different set of symptoms. The catatonic type of schizophrenia is marked by abnormal motor behavior; that is, limited or extreme body movement. The disorganized type has poor quality thinking, behaves aimlessly, and does not show appropriate affect. The paranoid type is abnormally suspicious and often misunderstands other people's behavior. The undifferentiated type does not fit in the above categories.

The course of schizophrenia varies from person to person. During the first, or *prodromal phase,* a person's behavior "slips" in a wide range of areas. Her friends might say, "She's not the same person anymore, her personality seems to have changed." The length of this phase varies greatly. Next comes the *active phase,* during which the person is subject to gross disturbances in thought, feeling, and behavior.

Perhaps as a result of successful treatment, the person reaches the *residual phase.* During it, functioning in most ways parallels the first phase, except that there is a remaining impairment in the person's ability to conduct day-to-day activities and he may still experience symptoms, though they will be less upsetting than before. From this point a return to full health is possible.

Researchers have not yet agreed about how frequently this desirable outcome occurs or, in contrast, how frequently people face recurring episodes of the disorder throughout their lifetime. And those who do suffer chronically face the possibility of ongoing difficulties ranging from problems in family and work life to bouts with depression and thoughts of suicide (Roy, 1986). It is known, however, that people are best off if they have opportunities to maintain their social competencies, their support network, and their work skills (Kiesler, 1982) and that successful readjustment is related to several factors including hospitalization history, compliance with medically prescribed regimes, and the level of social support available (Avison & Speechley, 1987; Ellison, Blum, & Barsky, 1986).

Scientists continue searching for the cause or causes of this disorder. Some researchers have directed their search to studying children of schizophrenics, who have a 10–15 percent risk of developing the disorder (Gottesman & Shields, 1982; Nuechterlein, 1986). Others have begun with a symptom, like hallucinations, and decided to focus on what might cause that symptom, such as how people with the disorder process information. For example, patients may spontaneously retrieve material from their long-term memory and then attribute that information to external sources, rather than to the self (George & Neufeld, 1985), thereby experiencing an hallucination.

Mood Disorders

Mood Disorders
Psychological disorders characterized by disturbances of affect, usually depression and/or elation.

"Mood" in psychology refers to prolonged emotions that shape one's outlook on life. **Mood disorders**—sometimes called affective disorders—involve disturbances in which people feel unusually depressed and/or elated for a period of time.

There is a need to differentiate between a normal life-crisis depression (for example, as a reaction to bereavement) and depression as a symptom of serious psychological disorder. When a recognizable event leads to a life crisis depression (e.g., failure in school, termination of employment, death of a parent), there is usually a normal state of sadness caused by the loss or by injury to our self-esteem. This reaction is appropriate, is time-limited, and gradually subsides. Sometimes, however, reaction to a life crisis may lead to more serious forms of depression.

Dysthymic Disorder

Dysthymic Disorder
A psychological disorder in which the person chronically suffers from a depressed mood, and also a variety of physical symptoms.

Dysthymic disorder is the problem we attempt to pinpoint when we describe someone as a "depressed personality." The person seems generally "down" or, in children and adolescents, "irritable." He or she feels worthless, listless, and hopeless about the future. In all likelihood, he or she suffers from decreased effectiveness in work and social relationships, and complains of a variety of physical symptoms (especially insomnia and fatigue).

The severity and duration of dysthymic symptoms and the degree to which functioning is impaired are considerably greater than what is seen in a normal life-crisis depression. The disorder is chronic, which is why it tends to be perceived as a feature of the personality (as opposed to an outbreak of illness). The feelings of depression may be persistent or intermittent. By definition they will have lasted for at least two years in the adult, or one year in a child or adolescent. In cases where depression is intermittent, periods of "normal" moods are relatively short, lasting a few weeks at most. The disorder is quite common at all ages, but is most often diagnosed in adult women. The problems caused by this disorder stem from its chronicity not its severity. Hence, while hospitalization is rarely necessary, eventually most sufferers' social relationships and work performance become impaired. A common complication is substance abuse, as those affected try to "lift their spirits" through "self-medication."

Major Depression

A diagnosis of **major depression** is made when a person has suffered a major depressive episode. These, by definition, last at least two weeks. During them people show a changed mood and/or an uncharacteristic loss of interest in and pleasure from most activities. While adults are sad and hopeless, in children and adolescents the mood may be either depressed or irritable. Other symptoms apparent during episodes include impaired sleep, eating, energy level, ideas of self-worth, and ability to make decisions and accomplish tasks.

Body movements and speech become slowed, and all the difficulties of life are exaggerated. Typical is the comment of a middle-aged woman who said: "I don't . . . I don't feel like I'm wanted. I don't feel at all that I'm wanted. I just feel like nothing. I don't feel anyone cares, and nobody's interested, and they don't care whether I do feel good or don't feel good. I'm pretty useless . . ." (Bart, 1970). In essence, the individual appears to give up, and may engage in or be disturbed by thoughts of death and suicide.

Major depression is apparently quite common: it has been called "the common cold of psychiatric disorders." It is often associated with chronic physical illness or with the important role losses that occur in transitional periods such as mid-life. It is estimated that twice as many women as men suffer from major depression. The course of the disorder is variable. In some cases it is chronic; in others it recurs after long periods of remission or is confined to a single episode.

Much research is being directed at discerning cognitive (thought process) and physiological causes of depression (Seligman, 1975). Considerable attention has also been paid to depression in children. Youngsters with parents who are depressed are at risk of developing this or other psychiatric disorders themselves (Beardslee et al., 1983), as are the many children in today's society whose parents separate or divorce (LaRoche, 1986; Wallerstein & Kelly, 1980).

Major Depression
A serious and persistent mood disturbance characterized in adults as a loss of interest in and enjoyment of most activities.

Depressed children are likely to make statements like these made by children aged 10, 12, and 8, respectively:

> "I am the biggest troublemaker in my family. I cry a lot and feel weird a lot."
> "I think I am the stupidest kid in class. . . ." "I feel ugly and like a dumbell. . . . Sometimes I would like to kill my friends or my own stomach or arm. . . . Friends make fun of me all the time." (Yahraes, 1978, p. 1)

Bipolar Disorder and Cyclothymia

Bipolar Disorder and Cyclothymia
Psychological disorders in which the person alternates between an elated, manic mood and depression.

People who suffer from **bipolar disorder** (formerly called manic-depressive disorder) or **cyclothymia** (its less severe counterpart) alternate between extremes of mood, cycling from manic to depressed and then back to either the manic or to the normal mood. The pattern in both disorders is this: In the *manic* mood (or "episode") the person becomes elated, hyperactive, and sometimes irritable. He or she talks loudly and rapidly, switching subjects abruptly, interrupting, and failing to wait for answers to his or her innumerable questions. The person is energetic, needs less sleep than usual, and experiences an inflated sense of self-esteem, claiming to be an expert on matters of which he or she knows little, or starting grandiose and unrealistic projects. Often he or she becomes sociable to the point of being intrusive and domineering. For example, a person in a manic episode may excitedly approach strangers on the street and offer advice or personal information. Or, seeking pleasure, the person can engage in poorly-considered activity with harmful consequences, like engaging in charge account spending sprees, risky sexual activity, or unwise, "get-rich-quick" business activity.

Depressions follow these manic episodes, within hours or days in some cases. In the *depressed* state, the individual takes little part in matters that would ordinarily interest him or her. He or she may feel worthless and guilty, hopeless, and "down in the dumps." Unable to sit still, the person paces, pulls at his hair or clothing, and complains. Appetite and sleep may be impaired. He is constantly fatigued, and may even be unable to get up in the morning.

Bipolar disorder is diagnosed if the individual's alternating moods significantly hamper functioning in work or social settings. Found equally often in men and women, many people with bipolar disorders experience two or more cycles a year without remission. However, the pattern of the cycles and the intensity of moods can vary greatly; people may spend long periods of time in one mood or the moods may alternate every couple of days. Likewise, there may be long time periods when their mood is not extreme.

Evidence suggests a genetic component is involved in bipolar disorders. If one twin is affected, there is an 80 percent chance an identical and a 20 percent chance a fraternal twin will also have it. Similarly, only 2 percent of the adoptive parents of people with this disorder also suffered from it, whereas the figure is 30 percent for biological parents (Kolata, 1986).

The Search for Personal Adjustment

Your Weather Report

"There is a sumptuous variety about the New England weather. . . . The weather is always doing something there . . . always getting up new designs and trying them on people to see how they will go," said Connecticut-born Mark Twain in an 1876 address.

New Englanders and other residents of the North Country are familiar with terms like "cabin fever" and "winter blahs." These describe the "blues" people feel when they grow tired of grey skies, mountainous snow piles, and spending seemingly endless hours indoors, often in tight quarters shared with others. Their distress is generally short-lived, however, and easily cured by sunshine and above-freezing weather.

In contrast, some individuals experience a clinically significant depression problem called *Seasonal Affective Disorder (SAD)*. It begins in the fall, when the days shorten, and lasts until spring when the days lengthen. During the winter those with SAD tend to oversleep, overeat (particularly carbohydrates) and gain weight. Some have gained relief from "light" therapy, either supplied artificially or by a trip to the Sunbelt.

1. Have you noticed any seasonally-related changes in your behavior?
2. Ask friends and acquaintances, particularly those from other parts of the country and world, if they themselves, or others they know have experienced seasonal changes in mood.
3. What adjustments do you make in your daily behavior to cope with the weather, climate, or seasonal changes where you live? Examples would include taking siestas to avoid oppressive heat and spading a garden as soon as it defrosts after a long, hard winter.   ▲

Scientists searching for genetic factors in bipolar disorders have examined members of an Amish community in Pennsylvania. This group, descendents of German immigrants who came to America from 1720–1750, live as their forbearers did 250 years ago. Their life-style is such that atypical behavior stands out most clearly. An Amish man with a bipolar disorder in the manic state, for instance, violates customary procedures by talking too fast and too boastfully, staying up too late, and driving his horse and buggy through the streets too fast. In the depressive state, his behavior is also noticeably different. One woman explains the clues she uses to detect her brother's depression:

> . . . he usually played with his children and was interested in his dogs. Now . . . he just sits after work and stares into space, he no longer laughs, and he does not pay attention to what is going on around him (Kolata, 1986, p. 576).

Cyclothymia is diagnosed if the manic and depressed moods affect the person less severely. Cyclothymia, equally prevalent in the two genders, often appears in adolescence or in early adulthood and tends to be chronic, sometimes developing into a bipolar disorder.

Personality Disorders

Personality disorders occur when personality traits that are inflexible and maladaptive cause distress or impair a person's social and occupational functioning. These traits usually appear in adolescence or early adulthood and cause persistent disturbances over most of the life span. The DSM-III-R groups more than 10 personality disorders into categories based on the predominant features. Those causing:

1. Eccentric or strange behavior. Jane has a paranoid personality disorder and consistently assumes others are trying to hurt or embarrass her. Since this is typically not the case, she appears odd when she challenges cashiers for intentionally trying to "steal" her money or when she hid behind the candy machine near her boyfriend's math class to check if he was "cheating" on her by flirting with other women.

2. Unpredictable, dramatic, and overemotional behavior. Grace has a borderline personality disorder. She is unsure of who she is, what goals or friends to have, and what values and sexual orientation to adopt. Unsure of herself, she dreads being deserted by others and frantically clings to established relationships. She behaves in dramatic, overemotional, and unpredictable ways. During the past 18 months she has made two suicide threats, abused alcohol and other drugs, had several shopping sprees, engaged in a good deal of casual sex, had recurrent episodes of binge eating, and was stopped for careless driving. The last time the man she had been seeing left her, she recklessly sought to build new contacts, a pattern typical of this disorder (Gunderson & Zanarini, 1987).

3. Behavior indicating anxiety or fear. Max has a dependent personality disorder and lacks self-confidence. Unable to make decisions, he constantly seeks encouragement and advice from others, often to the point at which they prescribe what he ought to do. Disturbed by and fearful of criticism, Max goes out of his way to please others, always picking up the check at the restaurant and being the first to volunteer for undesired duties. Such behaviors reduce his anxiety because they provide "protection" against others dislike or criticism.

4. Other behaviors or a mixture that bridges these types.

To further illustrate the nature of these disorders we next consider in more detail two types commonly diagnosed: the antisocial and the narcissistic personality disorders.

Antisocial Personality Disorder

People who are diagnosed as having **antisocial personality disorder** act irresponsibly without apparent regard for ordinary scruples or morality. For example, they lie, steal, and vandalize without compunction; they physically abuse and push other people around; they engage in aggressive sexual behavior and are generally irresponsible in relationships and at work. Often coming from deprived, poor, or unstable families, they themselves may have been victims of social or racial discrimination, maternal deprivation, and limited adult guidance. After the age of 30, in most cases, there is a decline in fighting and sexual promiscuity, but excessive drinking and use of drugs often continues.

While individuals suffering from antisocial personality disorder usually feel no guilt about mistreating others, they may experience tension and the distress associated with consistently having trouble holding jobs and sustaining close relationships with friends and sexual partners. People with this disorder who require institutionalization are often found in the penal system where, as a group, they may account for 40–50 percent of the prisoners (Reid, 1985).

Symptoms of what might develop into this disorder appear in individuals before they reach the age of 15. If the symptoms are noticed and the children are brought to the attention of the authorities, they will be labeled as having a conduct disorder. While many youngsters who behave antisocially (truancy, fighting with weapons, cruelty to animals and people, committing crimes like theft and robbery) adjust before reaching age 18, others do not and the label "antisocial personality" is applied. This disorder affects about 3 percent of American men and somewhat less than 1 percent of American females.

Narcissistic Personality Disorder

Narcissistic personality disorder is diagnosed more often now than in the past, possibly because of an increasing clinical interest in the problem of narcissism. People who suffer from this disorder are entirely impressed with their own importance. They lack interest in and empathy for others. Most of their energies are devoted to maintaining an exaggerated sense of self, and fantasies of unlimited power and success.

Their grandiose feelings of self-importance are fragile, however, and alternate with feelings of worthlessness. Further, they feel down in the dumps if they see signs of aging or other threats to their physical appearance. People with this disorder seek attention and assurances from others; they are eager to maintain appearances in the social world. However, they are unwilling to accept (and indeed unable to understand) the responsibilities involved in friendships and other human relationships.

For example, a person with narcissistic personality disorder will disregard the rights and integrity of others, while expecting special favors from them. He will tend to see others' misfortunes only as they affect himself. Thus the illness of a friend who was supposed to do a favor is viewed as an inconvenience: The person is angry at the friend's inconsiderateness, instead of being

Antisocial Personality Disorder
A psychological disorder in which a person acts without apparent regard for ordinary scruples or morality.

Narcissistic Personality Disorder
A psychological disorder in which the person is excessively impressed with his own importance and lacks interest in and empathy for others.

concerned about his illness. People who suffer from narcissistic personality disorder are by definition impaired or impoverished in their relationships. They feel that it is more important to be seen with the right people than to build good friendships.

Impulse Control Disorder: Pathological Gambling

Bert was much on his own during his adolescence. His parents worked long hours to pay for the wardrobes and new cars they purchased every year and to cover the mortgage payments on their very expensive home. Since they did not budget very well, they were always on the verge of financial disaster. Bert never understood his parents' financial situation or what they expected of him. Both parents were as "up and down" with Bert as they were with their financial situation. Sometimes they were harsh disciplinarians, other times they would say, "You're old enough to decide what you want."

During his college years Bert lived at home and worked part-time to help with tuition. While a sophomore, Bert organized a pool among the friends he had invited to watch the Super Bowl at his house. It went well so he held another one for the basketball playoffs. During his junior year Bert was organizing weekly pools on several sports, and had branched out to cover the Academy Awards and the primary elections in several states. Bert loved the excitement of betting.

But his urge to gamble kept growing. He began going to the track. And then he started cutting class, skipping social events, and calling in sick to his job so he could go to the races. As his habit grew more costly, Bert became preoccupied with earning money. But often when he put a few dollars together, he placed bets, hoping to double his money. Bert was on a course that was leading him to the disorder of **pathological gambling.**

Pathological Gambling
A psychological disorder in which the person is consistently unable to control the impulse to gamble.

Bert is not alone. Gambling is widely practiced in the United States. Custer (1987) estimates that 60 percent of adults are social or recreational gamblers who place one bet in a given year and that nearly 2 percent, or close to four million, are pathological gamblers. Pathological gambling is characterized by an emotional dependence on gambling. As Bert's case showed, it is a persistent, progressive disorder that eventually hampers the individual's family, social, and/or work life. More prevalent in males, the person experiences a "need" to gamble. Therefore, he misses other obligations in order to gamble, places larger bets to gain greater excitement, and will eventually encounter money problems from his losses.

Psychodynamic, cognitive, behavioral, group and family therapy, and chemotherapy techniques have been applied in programs designed to treat individuals with pathological gambling disorders. However, after reviewing the research, Taber and McCormick (1987) state "most people with gambling problems . . . probably can stop gambling with no more help than that offered by Gamblers Anonymous (p. 165)." And, these authors note, there are hundreds of chapters of Gamblers Anonymous operating in the United States.

Psychoactive Substance Use Disorders

In 20th-century societies, certain substances are consumed by people to modify their moods. It is generally considered socially appropriate for adults to "gear up" by drinking substantial amounts of caffeine-containing coffee, tea, and soda pop or to "unwind" by drinking alcoholic beverages. Of course, within societies, there are varying attitudes toward the use of psychoactive substances. While certain religious sects do not use either alcohol or coffee, members of other groups consider the consumption of even illegal substances acceptable for recreational purposes.

The **psychoactive substance use disorders** identified in the DSM-III-R result from ongoing, pathological use of one or more substances. A disorder is diagnosed only when the substance is creating difficulties such as impaired functioning in day-to-day activities or has the person "hooked" in the sense that he or she is unable to discontinue or reduce use, even though it is causing personal harm. The recreational use of a psychoactive substance, like alcohol, in reasonable quantities is not considered problematic. Neither is therapeutic use of physician-prescribed amphetamines or sedatives.

The DSM-III-R identifies 10 classes of psychoactive substances that can cause disorders. Included are alcohol, opiods (narcotics such as morphine and heroin), cannabis (marijuana), amphetamines (stimulants), sedatives, cocaine, hallucinogens, inhalants (chemicals found in glue, spray paint, cleaners, etc.), nicotine, and phencyclidine (known as PCP or angel dust) and related drugs. The disorders associated with the first five substances are discussed below.

Two levels of disorder are associated with the substances (except for nicotine where only Dependence is used): Psychoactive Substance Dependence and Psychoactive Substance Abuse. The "Dependence" categories are employed when the problem is more severe. Use may be out of control and the person's work and social life is affected. He may require increasing amounts of the substance to satisfy his hunger and may spend considerable time obtaining, taking, and recovering from its use. The "Abuse" categories are usually diagnosed in people who more recently started taking a psychoactive substance and in those who have a substantial but less severe problem.

Alcohol Dependence and Alcohol Abuse

Dan considers himself a social drinker, even though he often drinks alone each morning. Sometimes he goes on weekend binges, or even drinks heavily for several months. When he is drunk he often feels euphoric and talkative, but just as often he is irritable and depressed. His face is flushed, his speech slurred, and his coordination poor. Dan suffers from alcohol abuse.

When people drink too much, their behavior can become aggressive and violent. (Drinking is often a contributing factor in child abuse and spouse-beating.) Memory losses or blackouts are also common. In serious cases, the person requires daily drinking in order to function adequately and overcome the "shakes."

Psychoactive Substance Use Disorders
Psychological disorders in which the person makes unhealthy use of a psychoactive substance such as alcohol or marijuana.

The ingestion of great quantities of alcohol can result in hallucinations and deteriorating physical health. Malnutrition is common, as is increased frequency of liver and stomach inflammations (cirrhosis, hepatitis, and gastritis). Physical symptoms are also associated with any attempts that the person makes to break the pattern of abuse. In withdrawal the person experiences headaches, tremors, nausea, and other distressing sensations. Those who succeed in breaking the pattern of abuse usually do so in therapeutic or group-help situations.

In examining a cross section of Americans it has been found that, on the one hand, about 35 percent abstain from drinking altogether and, on the other hand, a little over 10 percent drink an average of more than an ounce of alcohol a day (American Psychiatric Association, 1987). Members of this latter group consume about half the alcoholic beverages sold.

Heavier "drinkers" expect greater benefits from the activity than do abstainers and lighter drinkers (Rohsenow, 1983). People with alcohol problems believe that drinking will improve their moods, decreasing anxiety and depression (Nathan, Titler, Lowenstein, Solomon, & Rossie, 1970), and expect it to make them more sociable (Lutz & Snow, 1985).

The incidence of alcohol abuse is very high. In the United States, almost 18 million people have drinking problems and better than 10 million of these individuals suffer from alcoholism (Lord et al., 1987). Approximately three million problem drinkers are teenagers. Among a sample of high school seniors, 6 percent reported that they used alcohol daily, and fully 41 percent said that they had consumed five or more drinks at least once in the two weeks before they were questioned (Reinhold, 1982). Although the great majority of adolescents use alcohol at one time or another, the problem drinker differs from his peers in drinking larger amounts and more often. Like adult abusers, the teenager also tends to drink by himself and expressly for the purpose of getting drunk (Rosenblatt, 1981).

Alcohol abuse is a significant factor in automobile accidents. Further, as long known (Batchelor, 1954), it often plays a part in suicide attempts, in accidental deaths in which the person drank and took drugs, and in causing damage to the body (see Figure 5.1).

Opiod Dependence and Opiod Abuse

Dottie took heroin intravenously about five minutes ago and is euphoric, a feeling that will last up to 30 minutes. Her pupils are dilated, her judgment is clouded, and her speech is slurred. Following this period Dottie faces several hours during which she will feel lazy, apathetic, and, perhaps, discontented, restless, or anxious.

When intoxicated with heroin, morphine, codeine, and certain other substances derived from opium (or that act like opium in the body), people feel "high" and removed from their daily troubles. They also experience disturbances in perception, attention, and psychomotor control. The substances are taken orally, intravenously ("shooting up"), or intranasally ("snorting"). Regular use of these substances builds tolerance in the body and means that larger

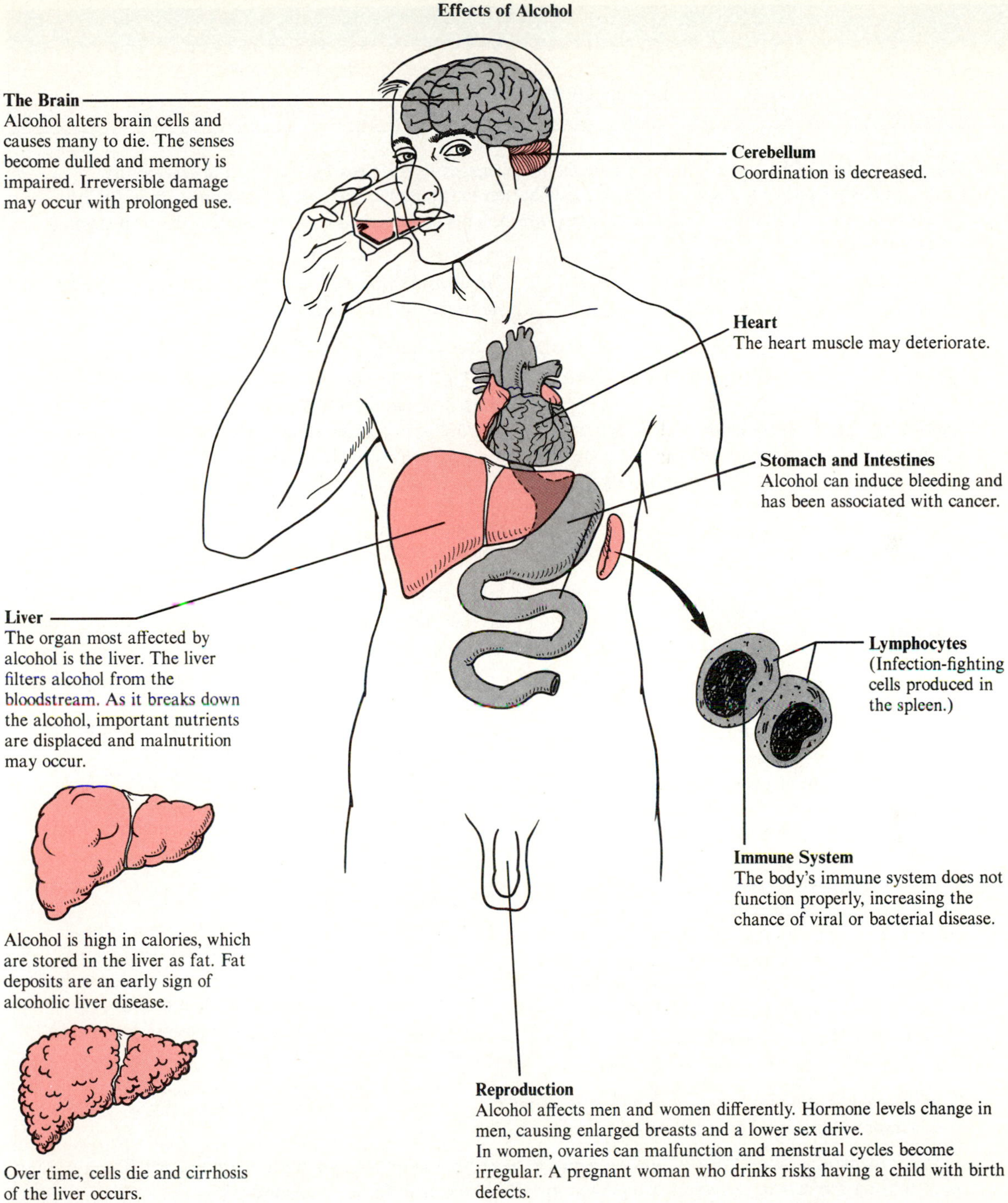

The Brain
Alcohol alters brain cells and causes many to die. The senses become dulled and memory is impaired. Irreversible damage may occur with prolonged use.

Cerebellum
Coordination is decreased.

Heart
The heart muscle may deteriorate.

Stomach and Intestines
Alcohol can induce bleeding and has been associated with cancer.

Liver
The organ most affected by alcohol is the liver. The liver filters alcohol from the bloodstream. As it breaks down the alcohol, important nutrients are displaced and malnutrition may occur.

Lymphocytes
(Infection-fighting cells produced in the spleen.)

Alcohol is high in calories, which are stored in the liver as fat. Fat deposits are an early sign of alcoholic liver disease.

Immune System
The body's immune system does not function properly, increasing the chance of viral or bacterial disease.

Over time, cells die and cirrhosis of the liver occurs.

Reproduction
Alcohol affects men and women differently. Hormone levels change in men, causing enlarged breasts and a lower sex drive.
In women, ovaries can malfunction and menstrual cycles become irregular. A pregnant woman who drinks risks having a child with birth defects.

Figure 5.1 The effects of alcohol.

Young People and Alcohol

The Ohio Department of Liquor Control sells alcoholic beverages in state stores. As a public service the Department publishes booklets about alcohol for distribution to the public. One title, "Communicating With Teenagers About Alcohol," makes suggestions about how parents can teach their youngsters to be responsible with alcohol. It suggests:

Parents Should Explain the Three Basic Alternatives Regarding Alcohol Use

1. Choose Not To Use Alcohol
   One-third of all adult Americans choose not to drink for a wide variety of reasons:
   —not liking the taste, or feeling sick if they drink
   —wanting full control over mind and body
   —religious or family traditions
   —fighting an existing or potential problem caused by alcohol abuse
2. Use Alcohol Safely
   Most moderate drinkers use alcohol safely and moderately. This means:
   —eating food while drinking to slow its effects
   —spacing drinks and limiting their number
   —knowing individual limits and respecting them
3. Abuse Alcohol
   People **who drink to excess** may:
   —drink to the point of losing control or getting drunk
   —drink frequently and often on an empty stomach
   —drink for negative reasons, such as to escape from problems; to ease the pain of loneliness, insecurity; to be "tough" or "adult"
   Adults and teenagers who continue to drink . . . even if it harms their health, family, schoolwork, and job . . . are alcohol abusers, and, if they cannot stop drinking, are alcoholics.

The Consumption of Alcoholic Beverages Is Widely Accepted In Our Society

Social drinking is enjoyed by many family, social, and business groups. In fact, seven out of ten adults drink at least occasionally.
Alcohol is so common that many people don't realize it's a powerful substance that can lead to disastrous effects **if abused.**

Parents Should Emphasize the Two Major Dangers Related to Teenage Alcohol Use

1. Drinking and Driving
   Alcohol-related automobile crashes are the leading cause of teenage deaths.
   —At least ½ of all drivers involved in fatal crashes have been drinking.
   —In 1985 alone, teenage drunk drivers killed 135 people in Ohio and injured 5,219.
   Avoid driving after drinking or riding with someone who has been drinking. Call parents or friends, walk or take public transportation. Wait until you can find a safe ride. Remember, **it's YOUR life.**
2. Drinking and Other Drugs
   Remember that even a moderate amount of alcohol, in combination with other drugs, often intensifies their effect. The interaction of alcohol and drugs **decreases an individual's ability to function and think clearly. The mixture can even be deadly!**

1. What is your evaluation of the information provided? If you were writing the booklet, what else would you include? Would you omit any of this information?

2. Is this information helpful to you now, or would it have been helpful to you at a younger age? If you were writing directly to teenagers, would you give the same or different information?

3. Do you think warning labels about the possible dangers in alcohol use should be required on labels of beer, wine, or liquor bottles?

4. Draft a booklet about alcohol use by teenagers that you would like to see distributed in your state. Send it to a public official.

▲

doses are needed to produce the "high." The danger of taking an overdose is ever present.

People become dependent on or abusers of these drugs in two ways. They may be introduced to them through peers or through a prescription and, over time, maintain their supply by seeking treatment from several physicians. The former means is the more common one among young people. Once "hooked," getting drugs becomes a central daily activity. People may turn to crime to obtain them or money to buy them.

Withdrawal is difficult for the individual, and causes symptoms that look very much like those associated with a severe case of the flu. However, the sweating, fever, vomiting, and tremors last for 10–14 days. The DSM-III-R estimates that 0.7 percent of American adults have experienced opiod dependence or abuse.

Cannabis Dependence and Cannabis Abuse

Corrie and Jack smoked a joint (a marijuana cigarette) some 10–20 minutes ago and are in a dreamy, carefree "high," state that will last for perhaps three hours. The couple is watching cartoons on television, eating "junk" food, and drinking diet pop to wet their dry mouths.

The substances in this category besides marijuana are hashish, chemically similar products manufactured synthetically, and purified delta-9 tetrahydrocannabinol (THC). These drugs are usually smoked, though they are sometimes mixed in food and taken orally. Marijuana is the second most popular recreational drug in the United States, preceded only by alcohol. It is more widely used by young people than by the population in general. One study indicated approximately one in nine of all American high school seniors were daily users in 1978. Since then, marijuana usage appears to have decreased, as indicated by the statistic that only 3.3 percent of high school seniors in 1987 reported using the drug daily (Facts on File, 1988).

The chemical responsible for the effects of marijuana is THC. Sensory perceptions (sight, smell, taste) may become more vivid, and the sense of time and space may be altered. There may be feelings of enhanced insight. At high dosages, these changes are intensified. In addition, the individual may experience rapidly changing emotions, fragmented thoughts, flights of ideas, disturbed associations, and an altered sense of personal identity. At very high dosages, distortions of body image, loss of personal identity, fantasies, and hallucinations occur.

Marijuana use impairs memory, specifically the formation of new memories that might be involved, for example, in learning a new list of words (Loftus, 1980). It also impairs the ability to concentrate, understand reading material, and solve mathematical problems (Brody, 1980). For these reasons, in part, marijuana use is sometimes associated with impaired school performance. Use also adversely affects psychomotor abilities, slowing reaction time and interfering with coordination and visual perception.

Some long-term health effects are also linked (though not conclusively) with frequent marijuana use. The drug is harmful to the respiratory system (Brody, 1980). In men, use is thought to increase sperm abnormalities and decrease sperm production.

The psychological effects of marijuana are controversial. Although it is not physically addictive, marijuana can create psychological dependence in the user. That is, the user may be unable to cope without the drug and may engage in compulsive drug-seeking behavior.

Heavy users may withdraw from social relationships and become uninterested in communicating with others. Some psychologists describe an "amotivational" (without motivation) syndrome in which heavy users lose interest in friends, schoolwork, and social activities.

Amphetamine Dependence and Amphetamine Abuse

Bonnie took speed (amphetamine pills) a few minutes ago and is feeling a "rush." She has a good sense of well-being and is self-confident, like she has "the world on a string." Although her speech sounds confused and incoherent, she believes she is expressing profound and creative thoughts. If Bonnie took too high a dose, she may soon have a headache, hear ringing noises, or think insects are crawling on her body. She may also become anxious and worry about paranoid feelings. The effects of amphetamines are similar to cocaine, but longer lasting. When the effects wear off, Bonnie will "crash." Feeling low and irritable, she will crave more amphetamines.

Amphetamines are synthetic drugs that stimulate or excite the central nervous system, including the brain. The drug, also called "pep pills," "diet pills," "uppers," and "speed," may be taken in pill form or intravenously. Amphetamines are used in the medical treatment of some psychological disorders. They are also used (with or without prescription) to treat depression and fatigue, and to suppress the appetite for the purpose of reducing weight.

The use of amphetamines appears to be increasing among young people, who take the drugs to produce a variety of effects. For example, students sometimes take them (as well as cocaine and other stimulants) to stay awake and alert in order to study for an important exam. The drug seems to give them increased energy; however, a survey of the research suggests that for tasks involving anything more than simple memorization or arithmetic operations, amphetamines do not seem to aid performance. In other words, learning does not take place at a faster rate.

Abuse occurs when the person becomes psychologically dependent on amphetamines. His body has built a tolerance to the drug, so it needs increasing doses to obtain the same physiological effects. Under the influence of the drug he appears nervous, talkative, overconfident, and alertly watchful. On discontinuing use, he typically feels very weak, depressed, and in great need of sleep. Usually, however, he is unable to sleep well. Especially if the amphetamine has been taken intravenously and in high doses, he may experience severe bouts of depression, paranoia, loss of self-control (including the acting out of sexual or aggressive impulses), and a variety of physical symptoms including muscle cramps, excessive hunger, and alternating feelings of hot and cold. Withdrawal symptoms appear very shortly after the drug is discontinued but are more gradual than is the case with heroin or morphine.

PCP, Barbiturates, and Cocaine

PCP or phencyclidine is commonly called "angel dust," "crystal," or the Peace Pill. PCP is an anesthetic, formerly used with both animals and humans but now illegal in this country. Often PCP is misrepresented as being THC by drug sellers.

The drug is usually eaten or smoked. It produces a "high," often accompanied by alterations in thoughts, a heightening of the physical senses, and behavior contrary to what is normal for the person. Being an anesthetic, PCP causes loss of feeling in the arms and legs, of which the person may be unaware, and has been a factor in car accidents, drowning deaths, and so forth. Severe paranoia sometimes occurs, and there is a risk of death from overdose.

Barbiturates, known as "goofballs" or "downers," are the most widely used sedative. About two dozen drugs are now on the market under such names as phenobarbital, Amytal, Nembutal, and Seconal. Barbiturates reduce anxiety because they act as a depressant on the brain. Although a small dose makes a person feel relaxed and sociable, larger doses can result in sluggishness, gloomy feelings, and antisocial behavior and, moreover, can lead a person to suddenly collapse and fall into a coma. Barbiturates are addictive: people who use them become tolerant and require larger doses to produce an effect. An addicted person who suddenly stops using them may die.

It is extremely dangerous to mix barbiturates with alcohol, another depressant, because the depressant effect is far greater when they are combined; even a small amount of both together can be fatal. Concerns also exist in connection with mixing alcohol and any drug and, for that matter, any combination of drugs taken without professional supervision.

Cocaine, called "coke," "snow," "toot," "C," and so forth, was an ingredient in Coca Cola and patent medicines before a 1914 law controlled its use. Cocaine can be ingested in many ways, but most often is snorted or smoked. The substance first produces a high, a euphoric feeling of confidence and well-being. Greater doses may bring bodily pain and unpredictable thoughts, perhaps enjoyable or perhaps scary. After cocaine intoxication a person may experience a "crash" and, as a result, feel tired, depressed, anxious, or irritable.

In recent years cocaine has been processed (or freed) from cocaine hydrochloride into cocaine alkaloid, a product commonly called "freebase." This purer product, also called "crack" and "rock," is the most potent and potentially most addictive and lethal form of the drug. When smoked, it quickly produces strong psychoactive effects in the user. Crack, however, can damage the lungs, the brain, and the heart, besides causing potentially unhealthy psychological effects. Besides being processed into crack, cocaine is sometimes added to heroin to create "speedball," a drug that is an immediate threat to the body as it depresses respiratory functioning.

Cocaine, once a drug used mainly by the wealthy, is now less costly on the streets and it has become a threat to members of all socioeconomic classes. Recent estimates suggest that some 22 million Americans have experimented with coke and that nearly 6 million use it regularly (Morganthau & Miller, 1988).

In 1983 a 24-hour hotline, 800 COCAINE, was established to serve the entire country, providing free and anonymous information or assistance. During the first three years of operation, its staff received over 1.5 million calls, or an average of 1,400 calls daily (Washton & Gold, 1987). Adolescents telephone to discuss, among other issues, drug-related school and work problems; arrests; drug-related brain seizures and other medical difficulties; family problems, including guilt from stealing from parents and siblings; and how to free themselves from cocaine habits.

Psychoactive Drugs and Problems in Adjustment

To state the obvious, alcohol and drugs can become a problem to any person, regardless of his background or station in life. This is no better illustrated than in a study conducted at the Pentagon.

In 1981 the Department of Defense developed a Pentagon Employee Referral Service to serve its 23,000+ workers when they encountered personal problems that affected job performance (Stein, 1984). By policy, the program maintains confidential records and participation and it does not affect an employee's job security. The distribution of problems for which people sought help is presented in Figure 5.2. The figure illustrates how much of a challenge we, as a society, are facing in this area: if alcohol and drug problems can strike so broadly at the adjustment of workers in the Pentagon, they present a costly and threatening problem for every institution in society.

Overall, psychoactive substance abuse is a significant problem in our society. As Bennett (1987) has stated, while it is difficult to estimate how many people are using each of the psychoactive drugs, we know the immensity of the challenge when elementary school pupils, in a Weekly Reader poll, identified drugs as the most serious problem in the schools. He went on to warn that although nonmedical drug use may have decreased in the 1980s, compared to the 1970s, it is still much more widespread than a quarter-century ago and remains at an unhealthy level. Scientists and policymakers studying how to cope with this problem have centered their work on examining sociocultural factors in communities, and factors in individuals that lead them to engage in nonmedical drug usage (Vetter, 1985).

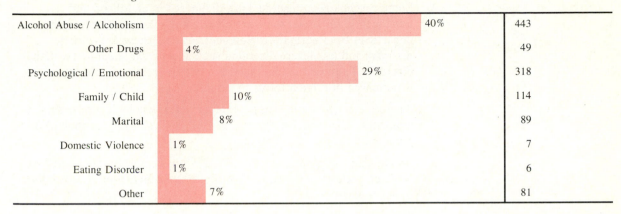

Source: Reprinted from R. Stein, "The Pentagon Employee Referral Service" in *EAP DIGEST*, July/August 1984, with permission of Performance Resource Press, Inc., 2145 Crooks Road, Suite 103, Troy, Michigan 48084.

Figure 5.2 This figure dramatically illustrates how costly alcohol abuse is to us as a society.

Psychological Disorders and Other Factors

We have discussed a range of psychological disorders—problems people face in their efforts to adjust to their environment. While scientists debate the causes of these disorders, research suggests that certain factors are associated with higher incidences of psychological disorders. Specifically, people most likely to experience psychological disorders are: younger rather than older; less happily married or single rather than happily married; less educated; unemployed or with low income; and lacking satisfying social contacts with relatives and friends (Leaf et al., 1984). In the chapters ahead we will discuss friendships, marriages, schooling, and work. But next, however, we examine several approaches to psychotherapy and the treatment of the disorders we just discussed.

SUMMARY

1. Psychological disorders are not uncommon. At any one time, perhaps as many as 32 million Americans suffer from relatively severe psychological disturbances.

2. Our understanding of psychological disorders is partly shaped by cultural factors. That is, our culture tells us what is within the boundaries of "normal behavior" and what is not.

3. *Diagnostic labels* given to psychological disorders reflect our current understanding of these disorders. The labels are imperfect, tentative, and changeable.

4. Some psychological disorders are diagnosed in childhood and adolescence. Of these, some are clearly age-related and represent departures from normal development. Among these are *autistic disorder* and less severe disorders such as *learning disabilities*. Other disorders diagnosed in childhood are not age-related in that they are experienced in related forms by adults.

5. *Anxiety disorders* are a major category of psychological disorders in adulthood. Examples are *phobic disorders* (such as agoraphobia) and *panic disorders* (anxiety attacks).

6. *Somatoform disorders* are expressed in physical symptoms that have no discernible physical cause. Examples are *conversion disorder* and *hypochondriasis*.

7. *Dissociative disorders* are disorders in which the person becomes dissociated or cut off from his usual self, to the extent of forgetting important facts about himself or adopting a new identity. Examples are *psychogenic amnesia* and *psychogenic fugue*.

8. *Schizophrenia* is one of the most common yet most serious mental health disorders. Its symptoms include a very disturbed sense of self, as well as severe disturbances of thinking and feeling (including delusions and hallucinations).

9. *Mood disorders* involve disturbances of the emotions that shape one's outlook on life. *Major depression* is a common mood disorder that is often associated with chronic physical illness, important role losses, or other substantial stressors.

10. *Personality disorders* are diagnosed when personality traits that are inflexible and maladaptive cause distress or impair functioning. Common personality disorders in our culture are the *antisocial personality* and the *narcissistic personality*.

11. *Psychoactive substance use disorders* involve regular and pathological use of a substance that impairs functioning. Physical or psychological withdrawal symptoms occur when use is discontinued. Commonly abused substances include alcohol and marijuana.

SUGGESTED READINGS

Beers, C. (1907/1966). *A mind that found itself.* Garden City, New York: Doubleday. An inspiring autobiography of a man who became mentally ill in the early years of this century and, after his recovery, helped to start the mental hygiene (health) movement.

Coles, G. (1987). *The learning mystique: A critical look at learning disabilities.* New York: Pantheon. This book challenges the widely held view that learning disorders are essentially biological in origin.

Goldstein, A. & Stainback, B. (1987). *Overcoming agoraphobia: Conquering fear of the outside world*. New York: Viking. This handbook, written in layperson's language, explains the roots of agoraphobia, and describes the drug-free treatment methods devised by the first author.

Gordon, B. (1980). *I'm dancing as fast as I can*. New York: Bantam. A sensitive, and at times humorous, portrayal of the problem of Valium addiction and a woman's crises when withdrawing from the drug.

Green, H. (1964). *I never promised you a rose garden*. New York: New American Library. A subtle and realistic novel about a schizophrenic adolescent girl's struggle to regain her sanity.

Greist, J., Jefferson, J., & Marks, I. (1986). *Anxiety and its treatment*. New York: Warner Books. This book provides an overview of anxiety and how the anxiety disorders (including phobias) can be treated.

Kesey, K. (1975). *One flew over the cuckoo's nest*. New York: Signet. A harrowing story of life in a psychiatric hospital, fraught with conflict between the need for individuality and the pressures to submit to the institutional way of life.

Kinoy, B. and others. (1984). *When will we laugh again?* New York: Columbia University Press. This paperback, to which members of the American Anorexia/Bulimia Association contributed, offers an insightful look into the eating disorders and how they affect the individual and her family.

McConnell, P. (1986). *Adult children of alcoholics: A workbook for healing*. New York: Harper & Row. The author offers step-by-step exercises to guide people with problems often found in adults who were raised in a home with an alcoholic.

Mothner, I. & Weitz, A. (1984). *How to get off drugs*. New York: A Rolling Stone Press Book/Simon & Schuster. The editors of Rolling Stone, after discussing the effects and risks of a range of drugs, suggest necessary steps to gain control of drug habits.

Schreiber, F. R. (1974). *Sybil*. New York: Warner. The story, based on an actual case history, of how the victim of an abusive mother and an ineffectual father develops multiple personalities as a defense against painful memories and conflicts.

Torrey, E. F. (1983). *Surviving schizophrenia: A family manual*. New York: Harper & Row. A practical volume describing the disorder and treatment options, including how and when family members can help.

6

Psychotherapy and Growth

- The value of informal help and "talking it out"—and cases where these may not suffice

- Frequently used psychological assessment tools, and the types of professionals who provide therapeutic help

- Common goals of psychotherapy, distinguishing features of the therapeutic relationship, and the way therapy generally progresses

- The many forms of individual psychotherapy (crisis intervention, psychoanalysis, behavior therapy, and so on) that are used in treatment

- Approaches that treat more than one person (family therapy, group therapy, and marital therapy), with the goal of alleviating individual problems or strengthening systems of interaction among members

- The difficulty of determining whether therapy helps and the even greater difficulty of determining which therapy works best

Marjorie had always wanted to become a geologist. In childhood she collected rock specimens, and visited natural history museums and geological formations whenever her family traveled. Even in elementary school she studied books on geological history. When she was called in for career counseling in high school, she impressed the counselor as "a woman with her mind made up." She knew which university she wanted to attend, and she was awarded the scholarship she needed. Her excitement was so great that she put out of mind a number of worrisome factors. She would be quite distant from her family and close friends (and Marjorie had always needed confidants). No one whom she knew attended the university. Although it had an internationally known geology department, she had heard that the campus resembled a "country club." The family could not afford to visit the campus or to accompany Marjorie to her orientation week.

Not long after Marjorie arrived she had a series of disappointing experiences. Her great hopes and excitement turned into distress and alarm about her future at the university. She found that her dorm-mates were intolerant of her studiousness, and puzzled by her career commitment. Her classmates in her most important courses were mostly male, and mostly aloof. Marjorie felt uncomfortable and shy. Although she tried to talk things over with a few students in her dormitory, this did not seem to help; she had never made friends easily. Calling home gave only temporary relief. Marjorie began to have trouble concentrating on her studies—a problem she had never before experienced and did not know how to handle. When she did not do as well as expected on her midterm exams, she became distraught. She went to the Dean's office to make arrangements for withdrawing or, as she was careful to say, transferring.

The Dean referred her to the Student Counseling Center, where she was immediately interviewed by a counselor. In the regular sessions that followed, Marjorie experienced relief and renewed confidence in her abilities. With the support of the counselor she transferred to a dormitory that housed primarily older in-state students and that had a reputation for "seriousness." There Marjorie was able to meet congenial people, study, and have fun. Marjorie was also encouraged to broaden her academic interests. Eventually, Marjorie's crisis was resolved. She avoided the sense of failure and frustration that might have resulted from her returning home. And she began not only to succeed as she had planned, but to enjoy other activities as well.

In Marjorie's case, short-term therapy provided the resources needed to cope with new problems in a new environment. In this chapter we will investigate the many situations that bring people to counseling or psychotherapy, the varieties of treatment available, and what is involved in a therapeutic relationship. We will begin by considering those nonprofessional relationships that most resemble therapy, the informal supportive relationships of people in our usual environments.

INFORMAL HELP: "TALKING IT OUT"

As we have seen, people engage in a variety of activities that help reduce anxiety and maintain emotional balance. Some jog. Some think their problems over and become calmer as they move toward solutions. Some get relief by expressing their feelings, perhaps by keeping a personal journal. Each person has his or her individual ways of coping with emotional emergencies. And yet there is one coping mechanism that practically everyone uses, the coping mechanism we call "talking it out" (discussed in Chapter 4).

Situational Supports
People in the environment who provide comfort, understanding, and advice to an individual who is experiencing psychological difficulties.

Most people who experience psychological difficulties seek out people in the environment who can provide comfort, understanding, and advice. Psychologists call these helping people **situational supports** (Aguilera & Messick, 1982). People commonly talk things out with close friends, spouses, and neighbors. Sometimes, however, the confidant is someone more removed from the person's day-to-day life: a distant relative, former teacher, physician, or religious counselor. The confidant may be someone who is simply a good listener like a waitress or bartender, or a commuter on the morning train.

Informal groups also offer people the opportunity to talk things out, for they bring together people with common experiences and difficulties. Young mothers on the playground benches help one another cope with illnesses and other emergencies of child rearing. Social groups for homosexuals help members cope with common social pressures, and so forth. Fathers who do not have custody of their children come together to help each other contend with difficulties over visitation rights and maintaining strong ties with their children. College students form their own support groups, usually a network of friends to whom they can turn when they are feeling "down," or when they need to talk with someone they trust.

The Search for Personal Adjustment

An important form of informal help is talking problems out with close friends. Psychologists call these people situational supports. They are there in a crisis—and they often make a difference.

Talking it out has many benefits. Usually there is relief in just sharing with another person the thoughts and feelings that are causing distress. Sometimes in the very act of talking, which is equivalent to thinking aloud, we begin to see the possibility of a solution to our problem, and that is all the relief we need to bring a crisis to an end. Also, we are likely to get emotional support from our listener and perhaps useful advice. We are fortunate when the person who is our situational support can inform us about sources of financial assistance, if that is needed, or guidance about health, family, career, sex, or relationships with a roommate.

Although many people indicate that situational supports have helped them significantly in the face of emotional difficulties (Bergin, 1971), such support is not always available. Some people do not have friends or sympathetic relatives to whom they can confide intimate problems. We are a population on the move; relocation, which often precipitates a crisis, leaves many people at a distance from their usual supports. Even if supportive people are available, they may themselves be too involved in the problem to view it with the necessary detachment and perspective. For example, another member of one's family is likely to be blind to manipulation within the family that victimizes one member. Similarly, a long-time confidant might discourage a friend from changing in ways that might jeopardize the friendship. And a spouse who needs to wield power might discourage his partner from resolving her difficulties in a way that might make her more independent.

Another problem is that our usual situational supports do not always provide the extent or type of help needed. They may be inadequate during a serious crisis, such as an attempted suicide or life-threatening illness. Even if they do provide relief, they are unlikely to help the individual develop new kinds of behavior or attain greater understanding.

How Supportive Are You?

Good therapists rely on training and experience for their effectiveness. However, they also follow certain rules or conventions. Below are some rules broadly adapted from a leading handbook for therapists. The examples may suggest ways in which you can be more supportive when listening to a friend in need.

Rule 1: Try not to act surprised, shocked, or horrified at a friend's confidence.
Example: "For some reason I panic whenever I'm alone with a date."

Not very helpful
   "You do *what?*"
   "That's ridiculous. There's nothing to be afraid of."

More helpful
   "I wonder why that happens to you."
   "That must be very upsetting on a date."
   "Do you want to talk about what happened last night?"

Rule 2: Try not to make moralistic judgments; avoid criticizing, belittling, or ridiculing.

Example: "My husband beats me whenever he has had a bad day. It's been happening for years. . . ."

Not very helpful
   "Your husband is no good."
   "You're crazy if you don't leave him."
   "You must be one of those people who enjoy being punished."

More helpful
   "It must be very hard for you to go on like this."
   "Tell me what happened last night, if you can talk about it."
   "Are you thinking of trying to change the situation?"

Rule 3: Don't dismiss a person's serious feelings with easy praise or flattery.

Example: "Lately I feel that I'm the ugliest, most awkward person in the world."

Not very helpful
   "Nonsense. You're great-looking. Take it from me."
   "You? Come on! I think you're fishing for compliments."
   "How can you say that? There are lots of people who are much worse looking than you. Look at [famous
      unattractive person]."

Source: From L. K. Wolberg. *The Technique of Psychotherapy* (3rd ed.). Copyright © 1977. Grune & Stratton, New York. Reprinted by permission of the Psychological Corporation.

More helpful
"You sound as if you're being very hard on yourself."
"Did something happen lately to make you feel that way?"
"What is it about your appearance that seems to bother you?"

Rule 4: Try to be open-minded with respect to the other person's beliefs or opinions; realize that you cannot impose your own viewpoint as a solution to another person's problem.

Example: "I'm thinking of breaking up with Chris. My father will be very upset if he finds out we've been living together, and the whole thing is making me a nervous wreck."

Not very helpful
"You're silly to worry about your father. It's your own life."
"If your father's upset—well, that's his problem."
"Sounds as if you're too dependent on your father's opinion."

More helpful
"Yes, I can see that you're in a difficult position."
"If only you could make your father understand. Have you tried talking to him about this?"

Rule 5: Do not use psychological terms to make snap judgments. (If you are a trained therapist, this is called premature interpretation; if you are not a trained therapist, it is usually a disservice.)

Not very helpful
"You just have an inferiority complex."
"The reason you have all these problems with women is your Oedipal conflict."
"You must be a masochist or something."
"Why don't you just stop being paranoid about this?"

Rule 6: Do not force a person to talk about something when he says he cannot do so because what happened is too painful, frightening, or traumatic. Especially do not press him if he appears to grow increasingly agitated without being able to talk about "it." Reassure him by showing that you will stay and listen even if he cannot talk about what is troubling him. If appropriate, suggest that he seek a counselor or other therapist who can help him overcome his agitation. (Do not tell him to go *talk the problem over* with a therapist, since that may not seem possible at first.)

Special caution: If a person threatens suicide in your presence, you must respond in a serious, thoughtful manner—that is, as if you fully believe that the person might take his life. Some people who threaten suicide simply need to talk it out. Others need professional attention, psychotherapy, even hospitalization. It is *not* your responsibility to know what is needed. It is your responsibility not to make matters worse.

Review the examples and responses above. Can you tell whether you are usually helpful when approached by a person with a problem? Do you see ways of improving your sensitivity? ▲

Finally, the person's usual supports may be insufficient when he or she is passing through a transitional period or crisis. When a gradual development culminates in a substantial change such as beginning school, leaving home, or becoming a parent, a person may be faced with the need to develop new resources. Many young adults who have gone away to college or established themselves in new jobs and apartments discover that friends from high school are no longer able to relate to their difficulties. A married person may come to feel the same way about confiding in single friends.

For a variety of reasons, then, the usual supports are not always adequate to help a person over a crisis. In cases where our emotional difficulties are greater than our ability to handle them, one solution is psychotherapy.

PSYCHOTHERAPY: A DEFINITION

Therapy (Psychotherapy)
A formal relationship between client and a trained person to bring about behavioral or personality changes and promote personal development.

Therapy, which we are here using as a shortened term for **psychotherapy,** is a form of treatment in which a trained person establishes a relationship with at least one client (or patient) for the purpose of applying psychological techniques to bring about sought-after behavioral or personality changes (Goldstein & Krasner, 1987). Therapy can also remove obstacles to an individual's potential in the academic, social, sexual, career, athletic, or artistic aspects of life. In the relationship the therapist functions as a helper, guide, teacher, and catalyst. The interaction between therapist and client provides the means by which the issues of therapy are confronted. The therapeutic relationship is a formal one in which certain features are defined at the outset: where it will take place, what the cost will be per session, what the goals are, and what methods will be used to achieve them.

The philosophic assumption underlying therapy is that people have the capacity to further their personal development, gain greater self-knowledge, make more effective decisions, and cope more successfully with the stresses and strains of their environment. Through those changes they experience a greater degree of personal fulfillment. A commonly held idea is that therapy is invariably a treatment or cure for emotional illness. In actuality, many individuals enter therapy to maximize personal growth, while others, at the opposite extreme, are involuntarily committed to state institutions where they receive therapy as part of a rehabilitation program. The sphere of attention in therapy is life itself, and all the life tasks that the individual is not able to accomplish unaided. Its need and popularity are attested to by the estimate that 34 million Americans are receiving psychotherapy or counseling (Brody, 1981).

GENERAL PURPOSES OF THERAPY

Virtually everyone who seeks therapy wishes, at some level, to improve the quality of his or her life. Therapy is supposed to *do* something. What exactly it is supposed to do varies from case to case, depending on the needs of the client and the orientation of the therapist. Despite the variety of therapeutic approaches, psychologists have identified some general purposes of therapy.

Some lawbreakers are provided with mental health services as part of their rehabilitation program.

Sundberg, Tyler, and Taplin (1973), for example, compared the work of numerous therapists and developed a comprehensive list of the goals that may be realized in therapy. Each goal on the list represents a different emphasis or theme. A therapist might be guided by different goals with different patients, or have varying goals with the same patient at different points in therapy. According to Sundberg, Tyler, and Taplin:

1. *Therapy can strengthen the client's motivation to do things that are right for himself.* It can help the client overcome the need to engage in unproductive or unhealthy behavior. For example, the therapist can work with the client to reduce the fear involved in freeing himself from an addiction, or alleviate the depression that is making it hard for the client to find a job or work productively. As a result of therapy, the person becomes (in his or her terms) a "better person."

2. *Therapy can reduce emotional pressures by facilitating the expression of feelings.* It has long been recognized that people experience sudden relief (or catharsis) when pent-up feelings are released. Therapy provides a "safe" and appropriate setting for the release of feelings. A client, for example, might express hostility toward a parent by angrily telling the therapist how unfairly he or she has been treated, or by hitting a pillow. After such a release, many clients report that a "great burden" has been removed (in most cases the burden of guilt).

3. *Another purpose of therapy is to release the client's potential for growth.* The inner obstacles that have inhibited the client from engaging in relationships with others, in a rewarding career, and so on, can be uncovered and overcome. For instance, a college woman who feels stupid because she has always been unfavorably compared to a sibling in intelligence and academic performance can learn that the comparisons were unfounded. Freed of this judgment internalized from her parents, she can begin to enjoy school and achieve academically.

4. *In therapy the cognitive structure of the individual can be modified.* A distorted conception about the world, about other people, or about one's relations to other people can be corrected. For example, a woman who interprets all attention she receives from others as charitable behavior can be made to realize that other people genuinely enjoy their relationships with her. ("I never thought of things that way," says the client.)

5. *In the course of therapy clients can be helped to achieve increased self-knowledge.* They become more aware of how they actually behave and what they are like. Thus, a person who habitually feels contemptuous of other people might come to realize that fear of rejection underlies the contempt. ("I never realized how afraid I was," is a typical insight. Another is: "I wasn't aware that I had *so much anger!*")

6. *Therapy promotes habit change.* With a sequence of planned learning situations, a client can be encouraged to give up an unproductive mode of behavior. The interaction with the therapist can promote this goal. For example, a man who is domineering can practice being flexible and cooperative toward the therapist, and eventually toward other people in his life.

7. *Therapy can improve interpersonal relationships.* The client's past and current relationships are examined, and recurring patterns of behavior are noted. The interaction of the therapist and client (or, in a group, members with one another) provides a situation in which interpersonal behavior can be dealt with as it takes place. Communication patterns are examined. The client may be asked, "Why do you take such a remark personally?" or "Did you mean to avoid responsibility for that remark?" The goal is to develop new and healthier ways of relating to others.

Sundberg, Tyler, and Taplin's list was updated in 1973. Since then, therapy, like other areas in psychology, has been enlivened by new ideas and techniques. Today, for example, some people enter therapy in order to learn relaxation techniques or develop greater awareness of and control over states of consciousness. Such goals were uncommon only 20 years ago. To the original list of therapeutic purposes, Korchin (1976) has added the following:

8. *Therapy can increase the client's knowledge and capacity for effective life decisions.* The client who is in a crisis is helped to make decisions on matters such as education, career choice, and living situation. The therapist, who retains a larger perspective on the choices available, is in a position to help the client be realistic in exploring the possibilities in his environment.

9. *Therapy can help bring about changes in the client's social environment.* Because therapists increasingly realize that a client's well-being depends on the effects of people or social institutions in his or her life, today they more often act (with their clients) to change social environments. For example, a common and very difficult task of a therapist is to provide necessary support to the young adult who must leave home because of a disturbed family situation.

10. *In some kinds of therapy, somatic (bodily) processes are altered in order to reduce painful feelings and/or increase body awareness.* For example, therapists can sometimes reduce extreme stress by means of relaxation techniques. Psychoactive drugs, such as tranquilizers, can be prescribed (by psychiatrists or by physicians working with therapists) to relieve distress and enable patients to engage in more conventional therapy. In addition, **biofeedback** and disciplines such as yoga are employed to achieve relaxation and to bring bodily sensations to conscious awareness.

11. *A relatively new purpose of therapy is to alter states of consciousness in order to extend self-awareness, control, and creativity.* Meditation techniques are used to turn a person's attention inward to discover additional internal sensations and resources, and presumably improve psychological health.

Biofeedback
A learning technique that enables individuals to gain information about bodily processes and to gain voluntary control over these bodily processes.

PSYCHOLOGICAL ASSESSMENT

In many clinical settings, the first step toward establishing therapeutic relationships is **psychological assessment.** The concept of "assessment" is familiar to us: by assessment we usually mean a procedure of collecting information about a person to predict his or her behavior. For example, we all make assessments informally when we try to predict who will do well in college, who will make a good date, or who will make a good teacher. In a clinical setting, such as a counseling center, assessment means the use of specific testing procedures to evaluate or differentiate individuals on the basis of certain characteristics. The characteristics most often assessed by psychologists are personality and intelligence.

Psychologists seek to determine characteristics of people because the data may help them, for example, to match clients with therapists or develop treatment plans. A variety of tests and interviews are used. Two requirements must be met before an assessment procedure can yield useful information.

Psychological Assessment
The use of diagnostic procedures to evaluate individuals on certain characteristics.

First, the procedure must have **reliability;** that is, it must measure a characteristic consistently. If you took two forms of a test at two different times and got very different scores, the test would be an unreliable measure, just as if you stepped on a scale twice in succession and got different readings, it would not be a reliable measure of your weight.

Second, a procedure must have **validity.** That is, it must measure the characteristic it was designed to measure. If you are using a test of intelligence, it is only valid if it measures intelligence and not other factors, such as aggressiveness, ethnic background, or socioeconomic level.

Assessing Personality

Personality is usually assessed through personal interviews, objective tests, and projective tests.

The Personal Interview

The interview, conducted by a skilled professional, can be a very versatile instrument for use in learning about an individual directly from that person. The sources of information are of two kinds: first, the self-reports made by the individual, such as "I have trouble making friends;" and second, the individual's behavior during the interview, such as the tendency to look away rather than at the interviewer, body in a tensed position, and speaking in an almost inaudible voice. Through verbal statement and body language, the client is conveying something about the nature of the problem.

Just how the interview is conducted depends both on the purpose of the assessment (what in particular is to be learned) and on the theoretical orientation of the psychologist. Some interviews are highly structured, with the psychologist asking a long series of prepared questions intended to obtain information deemed necessary for valid assessments. Others are highly unstructured interviews in which only a few broad questions are known in advance (e.g., "Tell me about yourself"). These may be followed by questions generated on the spot but which, too, are intended to encourage the client in his report of relevant information.

The interview is vulnerable to error. If we consider its components, we can recognize its potential weakness. To start off with, the psychologist asks some questions of the client. Are the client's answers biased in that he believes that the psychologist wants a particular answer? Do the questions ask about the client's experiences that are now in the hazy past, so that the answers would be unreliable? Are the psychologist's interpretations of the client's answers based on unfounded theory? Unfortunately, the answer to these questions must sometimes be "yes," which explains why many professionals take precautions to safeguard the quality of the assessment interview. Such precautions include the review of videotaped interviews by a more experienced professional, the use of duplicate questions at different points in the interview to see if the responses are consistent and, hence, reliable, and the building of trust to overcome a client's tendency to give only socially acceptable responses. Such care is exercised because the interview can be one of the most valuable instruments in assessment.

Objective Tests

One of the best examples of an objective personality test is the **Minnesota Multiphasic Personality Inventory (MMPI).** The test consists of 550 items to which the respondent answers "true," "false," or "cannot say." A series of scoring keys was developed so that the respondent can be placed in a diagnostic category on the basis of his or her responses. Among the diagnostic categories of the MMPI are hypochondriasis, depression, psychopathic deviate, and paranoia. Here are some of the questions from the MMPI:*

1. I like mechanics magazines.
2. I have a good appetite.
3. I wake up fresh and rested most mornings.
4. I think I would like the work of a librarian.
5. I am easily awakened by noise.
6. I like to read newspaper articles on crime.
7. My hands and feet are usually warm enough.
8. My daily life is full of things that keep me interested.
9. I am about as able to work as I ever was.
10. There seems to be a lump in my throat much of the time.

To develop the scoring keys, a large number of questions were administered to patients with a variety of psychiatric diagnoses and also to a group of so-called normals. Items that tended to be answered in the same manner by patients with psychiatric diagnoses and by normals were dropped. Items that were answered differently by normals and by those in different diagnostic groups were retained. Thus, if someone responded to an item in the same way as a diagnostic group, the person was scored as having a characteristic of that group. The MMPI has high reliability and validity and is often used as an assessment instrument. Recently, computerized personality profiles have been generated from MMPI data.

Projective Tests

In **projective tests,** respondents are presented with an ambiguous picture or vaguely defined stimulus and asked to report what they see. Because of the ambiguity of the item, what individuals "see" is what they *project* onto the stimulus, namely, their own private meanings, which are then interpreted by

Minnesota Multiphasic Personality Inventory (MMPI) An objective personality test, consisting of true-false statements about oneself, designed to yield diagnostic information.

Projective Tests Psychological tests in which the respondent is presented with an ambiguous stimulus and asked to describe what he or she sees.

---

*Reproduced by permission. Copyright 1943, renewed 1970 by the University of Minnesota. Published by the Psychological Corporation. All rights reserved.

Figure 6.1 Example of Rorschach inkblot.

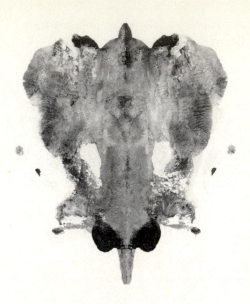

a trained examiner. Psychologists believe that such perceptions reveal underlying personality patterns and issues important to the respondent.

The **Rorschach Inkblot test** is one of the oldest projective methods. It consists of ten inkblots similar to the one pictured in Figure 6.1. Half are in color and half are black and white. Respondents are shown each card, one at a time, and then asked to describe what they see. The way the respondents interpret the ambiguous shape and color may shed light on their inner conflicts, preoccupations, and emotional responses as they deal with the world.

Another projective technique is the **Thematic Apperception Test (TAT).** The test is composed of a series of pictures, with each picture showing people involved in different situations. The respondent is asked to make up a story about each one. By evaluating both the structure and the content of these stories, as well as the person's behavior in telling them, the trained tester assesses the respondent's personality characteristics.

Assessing Intelligence

Intelligence has been defined in many ways: The ability to learn from experience . . . to adjust to the environment . . . to solve problems that require the use of symbols (e.g., verbal, mathematical, or geometric) . . . to succeed in school or college . . . to perform well on a job. More than 75 years since the earliest tests were introduced in modern times, the nature of intelligence is still a debatable issue. What is not debatable is the widespread use of intelligence tests, sometimes called IQ tests.

Mental testing was first used as long ago as the 3rd century, when the Chinese took into consideration the candidates' performance on mental tests in making appointments to the Imperial Court. By the 7th century they were

The Search for Personal Adjustment

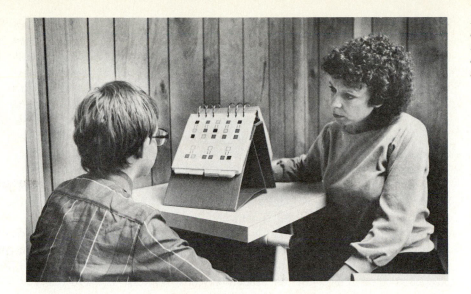

using types of items found in today's tests! One type is that of sentence completion, for example: The sun rises in the east and sets in the _____ . It is more surprising to learn that even then there was concern about the predictive value of tests. To frame the question the way they might have, those many centuries ago, we would ask, "Do those who perform well on our mental tests prove to be better members of the Imperial Court than those who do not do well on the tests?" (Vane & Motta, 1984).

Intelligence tests were first put to practical use in modern times in France as a means of determining which children needed placement in special classes because of their low academic aptitude. In the United States, both group tests, in which respondents write answers to printed questions on a standard form, and verbally-administered individual tests were developed. Most of us have experienced paper-and-pencil types of tests in school.

By and large, most of the tests have been shown to be reliable and valid for predicting academic success. In other words, those who do well on them in their early years in school tend to be successful in school. However, that outcome may be due in part to the fact that little is done in school on a protracted basis to overcome the initial disadvantages of those who do poorly on the tests. Some studies have shown that special training programs can improve an individual's academic performance as well as performance on the tests (Feuerstein et al., 1980; Schwebel & Maher, 1986). Even preschool programs of less than a year have been shown to have very worthwhile benefits through the school years and into young adulthood (Lazar & Darlington, 1982).

Some of the tests have been charged with being discriminatory against lower social classes and minority groups. Other ways of testing academic aptitude have been developed to overcome the limitations of the past. With these methods the psychologist structures the testing environment so as to inhibit impulsive responding or, first tests the individual, then teaches him the concept or skill that was not known, and finally tests the individual again. The latter approach gives an estimate of how well the individual functions both *before* being helped to overcome disadvantages and later *after* being helped (Feuerstein et al., 1979; Burhenne, Kaschak, & Schwebel, 1973; Schwebel & Bernstein, 1970). These approaches rest on the belief that testing is most worthwhile when it shows individual's intellectual potential and the kind of assistance needed to promote their fullest intellectual development.

A recent new approach does not limit intelligence to verbal and mathematical aptitudes. According to Sternberg (1985) who introduced the "triarchic theory," there are three aspects to intelligence, only the first of which has been given attention in the past. The componential aspect, analytical thinking, is the sort required on traditional IQ tests: if A is greater than B but smaller than C, how do C and B compare in size? The experiential aspect, creative thinking, is the sort that is required to take different components of experience and combine them insightfully. A person troubled by digestive problems makes a connection between a particular food, personal fatigue, and physical distress. The contextual aspect, "street smartness," is the sort needed to know how to play the game and manipulate the environment, such as in the role of political leadership (chairing a student group or organizing a fundraising project).

The most widely used individually administered test for adults is the **Wechsler Adult Intelligence Scale-Revised** (WAIS-R). Although the main purpose in administering this test is to assess intelligence, it can yield useful information about the examinee's personality. For example, a psychologist giving the WAIS-R will observe whether the examinee responds impulsively or thoughtfully, hesitantly or confidently. Does the examinee give up quickly or persevere as the items become more difficult? Does he or she try to please the psychologist? Such information is useful in an overall assessment of an individual's functioning.

Wechsler Adult Intelligence Scale-Revised
A widely used individually-administered intelligence test designed for use with adults.

Other Assessment Tools

Besides intelligence and personality tests, there are assessment tools used to evaluate interests, values, and aptitudes.

Interest tests are useful in career counseling. One frequently used interest test is the Strong Interest Inventory (Strong, 1974), which assesses the similarity between the interests of the respondent and the interests of successful people in a variety of occupations. If you have the same likes and dislikes as the people in a given occupation then you also might be interested in that field of work. Interest tests are not used to measure ability to perform the tasks connected with that field, but only possible interest in it.

Specialized aptitude tests for clerical work, mechanical occupations, and artistic and musical endeavors have been developed over the years to predict success in a specific occupation or training course. Such tests are useful, provided that they are well constructed and well evaluated, or, to use terms introduced earlier, provided they are reliable and valid.

More recently, psychologists in industry have developed a procedure carried out in assessment centers (Cohen & Sands, 1978). Job or promotion applicants are given a series of tasks similar to those they will perform on their jobs. Their performance is evaluated by several trained assessors, and predictions are made about future success on the job.

A study of psychological tests used in a variety of centers, clinics, and hospitals showed that the MMPI was the most commonly used. The WAIS-R, Rorschach, and TAT were also among the seven most frequently used assessment instruments (Lubin et al., 1986). Quality tests like these, used appropriately, can provide the assessor and the respondent with useful information.

WHO IS PROFESSIONALLY QUALIFIED TO PROVIDE THERAPEUTIC HELP?

A number of types of professionals have been trained to provide therapeutic help. Most have a doctoral degree that requires approximately four years of specialized study following the bachelor's degree. An essential component of the training is in the form of supervised practical experience known as "practicum." Either before the degree is granted or immediately afterward the newly trained professional undergoes at least one year of full-time supervised internship. That means the person engages in the practice that he or she has prepared for, but under the watchful eye of an experienced supervisor. The various types of professionals are discussed below.

Clinical psychologists are skilled in assessing an individual's personality, intelligence, and cognitive functioning, as well as providing a variety of therapeutic services (such as individual, family, or group therapy). They usually earn either a Ph.D. or Psy.D. In addition to academic and research training, they have completed at least a one-year supervised clinical internship, usually in a community mental health clinic, psychiatric hospital, or medical center. They may also obtain postgraduate training in therapy upon completion of their doctorate. Many work in mental health centers, hospitals, and clinics or in their own private practice. Some divide their time between professional practice in one of those settings and also university teaching and research.

Counseling psychologists typically work with normal or moderately maladjusted persons, individually or in groups. A Ph.D. or Ed.D., together with a one-year internship, is usually required. Counseling psychologists essentially function in an educational and preventive role, offering expertise in particular areas. They may help individuals with academic, career, social, marital, family, or health problems. The majority of counseling psychologists in the past were employed in colleges and universities, but now they are found increasingly in mental health or rehabilitation centers, hospitals, government agencies, industry, and private practice.

Psychiatrists have M.D.s with specialized medical training in psychiatry that enables them to diagnose and treat mental disorders. They are the only mental health professionals qualified to prescribe drugs and treat organic mental disorders. They have completed an internship and residency, usually in a psychiatric hospital. Some psychiatrists work in psychiatric hospitals, while others see individuals in private offices, clinics, and mental health centers. Some psychiatrists (called liaison psychiatrists) work in a general hospital as part of a treatment team that helps patients cope with chronic illness, surgery, and other medical intervention. Other specialists, child psychiatrists, work with children and adolescents and their families. Geriatric psychiatrists specialize in the problems of the aged.

Psychiatric social workers generally have a master's degree (M.S.W.); some may obtain a Ph.D. or D.S.W. (Doctor of Social Work) from a school of social work. Their education includes supervised field training in a mental health facility or social agency. Social workers are especially qualified to help clients with problems relating to the social system. For example, they may help clients cope with housing difficulties, legal institutions, difficulties with the police, foster care and adoption agencies, Medicare, and other entitlement programs. Some social workers are engaged in private practice and provide a variety of therapeutic services, including family and marital therapy. However, most social workers are associated with institutions serving the public welfare such as community agencies, psychiatric hospitals, penal institutions, child welfare agencies, and geriatric facilities.

Psychoanalysts are either psychiatrists, clinical psychologists, or psychiatric social workers who have undergone extensive postgraduate training at a psychoanalytic training institution and personal psychoanalysis. Psychoanalysts specialize in the exploration and treatment of unconscious conflicts, and follow some form of the procedures developed by Freud and modified by his followers. They are qualified to provide classic (long-term) psychoanalysis. Most psychoanalysts are engaged in private practice. They may teach at analytic institutions and serve as consultants in mental health projects.

Psychiatric nurses have a master's degree or other advanced training in psychiatric nursing. They are trained in diagnostic and treatment procedures, and participate in the operation and management of a hospital's psychiatric ward. Most practice in hospitals, geriatric facilities, and community health care clinics. They may also be involved in mental health consultations and community outreach programs, including making home visits and providing service at neighborhood centers.

THE THERAPEUTIC RELATIONSHIP

The central aspect of therapy is the relationship between the therapist and client, which is cultivated through the efforts of the therapist. This relationship is the medium in which the issues of the therapy are encountered. It is analogous to the paint with which the artist transforms the canvas or the instrument in whose tones the musician speaks.

Carl Rogers, the developer of the client-centered approach to therapy, and one of the most influential psychologists of the century, initiated research on the therapeutic relationship in 1949. To study the process of therapy scientifically, he introduced the practice of electronically recording therapy sessions. He and his associates set as their goal to establish the kind of relationship that would provide a safe psychological climate so that clients could feel secure enough to open up, explore threatening issues, and risk making changes. Three conditions are deemed necessary to create such a climate. The first is genuineness or realness: The therapist is himself, and puts on no professional front. The second is unconditional positive regard: No matter what emotion the client expresses, or what behavior is reported, the therapist cares about the client. The third is empathic understanding: The therapist senses the meanings and feelings that the client experiences and conveys understanding and acceptance to the client (Rogers, 1986).

An excerpt from a therapeutic session shows how Rogers ("Carl") interacts with a client ("Jan") who has just introduced an "age problem."

Jan: I feel that I am in a panic situation. I am thirty-five years of age, and I've only got another five years till forty. It's very difficult to explain. I keep turning around and I want to run away from it.
Carl: It's enough of a fear that you really—it really sets off a panic in you.

Jan goes on to say that the fear has affected her confidence, and that it only started in the last 18 months or 2 years. Rogers communicates her feelings to her and asks if there was anything that might have set it off at that time.

Jan: Not that I can recall, really. Well, my mother died at fifty-three . . .
Carl: Mm-hmm.
Jan: . . . and she was a very young and a very bright woman in many ways. But I think maybe that has something to do with it. I don't know.
Carl: You sort of felt that if your mother died at that early age, that was a possibility for you, too. [Pause] And time began to seem a lot shorter.
Jan: Right! (Rogers, 1986, pp. 200–201)

As Rogers himself comments, Jan feels safe enough in the relationship to begin to explore, and she comes to see a connection between her mother's death and her own fears. She has benefited from his genuineness, caring, and empathy. These characteristics, keystones to client-centered therapy, are widely regarded as important to effective therapy even when the methods employed are very different. Where there is a difference among therapists, it is not about the necessity for a positive relationship. Rather it is about controversial issues such as whether the more the therapist possesses those qualities, the greater the success of therapy (Patterson, 1984).

The therapeutic relationship resembles others, especially those with a trusted friend or family member. We talk, bare our soul, and seek support and advice. However, the therapeutic relationship is different in a number of respects. Therapists, because of their extensive education and supervised experience, have been trained to "listen with the third ear" to use an old phrase that means the therapist gets to the meanings behind the words. In the example above, Rogers sensed that something happened 18 months earlier that was related to her panic. Besides being sensitive to the feelings of the client, therapists are trained to be aware of their own feelings and values and to see that those do not intrude into the life and decisions of the client.

Another way the therapeutic relationship is different is that it exists solely in order for one person to help another. The therapeutic relationship is a *professional* one: As such, it is not reciprocal. The client will not help the therapist in the way the therapist helps the client. Instead the client pays a fee in exchange for a service. Moreover, unlike most friends or confidants, the therapist accepts hostility and irrational behavior. He or she avoids judging the client by the social conventions or moral standards that would ordinarily apply. Also, unlike a friend, the therapist might withhold comfort or remain silent if that seemed to promote the goals of therapy. Furthermore, therapy "provides a person with someone who pays attention to and accepts him *without responding in ways others close to him have always responded*" (Kovel, 1976, p. xv, italics added).

Finally, the relationship is a *formal* one. Before therapy begins both parties come to an agreement on the goals, therapeutic methods, fees, and frequency of sessions. Will the client sit on a chair or lie on a couch? Will therapy be individual or group? Will medication be used? Will the therapist interview members of the client's family? Any or all of these agreements may be changed after a designated period of time has elapsed, or at any other time if both therapist and patient agree (Ehrenberg & Ehrenberg, 1977).

The relationship of therapist and client ideally develops along identifiable steps. Although there are variations according to the different types of therapy and the differing needs of clients, the following stages seem to be typical.

Initial Stages

In the first stages of therapy a client who has been troubled by disruptive emotions experiences relief and a rise in morale (Frank, 1973); he or she now knows that someone understanding and accepting will be available to help. The client is likely to trust the therapist in a way that is unique. Generally, the more troubled and confused he is, the greater will be the reliance on the therapist (Wolberg, 1977). The client who is seeking primarily a growth experience may evaluate the therapist critically, to see if he has characteristics that the client values. At the other end of the spectrum, a disturbed patient waiting in an emergency room will usually become calmer merely on hearing that the person approaching him is a psychologist or psychiatrist.

The initial session is a crucial one. While the therapist is getting a first impression of the client, the latter is sizing up the therapist. A study gives us some preliminary ideas about how the first session relates to the outcome of therapy. It turns out that the experiences of the patient in the initial session in brief, time-limited (eight sessions) therapy are related to the success of therapy. In particular, patients who saw their therapists' emotional attitude toward them as more positive during the first session, showed greater improvement after four sessions than other patients. The improvement was assessed both by the patients themselves and the therapist. Also, the more positive the patient's assessment of the therapist's style of relating during the first session, the longer the patient stayed in treatment (Bottari & Rappaport, 1983).

As the therapy proceeds, the client tells the therapist details of his or her problem and its history. Accompanying these confidences are a release in tension and a loosening of inhibitions. The client "gets used to being in therapy." Putting the secrets of the past into words makes them seem less destructive—and certainly less abnormal. Talking about a current crisis, such as divorce or job loss, is beneficial for the same reasons. The therapist is calm, accepting. And the client has the reassuring feeling that he or she has heard this (or worse) before. Together the client and therapist are able to look at the confusion the client feels about his or her problems. Explanations for the client's motives and behavior are developed.

Growth of the Relationship

Gradually, in the safety of the therapeutic relationship, the client reveals to the therapist (and to himself) the painful details about present and past situations. The client focuses on matters, habits, or decisions that he or she was unable to confront before. Having the therapist's undivided attention is experienced as a great benefit (and clients are particularly resentful when the session is interrupted or canceled because of the therapist's vacation).

However, the therapy is also experienced as a form of punishment, or "benevolent ordeal" (Haley, 1963). After all, the client is asked to focus on the very sources of his or her anxiety. An extreme example: the person who is obsessively afraid of snakes may be made to view, touch, and eventually handle them—hardly a pleasant prospect at the outset. At the very least the person is encouraged to expose his or her most carefully guarded weaknesses to someone who, seemingly, has none. In family therapy, troubled family members must expose details of their miserable existence to someone who is perceived as a superior parent (Haley, 1963, p. 187). The therapist is sympathetic and benevolent; and yet he or she puts the client through a painful ordeal.

Not surprisingly, the client's feelings for the therapist can become very intense. The possibility of the relationship getting out of bounds is prevented by its limits in time and place (most therapists are opposed to seeing their clients socially). It is also free of complications that result from participants' knowing each others' friends and families. When freed from the usual inhibitions and treated supportively, the client comes to idealize the therapist and takes him or her for a model.

In this stage, the client often experiences complex emotions toward the therapist that are summed up in the word **transference.** The client transfers to the therapist some of the feelings he or she has experienced toward figures in the past (usually parents). In sessions, the client proceeds to *act out* feelings that originated in these past relationships. For example, winning the therapist's approval on minor points, hurting the therapist's feelings, or gaining an

Transference
A phenomenon in therapy in which the client transfers to the therapist feelings he or she has experienced toward other individuals in the past.

undue portion of his or her time may become important to the client. A common part of transference is the client's dependence on the therapist, which resembles the dependence on parents in early childhood.

Transference can be temporarily disruptive to therapy. The client may burst out with misdirected anger, because of his or her excessive needs, perhaps canceling appointments as a retaliation for a perceived injustice. However, unproductive as it may seem at times, transference is explained or otherwise used by the therapist to help the person move beyond the childhood pattern. For example, the therapist, by observing a client's dependent behavior in therapy sessions, can help him to develop insight about why he treats other people as if they were his parents. Moreover, the transference can provide a "corrective emotional experience" (Alexander, 1946): That is, old, disturbing emotions are relived in a new context and bring forth a different reaction from the listener.

Resolution

As therapy progresses the client gradually behaves less symptomatically, because the therapist responds so differently from the way that parents and others have always responded. For example, if the client is dependent and refuses to make his own decisions, the therapist does not gratefully make them for him (as a parent or spouse has done and then turn around, complain, and belittle). Instead the therapist subjects the dependent behavior to examination, and to the agreed-upon means of treatment. With the therapist's help, the client becomes able to recognize his real feelings and motivations. He recognizes his destructive patterns of behavior, as they merge in *new* life situations. And more and more, the client is able to avoid falling into those patterns.

Gradually the client learns to behave in new ways. The relationship with the therapist inevitably changes, as the client overcomes feelings of dependency and awe and begins to relate to the therapist as a human being with strengths, faults, and limitations. The client now longs to take a more active role in the sessions, and in life in general. At the same time he or she is usually afraid to dispense with the therapeutic session. Eventually the session begins to be viewed as something to fall back on. And finally, the client can do without it and is able to terminate treatment.

Of course, not all therapeutic relationships work this well. The client and therapist may be incompatible in personality or goals. The client may refuse to become genuinely involved in the therapy, or may cling to it—when it has ceased to be of further benefit—by falling back on old symptoms. On the other hand, the therapist may fail the client by losing interest in what he or she is saying, by imposing standards that are not the client's, or by discouraging the client from terminating in order to collect the fee. When any of these problems occur, and discussing them does no good, it is advisable for client and therapist to terminate the relationship (Ehrenberg & Ehrenberg, 1977).

Brief psychotherapy provided at a time of crisis can be a valuable aid to those trying to cope with the circumstances they face.

FORMS OF THERAPY

Crisis Intervention

A **crisis** is a changed condition in a person's life that produces acute stress. It often causes severe emotional upset and disorganized behavior. **Crisis intervention** is a relatively new form of therapy designed to help a person overcome such severe difficulties. The person may have suffered from external events such as rape or the death of a family member. Or great stress may have resulted from a deliberate change: going to college, leaving home, bearing or adopting a child, retiring from work, and so forth. In either case the individual is faced with a situation that demands coping and he or she may feel vulnerable and overwhelmed.

A crisis is, by definition, a temporary situation with an identifiable cause or causes. Usually the crisis lasts no more than four to eight weeks, by which time the individual makes an adaptation one way or another. Accordingly crisis intervention has a limited time span, and is oriented toward the present. Therapy is likely to consist of no more than eight sessions.

Because crises are "turning points," timely intervention can be crucial. Psychologists point out that failure in handling any of the developmental crises can have serious effects on the growth of an individual. Among these effects are immaturity and inadequate personality development, as well as more serious psychological illness (Zimet, 1979). It has been shown that in many patients suffering from mental disorders, significant changes in personality appeared to have taken place during fairly short periods of crisis (Caplan,

Crisis
A changed condition in a person's life that produces stress and often causes emotional upset and disorganized behavior.

Crisis Intervention
A form of brief therapy designed to help a person overcome sudden and severe difficulties caused by changed conditions.

Resources

It is often said that the time to seek out a physician is when you are well; only then do you have the time to evaluate your needs in a medical relationship. By the same reasoning, the time to learn about mental health services in your community is when you are not in immediate need of them. It makes good sense to know in advance how you could be referred to a mental health professional during a sudden life crisis, or at any other time when your ordinary coping skills were ineffective.

You should also be aware of available services because you may become involved in somebody else's crisis. For example, you might be supportive to a depressed friend by letting her know of the services available at the Student Counseling Center. Or you might be supportive to a friend who has a drinking problem by encouraging him to contact an alcoholic abuse intervention program.

1. Physicians (for example, your family doctor, internist, or gynecologist) can refer you to a psychologist or other mental health professional. If you have a physician to whom you would go for a referral, check your address book to be sure you have his or her telephone number.
2. Clergy provide counseling and may refer people to mental health professionals. If you have a clergyman who could help you in a crisis, check your personal address book to be sure that you have his number.
3. Colleges and universities usually maintain student counseling services. If you attend a college or university, find out about the counseling service and record the full name of the service, its location, the hours it is open, and the procedure for referral.

1964). On the other hand, successful responses to crises can, in a short time, broaden a person's potential and increase maturity and independence. Caplan illustrates this point by explaining that combat, for some soldiers, produced psychological incapacitation; others became stronger and more self-reliant. Crisis intervention attempts to tip the outcome toward psychological health (Aguilera & Messick, 1982). In dealing with the emergency the goal of crisis intervention is "to reach people in acute stress and provide them with enough support to prevent them from becoming the 'chronics' of the future" (Phares, 1988, p. 505).

Crises are viewed as experiences that happen to normal people; their origin is in life circumstances, and not in character or personality disorders (Whitlock, 1978). Therefore crisis intervention does not attempt to reconstruct the personality or treat the disorder. It focuses on the situation at hand and is goal-oriented. It is designed to marshal the client's best resources and

4. If you are not in school, or if you prefer not to rely on school-related services, the mental health association of your county can give you information about existing services and provide a referral. Obtain the telephone number of the association.

5. Many specialized counseling services and "hot lines" probably exist in your community. Explore your telephone directory until you know where you would find listings for rape and crime victim counseling; child abuse services (e.g., Parents Anonymous); services for battered or abused women; abortion counseling; marriage and family counseling; alcohol and other drug abuse intervention programs; and suicide-prevention hot lines. Some of these listings will probably appear at the beginning of the directory, along with other emergency numbers. Other listings may appear in alphabetical order, under type of crisis (e.g., under "r" for "rape"). Make sure that you know where important counseling services are listed.

6. Check the telephone listings of the hospital center nearest you. Familiarize yourself with any special mental health clinics or services that are affiliated with the hospital.

7. Some health or hospital insurance plans cover selected forms of mental health or psychiatric services. If you have a health or hospital insurance plan (or if you are covered as a dependent), determine what kinds of mental health care would be covered for you. ▲

coping methods, and to help him or her acquire new ones. It attempts to bring the client back to his or her ordinary level of functioning and possibly beyond. The therapist actively directs the sessions to keep the focus on the crisis and freely offers reassurance and support.

Crisis intervention is provided by psychologists, counselors, and social workers, as well as by physicians, clergymen, nurses, and police officers. In some cases paraprofessionals with special qualifications are trained to do crisis intervention in its initial stages. For example, trained volunteers sometimes staff telephone "hot lines" for victims of violent crime or for potential suicides. This form of service has become prominent and in a review of studies on telephone counseling effectiveness, Stein and Lambert (1984) concluded that lay telephone counselors are effective and that clients who use the services give them high ratings.

Crisis intervention sometimes leads to other forms of therapy, as in the following two examples. On the night before an important midterm Rick, a sophomore computer science major, drank a six pack with his roommate and then took street drugs. Afterwards, he started having a "bad trip." Friends drove him to a crisis center. Scared by the night's experiences and pleased by the counselor's warmth, Rick joined a drug-free support group. Sandra, a 26-year-old school teacher frantically called the crisis unit of a county mental health center. During her first visit she explained that the man she was living with decided to see other women as well. For four days she had been crying, unable to eat or sleep. The counselor recognized (and explained to Sandra) that while the man's decision had precipitated the crisis, the problem was deeper than that. More important was her need to pass successfully through the transition period of young adulthood in which one learns to achieve a lasting intimate relationship. And so, instead of concentrating on the man and what he did to her, Sandra turned her attention to what exactly she wanted in a relationship, whether the present one satisfied her needs, and what resources she had to change the quality of her life (Golan, 1980). These examples show that crisis counseling not only addresses crises; it is also an entree to services that can help people cope with more pervasive problems.

Counseling

When a person has a rather specific problem to face or decision to make, but one not so acute as to bring about a crisis, **counseling** may provide the needed help. In most colleges and universities, counselors are available to help students choose majors and plan for careers. In hospitals, rehabilitation counselors help disabled people overcome obstacles to independence and productive work.

Although the term "counseling" is often used loosely, the customary definition is a "form of interviewing in which clients are helped to understand themselves more completely in order that they may correct any environmental or adjustment difficulties" (Wolberg, 1977). Unlike therapists (who are experts on "people in general"), counselors are ordinarily experts in the specific field in which they are consulted: health programs, employment opportunities, social programs for veterans, and so forth. In their fields, counselors provide information and other resources. In addition, they help clients evaluate personal goals in light of their strengths and weaknesses. In some cases they administer tests (for example, in vocational skills). Even when counselors deal with more complicated situations, for example, the interrelationships of family members, their activities are generally restricted to considering an individual's relation to, or participation in, one phase of life.

One of the major responsibilities of educational and vocational counseling is to help people, especially those who are young, through the sometimes difficult process of establishing their identity. Teenagers and young adults must make decisions about personal goals, plan for further education or training, choose a career (and other life objectives as well), prepare for, enter, and progress in the career. Many adults, by choice or necessity, change career directions and seek professional assistance from counselors. Research shows that clients benefit from counseling. From it, they are better prepared, for example, to make decisions, choose more appropriate career preferences, improve their attitudes about study, and reduce test anxiety (Myers, 1986).

When educational-vocational counselors find that their client's problems are broader or deeper, they explain their finding and prepare the client for referral to a therapist.

Psychoanalysis

In Vienna in the 1880s, Sigmund Freud became acquainted with a physician, Josef Breuer, who was treating a young woman for paralysis and difficulty in seeing. When Breuer hypnotized his patient (whom he called "Anna O"), she was able to recall events of which she had no conscious memories. After the hypnotic sessions in which she related these emotionally charged experiences, her physical symptoms were relieved. She regained feeling in her arm and leg, and her sight became clearer. Freud and Breuer proposed the existence of the unconscious, the part of the personality that, while powerful, evades our notice.

Freud soon abandoned the use of hypnosis in therapy, but he continued to believe that the key to treatment resided in the unconscious. He found that if he listened with full attention to everything his patients said—even dreams and associations that seemingly made no sense—he would eventually approach the unconscious material. He instructed his patients to withhold nothing. He began to realize that *whatever* they told him was meaningful, and that he had merely to wait for the productions of their own minds to illuminate those conflicts of which they were unaware (Schur, 1972).

At about the same time, Freud began to subject his own thoughts to a similar process. As with his patients, he examined both dreams and conscious mental productions. During this highly creative period, he spent much of his time in "peculiar thoughts not accessible to consciousness, twilight thoughts, veiled doubts," waiting for new material to emerge from the unconscious. He wrote, "I have to wait until things start stirring inside of me and I come to know them" (quoted in Schur, 1972, pp. 114, 135). As a result of this process Freud was able to reconstruct childhood events that had been lost to his conscious memory. And he was able to bring to consciousness desires that he had repressed, for example, murderous wishes toward parents and siblings.

Freud found that confronting these early experiences helped him understand and overcome certain current difficulties in his life. For example, he was able to see how his guilt over the death of a younger brother had helped determine the "neurotic side" of his later friendships. Freud made similar breakthroughs in his treatment of patients.

The therapeutic method that developed out of Freud's experiences is called **psychoanalysis.** In classic psychoanalysis the patient and analyst attempt to bring into awareness the unconscious experiences and passions that have formed the personality. The basic rule of treatment is the rule Freud first imposed: withhold nothing, engage in **free association.** With a minimum of outside stimuli and a minimum of conscious control and editing, the analysand (the person who is being analyzed) attempts to say whatever comes to mind.

Psychoanalysis
A therapeutic method developed by Sigmund Freud, in which the patient and analyst attempt to bring unconscious material into awareness and deal with internal conflicts usually rooted in childhood.

Free Association
A therapeutic method used by classical psychoanalysts in which a person says whatever comes to mind with as little editing as possible.

What he or she says cannot help but be greatly influenced by unconscious forces, which slowly reveal themselves. The analysand is encouraged to relate dreams, which, of course, are created outside of consciousness.

Psychoanalysts are less active than other therapists. They do not give patients advice; they do not disclose information about themselves; they do not interact with clients in any usual way. Often they wait silently for the meaningful material to emerge. Sometimes they ask questions, stress the importance of some material, and interpret behavior in terms of material that is just beginning to become conscious. Most important, they examine and attempt to dissolve the various forms of **resistance** that patients exhibit when revelations become painful. For example, a patient may resist mentioning her mother while free associating, even when there are obvious logical or natural connections. The analyst would then focus on what is *unsaid*: hidden or repeatedly "edited out" of the client's associations.

Resistance
In psychoanalysis, the client's efforts to avoid painful revelations that are beginning to enter consciousness.

Transference is especially dramatic in psychoanalysis. Often it reaches such an intensity that it is described as "transference neurosis." In other words, the relationship with the analyst has dramatically reproduced the original disturbed relationship with the parent or other significant figure. The patient struggles with the analyst to achieve frustrated childhood desires. In the analysis these desires are recognized and worked with. The treatment is not completed until the transference is resolved, and the patient truly sees the therapist as another person, with limits as to power and excellence.

In classic psychoanalysis, the patient reclines on a couch, with his or her back to the analyst. This arrangement is thought to facilitate free association. (The patient is not distracted by the analyst's facial expressions, and he or she can readily project imagined emotions and characteristics onto the analyst, as onto a blank screen.) Sessions ideally take place three to five times a week, usually for at least three to five years. Obviously psychoanalysis is a time-consuming, expensive, and sometimes painful procedure. On the other hand, it offers the patient the possibility of knowing himself thoroughly, and with that knowledge transforming or reconstructing his personality.

Psychoanalytically Oriented/Psychodynamic Therapy

Of the many people who are in therapy, few are engaged in what we have just described, a classic psychoanalysis. Most cannot afford the time, money, and long-term commitment that such treatment requires. Moreover, relatively few therapists undergo the long training necessary to practice psychoanalysis. Perhaps most important is the fact that few people enter therapy with the long-range goal of reconstructing their personalities. Most seek immediate relief from emotional distress, which psychoanalysis cannot offer.

Many therapists who share Freud's goals and have the same understanding of personality structure and development perform treatment within a modified context that does not require so much time and expense. Patient and therapist meet once or twice a week. They sit face to face while the client talks about everyday events and feelings, as well as about dreams and childhood experiences. Using this material, they explore the unconscious.

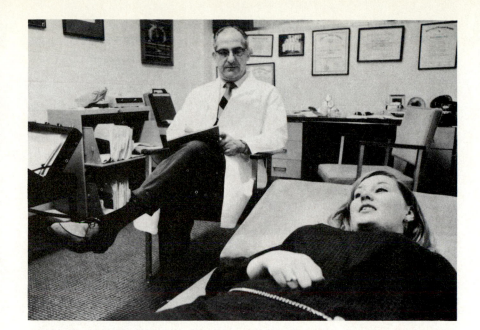

This patient in analysis may be describing childhood experiences, dreams, or other concerns.

Many psychoanalytically oriented therapists are neo-Freudians, who emphasize interpersonal relations and conscious experience (over the unconscious ones), and social and cultural factors (over instinctual ones). Even so, these therapists accept many of Freud's ideas: they emphasize the presence of inner conflict, the importance of childhood experience, and the usefulness of verbal methods in analyzing current experience to determine underlying forces in the personality (Kovel, 1976).

In the therapy conducted by neo-Freudians, the interaction between patient and therapist is of central concern. The therapist intervenes more often, directing the therapy and sometimes giving advice. Attention is given to the patient's life, to self-esteem, and to the attainment of immediate goals. It is adapted more to the solution of acute and temporary problems than to full-fledged definition of underlying conflicts. "The techniques and strategies of living—what might be called our adaptation to the world and the feelings of self-evaluation connected with adaptation—become the centerpiece of what is altered" (Kovel, 1976).

Existential-Humanist Approaches to Therapy

Rollo May, who brought existential therapy to the United States, wrote that existential therapy "is not a system of therapy, but an attitude toward therapy; not a set of new techniques, but a concern with the understanding of the structure of the human being and his experience that must underlie all techniques" (May, 1961).

Existential and humanist therapies do not systematically investigate the unconscious. Instead, they are concerned with values, having developed them from a number of sources like Freud, European existentialists, and American pragmatism. And they are concerned with growth and health, as opposed to illness and cure. Therapists call the people they work with "clients," not "patients" as the psychoanalysts often do. In the therapeutic relationship, clients are treated as partners rather than as objects of treatment. Therapists consistently communicate positive feelings for their clients—for what they are and can be (even if not for what they do at the moment). This attitude, called **unconditional positive regard** by Carl Rogers, is the essential and health-giving element in the relationship (Rogers, 1951). Existential and humanist therapists convey the underlying conviction that all people are essentially good, worthy of respect, and capable of growth.

In practice, these therapists deal with their clients' immediate experiences. Instead of analyzing the personality to determine its conflicting parts, as do Freudian therapists, they encourage clients to experience their wholeness. Clients are helped to achieve their potential, to become more fully who they are. They are encouraged to accept all their experiences and feelings as belonging to themselves. In some cases the therapist will encourage the client to deliberately broaden his experiences. However, clients themselves make decisions about the meaning that their lives have for them.

According to some existential and humanist psychologists, the qualities of the therapist are more important than any particular techniques. Carl Rogers, for example, finds that therapists must be open, honest, and undefensive with clients. They must communicate what they feel, and what they feel must be respect and liking. Therapists must sincerely experience unconditional positive regard for the client, as well as "empathic understanding" for the client's feelings. It is the relationship with the therapist that enables a client to overcome doubts and self-hatred, and consequently to grow as a person. Often the period of therapy is a year or less, with sessions once a week.

Gestalt Therapy

Gestalt therapy is a form of existential-humanist therapy. Introduced in the early 1950s by Frederic Perls, gestalt therapy is important in its own right and also because many of its diverse methods have been borrowed by other forms of therapy.

The German word "gestalt" means shape or totality. Perls believed that people go through life with gestalts that are not completed and this lack of closure affects how they feel and behave. He wrote, "Let's say if you had a fight, you really got angry at that guy, and you want to take revenge. This need for revenge will nag and nag until you have become even with him" (Perls 1973, p. 119).

In therapy, Perls concentrated on clients' awareness in the here-and-now and their taking responsibility for their feelings, thoughts, and actions. The gestalt therapist expects that through awareness of personal experience at the moment and acknowledging responsibility for it, the client can begin to get

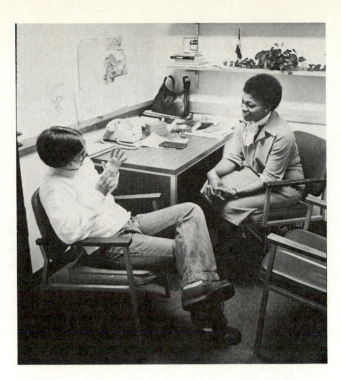

feelings of closure. That happens when a college student says, "I must admit now that I'm the one who provokes fights with my parents whenever I go home. I always blamed them. I don't like to admit it, but it's so." Clients become aware of desires and feelings that they have disowned but are very much a part of them: "Yes, I act like I'm very shy but underneath it all I *do* want to be the center of attention." They also find they are trying to live by values they borrowed or felt they had to adopt from others, instead of their own (Nietzel & Bernstein, 1987).

The gestalt therapist's attention to nonverbal behavior, as in the following excerpt, shows how the client is made aware of parts of the self in the here-and-now that have been hidden.

Therapist: How are you feeling?
Patient: I'm calm; I feel good.
Therapist: Are you really?
Patient: Oh, yes.
Therapist: Why are you sitting so stiff, like a ramrod?
Patient: I'm not!
Therapist: Check yourself. See your legs, feel your back against the chair.
Patient: I see what you mean.
Therapist: Let the stiffness talk. What is it telling you?
Patient: I'm afraid to let go. I feel like I'm trying to control myself (Phares, 1988, p. 420).

The therapist's observations about the patient's behavior allowed the two of them to get down to the really important feelings in the here-and-now.

Gestalt therapy has a diversity of methods and points of view, so that it is not easy to pin it down. "Gestalt therapists do not agree among themselves, and at times they even seem to revel in their lack of agreement" (Phares, 1988, pp. 418–419). However, they do agree on focusing on the present and on client responsibility.

Behavior Therapy

A high school class attempted to alter the behavior of their teacher. They agreed to look interested and to respond to his questions when he was on the side of the room near the door, and to look bored and talk among themselves when he was distant from the door. Little by little, they hoped to get him to the door and out of it. What the students attempted, a form of behavior modification, was based on their understanding of the ideas of behavioral psychologists and therapists.

Behavior Therapy
A form of therapy in which, through relearning, a client acquires new behaviors or responses and eliminates old ones.

In the broadest terms, **behavior therapy** is relearning: A new response or conduct is acquired, and an old one is eliminated. The students attempted to teach their teacher not to teach them. The point must be made that the behavioral therapist does not engage in subterfuge like that and usually uses relearning techniques to help clients achieve *their* goals, not the therapists.

In the first step of behavior therapy, the problem to work on is identified. A means by which progress can be gauged is then formulated. In the case above, the teacher's distance from the door provided such a gauge. Then an appropriate technique is used to associate a desired behavior with gratification (the reward of the students' attention) or, in another type of approach, to break a person's association between an object or experience and the fear that it engenders.

Behavior therapy emphasizes the removal of symptoms, which are seen not as evidence of illness, but as examples of maladaptive or undesired behavior. Behavior therapists do not address what others call "the whole person." They concentrate on symptoms alone. (Thus, John is not "ill"; he has a drinking problem that can be described objectively.) The inner experience of the individual is not attended to, except when it can be manipulated and reported. In most cases the therapist is directive—that is, he or she tells the client what to do in order to eliminate the undesirable behavior, and what the rewards for doing so will be.

Systematic Desensitization
A behavioral technique for treating phobias, in which the client is increasingly exposed to the feared object or situation under conditions that defuse anxiety.

Systematic desensitization is one of the most widely used behavior therapy techniques. It is used to reduce learned anxiety, as in the case of phobias like claustrophobia (dread of being in a closed room), or similar strong reactions to any one of a countless number of aversive objects including animals, noise, dirt, men, women, and so forth. The therapist elicits a response from the client that is incompatible with the anxiety. Joseph Wolpe (1982), who first described systematic desensitization, selected three types of anxiety inhibitors: deep muscle relaxation (the most widely used one), interpersonal assertiveness (used especially in connection with interpersonal anxiety), and sexual arousal (used when anxiety interferes with sexual activity).

Before desensitization treatment begins, the client, assisted by the therapist, prepares a hierarchical list of events that make him anxious and trains him in progressive relaxation to learn how to achieve deep muscle relaxation. In this training, the client tenses each of 16 sets of muscles for a few seconds and then releases them while focusing on the feelings of relaxation experienced after the release. In other words, the therapist gets the client to feel tense and then to feel relaxed and, in time, to gain control over that process. When the client reaches that level of control, the therapist introduces an anxiety-arousing stimulus in a gradual hierarchy, starting with the least anxious to the most. Anxiety is defused by having the client use the relaxation technique whenever necessary. The anxiety-arousing stimuli that have been set up in a hierarchy may be "imaginal," in which case the client visualizes them when they are called for by the therapist. When the client can tolerate scenes in imagination without anxiety, he or she is directed to seek out counterparts in the real world.

Applying the method to a concrete case, a man who becomes extremely anxious when trying to have sexual relationships with a woman will be introduced to sexual experiences that at first do not provoke a high level of anxiety. He may first imagine factual material on female sexual organs. Then he may be directed to visually examine his partner and himself in a leisurely way, massaging his partner, sleeping with her *without* having intercourse, and so on. Each exposure is potentially more threatening; in each case anxiety is overcome with the support of the therapist. Eventually, the sexuality of his female partner loses its capacity to make him anxious. Desensitization is sometimes called counterconditioning, because it disrupts the association between the object and the anxiety that was the result of past conditioning.

Another behavioral technique is **aversion therapy,** in which the therapist administers an aversive stimulus (or punishment) to inhibit an unwanted emotional response, thereby breaking an undesired habit (Wolpe, 1982). Best known is the treatment of alcoholism in which a substance is administered that produces nausea when the patient takes a drink. The punishment, the nausea, is experienced only when the undesired behavior, the drinking, occurs. In another aversion therapy an older child who habitually wets his bed is awakened by a mild electric shock or some other aversive stimulus as he wets the bed. Eventually the child learns to avoid the shock by awakening before he needs to empty his bladder.

Perhaps the most systematic approach to changing behavior is the **token economy** (Ayllon & Azrin, 1968). This technique, based on the principles of operant conditioning, seeks to change the behaviors of people who live in a controlled environment, such as a psychiatric hospital. Quite simply and mechanically, tokens are given to patients when they perform "target behaviors." For example, a patient may receive a token for bathing at a designated time, or for participating in an exercise class twice a day. Tokens can be saved up and used to purchase passes, cigarettes, special foods, and so forth. Although the use of token economies is controversial, such programs have been as successful as, if not more successful than, other therapy programs in similar environments.

Aversion Therapy
A behavioral treatment approach, designed to break an undesirable habit, in which a punishment is administered to inhibit the person's usual response.

Token Economy
A behavioral approach in which people who live in a controlled environment are given tokens when they perform target (desired) behaviors.

In some homes and schools, a token economy system is employed. Poker chips, gold stars, or other currencies are earned by desirable behavior and can be spent to purchase "rewards."

Self-Directed Change
A behavioral technique in which a person identifies behaviors he or she wishes to acquire or eliminate and then carries out a plan for change.

Contingency Management
In behavior therapy, a technique that seeks to control behavior by manipulating its consequences.

Biofeedback Training
Through the use of electronic equipment, individuals can observe certain on-going changes in their physiological functioning. They can learn to use this information to reduce tension and relax.

At the opposite extreme, the behavioral approach can also be used to achieve **self-directed change.** An individual can devise a program to acquire new target behaviors of his or her own choosing, or to gradually overcome a fear or bad habit. For example, a student might be able to overcome a fear of speaking in class by first answering easy questions in a small class, and by gradually speaking about more difficult matters in larger, more threatening situations. Self-directed change usually requires that a person take great care in identifying his or her target (desired) behaviors, work out a plan for acquiring the new responses, and monitor it closely to see if it works.

Today behavioral techniques are used in many different contexts including relaxation therapy, assertiveness training, sex therapy, and programmed instruction. Behavioral techniques are also sometimes incorporated in nonbehavioral therapy. For example, when a therapist praises a client for displaying some sign of growth, the praise can be viewed as reinforcement. Behavioral therapy has also been applied to one of the major health and social problems, alcohol and drug abuse. Although the studies assessing its effectiveness have, for the most part, not been adequate to give conclusive evidence, the results thus far show that many of the behavioral treatment interventions are promising (Childress, McLellan, & O'Brien, 1985).

Biofeedback

Contingency management is a behavior therapy technique that seeks to control behavior by manipulating its consequences. **Biofeedback training** can be understood as "a unique version of contingency management" (Nietzel & Bernstein, 1987, p. 271) and as a type of behavior therapy.

Biofeedback is an important addition to the approaches available to the therapist. While it can be used independently of any other form of treatment, in general this physiological approach is combined with "talking therapy." How

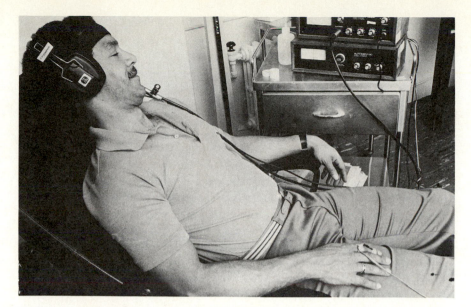

This client sought biofeedback to help him learn to be more sensitive to his body's own messages.

does it work? Through rather sophisticated electronic equipment, the individual gets feedback about her physiological functioning. For example, a galvanic skin response device may be attached to her fingertips, and the more her sweat glands open, the louder is the sound of a buzzer. The *feedback* that she gets about her biological functioning tells her how anxious or tense she is at the moment. Her task, with the help of her therapist, is to reduce the pitch of the sound, which means her anxiety or tension has been reduced, and the sweat glands in her fingertips are more closed than they were initially. She uses some mental or physical strategy to reduce tension and to relax, maybe visualizing a restful country or seaside scene.

Biofeedback can provide a person with information about other biological conditions, including blood pressure, heart rate, muscle tension, and brain wave activity. Such information can enable the person to assume greater responsibility in maintaining his own health. In fact, as Fuller-von Bozzay (1986) says, "the underlying philosophy of biofeedback involves returning responsibility to the individual" (p. 295) rather than having it rest with the physician to cure illness through such interventions as drugs and surgery. Through it people come to appreciate the close relationship between their psychological state (e.g., emotional responses, interpersonal relations, or environmental pressures) and their physiological state (e.g., blood pressure, back pains, or migraine headaches).

Favorable results in the use of biofeedback show it to be a very promising approach (Fuller-von Bozzay, 1986; Wentworth-Rohr, 1984). It has reduced the effects of several psychosomatic problems such as essential hypertension (high blood pressure), Reynaud's disease (a problem of reduced blood flow that can lead to gangrene in hands or feet), and tension headaches. There have been encouraging results in treating insomnia, seizures, and neuromuscular disorders (Phares, 1988). In the treatment of mental disorders its use thus far appears to be limited. Nonetheless, biofeedback has been helpful in modifying physiological responses in highly anxious patients, and it has helped some suffering from schizophrenia and anxiety disorders to achieve physical and mental relaxation. While biofeedback is not the primary treatment procedure for mental disorders, the evidence shows it to be a useful adjunct (Futterman & Shapiro, 1986).

Cognitive-Behavior Therapy

Cognitive-Behavior Therapy
A form of therapy based on the idea that emotional problems are the result of faulty cognition. The client is encouraged to identify and test his or her negative assumptions.

Cognitive-behavior therapy rests on the assumption that an individual's emotions and behavior are largely determined by the way he structures the world. That is, they are determined by the perceptions and thoughts (the "cognitions") with which he formulates his experiences. For example, a person may be disturbed because he thinks he is an object of disgust, or because he assumes that unless he does everything perfectly he is a failure. The therapist works with the patient to identify his faulty assumptions and to help him test these assumptions in a systematic way. For example, if a patient believes that everyone he meets turns away from him in disgust, the therapist might help him set up a system for judging other people's reactions by making objective assessments of people's facial expressions and bodily movements in his presence (Beck et al., 1979).

Cognitive therapy is regarded as an independent form of therapy and described very much as we have described cognitive-behavior therapy. However, we use only the combined form because cognitive therapists tend to use behavior concepts as well as cognitive ones. The therapy they practice is very much like that of cognitive-behavior therapists. The differences even between "pure" behavior therapists and cognitive-behavior therapists are beginning to narrow. This is apparent when a world renowned British behavior therapist, H. J. Eysenck (1987) insists that behavior therapists are interested in more than just behavior, that they are interested also in patients' beliefs, attitudes, and thoughts.

Cognitive-behavior therapy, like behavior therapy, is used to treat phobias. The emphasis is on the thoughts of the client, as in the following case. A young woman overwrought with anxiety when a dog appears is helped by having her specify what exactly it is that she fears. Her thoughts turn out to be about being bitten and chewed up—something really calamitous. She is helped to realize how unlikely such an occurrence is, and that even if she were bitten it would not be the end of the world.

The versatility of cognitive-behavior therapy is evident in the fact that it has been found to be effective with patients suffering from depression (Kovacs et al., 1981; Murphy et al., 1984). The therapist finds that because of the dominance of certain cognitive patterns, depressed patients regard themselves, their experiences, and their futures in a negative way (Beck, 1979). The goal of therapy is to help patients recognize, test out, and correct those destructive beliefs about themselves.

Rational emotive therapy, known as RET, is recognized as a form of cognitive-behavior therapy, although it was formulated by Albert Ellis in 1955, long before cognitive-behavior therapy came upon the scene. His dissatisfaction with psychoanalysis, in which he had been trained and practiced, led him to search for a more effective form of treatment.

According to the theory of RET, virtually all people, no matter how intelligent, are sometimes irrational. Their irrationality shows up under the following circumstances: They make demands on themselves (I must always be the best), on others (people will flock around me at parties), or the world (career opportunities I want will always be available). When the demands are not met—and those usually cannot always be met—they put themselves down. These put-downs are like the following: I'm incompetent . . . irresponsible . . . bad . . . not worth much (Ellis & Dryden, 1987). Fortunately, people have the capacity to change their irrational thinking, and the methods of RET are used for that purpose.

RET is an active, educational type of therapy in which the therapist, who directs the course of the session, is alert to such self-demanding words as "should" or "ought." Clients who seek help to overcome severe anxiety in social situations may say, "I felt like a fool. I should have said something very clever." The therapist will help this person recognize the underlying irrational beliefs about "top performance" that are creating the anxiety. The aim of RET is for clients to recognize these beliefs as destructive and to replace them with effective coping beliefs—"I would like to be clever in conversations, but nothing says I must." Another aim of RET is for clients to be able, on their own, to recognize and replace their irrational beliefs so that they may become their own RET therapists.

Bridging the Therapies

We have presented separate sections on each of the various forms of therapy in order to convey their unique character. This approach may give the impression that each therapy is "pure" in the sense that it is distinctly different from all others. The fact is that a considerable amount of cross-fertilization has occurred so that many behavioral therapists no longer restrict themselves to observable and measurable behavior but are attuned as well to the client's cognitions, such as thoughts about themselves and others. Cognitive therapists are not at all indifferent to the client's behavior. Even the psychodynamic therapies are not immune to influence by other points of view (Wachtel, 1982). There is, in other words, almost a sibling relationship between therapies.

Currently, scholars on the subject are debating issues about bridging therapies. The debate is not whether, for example, behavior and cognitive therapies have something to offer those who are dynamically oriented, but rather to what degree the various therapies can draw on each other and still retain an identifiable therapeutic approach (Messer & Winokur, 1980; Messer, 1986).

Eclectic Therapy

As the dictionary definition of eclectic suggests, **eclectic therapy** borrows freely from others. Eclectic therapy is now widely used. In the opening chapter of a handbook on eclectic therapy, Norcross (1986) explained that eclecticism has come into its own as a clear area of interest since about 1960. This has happened because therapists whom he called "adventuresome" began to use therapeutic strategies regardless what theory or school of therapy these strategies were associated with. They began to do what their experience was dictating to them: No one theory or set of methods was appropriate for all kinds of problems.

An eclectic therapist uses a variety of techniques (e.g., drawing from behavioral, cognitive, humanistic, and psychoanalytic approaches) to suit the needs of a particular client. Such therapists have integrated their own conception about practice, drawing freely from ideas and techniques identified with old and new therapy orientations. Arnold Lazarus, an early behaviorist, now argues that every therapeutic technique that might help the client should be used. He makes a distinction between two forms of eclecticism: theoretical, in which different theoretical ideas are mixed in unsystematic ways, and technical, in which techniques that are found to work are adopted no matter with what therapy approach they are identified.

A technically eclectic approach developed by Lazarus, **multimodal therapy,** views clients as people with diverse needs and problems, who must be assessed within several different frameworks (or "modalities") before an individualized treatment plan can be developed. In treatment, the multimodal therapist uses a variety of techniques, including assertiveness training, cognitive restructuring, relaxation training, and drug and physical therapy. Because, as Lazarus maintains, there is no single cause for the client's problem, a comprehensive and eclectic approach will serve him or her best (1981, 1987). The multimodal approach has been applied to group, marriage, family, and sex as well as individual therapy. With varying degrees of success it has been used in connection with a whole range of mental health problems such as obsessive-compulsive behavior, shyness, alcohol abuse, obesity, insomnia, and schizophrenia (Lazarus, 1986).

Other types of therapy, along with brief descriptions, are given in Table 6.1.

Brief Therapy

One of the biggest changes in the mental health field is the availability today of what is known as brief or short-term therapies. In one sense this is not new, because Freud himself did not usually go on for years with his patients. He is said, in fact, to have treated George Mahler, the distinguished composer, during a four-hour walk through the Vienna woods (Trujillo, 1986). However, only with the development of the behavioral, cognitive, and interpersonal therapies, mostly in the 1960s and later, did short-term therapy really become available. More recently, brief psychoanalytically oriented therapy has been introduced and can be expected to be widely used.

The Search for Personal Adjustment

TABLE 6.1 *Some Other Types of Psychotherapies and Growth Experiences*

Therapy	Founder	Approach
Reality therapy	William Glasser	Promotes responsibility and moral behavior by clarifying basic values through an examination of present behavior and future goals. Stresses the development of realistic behavior as a way of overcoming personal problems.
Jungian therapy	Carl Jung	Emphasis is on supportive therapy and practical advice. Stresses a warm, positive relationship with the therapist, and imaginative discussion of dream content as a vehicle for exploring the unconscious.
Primal therapy	Arthur Janov	An attempt to reactivate repressed early painful memories, which are viewed as the source of personal conflicts. Through regressive relaxation techniques, and direct confrontations to elicit childhood memories, an intense emotional catharsis (primal scream) is achieved.
Transactional analysis (TA)	Eric Berne	Examines and analyzes transactions between people according to one of three ego states: parent, adult, or child. Attempts to make people aware of the roles and games they play and, through confrontation, tries to promote rational and appropriate adult patterns of communication.
Psychodrama	J. L. Moreno	A type of group therapy that emphasizes role playing in which other group members assist in enacting problem situations. Emotional catharsis, feedback, and group discussion follow spontaneous dramatization. The therapy attempts to enhance self-awareness and improve interpersonal relations.
Bioenergetics	Alexander Lowen	Regards conflicts as a disruption of the natural functioning of the body. Tries to release emotional blockages through exercise, physical manipulation, and emotional expression.

Source: Adapted from (1) E. Ogg, *The Psychotherapies Today.* New York: Public Affairs Pamphlets, August 1981; (2) J. Kovel, *A Complete Guide to Psychotherapy.* New York: Pantheon (1976).

The interest in short-term therapy is not accidental. Changes in our country brought it about. The public wants and needs therapeutic services; many people cannot afford long-term treatment; agencies that help pay for such services, such as the federal government through Medicaid or Medicare, and insurance companies, want to limit costs; finally, the brief therapies have been found to be effective. Trujillo (1986), referring to some myths about the short-term therapies, says it is not limited to a narrow range of patients and problems.

According to Phares (1988) there are now several hundred types of brief therapy. Because that variety may appear to make the choice of a therapist very formidable, we do want to point out that most of the several hundred fall within one or another of the broad categories of therapies already discussed. They are crisis oriented, existential-humanist, behavioral, cognitive-behavioral, or eclectic. Most surprising, many come from the psychoanalytic tradition known for its long-term treatment. Therapists with that orientation are discovering that they can be highly active and introduce, even in the first session, some concepts, like transference, that would not ordinarily come up for weeks or months (Goldin & Winston, 1985).

Perhaps, as Phares said, brief psychotherapy is a state of mind. Both client and therapist know it will be short-term and they think and work accordingly. This condition is likely to encourage technical eclecticism, as Lazarus (1987) calls it, so that therapists will retain their basic orientation (e.g., psychodynamic or behavioral) but draw upon any helpful techniques. And, as Gustafson (1986) suggests, therapists will be encouraged to look at human problems from all the different therapeutic perspectives. Any method, he points out, is workable in some situation, that is, with some patients, but none is workable with all.

Family Therapy

Although therapists in many traditions attempt to discover how parents and other family members affect a client's adjustment, most are restricted to their client's indirect reports. Family therapists, however, work *directly* with the whole family. They deal not with the problem of any one family member, but with problems as they affect the family system. In a relatively short time the therapist attempts to establish more satisfying ways for family members to relate among themselves and to the outside world.

The theory underlying **family therapy** is that the problem or illness of a family member, especially that of a child, has adaptive value within the family system. In other words, it plays a part in maintaining the interrelations within the family. If there is a "sick" wife, there may be a husband whose special role is caring for and putting up with her. If there is a "crazy" child, there are also parents who need his or her illness to distract them from their own problems, to draw them closer together in their concern, or even to give them an issue to argue about that is symbolic of their own conflicts. For example, children who soil themselves past toddlerhood are sometimes expressing parental disagreements or inconsistencies about the allowability of messy or "dirty" (sexual) behavior (Mainprice, 1974).

In such cases the underlying problem is not really solved by treating the person whom the family identifies as the "sick" member. For, if this person succeeds in overcoming illness, the equilibrium of the family, its homeostasis, is destroyed, and a more pervasive disturbance may appear. For example, if the "sick" wife recovers from her migraine headaches, the long-suffering husband is confronted with the opportunity to resume sexual relationships, whereupon a conflict-ridden area of the marriage comes to the surface. If the "sick" child becomes well, parents may be forced to look at their own long-buried conflicts rather than at the child, and may quarrel and separate. Consequently, parents, child, and other family members tend to resist change. They hold onto their usual ways of behaving—bemoaning the child's or spouse's problem, but acting in ways that make it necessary for that problem to exist.

The Search for Personal Adjustment

To the family therapist, it is the family, and not the identified client, that is "sick." The individual who is brought in with symptoms is only an emblem of the family's disorder. The problem identified with a family member is understood by the therapist as part of the interactions this person has with other family members. Family therapists see a symptom like "depression" or "phobia" as a contract between family members that helps sustain them (Haley, 1987). A particular family member's tendency to be "blue" or highly fearful is the glue that keeps the family together. Therefore, although the family may enter therapy solely because of the problems of a single member, the therapist meets with the entire family. He or she determines how the initial problem or illness is connected to the network of family relationships by learning family rules and culture, the ways in which family members react to outsiders, the coalitions that exist among members, and the ways in which members interact.

The therapist discusses and monitors the communications within the family and moderates conflicts among members without taking sides. Sometimes he or she manipulates the system to create disturbances to which all family members will react. Intervening in the midst of the reaction, the therapist gets them to "change the rules," to discard old patterns of behavior for new. For example, if the mother continually offers herself as an "expert" on the child's problem, the therapist may turn to the father and ask him to explain things. If the parents seem to have focused their marital life entirely on the child's problem the therapist may point to progress in him, commend the parents, and suggest that they give themselves an evening or weekend alone as a reward (Haley, 1976). The family is made to relate in new ways and confront hidden as well as overt problems.

As we can see in these examples, family therapy is directive; that is, the therapist is more active than passive. Like many other forms of therapy, it fosters increased knowledge of the individual's real feelings. However, the primary emphasis is not so much on beliefs and feelings as on behavior, especially communication. The family therapist focuses on the way the family members "negotiate" with each other to obtain their goals instead of on the abstractions that are dear to the family (being caring parents, having a smooth marriage). Family therapy uses one-way mirrors, videotaping, role-playing, and other techniques to vividly portray to family members how they behave and what behaviors need to be changed. In some cases co-therapists (male-female) are used to provide role models for the parents.

Many of the methods used by family therapists are similar to those in individual therapy. For example, "positive reframing" may be employed to help parents see their child in a more positive and constructive way, so that a "noncompliant" son is presented as one who is "deficient in attending skills," but who could learn them (L'Abate, Ganahl, & Hansen, 1986, p. 60). Other methods of family therapy include the use of written contracts (e.g., the 15-year-old daughter promises to do the chores and her homework and respect the curfew hours, and her parents promise to increase her allowance and extend

curfew times); and training in clear and direct communication skills (e.g., instead of hiding wishes in a question—"Would you like to go out to a movie tonight?"—Family members are taught to be forthright about wants—"I would like to go to a movie tonight") (L'Abate et al., 1986).

When we think about our personal lives we become aware of the influence a grandparent, uncle, aunt, or cousin has had in our own family, maybe on our own life. This fact has led family therapists to extend their thinking and even their methods. Some therapists will arrange to bring together a large portion of the extended family, at least for a single session. More typically, therapists bring them into the sessions in nonphysical ways, for example by developing a "genogram." A genogram is "a format for drawing a family tree that records information about family members and their relationships over at least three generations" (McGoldrick & Gerson, 1985, p. 1). The genogram is then used extensively in therapy to help point out such significant troublesome relationships as a three-generation triangle in which a grandparent and grandchild are allied against the parents. The family in therapy can then work at understanding why this triangle has developed and how to go about changing it, to the benefit of all concerned.

Family therapy has been used with families in which one member is schizophrenic. There is little evidence that family interactions are a causal factor in the development of this disease. However, there is enough evidence from several controlled studies to suggest that such families are different in some respects from other families, that those differences may have an effect on the course of the illness, and that intervention may be helpful. A recent review of work in this field reports that family therapy, combined with drug therapy, appears to reduce the likelihood of relapse in some schizophrenics, at least in the year following hospital discharge (Waring, Carver, Moran, & Lefcoe, 1986).

Marital Therapy

Marital or **couples therapy** is sometimes considered a field within family therapy. As with family therapy, the marital therapist concentrates on relationship issues, that is, problems between the people rather than those of one individual or the other.

The issues confronted in marital therapy are "give-and-take" issues. They include power, level of intimacy, and inclusion (who else is heavily involved with the couple—parents, friends?) (Berman & Lief, 1975). Conflicts result when partners desire incompatible levels of these variables. For example, many marital conflicts in recent years have involved the need of women to assert themselves and wield more power in their marriage, and the incompatible need of their husband to maintain the male-dominant status quo. Complications occur as partners send out ambiguous and misleading messages about their needs. A husband, threatened by his wife's desire for more independence, may act to sabotage her attempts, even while he intellectually and verbally approves them. In marital therapy, the therapist attempts to clarify what each partner wants and to discover what behaviors must be changed if both are to be satisfied. When hostility occurs, the therapist tries to focus it on real and not imagined issues.

Marital therapy can take place in a variety of settings. In *collaborative therapy* partners are seen by separate therapists, who discuss the couple between themselves. In *concurrent therapy* both partners are seen individually by the same therapist. In *conjoint therapy* (the most frequent couples therapy) the partners are seen together by one or more therapists, and the focus, as in family therapy, is squarely on the relationship.

Couples therapists are handicapped by the fact that there is no comprehensive theory that explains what makes good or poor marriages (Sager, 1986). This makes diagnosis and prediction difficult and not very reliable. One experienced couples therapist, who works as co-therapist with his wife, said that by now, after a few sessions, the two of them should be able to predict which couples would make successful use of therapy and make a go of it together. Instead, their predictions turned out to be poor, so that couples that looked hopeless ended up with vital marriages, and those that looked like sure bets got nowhere (Framo, 1986). Despite this handicap marital therapy seems to be effective, at least if maintaining a marriage is an acceptable criterion of its effectiveness.

In one study of couples five years after completing conjoint therapy, 56.4 percent were still married, and 76 percent of them said the outcomes of the therapy were either good or moderate (Cookerly, 1980). For the real meaning of these results one would need to compare the percentage still married with that of comparable couples that did not avail themselves of therapy. The impression is that the result would still be favorable. More conclusive results come from a controlled study that found the following difference between those couples that had therapy and the control couples that did not: The treated couples (eight sessions for each) showed significant gains over the controls on such measures as marital adjustment, reduction of the target complaints about

Marital Therapy
A form of therapy in which problems in the spousal relationship are investigated.

their marriage, and increased level of intimacy (Johnson & Greenberg, 1985). Together, these studies and others reported in the *Handbook of Marital Intervention* (L'Abate & McHenry, 1983) show the value and promise of couples therapy and the need for further research.

Group Therapy

When Barbara's mother was suddenly widowed at the age of 52, she began to show uncharacteristic symptoms of emotional disturbance. Her self-esteem was shattered. She felt that her friends no longer valued her for herself. Even several months after her husband's death, she refused to get together with married friends, claiming she would be "a fifth wheel."

Probably the most disturbing development, from Barbara's viewpoint, was that she, Barbara, was put in the position of having to advise and even nag her mother. Surely her mother knew how and when to balance the checkbook. And hadn't she always paid the bills on time? Why not now? Barbara finally lost patience when she discovered that her mother had let her regular doctor's appointment lapse and declared herself no longer interested in monitoring her slightly elevated blood pressure.

At about this time Barbara heard about a new group that was forming at a downtown church. The group was for the recently widowed and was led by a psychologist who was a widower. Barbara's mother offered many reasons for not going. She didn't want to meet a lot of depressed people. She especially didn't want anyone to think that she was interested in meeting men. Most of the people would be older. To her exasperation Barbara found herself arguing reasonably, as her mother used to do with her, and with the inevitable result. Her mother agreed half-heartedly to attend the group just to prove it was "all wrong" for her.

Initially, it was. Barbara's mother was uncomfortable. But she soon discovered that others who attended were uncomfortable for many of the same reasons. She also discovered that the feelings of guilt she had been having, which had incapacitated her, were by no means unique. Even women whose husbands had been much older and in poor health blamed themselves for not doing more. And they blamed themselves, as she did, for feeling angry at the departed spouse, and at everyone who tried so hard to help. Naturally, after the meeting Barbara pumped her mother for information on what the group was like, and at first her mother seemed eager to tell her. In fact they talked half the night.

After the second session, however, Barbara's mother cut short the discussion with the remark that "one of the things we *all* agree on is that it is not fair to burden our children. Besides," she added, "you need more sleep, if you are going to spend all your weekends and evenings out, and get up early, and. . . ."

"Etc., etc.," said Barbara wearily, but a little gratefully for once.

Barbara's mother (and Barbara) benefited from this developmental task group designed to help people cope with a normal life crisis. Developmental task groups are one of many forms of group therapy that are available to help people through emergencies, or to treat them for emotional problems.

Group therapy acknowledges that through social interactions people become emotionally disturbed or ill, and holds that through group action they can be helped to overcome their disturbances. Group therapy views people "not from the vantage of their individual subjectivities, but within a system of relationships with others" (Kovel, 1976, p. 163). The group is a cohesive unit of "intimate strangers" who provide hope, support, and feedback for each other. While helping each other, group members help themselves.

Group Therapy
Therapy conducted in a group setting, with the purpose of providing members with hope, support, improved socialization techniques, and other benefits.

Psychodynamic and Other Group Therapies

Group therapy arose when psychoanalytically oriented therapists adapted techniques from their one-to-one therapy to group work. Some clients were referred to group therapy only; others met with the therapist individually and in a group, where the therapy dealt more directly with such matters as peer relationships, interaction with authority figures, social isolation, and the development of social skills.

In a group, members provide for each other many of the supports that a therapist provides for the client seen individually (Yalom, 1970). Some special supports of group therapy, identified by Yalom, are:

1. *Hope.* The group member learns that other group members have made progress with their problems and sees that they continue to progress during the life of the group. The member feels confidence about the treatment and becomes more hopeful about himself. The therapist strengthens these effects by setting up the group so that members are at different stages in development and treatment, and by calling attention to the improvements that group members are making.

2. *Universality.* Group members see that other people have problems, just as they do. They are not uniquely stricken or miserable. This recognition tends to speed up the progress made upon entering the group.

3. *Support.* Group members receive encouragement and support from one another. For example, members point to the strengths and assets they discover in others. In fact, the group develops the common purpose of supporting its members. By participating on both sides of supporting relationships, members feel less isolated and also more capable.

4. *Corrective recapitulation of the family.* In its composition the group approximates a family: there are siblings (members) and a parent (therapist), or even two parents (if the group is led by a man and a woman therapist). Because the group is protected by its artificiality and separateness from members' everyday lives, family conflicts can be replayed with vividness, but under more favorable conditions. Feelings associated with sibling rivalry and parental authority can be reexperienced, questioned, and examined.

5. *Development of socialization techniques.* For people who do not have many friends, the group provides much-needed interpersonal feedback. Group members find out how other people understand and respond to them. For example, one member will point out that another seems arrogant, or fails to look at people directly. Problems in communication are brought to the fore.

6. *Experimentation with new behavior.* The group experience enables members to try out new behaviors in a safe setting. Someone who has never expressed hostility can do so *and* discover that the rejection he or she anticipates does not necessarily occur. Being able to behave in a new and desired way is often described as a "breakthrough" by the group member. Also important is the opportunity to try out the behaviors of other members who have been closely observed. This helps dissolve rigid patterns of behavior, even when the experimentation is only temporary.

7. *Development of social relationships.* In the group, an isolated person has the chance to engage in friendship, to express and receive affection, and finally to become more trustful of others.

The therapist, in setting up and guiding the group, acts to promote its cohesiveness. The more the group develops a life of its own, the more therapeutic is its effect (Yalom, 1985). Toward this goal the therapist establishes norms ensuring, for example, that everyone has a chance to speak, or that self-disclosure is practiced. Often the therapist comments on the interactions in the group and generally intervenes to prevent disruption or to defend someone who is being made a scapegoat.

What Kind of Group Therapy Would I Choose?

Group psychotherapies are different both in theory and method. One useful way to classify them is by noting what the therapist focuses on. Using that method to classify the group therapies, Thompson and Kahn (1988) presented three types, each of which is explained and illustrated using the example of John.

John, age 21, is in a group set up for college students. During this session, the fifth weekly meeting of the group, he says laughingly, "No one's interested in what I have to say."

In the first type of group therapy John's statement is considered to be the result of what is going on inside him. The activity taking place at the *intrapersonal* level is the most relevant. The group therapist will work with John directly, trying to elicit whatever it is in him from the past that leads him to belittle his own ideas. The role of the other group members is mainly to give John support, maybe by sharing similar feelings or complimenting him for speaking up about his feeling.

In the second type of group therapy John's statement is considered to be the result of his interactions with one or more persons in the group. The activity taking place at the *interpersonal* level is the most relevant. The therapist and group members will encourage John to tell what interactions, and with whom, have led him to feel this way. He will then have the opportunity to hear from group members whom he claims have been unresponsive to him. If his feeling that no one is interested in him is validated, he can learn why that is so (for example, does he tend to turn people off by boasting?). If they are not validated he can learn from others and from himself why he, nevertheless, feels as he does.

In the third type of group therapy John's statement is considered to be the result of all the transactions in the group. The activity taking place at the *intragroup* level is the most relevant. The focus of discussion is on what has occurred in the group to precipitate those feelings in John. Perhaps they will find a tendency for the group to subdivide psychologically into two subgroups with John excluded from both. If that is so, they can examine the reasons for his exclusion.

1. Put yourself in John's position. Which of the three approaches would be most helpful to you:
   *focus on you alone
   *focus on you and one or two group members
   *focus on you and the entire group
   Explain the reasons for your choice.
2. A member of your family plans to join a therapy group and asks your advice. Think of one family member and advise him or her which of the three types you would recommend. Give three reasons for your choice. ▲

Besides the psychoanalytically oriented group therapies, others have been introduced by the various therapeutic schools of thought. Specifically, the cognitive therapists have applied group therapy to the serious problem of depression, and with "reasonably satisfying outcomes" (Beck, Rush, Shaw, & Emery, 1979). So have rational emotive (see Table 6.1 for a brief description) (Ellis & Grieger, 1986) and transactional analysis (see Table 6.1) therapists (Dusay, 1986).

Encounter Groups
Groups formed with the general goal of enriching the lives of the members through personal growth experiences and open expression of here-and-now feelings.

Encounter groups, which flourished in the 1960s, were formed in the spirit of humanist therapy, especially that of Carl Rogers. They are sometimes organized for reasons as specific as reducing racial tensions, overcoming obesity, or promoting harmonious relations among coworkers. However, they have become better known for their more general goal of enriching their participants' lives through personal growth, greater accessibility to personal relationships, and peak experiences. One of the leaders in the field, Schutz (1986), defined the encounter as "a method of human relating based on truth, self-determination, self-awareness, awareness of the body, attention to feelings, and an emphasis on the here and now" (p. 365). An encounter group is therapeutic in the sense that it seeks to remove blocks to improved functioning, and, he adds, it is educational in the sense that it tries to create conditions that lead to optimal use of one's capacities.

Groups typically consist of eight to twenty members. They are limited in time to a small number of sessions or sometimes to a several-day marathon. And they deal almost exclusively with the present. Participants are encouraged to act spontaneously, to confront each other with direct expressions of love, anger, and hostility. Conspicuous are nonverbal techniques such as the "blind walk," in which a seeing member guides another whose eyes are shut; or the touching of the faces and bodies of other participants, with the purpose of conveying feelings of closeness and trust. Other activities are designed to overcome socially induced inhibitions, and to enable people (during sessions at least) to act as they feel: to scream, to hug strangers, and, in some groups, to disrobe.

Obviously, encounter groups are very different from traditional therapy groups. Leaders do not, in some cases, have skills beyond those that members of the group may themselves acquire during the sessions. Most participants do not think of themselves as ill or needing help. Instead they are seeking to become more effective in interpersonal relationships, to enrich their emotional lives, or to have fun (many marathons are held at resorts).

In their heyday, reactions to encounter groups were of two extremes, so that they were either praised or vilified. After a long decline, a renewed interest is evident, particularly in organizations seeking to increase productivity and improve morale (Schutz, 1986).

Developmental Task Groups

Some groups are organized to help people through a life crisis, and members consist of people who are attempting to master the same life task. For example, the group that Barbara's mother attended sought to help people cope with widowhood. Other groups help members learn to raise children, prepare for retirement, deal with a terminal illness, and so forth. In such **developmental task groups,** people share their experiences and feelings, support one another emotionally, and give one another practical advice and assistance. Together they overcome feelings of isolation and hopelessness. There are groups of single

Developmental Task Groups
Groups composed of people who have shared or share a particular life crisis. Members share feelings and offer mutual support and advice.

TABLE 6.2 *Representative Major Psychotherapeutic Drugs*

Therapeutic Use	Generic Name	Brand Name
Antianxiety (minor tranquilizers)	Diazepam	Valium
	Chlordiazepoxide	Librium
Antidepressant	Amitriptyline	Elavil
	Phenelzine	Nardil
Antipsychotic (major tranquilizers)	Chlorpromazine	Thorazine
	Haloperidol	Haldol
Antimanic	Lithium	Eskalith

parents, for example, where members talk about the difficulties they have in trying to raise children and work at the same time or about their loneliness in no longer having another adult with whom to share tasks and experiences. The group members may exchange information about vocational programs and day-care facilities, and even take care of children collectively (Zimet, 1979).

Developmental task groups are a relatively new concept in therapy. They are organized by social agencies, special-interest groups, religious organizations, and so on. They are often short term, although some change and continue as their participants' needs change. Often they have no leaders.

Drug Therapy: Psychopharmacology

Substances of one kind or another have been used to influence mental functioning and behavior in virtually every society in the world, in the past as well as the present. Among others, people have used alcoholic beverages, tobacco, coffee, and marijuana. The scientific study of how drugs relate to mental and emotional experience is known as **psychopharmacology.** In the mid-1950s the development of new drugs, particularly the "tranquilizers," had remarkable positive effects on psychiatric patients, allowing a great many who had been hospitalized to be treated on an out-patient basis. This first breakthrough was followed by new types of drugs (Klerman, 1986).

Psychopharmacology
A field that includes the scientific study of drugs and how they can be used to treat people with mental health disorders.

Drugs can be classified in terms of their chemical composition and in various other ways. For our purposes we have chosen a classification system based on the problems of people for which the drugs are prescribed. The four types—antipsychotic, antidepressant, antimanic, and antianxiety—indicate that they are used respectively to counteract psychotic behavior, depression, manic behavior, and anxiety. Table 6.2, presents each of the four types of drugs, accompanied by examples of generic and trade names of the drugs.

Most of the *psychotropic drugs,* as these are called, are prescribed by the patient's general medical practitioner and not by a psychiatrist. This is understandable when one learns that about 50 percent of the patients who receive antianxiety drugs suffer from some medical illness, and the drugs are given to reduce the emotional consequences of that illness.

Drug therapy for psychological problems has been used on its own and in combination with psychotherapy. The question about the comparative efficiency of drug therapy alone versus psychotherapy alone versus the two in combination is far from answered. Some of the results have even been contradictory. Kendall (1984), after reviewing many studies, concluded that in the treatment of depression the psychotherapies were more effective than the drug therapies. Klerman (1986) found the two to be about equally effective with depressed patients. He also pointed out that the results of studies involving many types of psychological problems are inconclusive. Of course, we would prefer to have some clearcut conclusions. For the present, however, we must recognize that pharmacology has already made great progress in alleviating the very distressing symptoms in the four categories shown in Table 6.2, and look forward to new developments in the future.

CHOOSING A THERAPIST

At some time in life most of us are involved in choosing a therapist for ourselves, our child or family, or in assisting a relative or friend to do so. The following points may be helpful.

1. Define as clearly as possible what you consider to be the problem. Preferably write a very brief description of it for yourself.

2. Obtain the names of three licensed therapists from sources like the following:
   a. state association of psychology, psychiatry, or psychiatric social work
   b. nearby mental health center
   c. university mental health clinic
   d. "satisfied customers" (friends or acquaintances who feel they have been successfully treated by a therapist)

3. Make the first session a trial one. If you are not content with your first choice, arrange to see the second, and if need be, the third on your list until you have a feeling of confidence about therapy.

4. Be sure before the first session is completed that you understand the goal of therapy for you, the plan that will be carried out, the approximate number of sessions and the fee. The therapist may reasonably say he or she needs another session with you to be able to finalize the plan and determine the number of sessions.

5. Bear in mind in making your selection of a therapist that his or her theoretical orientation will have considerable influence on your therapeutic experience. We recapitulate here in capsule form what you might expect from therapy in each major category:

   Psychodynamic: exploration of your unconscious through childhood experience, dreams, and everyday experience.

Existential-humanist: encouragement to be open, accept and take responsibility for your feelings, values, and behavior.

Behavior: "unlearning" your ineffective responses and learning effective ones by a reconditioning process directed by the therapist.

Cognitive or *cognitive-behavior*: exploration of your cognitions to identify and eradicate irrational beliefs and ineffective ways of thinking.

Eclectic: use of any of these in accordance with the therapist's understanding of your problem.

Family: your family, rather than you, is directed to search for the "rules" of behavior that maintain the problems, and to change them.

Group: through your interactions with the group you are helped to recognize maladaptive feelings and behavior and are encouraged to replace them.

6. Be open about your problem both with yourself and the therapist. Remember that the success of therapy and the speed with which it can be completed successfully depends, at least in part, on your behavior. Holding back information from a therapist is comparable to going to a dentist and refusing to indicate which tooth is painful.

7. If you have concerns about how the treatment is working out for you, discuss them frankly and fully with your therapist. It is not wise to make a decision to leave therapy before one has held such a discussion, and not wise to stay on for a lengthy period of time if the dissatisfaction persists after the discussion. Be aware that sometimes the reservations you have may reflect a tendency to avoid some of the personally painful topics that are raised in therapy.

8. The professional state and national associations with which most therapists are affiliated and the state licensing boards maintain regulations and guidelines for professional behavior. For example, all psychologists are expected to observe the American Psychological Association's Ethical Principles For Psychologists, available in a 1981 publication by that name. These guidelines emphasize the high quality performance and conduct expected of a professional. For the most part, therapists succeed in keeping such standards. Unfortunately, there are exceptions. If you should find questionable behavior on the part of your therapist, such as evidences during sessions of the consequences of substance abuse or sexual harassment, you should terminate treatment. It would be helpful if you would also bring the incident to the attention of the appropriate state association ethics committee or to the state licensing board.

9. Think of therapy as a learning experience. If it is really successful, you will be better equipped to cope not only with the particular problems that led you to seek help but with others as well. It will help you not only with today's problems but also with those in the future.

EVALUATING THERAPY

Of the several hundred forms of psychological intervention that have been identified (Herink, 1980), we have focused only on the most prominent. In the effort to help people in need, professionals have introduced various types of art therapy, dance therapy, play therapy, and bibliotherapy, among others. Perhaps less well known is the use of animal therapy. A dog's or cat's companionship represents an adjunct to established methods of psychotherapy, or may actually be the therapeutic agent. In the latter case, the warmth, touch, and loyal companionship of the animal are a source of security and an inducer of relaxation (Levinson, 1984). Undoubtedly, many new forms of therapy will be developed in the future.

How effective is therapy? Numerous studies are undertaken each year. In an earlier review of the research, Bergin concluded that "there remains some modest evidence that psychotherapy works" (1971). While most review studies do not provide definite conclusions, the number that support the effectiveness of therapy is greater than what would be expected by chance. One study involving nearly 475 controlled evaluations found that on the average the typical therapy client is better off after therapy than 80 percent of the individuals who need but do not receive therapy (Smith, Glass, & Miller, 1980). Others have stated that family therapy seems to show the most consistently positive results (Epstein & Vlok, 1981).

If it can be concluded that therapy is likely to help, what form of treatment ought to be chosen? Which, in other words, is most effective?

Studies show that no real conclusions can be drawn beyond stating that the behavior and cognitive methods have been more effective with problems such as phobias, compulsive behavior, and problems like childhood aggression (Lambert, Shapiro, & Bergin, 1986). With other difficulties, in fact, some researchers find that the type of therapy actually matters very little (Smith et al., 1980). What may be more important are the personal qualities of the therapist. If the therapist is warm, experienced, and skillful, this, rather than any particular orientation, will influence outcome (Adams, 1979). Other investigators report that the greatest gains were achieved by those patients who maintained a positive attitude toward the therapist and the work of therapy (Marziali, Marmar, & Krupnick, 1981). It is not surprising, therefore, that meta-analytic studies (that is, the global study of studies) of therapy have failed to detect "appreciable differences between the various therapies in the nature or degree of benefits effected" (Parloff, London, & Wolfe, 1986).

An exception to this rule might be that the behavior and cognitive methods have been more effective with problems such as phobias, compulsive behavior, and problems like childhood aggression (Lambert, Shapiro, & Bergin, 1986).

Two issues of a different sort, important in their own right, are still at an early stage of investigation. These are about the relevance of the sex and race of the therapist to the effectiveness of the therapy. Research on these is complex, as can be seen when we raise the following questions about therapist gender. Are therapists more effective with same sex or opposite sex clients? If they are more effective with one of these, does this apply across all age groups (children, adolescents, young adults, etc.) or only some of them? Does it apply to all client problems (school failure, marital, family, neurosis, psychosis) or only some of them? Does it apply to all types of therapeutic approaches (psychoanalytic, behavioral, etc.) or just some of them? And, since client choice is a variable that cannot be ignored, what are the preferences of clients as to the gender of their therapist? And do those preferences vary by age group, type of problem, etc.?

As you can see, the simple question about the sex of the therapist (and the very same about the race of the therapist) opens up a Pandora's box. No wonder that, after reviewing research studies and clinical writings on the subject, Mogul (1982) concluded that because of the many client, therapist, and therapy variables involved, quantitative studies on the effects of therapist gender have little to offer, and are not likely to be more effective in the future. However, she adds that the sex of the therapist can be important in individual cases, not only because clients have preferences but also because certain problems may be more soluble with a same- or different-gender therapist.

In the 1960s, discussions about the relevance of the race of the therapist referred almost exclusively to how the white therapist related to members of other races. Since then, more therapists from minority groups have been trained. In a review of the literature on the subject, as it applies to black and white therapists and patients, Griffith (1977) found more positive relationships, better rapport, and more self-disclosure when the two are of the same race. That is not a hard and fast conclusion, he added, providing the therapist is knowledgeable about the client's cultural background and is sensitive to conditions that give rise to problems.

Besides the qualities of the therapist and the relationship, another key factor in the outcome of therapy is the condition of the client at the very outset. As in the case of physical health, clients who are in a better state of mental health when they enter therapy are likely to obtain greater benefits from treatment than those who are deeply troubled. "The rich get richer" in therapy as in finance, according to one authority (quoted in Adams, 1979).

Finally psychologists have examined negative outcomes in psychotherapy to find out the extent and the cause of them. By negative outcome they mean a decline in the patient's functioning that appears during therapy and persists for substantial time thereafter (Mays & Franks, 1985). Although those who receive treatment, in general, fared better than those who did not, some patients experienced negative outcomes because of:

Patient characteristics   those with a less firm grip on reality are
    more likely to experience negative outcomes than the general
    patient population;
Therapist characteristics   low levels of therapist genuineness,
    positive regard, and empathy are related to negative outcome;
Extratherapeutic factors   life strains such as those set off by a
    difficult transition, like leaving home for college, or by the death of
    a parent or spouse, combined with a high-risk disorder, can lead to
    negative outcome.

The difficulties of evaluating therapy are formidable. Nevertheless, research seems to indicate that the effects of therapy, including group treatment, are modestly impressive (Bergin, 1971) or even clearly beneficial (Smith et al., 1980), especially in raising patients' self-esteem and reducing levels of anxiety.

SUMMARY

1. People who experience psychological difficulties are often helped by supportive people in the environment, called *situational supports*.

2. *Psychotherapy* or *therapy* is a formal relationship between a trained person and at least one client, for the purpose of applying psychological techniques to bring about sought-after behavioral or personality changes, or to otherwise promote personal growth and development. A variety of psychological tests may be used to assess the client's personality and intelligence.

3. Among those qualified to provide therapeutic help are clinical psychologists, counseling psychologists, psychiatrists, psychiatric social workers, psychoanalysts, and psychiatric nurses.

4. In therapy, the client reveals painful details about past or present situations, focusing on matters he was unable to confront alone. The client may transfer to the therapist some of the feelings he had for important figures in his past, a phenomenon called *transference*. As therapy progresses the client learns to behave in new and more adaptive ways.

5. One form of therapy is *crisis intervention,* which helps clients cope with temporary, stressful situations.

6. *Counseling* provides help in solving a specific life problem, such as choosing a vocation or overcoming a handicap.

7. *Psychoanalysis* is the method of therapy developed by Sigmund Freud. The client engages in *free association,* the goal being to discover unconscious material and help the client to understand the forces that have shaped his personality. Classic psychoanalysis is a long-term undertaking that aims at transformation or restructuring of the personality. Today briefer forms of psychoanalytically oriented therapy are available.

8. *Existential-humanist therapy* focuses on growth, health, and creativity; on immediate experience; and on the building of self-esteem. The therapist actively seeks to communicate respect and liking for the client, who is thereby encouraged to accept all his experiences and feelings, to become more fully himself.

9. *Behavior therapy* may be described as relearning. The therapist tells the client what he must do to eliminate undesirable behavior. Some techniques commonly used are *systematic desensitization* (a method for overcoming phobias) and *aversion therapy* (in which punishment is used to inhibit an unwanted response). The behavioral approach can also be used to achieve *self-directed change*.

10. *Biofeedback* is a learning method which, through the use of sophisticated electronic equipment, helps clients become aware of and control certain physiological processes. Generally it is employed in combination with one of the verbal therapies.

11. *Cognitive* and *cognitive-behavior therapy* assume that the client's emotional or behavioral difficulties are the result of faulty perceptions and thoughts. The cognitive therapist helps the client to identify faulty assumptions, test them systematically, and correct them.

12. *Eclectic therapy* is not based on a single theory or set of practices but rather on a combination of ideas and methods that suits the individual therapist.

13. *Brief therapy,* sometimes called short-term therapy, is explained by its name: some problems formerly treated over long periods of time are now dealt with during a short, predetermined period.

14. *Family therapy* is often begun when a family member is identified as having a behavior problem. Instead of treating the disturbed member, the family therapist treats the entire family (the family system). The family is directed to relate in new ways and to confront underlying problems.

15. In *marital therapy* both partners are treated, usually together. Emphasis is on issues such as power, sex, and communication.

16. *Group therapy* involves a small number of members who are guided by a therapist. Group members provide one another with various supports, are helped to develop social skills, and experiment with new behaviors. Developmental task groups are formed to help people through normal life crises. Encounter groups have the general goal of enriching the lives of members through personal growth experiences.

17. *Drug therapy* has a history of little over 35 years during which it has contributed enormously to relieving symptoms of many mentally ill patients.

18. To scientifically *evaluate the effects of therapy* is very difficult. From the existing evidence, we can conclude that most therapy clients are better off after therapy than individuals who need but do not receive therapy. No general conclusions can be drawn as yet about the relative effectiveness of the different forms of therapy.

SUGGESTED READINGS

Beck, A. T. (1979). *Cognitive therapy and the emotional disorders.* New York: New American Library. Written by one of the founders of cognitive therapy, a clear exposition of its theory and practice, illustrated by use of case material.

Chapman, A. (1975). *It's all arranged: Fifteen hours in a psychiatrist's life.* New York: Putnam. Chapman offers a fascinating look into the workday of a psychiatrist.

Ehrenberg, O. & Ehrenberg, M. (1986). *The psychotherapy maze.* New York: Simon & Schuster. This paperback contains insightful discussions of how to choose a psychotherapist and make the process more likely to work.

Ellis, A. & Harper, R. (1975). *A new guide to rational living.* Hollywood, CA: Wilshire. Application of the principles of rational emotive psychotherapy to the problems of coping with daily living.

Frank, J. D. (1969). *Persuasion and healing.* New York: Schocken. An insightful examination of the art of psychotherapy and individual healing processes.

Lazarus, A. (1981). *The practice of multimodal therapy.* New York: McGraw-Hill. The book describes an eclectic (drawn from several theories) approach to psychological assessment and treatment.

Malcolm, J. (1981). *Psychoanalysis: The impossible profession.* New York: Alfred A. Knopf. Malcolm's book is a superb exposition of the psychoanalytic process, presented through questions posed to an orthodox Freudian.

Moursund, J. (1985). *The process of counseling and therapy.* Englewood Cliffs, NJ: Prentice-Hall. This book provides an excellent overview of how one-to-one, couple, and group psychotherapy proceed.

Perls, F. (1973). *The Gestalt approach & eyewitness to therapy.* Palo Alto, CA: Science & Behavior Books. This volume contains Perls' last statement of his theory and transcripts of sessions conducted by Perls.

Williams, E. (1976). *Notes of a feminist therapist.* New York: Praeger. This book provides an excellent introduction to feminist therapy and how men's and women's behavior is shaped by societal expectations and teachings.

Personal Adjustment through the Life Span

Challenges in Infancy, Childhood, and Adolescence

- ▶ The idea that life even before birth affects emotional adjustment, and new approaches to childbirth that may benefit infant and parents
- ▶ The forging of the first attachment to another person, and factors involved in determining the quality of that attachment
- ▶ The normal developmental crises experienced by children and adolescents, with favorable outcomes in our culture being trust, autonomy, initiative, industry, and ego integrity
- ▶ How reactions to siblings, peers, and school are based on past developmental experiences that can either promote growth or create new difficulties
- ▶ Crises that are unusual rather than a part of normal maturation, and the varying ways people are predisposed to cope with them

*H*ans Selye, the stress researcher, likes to tell the story about two sons whose father suffered from alcoholism (Selye, 1980). One son grew up and became a teetotaler, a person who would not take an alcoholic drink under any circumstances. The other grew up and became an alcoholic who was drunk most of the time. When asked to explain their drinking habits, both replied, "With a father like that, what do you expect?"

The story makes two points. The first is that our parents and family experience can influence our adjustment as adults. The second is that there are significant differences in the way individuals cope with the same family experience. In Selye's words, "it is not what we face but how we face it that matters. Though internal and external factors influence or even determine some responses, we do have limited control over ourselves" (Selye, 1980, p. 143).

Maturational Crises
Normal, age-related crises that an individual experiences in our culture as he or she undertakes new developmental tasks.

In this chapter we will examine personal development as it emerges from childhood experience. First we will discuss the normal crises, or **maturational crises** that most children in our culture experience. We will describe the stresses that are usually involved in undertaking new developmental tasks, from infancy to adolescence. For example, we will examine what is involved in becoming attached to a parent, and in learning to function independently in peer groups and at school. We will then examine the role of **situational crises** in our development—crises that are not an expected part of life, but are experienced as accidents or special circumstances.

Situational Crises
Emergencies or special circumstances that occur in an individual's life, whose outcome will depend on age, ego strengths, and other factors.

The extent of the challenges individuals face growing up in a 20th century industrialized nation is well illustrated by statistics. Researchers estimate that today from 5–23 percent of American children and adolescents suffer from a diagnosable mental health disorder (Namir & Weinstein, 1982). To obtain the full picture one can add to this number the nearly 6 million considered maladjusted by their teachers, the 3 percent, or 2.5 million, of these age groups who are mentally retarded, the 1 million who are physically abused, and the 2 million arrested each year (Levine & Perkins, 1987).

Youths also encounter sexual and substance abuse problems. Thirty-six percent of rape victims are under 19 years of age (U. S. Dept. of Justice, 1985). Social scientists estimate that each year approximately 300,000 children are sexually abused, more than half by people they know (Pettis & Hughes, 1985). As many as 20 percent of these children will suffer long-term harm (Goodman, 1984). One survey conducted in a New York high school indicated that 11 percent of the students felt they were dependent on alcohol and more than one-quarter abused alcohol at least six times a year (Barnes, 1984). As discussed in Chapter 5, other psychoactive drugs also present major problems.

While parents, siblings, and members of the extended family are a child's first line of support in coping with the problems of life, these people cannot always provide the child with what is needed. The parents, for instance, may be coping with personal inadequacies, poverty, and unemployment, marriages being terminated by divorce, and so forth. And sometimes the parents are themselves adolescents who, due to poor judgment, had an unplanned child. Finally, there are instances, such as child abuse, in which parents are the direct cause of a child's adjustment difficulties.

Social agencies and institutions stand behind the home to help children in need. Approximately 15 million youths are involved with special programs in schools or in the courts (Levine & Perkins, 1987). Even so, not all children in need of service receive it. Estimates of the percentage of children needing mental health services who are actually served vary from 10 percent (Namir & Weinstein, 1982) to 33 percent (Knitzer, 1984). Further, Namir et al. (1982) report that youths may encounter barriers in obtaining necessary assistance because of their race, social class, or ethnic backgrounds.

Although children and adolescents encounter difficult challenges during this stage of the life span, most find acceptable ways of adjusting. For those who have had the most difficulty, large scale efforts like the Head Start program have been successful. This program, for instance, was effective in reducing the number of people with educational disabilities and often-associated social disabilities, such as unemployment, mental illness, and problems with the criminal justice system (Berrueta-Clement et al., 1984; Iscoe & Harris, 1984).

We turn next to a consideration of maturational crises individuals encounter following, as closely as possible, the stages of development suggested by Erikson (1963).

LIFE BEFORE BIRTH

We do not know a great deal about the beginnings of life—those months in the uterus—at least not from the unborn child's viewpoint. Some psychologists have imagined that the prenatal (or pre-birth) environment is a state that requires no exertion or adjustment at all, and is equivalent to "being at one with the universe."

However, others believe that the process of adjustment begins in the uterus. "We no longer think of the newborn as a blank slate," says one specialist in the new field of infant psychiatry. "At birth the newborn is already the veteran of an intimate set of interactions between itself, the mother, and the placenta, which affect both physiology and psychology" (quoted in Sobel, 1980, p. C1).

When personal adjustment begins is a matter for speculation. We do know, however, that the unborn child or fetus "behaves" in the sense that it reacts to stimuli in the environment. From physiological measurements we know that loud noises make the fetal heart beat faster, and that hormones produced by the mother under stress may cause the fetus to move about excessively. A classic study found that women who suffered severe stress during pregnancy tended to have active, irritable infants who had difficulty adjusting to feeding and sleeping schedules after birth (Sontag, 1941).

Since then psychologists have paid increasing attention to the social environment that surrounds the pregnant woman, and her fetus. As Grossman et al. (1980) said, "Pregnancy is indeed far more than just a biological event. In fact, the experience and comfort of pregnancy seem influenced by psychological and environmental variables which are unrelated to the actual biological situation (p. 42)."

Each unborn child is part of a social situation, part of a family, a couple, a mother and perhaps, grandparents and an extended social network (Gottlieb & Pancer, 1987). These other people will exert their influence. Research suggests women who adjust poorly to pregnancy, perhaps because of a lack of social support, experience anxiety and stress and are more likely to have complications during labor. Similarly, expectant mothers who encounter significant discord with the baby's father may give birth to infants who are as healthy as their peers, but who lag behind developmentally and show behavioral disorders.

The social environment can have health-promoting impact as well. Some children are conceived after years of waiting and planning. Their mothers are delighted, joyful about the future and confident, typically sharing a sense of accomplishment and security with an equally pleased father (Rayner, 1986). These babies' entrance into the world will be different, though perhaps not ultimately more joyful, than that of the unplanned child born to a large family in economic need. And some children are actually unwanted from the start. This may come to influence their self-concepts and adjustment. A large number of patients with psychological or psychosomatic problems begin by telling the therapist, "My mother never wanted me," or even, "I was a mistake." Others speak of having failed their parents in being of an undesired sex or for "having caused" a difficult pregnancy. The point is that the parent begins to relate to the idea of the child before birth, and that this early attitude can have a significant effect on adjustment.

A second and more subtle point is that the parents' relationship to each other affects and is affected by the unborn child. Some children are created as an expression of marital love; others are conceived to save a marriage. Often the role of the child in the parents' marriage is felt early. For example, the novelist and poet D. H. Lawrence, born to a long-suffering mother and an apparently brutal alcoholic father, told a friend that "I was born hating my father. . . . He was very bad before I was born" (Lawrence, 1910, 1979). This is an extreme and retrospective statement, but it emphasizes a basic human truth. The child is born to a couple that is expecting him or her, and from the beginning becomes part of their emotional life.

The physical environment that surrounds the unborn individual is also of obvious importance. One aspect of it, what the mother ingests during pregnancy, has been the subject of scientific research and changing opinion in recent decades. During World War II the German army surrounded Leningrad, cutting the supply line to the city. Severe shortages ensued, forcing the Soviet residents to ration food and cut their daily intake drastically. Comparing the rates of premature births, stillborns, and infant death before, during, and after this period, Antonov (1947) found substantial differences: Significantly greater numbers of the births during the siege were stillborn (5.6 percent) or premature (41 percent); further, an abnormally high number (30 percent) of the premature and nearly 10 percent of the full-term babies died before their first birthdays. Smith (1947) made comparable observations in the Netherlands.

In recent years it has become more commonly known that the intake of tobacco smoke, alcohol, and drugs can have adverse affects on the developing fetus. The risk of miscarriage is higher in mothers who smoke and their baby's birth weights and growth rates are lower and slower than their peers (Naeye, 1981; Witter & King, 1980). Even if a pregnant woman is a nonsmoker, being exposed to substantial amounts of smoke could adversely affect her fetus (Bottoms, Kuhnert, Kuhnert, & Reese, 1982). Like the chemicals contained in smoke, the alcohol in beverages also crosses the placenta. It intoxicates the fetus, who will likely remain in that state for a longer time period than the mother (Brien, Loomis, Tranmer, & McGrath, 1983). If a pregnant woman drinks heavily during pregnancy her baby may be born with the fetal alcohol syndrome, characterized by mental retardation, poor physical coordination, and physical abnormalities. Drugs, of course, can cause a variety of problems for the developing baby and should be taken by pregnant women only under medical supervision.

INFANCY: ATTACHMENT AND TRUST

The Crisis of Birth

Birth is the first observable crisis in our lives—and it is a dramatic one. It has been assumed that the birth event represents trauma (psychic injury), or at least a massive call for readjustment (Rank, 1929). Today, however, there is a tendency to consider birth as a potentially more satisfying experience. Health care providers manipulate the birth environment so that it is less startling to the infant. And they now promote fuller participation by the mother and father.

Many hospitals and other organizations offer courses in preparation for parenthood. Usually these courses teach the essentials of fetal development and childbirth so that expectant parents become aware of the physiological events occurring before and during birth. Prepared, or natural, childbirth, the Lamaze method, teaches techniques and exercises designed to increase the mother's participation and minimize her discomfort during pregnancy and labor (Lamaze, 1972). The father serves as coach and provides emotional support during labor and birth by assisting in the mother's breathing exercises and being present during delivery. The father's participation in the Lamaze method seems to affect his feelings about the birth.

Advocates of natural childbirth believe *bonding,* or the formation of close attachments between baby and parent, is facilitated by early physical contact. Obviously, bonding is important to the survival and growth of an infant. Some experts argue that the bonding process is set into motion by newborns' large eyes, high forehead and cuddly, helpless appearance. These characteristics lead adults to be attracted to infants and to provide them with nurturance and care.

In fact, parents enjoy the opportunity to bond immediately after birth and, months later, mothers who have had early physical contact touch, hold, and look at their babies more than other mothers (Winberg & de Chateau,

1982). Fathers are affected in a positive manner if they are present at the birth or in the presence of their baby soon afterwards: They experience elation and want to hold and gaze at their infant (Greenberg & Morris, 1974). It should be noted that early contact, or the lack of it, has not been found to have permanent effects on the child (Chess & Thomas, 1982; Winberg & de Chateau, 1982) and, of course, as parents who have adopted can attest, bonding between parent and youngsters can take place at any point in childhood.

The Leboyer method has grown out of an attempt to see birth from the newborn infant's perspective (Leboyer, 1975). It calls for changes in the delivery room environment. The goal is to minimize birth trauma by providing a kind of "halfway house" between the uterine environment and the external world. The lights are dimmed, loud noises eliminated, and sometimes soft music is played. The newborn is placed gently on the mother's abdomen. (The umbilical cord that connects the infant to the mother is not immediately cut.) Shortly thereafter, the father administers a warm water bath that is reassuringly similar to the uterine environment. The desired result is a gentle birth— a relaxed, even serene, experience for the infant in which there is immediate warm contact with the parents.

To date there is only preliminary research on the effects of the Leboyer birth experience. However, it seems clear that the experience favorably affects the way the parents perceive the infant. For example, Rapoport (1976) studied 120 families in which a baby had been delivered by the Leboyer method. The children—at ages one, two, and three years—were described by their parents as "easy," "delightful," and "unusually flexible." Indeed, the parents found that the child delivered by the Leboyer method was "much more adaptable" and experienced relatively fewer eating or sleeping difficulties than other children in the family who were born in traditional ways.

Another project compared "gentle" conventional deliveries with Leboyer deliveries, randomly assigning consenting mothers to one or the other condition (Nelson et al., 1980). The researchers took many measures, but found only two significant differences: mothers experiencing Leboyer deliveries had shorter periods of labor and, eight months after giving birth, they were more likely to think the Leboyer delivery had positively affected their baby's behavior. No significant differences were found between groups in measures of mothers' attitudes and adjustment or in assessments of the babies' behavior during the first hour after birth and at one day, three days, and eight months. And no differences were found in the health of the mothers and babies, leading the researchers to conclude that the Leboyer method yields no substantial benefits beyond those provided by gentle, conventional deliveries.

As research is done, psychologists will learn more about the initial adjustment we call birth. At this point, however, evidence suggests that from the mother's perspective, the presence of the father (or a supportive companion) during labor and delivery seems to reduce the incidence of problems and her level of medication and pain while, at the same time, making childbirth more of a "peak" experience (Parke & Tinsley, 1987).

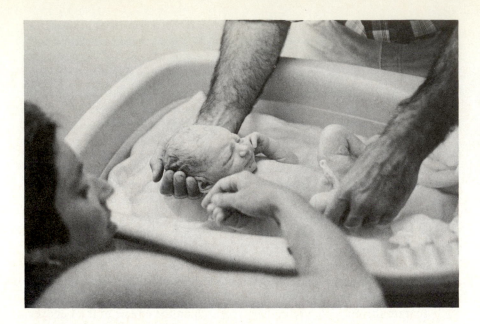

Individual Differences and Early Adjustment

At birth, after the well-known "spank" on the bottom is delivered, the new-born's backbone, naval, mouth, feet, sex organs, and anus are checked for congenital defects (Kunz, 1982). The Apgar Scale (Apgar, 1967) is also administered in most hospitals at one and five minutes after birth. With this instrument, the baby's status is rated on a two-point scale in each of five areas: body color, heart rate, muscle tone, reflex reaction, and respiratory functioning (see Table 7.1). The second assessment is the more predictive and most babies who have a low score at one minute improve substantially by five minutes (Koops & Battaglia, 1987). Although caution is needed in interpreting Apgar scores, newborns with low scores are more likely to have serious difficulty adjusting to life outside the womb (Koops & Battaglia, 1987).

The newborn is equipped with many reflexes (Caplan, 1981), some of which are essential to adjustment and others which are not. The *sucking reflex* leads the infant to suck when a nipple, finger, or object is placed in her mouth. When the area near the mouth is touched, the *rooting reflex* leads her to move toward the touch, thus facilitating feeding. Besides the role these reflexes play in terms of biological survival, cognitive theorists, like Piaget, have argued that the baby first learns about the environment through the use of certain reflexes. For example, Piaget explains that by sucking on objects as varied as mother's nipple or her own finger, and as a soft doll and hard wooden block, she learns about important differences between objects.

In contrast to these reflexes, others seem to have little adaptive value today. With the *palmar grasp,* for instance, the baby's hand closes to hold an object that has touched the palm. With the *plantar grasp,* the toes curl when the bottom of the feet are touched. Finally, the *walking reflex* leads the baby

"Chapter 1: I Am Born"

"Whether or not I shall turn out to be the hero of my own life, or whether that station will be held by anyone else, these pages must show. To begin my life with the beginning of my life, I record that I was born (as I have been informed and believe) on a Friday, at twelve o'clock at night. It was remarked that the clock began to strike, and I began to cry, simultaneously. . . ."

So begins the great novel *David Copperfield,* by Charles Dickens. Writing in the voice of his hero, Dickens relates all the details of his birth, for these are the details that set the novelistic stage for everything that happens.

Life may not be so neat as art; nevertheless, the circumstances of a person's birth do set the stage for what happens in the long novel of his life. If you were to write an autobiographical novel, what details would you put in "Chapter 1: I Am Born"? The following questions may help you re-create the circumstances of your birth.

1. Where were you born? In what city or town? At what hospital? If you were to re-create the setting in a novel, what adjectives would you use?
2. If you were adopted, what do you know about the circumstances of your birth and early care? What do you know about your natural mother or father, and the reasons for their inability to care for you? What do you know about the social agencies that may have intervened in your early life, for example, the foster mother, the adoption agency, the family court? At what age were you placed with your adopted parents?
3. Have you seen photographs of your mother and/or father that were taken shortly before you were born? If so, how would you describe them at this time?
4. How old was your mother at your birth? Describe if you can her situation at that time. (For example, how much education had she completed? What jobs had she held? What were her relationships with her parents?)
5. How old was your father when you were born? Describe if you can his situation at this time. (For example, how much education had he completed? What jobs had he held? What were his relationships with his parents?)
6. What do you know about the relationship between your parents at that time? (For example, were they not married, recently married, married for some years and the parents of other children? Were they very happy together? Experiencing difficulties? Coping with financial problems?)
7. Before you were born, how did your mother and/or father relate to the idea of you? (For example, do you think your parents planned or hoped to conceive a baby at the time you were conceived? Did your parents hope for a baby of the gender that you turned out to be? If they were disappointed, how did they adjust to it?)
8. Have your mother, father, or grandparents said anything significant about their feelings when you were born? If you have an older sibling, do you know anything about his or her reaction?
9. What have you heard about the medical details of your birth? For example, how long was your mother in labor? What was the family reaction to your weight? To your appearance?
10. How did you get your name? If you were named for someone, can you say why the name was given? (For example, what ethnic, religious, or family customs entered into your naming?) How do you feel today about your name?
11. Was there anything significant about the timing of your birth? Were you premature or postmature (past due)? How did this affect the feelings of your family?
12. If you have had children yourself, did feelings about your own birth affect the way in which you prepared for the birth of your children? ▲

TABLE 7.1 *The Apgar Scale*

	Score		
	0	*1*	*2*
Heart rate	Absent	Slow—less than 100 beats per minute	Fast—100–140 beats per minute
Respiratory effort	No breathing for more than one minute	Irregular and slow	Good breathing with normal crying
Muscle tone	Limp and flaccid	Weak, inactive, but some flexion of extremities	Strong, active motion
Body color	Blue and pale	Body pink, but extremities blue	Entire body pink
Reflex irritability in response to stimulation	No response	Grimace	Coughing, sneezing, and crying

Source: From Virginia A. Apgar, "A Proposal for a New Method of Valuation of a Newborn Infant" in *Anesthesia and Analgesia,* 32, 260–267, 1967. Copyright © 1967 International Research Society, Cleveland, OH. Reprinted by permission.

to "take steps" if supported securely and held appropriately, with feet touching a solid surface. However, the absence of these reflexes or others might indicate a medical problem.

Normal newborns in a hospital nursery at any one time vary widely in wakefulness, crying, and general activity levels. Some lie relatively still, while others kick and wave their arms and legs; some cry a lot, while some contentedly suck their thumbs; some sleep all the time, while others seem unable to relax at all.

Moreover, it appears that even at birth, individuals differ in irritability and in their need to avail themselves of *others* in seeking comfort (as opposed to comforting themselves). Some differences in styles of adjusting to the environment can be attributed to constitutional differences in temperament, the pattern of reactions to which an individual seems predisposed. A person's temperament effects the nature and level of his or her emotionality, activity, and sociability (Plomin, 1986).

For example, one temperamental difference easily observed in babies is "cuddliness," a quality so pronounced that Korner (1971) classified the infants she studied into two groups, the cuddlers and the noncuddlers. Cuddlers tend to be more composed; they require more sleep, and are likely to form strong specific attachments earlier than noncuddlers. In contrast, noncuddlers tend to be more restless and active, and less tolerant of any type of physical restraint.

Perhaps the most comprehensive studies of temperamental differences in infancy and their effects on later adjustment were conducted by Thomas and Chess and their associates (Thomas et al., 1963; Chess & Thomas, 1987). This research, sometimes called the New York Longitudinal Study, documents what many parents had long suspected. From birth, infants show significant differences with respect to mood, responsiveness to people, attention span, persistence, and adaptability to new situations. These differences might be no more than material for family anecdotes, if it were not so evident that they affect the infant's first relationships. In actuality, temperament has some role in determining the kind of parental care a child receives. The "easy" child—the one who adjusts to things without a fuss, who eats well, and is perhaps a cuddler and a smiler—makes the parents feel equally content. Parents with such children will be eager to play with them in infancy, to teach them songs and stories as they grow. The "difficult" child—the child who is a stubborn noncuddler, who balks at new situations and seems never to sleep—can frustrate his or her parents. They may feel like failures as parents and experience a helpless anger.

Of course, the effects of an infant's behavior depend largely on the parents' understanding and expectations. What one set of parents considers "difficult" behavior is accepted as natural or desirable by another couple. For example, Thomas and his associates studied the early adjustment of two little girls, both of whom, by temperament, were low in distractibility:

> One girl's parents were well accustomed to the trait, having themselves a marked capacity to become absorbed and even buried in what they were doing. They were pleased by their little girl's tenacity, appreciated her ability to amuse herself, and took calmly the occasional inconvenience of prying her away from a deep preoccupation that interfered with routines. The other parents seemed remarkably different from their daughter. Lively, expressive, and enthusiastic, they were puzzled by the child's solemn determination, her protracted work on jigsaw puzzles, her unsmiling struggle when only three to sew a button on a piece of cloth. They felt that she ought to be more relaxed and joyful, and they were frustrated by her lack of overt emotion, which they interpreted to mean that she was unsatisfied with the things they did for her. The little girl lost out in parental favor to her two more distractible but more responsive brothers and became in effect a rejected child (Thomas et al., 1963, pp. 41–42, as summarized by White, 1972, p. 174).

Generations ago, authorities put the responsibility for a child's behavior squarely on the child (his or her genes, or inborn "character"). By the 1940s, scientific opinion had shifted. People were told that what went wrong with children was all their parents' fault. During this era parents were taught that even the earliest interactions with their youngsters, if handled improperly, could cause later problems and that too much discipline would lead children to repress feelings and grow into neurotic adults. Given such beliefs in the scientific community, how could the average person know how to act as a parent? Dr. Benjamin Spock's (1946/1985) influential "Baby and Child Care" provided answers. He reassured generations of parents, telling them a simple message: be yourselves, you know more than you think about childrearing. Your parents and grandparents probably read Dr. Spock's book and were told that you, their child, wanted to be good and, if you were loved, you would undoubtedly develop into a responsible, healthy adult.

What Is Your Temperamental Style?

Chess and Thomas (1987) described nine categories of temperament and provided typical examples of high and low ratings on each. To the best of your recollection (or after consulting with your parents), which of these descriptions fit you as a 12-year-old child?

Nine Categories of Temperament

	Describes Me	Doesn't Describe Me	I'm Not Sure Whether It Describes Me
1. Activity Level motor activity and the proportion of active and inactive periods			
High activity "When she comes home from school, she is immediately outside playing an active game."	____	____	____
Low activity "Typically she gets involved with a jigsaw puzzle and sits quietly working at it for hours."	____	____	____
2. Rhythmicity (Regularity) the predictability or unpredictability of the timing of biological functions, such as hunger, sleep-wake cycle, and bowel elimination			
Regularity "She awakens like clockwork each morning; I never need to wake her for school."	____	____	____
Irregularity "Sometimes her big meal is lunch time, sometimes it's dinner, I never know."	____	____	____
3. Approach or Withdrawal the nature of the initial response to a new situation or stimulus—a new food, toy, person, or place. Approach responses are positive and may be displayed by mood expression (smiling, speech, facial expression) or motor activity (swallowing a new food, reaching for a new toy). Withdrawal reactions are negative and may be displayed by mood expression (crying, fussing, speech, facial expression) or motor activity (moving away, spitting new food out, pushing new toy away).			
Approach "She came home from her new school the first day talking as if all the other pupils were already her friends."	____	____	____
Withdrawal "The class just started fractions. As usual, she is sure she will never learn it. I reminded her that she always says that with a new subject, but then she masters it well."	____	____	____
4. Adaptability long-term responses to new or altered situations. Here the concern is not the nature of the initial responses but the ease with which they are modified in desired directions.			
High adaptability "She went to a new summer play group this year. Although it was a totally new type of schedule, and she felt uncomfortable at first, it took her only a few days to get involved and feel comfortable."	____	____	____
Low adaptability "We moved to a new neighborhood three months ago, and she is only just now beginning to make friends."	____	____	____

Nine Categories of Temperament	Describes Me	Doesn't Describe Me	I'm Not Sure Whether It Describes Me
5. Sensory Threshold the intensity level of stimulation necessary to evoke a discernible response, irrespective of the specific form the response may take.			
High threshold "She came home from playing soccer with a blistered heel and hadn't noticed it, and didn't complain at all."	____	____	____
Low threshold "She is the first one in any group to notice an odor or feel a change in room temperature."	____	____	____
6. Quality of Mood the amount of pleasant, joyful, and friendly behavior and mood expression, as contrasted with unpleasant crying and unfriendly behavior and mood expression			
Positive mood "She never objects to home chores and does whatever she is asked with a smile."	____	____	____
Negative mood "School just started last week and she already has a list of grievances about each teacher."	____	____	____
7. Intensity of Reactions the energy level of response, positive or negative			
High intensity "In the restaurant she couldn't get the food she wanted and screamed and made a big fuss."	____	____	____
Low intensity "I know she was very upset at failing the test, but outwardly she appeared only a little subdued."	____	____	____
8. Distractibility the effectiveness of an outside stimulus in interfering with or changing the direction of the child's ongoing behavior			
High distractibility "Her homework takes a long time, as her attention repeatedly gets sidetracked."	____	____	____
Low distractibility "Once she starts reading a book, we can't get her attention until she gets to the end of the chapter."	____	____	____
9. Persistence and Attention Span These two categories are usually related. Persistence refers to the continuation of an activity in the face of obstacles or difficulties. Attention span concerns the length of time a particular activity is pursued without interruption.			
High persistence "If she has a hard arithmetic problem for homework, she keeps after it and insists she has to figure it out herself."	____	____	____
Long attention span "If she has a part in a school play, she can rehearse it for hours."	____	____	____
Low persistence "She tried to learn to ice-skate, but after she fell a few times, she gave it up."	____	____	____
Short attention span "She likes to read, but only a half hour at a time."	____	____	____

What Is Your Temperamental Style? (Continued)

1. Chess and Thomas identified three types of children, all normal, but with differing temperaments or ways of relating to the world: the easy child, the difficult child, and the slow-to-warm-up child. These categories describe 40 percent, 10 percent, and 15 percent of children, respectively. Considering how you answered the questions above, to what extent did you, as a 12-year old, fit into a category?

   the easy child: tends toward regularity (2), positive approaches to newness (3), high adaptability (4), positive moods (6), and low to moderate intensity of reactions (7).

   the difficult child: tends toward irregularity (2), withdrawal from newness (3), low adaptability (4), negative moods (6), and high intensity of reactions (7).

   the slow-to-warm-up child: tends toward withdrawal from newness (3), low adaptability (4), mild intensity of reactions (7).

2. Each temperamental quality and particular combination can be an asset or liability for a person in regard to given tasks. Examples are provided and you are invited to finish the sentences below with ideas of your own:

   a. Maria is persistent (9), distractible (8) and has low threshold (5). She might complete course assignments but tends to hand them in late and she. . . .

   b. Hank has low persistence (9) and high distractibility (8). He might promise and plan to have your notes copied by the weekend but will not actually get around to it and he. . . .

   c. Judy has a high activity level (1) and is high on persistence and attention span (9). She might be an excellent candidate to train for a marathon race and. . . .

3. Some psychologists would argue: Temperament is one factor that helps shape the developing personality in children. If parents became aware of and understood the concept of temperament they could better understand their child's needs, his reactions to events, and his interactions with others. Would you support the spending of tax dollars for a public service television campaign to educate parents about the concept of temperament?   ▲

By the 1970s research began offering a more balanced view (Murphy & Moriarty, 1976). Constitutional factors, like genes and temperament, were recognized as important, as were environmental factors, including the quality of parenting. However, researchers noted that it is not only parents who train and educate; babies, too, exert influences which, from birth, affect the nature of the parent/child relationship. But the responsibility cannot really be shared. Usually, parents have acquired, through education or experience, the understanding that helps them with a "difficult" infant. Infants have no similar understanding of the rage or rejection their behavior could cause.

The First Attachment

Physical closeness between mother and child obviously begins during pregnancy. The fetus is provided with nourishment and oxygen by means of the umbilical cord and the placenta. When the cord is cut infants seek attachment with a nursing mother or a nurturing mother substitute.

The rooting and sucking reflexes (page 294) are present the first time a mother holds her newborn infant. They help establish the initial infant-mother bond. Even if the mother has never nursed (or even observed someone else doing so), the infant held to her breast will reflexively root around, grasp the nipple, and begin to suck. The act of breast-feeding naturally fosters contact, warmth, and attachment. Of course, a person who holds a baby lovingly while feeding with a bottle can also establish a warm mutual attachment.

The nursing experience is only the first in a developmental sequence that results in the infant's attachment to the mother or some other "human partner." There is no one moment in which the attachment is forged. Yet by the time human infants are eight or nine months old, they demonstrate this attachment by producing all the characteristics we associate with human love (Fraiberg, 1977; Bowlby, 1969). "He shows preference for his mother and wants repeated demonstrations of her love; he can only be comforted by his mother, he initiates games of affection with her, and shows anxiety, distress, and even grief if a prolonged separation from her takes place" (Fraiberg, 1977, p. 56). Such an attachment is absolutely critical to normal development, and almost always takes place, without any reflection or planning on the parents' part. Certain behaviors of the infant virtually guarantee it.

At first infants can only cry. This primitive communication brings mother or father to the cribside. A "dialogue of 'need' and 'answer to need' " unfolds, as infant and parents learn to read each others' signals (Fraiberg, 1977). The staring of infants also serves to draw parents' attention: infants sometimes mesmerize adults by gazing solemnly into their eyes. Finally there is smiling, a signal that appears invariably in infants of all cultures, and even in the blind (Wilson, 1978). If the smile is an innate response, somehow programmed into the infant, it is easy to see what survival purpose it might serve. The smile draws the parents with its statement of pleasure, and its suggestion of reciprocal love (Rayner, 1986).

Satisfaction of Early Needs

The attachment to the mother or some other human partner is made in infancy, usually without crisis. However, the quality of the attachment that is formed varies from person to person. This quality seems to depend on the manner in which the earliest needs and satisfactions are experienced.

The infant has limited intellectual (or cognitive) understanding of her environment. She lacks the capacity to differentiate herself from her mother; that is, she does not realize that she is in any way separate from this all-encompassing maternal person. Her ability to adjust is comparably restricted. For example, if her mother does not often comfort or feed her when she cries, she cannot be in a temper at her mother specifically, nor can she wish her mother to act differently. She can only feel a general undirected rage and dissatisfaction. Similarly, if the mother is regularly attendant but highly anxious, the infant is not in a position to understand, compare, and excuse. It is the world that is anxious.

Oral Needs

In the first year of life the baby's security is intimately related to sustenance and the process of feeding. Because the infant's feeding experience represents the first interaction with the environment, it has been given attention by virtually all psychologists studying personal adjustment.

Freud, for example, saw the "oral state" as the first psychosexual stage of development. At first, the lips, gums, and mouth are the main areas of physical pleasure. Sucking absorbs a large part of the infant's energies. Later, as teeth appear, biting and chewing become pleasurable.

Tactile Needs

Even as adults when we are immersed in personal difficulties, the touch of a friend or a group member or therapist, often acts to release tension. In infancy the effect of being touched, held, or protected is especially obvious. Most parents have observed, for example, that unhappy or uncomfortable infants will stop crying when they are picked up and held close even without being offered the breast or bottle.

Evidence of an infant's need for physical closeness to a mother figure was provided by Harry Harlow's classic experiments on the attachment behavior of rhesus monkeys separated from their natural mothers (Harlow, 1958; Harlow & Harlow, 1969). In one experiment half the monkeys were "nursed" with milk from bottles attached to surrogate mothers covered with terrycloth; the other monkeys were "nursed" by mothers made of unupholstered wire. As the infants developed, those who had been "nursed" by a wire mother spent increased periods of time clinging to the cloth mother, even though it provided no nourishment. This result suggests that attachment behavior is not exclusively a search for nourishment but also an attempt to find warm and comfortable physical contact. It has been suggested that the human infant, like the monkey, has a basic need to cling to the mother or other attending adult (Bowlby, 1969).

"Trust versus Mistrust": The First Psychosocial Crisis in Erikson's Theory

As babies build up a repertoire of attachment behaviors, they establish what Erikson calls "the cornerstone of the healthy personality" (1968, p. 97): they resolve the developmental crisis between basic trust and mistrust. In other words, if the basic needs for food, comfort, and attachment are regularly met, the baby comes to believe in the continuity of care, the continuity of mother, others, and self, and lays the foundation for trust in interpersonal relationships.

Trust
A favorable outcome of Erikson's first stage; a sense of trust in others that develops if the individual's basic needs were sensitively and reliably met by the caregiver.

A favorable outcome in infancy does not require that every need be immediately met. Frustrations are inevitable, even desirable. To Erikson, **trust** results from the quality and conviction of the early relationship, from "the kind of administration which . . . combines sensitive care of the baby's individual needs and a firm sense of personal trustworthiness within the trusted framework of a culture's life style" (Erikson, 1963, p. 249). Infants who feel fundamentally safe in the world develop the enduring ego strength of "hope." They reach out to the environment with wonder and interest (Maslow, 1968) and are delighted, rather than frustrated, by the new experiences that await them.

Some infants emerge from infancy with an unfavorable outcome, and an attitude of basic mistrust. They feel abandoned, empty, and "no good" (Erikson, 1959). A lack of sustaining attachment and love from another person may cause them to become withdrawn, angry, fearful, and consequently unable to take the risk of moving on to the next stage of development. In cases of extreme deprivation when infants lose their mothers and are not provided with a substitute (Wenar, 1989), or when they are placed in impersonal institutional care, a "reactive depression" sets in (Spitz, 1945). Abandoned infants lie listless, with blank expressions. Their mental and physical processes quickly deteriorate, and they are unusually susceptible to disease and death.

Individuation

In the first few months of life, the mother and infant are closely bonded. (Bonding may also occur with the father, a grandparent, or other person who is primarily responsible for child care. In this and subsequent sections, reference will be made to the mother because in the majority of cases she spends the most time with the child.) Indeed, some psychologists speak of a "oneness" with the mother, or a "human symbiosis," that is, a relationship of mutual benefit (Mahler, 1972). However, this cannot last for long.

From about the fifth month on, the infant resists being totally "at one" with the mother (Mahler, 1970): a growing sense of autonomy propels the child out of mother's lap. This process of separation is sometimes called **individuation.** Often it represents a small crisis for the mother and infant. Both must face the loss of the emotional security that came from being "one," in order to achieve the more challenging love that can take place between two people.

The individuation process reverberates throughout the life span. From the moment of birth we begin a gradual departure that ends when we become a normal adult, "both fully 'in' and at the same time basically separate from the 'world out there' " (Mahler, 1972, p. 333). The beginning of this process Mahler calls **differentiation.** Infants are now awake for more hours during the day. They are aware of the mother as something that exists apart from themselves. They are, so to speak, "hatched" from the contained circle of the early mother-infant relationship. Babies at this stage pull people's hair, grab their eyeglasses, hold onto their nose—in technical terms, they manually and tactilely explore anything that comes within reach.

At approximately ten to fifteen months, babies enter the **early practicing stage.** They crawl or hitch themselves along the floor, stand up holding onto furniture or walls, and "get into everything." They carry on a "love affair with their personal environment." Like all such affairs, this one is sometimes rocky. Parents may find it difficult to stand back as the baby tumbles, fumbles, and explores everything in the vicinity.

Individuation
A process, beginning at about five months of age, in which an infant displays a growing need for autonomy and seeks some degree of separation from the mother.

Differentiation
A process, generally occurring between ages five and ten months, whereby the child becomes aware of existing apart from the mother.

Early Practicing Stage
A stage, occurring roughly between ten and fifteen months of age, when a child begins to aggressively explore the environment but also frequently returns to, and demands attention from, the parents.

The first independent explorations are tentative and short. At this point infants are only "practicing." They return often to mother or father, touching them for reassurance or "emotional refueling." When infants become full-fledged toddlers (by eighteen months or so), they can separate themselves from their caretakers more easily. Surprisingly, what they most often choose to do is follow their mothers from place to place. Apparently, as toddlers become increasingly aware of mother's separateness, they have an increased desire that mother share things with them. At this stage there is also a greater interest in fathers (Mahler, 1972). Children will typically insist that father do for them something that mother has always done; for example, pour their cereal or bathe them.

This period is characterized by a basic ambivalence that Mahler sees as the hallmark of human development. Toddlers go forth to explore the playground, but not without many a backward glance to be sure that mother is still sitting on the park bench. A toddler may quite independently make a mud pie, but then insist that mommy sit down in the mud and share it. Mahler summarizes this basic struggle of human growth as a slow transition from oneness with the mother to mature, independent functioning as an autonomous person.

CHILDHOOD: THE SELF IN THE SOCIAL WORLD

"Autonomy versus Shame and Doubt": The Second Psychosocial Crisis in Erikson's Theory

In the early months of exploring, children benefit from the continued presence of parents who encourage their wider range of activity without undue correction or reproof. According to Erikson, the crisis of toddlerhood is between **autonomy** on the one hand and shame and doubt on the other. The emerging ability is self-control or willpower. From the parents' viewpoint, the recurring disaster of this period is the temper tantrum, that seemingly most willful and least controlled of human behaviors. Also characteristic is negativism: it seems as if toddlers seek to differentiate themselves from parents by always opposing them.

At issue is the toddler's increasing self-control and control over objects in the environment. Toddlers gain the ability to hold or release objects at will. They alternately cling to treasured objects and throw them out of the crib or playpen. This hold-on-and-letting-go behavior, resulting primarily from the toddler's increased muscular control and new found autonomous will, is a source of conflict between parents and child.

The area where these two conflicting patterns of holding on and letting go is most strikingly brought into play is bowel and bladder function. Whereas infants simply empty their bowels and bladder when they are full, toddlers, having developed the appropriate neural connections, learn to control this emptying behavior. They are encouraged to tell adults when they need to be brought to the bathroom and are eventually expected to be able to postpone the pleasure of letting go, as necessary. The learning of these behaviors (or, we might say, the teaching of them) is called toilet training.

Autonomy
A favorable outcome of Erikson's second stage; a sense of independence or ability to stand on "one's own two feet" that a child acquires if parents allow him/her appropriate levels of control and freedom.

In the early practicing stage, toddlers make their first independent explorations of the environment, but return to their parents for reassurance. A successful resolution of this stage results in the development of autonomy.

In this stage, as in infancy, the parents' behavior and expectations are crucial. If toilet training is begun too early or is too rigid, children may feel deprived of the chance to willingly control their excretions, and may become engaged in a struggle for autonomy against the parent. Ideally, parents help children to feel capable of doing many things independently during this stage, while still protecting them from dangerous or frightening experiences. If they do, children will gain self-control without the loss of self-esteem.

An unfavorable outcome at this stage is shame and doubt. Children who emerge from toddlerhood feeling shame and doubt have come to believe in the inevitability of their own disgrace. They may strive to be perfect (perfectly clean or perfectly organized) but they feel incapable behaving adequately through their own will. Any mistake may bring an excess of shame. Unfavorable outcomes in this period are not the result of conflicted toilet training alone. The parents' attitudes are generally reflected in other areas, for example, in eating habits and play. If children are constantly scolded for doing things that seem perfectly reasonable to them, such as playing with mud or dropping toys over the side of the crib, they may emerge from toddlerhood with a feeling of insecurity and the belief that very little they can do is right.

Children who tested as secure in their attachment to their mothers were compared with those who scored as anxious (Slade, 1987). Significant differences were found between these groups in the quality of their free play during bimonthly observations at ages 20–28 months. Specifically, when playing alone, secure children played for longer periods of time and, in the later months, more often engaged in higher quality symbolic play. When mothers joined their children in play, the same patterns persisted, indicating maternal involvement facilitated the functioning of secure children much more than anxious ones. Slade's findings support the view of attachment theory, which explains that children's interest and effectiveness in exploring the environment is greater if they believe their basic needs will be met by the primary caregiver (Bowlby, 1969). Other research has shown links between the security of attachment and competency in social (Bretherton, 1985) and in challenging situations (Belsky, Garduque, & Hrncir, 1984).

"Initiative versus Guilt": The Third Psychosocial Crisis in Erikson's Theory

By the age of four, children have improved their locomotion and coordination considerably. They can dress themselves, use scissors, run, climb, throw, ride tricycles, and even catch. They can sing songs and tell stories. All of these are valuable skills that preschoolers use to extend their exploration of the world and their relationship with people. Although they often imitate adults (through fantasy, dressing up as grownups, or adopting adult mannerisms), a major development at this stage is the ability to initiate activity themselves.

Four-year-olds are suddenly more loving, brighter in their judgments, and more relaxed (Erikson, 1963). They "reach out" in a charming way—full of the pleasure of attack and conquest. In Erikson's view, this period is marked by a crisis between **initiative** and guilt. Children can proceed purposefully toward adult roles, manipulating the environment, utilizing their newly acquired motor and verbal skills, and carrying through a wide variety of group activities. However, if overrestricted or belittled, children may inhibit their motor activities, deny their needs, and succumb to feelings of littleness and guilt.

Initiative
A favorable outcome of Erikson's third stage; the ability to comfortably create play, fantasies, and various activities that develops in a child if he is not harshly criticized in this stage.

Consider how the struggle between initiative and guilt might surface in a child in the area of play. Research (Etaugh, 1983) has shown that girls and boys are provided different toys in infancy, and beyond, and that parents play differently with sons and daughters. And sex difference in play and preferences in toys are apparent as early as from 12–18 months of age. Girls choose dolls and doll equipment. Boys select balls, plastic robots, and transportation toys.

By age 3–5 years, another difference is apparent. Boys play outdoors more, in active, aggressive games, while girls tend to engage in quieter, more nurturant play, indoors. The differences can be attributed to biological differences (Haraway & Moss, 1983) and to a number of social factors. Regardless of the cause (Etaugh, 1983), teachers, peers, and family members react to children in differing ways, depending on the toys they are playing with or the games they propose. In other words, children's choices in play may bring them the approval of important adults or they may not; either way the choices affect the children's struggle between initiative and guilt.

Parents

Classic psychoanalysts see this period as one in which a family sexual drama is enacted. According to Freud, the child's libido (sexual energy), which had at first been centered in the mouth and later in the anal region, now focuses on the genital organs. The sexual feelings, vague and confusing as they may be to young children, are directed primarily toward the parent of the opposite sex. With them come new feelings of resentment, jealousy, fear, and guilt concerning the same-sex parent, who is now seen as a rival. Children also fear bodily harm, which they unconsciously believe may come as punishment for their desires. More generally, they feel a threat to their self-esteem as they recognize their parents' strength and feel the parents are giving each other first priority.

In Freud's classic theoretical description, the small boy falls in love with his mother and consequently feels himself in deadly rivalry with his father. This predicament Freud called the **Oedipus complex,** or the Oedipal conflict, after the Greek drama in which the young prince Oedipus unknowingly (unconsciously) kills his father and marries his mother. Freud believed that this "family romance" is universally played out in the unconscious lives of all normal boys. Girls experience a variant of the Oedipus complex (sometimes called the **Electra complex**) that involves a romantic attachment to the father, accompanied by anxiety over the possible loss of their mother's love.

The Oedipal conflict is said to be resolved as the child begins to make a transition in his affections, one that will ultimately lead to a suitable love object. As an alternative to "marrying" or otherwise possessing his mother, the boy strives to be more like the person who has achieved these things—namely, his father. He will grow up and have a wife of his own. Especially if the father is benevolent and has not harshly interfered with the mother-child relationship, the boy will overcome feelings of resentment and jealousy toward his father.

Oedipus Complex and Electra Complex
In psychoanalytic theory, a stage of psychosexual development when a child experiences sexual feelings toward the opposite-sex parent and resulting emotions of jealousy, fear, and guilt toward the same-sex parent, now viewed unconsciously as a rival.

Sibling Relationships

In many families, a second child is born at about the time the first child is experiencing the "family romance" conflict and resolving the crisis between initiative and guilt (Lidz, 1976). This event is likely to provoke much jealousy, for the new infant occupies a great deal of the parents' attention. The older child may feel displaced by the infant. Moreover, the infant may be somewhat disappointing to the child, worthless as a companion because he or she is unable to walk, talk, or play. It is thus natural for children to express unhappiness over the new addition to the family and possibly ask their parents to send the unentertaining, attention-stealing infant "back." The older child may take the infant's toys or even try to harm him or her. This reaction may, in turn, cause family problems as the parents must protect the helpless infant, thereby feeding the child's suspicion of favoritism.

Since Sir Francis Galton noted, over a century ago, that only and first-born sons were overrepresented among noted English scientists, researchers have studied possible links between birth order and intelligence, mental health, social skills, conformity, and a wide range of other factors (Weiss, 1981). Studies have suggested that the experiences children have with respect to the birth of younger siblings (that is, experiences determined by birth order) affect later personal development. For example, firstborn children begin life with only adults as models and information-bearers. They are exposed to a fairly

The Psychologist and His Brother

This photograph, taken in 1900, shows two very famous brothers. The man on the right is William James, the American pragmatist philosopher and one of the founders of the modern discipline of psychology. The man on the left is Henry James, the novelist who wrote *Portrait of a Lady, The Ambassadors, The Wings of the Dove, The Turn of the Screw,* and many other celebrated works.

What does this photograph say about the relationship between the two brothers? See if you agree with literary critic Richard Hall, who has analyzed the photograph, drawing upon the work of Leon Edel, the renowned Henry James biographer, and other scholarly sources.

1. Note that William James, the older by fifteen months, stands with his arm thrown comfortingly around Henry's shoulder. What does this convey? William's writings show that he believed his eminent brother to be a helpless sort of person, in need of brotherly protection.

2. The two brothers appear to be of the same height, but which stands taller and looks more like a "pillar"? Henry wrote: "I have always regarded him as the pillar of my family life."

3. In the photo, Henry has tilted his head affectionately toward his brother. What does this attitude convey to you? Hall states: "The whole effect is one of dependence and passivity." It might also be a kind of deferral to the older brother's greatness. Henry James wrote: "I never for all the time of childhood or youth in the least caught up with him or overtook him." The biographer Edel noted that at the time this photograph was taken, Henry's writing reflected the old emotions of love and anger—emotions of "the little Henry who yearned with all the intensity of his being for acceptance by his brother."

Look through your family album and select a photograph of yourself and a sibling. Choose a photograph that is similar to many others you have, but that you have always thought was a "good one" of both of you. (If you do not have a sibling, you can work through this exercise using a photo of yourself and a parent.)

1. What does the photo say about you? About your sibling? About your relationship? For example, who dominates the photograph? Who is more attractive, or appears to have a self-concept of greater attractiveness? Which person seems to be having a better time?

2. If possible, show the photo to someone who does not know you or your sibling very well. What sense of your relationship does this more objective person gain from the photo? Is his or her interpretation consistent with yours?

3. Have you had any reason to examine the assumptions that underlie *your* relationships with a sibling? Have these assumptions been contradicted by experiences you have had since you established your identity as an adult beyond the family circle?

Source: Excerpted from R. Hall. "An Obscure Hurt: The sexuality of Henry James," in *The New Republic,* April 28, 1979, pp. 25–31; and May 5, 1979, pp. 25–29. Copyright © 1979 The New Republic, Inc.

Hall, who found so much to say about this photograph of William and Henry, has looked at other photographs of Henry taken during this period. It seems that when Henry is photographed without his brother he looks very different: he is "upright, squat and powerful." And this corresponds to the facts as we know them: Henry at this time in his life was an internationally famous author, and a powerful presence in the London society in which he moved. Henry was neither helpless nor dependent. In other words, the assumptions underlying the relationship between the brothers were contradicted by the evidence of the real world. In late middle age, Henry came to understand this, and was to some degree liberated from the presence of his brother.

4. Consider reading *Becoming William James* by Howard M. Feinsten (Ithaca, N. Y.: Cornell Univ. Press, 1984). This book offers insight into family life and how it affects the individual's development across the life span. ▲

orderly world, and receive a great deal of intellectual stimulation. Younger siblings, on the other hand, derive much of their information and experience from older children, who naturally display the inconsistent thoughts and impulsive behaviors of children. However, their parents are more secure in their role and tend to discipline them less than they did the firstborn.

There is some evidence that firstborn (and only) children are intellectually superior to later-born children, push themselves harder to achieve, and are more likely to earn note, such as being elected to Congress or be included in Who's Who (Bradley, 1982). However, the experience of losing the parents' exclusive attention may also have negative effects. Firstborns may try to adjust to their changed circumstances by "growing up" fast. Based on Leman's (1984) review of the research, firstborns feel more pressure to please others, even if self-sacrifice is involved, and they strive for perfection. (Although, Leman points out, they may protect their self-view by being sloppy when they cannot be perfect.) From childhood to adulthood, these characteristics tend to make the firstborn sensitive, anxious, and pessimistic. He or she wants to know "the rules," so he can follow them, and hesitates to discuss his true thoughts or feelings for fear that he will be rejected (Leman, 1984).

Later-born children, who have never enjoyed the position of "only child," do not suffer so great a loss when new children enter the family. Unlike the firstborn, from birth they have had to learn how to relate to and compete with others. Perhaps for this reason, younger children tend to be characterized as "popular" and sociable and attracted to activities and professions that require interaction with others (Leman, 1984).

In sum, the birth of a younger sibling represents a crisis for the child, particularly for the firstborn; whether and how this crisis affects personality depends on the older child's developmental level. If the birth occurs when the older child is three or four years older he or she will probably react with the jealous striving that is characteristic of this stage. If it occurs earlier or later, the effect will be different. For example, children of seven or eight are generally less resentful of a new infant, for they have already succeeded in becoming somewhat independent of parents and have developed peer relationships outside the home.

School and Peers

As children grow older, they spend less time with the family and more time with children and adults outside their homes. Accordingly, their interactions at school and with peers play an increasingly large part in the developmental process.

Parents, social scientists, and public policymakers have been debating the merits and consequences to young children of home care versus day care. The significance of their consideration is clear. Because over 50 percent of children in the United States currently receive child care from others besides their parents (Phillips, McCartney, & Scarr, 1987), the question arises as to how their social development is effected. Evidence collected thus far suggests

that day-care enrollees, in contrast to their peers at home, mature socially at an earlier age (Clark-Stewart & Fein, 1983). As a result, they show negative social behaviors sooner, like aggressiveness and resistance to adult directives, as well as positive behaviors, like social confidence and the ability to work cooperatively. The quality of a day-care center, as measured by several factors, including caregiver-child verbal interactions, is an important determinant of a child's social growth while at the facility (Phillips et al., 1987).

The elementary school classroom, like the child care center, differs from the family in a very basic way: it is an institution whose sole purpose is to educate and socialize children. At home, children are most likely to be loved simply for being their parents' offspring. In school, children are valued and praised chiefly for their achievements. School, therefore, contributes to a child's ego development by presenting a new, objective measure of self-worth. It gives children experiences that counteract, and may correct, some of the more idiosyncratic notions they have acquired at home.

At school, children become part of a peer group. Such relationships are different from those within the family structure because the peer group contains members similar to each other in age, size, and ability. An interesting aspect of elementary school interaction is the separation of the sexes that normally occurs. Girls and boys tend to isolate themselves, mainly to reinforce their own positive feelings about their gender identity.

In the school environment, children learn skills that will be important in future life adjustments. For example, attitudes toward competition and compromise develop in this period, as does the quality of personal ambition. School-age children learn how to behave toward figures of authority who are not their parents. And within the peer group, children learn the difficult business of social exclusion—what is involved in being "popular" and what it feels like to be the last one chosen for the team. In such situations children have the opportunity to develop empathy for their peers.

Some children adjust easily to school and are successful in that they seem to work up to their abilities and are well liked by teachers and their peers. Other children encounter difficulties in school: they are lonely; they are said to have "behavior problems"; they are "underachievers," not earning the grades they could. What accounts for different outcomes in school?

Not surprisingly, the ability to cope with school grows out of one's temperament (Terestman, 1980), and the general coping skills developed in the preschool years. In addition, there appear to be specific skills or experiences associated with school success. The following experiences have been identified by Brown (1973) as those that prepare the child to cope with school and other social environments encountered during the school years.

1. *Ability to handle closeness and separation:* Through day-to-day experiences, the child and the family can develop mechanisms for coping with separation. Effective coping skills tend to be developed if parents clarify the reasons for their departures, attend to children's feelings of loneliness, and inquire about the activities that have occurred in other family members' lives during an absence. If separation has been poorly managed, children may become clinging and demanding, and may be unable to function autonomously in school or elsewhere.

   If children have had good experiences with closeness the basic trust they have makes them willing to invest themselves in a new and different type of relationship with their teachers. Children who have not had sufficient experience with closeness may resist any relationship with the teacher, often becoming restless, uncommunicative, and hyperactive in the classroom.

2. *Ability to communicate emotions:* The ways in which emotions are communicated and received within the family teach children how to handle emotions in peer groups and in school. When the family has developed mechanisms for sharing even difficult emotions (such as anger and frustration), children learn to accept their own emotions as a normal part of life. They develop the "constancy of inner emotions" that allows them to keep their attention focused on learning. If they do not achieve this, they may be distracted from their tasks by disturbing or unexpressed feelings. For example, a boy may avoid reading a story because he is upset by the events that it relates.

3. *Ability to communicate perceptions:* In the family, children are first encouraged to communicate about what they hear, see, and touch. They learn to find pleasure in the exercise of their perceptual abilities—but only if they are continually rewarded for

communicating their perceptions to other family members. This effective sharing of perceptions has long been understood to foster good learning abilities. (It is probably for this reason that many educational television programs, rather than simply informing, show close-ups of objects and ask children to guess how they look or feel.)

4. *Ability to communicate ideas*: As toddlers, children also begin to communicate their ideas, through talk, questions, and play. How the family receives these communications—and how other family members communicate themselves—becomes important.

5. *Ability to use language*: In some families, language is used in a primitive fashion—"just enough to get across the basic feelings, but not enough to refine them" (Brown, 1973, p. 26). This makes the sharing of feelings very difficult, and it may lead to misunderstanding, fear, and insensitivity. When families use language effectively, they are able to refine and fully formulate their ideas and feelings. And this helps children to develop abilities that will greatly aid their adjustment to school and other social settings.

6. *Ability to experience bodily freedom and pleasure*: As toddlers, children show natural curiosity about their bodies. As they develop, they learn either to accept their bodily functions and pleasures, or to be self-conscious, guilty, and ashamed of them. It appears that when children feel uncomfortable with their bodies, they may be excitable, distractible, and unable to concentrate on formal learning.

7. *Ability to clarify reality and fantasy*: As we have seen, children have a different idea of reality than adults. It is helpful to children if parents talk about ghosts, spacemen, or television dinosaurs, helping the child sort out the real from the unreal. When a child has unrealistic expectations or fears, family members need to address them, being careful to listen to and respect the child's view. In less favorable situations, the parent does not help the child differentiate between reality and fantasy. Sometimes, the parent plays on the fantasy to frighten the child into better behavior, saying, "The bogeyman will get you." The child who has good experiences in clarifying reality and fantasy is better prepared to engage in imaginative sharing of activities in school.

8. *Ability to resolve interpersonal conflicts*: The abilities to empathize with and listen to others will help the child adjust to the school environment. However, if a girl has experienced ineffective ways of resolving conflicts at home—if her parents typically shame, rigidly punish or engage in childish confrontations with her—she will be less prepared to handle conflicts with peers at school. She may withdraw, or insist on having her way in any play situation.

We are not born with social
skills; we must learn them. For
some individuals, this learning
comes more easily than for
others.

9. *Ability to fulfill goals and complete projects*: The child's
participation in family projects and experiences in working toward
fairly distant goals prepares him to become involved in organized
activities in school. In some families this is achieved through
participation in athletic or camping activities; in others, family
members work together on household maintenance projects. What is
important is that the child learn to engage in activities that lead to a
gratifying result. When a child's family is too disorganized or
demoralized to do this, he is not well prepared to complete schoolwork
or participate in group learning activities.

10. *Ability to use memory effectively*: Positively recalled family events
help the child construct an identity; they also give him a positive
attitude toward the mastering of present experience. It is probably for
this reason that nursery school teachers often ask children to bring in
photographs of themselves as babies; the photos are shared and
perhaps pasted on the bulletin board or cubby holes in the first week
of school. Of course memory is not always used in this pleasant way.
When memory is consistently used to remind the child of past
failures, it contributes to anxiety and perhaps to a negative attitude
toward learning in the new setting.

11. *Ability to use roles flexibly*: Under favorable circumstances children develop good one-to-one relationships with a variety of people in their social environment. If they do, they likely take on many different roles and will be well prepared to form good relationships with teachers and peers at school. However, if a child is rigidly required to perform only one role in the family, difficulties will probably be experienced in school. Thus, the child who is set on being Daddy's Little Girl at home may be so concerned with gaining praise at school that she is unable to make friends or invest herself in the learning process.

Brown's points are interesting because they show how early family experience can affect the child's ability to adjust to school. It should be remembered, of course, that the school is one part of the child/school relationship, and sometimes it too has inadequacies. The teacher, for example, may suffer from being too rigid herself. The point is that the child who has a supportive family and has developed the strengths and coping skills described above will be best equipped to cope with an unfavorable as well as a favorable school situation, and will be less vulnerable to failure.

Schools are designed to prepare youngsters to live in society. Children enjoy attending because it provides opportunities to learn, but the major attraction for them is their peers (Fishbein, 1984). Children seek friendships and their success or failure in this enterprise is quite clear, as Beck, Neeper, Baskin, and Forehand (1983) demonstrated when they asked elementary school children to rate how popular they were in their classroom. The children knew whether they were among the most or least popular in the class or whether they fell in between.

Social skills and academic success are related to popularity in the lower grades (Beck, Collins, Overholser, & Terry, 1985; Bossert, 1979). Bossert found, in fact, that children who were friends in the third grade ended their association in the fourth grade if differences in academic achievements became apparent.

Several approaches to training children in the social skills necessary for making friends have proven effective. They have ranged from teaching problem-solving techniques and reducing a child's aggressiveness to asking a child to advise the experimenter as to what he might tell a friendless child (Urbain & Kendall, 1985). Oden and Asher (1977) coached socially isolated students by teaching them friendship skills (see Table 7.2). After a lesson, they had the subjects play with peers and participate in postplay reviews of their play session with their coach. Following the month-long study and one year later, these subjects were identified by peers as possible playmates more often on a questionnaire than they had been before the coaching. The topic of friendship is discussed in considerably more detail in Chapter 8.

TABLE 7.2 *Training Children in One Social Skill Necessary for Making Friends*

The following dialogue includes an example from the basic script used to coach the concept of cooperation and illustrates typical responses given by children.

Coach: Okay, I have some ideas about what makes a game fun to play with another person. There are a couple of things that are important to do. You should *cooperate* with the other person. Do you know what cooperation is? Can you tell me in your own words?

Child: Ahh . . . sharing.

Coach: Yes, sharing. Okay, let's say you and I are playing the game you played last time. What was it again?

Child: Drawing a picture.

Coach: Okay, tell me then, what would be an example of sharing when playing the picture-drawing game?

Child: I'd let you use some of the pens too.

Coach: Right. You would share the pens with me. That's an example of cooperation. Now let's say you and I are doing the picture-drawing game, can you also give me an example of what would *not* be cooperating?

Child: Taking all the pens.

Coach: Would taking all the pens make the game fun to play?

Child: No!

Coach: So you wouldn't take all the pens. Instead, you'd *cooperate* by *sharing* them with me. Can you think of some more examples of cooperation? [The coach waited for a response.] Okay, how about taking turns . . . Okay, I'd like you to try out some of these ideas when you play [name of new game] with [other child]. Let's go and get [other child], and after you play I'll talk to you again . . . and you can tell me if these things seem to be good ideas for having fun.

(The child plays a new game with another youngster.)

In the 3–5 minute postplay review, the coach asked the child, Did you get a chance to try out some of the ideas we talked about? [The coach waited for a response.] Do you think that [other child] liked playing the game?

Source: From S. Oden and S. Asher, "Coaching Children in Social Skills for Friendship-Making" in *Child Development* 48: 495–506, 1977. Copyright © 1977 The Society for Research in Child Development, Inc. Reprinted by permission.

Television

Children born after World War II face a challenge unimagined by those who preceded them. It first appeared when your parents and grandparents congregated in the only house in the neighborhood that had a television. Huddled around the set that may well have had a magnifying glass affixed to its screen, they watched with marvel the first broadcasts. Now television is an important part of nearly all children's daily activities. And, through programs and commercial messages, they are exposed to ideas, characters, events, and a quick pace they rarely experience in their "real" lives.

Television sets play up to six hours a day in the typical American home and preschoolers watch as much as 3–4 hours of it (Pearl, Bouthilet, & Lazar, 1982). By about age nine, among the best predictors of whether a child sees the world as "scary," and whether a teacher rates the child's behavioral adjustment to the classroom as poor, is determined by: (1) how frequently the youngster watches action adventure programs (like detective shows); and (2) how television is used in the home (the number of sets, their accessibility to the child, and the availability of cable programs).

Based on their research, Singer and Singer (1986) state that too much television viewing can effect children's behavior, making them more prone to act aggressively and to feel restless, discontent, and anxious. Further, Schwartz (1982), argues that in many homes television has superceded the family and school as a major socializing force. Youngsters are finding answers to questions they have regarding personal relationships, sexuality, health, and their careers in programs and commercials.

Sex Roles

Historically, societies have assigned men and women particular behavior roles. The assignment has been based on societal needs, physical differences in the bodies of the sexes, and other factors (see Self-Knowledge Box). In our society for instance, assignments have been shaped by assumptions about psychosocial differences (women being more caring, interested in their personal appearances, and less interested in power) thought to stem from biological factors. Scientists are questioning those assumptions, suggesting that societal teachings as well as biological imperatives are involved in producing observable differences in the current behavior of the sexes (Hyde & Linn, 1986).

When people speak of "sex roles," they are referring to cultural expectations about appropriate behavior for men and women including, but not limited to, the personality traits they should show and the tasks and responsibilities they should assume. The traditional male sex role indicates men should be strong, emotionally controlled, and successful, providing for their dependent wife and children. The traditional female sex role indicates women should be attractive, nurturant, and dependent on their husband's income, focusing their efforts on maintaining the marriage, raising the children, and creating a happy home.

Children acquire knowledge about sex roles, and what behavior is appropriate for them, in various ways. They observe their own families and parents, who serve as models. They are taught directly, in straightforward terms: "Gentlemen do . . . Ladies . . ." and indirectly. For example, girls are often inadvertently taught to be timid when deprived of opportunities to explore the environment by misdirected parental helpfulness (Block, 1984). Sometimes parents limit their daughter's activities because of overconcern of safety. Other times parents overprotect their daughter from the risk of failure, unintentionally teaching the girl to shy away from, rather than accept, appropriate challenges. Mothers, for instance, may provide excess, unneeded help to their daughter's efforts to solve a problem with her girlfriends (Block, 1984). An unintended consequence of such parental intervention is to deprive her child of opportunities to develop determination, by trying alternative problem-solving approaches until one works, and to build self-confidence as a result of mastery.

Defining Male and Female Activities

How much of your masculinity and femininity do you understand and accept? To help you to determine the answer to this question, list below the "typical" male and female chores and activities that you routinely perform:

Male Chores and Activities

1.
2.
3.
4.
5.
6.
7.
8.
9.
10.

Female Chores and Activities

1.
2.
3.
4.
5.
6.
7.
8.
9.
10.

Would you want to do away with one of these lists? Why?

Are there any actions on either list that you would be embarrassed to perform in front of males? Females? Why or why not?

Are there any chores or activities on your lists that should be performed by males only? Females only? Why?

The answers to these questions will help you decide whether or not you are comfortable with both the masculinity and femininity in your personality. You should be aware of how you express both your maleness and your femaleness (i.e., your humanness) and be comfortable with that expression.

Besides learning from family, television broadcasts, day-care/school influences, and other sources, children's peers help teach children about sex roles. In the elementary school years children seek same-sex friends. Serafica and Rose (1982) explain that such choices both demonstrate children's desire to learn sex-appropriate behavior (behavior for which they will be rewarded) and help them master this type of knowledge. Part of what children are learning, of course, are **sex role stereotypes.**

Sex role stereotypes are widely held assumptions and beliefs about personality traits, characteristics, and skills of men and women, in general. One is responding to a stereotype by drawing conclusions about a person's traits

Sex Role Stereotypes
Widely held assumptions about personality traits, characteristics, and skills of men and women, in general.

based on his or her sex alone, without any other information about the person as an individual. This may be true even if one draws a conclusion about which there are real differences. For instance, males are generally superior to females in tasks requiring visual-spatial ability. An employer would be reacting to a stereotype if he or she hired a male applicant over a female one for a job requiring such abilities, without testing or interviewing the candidates. And that points to some of the major concerns with stereotypes: they cause unfairness, they limit the potential of individuals, and they damage society in ways ranging from limiting the productivity of the labor force (due to non-optimal use of human resources) to hampering the mental health of its members.

We often think of femininity and masculinity as opposite ends of a continuum, like day and night or white and black. Such thinking means that characteristics like leadership or sensitivity have to be assigned to one sex or the other. If leadership is seen as masculine and sensitivity as feminine, then no one person could have both traits. If, however, masculinity and femininity are instead viewed as two separate dimensions, then a person could have traits from both dimensions.

The term "androgyny" comes from the Greek words, *andros* and *gynes,* meaning man and woman, respectively. A person who comfortably behaves in ways that have traditionally fallen within the sex roles of both men and women can be described as androgynous. This individual has great flexibility in adjusting to the demands of a particular situation, being able to react sensitively or assertively, or in whatever way required with equal comfort (Bem, 1974).

Conscience and Moral Behavior

In the early school years, children begin to identify with parents of the same sex and consciously and unconsciously model their behavior after him or her. For example, they imitate aggressive behaviors and pick up manners of talking and behaving in social situations. By this time they have also come to understand what is right and wrong, or at least what one is praised and punished for. In this primitive way children develop a sense of moral responsibility and conscientious behavior.

In the middle school years, conscience develops further. The child has internalized many of the values and restrictions of the parents. In Freudian terms, the child has developed a superego that is in a preliminary stage of morality, preliminary because it does not really indulge in serious self-criticism, but reacts mainly to threats of external punishment (A. Freud, 1936/1966).

Piaget and Inhelder (1969) are among cognitive psychologists who have studied conscience and moral behavior and who have found that these behaviors are not simply the outgrowth of social learning. They also depend on cognitive or intellectual development. Until children can think abstractly (which most cannot do before adolescence), their good behavior can be motivated only by a desire to conform and maintain the social order as they perceive it (Kohlberg, 1963, 1968). School-age children, if asked to explain their "bad" behavior, will typically say that they meant well or were only doing what everyone else was doing. At this stage, children's behavior is most influenced by the need to have approval or avoid punishment.

As children near adolescence, they begin to understand cooperation as a value in its own right. They come to appreciate the need to be "democratic" and to understand the informal "social contracts" that exist to protect one another's rights. The growth of moral understanding affects adjustment to life in numerous ways. As children move from a "good child"-"bad child" orientation into the social-contract world of adolescence, their ideas about themselves change. They are better able to compromise. Their interpretation of events becomes more rational and less egotistical as they see what people "should do" for the common good. This growth in understanding also prepares children for one of the most positive upheavals of life, the questioning of parental values, and the taking of one's own moral stand, in adolescence.

"Industry versus Inferiority": The Fourth Psychosocial Crisis in Erikson's Theory

How do children emerge from the elementary school years? Erikson describes these years as being characterized by the child's conviction, "I am what I learn" (Erikson, 1959). Children gain a sense of **industry** when they are able to successfully complete the projects they undertake, such as helping with the laundry, finishing a painting, or solving an arithmetic problem. They experience the pride of being part of a productive group. As a result, they emerge with a sense of industry that allows them to take setbacks and short-comings in stride (a facility that is favorable to future adjustment, for obvious reasons). Of course,

Industry
Favorable outcomes of Erikson's fourth stage, the abilities to be productive, to follow rules, and to do work, develop if a child is encouraged to undertake and complete tasks.

some children emerge with a less favorable outcome. What they experience in the school years only builds upon what they have experienced earlier: it convinces them that they are inadequate and inferior. They take even small difficulties as personal defeats, become dependent on others, or find uneasy refuge in conformity.

Erikson thought that the stage during which the child struggled with industry versus inferiority was socially a most decisive stage. At least one important study supports this view. The study, which followed 456 inner-city white men for 35 years, found that industriousness, the willingness and capacity to work hard in childhood, was the most important factor in predicting adult mental health. Industrious children grew up to have the most successful work lives and the most satisfying personal relationships (Vaillant & Vaillant, 1981).

ADOLESCENCE: THE TRANSITION TO ADULTHOOD

All the stages of the life span can be regarded as transitions, periods in which the individual must accomplish certain tasks, resolve certain maturational (normal) crises, and progress from one level of development to the next. Adolescence above all seems to be a transition between two major periods of life. It is, therefore, rightly considered an unusually critical period of adjustment. We begin this stage of life as "children at play, dependently attached to [our] parents and with [our] futures unshaped." We leave this stage as young adults, "responsible for [our] selves, [our] personalities patterned, [our] future direction indicated" (Lidz, 1976, p. 307).

"Ego Identity versus Role Confusion": The Fifth Psychosocial Crisis in Erikson's Theory

The developments of adolescence are not confined to physical and sexual maturation. Young people between the ages of 12 and 18 experience marked intellectual and cognitive growth as well. Not only do they assimilate an enormous amount of information and acquire a wide variety of skills, but they develop many new ways of observing the world and thinking about it. What Piaget has called "formal operations" become possible in adolescence, and this opens up the whole range of logical and abstract thought. Adolescents are able to cope with their world on new terms. They tend to philosophize and theorize, to hold reality up and measure it against the ideal formulations they imagine. Further, they are often able to think about themselves with greater objectivity than before. Erikson has described adolescents as involved in a process of simultaneous reflection and observation, on all levels of functioning. They are judging *themselves* the way they perceive others judge them, and they are judging the *community* for its way of judging them (Erikson, 1968). Through this continuing process, the individual attempts to form an identity that "works" for both the inner self and the outer environment.

Crucial to the development of identity is the adolescent's ability to integrate new experiences (for example, sexual and intellectual experiences) into the personality that has been developing all along. It is difficult to build on a foundation that does not include the trust, autonomy, initiative, and industry of Erikson's earlier stages, for all of the earlier crises are reworked at the level of adolescent needs.

Just as developing infants struggle with the need for basic trust, so too do adolescents. Adolescents must learn again to trust their bodies, the continuity of their personalities, and their physical needs. They must find people and ideals to have faith in, then try to prove both to themselves and to those they respect that they are trustworthy. Adolescence also brings a new desire for autonomy. Adolescents need to feel unconstrained by arbitrary parental power and there is much rebellion in these years. Initiative and industry are also necessary tools for the adolescent, who must now begin to formulate and work toward future goals.

During the identity crisis, individuals may feel vulnerable, at risk, in danger of "falling apart or diffusing into nothingness" (Keniston, 1970, pp. 639–640). Usually these are temporary, "typical" feelings. In some cases, however, young people are rather severely inhibited by "role confusion," the failure to find (even temporarily) a comfortable and positive identity. This confusion may be due to a sexual identity crisis, or it may have to do with future goals. In our culture, for example, confusion about the choice of an occupation or profession is particularly common in adolescence, yet it is usually resolved (if only temporarily) by the end of this period.

Although adolescence is normally a period of personal crisis and may appear to be more disruptive to the individual than earlier periods, adolescents are on the whole better equipped to handle identity issues than younger children. For one thing, they are intellectually more advanced and can observe themselves more objectively. For another, they have more social resources. An example: some adolescents cope by identifying themselves with a group, thus constructing a "transitional identity." Group participation, such as club memberships, affiliations with political or religious organizations, and athletic teams, all give the adolescent a sense of belonging to something that provides a support system and at least a temporary identity.

To summarize, the adolescent crisis involves the person's identity as an individual. The adolescent asks some basic questions: "Who am I? How does the person I seem to be now connect with the child I remember being long ago, or with the person I imagine myself becoming as the future unfolds?" If the new aspects of the adolescent's experience come to feel comfortable, the outcome will be the formation of a strong **ego identity.** If not, if the person experiences discord between different aspects of his or her personality, then *role confusion* results. Adolescents may swing back and forth between independence and dependency and try new styles and new manners as well as new friends and new ideas with a dizzying inconsistency. The object is to emerge with a strong sense of oneself and a true sense of direction in charting the rest of one's life, no small task, as most adolescents and their parents would agree.

Ego Identity
A favorable outcome of Erikson's fifth stage; an individual's gradual definition of who he or she is that is acquired if he has support from others.

Puberty and Sexual Development

Adolescence begins with the onset of puberty at age 12 or 13, and lasts until the age of 18 or 19. Spanning the teen years, in our society this period is said to last until the individual attains economic or social independence (entering the job market, going to college, getting married, or reaching legal majority).

The most obvious changes that take place in adolescence are physical. In early adolescence there is a dramatic growth spurt that coincides with sexual maturation. In girls, the breasts begin to develop and the menarche, or first menstrual period, occurs. Pubic hair appears, and hips and breasts enlarge as additional fat is deposited in the adult pattern. Boys experience the growth of facial hair, an increase in musculature, a deepening of the voice, maturation of the penis and scrotum, and the first ejaculation. Less obvious, but just as important, are the endocrinological (hormonal) changes that are responsible for the appearance of these sexual characteristics. Hormonal change may contribute to emotional and behavioral changes; for example, to irritability, mood instability, or unaccountable bouts of aggression and depression. In short, changes in the body and its sexual functions upset the relative quiet of the earlier school years.

Puberty usually brings with it a reawakening of the sexual drives, as well as (according to Freudian theory) the old Oedipal feelings. This time the Oedipal feelings occur under more threatening circumstances. For example, the daughter is now more realistically her mother's rival, and she may appear startlingly attractive to her father. For daughters and sons, the conflict must again be resolved, usually through the selection of a more appropriate partner. Most adolescents seek sexual satisfaction from peers of the opposite sex. The focus of sexual desire and satisfaction becomes genital—more or less permanently and exclusively centered in the genital organs. The sexual instinct begins to direct itself toward the act of coitus, and therefore toward the biological aim of reproduction.

The timing of sexual development varies considerably. Throughout childhood, individuals display different rates of physical growth, largely because of inherited growth patterns. At early adolescence, differences in rates of growth become conspicuous. Maturing sexually very early or very late relative to one's friends has social and sometimes psychological consequences (Clausen, 1975).

Most research suggests that the early-maturing boy is at a social advantage. He is bigger and stronger, and because of this he often achieves a position of leadership in sports, becoming captain of the football team, for example. The early-maturing boy receives early assurance of his masculinity. He is expected to behave in a more adult manner than his less mature peers (Duke et al., 1982). He tends to be perceived as more relaxed and confident in social situations, such as dating and relating to adults and is often poised and relaxed (Siegel, 1982). Jones (1957), who followed subjects longitudinally into their 30s, found most of these differences between early and late maturing males disappeared over time.

Maturing later is usually difficult for the adolescent boy. Because he appears to be less adult than his peers, he sometimes develops feelings of inadequacy. He may wonder, "Will I ever grow up, be attractive to girls, and earn the respect of parents and other adults?" Sometimes the coping mechanisms of the late-maturing boy are compensatory, as if he is saying, "I'm small, but please notice me." For example, he may be overly talkative, engage in attention-getting behaviors, or set unrealistic goals in an effort to demonstrate superiority in some area. Feelings of inadequacy may persist into adulthood. However, some of the coping mechanisms developed by late-maturing boys may serve them well in adulthood. These boys appear to be more willing to face their feelings and, as adults, they are described as more insightful than early maturers, and as having more flexible personalities (Jones, 1957).

The social and psychological effects of early and late sexual maturation in girls are less clear (Siegel, 1982). In the 1940s, researchers found that early maturation was a disadvantage. Today, however, it cannot be consistently regarded as a disadvantage or an advantage. The girl who matures much earlier than her friends may feel conspicuous and socially awkward. Likewise, the girl who matures much later than her friends may experience anxiety about whether she will ever become womanly, attractive, and popular with boys. However, few of these effects persist into adulthood.

Family Relations

Adolescents' relationships with their family are characterized by the need to sever childhood bonds in order to establish themselves as independent people. Important in this process is the reevaluation of parents and their values, with the aim of making adult, independent choices. In adolescence the person comes to question the powerful assumption that "there is only one way to do things—the parents' way" (Gould, 1978). Adolescents gradually come to understand that doing things their parents' way will not protect them from failure. At the same time they see that acting in opposition to their parents' beliefs will not bring the expected disaster or disgrace that it used to. Thus adolescents begin to develop their own standards.

One area in which "the-correct-way-to-do-things" assumption has been strongly questioned is the definition of sex roles. In the past, most parents, and society as a whole, held firm expectations about how males and females should behave, what work they should do, and what personal attributes they ought to have. Today, there is considerable experimentation in sex roles, and some recognition that a well-adjusted person may possess personality attributes that are both "masculine" and "feminine" as traditionally designated. In our present environment of changing sex roles, maturing adolescents typically have a need to develop their own role identities. In doing so they question their parents' assumptions about the "correct way to do things" for a man or woman.

Often this involves a conscious need to differentiate oneself from the same-sex parent. For example, a young woman may reject her mother's advice on dress and "the way to behave with boys" as well as her ideas about what constitutes a fulfilling career for a woman. At the same time this adolescent must cope with fears that if she does not follow her mother's advice, she will indeed be rejected by men and become "too successful" at her job to be really happy. In defining new sex roles, as in the questioning of other parental values, the adolescent may experience a temporary loss of security. The loss, though necessary as part of growth, is real: "The idea that there is only one right way, and that we can find a magic key to the complex processes of reality, is a lifelong hope as we try to guarantee our future and erase the terror of the unknown" (Gould, 1978, p. 88).

Not surprisingly, there remains in the adolescent a longing for childhood dependence. This may cause a conflict for adolescents who find that their fight for independence is followed by a sense of loneliness and the wish to revert to a dependent and comforting state. In some cases adolescents cope with this by propelling themselves forward, returning only now and then for "emotional refueling." In other cases, they rebel totally against their need for dependence, and deny having any reliance on parents or other family members. In most cases, adolescents express an ambivalent attitude toward their parents. They seek psychological detachment from them but at the same time want to "remain on good terms." They are often heard to say that their parents do not understand them, but at times need to be reassured of their parents' love and understanding (Goleman, 1980).

Regardless of the clarity of parental-adolescent communication at the time, as young adults make the separation, they take with them the skills and tools of life they developed over the years at home. They also carry a set of attitudes that were fostered there. Adolescents who grew up in a supportive home—who enjoyed family members and felt they were listened to and respected—are among those who will likely move onward with healthier self-esteems (Hoelter & Harper, 1987).

The Peer Group

Interactions within the peer group can have a powerful socializing influence on the adolescent. The peer group often provides a source of support, security, and identity for the adolescent who no longer seeks these things exclusively from the family. It can also take on former parental functions—everything from choosing clothes to making moral judgments. Since friends usually come from similar backgrounds, the peer group often endorses values similar to the teenager's parents (Siegel, 1982). However, in some cases, the group may discard parental morals completely and pressure its members to assert their adult status through sexual activity or the use of alcohol or drugs. In fact, one school of thinking (Oetting & Beauvis, 1987) maintains that the peer group is the most powerful factor regarding the adolescent drug-use decision. Peers help form attitudes about drugs, supply the drugs, host the setting in which drugs are used, and provide a rationale for the decision to consume drugs.

Teenagers who have a strong identity and are secure with who and what they are will tend to exercise their own sense of judgment and not succumb to peer pressure. They come to assert their independence from peers, as they earlier asserted independence from their parents.

America has been described by Packard (1972) as a nation of strangers. More than 42 million people moved in the year ending March, 1987 (USA, May 11, 1989, p. 3A). To the vast legions of children who begin the fall term in new neighborhoods and new schools, building and maintaining friendships present a special challenge. One study examined the impact on children's social lives of family relocation initiated by corporate transfer (Brett, 1982). The data indicated that teenagers in the 15–18-year-old bracket were most affected, missing old friends more than younger boys and girls, and having greater difficulty in making new ones.

SITUATIONAL CRISES

In this chapter we have seen that individuals in our culture pass through certain normal and expectable crises. However, as we all know from observation of the many lives around us, individuals also experience crises that do not emerge from the normal process of maturation, but are more like accidents, emergencies, or special circumstances. We call these occurrences **situational crises.** Like the normal crisis, the situational crisis represents both an opportunity and a danger. The person may emerge from the crisis with enhanced coping abilities, or may be overwhelmed and turn back to less mature or ineffective coping mechanisms. The outcome of a situational crisis depends on the interplay of a number of factors, among them the age (developmental level) of the person when the crisis situation is encountered; the ego strengths that have been developed so far; the person's experience with other crises; and the kinds and quality of supports that exist in the person's environment.

Situational Crises
Emergencies or special circumstances that occur in an individual's life, whose outcome will depend on age, ego strengths, and other factors.

We can see how all these factors interact to create a unique life history if, for example, we develop the story of the two sons with which this chapter began—one who became a teetotaler and the other an alcoholic. Let us arbitrarily assume that Son 1 is three years older than Son 2. What might account for the different outcomes of the two sons in young adulthood?

First, the sons may have emerged differently from the same maturational crisis of trust versus mistrust. Let us say, for example, that in infancy the sons encountered very different family situations.

When Son 1 was born, his father held a good job, and though he had had problems with alcohol in the past, he was not drinking then. The mother was optimistic about life and thrilled with the birth of a first child who was a son, just as she had hoped. The maternal grandmother was on hand to help with the new baby, who was widely acknowledged to be an "easy" baby—cute, cuddly, an early smiler and talker.

Son 2 was born just after his father lost a good job. During the first six months of his life, his father was at home all day, and the house was full of tension. Son 2 suffered from recurrent gastrointestinal distress, and his irritability and crying made matters worse for everyone. His mother was overworked and worried about the family's financial situation. The maternal grandmother was then too crippled by arthritis to be much help with the new baby, and in fact her complaining added to the mother's burden. The mother felt isolated from her husband, and though she did not admit it, she was depressed at the thought that she would never have a daughter. About the only bright spot in the family was Son 1, who was adjusting beautifully. Things improved when the father found a job. However, it proved to be not as satisfying as the job he had lost, and he began drinking heavily again.

On the basis of this information, we could not have said for certain what the outcome for these two sons would be. But it seems clear that Son 1 was more likely to emerge from infancy with a strong attachment to his mother and with basic trust in the world.

What about situational crises that might have occurred when the sons were older? Let us suppose that when Son 1 was eleven years old and Son 2 was eight, the father disappeared for several months and upon his return was hospitalized briefly for treatment of alcohol-related diseases. During this period the family functioned as a single-parent family.

In this situation Son 1 was able to draw upon a number of strengths in addition to "basic trust." An early experience with an eye problem, requiring minor surgery and hospitalization, had helped him develop coping mechanisms that were effective in the present crisis. He knew how to ask for help and how to talk about his feelings. He had, moreover, some understanding of hospitalization, so it was not a foreign concept to him. During the time his father was absent, Son 1 also had a variety of social supports, including a teacher who took a special interest in him, and his ophthalmologist who functioned as a kind of father figure to him. Also, Son 1 was old enough to hold an after-school job delivering advertisements. He felt that he was helping out by earning money for his lunch and school supplies. Because he was so responsible, his mother allowed him some independence. For example, she felt

Situational Crises in Your Life

Johnson and McCutcheon's (Johnson, 1986) Life Events Checklist is presented below. It contains 46 events, most of which can be experienced as situational crises or milestone points during childhood and adolescence. It also provides space for respondents to enter items not already listed.

The Life Events Checklist

Instructions: Below is a list of things that sometimes happen to people. (A) Put an X in the space by each of the events you have experienced during the past year (12 months). (B) For each of the events you check circle whether you would rate the event as a *Good* event or as a *Bad* event. (C) Finally, indicate how much you feel the event has changed or has had an impact or effect on your life by placing a circle around the appropriate statement (no effect, some effect, moderate effect, great effect).

Please read over the entire list. Then respond to those events you have actually experienced during the past year.

Event	Type of Event		Impact or Effect			
___ 1. Moving to new home	Good	Bad	no effect	some effect	moderate effect	great effect
___ 2. New brother or sister	Good	Bad	no effect	some effect	moderate effect	great effect
___ 3. Changing to new school	Good	Bad	no effect	some effect	moderate effect	great effect
___ 4. Serious illness or injury of family member	Good	Bad	no effect	some effect	moderate effect	great effect
___ 5. Parents divorced	Good	Bad	no effect	some effect	moderate effect	great effect
___ 6. Increased number of arguments between parents	Good	Bad	no effect	some effect	moderate effect	great effect
___ 7. Mother or father lost job	Good	Bad	no effect	some effect	moderate effect	great effect
___ 8. Death of a family member	Good	Bad	no effect	some effect	moderate effect	great effect
___ 9. Parents separated	Good	Bad	no effect	some effect	moderate effect	great effect
___ 10. Death of a close friend	Good	Bad	no effect	some effect	moderate effect	great effect
___ 11. Increased absence of parent from the home	Good	Bad	no effect	some effect	moderate effect	great effect
___ 12. Brother or sister leaving home	Good	Bad	no effect	some effect	moderate effect	great effect

SOURCE: From "Assessing Life Stress in Older Children and Adolescents: Preliminary Findings with the Life Events Checklist" by J. J. Johnson and S. M. McCutcheon in *Stress and Anxiety*, 1980. Copyright 1980 Hemisphere Publishing. Reprinted by permission.

he was old enough to go alone to meet his friends at the community center and the roller rink.

Son 2 experienced his father's absence very differently. Though he knew (intellectually) that it was not so, he feared that he was somehow responsible for his father's leaving home. Because his ideas about hospitalization had been formed when his grandmother entered the hospital and did not return, he also had vague fears for his father's life.

Event	Type of Event		Impact or Effect			
___ 13. Serious illness or injury of close friend	Good	Bad	no effect	some effect	moderate effect	great effect
___ 14. Parent getting into trouble with law	Good	Bad	no effect	some effect	moderate effect	great effect
___ 15. Parent getting a new job	Good	Bad	no effect	some effect	moderate effect	great effect
___ 16. New stepmother or stepfather	Good	Bad	no effect	some effect	moderate effect	great effect
___ 17. Parent going to jail	Good	Bad	no effect	some effect	moderate effect	great effect
___ 18. Change in parents' financial status	Good	Bad	no effect	some effect	moderate effect	great effect
___ 19. Trouble with brother or sister	Good	Bad	no effect	some effect	moderate effect	great effect
___ 20. Special recognition for good grades	Good	Bad	no effect	some effect	moderate effect	great effect
___ 21. Joining a new club	Good	Bad	no effect	some effect	moderate effect	great effect
___ 22. Losing a close friend	Good	Bad	no effect	some effect	moderate effect	great effect
___ 23. Decrease in number of arguments with parents	Good	Bad	no effect	some effect	moderate effect	great effect
___ 24. Male: girlfriend getting pregnant	Good	Bad	no effect	some effect	moderate effect	great effect
___ 25. Female: getting pregnant	Good	Bad	no effect	some effect	moderate effect	great effect
___ 26. Losing a job	Good	Bad	no effect	some effect	moderate effect	great effect
___ 27. Making the honor role	Good	Bad	no effect	some effect	moderate effect	great effect
___ 28. Getting your own car	Good	Bad	no effect	some effect	moderate effect	great effect
___ 29. New boyfriend/girlfriend	Good	Bad	no effect	some effect	moderate effect	great effect
___ 30. Failing a grade	Good	Bad	no effect	some effect	moderate effect	great effect
___ 31. Increase in number of arguments with parents	Good	Bad	no effect	some effect	moderate effect	great effect
___ 32. Getting a job of your own	Good	Bad	no effect	some effect	moderate effect	great effect
___ 33. Getting into trouble with police	Good	Bad	no effect	some effect	moderate effect	great effect
___ 34. Major personal illness or injury	Good	Bad	no effect	some effect	moderate effect	great effect
___ 35. Breaking up with boyfriend/ girlfriend	Good	Bad	no effect	some effect	moderate effect	great effect

Unlike his brother, he had not had experiences that had taught him how to talk about his feelings or to ask for help. After school Son 2 had taken to watching a lot of television—anything that was on. Because he was too young to hold a job or meet friends independently, he spent a great deal of time at home, even when his mother was at work. He thought a lot about bringing off some dramatic event that would change the family situation, for example, winning one of the sweepstakes advertised on television. He also dreamed about writing a song that would be accepted by a rock group on the rise.

Situational Crises in Your Life (Continued)

	Event	Type of Event		Impact or Effect			
___ 36.	Making up with boyfriend/ girlfriend	Good	Bad	no effect	some effect	moderate effect	great effect
___ 37.	Trouble with teacher	Good	Bad	no effect	some effect	moderate effect	great effect
___ 38.	Male: girlfriend having abortion	Good	Bad	no effect	some effect	moderate effect	great effect
___ 39.	Female: having abortion	Good	Bad	no effect	some effect	moderate effect	great effect
___ 40.	Failing to make an athletic team	Good	Bad	no effect	some effect	moderate effect	great effect
___ 41.	Being suspended from school	Good	Bad	no effect	some effect	moderate effect	great effect
___ 42.	Making failing grades on report card	Good	Bad	no effect	some effect	moderate effect	great effect
___ 43.	Making an athletic team	Good	Bad	no effect	some effect	moderate effect	great effect
___ 44.	Trouble with classmates	Good	Bad	no effect	some effect	moderate effect	great effect
___ 45.	Special recognition for athletic performance	Good	Bad	no effect	some effect	moderate effect	great effect
___ 46.	Getting put in jail	Good	Bad	no effect	some effect	moderate effect	great effect
	Other events which have had an impact on your life. List and rate.						
___ 47.	_____ _____	Good	Bad	no effect	some effect	moderate effect	great effect
___ 48.	_____ _____	Good	Bad	no effect	some effect	moderate effect	great effect
___ 49.	_____ _____	Good	Bad	no effect	some effect	moderate effect	great effect
___ 50.	_____ _____	Good	Bad	no effect	some effect	moderate effect	great effect

1. Take the checklist and score it as follows. Counting 0 points for "no effect," 1 for "some effect," 2 for "moderate effect," and 3 points for "great effect," tally points for the positive (good) and negative (bad) events you encountered during the last year.
2. Johnson (1986) reports that high negative scores have been related to reports of physical health and personal and psychological problems. People with high positive scores tended to have fewer medical visits than those with lower scores. Do these findings make sense to you?
3. Re-examine the checklist and count how many of these events you have experienced to this point in your life. What new coping skills or personal abilities did you develop as you sought to deal with each event you experienced?
4. Re-examine the list one more time and identify those events which you believe fall into the category of situational crisis. ▲

The information in this case does not enable us to say for certain what would happen in the lives described. But if we were to meet these two sons as adolescents, we would not be surprised to learn that Son 1 had many friends (but had resisted peer pressures to drink and take drugs), that he had become an unusually hard-working student, and that he had begun to talk to his vocational counselor about the possibility of becoming an ophthalmologist. Nor would we be surprised to learn that it was Son 2, without friends or realistic plans for the future, who began to blot out the pain of adolescence with alcohol.

From the preceding case example we can see that maturational and situational crises interact in a unique way to shape an individual's life. Because each case is different, we cannot easily generalize about the role of situational crises in our lives. The most we can do, in coming to understand our own lives, is to examine the situational crises we have experienced, noting when they occurred, how well we were prepared by earlier experiences to cope with them, and what special supports we had or did not have.

Some stressful events that often contribute to or are experienced as situational crises are given in the self-knowledge exercise presented here. Note that the meaning of these situational crises to an individual will vary with age. For example, moving may not be experienced as a large crisis by a 3 year old who has formed no attachments to other children in the neighborhood; however, it may be very stressful to a high school junior who is getting ready to enjoy a year of graduation activities with her friends. Similarly, the crisis of divorce presents different problems and challenges to a 4 year old, a 10 year old and a 16 year old. The 4 year old may have difficulty understanding the divorce process, and as a result feels responsible. He may also feel divorce is in some way equivalent to death of, or desertion by, the parent who did not obtain custody. The 10 year old will have a better understanding of custody arrangements and the politics of "taking sides." The 16 year old may be worried about how the divorce will affect her growing independence and future education plans.

GROWTH TO ADULTHOOD

We study the events and developments of our early years because we expect that they will influence our adjustment as adults. And this, of course, is true. The basic trust we establish in infancy is the foundation for our relationships in adulthood; the identity we forge in adolescence is the material with which we begin to construct our adult occupations and family roles. Unfavorable outcomes of these periods make it more difficult to achieve positive mental health in adulthood.

Children inevitably face adjustment crises, leading theorists and researchers to search for protective factors that enable individuals to deal most effectively with them. In quest of such factors, ones that insulate youngsters from negative outcomes when exposed to harsh stressors, investigators have studied individuals raised in high-risk environments but who emerged successfully, competent and strong. Garmezy and his colleagues (1983) collected data pertaining to residents of a poor section in London, England, and surveyed research reports published about competent black children raised in American inner-cities. They sought to determine what provided resiliency to these children who had to cope daily with the stressors of poverty and also, in

the latter case, of prejudice. Results pointed to three factors, possessing: a temperament or disposition characterized by flexibility and a positive mood, a warm, supportive and cohesive family environment, and helpful people in the school and community with whom the child can identify.

In contrast to those who become resilient, some individuals become alienated during their youth, and, as a result, feel uninvolved in the world about them, powerless in situations, and threatened instead of challenged by the possibilities before them (Maddi, Hoover, & Kobasa, 1982). Alienated persons are less motivated to explore opportunities for personal growth and development, accordingly limiting themselves. When confronted with a negative life event (e.g., being dismissed from a part-time job), their outlook differs dramatically from those who believe social support is available to them. Alienated individuals, in contrast to those "buffered" by their support group, can cope less well with negative events and are more likely to have them lead to unfavorable consequences, such as being converted into physical symptoms (Cohen & Hoberman, 1983).

However one emerges from youth, it should be noted that adult life presents many opportunities to "try again," to rework earlier challenges and emerge with a more favorable outcome. For example, people who were unable to develop basic trust in infancy may learn to trust in a relationship with an exceptional teacher or someone they fall in love with. Alternatively they may enter into therapy and, with the therapist, engage once more in the struggle between basic trust and mistrust. In a second attempt, whatever form it takes, they may emerge with a favorable outcome. As noted at the beginning of this chapter, it is not our early experiences per se that are crucial in determining our development; it is how we cope with them. We have the opportunity to cope again with similar challenges, at many later points in our lives.

SUMMARY

1. Children in our culture normally experience *maturational crises* as they undertake new developmental tasks, and may undergo specific *situational crises* as well.

2. Some psychologists believe that the process of adjustment begins before birth, in the relationship between the mother and the fetus. For example, they feel that stress experienced by the mother during pregnancy may affect the child's development.

3. Birth has usually been thought to represent a trauma for the infant. Today, however, newer approaches to childbirth, such as the Leboyer and Lamaze methods, attempt to make the process more emotionally satisfying for the infant and parents.

4. In infancy, individuals differ greatly in activity level, responsiveness to people, and many other temperamental characteristics. The quality of the parent–child relationship is affected by the parents' acceptance or rejection of the infant's temperament.

5. The infant engages in many behaviors, such as crying or smiling, that result in an attachment to the mother or other nurturing person. The quality of the attachment depends largely on the manner in which the infant's earliest needs are satisfied. Especially important is the satisfaction of oral and tactile needs.

6. According to Erikson, the infant develops an attitude of trust or mistrust, depending on whether basic needs for food, comfort, and attachment are consistently met.

7. In about the fifth month, the infant begins the long process of *individuation,* or separation from the mothering figure. At the toddler state, according to Erikson, self-control is a major issue and the child may experience either autonomy or shame and doubt.

8. By the age of four the child has greater freedom of movement and can begin to initiate activities. According to Erikson, the child at this point experiences a crisis between initiative and guilt. Freud emphasized the child's struggle with the Oedipal conflict at this stage.

9. Birth order can affect a child's emotional development and his orientation toward others.

10. As children grow older, their interactions at school and with peers play an increasingly important part in the development process.

11. In the middle school years, children develop a sense of "moral responsibility" that is based on rewards and punishments. According to Erikson, children at this point experience a crisis between industry and inferiority.

12. Adolescence is a period of transition between childhood and adulthood. Puberty brings dramatic physical growth, the emergence of mature sexual characteristics, and marked intellectual growth. The adolescent, in Erikson's terms, struggles against role confusion and tries to form a strong ego identity.

SUGGESTED READINGS

Bank, S. & Kahn, S. (1982). *The sibling bond*. New York: Basic Books. This volume examines the links that tie siblings together, ones that take years to develop and typically last a lifetime.

Chess, S. & Thomas, A. (1987). *Know your child*. New York: Basic Books. Based on years of research by the authors, this book examines individual differences in the developing child and how families can best manage the differing styles of its members.

Coles, R. (1964). *Children of crisis*. New York: Delta. An exploration of the attitudes and reactions of children caught up in the process of racial conflict.

Elkind, D. (1978). *A sympathetic understanding of the child: Birth to sixteen* (2d ed.). Boston: Allyn & Bacon. An excellent developmental perspective on the normative behavior patterns of children and adolescents.

Elkind, D. (1981). *The hurried child*. Reading, MA: Addison-Wesley. A fascinating perspective on how, in Western countries, families, schools, and the media are now rushing the process of growing up.

Galinsky, E. (1981). *Between generations: The six stages of parenthood*. New York: Quadrangle (Time Books). An analysis of the effects of the developing child on the psychological growth and development of the parent.

Kaplan, L. J. (1978). *Oneness and separateness: From infant to individual*. New York: Simon & Schuster (Touchstone Books). An eloquent and touching view of the mother–child relationship, and the psychological birth of the individual.

Kaplan, L. J. (1984). *Adolescence: The farewell to childhood*. New York: Simon & Schuster. This book provides an insightful look into the inner and outward worlds of the teenager.

Schaffer, K. (1981). *Sex roles and human behavior*. Cambridge, MA: Winthrop Press. In textbook length chapters, this book offers practical information about sex roles and how they shape day-to-day lives.

Weiss, J. (1981). *Your second child*. New York: Summit Books. With so much effort and attention paid to preparing parents for the birth of their first child, this book contributes much-needed understanding of the process of adding the second.

Friendship, Loneliness, and Love

8

- The process through which people choose their friends, and ways to examine and understand people's interactions in developing friendships

- How children progress hierarchically through stages in the understanding and practice of friendship, and how friendship patterns vary over the life span

- Social and personality factors that can cause loneliness, and how people emerge from this state

- The process of dating: common patterns, common problems, and the differing views of men and women

- Theories of why people need love, characteristics of love and some common types of lovers, and the personal challenges posed by the end of a relationship

*A*lthough Kelly had gone to bed well before midnight, she was still wide awake, reviewing her day. Before breakfast she and Susi, who lived downstairs, began the morning comparing the calculus home-work. After breakfast, Bob came by as promised, and drove them to school.

After a morning of classes, Kelly walked with Nancy to the cafeteria. There they joined some fellow reporters from the campus newspaper. The group spent most of the lunch hour planning a party for the senior editor, who would soon graduate.

Kelly left to go to the Burger Den, where she worked afternoons. Hope had to leave then, too, and offered Kelly a ride.

After spending the afternoon catering to a never-ending line of people buying double burgers and thick shakes, she was exhausted. But when Bob dropped by with a group of friends, she found new energy. They decided on an evening of dinner and bowling.

When Kelly finished reviewing her day, she thought: "Time for sleep. Just thinking about all I did tires me." What did not occur to Kelly, however, was that she had spent almost every waking moment of her day interacting with people. Kelly had hardly had one minute alone.

As Kelly's day shows, people live together, work side by side, and spend much of their leisure time in the company of others. However, while the basic nature of human beings is social and people strive to establish meaningful, satisfying contacts, the tasks of building friendships and love relationships are not necessarily easy.

The focus of this chapter is on how individuals meet the challenge of maintaining social relationships across the life span. Topics covered include how children learn social skills and how adults build acquaintanceship into friendship and love. As we explore the processes involved, we will identify factors that support or inhibit individuals in their personal quest to establish a social network. Obviously, not everybody is satisfied with his or her success in this area of life. Perhaps because of the complexity of our industrial, urban society, most people some of the time and some people most of the time feel lonely, even when they are surrounded by others. Between our discussions of friendships and love relationships, we consider the topic of loneliness—the experience of feeling a lack of meaningful social contact—and what can be done to combat it.

FRIENDSHIP

Defining Friendship

Four professors, a physicist, a mathematician, a psychologist, and an educator, were speaking informally at their faculty club, when one mentioned something that had happened in his daughter's junior high school class. Instantly, the tempo of the discussion quickened and each took a turn to assert how he or she thought the junior high school teacher should have handled the matter. Afterwards, the education professor commented: "I would never think of arguing with a physicist about his theories, but when you talk of education, people all have their own notions and are willing to argue with you."

What the education professor stated also holds true about some areas in psychology. For example, one topic almost everybody has had personal experience with, and is willing to offer thoughts on, is friendship. People have definite, common-sense, experience-based ideas about how friends are made, and theories to explain successes and failures. However, research and theoretically-based concepts allow us to go beyond our common-sense understandings of friendship and to systematically assess the role it plays in personal adjustment.

We begin the exploration by accepting a definition of friendship and recognizing that the friendship relationship can take many forms. Reisman (1981, p. 206) defined friendships in a manner that certainly fits notions most of us hold, and categorized them into three levels: "(A friend is) someone who likes and wishes to do well by someone else and who believes those feelings and good intentions are reciprocated."

Associative friendships are widely found in adults. These develop and are sustained by the fact that two people work together, live nearby, or are members of the same group. When circumstances change, neither party invests much energy into maintaining contact.

Reciprocal friendships are close and intimate bonds formed between people who regard each other as equals and who are loyal and committed to each other.

Receptive friendships link individuals of different status, with one person tending to give more than the other (such as teacher-student, employer-employee, and leader-follower relationships).

These people have an associative friendship. Linked by the circumstances of their job, their relationship will end when one of them leaves the company.

Support System
A group of people—comprised of friends, family members, and others—who help satisfy an individual's need for affection, intimacy, and self-esteem and provide support during psychological and physical crises.

Common-sense notions tell us that people want friends because they enjoy companionship. In essence, we think of making friends as a natural activity that apparently satisfies a human need for social contact. This need is not solely ours. It exists, for example, in apes and rats. These animals, according to Werner and Latane (1974), are gregarious and pursue opportunities for "social interaction" simply for the satisfaction they gain from it.

Besides being partners for companionship and recreation, friends of the three types listed above can also serve as members of a person's support system. A **support system** is a group of people who help an individual meet the "variety of needs that demand satisfaction through enduring interpersonal relationships, such as for love and affection, for intimacy that provides the freedom to express feelings easily and unself-consciously, for validation of personal identity and worth, and for support in handling emotion . . ." (Caplan, 1974, p. 57). Besides friends, those in an individual's support system usually include family members. They may also include a person whom he or she is dating; work colleagues; fellow members of religious, social, recreational, and political groups; physicians; teachers; clergymen; and others.

Support system members, including friends, help individuals when they encounter the inevitable psychological and physical crises that occur over the life span. The extent of the helpfulness is well illustrated by one study (Cobb, 1974) involving men who were scheduled to lose their factory jobs. Among other findings it was reported that men with social support from family, friends, and so forth were less stressed (as measured by the amount of uric acid and cholesterol in their blood) than their counterparts, even some twelve months after the plant's closing. Another project studied women in nonconflicted marriages (Monroe, Bromet, Connell, & Steiner, 1986). They found that women

How To Win Friends and Influence People

The advice Dale Carnegie (1936/1981) offered in "How to Win Friends and Influence People" can be summarized into six rules (p. 103):

Rule 1: Become genuinely interested in people.
Rule 2: Smile.
Rule 3: Remember that a man's name is to him the sweetest and most important sound in any language.
Rule 4: Be a good listener. Encourage others to talk about themselves.
Rule 5: Talk in terms of the other man's interest.
Rule 6: Make the other person feel important—and do it sincerely.

1. Do these rules fit with your social experiences?
2. Do you think that by following these rules one would build quality friendships?
3. Would you want your spouse to follow these rules in interacting with you?
4. Which rule do you think is most useful, which the least?   ▲

who reported receiving adequate support from their husbands were less likely than those reporting less adequate support to experience psychological symptoms of depression.

And additional research continues to suggest that having close relationships helps people adjust to stressful situations (Mitchell, Billings, & Moos, 1983; Turner, 1983) and buffer people from some of the ill effects from negative life events, like the loss of loved ones, accidents, family problems, and so on (Cohen & McKay, 1985; Barrera & Ainlay, 1983).

Making Friends

Some people find it easy to build a friendship and to fill their social calendar with activities. Others have more difficulty reaching out to peers. Among these people are individuals who are satisfied with their level of social contact and individuals who are not. People wishing to broaden their friendship circle can learn how to be more effective in building relationships.

Over many decades millions have sought to learn "How to Win Friends and Influence People" by reading Dale Carnegie's famous self-help book (1936/1981). While that long-time best seller offers sage advice, research conducted since its publication has broadened our understanding of the friendship-building process and provides a sounder basis for advising people who wish for more social effectiveness. Next, we examine that research and theory.

Because of the design of this building, the residents whose apartments are adjacent are more likely to establish friendships.

Proximity

"Propinquity is preemptive," Professor Don Glad of Louisiana State University would tell community people endeavoring to better their neighborhoods. He used these very words because the idea, phrased this way, is not easily forgotten. When puzzled looks came across faces in his audience, Glad would explain: The physical nearness of people increases the number of opportunities they have for contact and, as the frequency of unintended contacts increases, so does the likelihood that a relationship will develop. Therefore, people living in the same dormitory, or attending the same church, or enrolled in the same school may become friends because the first and most necessary and powerful (i.e., *preemptive*) condition for relationship-building is met, the physical nearness of two or more people (**propinquity**). Glad would also introduce "functional distance," a concept that involves the possibility for contact between people. Hence, married students in adjacent units who share a common parking area are more likely to have unintended contact and become friends than couples in equally-distant adjacent apartments who do not share this.

In a classic study, Festinger, Schacter, and Back (1950) discovered that couples assigned apartments within about 20 feet of each other were likely to become friends. This was much less likely if they were assigned places 90 feet apart. The power of physical proximity in shaping friendships also has been demonstrated in the elementary school classroom where teacher-assigned seat locations affected who children reported liking (Schwebel & Cherlin, 1972), among police trainees who were seated in alphabetical order and tended to befriend those with a surname near theirs in the alphabet (Segal, 1974), and among senior citizens living in a housing project (Nahemow & Lawton, 1975). When asked to identify their friends, about 50 percent of the elderly residents first chose somebody on their floor while 88 percent, in total, first named a person in their building.

Propinquity
The physical nearness of people to each other.

Attraction

Theorists have treated "interpersonal attraction" as an attitude—one person's positive or negative attitude toward another (Berscheid, 1985). As an attitude it has three components: *cognitive,* or person A's beliefs and ideas about person B; *affective,* person A's emotions and feelings pertaining to person B; and *behavioral,* the actions person A directs toward person B. If person A has a positive attitude (is attracted) to person B, she may have positive thoughts (she's nice) and feelings (comfort) and may approach and begin conversation (behave toward) with person B.

Two major approaches have proven most useful in explaining the process of interpersonal attraction (Berscheid, 1985). First, the cognitive consistency theories argue that individuals strive to maintain consistency in their thoughts (or cognitions) and in their interactions with others in the environment. People perceive and process information, these theories hold, in ways that allow them to maintain these consistent views. Thus, in a simplified form, if person A likes cheerleaders and meets person B, a cheerleader, person A may well perceive and interpret person B's behavior in a more positive way than that same behavior from a noncheerleader. This helps person A maintain consistency. By the same token, if you dislike Democrats (or Republicans), you may mishear or quickly distort in memory a candidate's speech, reshaping his remarks so they fit your political views. Alternatively, you might have to alter your view of your favored political party.

Second, reinforcement theories maintain that interpersonal attraction is shaped by the rewards and punishments associated with interacting with each particular other. A concrete example of this: we are rewarded by being associated or "seen" with the physically attractive, the intelligent, the football hero, and other people of high status. Men, for instance, accompanied by beautiful women find themselves more highly regarded by others (Sigall & Landy, 1973). And groupies will make considerable sacrifices to gain rewards (autographs, a handshake, a kiss, etc.) from their heroes.

Going a step further, reinforcement theories suggest that the nature of exchange of reinforcements is important in attraction. Attraction is strongest when fairness or equity prevails. For example, people will be more attracted if they take turns buying lunch, rather than one always paying, or if one person is a good talker and the other a good listener. These theories correctly predict the **matching hypothesis,** that friends tend to be equally attractive physically, and argue that attraction would be weak if there is an unjust distribution of costs and benefits. In this case, the underbenefitted party would likely withdraw.

Matching Hypothesis
A research finding showing that individuals associate with same and opposite sex people who are approximately as physically attractive as they.

Impression Formation

Generations of parents have admonished their children: "Tuck your shirt in. First impressions are important. Make a good one." Research data bear out the truth in this age-old wisdom, showing that impressions are formed quickly. It seems that data like a "hanging shirt tail" *are* used, and first impressions can be hard to change. In fact, the sequence of observing another person and drawing conclusions begins after only moments of interaction. Then, in but a few more minutes of conversation, additional judgments are made about the other's personal qualities. These judgments, in turn, lead to a decision about whether or not to continue contact.

How this decision-making process unfolds can be illustrated with a familiar classroom situation. Mary, a college sophomore, arrived early at her 8:00 A.M. class the first day of the term. After entering and surveying the vast lecture hall, she elected to sit one seat away from the only other person in the room. The occupant of that desk, a middle-aged woman, did not glance up from the school newspaper until Mary addressed her: "Did you buy the textbook yet?"

Simply on the basis of their behavior to this point, Mary and the woman had generated a good deal of information each could use to assess the other. Looking at the interchange from Mary's perspective, she first made a judgment that the woman was approachable and would respond to her question. In making this decision Mary undoubtedly took into account factors like the person's sex, age, appearance, sitting posture, student status, and the fact that if she (Mary) wanted to talk, this woman was the only person available. To Mary's question, the woman responded: "Yes, I bought it at the campus bookstore. Did you have trouble finding a copy?" Mary then had much more information. The woman's accent suggested a New York City background, and her posture when speaking, the way she tilted her head, and her direct eye contact, were signs of a self-assured person. The tone of her voice and the way she held her arms suggested she was open and warm. Finally, the response she chose and her wording of it provided additional clues to her character.

So Mary had much information about the other woman and, as all of us do, used it to make judgments or attributions about her personality. Whether these attributions were accurate or not, they guided Mary in her interactions with the woman, at least in the next few weeks as Mary got to know her better.

Why do people make these quick judgments? One explanation is that such assumptions are necessary to keep us from being overwhelmed by masses of data. By taking input and transforming it into a few judgments, we simplify both the memory task and that of deciding how to relate to the other person at each point of choice.

Psychologists have attempted to describe the process by which we form impressions. Below is a simplified version of Schneider, Hastorf, and Ellsworth's (1979) step-by-step model of what happens in the short period of time when person A meets person B and makes judgments about B's personality. The authors suggest that this sequence of six steps is commonly but not inevitably followed. In other words, certain people in some situations may well deviate from the order and may skip steps:

| *Step 1:* | Person A attends to person B's appearance and behavior and the context in which the behavior takes place. | Alice watches good-looking, 6'5" Zack doodle in his notebook instead of listening to the lecture. |

Step 2:	Person A makes stereotyped snap judgments about person B and feels attracted to or repelled from person B.	Alice decides Zack is a "dummy" and a "jock" and thus is not attracted.
Step 3:	Person A makes attributions about why person B behaved as he or she did in that situation.	Alice decides Zack is good in athletics but not in academics, and probably is unable to keep his mind on classwork.
Step 4:	Person A attributes a personality trait in person B that would explain what person A has observed, and person A hypothesizes that certain other traits also exist in person B.	Alice decides Zack is a goof-off type (fun-loving, not serious, beer-drinking fraternity man) who has a basketball scholarship and has dozens of women chasing him.
Step 5:	On the basis of the traits person A has attributed to person B, person A forms a general opinion of person B and decides whether he or she is likable.	On the basis of the above traits, Alice decides Zack takes nothing seriously and is not likable to her.
Step 6:	Person A, using all the information, thoughts, and judgments available to him or her, predicts how person B will react in certain situations in the future.	Alice figures Zack would not make it outside of the sports world. Further, Alice decides that if Zack ever dated her, she would not like the way he acted.

Psychologists use the term **impression formation** to refer to the process through which people gather and integrate information about others. As individuals pass through these six steps, what helps them to infer personality characteristics in others and to piece these characteristics together to form a meaningful picture? Research suggests that individuals each have their own *implicit personality theory* and employ that theory in the impression-formation process. A person's implicit personality theory serves him or her as a formally developed personality theory serves the scientists. Both "indicate" how one behavior or trait is related to another behavior or trait, and both allow the holder of the theory to predict that if person A behaves in fashion B, then person A is likely to possess characteristic C.

Some practical lessons can be derived from the impression-formation field of research. Specifically, the findings suggest that we can be more successful in interactions if we: (1) train ourselves, particularly in important situations, to refrain from making premature judgments, waiting instead until we have ample information; (2) avoid stereotyping others, and instead work toward understanding them as individuals; (3) ask questions and direct conversation toward the goal of learning what we need to know about others, given the intended purpose of our contact. For example, asking a set of relevant questions to judge an auto mechanic's honesty and skill would be a better practice than looking at him, his uniform, and his shop and then, on the basis of these observations, leaving with him a car needing major repair work.

Impression Formation
An area of psychological study that investigates the ways in which individuals gather information about people whom they encounter and infer personality characteristics from that information.

The Developing Friendship

Most of the research on interpersonal attraction and the development of friendships has focused on the earliest stages of acquaintance-building. This portion of the process presents the fewest obstacles to investigators. Strangers can be brought together in a laboratory and experimental techniques can be creatively applied. Issues of privacy, of ethics, and of finding effective research methods that sort out the complex of variables have meant that the understanding of the later stages is sketchier.

Acknowledging that fact, we next ask why Mary, the sophomore in the lecture hall, addressed the only other woman in it while Alice, in contrast, elected to not acquaint herself with Zack. In each of the cases, Huston and Levinger (1978) would suggest, each person considered: "a) the degree to which he finds the attributes of the potential partners attractive, and b) the degree to which he anticipates they would find his attributes attractive and hence respond favorably to his initiative" (p. 126). Beyond this, of course, individuals are guided by norms so, for instance, traditionally-oriented women, even if these two conditions were met, might hesitate to initiate interactions with the man.

When contact is made and friendships develop, those working in the field suggested the following changes may take place in people's interactions, depending on the goals people hold for the relationship (Burgess & Huston, 1979, p. 8):

1. They interact more often, for longer periods of time, and in a widening array of settings.
2. They attempt to restore proximity when separated, and feel comforted when proximity is regained.
3. They "open up" to each other, in the sense that they disclose secrets and share physical intimacies.
4. They become less inhibited, more willing to share positive and negative feelings, and to praise and criticize each other.
5. They develop their own communication system, and become ever more efficient in using it.
6. They increase their ability to map and anticipate each other's views of social reality.
7. They begin to synchronize their goals and behavior, and develop stable interaction patterns.
8. They increase their investment in the relationship, thus enhancing its importance in their life space.
9. They begin increasingly to feel that their separate interests are inextricably tied to the well-being of their relationship.
10. They increase their liking, trust, and love for each other.
11. They see the relationship as irreplaceable, or at least as unique.

Examining Interactions Between People

Transactional Analysis

To gain deeper understandings of what people experience as they develop and maintain friendships, we need to be able to put their interactions "under the microscope." One way to do this is to apply **transactional analysis,** sometimes called TA for short. The approach was introduced by Eric Berne in *Games People Play* (1964) and has been the subject of many other books, including Harris' invitingly titled *I'm OK, You're OK* (1967). Although TA's popularity peaked some twenty years ago, it is still a most useful tool in the study of interactions between people.

The Three Ego States   TA theorists believe that during childhood we all form three personality parts, each complete with feelings, attitudes, and perceptions that produce certain thoughts, behaviors, and ways of relating to others. The three personality parts, or "ego stages," are:

> *The Parent Ego State:*   This is a system of rules for living. In this state people react, behave, and feel just like their parents. When in the Parent Ego State, people do not need to think through what to do in a situation: what is right, good, and should be done is obvious. This ego state can be warm and supportive or harsh and overcontrolling.
> *The Adult Ego State:*   This part of the personality stores information and makes rational decisions after assessing all available data.
> *The Child Ego State:*   In this state, a creative, joy-loving mode, people behave, think, and feel the way they did in childhood. The Child Ego State appears in adults not only in recreational settings but also sometimes in the classroom or boardroom, when someone cracks a joke and people "take a few moments off." The Child Ego State can be impulsive, hateful, angry, happy, or despairing.

Ordinarily, in transactions between acquaintances and casual friends, the rational, information-gathering Adult Ego State and the fun-loving, emotional Child Ego State predominate. However, all three ego stages are important in moment-to-moment functioning, and normally, as people interact, they seek to use the three states in a healthy, balanced way.

As Figure 8.1 illustrates, the shift from using one ego state to another can produce dramatic changes in the nature and quality of the interactions between people. Transactions like 1, 2, 3, and 6, which begin and end the conversation, are called complementary because the addressed ego state in Person B (Gary) responds back to the ego state in Person A (Lisa) that initiated the transaction. These transactions generally promote effective interactions and good relationships between people. For example, in the Figure 8.1 dialogue, Lisa and Gary use **complementary transactions:** to seek agreement about Parent Ego State values (Transaction 1); to logically consider options as equals (Transaction 2); to share playful fantasy (Transaction 3); and, to ask for and offer to provide help (Transaction 6).

Transactional Analysis
An approach to understanding human interactions that identifies three ego states from which a person may be operating; ways in which people seek "strokes," or recognition from others; and as explained later, ways people structure their time, ranging in quality from intimacy to self-defeating game-playing.

Complementary Transaction
A verbal exchange in which person B follows the ego state pattern initiated by person A.

Figure 8.1 A sequence of transactions: Parent, adult, and child ego states.

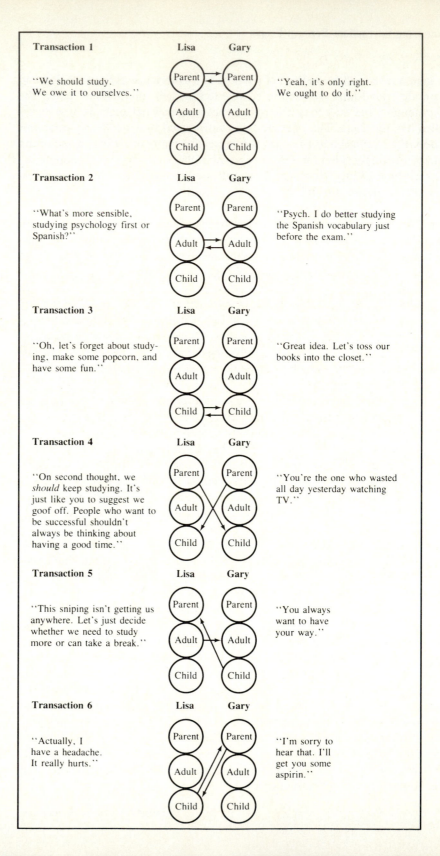

Transaction 1   Lisa   Gary

"We should study. We owe it to ourselves."

"Yeah, it's only right. We ought to do it."

Transaction 2   Lisa   Gary

"What's more sensible, studying psychology first or Spanish?"

"Psych. I do better studying the Spanish vocabulary just before the exam."

Transaction 3   Lisa   Gary

"Oh, let's forget about study-ing, make some popcorn, and have some fun."

"Great idea. Let's toss our books into the closet."

Transaction 4   Lisa   Gary

"On second thought, we *should* keep studying. It's just like you to suggest we goof off. People who want to be successful shouldn't always be thinking about having a good time."

"You're the one who wasted all day yesterday watching TV."

Transaction 5   Lisa   Gary

"This sniping isn't getting us anywhere. Let's just decide whether we need to study more or can take a break."

"You always want to have your way."

Transaction 6   Lisa   Gary

"Actually, I have a headache. It really hurts."

"I'm sorry to hear that. I'll get you some aspirin."

But, sometimes people have **crossed transactions.** In these, person B does not follow the lead of person A, but instead directs the transaction in a different direction. Figure 8.1 visually demonstrates that in crossed transactions the arrows on the charts are not parallel. In Transaction 4 Lisa's Parent Ego State (which can range from nurturant to hateful) harshly criticized Gary's Child Ego State. His Parent Ego State then struck back at her Child Ego State. In Transaction 5, Lisa tried to move the conversation back to issues of planning the day but Gary, responding from his Child Ego State, voiced a criticism of Lisa. Crossed transactions are associated with ineffective communication and other problems between people. In troubled and strained relationships these transactions occur frequently.

Strokes Eric Berne, in "Games People Play," theorized that just as people need food, water, and shelter to live, they also need **strokes;** that is a recognition by others of their existence. Strokes can be given verbally or nonverbally and can come in forms ranging from a smile, a hello, a compliment, a hug, a neutral comment, or even a frown or criticism.

While everybody has an unlimited supply of strokes available to give, because of training and habit, many people are stingy in providing strokes to friends, loved ones, and, for that matter, to anybody they encounter. As a result, many individuals feel dissatisfied with the number they receive. Some deal with this deficiency by "giving up" on earning positive strokes like hellos, smiles, compliments, affection, and love and settle for more easily earned negative strokes, such as having others yell at or be critical of them. For instance, you may remember the class clown who earned strokes by getting into trouble and being sent to the principal's office. People may settle for negative strokes because they at least provide them with the satisfaction of knowing their presence is recognized and acknowledged.

Self-Disclosure and Johari's Window

The role self-disclosure plays in relationships has been widely studied. Researchers have assumed that as relationships develop, each person shares personal and intimate information about him or herself. While there is little knowledge about how self-disclosure operates in relationships on a day-to-day basis, laboratory studies have suggested that self-disclosure is highly valued by friends (Berscheid, 1985). When individual A shares personal information, individual B is likely to reciprocate with information approximately as personal. Further, after the exchange, A and B are likely to see each other as being more attractive.

While speaking to groups of students about friendships and self-disclosure, psychologists are frequently asked: "How does an acquaintanceship progress into a friendship? Why does talking about personal things make you feel closer? What happens when people get closer?" Responding to these queries is not simple because the answers partly depend on the individuals themselves—their personalities, goals, value systems, and so on. However, meaningful, personal conversation can never begin until the comfort level between people permits such interchanges, and that usually occurs only after

Crossed Transaction
A verbal exchange in which person B does not follow the ego state pattern initiated by person A.

Strokes
Acknowledging another person by making contact visually, physically, or through words.

Figure 8.2 Johari's window.

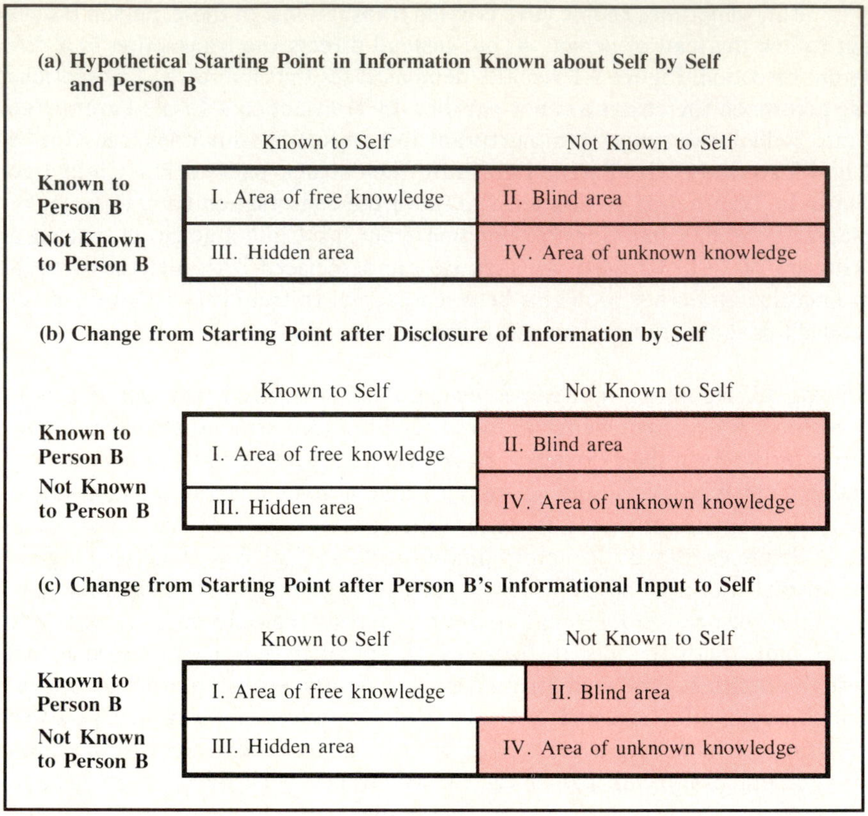

(a) Hypothetical Starting Point in Information Known about Self by Self and Person B

	Known to Self	Not Known to Self
Known to Person B	I. Area of free knowledge	II. Blind area
Not Known to Person B	III. Hidden area	IV. Area of unknown knowledge

(b) Change from Starting Point after Disclosure of Information by Self

	Known to Self	Not Known to Self
Known to Person B	I. Area of free knowledge	II. Blind area
Not Known to Person B	III. Hidden area	IV. Area of unknown knowledge

(c) Change from Starting Point after Person B's Informational Input to Self

	Known to Self	Not Known to Self
Known to Person B	I. Area of free knowledge	II. Blind area
Not Known to Person B	III. Hidden area	IV. Area of unknown knowledge

they have shared sufficient time. During the hours they spend together they talk and learn about each other and a trust develops. In a step-by-step fashion, each self-discloses increasingly personal information and each tells the other more of his reactions to the other's thoughts and behaviors. Johari's Window (Luft, 1984) is a model illustrating how this information exchange between person A and person B produces change as their relationship grows.

Johari's Window (a term coined from the names of its developers, psychologist Joe Luft and his colleague Harry Ingham), shown in Figure 8.2, assumes the more person A and person B know in common about person A, and vice versa, the richer will be their interactions.

Note how the four cells, or windowpanes, depict who knows information about a person (the self in this diagram). In the first column, cells I and III, the two types of information known to the self are presented: that known to both person B and oneself and that known only to oneself. If the self discloses personal information previously unknown to person B, then cell I enlarges and cell III is accordingly reduced, as in diagram (b). An example of this might be a person saying, "My political views are quite liberal. I believe in equal rights for all, regardless of sex, age, race, creed, or national origin." Or he might invite person B to a party and reveal how uninhibited he is on the dance floor.

The second column of Johari's Window, cells II and IV, represents the information not known to the self. Assume that diagram (a) is the beginning point. If person B provides information or gives **feedback** to the self that had been previously unknown, then cell II is reduced and cell I is correspondingly enlarged. This is depicted in diagram (c). Examples of the information that would cause such a change range from person B saying "I really enjoy your uninhibited dancing" (when the dancer thought himself inhibited) to "since we know each other pretty well now, I want to point out that you end many statements with tag questions like 'Is that okay?' or 'Don't you agree?' You'd be more effective in class and socially if you dropped those tag questions and were more assertive." Generally as friendships grow, cells II and III become smaller, while cell I becomes larger. Cell IV represents information not known to either person, like the self's unconscious.

Of course, Johari's Window model can be rearranged to show what happens if person B discloses personal information or is given information by the self.

While self-disclosure and input from others naturally occur as people spend time together, share experiences, and build friendships, this model also suggests the benefits of investing extra effort in the deliberate sharing of information in personal interchanges. In this way people may speed the "getting-to-know-you" process and move more quickly to a deeper level of conversation and a fuller relationship.

Another tool that has been used to examine interactions among people in **sociometry.** Sociometry is discussed in the Self-Knowledge Exercise on page 350 and illustrated in Figure 8.3.

Friendship Over the Life Span

In our study of friendship we next look across the life span, examining how individuals at various ages meet the challenge of linking with others and building a circle of friends and acquaintances.

Infancy: The Foundations of Friendship

Newborn infants, as noted earlier, seem unable to tell the difference between themselves and other people. For example, a breast-feeding newborn needs to learn that the nipple in her mouth is not part of herself but rather of her mother, who is a separate person. Such knowledge is acquired in a stepwise fashion as newborns interact with their mother and others in the environment. Using age only as an approximate guideline, we can identify some early learning experiences that serve as benchmarks in this growth process and some of the skills infants master as they become more mature social beings.

During the first month of life for some, and by the third for nearly all, maturation and learning enable newborns to take an important, basic step: the visual recognition of their own mother or other primary caretaker. Upon seeing her, they show excitement and make movements toward her, behaviors that are not displayed with other people. While it is not until this point that infants recognize their mother as a separate entity, by three days of age they can

Feedback
A term used to describe the information one person or several people give to another person about his or her behavior.

Sociometry
The study and measurement of interpersonal relationships in a group of people, usually applied to the investigation of friendship patterns.

Sociometry

In the 1930s J. L. Moreno introduced sociometry, the study and measurement of how group members think and feel about others in the group. Over the years sociometry has been used both for research purposes and to address immediate problems in settings ranging from children's summer camps to military units and correctional institutions. Perhaps its most frequent application has been to study friendships in elementary school classrooms.

In the example below Mrs. Campbell administered a sociometric questionnaire to her sixth grade class. It asked the children, "Name three students you want in your study group." Mrs. Campbell organized her data into what is called a sociogram. This alerted Mrs. Campbell to several issues:

1. Ann, Delores, Joyce, and Shirley have a clique. Mrs. Campbell will observe these four carefully to determine whether they exclude "outsiders."
2. Hendrix, who was popular among his peers, made two intersex choices. When Mrs. Campbell suggests co-ed spelling bee groups and the children resist, she will appoint Hendrix as a team captain.
3. Since physical proximity fosters social interaction, Mrs. Campbell will use her data to rearrange the seating chart and to promote the involvement of all children in the social networks. After employing the new seat assignments for a month she will retest the children and determine the success of her intervention.

Using a Sociogram Yourself

1. List eight to ten high school classmates (or, if it's been several years since high school, members of another group you belong to, such as a club or church organization).
2. Leaving yourself out, make a sociogram by imagining the three choices each of the people might make for his or her best friends.
3. Imagine where you would be in the sociogram. What feelings come to you? What thoughts?
4. If you can administer a sociometric questionnaire to a group of people without worrying them unduly, try your hand at it and develop a sociogram. To make the situation less threatening, perhaps ask them to name people they would like to be in a class with, or choose to sit with in a cafeteria.
5. Delineate how the data you collected might be used to help the people who participated.

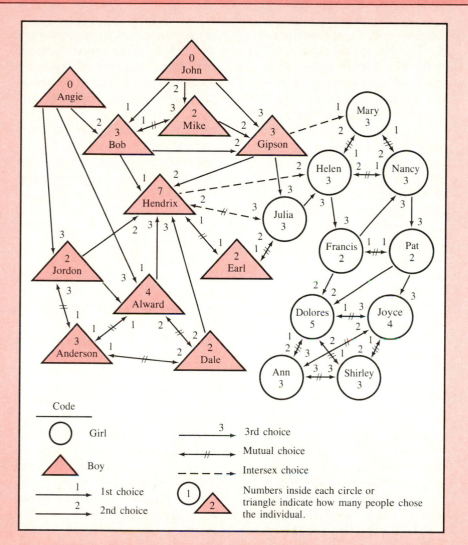

Figure 8.3 A sociogram.

Code

○ Girl

△ Boy

——1→ 1st choice

——2→ 2nd choice

——3→ 3rd choice

←—#—→ Mutual choice

——–—→ Intersex choice

① △2 Numbers inside each circle or triangle indicate how many people chose the individual.

distinguish their mother's from other female voices and will suck in a particular way in order to have her voice played on a tape (DeCasper & Fifer, 1980). Further, other researchers suggest that as early as one week of age, infants can recognize the smell of their mother's breast pad or recall previously having heard her voice (Olson, 1981).

By three months of age, most infants not only show a special reaction to their mother's visual presence and her voice, but also protest at her departure, usually with special vigor. Another new skill in their social repertoire is the smile, which they readily offer to the several people they now recognize. At four months, infants begin to convey moods by using a variety of vocalizations. For example, they laugh while interacting socially, but announce displeasure when their play is interrupted.

At about the half-year mark children smile at other youngsters, turn when called by name, and are able to play games such as peek-a-boo, "come-and-get-me," and "bring me the rattle." Further, they imitate others' facial expressions, this being an important step in mastering the socially important skill of nonverbal communication. Around seven months, babies recognize the difference between anger and friendliness in another's voice, and they display humor and the ability to tease. They also gain the ability to tell people apart, which means strangers can cause fear and evoke crying.

At approximately nine months, newly developed social skills enable infants to initiate simple ball games and "pat-a-cake," to begin to assess the moods of others, and sometimes to fight for a desired toy. At ten months, children's ability to relate to others shows new dimensions. They understand the meaning of "no," obey commands, and seek approval. They also refuse to cooperate at times, and display indications of guilt. While playing *together* with another child is still outside the scope of their ability, two or more children can *each play separate games* in physical proximity to each other. This is called **parallel play** and is an important step in the development of social relationships.

In a year's time babies have made remarkable progress. Besides displaying affection, a sense of humor, and a preference for certain people's company, year-old children test and master ways of exerting personal power in getting what they want. Their repertoire of resistance includes the ability to use temper tantrums with dramatization suitable to a Broadway stage and the power of locomoting themselves away from parents. In the first 12 months they have indeed built a foundation and are ready for the rapid growth in their social skills that will unfold in the years that lie ahead.

At about age three, children develop physically and psychologically to the point where they are first able to have and to be a friend. Three year olds have approximately the same number of contacts each day with children as they do with adults and, even at this age, have more same-sex playtime (Feiring & Lewis, 1987). What follows is a discussion of the decade-long growth in children's understanding and practice of friendship.

Parallel Play
When two or more children play in proximity to but not with each other.

Stages of Friendship in Childhood: A Cognitive Perspective

Some clear evening when you are driving in a car with a three-year-old child, ask him or her what the moon is doing. The odds are that you will hear an excited youngster respond, "It's following us." Try as you may, you will be unable to *truly convince* the child otherwise. Perceptual information proves the point to a young mind, and the moon appears to be following the car.

It was once believed that children were simply "miniature adults" and that their thinking and logic were similar to their elders', only less well developed. Developmental psychologists like Jean Piaget, however, have discovered otherwise: Children's thinking is qualitatively different. Knowing this fact has helped psychologists to study how youngsters at different stages of development reason and interpret various phenomena in their world.

Some research by developmental psychologists that is particularly relevant is Selman and Selman's (1979) study of how people change in the practice and understanding of friendship. They gathered their data by posing hypothetical interpersonal dilemmas to individuals from three to thirty-four years of age. Here is an example of a situation they presented to their subjects:

> Kathy has been asked by Jeannette, a new girl in town, to go to an ice-skating show with her the next afternoon. But Kathy has already made a date with her long-time best friend, Debby, to plan a puppet show. To complicate matters, it is clear that Debby does not like Jeannette.

In a one-to-one interview, the subject was asked questions about the dilemma that dealt with his or her understanding about: (1) how friends are made; (2) intimacy in friendships; (3) trust and give-and-take; (4) jealousy and exclusion of others from friends' interactions; (5) conflicts and how they are resolved; and (6) how friendships end. The researchers were interested in more than simple yes/no answers; they wanted responses that would convey the nature of the thinking behind the subject's decision in each particular situation. In analyzing such responses, researchers must guard against making assumptions about what subjects are intending to convey. For example, a five-year-old and a fifteen-year-old might both report that, if they were Kathy, they would plan the puppet show with their close friend. However, the fifteen-year-old would most likely define "closeness" in terms of shared values, while the five-year-old would more likely mean that Debby lives nearby and plays with Kathy frequently. In this type of study, the investigator must make certain exactly what meaning the subject intended.

After collecting a substantial amount of data, the Selmans were able to propose five stages they theorize individuals pass through as their understanding and practice of friendship approach those of a mature adult. Note that an approximate age range is associated with each. While youngsters vary in the speed with which they proceed up the ladder of stages, the order of the stages is invariable. In other words, to reach Stage 2, a child must pass through Stages 0 and 1.

Stage 0 (3–7 years of age) is called the *Momentary Playmateship Stage*. During this stage a child befriends another because of physical proximity (he lives next door) or material possessions (she has a brand new doll I like to play with). Relationships between peers are handicapped by the fact that children do not realize their viewpoint differs from others.' When they want a truck they cannot imagine a playmate would wish otherwise, and thus do not expect the reaction they get after grabbing it away from the playmate.

Stage 1 (4–9 years of age) is called the *One-Way Assistance Stage*. Youngsters can now differentiate between their perspective and that of a playmate but do not yet comprehend the need to contribute a fair share in a give-and-take friendship. For instance, children in Stage 1 know when another youngster wants a turn on the swing, but are unable to understand why they should release the swing to provide that turn. Unable to participate in give-and-take exchanges and to create a system of sharing, children define a good friend as one who follows their lead or does things as they wish. A boy might declare: "Mary is not my friend now 'cause she won't play trucks."

Stage 2 (6–12 years of age) is the *Two-Way Cooperation Stage*. Youngsters can now engage in reciprocal give-and-take, weighing both their perspective and that of peers. While Stage 2 children are concerned about what playmates think and how playmates feel about them, the relationship is limited because each takes care of his or her interest rather than their mutual interests. For example, one child says, "I'll go first." The second suggests, "I'll go next." Neither proposes a plan that takes both their interests into account simultaneously, such as: "Since I went first yesterday, you go first today. That is fair to both of us." Nonetheless, they do recognize that both must participate

for a friendship to work. As one of the Selmans' subjects put it, "We are friends. She likes me and I like her. We do things for each other."

Stage 3 (9–15 years of age) is the *Intimate, Mutually Shared Relationship Stage.* Youngsters now grasp their own perspective, that of a friend, and that of somebody outside of their relationship. With the ability to do the latter, the child can see friendship as an ongoing phenomenon that a third party experiences differently from the friends. Also, the child understands how a third person feels when excluded from the activities of two friends. Further, the child now can consider the mutual interest of both parties and can work toward shared, common goals. Friends at this stage share secrets, plans, feelings, and personal problems, and can discuss conflicts and work together toward their resolution. Another new development is an exclusiveness in a close friendship and the associated possessiveness of one youngster toward another. A typical view of Stage 3 "good pals" was provided by one Selman subject: "He is my best friend. We can tell each other things we can't tell anyone else; we understand each other's feelings. We can help each other when we are needed."

During *Stage 4* (12 years and beyond), the adolescent and adult recognize that both dependency and autonomy are necessary ingredients in a healthy friendship. This period is called the *Autonomous Interdependent Friendship Stage.* While Stage 4 persons need to be able to depend on a friend for support at certain times, they also recognize the importance of cultivating other relationships in order to support the broadest possible personal growth and fulfillment. At this stage people recognize what one of the Selmans' subjects verbalized: "One thing about a good friendship is that it's a real commitment, a risk you have to take. You have to be able to support and trust and give, but you have to be able to let go, too."

Table 8.1 demonstrates how an individual's views and thoughts about friendship change with development in one area important to friendship.

As with other areas of human development, such as the growth of intelligence, the understanding and practice of friendship develop step by step in a hierarchical fashion. That is, the insights of a new stage build upon earlier understandings. It is interesting, however, that the new sets of understandings do not replace the old; rather, they coexist. Thus, the adult generally has access to the thinking associated with all previous stages, and may well put all to use. For example: Rich and Ellen happened to sit next to each other in their English Composition class. After a quick exchange of glances, each evaluated the other's physical attributes, making a Stage 0 assessment of the value their association would provide. After class they went for coffee together and shared views about school, college life, and hobbies. In a Stage 1 manner, Ellen felt that Rich would follow her lead if she suggested pursuing her favorite activities. In a Stage 2 manner, Rich felt that Ellen was bright and might help him with his science homework and perhaps be an attractive date to take to an upcoming party. As Rich and Ellen began seeing each other regularly, they made a longer-term commitment and, as in Stage 3, began to form an exclusive relationship and share a great deal. Finally, in time, they became a couple, with their interactions guided by Stage 4 characteristics.

TABLE 8.1 *Trust in Friends of Different Ages*

Issue: The first individual has a special tricycle or bicycle that the second individual wants to ride.

Second Individual Asks	*First Individual's Response and Rationale for Trusting Second Individual*
Stage 0: "May I ride your tricycle?"	"Yes," thinking I trust her because she is not physically big enough to break it.
Stage 1: "May I ride your bicycle?"	"Yes," thinking I trust her because she will ride it where I tell her she can go with it.
Stage 2: "May I ride your bicycle?"	"Yes," thinking I trust her because she will let me ride hers.
Stage 3: "May I ride your bicycle?"	"Yes," thinking I trust her because she is my friend.
Stage 4: "May I ride your bicycle?"	"Yes," thinking I trust her based on my knowledge of her personal characteristics.

Friendships: Psychoanalytic Perspectives

Harry Stack Sullivan and Erik Erikson are two other developmental theorists whose work is relevant to our consideration of friendship. Each identified a step he believed was crucial in the transition that enables an individual to have mature, adult-like friendships.

According to Sullivan (1953), people enter what he calls the preadolescent period (somewhere between ages eight-and-a-half and ten) when they have made a "chum," a person of the same sex with whom they form an intimate relationship. The child who does not find a chum, Sullivan theorizes, will experience lifelong loneliness.

Children at this age make promises to each other and share secrets of the kind they would never consider telling an opposite-sex peer, a person who, by definition, they would think of as untrustworthy (Rotenberg, 1986). Besides sharing secrets, they share activities and, for the first time in their lives, relate to another person in a reciprocal, equitable manner. As they interact, each chum develops "a real sensitivity to what matters to another person . . . [learning what I should] do to contribute to the happiness or to support the prestige and feeling of worthwhileness of my chum" (Sullivan, 1953, p. 245). In other words, preadolescents experience intimacy with a chum and as a result validate their own worth. At the same time that they are mastering the skills of building a quality relationship, they are also preparing themselves to someday make a lifelong commitment to another person.

In Erikson's theory (1968) key steps in preparing for mature friendships are taken in Stage 5, identity versus role confusion and Stage 6, intimacy versus isolation. In Stage 5, which roughly corresponds with adolescence, the individual faces an identity crisis, encountering the questions of "who he is," "where he's going," and "how can he be comfortable in his body." Once people have

Sullivan believed that the experience of having a chum in preadolescent years—with accompanying practice in sustaining an intimate relationship with another— lays the groundwork for rewarding friendships and involvements in later years.

achieved identity, they become ready to fuse that identity with others.' They have developed to the point where they are prepared for intimacy, being able to commit themselves to a partnership with others, even if they themselves must make sacrifices. Those who cannot find intimacy at this point in their development face the danger of isolation and loneliness.

Friendships in Adolescence and Adulthood

During the teenage years considerable time is available for friends. Coates (1987) studied the social networks of young adolescent blacks (mean age = 14.8) and found that females estimated having larger networks than did the males. While the females reported feeling close to members of both sexes, the males did not, indicating that they were close only with males. In reviewing her results, Coates concluded that the females, in contrast to the males, had older peers, spent more time with them, and tended to meet in smaller, more private groups.

The members of Coates' sample were entering their teens, an important transition point at which individuals begin the process of literally moving away from their parents and their influence. At this point, friends and associates have increased significance. For instance, the peer group serves as a socializing agent, providing support and security and directing adolescents in how to gain approval through behavior, speech, and dress. In this way, peer interaction plays a major role in shaping an adolescent's self-view and plans for the future. And friends help individuals adjust to the changes teenagers encounter in areas ranging from sexuality to the new expectations adults have of them.

Gender-related differences in friendship patterns are marked during adolescence. For instance, Dickens and Perlman (1981) concluded that while both young men and young women depend on same-gender friends to help them explore new feelings and thoughts, females tend to be more intimate, sharing and seeking support for their feelings and anxieties. Similar gender-differences continue into and throughout adulthood (Williams, 1985).

Probably because of their sex-role training, throughout adulthood women tend to have more friends than men. Women friends join in more spontaneous activities in their relationships than their male counterparts and are more intimate and self-disclosing (Baron & Byrne, 1981). Further, women are able to be closer to and more caring toward a greater number of people. In contrast, American men appear to be constrained by their sex-role dictates and, as a result, tend to direct all their loving feelings for adults toward one person—their spouse or significant other (Bell, 1981). The sex difference in the expression of warmth and love is at least partly cultural, and not biological. Southern European and Middle Eastern men, for example, are much freer in touching and expressing warmth to other men.

Teenagers spend a great deal of time in school and classmates often become the center of their social networks. From the pool of fellow students, individuals often find people to date and same-sex people to befriend. Same-sex schoolmates, besides having ample opportunity for contact, may be involved in the same activities, encounter similar challenges, and have common hopes for the future. As a result, they are well-suited to serve functions ranging from study partners or "fishing buddies" to confidantes. In contrast to opposite-sex friends, same-sex friends tend to be more helpful and loyal (Rose, 1985).

At the end of the high school career and, again, after the college years, friendship circles change. In both cases the individual encounters a challenge: While some contact with old acquaintances will be maintained, new interests, new life tasks, and a new residence in perhaps a new geographic area mean that people must generally start over, building new friendships and establishing a satisfying social network.

Five years after their college graduation, people are searching for somewhat different qualities in friends (Tesch & Martin, 1983). Whereas undergraduates seek trust, acceptance, respect, and the opportunity to confide in friendships, their 25-year-old alumni counterparts tend to value individuality and the ease of communication more highly. It makes sense that as people's lives change (completing their formal education, entering the work force, and, perhaps, marrying), so do what they want in companions.

Friendship needs persist in both sexes throughout adulthood, though there are changes in how they are expressed. During the young adult years, typically three to four close friendships are established (Haan & Day, 1974). One way

In the middle adult years, people tend to spend more leisure time with a smaller group of friends than when they were younger.

people create a bond between them during these years is to share such experiences as going to the movies, having lunch together, and so forth. In time friends not only enjoy the present, but can look back and contentedly discuss their "shared history," which includes favorite films, the time they had a flat tire in the middle of nowhere, and that funny blind date Al had at Kerry's party.

In the middle adult years, people tend to spend more of their leisure time with a smaller number of friends rather than, as they likely did earlier, with a broader group of acquaintances (coworkers, neighbors, etc.). While good friends made during this life stage need regular visits and shared time with each other, close ties between geographically separated friends from earlier years can be adequately maintained by occasional but regular contact.

Another important issue through the young and middle adulthood years is the gender of friends. With marriage, husbands and wives often give up individual friends and form a unit for social activities and friendships (Brown, 1981). They may become part of a group of couples who regularly share entertainment, recreational activities, and personal matters (Bell, 1981). Thus, except in the case of couples who are friends with other couples, married people are discouraged from having close friends of the opposite sex: Married women generally limit their friendships to women, and men to men. During middle adulthood, married couples usually develop close friendships with other couples from similar occupations and, if they have children, with people who have offspring about the same age as theirs. These factors offer a common interest for people and provide a more important bonding agent for friendship than the ages of the people themselves.

Through most of adulthood people generally have a fairly constant number of friends, a number that generally matches the optimal number they can comfortably handle. Whatever an individual's number might be—and three or four is typical—if he or she moves from one city and loses regular contact with four friends there, the odds are that in time the person will find four new close friends in the new locale (Hess, 1972). This does not necessarily hold true in the later years, because older people may become less able or willing to keep as many friends. One issue is access. Due to problems with mobility, older people's options for social participation may be limited to those next door or on the same block (Maas, 1984). However, those who were part of an active social network in earlier years often manage to keep many friends, while their counterparts who were more isolated tend to remain so in their later years (and may well be satisfied with spending most of their time alone).

Friendships among older people are distinctive in some ways. While young friends may visit daily, the frequency of contact among older friends may be once a month or less. Similarly, while younger people build their intimacy by emphasizing what they and their friends are doing now, more senior friends relate intimacy to length of acquaintance. As one 81-year-old man said, "Of course I consider Jack my friend. We grew up on the south side of town together. I've known him nearly all my life. We've been through a lot together, grammar school, high school, the depression, the war, you name it." As this statement illustrates, the older person finds that a long-time friend has become part of his life, through having known his family and through having shared many of his formative experiences.

Retirement villages and other age-segregated living accommodations are important to any discussion about older Americans and their friendship patterns. Recent arrivals at such housing face the process of making new friends and, like their younger counterparts, look for people with certain interpersonal qualities and personalities to befriend. In a well-administered facility, their task may be simplified because of planned activities designed to promote and sustain friendships. In such centers the staff recognizes that even in one's later years the need for friendship remains and is related to one's happiness and well-being (Antonucci & Akiyama, 1987). Roberto and Scott (1986) point out, after studying 110 people ranging from 64–91 years of age, "Through friendships individuals find acceptance, support and companionship that is vital to a sense of personal worth and fulfillment in later life" (p. 108).

Before turning to the next topic, roadblocks in friendships, we can summarize the research on friendship in adults by making these points (Reisman, 1981):

▸ Females tend to value friends as confidantes.

▸ Males tend to value friends as companions with whom they enjoy activities.

- Many of people's closest friends are made in young adulthood but, over the years, the frequency of contact with them is reduced.

- Friends are important throughout adulthood but the priority of cultivating these relationships tends to be lower than that of investing time and energy in one's family and one's career.

Roadblocks in Friendships

As in every aspect of life, people unhappy about their friendship circle or social situation can take steps to make the kind of changes that will bring satisfaction. For example, those overwhelmed by their social life can trim their schedule, while those feeling a need for more contact can reach out to others. People who believe they cannot take appropriate action alone should consider seeking assistance from family members, a pastor, or a mental health worker. Noncredit courses offered in many communities and how-to books are additional resources.

Applying Research Findings

Research findings shed light on the friendship formation processes and how people can overcome problems in making friends. This knowledge is essential to counselors and clinicians. To illustrate how research can be used by practitioners, we singled out three studies that produced results with direct applied value.

Problems in Individuals   The first study was conducted by Fenigstein (1984) and its results might aid Mary, a client who notices people giggling at parties and then convinces herself that she is the target of their fun. In one condition of his investigation, just before returning blue book exams, professors told the students in their psychology classes that there was one especially bad test in the pile, among the worst that had ever been handed in. In other classes the professors instead spoke highly of one outstanding exam. Next, the professors asked class members to anonymously estimate the probability that theirs was the one that had been singled out. Taking into account the grades students expected to earn, Fenigstein found statistically significant results indicating that the subjects were more likely to believe the exam in question was theirs, not a classmate's, with the result being stronger with the poor exam.

This study and others illustrate a common cognitive bias: people tend to overperceive themselves as the one person being "singled out." Mary reacts in this way when she sees others laughing and she would benefit from knowing about this study and related research that suggests the normalness of her reaction. A therapist or counselor could teach Mary cognitive strategies to help her overcome or manage this problem.

The second study might help Terry, a client who fears his scheduled interview for membership in a fraternity. Those conducting it are people with whom he very much wants to become associated and that, he believes, will make him self-conscious of his every statement. In this research, Carver and Scheier (1978) administered a sentence completion test (e.g., "Right now I feel. . . .") under several conditions: subjects had a mirror on the desk they used, subjects had another person present while they worked, and subjects completed the instrument privately, with no mirror present. Comparing performance, the researchers found that the presence of the mirror and of the observer made subjects more self-conscious or intensely aware of themselves.

The results of this and related studies suggest that Terry could profit from stationing himself in front of a mirror and practicing answering the questions he expects to be asked. During such practice Terry would likely become self-conscious and experience feelings similar to those he would be encountering during the interview. The practice might enable Terry to learn how to perform at a high level during the interview.

Mick has minimal confidence in his ability to impress Jane, a fellow student from the same hometown. Mick is driving her back this weekend and hopes to generate the courage to invite her out for a movie. The third study might help him. Jones, Rhodewalt, Berglas, and Skelton (1981), in one condition, instructed subjects to be self-enhancing in a role-played job interview. More specifically, subjects were told to give a positive impression by thinking about themselves in a good mood on a good day and by remembering their positive qualities.

After a role-playing was completed in the laboratory, subjects were tested and found to have increased self-esteem. In contrast, other subjects who were led to be self-deprecating experienced lowered self-esteem. Mick can be told of this and related studies and could be "given permission" to present himself positively during the drive. If he carried through, such a self-presentation might improve Mick's self-view, the probability he will ask Jane out, and the chances for positive outcomes.

Communication Problems

Misunderstandings   A paper entitled "The Fateful Process of Mr. A Talking to Mr. B" (Johnson, 1974) details the difficulties inherent in this deceptively simple act. Consider for a moment the process of speaking. To have another person know what we are thinking and feeling, we must first accurately identify what we are experiencing and then code it faithfully into comprehensible words and nonverbal signs. The other person must hear and see our utterances and cues and transform them accurately into a perception of our communication.

Perhaps because communication is more complex than it appears, friends, parents, children, lovers, and business associates frequently experience what they call "communication problems"; that is, difficulty in conveying their thoughts and desires to another person. There are many useful how-to books in public and college libraries that offer techniques to improve communication. Three widely recommended guidelines are: (1) send clear messages,

(2) listen actively, making a sincere effort to understand the speaker's thoughts and feelings, and (3) check for accuracy by asking questions and putting into your own words what you thought the speaker said.

Value Differences and Related Sources of Interpersonal Conflict Many times close examination reveals that what appeared to be a communication problem between people has a more basic cause. For example, Benita, a college sophomore who lives at home, told her friends that she just couldn't talk to her parents. "We just don't agree about anything." Her parents feel the same way. The problem is not communication, because they are able to exchange thoughts accurately. The problem is that Benita and her parents have different needs and values.

Nye (1973) discusses five causes of basic differences between people that hamper the growth of relationships. They are (1) competitiveness; (2) domination or attempted domination of one by the other; (3) failure to reach goals, which one (or both) blames on the other; (4) constant provocation by one (or both) of the other, preventing any harmony from developing; and (5) value differences in matters that are important (as was the case with Benita and her parents). Interpersonal conflicts can also occur, according to Grasha and Kirschenbaum (1980) because people hold incompatible goals, hold common goals but wish to pursue them in different ways, disagree about proposed uses of limited resources, or have different notions about appropriate behavior. Honest discussion, perhaps guided by a neutral third-party, is a most effective way to cope with problems such as these, if those involved are willing to work cooperatively toward solutions. In such cases, tolerable, if not ideal, solutions are often found.

Psychological Games

Games (which should not be confused with healthy playfulness) are another transactional analysis (TA) concept. **Games** are defined as a repeatedly played set of transactions in which people take roles. Because the players are following a "script," instead of being themselves, they are not relating to each other in straightforward ways (Steiner, 1981). Although people may play a game repeatedly, they are generally unaware of their participation in it and of the motives and payoffs in playing. Nonetheless, by game's end one or more of the players will usually feel bad. The "Why Don't You—Yes But" game illustrates many of these points.

Games
A term in transactional analysis used to describe an interaction in which people take roles and follow a script, as they relate, instead of being themselves and straightforward with each other.

Background: Daniel has been feeling that his three roommates (Abe, Barry, and Charles) are ignoring him lately and leaving him out of things. Without full awareness, for the third night in a row he is seeking attention from them by taking center stage and focusing the dinner conversation on his apparent request for help.

Scene: Dining room, 6:00 P.M., Thursday night.

Games Friends Play

Since repetitive game-playing can strip enjoyment from interactions, make the players feel bad, or cause one person to withdraw from a relationship, friends should try to avoid engaging in games. How? One step is to identify games they play. Friends can ask themselves: What happens repetitively and leaves us with sour feelings? How does it begin? Then what happens? How does it end? The simple process of engaging in this line of thought should strengthen the bonds between friends and assist them in avoiding game-playing. Toward that end, examine the list of games below (James & Savary, 1976, pp. 128–129).

Name of the game	Theme of the game
"Harried"	Being "too busy" and having no time to develop closeness
"Kick Me"	Continually doing things to get a friend's disapproval
"Poor Me"	Complaining and complaining to get sympathy
"Why Don't You . . ."	Giving more and more advice that is not wanted
"I'm Only Trying to Help You"	Continually being available, but only as a helper
"Blemish"	Being a nitpicker; finding all the little things that are wrong
"Now I've Got You"	Waiting for a friend to make an error, then pouncing on him or her

1. Do you and your friends play any of these games, or other games you can identify?
2. Choose one of the listed games and write an imaginary exchange of conversation between two game-players. Let each of them make eight to ten comments in the interchange. ▲

Daniel: My history midterm is coming up Monday and I'm way behind.

Abe: Well, you can study tonight.

Daniel: Yes, but I promised I'd fix Barry's car tonight.

Barry: Oh, that's all right, you can fix my car Sunday. I'll walk to school tomorrow.

Daniel: Yes, but Sunday afternoon I have a date.

Barry: You can work on the car Saturday, then.

Daniel: Yes, but that's when Mark is lending me his notes.

Charles: Well, you could borrow my notes instead and study tonight or Saturday.

Daniel: Yes, but I haven't read the textbook yet.

Abe: I'll trade hours with you at the garage so you won't have to work until after the exam. That'll help, won't it?

Daniel: Yes, but. . . .

No matter what solution is proposed by any of his roommates, it meets with the same reaction: rejection. Daniel was playing "Why Don't You—Yes But" to win attention, sympathy, and other strokes. He drew his roommates into the game, and each played a rescuer-type role. At the apparent level of exchange, the conversation appeared to be transactions between Daniel's Adult Ego State and his roommates' Adult Ego States. However, the "game" part,

TABLE 8.2 *Techniques for Ending Games*

You Can:	This May Work For You Because:
1. Make an honest statement such as, "I don't like it when you phone me daily and talk for so long."	You are turning unsatisfying routine into a discussable problem that friends can solve.
2. Give an unexpected response such as "I'll go to any movie *you* want to see. Just name it."	This breaks up the ritualized flow of a game and frees both parties to think about what is happening (e.g., every film you suggested has been rejected).
3. Stop exaggerating your own weaknesses or strengths.	Exaggerating weaknesses invites another to bail you out (not to *help* you as an equal). Exaggerating strengths invites others to continually ask you to bail them out.
4. Stop exaggerating the weaknesses or strengths of others.	Again, exaggeration invites a bail-out process rather than a helping one.
5. Freely give and receive positive strokes.	If sufficient positive strokes are exchanged, a person may cease playing games to receive negative or "tainted" strokes.
6. Structure more of your time with activities and intimacy.	Time used in these productive ways will be satisfying, and thus game-playing is less likely to be needed.
7. Stop playing Rescuer (i.e., stop helping those who don't really need help).	Instead of getting into a game, you can determine what is wanted—help or strokes. Either can be asked for and provided straightforwardly.
8. Stop playing Persecutor (i.e., stop giving nonconstructive, person-targeted criticism).	Instead of getting into a game, you can determine what is wanted—constructive criticism or strokes. Again, either can be asked for and provided straightforwardly.
9. Stop playing Victim (i.e., stop acting helpless or dependent when you are really able to stand on your own two feet).	Instead of getting into a game, you can determine what you want, help or strokes, and request these things more directly.
10. Withdraw physically or psychologically.	This breaks up the ritualized flow of a game and provides an opportunity to think about what is happening.

From M. James, *Born to Love*. Copyright © 1973, Addison-Wesley Publishers, Reading, Massachusetts. Reprinted by permission of Muriel James.

of which they all were probably unaware, was Daniel's helpless Child Ego State "serving up a request" for attention and ideas from his roommates' Parent Ego States, and their Parent Ego Stages "returning the ball" by transmitting messages assuring Daniel's Child Ego Stage that they cared about him. However, because Daniel rejected their true, nongame, self-sacrificing offers, the roommates probably became annoyed at him by the game's end and may in fact have paid less attention to him after that as punishment for his lack of appreciation of their generosity.

At any point during "Why Don't You—Yes But," a roommate could have ended play by identifying the pattern: "It seems none of our ideas make sense to you. Perhaps we can't help with this one." For his part, Daniel would have been more likely to get what he really wanted had he avoided the game altogether and said: "Frankly, I've been feeling left out of things here lately. Is that my imagination or what?"

There are many ways to stop a game, as Table 8.2 shows.

LONELINESS

People feel lonely because they have had difficulty establishing the kind and the number of satisfying relationships they desire. By their very nature, humans are social beings, and thus friendship should come easily to them. But frequently this does not happen, leading us to ask, as did the Beatles, "All the lonely people—where do they all come from?" In fact, estimates suggest that about 10 percent of children, a higher percentage of teenagers and, perhaps, as many as 50 million Americans, or about 20 percent, of the population feel some degree of loneliness (Meer, 1985). Loneliness affects people from all walks of life and, as you can see, is represented at all points in the life span.

It is useful to make a distinction between chronic and situational loneliness. Situational loneliness, as the name suggests, is a more temporary problem and one that you may have noticed is prevalent on college campuses, particularly among new students at your school. Cutrona (1982) found that over 50 percent of the freshmen she tested in a fall term experienced situational loneliness. By spring these individuals no longer tested as being lonely—they had built a satisfying social network. In contrast, another 13.5 percent of the freshmen tested as lonely in both the fall and spring terms and were categorized as chronically lonely. Many of these individuals made some friends during the school year, but after nine months on campus, they still felt dissatisfied with their social network.

There can be many aspects in a person's social network: friends, spouse/ significant other/romantic partner, family members, and associations with the larger community. Schmidt and Sermat (1983) explain that an individual having many good friends, for instance, still might feel lonely because of a lack of a certain type of relationship in his social network. For example, Jason has only one male friend and that suits him fine. He feels lonely, however, because he wants a relationship with a woman. In contrast, Jackie, a classmate of his, has several good friends she shares time with, but feels lonely because none of those relationships provide the level of intimacy she seeks.

Jackie's experience is consistent with research findings suggesting that lonely college freshmen, as indicated by their score on a paper-and-pencil test, have as many "good friends" as their non-lonely counterparts, but have lower levels of intimacy in their "best-friends" relationships (Williams & Solano, 1983). Along this same line, these investigators also found that, when asked, the lonely subjects listed as many friends as other subjects, but those they listed did not reciprocate as frequently as did the friends listed by non-lonely subjects.

Causes of Loneliness

Personal Factors

Two kinds of personal qualities inhibit the development of friendships; those, like hostility or deviancy, that make a person unattractive to others; and those, like shyness, low self-esteem, lack of social skills, and nonassertiveness, that prevent others from realizing that an individual would like to attract them.

Since shyness is now affecting 40 percent of Americans and has affected an equal number at earlier points in their lives (Zimbardo, 1977), we will examine it as an example of how personal qualities can inhibit the building of a social support network.

Zimbardo defines *shyness* as "a tendency to avoid social situations, to fail to participate appropriately in social encounters, and to feel anxious, distressed and burdened during interpersonal interactions" (1979, p. 510). About half of a group of shy students Zimbardo studied experienced increased pulse, blushing, perspiration, "butterflies in the stomach," and heart-pounding. The great majority reported feeling self-conscious, and most also expressed concern about the impression they made, worried about how they were evaluated socially, had a negative self-evaluation, and found social situations unpleasant. Their overt behaviors were characterized by frequent silence and, in about half those studied, avoidance of eye contact, avoidance of others, a tendency not to take action, and a low speaking voice. As these reactions suggest, most shy people do not like being shy and find it causes them problems.

Shyness reduces an individual's opportunities to make social contacts and, over time, this hampers a person's efforts to build a social network. Such an effect was well-illustrated in a research study. The investigators (Cheek & Busch, 1981) tested the level of shyness in introductory psychology students at the beginning of the semester, and their loneliness at the beginning and the end of the term. The finding—that the shy students were significantly lonelier than their unshy counterparts at the end of the semester—confirmed what you might have expected. Personality characteristics, like shyness, can have a major impact on students and their feelings of connectedness with others on campus.

Psychologists have identified several factors that could cause shyness. These include being raised in a cultural background where such qualities are valued (such as in a traditional Oriental home) and having parents who acted as models for shy behavior. Of course, some people may deliberately choose to withdraw in order to protect themselves from rejection by others, perhaps because they have a negative self-concept or because they experienced an embarrassing situation.

Zimbardo believes that the shy can learn not to be shy:

> You have chosen to be shy and learned to act like a shy person. You can now choose not to be, if you are willing to unlearn those old habits and substitute ones that work for your best interest. You are free to do X, even when others say you cannot; you are free to refuse to do X, even when others say you must (1977, p. 205).

To help clients overcome shyness, Zimbardo stresses these points: "You have control over what you feel and do. You are responsible for those feelings and actions and for creating the consequences you want."

Zimbardo recommends that the shy take steps to make themselves more physically attractive and that they experiment with different behaviors to determine which yield the desired social rewards. Some of the behaviors he suggests are: saying hello to strangers on campus, starting conversations in places like a grocery store line, giving compliments to an acquaintance, and practicing and telling jokes.

Besides shyness, factors that predispose individuals to loneliness include self-consciousness, introversion, lack of assertiveness, and a belief that luck rather than personal efforts control one's social life (Perlman & Peplau, 1984). People's cognitions (thoughts and how they explain events to themselves) are also a factor. Those who scold themselves, "It's Saturday night and I should be out," will feel lonelier than those who reason, "It's okay to study this Saturday night. I can go out another night." Similarly, people who blame themselves for having no plans will feel lonelier than those who recognize that the situation, the fact that they are new on campus, has made a difference and that in time their social network will broaden.

Social Factors

Another force that inhibits the formation of relationships is today's world. As one author observes, we like things that keep us apart (Keyes, 1973). We drive our own car instead of riding the bus, we prefer our houses spaced away from those of our neighbors, and we watch the latest movies on videotapes and cable television instead of going to the movie theater and watching with others. Even our jobs may force us to work in isolation or in competition with colleagues whom we might otherwise befriend.

We do not have the same friendship opportunities our forbearers enjoyed. We go to the supermarket instead of the neighborhood grocery store. We bank by mail. Men have forfeited the sociability of the daily barbershop shave for the efficiency of the electric or disposable razor. We move a lot.

Packard (1972) indicates that the typical American has 24 addresses during a lifetime, and recent data suggest that about 43 million will move at least once in a given year, a figure that includes about one-third of people in their 20s (U.S. Census Bureau, 1987).

Loneliness Is a Widespread Problem

While **loneliness** is not a sign of psychological disorder, research indicates it can be associated with low self-esteem, high anxiety, feelings of helplessness, a reduced appetite, and physical ailments. Moreover, a lonely person can inflict further pain on himself by engaging in self-defeating behaviors. For instance, loneliness can cause a person to have sex with another simply to obtain another date, to enter into an ill-advised marriage, or, in extreme cases, to commit suicide.

In order to determine how widespread loneliness is as a problem, psychologists have developed research tools to detect its presence and to determine the magnitude of the problem in a person. Sample items drawn from one of the available "loneliness scales" (Russell, Peplau, & Ferguson, 1978) are presented below.

Respondents are asked to consider each item and indicate whether it "often," "sometimes," or "never" describes how they feel.

I am unhappy doing so many things alone.
I have nobody to talk to.
I find myself waiting for people to call or write.
There is no one I can turn to.
My social relationships are superficial.
No one really knows me well.
It is difficult for me to make friends.
People are around me but not with me.

Using scales like this one and other measures, social scientists have shown that loneliness, as mentioned earlier, is a widespread problem. Findings suggest that unmarried people encounter more loneliness than married, and that the poor and those in ill health experience more than their better-off counterparts. Of course, divorce and the death of a spouse are other causes of loneliness.

Contradictory results have been reported with regard to gender. After studying the published research literature on this matter, Borys and Perlman (1985) concluded that: When asked directly, women are more likely to label themselves as lonely. When asked indirectly, such as through the widely-used UCLA Loneliness Scale, men are more likely to score as being more lonely than women. There are many possible explanations for this pattern, including the fact that sex-role training has taught women to be more open and men to be more secretive about feelings and personal difficulties. At this point in our knowledge, we lack a full understanding of how loneliness differentially affects men and women.

Loneliness
A condition experienced by a person when he or she lacks the number and type of satisfying social relationships he desires.

Finally, although loneliness is often imagined to be a problem that increases with age, people are perhaps most vulnerable to it during their teenage years and early 20s. As Revenson and Johnson (1984) found, the prevalence of loneliness actually decreases over the life span. Using survey data collected from over 2000 people ranging in age from 18–89, they discovered those over 65 were the least lonely and the most content with the relationships they had. Although one can easily imagine a retired, widowed senior-citizen rocking alone on his front porch and assume that he is lonely, he is probably not. Schultz and Moore (1984) found that their 65-year-old subjects averaged only 1.5 bouts of loneliness a month that lasted about 7.2 hours each.

Coping with Loneliness

People suffering from loneliness often withdraw from others, sometimes busying themselves with what can be thought of as the pseudo-companionship provided by television. Rubenstein and Shaver (1982) found that 61 percent of the 18–25-year-old Americans they sampled viewed television to remedy loneliness. Similarly, lonelier senior citizens watch more television than their peers (Perlman, Gerson, & Spinner, 1978).

Instead of retreating, people can deal with their loneliness by taking two sometimes difficult but often rewarding steps. First, recognizing that their loneliness is not unique, that all people spend time alone and may occasionally feel lonely, they can choose to capitalize on this time, using it productively to develop greater self-acceptance. Second, they can devote time and energy to building new relationships with others and to rekindling and strengthening old ones. A surprising number of people make little effort to do this.

Those who feel they cannot develop a plan by themselves to overcome loneliness can seek assistance. Aid can come from family members, pastors, counselors, psychotherapists, or others in the community. One way professionals can help is by teaching the social skills involved in holding another's attention. For instance, Jones, Hobbs, and Hockenbury (1982) used audiotapes to teach lonely male college students how to make statements about the other person and how to ask effective questions in a social conversation. Results indicated that the students learned these skills and, in turn, became less shy, less lonely, and began to feel better about themselves. Assertiveness training is another technique that professionals use to help people overcome shyness and loneliness (see the Self-Knowledge Exercise).

Ralph's and Henrietta's experiences illustrate the value developing a plan can have in overcoming loneliness. Ralph, a 19-year-old who had recently separated from his woman friend, felt lonely and isolated. Although surrounded all day by fellow students, he approached nobody, except when essential. Like most people his age, he experienced greater daily fluctuations in feelings of loneliness than do older people, and he was especially lonely on weekends. But he felt too immobilized to make arrangements for Friday or Saturday nights until he was motivated to action by a conversation he had with his older sister. She explained how, some three years earlier, she had encountered the same problem. To remedy it she eventually developed a plan that included studying

in the library, going to social events with women-friends, and, once every other week, asking a man to dinner with her at a nearby restaurant. Within the first few months her problem was solved. Ralph adopted a plan somewhat similar to his sister's, and almost immediately felt less lonely.

Henrietta, a widowed 68-year-old woman, also dealt with her loneliness, although she approached the matter quite differently. For two months after her last daughter moved away, all Henrietta did was mope around the house. She really wanted to spend time with others, but she was afraid to reach out. She told herself, "I don't know how to develop a new social life anyway." As the weeks passed, Henrietta realized that the best way for her to cope effectively with loneliness was to plan ways of acquiring the contacts she needed.

Henrietta began by making "safe" contacts with others. She invited a salesperson to show her a new security system for her house. She began to regularly telephone a radio talk program and offer her opinions. Both these involvements were enjoyable to her and provided some relief from her loneliness, but they were not enough. Henrietta finally decided to take a risk and joined a singles group for older people in a nearby church. In time, she made a few good friends and developed some sense of attachment and community. Encouraged by a member of the church group, she decided to spend one day a week as a volunteer at the local hospital.

When Henrietta tells others about how she overcame her loneliness, she says: "In June I was worried about spending Christmas alone. By December I had so many kind offers I was afraid of hurting somebody's feelings because I couldn't spread myself that thin."

Humans are social beings and need to form bonds with friends and those they love. Though people often encounter difficulties in building and maintaining relationships, with a degree of effort, and sincere interest in the people they meet, they can generally be successful. In the next section we look at the topic of love and how it relates to friendships and loneliness.

Assertiveness

Assertiveness trainers explain that all individuals have a right to feel like they are in charge of themselves and that they have the personal power to gain their rights without apology or asking permission for what is theirs. Assertive persons have learned a system of values and behaviors that lead them to act in self-affirming ways that reflect their genuine feelings.

Those who are not assertive can learn to be so by teaching themselves, perhaps with aid from a book, or by enrolling in an assertiveness training program. Such offerings help students learn to accept themselves, their rights, and the fact that being nonassertive is both frustrating and, over time, harmful to the self and others (Doty, 1987). Assertiveness training helps students learn how to communicate verbally and nonverbally in open and appropriate manners that reflect their needs and feelings, to develop more fulfilling relationships, and to pursue those activities that interest them most.

Training programs use behavioral and cognitive techniques to teach assertiveness. For example, reinforcement and shaping (reinforcement of increasingly correct behavior) can be used along with observational learning (watching models act assertively). Students can also be taught to challenge their own irrational beliefs (I can stand up for my rights and ask my roommate to be quiet after 11 P.M.) and to use behavioral rehearsal (by role playing a conversation in which "the roommate" is asked to be quiet after 11 P.M.).

It is important to differentiate assertiveness from aggressiveness, an interpersonal strategy through which people try to gain what they want in a way that violates others' rights or needs. After taking an aggressive action, most people feel badly, perhaps guilty or embarrassed. After being assertive, most people will feel better about themselves and, in turn, they will be able to offer more to others. It is also important to contrast assertiveness with passiveness, an interpersonal strategy used by people who feel powerless and uncertain of themselves. Notice the differences in the style the three students below used to achieve the same goal:

Student 1: Passive approach in a timid voice—"Uh, I was wondering if you would mind, uh (looking down), be willing to take the time to show me, if you could, how to do this problem?"

Student 2: Aggressive approach in a harsh voice—"I've come by your office three times and (glaring at the instructor's eyes) you haven't been there to explain to me how to do this problem."

LOVE BETWEEN ADULTS

The Need for Love

Since 96 percent of Americans marry, one could assume that nearly every adult has fallen in love at one point or another. Why does this happen? Psychologists agree that falling in love fulfills a human need. But what need? Theorists propose different ideas.

Psychoanalytically oriented theorists argue that falling in love is one way in which adults can meet their id's need to maximize their happiness. Being in love, like doing satisfying work, is a form of sublimation that enables a person to harness instinctual energies in a socially appropriate and adaptive manner. According to psychoanalytic theory, people who build a successful

Student 3: Assertive approach in a relaxed but firm voice—"Professor Jones (looking at him in a friendly way), I want to set up an appointment with you this week so you can help me learn how to solve this problem."

1. How assertive are you: Very assertive, somewhat assertive, not at all assertive?

2. Which two of your friends are most assertive? Ask them when and how they learned to become assertive. Ask them what they think are the advantages and disadvantages of their assertiveness.

3. Fogging is a technique taught by assertiveness trainers. Fogging involves focusing on the important point in the other person's comment (ignoring the rest of it), paraphrasing the essence to indicate an understanding, and then stating your disagreement. Using fogging in Peggy's comments, finish this conversation between Peggy, 21, and her mother, by writing three lines for each.

Peggy: I've been invited by Dan to his fraternity beer blast! I'll be back by 2:00 A.M. or so.

Mother: No way. No daughter of mine is going to be involved in a wild orgy with those animals. They'll probably be smoking dope and who knows what else. You're not going there.

Peggy: You're afraid the guys are going to get out of hand, but you know I am a responsible person and I can take care of myself.

4. Broken record is another technique taught by assertiveness trainers. Broken record involves persistent repetition of a message in a firm, clear manner. By rephrasing and repeating your wishes, the resistance of the other person may wear down. Create a realistic dialogue between Ken and Rick, freshmen roommates, who want to meet some people on campus. Have Rick use the broken record technique and have the decision-making end with Ken understanding Rick's position and agreeing to a compromise: they go to the party for an hour or two and then to the movies.

Rick: Let's go to the party and try to meet people.

Ken: Let's go to the movies. I don't think there will be many freshmen at the party.

Rick: C'mon, let's walk over to the party and see who we run into.

love relationship must direct some of their instinctual sexual energy away from seeking immediate gratification and toward longer-term strengthening of the relationship. By forming an enduring emotional tie with another, a person can both gratify sexual instincts and obtain intense healthy pleasure.

Humanistically oriented theorists, like Carl Rogers and Abraham Maslow, take a different view. They argue that adult love partially satisfies the human need to become more fully actualized. Maslow, for example, believed that there is an innate human drive toward health and that individuals seek partners who will facilitate and support their growth.

Finally, social learning theorists such as Albert Bandura view falling in love as behavior learned from important childhood models. The needs people seek to fulfill through adult love include meeting the expectations of others and achieving the status associated with being in love. Social learning theorists further argue that the ways people fall in love, and the ways they tell their partner and the world about it, are with behaviors learned from models at home, on the television screen, and in their friendship circles.

The Art of Loving

Erich Fromm, in his book *The Art of Loving* (1956/1974) expresses his belief that love is an art. People are often disappointed in love because they fail to recognize it as an art that they must master in the same way the pianist, carpenter, and physician master their art, that is, by acquiring knowledge and making efforts. Although Fromm's view is not a very romantic one, it fits with available research data and is reflected in the experiences of many people we know personally.

An important part of achieving love is to develop one's personality and to become what one is capable of. In doing that, the capacity to love others is developed. Fromm maintains that it is important to consider three issues.

First, there is a distinction between *being loved* and *being loving*. Those who desire love generally believe that they will be loved if they make themselves lovable. They buy clothes, exercise their bodies, and cultivate conversational skills. However, it is as important for people to develop the ability to love.

Second, people search for the "perfect" mate. They think that love will happen when they find the right person. In fact, love grows only when people have developed the art of loving.

Third, people confuse *falling in love* with *being in love*. Falling in love is the simpler of the two. But when the infatuation passes, the excitement that accompanied it must be replaced with other satisfactions, if the couple is to be in love over a period of time.

Fromm identifies five forms of love. There are (1) brotherly (sisterly) love—a nonexclusive, "love thy neighbor" orientation; (2) motherly (fatherly) love—a nonpossessive, unconditional form that parents have toward their children; (3) erotic love—an exclusive type seen in people who seek oneness with their partners; (4) self-love—a necessary form that enables one to love others; and (5) love of God.

Because of the great satisfaction love can provide and the great frustrations and unhappiness that can stem from problems in love relationships, our society eagerly seeks advice from experts about this subject. Although Fromm thoughtfully discusses "building love," he forewarns his readers not to expect easy-to-follow instructions. His warning is a sensible one. There is much to learn about love and loving, as you will see in this chapter. Nonetheless, there are no easy solutions. We begin our study with the topic of dating, the social situation in which love often develops.

People have differing reasons for dating, ranging from physical attraction to a desire to have a partner for social activities. Other benefits are also intrinsic to dating: the improvement of social skills and the evaluation of the importance of different personality characteristics encountered.

Dating

Dating can be viewed as a specialized case of the friendship-building process. Most of the principles discussed earlier under the category of friendship apply. For example, physical proximity is essential at the outset, self-disclosure grows with the developing relationship (Rubin, Hill, Peplau, & Dunkel-Schetter, 1980), and communication problems can make day-to-day living difficult for the couple. However, dating relationships do differ from same-gender friendships in obvious ways.

Two people generally date to have fun and with the hope that they will become better acquainted or find romance. Dating also serves varied social purposes; for instance, a date provides both parties with opportunities to learn from their interactions. Specifically, they can sharpen their social skills, discover what is necessary to attract and relate to members of the opposite sex, and begin to determine the qualities they want in a lifelong mate. Those who date also have a chance to test adult roles, including stereotyped sex-role behaviors that were accepted in the past but are changing now. For example, men test the assumption that they must initiate contact by asking for a date, while women examine how they feel about the traditional "passive" way of attracting men. Finally, through the process of dating, people do the important work of selecting a spouse.

"Fair" Dating

It is commonly believed that a good relationship between two people requires give and take. Some social scientists have developed this idea into **equity theory,** a theory that suggests interpersonal attraction is influenced by principles of fairness. Researchers have developed instruments to study the role equity

Equity Theory
A theory that suggests people's attempt to maintain equity in their relationship so that each is receiving a fair payback for what he or she is putting in.

(whether individuals achieve equal relative gains) plays when people are seeing each other, either as friends or lovers (Hatfield & Traupmann, 1981; Thibaut & Kelley, 1959; Walster, Berschied, & Walster, 1973), and have found some support for the theory.

One important issue to a person who steadily dates another is whether the benefits of being a couple are equal to or exceed the costs. What constitutes benefits or rewards may vary from person to person but generally include gaining approval, attention, support, physical contact, and sex. Costs also vary, but they generally include the discomfort associated with arguments, the time and money investment necessary, and so forth. Since men and women who date each other do not always hold the same goals, sometimes they "make a trade," as Collins' (1974) study illustrates. While Collins' female subjects reported dating primarily to gain affection and closeness and to build a good relationship with someone else, the males were more oriented toward achieving sexual intimacy. As they date, people make an exchange, and each gets some of what he or she wants. If they build a quality relationship, eventually each person can also enjoy and benefit from the pleasures the other initially desired.

Another important "fairness issue" is whether each person is receiving an equitable share of what the relationship yields. Those who find themselves in a situation they believe to be inequitable will take one of several courses. First, they may try to restore equity. For example, the man may have chosen activities and paid for them during a couple's first three evenings together. This time they agree that the woman will make the plans and cover the expenses.

A second alternative is for the partners to convince themselves that they have equity. For example, an engaged couple spent both Thanksgiving and Christmas with the woman's parents. The two concluded that this was fair because the man's parents did not have enough room for visitors in their apartment.

Third, if the inequity cannot be corrected or justified, one or both may end the relationship. For example, if a woman feels a relationship is fair but a man believes she has been "using him," he is likely to break off with her.

Social exchange theory, like equity theory, provides a tool for examining interpersonal relationships. **Social exchange theory,** developed from learning principles, holds that social interactions are based on the expectation of rewards and the belief that if one acts in a certain way toward another, he or she will reciprocate, and react in the same way. Social exchange theory postulates that interactions between individuals are based on an exchange of benefits that include love, sex, attractiveness, kindness, a classy automobile, and so forth.

The social exchange model suggests that there is a social "marketplace," full of competition, in which each person offers his or her assets for trade. As long as benefits for each person in a relationship outweigh the costs involved in the exchange, the relationship continues, since it is satisfying the needs of all parties.

Social Exchange Theory
A theory that suggests interpersonal relationships are guided by an exchange of benefits between people.

Personal Adjustment through the Life Span

To the observer, not all enduring relationships appear like each partner is receiving adequate benefits. When this seems to be the case, there are probably factors affecting the relationship not readily apparent to those outside of it. To illustrate, one partner may have low self-esteem. Since he believes he has little market value, he will not demand as much as somebody else might from a friend, a date, or a spouse. Further, as the case of Diane illustrates, he might put in more effort as a way of "compensating" for what he perceives as personal lacks.

Diane, an extremely overweight 19-year-old woman, sought help at a community mental health center, complaining of listlessness and discontent. After several sessions with a counselor, Diane came to realize that much of her distress stemmed from what was happening in her first serious love affair. The man she was involved with, John, was a 27-year-old trucker. Their relationship was inequitable in several ways. Diane suspected that when John was on the road he saw other women, but she was afraid to ask. When he wasn't traveling he expected Diane to wait on him. She did, and even cut classes when he asked her to.

Although missing classes bothered Diane, John would say, "What's the difference? You'll never do anything with your degree anyway." Because of Diane's feelings about her figure and her attractiveness to men, she felt she was not in a position to demand or even bargain for changes. Instead she decided to be sweet, tolerant, and faithful, and hoped he would treat her in the same way.

Working with the counselor, Diane recognized that she was acting as if she had only two choices: an unsatisfactory relationship with John or no man at all. She had accepted the situation and stayed with John because she wanted love and feared that she could not find it with anyone else. After several months and many sessions, Diane decided to take a chance. She broke up with John, began a diet, and joined several campus groups. Through insight gained in counseling, Diane raised her self-view and expected more in her social relationships.

Dating Habits and Problems   Norms, codes, and styles in dating, or "going out," vary from decade to decade. Regardless of what is popular at a given time, drive-in burger joints and convertibles, discos, group dates, or women asking men, over the years certain patterns have persisted. For instance, high school students tend to date more people than college students; in college there is a greater tendency to see one person exclusively; upper classmen tend to have more dates than freshmen. An anonymous 35-item survey designed to assess dating behavior patterns and commonly encountered problems was given to about 200 undergraduates (Klaus, Hersen, & Bellack, 1977). The data indicated that both males and females had about 5.5 dates per month (some respondents may have exaggerated) and that freshmen tended to have fewer dates than upperclassmen.

The dating problems people encountered were associated with their gender and year in school. Specifically, freshmen reported significantly more difficulty than upperclassmen in finding dates and in initiating sexual activity. Men identified calling to ask somebody out as a problem, and women indicated the following difficulties: finding dates, getting men to ask them out a second time, maintaining conversation and feeling comfortable during a date, and ending it when they felt ready. The survey also indicated that women were willing to talk about "inner" personal feelings earlier than men, but there were no gender differences in readiness to speak about sex, family matters, or marriage. Men were prepared to "pet" and have sexual intercourse sooner than women were.

These researchers also looked at their data in another way, comparing low-frequency and high-frequency daters. Analyses indicated that the low-frequency daters desired significantly fewer dates, felt they had less adequate dating skills, experienced more difficulty in contacting possible dates, and more problems in various areas of socializing (for example, in maintaining conversation).

Dating Anxiety

There are many reasons why people date infrequently. Some are in a situation where they have little contact with prospective dates. Others prefer spending time on academic work, perhaps because of an achievement-oriented upbringing. The most prevalent reason, however, is that they have anxiety about dating.

A survey of randomly selected University of Arizona undergraduates indicated that about one-third of the respondents were "somewhat" or "very" anxious about dating (Arkowitz et al., 1978). Further, half of the 3,800 students involved in the study expressed interest in participating in a program directed toward aiding them in dating.

The Arizona researchers also found marked sex differences in the responses to their survey: 37 percent of the men in contrast to 25 percent of the women reported being "somewhat" or "very" anxious about dating. Similarly, 56 percent of the men compared to 43 percent of the women expressed interest in attending the dating program. The sex differences, it was theorized, might be due to the fact that males, because of stereotyped sex roles, have to take the risk of asking, and this causes dating anxiety in them.

Since dating anxiety is a pervasive problem and one that can hamper individuals in their adjustment to adult life, many college counseling centers offer treatment programs for those affected. Program designers have used four models to guide them in addressing dating anxiety and the problem sometimes called "minimal dating." Each model assumes one factor is the key to the difficulty, though in fact several may be playing a role in any given person's behavior (Arkowitz et al., 1978).

The *social skill deficit model* assumes people are anxious about dating because they lack certain social skills. Without these abilities, their efforts at dating meet with failure and feelings of rejection. Some data suggests that

Dating: Men's View, Women's View

1. What advantages and disadvantages are there for you in the traditional "boy calls girl" dating system?
2. *Women:* Would you call a man to ask for a first date? Why or why not?
   Men: How would you react if a woman asked you for a date?
   What advantages and disadvantages are there for you in sharing the cost of dates?
3. Predict how a particular person of the opposite sex would answer Question 1. When you get a chance, ask him or her.
4. Suppose a new male student on campus asked you to name five obvious places (student union, dormitory parties) and five not so obvious places (laundromat, camera club) where he could meet single women. What would you advise him? What reasons would you give?
5. Suppose a new female student on campus asked you to name five obvious and five not so obvious places where she could meet single men. What would you advise her? What reasons would you give?
6. Are your answers to question 4 and question 5 different? If possible, compare your answers with those of others in your class or discussion group. What differences of opinion, if any, do you discover?
7. Identify mistakes you or a friend have made in arranging for dates. For example, he, afraid of rejection, asks: "What are you doing Friday?" She, wanting to sound popular, exaggerates: "I'm going out." Net result: They both sat home Friday. ▲

dating-anxious women, more than their male counterparts, tend to have social-skills deficits. A treatment strategy suggested by this model is to provide training in basic social skills such as, how to begin conversations, speak competently on the telephone, interact confidently, communicate nonverbally, and deal with conflicts and handle criticisms.

The *conditioned anxiety model* assumes a person has been conditioned through past learning to become anxious in dating situations. The anxiety is inappropriate, since the individual is assumed to have adequate social skills, and the indicated treatment is to teach the person to be less anxious (for example, by systematic desensitization).

The *cognitive model* assumes people are anxious because they are overly critical about their own behavior in the dating situation. They may have set extremely high standards for themselves and may make unjust self-accusations about their functioning in dating situations. In other words, since they think they perform inadequately (whether they actually do or not), they are anxious. Since their social skills are assumed adequate, treatment is aimed at modifying people's self-evaluations and the "things they tell themselves."

Finally, the *physical attractiveness model* assumes people are anxious about dating because their looks lead others to treat them as undesirable prospective dating partners. The indicated treatment is to help individuals improve their appearance. Also useful would be assisting them in developing other strengths that would make them more appealing as a prospective date.

One treatment approach (Haemmerlie & Montgomery, 1982) was tested at a university in which males outnumbered females, 5 to 1, and provides an example of how dating, or heterosocial anxiety, can be reduced. Following Bem's (1972) theory that people observe their own behavior and from it infer their attitudes and emotions, the researchers prearranged it so men who had recently averaged about one date a year found themselves in 12-minute-long, one-to-one conversations about impersonal and campus topics with 12 different women. In these prearranged meetings the women, working for the experimenters, were pleasant and accepting and the subjects evidently functioned in socially adequate ways. The subjects and the women-helpers did not realize the purpose of the conversation or the research. Following the talk-sessions, measures indicated that subjects were less anxious and more self-confident about interacting with women and, indeed, when they spoke individually with still another woman, a campus queen nominee, the men showed improved conversation skills. Follow-up tests six months later were also impressive: The subjects were having more dates and maintaining their lowered level of anxiety. In summary, the prearranged, pleasant conversations with the women students had the power to lead subjects to change their thoughts, feelings, and behaviors in healthy ways.

These models and treatment programs suggest ways to understand and help those who date infrequently. However, the important issue is not how frequently people date but rather whether they are satisfied with this aspect of their life. If an individual is bothered by dating anxiety or is dissatisfied with his or her dating frequency, steps can be taken. That person can develop a plan for change and perhaps seek the assistance of others.

Liking and Loving

There is a great similarity between love relationships and good-friend relationships (Davis, 1985). In both, there are high levels of trust, mutual respect, and acceptance. Further, the interactions between the people involved are characterized by high levels of understanding, assistance, and confiding. Nonetheless, however, the love relationship, with its greater depth of caring and exclusiveness, typically generates greater power. As a result it can affect individuals more, having the potential to meet a broader sweep of human needs or to cause greater frustration and distress.

During the dating process, couples sometimes discover that liking has turned to loving and friendship to romance. Is it difficult to recognize this change? If you asked a sample of people on campus whether they knew what love was, how many do you think would answer affirmatively? In all probability, most would say that they knew or thought they knew. Only a small percentage would be uncertain.

While most people have a good sense about what love and liking are (and the differences between relationships involving the two), research psychologists need concrete tools that can measure these phenomena reliably. One contribution in this area was the "love" and "liking" self-report scales developed by Rubin (1974).

Sample items on the love scale were:

I feel I can confide in _____ about virtually anything.

I would do almost anything for _____ .

I feel responsible for _____ 's well-being.

Sample items on the liking scale were:

_____ is one of the most likeable people I know.

I have great confidence in _____ 's good judgment.

_____ is the sort of person who I myself would like to be.

Subjects were asked to respond to each item by picking a number on a scale ranging from 1 ("not at all true; disagree completely") to 9 ("definitely true; agree completely").

Rubin tested these two instruments with 182 dating couples who answered both scales, first about their partners and then about a same-sex close friend. To promote frankness, partners were asked not to sit near each other. When the responses were collected and analyzed, Rubin was able to compare the ratings that dating partners and friends had been given.

The data indicated that men and women issued their "steadies" nearly the same number of points on the love scale. The scores that the subjects issued their same-sex close friends were expectedly lower than those earned by their dating partners. However, the women were somewhat more generous with their friends on the love scale and a great deal more on the liking scale than were the men. Sex-role teachings can explain these differences. Women have traditionally been given greater freedom than men to build closeness with same-sex friends and to express it.

Understanding Love

Since the beginning of thought, humans have undoubtedly been struggling to understand love. Poets, blushing maidens, and cavalier Don Juans strumming guitars beneath their angels' balconies have all tested their wits with this endeavor. And, out of their efforts have come beautiful thoughts. Ponder for a moment two lines from George Chapman's 1605 work, *All Fools*:

I tell thee Love is Nature's second sun,
Causing a spring of virtues where he shines.

Psychologists have been involved too, directing efforts toward a scientific definition of love. Sternberg (1986), for example, has suggested a triangular theory, arguing that love has three components:

▶ **Intimacy,** which encompasses the feelings of closeness, connectedness, and bondedness one experiences in loving relationships

▶ **Passion,** which encompasses the drive that leads to romance, physical attraction, and sexual consummation

▶ **Decision/commitment,** which encompasses, in the short term, the decision that one loves another, and in the long term, the commitment to maintain that love (p. 119).

In order, these three components contain the feelings, motivations, and cognitive aspects of relationships. Sternberg (1986) believes that the amount of love experienced depends on the overall strength of these components, while the nature of the relationship is shaped by the relative strengths of the components (i.e., a couple high on passion and relatively low on commitment could have an intense summer romance that would end when each returned to college in towns 100 miles apart).

The Feeling of Love

Warning! If one enchanted evening you go to a chiller movie with somebody special or on a trip through a fun house featuring spooky creatures jumping out of the wall, beware. If your companion attributes sweaty palms, a pounding heart, and stomach butterflies to your presence, this special friend may decide he or she is in love with you.

To understand how this connection works we go back more than 25 years when Schacter (1964) proposed an explanation that sheds light on human emotional responses. The two-component theory he developed suggests that two factors must be present for us to experience emotion: physiological arousal and a reasonable "emotional" explanation for the feelings we sense. In the case of a horror movie, for instance, your date can attribute the aroused state to the effects of the movie or to the emotion of love evoked by your physical proximity.

Berscheid and Walster (1974) applied Schacter's concept to the area of passionate love. They explain that a highly aroused person, regardless of what caused the state, can accurately or mistakenly attribute the feelings to love and studies have verified this. For example, White, Fishbein, and Rutstein (1981), using exercise, comedy, and horror tapes to arouse men, found that they liked an attractive woman more than their nonaroused counterparts. Why? Because they attributed their arousal to the woman. When an unattractive female was employed, the aroused men, in contrast, attributed their state to the exercise or tapes.

Additional research projects have demonstrated that people's attraction to others can be manipulated through fear (having subjects meet an attractive person on a swinging bridge high above a river gorge), artificial feedback about

When dating, you may be likely to attribute the state of arousal caused by attending a horror movie or riding a roller coaster to your feelings for your companion.

bodily reactions (telling male subjects that their heart is beating faster when they view certain photos from Playboy), and through similar techniques. Taken as a whole, these studies suggest that arousal caused by jealousy, rejection, or dealing with a hard-to-get partner, like arousal caused by sexual activity, can lead a person to feel that he or she is in love.

Intimacy

A love relationship provides a setting in which people can be intimate, both psychologically and physically. Although most people have a good common-sense notion of what intimacy is, psychologists have not been able to identify and agree upon one good way to measure its presence in a relationship. Many researchers, for instance, have tried to assess the level of intimacy in a relationship by examining the amount and depth of self-disclosure between partners or by the nature of their sexual relationship. Less commonly, social scientists have evaluated intimacy by determining the amount of caring in or commitment to the relationship, or by ascertaining one person's ability to take the perspective of the other.

You will recall that Erikson's sixth stage of psychosocial development, young adulthood, poses the crisis of "Intimacy versus Isolation." The optimal outcome of this stage is to meet its challenge by committing oneself to another and building a sexual love.

As Erikson's theory suggests, people are not born with the ability to be intimate. They must learn. One investigator (Fischer, 1981) reported that young women, toward the end of adolescence, master the skills of intimacy from their interactions with female peers and, later, teach these to their boyfriends and men friends. Another team (White, Speisman, Jackson, Bartis, & Costos, 1986) who has been studying young married couples, believe that the ability to be intimate develops over time and can continue to grow after an individual marries.

How People Select Mates

What factors determine how people pair and choose marriage partners? This question is of both theoretical and practical interest to single adults. If you are a junior at a college in Salt Lake City, the probability is greater that you will marry someone at your school rather than a person working at a bank a hundred miles away. Further, if you were to marry a fellow student, of all potential spouses there are some you would be more likely to select than others.

While people frequently say "opposites attract," when it comes to couples, in fact, individuals tend to marry people similar to them on variables such as age, race, ethnic background, religion, socioeconomic status, mental abilities, attitudes and opinions, height, weight, and personality characteristics (Buss, 1985). The term **homogamy** is used to describe human beings' tendency to marry others who have similar personal characteristics.

Homogamy
The tendency in people to marry another who has similar personal characteristics.

The question of how people actually go through the process of selecting mates has interested researchers. Adams (1979), who summarized the literature in the area, has proposed a set of sorting steps people take in mate selection. Obviously, the first one is to come into contact with eligible single people. Here, propinquity—nearness in place—is an important factor. The power of propinquity was well illustrated by Clarke (1952), who found that 37 percent of his sample of over 400 couples lived within eight blocks of each other and 54 percent within sixteen blocks. Many people, upon questioning their parents and grandparents, find that they lived near each other when they had their first date.

While automobiles, social changes, and new life-styles and economic conditions have made us more mobile than our parents and grandparents, and thus more likely to marry an "out-of-towner," we are still likely to select a mate from the same social category. This is true because individuals of similar religions, races, and educational backgrounds tend to spend more time together. Propinquity provides opportunity, and statistics indicate that the vast majority of people marry those belonging to the same major religious group and the same race.

TABLE 8.3 *Characteristics Commonly Sought in a Mate*

Rank	Characteristics Preferred by Males	Characteristics Preferred by Females
1	kindness and understanding	kindness and understanding
2	intelligence	intelligence
3	*physical attractiveness*[a]	exciting personality
4	exciting personality	good health
5	good health	adaptability
6	adaptability	*physical attractiveness*
7	creativity	creativity
8	desire for children	*good earning capacity*
9	college graduate	college graduate
10	good heredity	desire for children
11	*good earning capacity*	good heredity
12	good housekeeper	good housekeeper
13	religious orientation	religious orientation

[a]The sex differences in ranking are significant beyond the 0.001 level (n = 162) for characteristics in italics.

Reprinted by permission, *American Scientist, Journal of Sigma Xi,* "Human Mate Selection," by David M. Buss, AM. SCI. 73: 47–51, 1985.

Having met each other, people may or may not experience what Adams calls early attraction. In the manner described earlier (impression formation), each person judges the other on the basis of the most immediately obvious information. If each "passes" the other's test, the two may spend time together, revealing more about themselves and assessing each other further.

The next sorting step encountered is whether the couple develops what Adams calls deeper attraction. Many ideas have been suggested about what factors keep people together at this point. Deeper attraction depends partly on how potential mates assess the "fit" of their personalities, values, future goals, and desired life-styles. One notion is that people with similar personality characteristics and backgrounds seek out and are happiest with each other. A good example of this is a man and woman from the same ethnic group. If they are attracted to each other, they have the advantage of a shared cultural perspective and therefore may better understand each others' behaviors and motives.

Table 8.3 shows the kinds of characteristics men and women typically seek in a partner. The list was developed by Buss (1985) who asked subjects to rank order items he supplied. As the table shows, the two major gender differences in the rankings were that men gave more priority to physical attractiveness, while women gave more to earning capacity.

Friends and relatives of the two individuals can be another force affecting the extent of the couple's romantic involvement. Parks, Stan, and Eggert (1983) found that couples became more deeply involved if there was support for their relationship in the individuals' networks of family and friends. However, opposition to the partner selected can also draw a couple together, as in the Romeo and Juliet effect (named after Shakespeare's characters). Specifically, every generation of parents expresses opinions about what types of mates are suitable for their adult children, and their children either ignore or oppose them. Driscoll, Davis, and Lipetz (1972) assessed how perceived parental interference in mate selection affected couples' level of romantic love. The data indicated that parental interference heightens a couple's feelings of love, and if parents stop voicing objection, the couple's level of love suffers.

A final sorting step is for each individual to acknowledge, by thought or action, that the partner is "right for me" or "the highest quality I am capable of attracting." As people grow older, they tend to be more likely to "settle," perhaps because they are more realistic or because they are hesitant to start over again in the search for a new partner.

Six Types of Lovers

Hollywood films of earlier decades suggest that being in love means red-hot passion, vintage wine, the glow of candles, and moonlit trysts on warm tropical beaches. That appealing stereotype is deceiving, however. Research suggests a great variation among people in their styles of expressing love and how they experience the many facets inherent in their relationships. Lasswell and Lasswell (1980), who have studied over 1,000 subjects in their research program, have identified the six types presented next. While pure types are described here, in actuality most people display characteristics of more than one type.

The Romantic Type

Romantic-type lovers put a high priority on the processes of falling and being in love. They are convinced that love makes them "glow" and believe it is the state in which people were meant to live. Romantic types treasure "love at first sight" and remember all the "firsts" with their partners: how and when they met, how they both looked, how they spent their first evening together, their first kiss, and so on. These lovers like everything about their partners, from the color of their eyes to the tone of their voice, and are always interested in learning more about them. Similarly they reveal everything about themselves, covering the range from early childhood recollections to last night's dreams and today's feelings and thoughts.

When two Romantic types find each other, everybody knows. They gaze at each other, select the same meals when they dine at a restaurant, and are sure to be seen walking hand in hand. Since they share as much time as possible, jealousy is unlikely. Further, since they enjoy pleasing each other, they delight their partners with special gifts, by cooking favorite dinners, and so on.

Romantic types generally have been raised in secure and happy homes by parents they believe have good marriages. They themselves may go without love partners for extended time periods but, when they find somebody, they invest full energy and do their best to make the partnership prosper. Just as they fall in love totally and quickly, breaking up is a total, painful, and perhaps explosive event.

The Self-Centered Game-Player Type

As the name suggests, Self-Centered Game-Players toy and strategize at love as most would at chess, planning steps carefully to bring them what they believe to be the greatest benefits at the least perceived cost. As a result, they may have ongoing relationships with a number of lovers simultaneously, avoiding commitment to (or from) any.

Self-Centered types neither reveal themselves nor ask their partners for revelation. Instead, they keep relationships at a shallow level, avoiding dependency in either direction. If a relationship becomes serious or a problem develops, rather than trying to cope, they prefer to search for new partners.

Self-Centered lovers are not possessive or jealous. Instead, they seek nondemanding, self-sufficient partners who do not ask them to change. For example, they often have only one sexual routine. If it fails to satisfy, or if a partner suggests a different technique, they may leave the person. Put in different terms, sex is self-centered and perhaps exploitative and is not directed toward binding the couple into a committed relationship. Self-Centered Lovers sometimes pursue what is referred to as "one-night stands."

Nevertheless, wine, flowers, and specially chosen greeting cards are all part of the Self-Centered Lover's strategy for making encounters romantic and enjoyable. Such strategies, combined with this person's good self-concept and success in many aspects of life, can make this type fun to be with during an evening.

The Totally Lover-Centered Type

The Totally Lover-Centered type does not fall in love but instead has love available to give those who are willing to receive it. These people place the highest priority on their lovers' happiness and on taking care of them, even if that means, in an extreme case, waiting for them to be released from prison or to recover from a substance-abuse addiction.

Totally Lover-Centered people are both fully supportive and extremely forgiving of their partners. For example, they would arrange a partner's medical appointment to treat a case of sexually transmitted disease contracted during an affair with another. Instead of being angry and seeking retaliation, they would provide help because they are likely to think of their partner's action as a mere lapse or a yielding to another's pressure.

The Possessive-Intensely Dependent Type

Possessive-Intensely Dependent types of lovers center a great deal of energy on their partners, generally in ways unhealthy to themselves psychologically. More specifically, they think endlessly about their loved one and the relationship, sometimes to the point where it upsets their eating and sleeping habits and leaves them in alternating states of extreme highs and extreme lows.

Lovers of this type generally are highly anxious about intimacy with others and frequently suffer from a poor self-image. Their anxiety can foster sexual problems, produce irrational jealousy and worry about their lover's faithfulness, and make it difficult for them to maintain relationships with more self-sufficient partners. When love affairs end, they view the experience as a personal rejection. They feel crushed, become anxious, and carefully go over events trying to figure out exactly what went wrong.

The Logical-Sensible Type

Logical-Sensible types shop for love as they do for other commodities. After realistically assessing their own "market value," they attempt to attract the highest-quality partner possible. Sometimes, in fact, these people will postpone their search until they have achieved a goal that makes them more desirable, such as completing college or owning a house. So pragmatic are lovers of this type that they carefully check future in-laws and assess the potential for hereditary defects in future children. However, once they decide on a "deal," they fall in love and remain faithful.

A logical-sensible quality permeates their relationships. They seek sex not necessarily because of love, but rather to relieve sexual tension and to ease them into sleep. They plan families carefully. For example, if a Logical-Sensible type is a schoolteacher, she will make sure conception takes place in the fall so that the baby's arrival will coincide with the summer recess.

Lovers of this type help their partners receive what they want (such as a job promotion) and deserve (such as proper attention from auto mechanics). However, when the other person's balance of assets changes (perhaps through

What Is Your Style of Love?

One of the authors asked students in his class, after they read about Laswell and Laswell's (1980) types, to describe their style as a lover. Abbreviated versions of five of these descriptions are presented below (with permission from the students). Read these and then write a description of your love style (or a friend's). Are you one type or a combination?

Student A: The six types of lovers hit me hard. It bothered me to be in the category I'm in, but it's me. It's exactly me in relationships yet it bothers me to be referred to as a "Self-Centered Game Player" . . . but I guess the truth hurts. . . . I always try to keep a relationship casual. If I see it's getting serious (well, he is), and I'm not getting much room, I end it. I also don't feel that I should really have to change too much for a guy. . . . This will sound awful: if a guy becomes insecure and begins to wonder about where the relationship is going, I'll do something for him to keep him a while longer, until I'm ready to end it. It reassures him. . . . I do feel bad about being this way. I really don't know why I am and I really wish I knew, because it is a crummy way to treat a person. . . . Someday I hope to figure out my problem so I won't treat guys like I do. I hope so, because even though I have fun, in the end I feel bad.

Student B: As I approach my middle twenties I have become a logical-sensible type of lover. . . . Before I even go out on a date with someone I analyze her, thinking whether she would be compatible with me. I consider how physically attractive she is because no matter how many other good characteristics she has, if she is not attractive, I will not be able to develop strong feelings toward her. Second, plain and simple, how likable is she? Is she thoughtful and is she just fun to be with? For me the ability to have fun is a very high priority. Life is to be enjoyed. Third, she must be intelligent. If a person passes these requirements, I ask her out on a date. And if something happens between us, that's great, but I don't expect it.

Student C: I had many boyfriends in high school and with each one, I said that I loved him. I remember everything about each guy—how we met, the color of his eyes, the first date. While dating a guy, I would spend a great deal of time with him. I wrote poems and letters that revealed personal feelings and thoughts to the guy I was dating. Breaking up with a boyfriend was always a painful event for me. I became depressed, hurt, and uninterested in other activities. It was difficult to pull out of these moods, but, soon I would be over it and find another love.

Student D: My sister Jill, and her ex-boyfriend are examples of life-long friends. It wasn't until after two quarters of being dorm neighbors that they saw each other as more than friends. Even in the more intimate relationship, they were happy and comfortable. While they argued, they stayed together and learned from it. . . . Being separated from each other was not a big issue, and, if anything, it helped them.

Student E: Mindy has been dating Bill for over a year and is an example of passive-intensely dependent type. Now they live in different towns but call each other everyday. They have to know what the other person did every minute. Mindy is jealous of Bill's ex-girlfriends and is always trying to find out more about them.

Mindy's life revolves around Bill. Her area of the dorm room is decorated with pictures of him . . . often Mindy's moods are controlled by Bill. If he is coming for the weekend, for example, she gets very excited. Whenever he isn't around she is a pretty "mellow" person. Mindy has not made an effort to meet anyone at school. She doesn't have any friends other than her roommates. She doesn't care to meet anyone because she has Bill and that is enough for her.

▲

job loss or the fading of an attractive appearance), they can become dissatisfied and seek another partner. Even so, practical issues may delay action. For example, they would postpone a separation for a year if their child were a high school senior.

The Lifelong-Friends Type

Lovers of the Lifelong-Friends type build what they view as a permanent love relationship on a foundation of friendship. As a result, they may suddenly discover that they have been in love for some time. For this reason sexual intimacy tends to come later for them than for others, but it is as they like it: enjoyable, predictable, and comfortable.

Relationships with their lovers are sibling-like in several ways. First, they do not accept arguments as an indication of dislike, incompatibility, or anything that infringes on their love. Second, when they reach a point of maturity, they see their partner as irreplaceable, much in the way a sibling is. Third, they value the comfort and security of the home routine and the predictability of a partner's behavior.

Lifelong-Friends Lovers build an interdependent relationship and work to fulfill mutual needs. Temporary separations are an inconvenience to them but not an issue. They generally do not fantasize about finding new lovers and trust that their partners would do nothing to harm their relationship. However, if they divorce, they generally remain good, caring friends who exchange advice, even about their new love affairs.

Most of us are not "pure" examples of one type or another, but rather have a "hybrid" style of loving, exhibiting elements from two or more categories. Prasinos and Tittler (1984), who administered Lasswell and Lasswell's (1980) instrument to undergraduates, discovered that there were aspects of the possessive-intensely dependent type in most people's style of loving. They further noted that if this style is allowed to assume a central dominant role, the behavior it fosters can have negative consequences for both the possessor's psychological health and for his relationship.

Problems Couples Face

In contrast to two friends, those in love face some unique problems (deciding when to take steps like engagement, marriage, and so forth), some similar ones (communication, differences in values, and so forth), and some similar but often more intense ones (jealousy and the end of a relationship).

Jealousy

Jealousy is an emotion familiar to all, if not from direct experience, at least through novels, television programs, and movies. Romantic jealousy is more powerful than the envy people may have for others' coveted possessions, because it includes that envy and goes beyond (Salovey & Rodin, 1986). Specifically, romantic jealousy carries the additional stress associated with the

Jealousy is an experience familiar to everybody. Personal adjustment involves learning to manage this very human emotion.

threat of losing an important relationship and often involves feelings of having been betrayed and perhaps deceived. Thus, the nearly universal feeling of romantic jealousy provokes a host of negative feelings focused on the lover, the self, and the perceived rival. And it can be very destructive in relationships.

At least two factors need to be present for romantic jealousy to develop. First, an individual must perceive a relationship as valuable and, second, the partner's behavior, real or suspected, must be seen in conflict with the jealous individual's definition of the relationship. Studies have helped explain the role jealousy can play in relationships. Hansen (1985) administered questionnaires to college students that asked how they would react to five hypothetical situations: they ranged from a dating partner spending a large portion of free time alone with a hobby to one in which he/she went out of town for a weekend and had a one-time sexual encounter with somebody else. The results indicated that women tended to be more jealous than men over their partner's time with hobbies and family members and that "traditionally-oriented individuals" experienced the most jealousy. They also found that a substantial number of subjects, perhaps to avoid feelings of jealousy, expected sexual exclusivity and avoidance of close opposite-sex friendships.

In another study, almost 25,000 *Psychology Today* readers, mostly in their early 30s, responded to Salovey and Rodin's (1985) invitation to respond to a questionnaire that asked about romantic jealousy and envy. Not unexpectedly, the results indicated that romantic jealousy grew in subjects as the potential threat of the loss of their relationship increased and that jealousy was more likely in persons having low self-esteem and less commitment from the partner (such as when couples cohabitate instead of marry). Among the respondents, single and divorced people were more likely than married to experience jealousy and to act on that feeling by calling lovers unexpectedly, listening in on their phone calls and looking through their belongings.

These authors also reported a study that, in part, examined how people deal with romantic jealousy. They found that three approaches were used. They called the first self-reliance. With this technique people depended on their own strengths, holding in feelings of anger, embarrassment, and sadness and becoming further dedicated to the relationship. The second, selective ignoring, involved deciding the relationship is "just not that important." This technique was somewhat less effective than the first. Finally, the third, self-bolstering, involved thinking about one's own positive qualities and doing something for oneself. It was generally ineffective for the subjects.

Changes in Love

An underlying theme in psychological studies of the life span is that change is inevitable and provides impetus for personal growth. In other words, as one psychologist put it, "Human beings go through life changing and creating change" (Buhler, 1933). As a result we constantly face adjustment to new circumstances and new objectives to work toward. Even love, which we think of as stable and ideally everlasting, is no exception: It changes over time. Consider what "adjustment" student John observed in a relationship between his longtime best friend, Neil, and "lifelong buddy" Vicki:

> During Neil's junior year in high school he was good friends with a group of several girls. As the year progressed you could sense that he was singling Vicki out as his favorite. During Neil's senior year Vicki and Neil did many things together, but only as friends.
>
> About one month before Neil left for State they finally went out on a 'date.' And, much to both of their surprises, they kissed and found something more than just friendship was present. They went steady and did not date others that year. But, when Vicki entered college she decided within a few months that she wanted to go out with others.
>
> Neil accepted this but, however, not very easily. Today, a few months later, they are pretty much "broken up," but still remain friends. And, although Neil does not agree with, or necessarily believe, what Vicki says she is doing, Neil no longer becomes angry. He tries to accept what is happening and put it behind him so that a friendship can remain, no matter what.

The changes that take place in love are most obvious at the beginning and end of a relationship. People who have recently fallen in love feel lost when physically apart. They find themselves preoccupied with thoughts of the other and their desire to share time and as many activities as possible. In evaluating the new loved one, they are typically blinded by affection, overrating his or her positive qualities while underrating negative ones.

Social scientists have explained how such "blind love," combined with passion, naturally bonds partners while they build and concretize their relationship (Malone & Malone, 1988). With regard to newlyweds, for instance, while they are learning to live together harmoniously, they are bound together by the excitement of romantic love and the availability of unlimited sexual activity in a socially legitimized relationship. While sex is serving as this cementing function, the couple has the opportunity to generate companionship ties (children, a history of shared experiences, a home, etc.) that they will need when their level of sexual activity begins to decline. Put another way a general pattern in a couple's love is a shift from romantic love at the outset toward a more companionship type of love.

The End of a Relationship

At one point or another most people encounter a difficult personal challenge: coping with the end of a significant love relationship. A leading person in the area of relationships has said, "There is very little pain on earth like the pain of a close long-term personal relationship that is falling apart" (Duck, 1988, p. 102).

When a relationship ends, the decision is usually not a mutual one, and whoever is "left" by a lover typically has the more difficult adjustment task. Of more than 100 college student couples studied by Hill, Rubin, and Peplau (1976), only about 7 percent had mutually decided to break up. Interestingly, these couples generally differed in how abruptly they wished to end their relationship and also on what they felt was the cause of their troubles. Women tended to define the problems as interpersonal, citing one partner's desire for independence, differences about getting married, or conflicting personal interests and goals. Men were less certain about the nature of the problem, but tended to blame external factors such as geographic separation.

Studies have identified four types of strategies people use when they grow dissatisfied with a romantic relationship (Rusbult, Zembrodt, & Iwaniszek, 1986). They are: (1) exit—a person threatens to or physically separates from the partner and ends the relationship; (2) voice—taking action to improve the situation by discussion, seeking help from a counselor, making suggestions and offering compromises, etc.; (3) loyalty—waiting with the hope that matters will improve; (4) neglect—ignoring the partner and waiting for matters to deteriorate, criticizing the partner without allowing discussion, or treating the partner poorly. Rusbult's team views loyalty and neglect as passive approaches in contrast to the more active voice and exit. Further, they see voice and loyalty as constructive and the other two as destructive approaches.

While the specialness of a relationship can end after only a handful of dates, it also can remain for nearly a lifetime, declining only after a husband and wife have completed the job of raising six children and are about to enter their retirement years. Either way, when a committed person discovers the relationship is over, pain and what amounts to a period of mourning lie ahead.

It helps a sufferer to recognize that the pain will dissipate in time, even if he or she feels immobilized and does nothing. Of course, doing nothing is not an effective strategy. Although taking steps to cope does not supply immediate, total relief, it can be of substantial benefit. Examples of useful steps are talking to friends, planning satisfying activities, and finding new social outlets. People who cannot energize themselves are fortunate if those in their support system coax or are insistent in drawing them into such undertakings.

Individuals who have been harshly affected by the loss of a lover should recognize that the following symptoms are common (based on Wanderer & Cabot, 1978). The person may:

1. Be unable to concentrate.
2. Watch the telephone and jump expectantly when it rings (hoping it is the "ex").
3. Spend long hours devising scripts of imaginary conversations with the "ex."
4. Talk about the lost love and seek consolation, support, and advice.
5. Question and probe friends for information about the "ex."
6. Go by the "ex's" dormitory, house, school, or place of business.
7. Sleep excessively.
8. Not want to go anywhere or do anything.
9. Cry a lot.
10. Be afraid that he or she will now be alone forever.
11. Want to run away.
12. Feel it necessary to be with someone all the time.
13. Have attacks of heartburn or diarrhea.
14. Wake up in the middle of the night.
15. Feel as if everything gives him or her physical ailments.
16. Get irritable at the slightest provocation.
17. Be thrown into a panic when little things go wrong.
18. Be careless and have accidents.
19. Find it increasingly hard to fall asleep.
20. Find it difficult to eat.

Identifying the symptoms that develop at the end of a love relationship can alert a person to take action and suitably cope with the loss that has been endured. People recover more rapidly if they realize that they themselves must work to overcome grief, reestablishing their priorities, and in a reasonable amount of time resume their normal day-to-day responsibilities. If they need assistance and the people whom they know are unable or unwilling to help, mental health workers can provide the needed support. There is also the possibility of self-help books and other written resources.

In one such book, "How to Break Your Addiction to a Person," a healthy relationship, in which a person "freely chooses" to be with a loved one, is contrasted with an unhealthy one. The latter type, called "addictive" by author Halpern (1982), is characterized by a person being compulsively attached. This individual feels he or she must stay with the lover, experiencing panic at the thought of the relationship's end. If the couple separates, however, after experiencing "withdrawal symptoms" (weeping, physical pain, depression, and the desire to get back together), the formerly-addicted lover feels a sense of triumph and liberation (in contrast to the slow healing that follows the termination of a healthier relationship).

Halpern suggests a cognitive approach to help addicted individuals survive a break up: He instructs them to repeat aphorisms to themselves when sensing anxiety, pain, or intrusive, unpleasant thoughts. Examples are:

1. You can live without him/her (probably better).
2. Love is not enough (to make a positive, lasting love relationship).
3. Love doesn't necessarily last forever.
4. You can't always work it out, no matter how much you may want to.
5. The pain of ending it won't last forever. In fact, it won't last nearly as long as the pain of not ending it.

An unhappy picture has been painted of people's response to a partner's departure. But however painful the end of a relationship is, not only do people overcome it, but in a relatively short period of time they seek out new partners. Evidence of this is found in the fact that a high percentage of individuals remarry within two years of divorce.

That the joy and fulfillment experienced during a relationship compensates for pain at its end was borne out in a study by Kephart (1970). He reported that at least 70 percent of men and women students responded that having been in love (including short-term infatuations) had left them happier afterward. Given this statistic, one could conclude that most would endorse the spirit of Tennyson's lines:

'Tis better to have loved and lost
than never to have loved at all.

SUMMARY

1. Human beings are social by nature, and nearly all value friendship. Everyone has common-sense notions about how friendships are built and maintained. Researchers have studied these issues and also have demonstrated the benefits provided by a support system.

2. Theorists have explained the process of interpersonal attraction by describing it in terms of an attitude one forms and holds toward another.

3. *Impression formation* is the process by which two people, on first meeting, quickly gather information about each other. On the basis of these data each decides whether to continue with the other.

4. *Transactional analysis* (TA) is one way of understanding interactions between friends. Three ego states are identified: parent, adult, and child. TA theory suggests that people need strokes—recognition from others—just as they need food, water, and shelter.

5. As a friendship develops, there are shifts in the amount of knowledge each person has about the other—a concept illustrated by the Johari's Window model.

6. During the first twelve months of life, an infant makes remarkable progress in the area of social learning. For example, the child learns the difference between the self and others and begins to recognize the difference between friendliness and anger in another's voice.

7. From about age three to the teenage years, an individual passes through five developmental stages in practicing and understanding friendship. In the first stage, a child befriends another because of physical proximity or material possessions. By the last stage, the individual has come to recognize the need for both dependency and autonomy in a healthy friendship.

8. Probably because of sex-role training, throughout adulthood women tend to have more friends than men and are more intimate and self-disclosing in their relationships. Friendship needs persist in both men and women throughout adulthood, although there are changes in friendship patterns over the years.

9. People may encounter roadblocks in the process of building and maintaining friendships. For instance, individuals' self-views may discourage them from reaching out to others and communication problems and conflict can develop between people, threatening their relationship.

10. Loneliness is a widespread problem in our society. Some people are lonely because they have shy, nonassertiveness personalities and do not reach out to others. Others are lonely because changes in our society have reduced opportunities to interact. People interested in overcoming their loneliness can be taught certain helpful techniques.

11. Dating, which generally begins during adolescence, is sought for friendship-building, romantic, and recreational purposes. Many college students experience dating problems, some of which are related to their sex and year in school. Men and women tend to identify different problems. A significant percentage of undergraduates is anxious about dating. A deficit in social skills is one of the many explanations proposed for this anxiety.

12. After a period of dating, a couple may fall in love. Psychologists believe being in love satisfies a human need, although theorists from different perspectives disagree about what that need is.

13. Lovers have different styles of relating to their partners. One team of researchers identified styles that ranged from the Self-Centered Game Player to the Romantic and Lifelong-Friend types. Over time, most partners experience a decline in romance and passion and an increase in companionship.

14. Coping with the end of a love relationship can be very difficult. A person often goes through what amounts to a mourning period. Constructive coping can relieve some of the stress.

SUGGESTED READINGS

Burns, D. (1985). *Intimate connections*. New York: A Signet Book. A practical book with many self-help forms designed to acquaint the reader with information about loneliness, self-love, connectedness, and getting close to others.

Colgrove, M., Bloomfield, H. & McWilliams, P. (1976). *How to survive the loss of a love*. New York: Bantam Books. This easy-to-read manual provides ideas that might be useful to an individual in adjusting to the end of a significant relationship.

Harayda, J. (1986). *The joy of being single*. Garden City, New York: Doubleday & Company. This book discusses how to be a happy single person, covering topics ranging from building friendships with members of both sexes to the need to rally 'round rituals' (celebrating Thanksgiving with an appropriate dinner) and find ways to nurture the next generation.

Huffine, L. (1986). *Connections with all the people in your life*. San Francisco: Harper & Row. The book presents 64 techniques to better interpersonal communication and improved relationships.

Kleinke, C. (1986). *Meeting and understanding people*. New York: Freeman and Company. The book examines the social psychological research literature and shows how it can be applied in people's day-to-day life.

Malone, T. & Malone, P. (1987). *The art of intimacy*. New York: Prentice Hall. The book explores the problems people encounter in relationships and explores how people can build intimacy and love in relationships.

Miller, S. (1983). *Men and friendship*. Boston: Houghton Mifflin Company. Explores how factors like competition, careers, and family obligations make it difficult for men to achieve true friendship with each other.

Rubenstein, C. & Shaver, P. (1982). *In search of intimacy*. New York: Delacorte Press. Guided by survey data and findings from interviews, these authors explore people's loneliness at each stage in the life cycle and offer suggestions about how individuals can work to find intimacy.

Rubin, L. (1985). *Just friends: The role of friendship in our lives*. New York: Harper & Row. Based on interviews of 300 subjects, the author explores the many aspects of many types of friendships.

Sexuality

9

▸ Sexuality as one area in which a person adjusts to adulthood, finding enjoyment but sometimes confusion or conflict as well

▸ The pioneers in studying sexuality, who have reshaped our views and gathered objective data that have surprised many people

▸ The varied forms of sexual expression, some wholly approved by society and others commonly practiced but associated with mixed feelings and value conflicts

▸ How sensuality begins in infancy and proceeds—sometimes gradually, sometimes by leaps and bounds—to develop into adult sexuality that can be enjoyed into the elderly years

▸ The difficulties presented by some aspects of sex: sexual dysfunctions, decisions about birth control, sexually transmitted diseases, occurrences of rape

▸ How the sexual revolution has helped some people and created new difficulties for others

*I*t was Jerry's first month in college, and he sat listening intently to a speaker from the counseling center discussing the subject of "Sexuality and You." The men in Jerry's group had laughed before the meeting, one remarking that he hardly needed this because he had passed high-school hygiene with flying colors. Yet Jerry knew that there was much about sexuality he could learn. He was not alone; most of the men in his group were aware of gaps in their understanding.

Jerry listened calmly to the speaker's introduction, but when the speaker turned to the physical details of sex, Jerry began to feel uncomfortable. Jerry's surreptitious inspection of the audience told him that others were uneasy too. The speaker went on to discuss common problems that may hinder a couple's sexual satisfaction, citing research findings that suggested possible causes and solutions. Jerry had heard talk about all these subjects but was very surprised to hear that there were scientific opinions on them.

After more "basics" were discussed, the speaker suddenly announced he was going to spring a quiz. "It won't be graded or even collected," he added quickly. "I just want you to have an idea of how knowledgeable you are about sex and to identify myths you believe."

Jerry skimmed through his three-page-long quiz, getting an overview of what was covered. Returning to the first question, "Where did most of your information and attitudes about sex come from?" he closed his eyes and tried to formulate a response. After some thought he wrote:

My parents were very straightforward and very open. But while we spoke about nearly everything, sex was the exception. I learned the facts of life from books and from friends, yet I do consider myself fortunate because I believe I developed healthy attitudes about the opposite sex. I am not a male chauvinist.

As Jerry and his friends left the auditorium and headed for a coffee shop, they sensed that the evening's program had been very helpful. They had gained useful information, explored their attitudes, and in the process, helped further prepare themselves for one important area of human life—their sexuality. The purpose of this chapter, like the purpose of the lecture Jerry attended, is to provide accurate information about human sexuality and to highlight attitudes and varying moral perspectives that people hold toward sex and toward their own sexual behavior.

Coming to terms with one's sexuality is an important part of making a healthy adjustment to adulthood. For most adults, one hallmark of happiness is an ability to express themselves sexually, both physically and emotionally, and in ways that are fully consistent with their life goals. For example, many people seek a lifelong commitment to a mate and choose to satisfy their sexual needs in the context of this relationship. In this case, the sexual exchange brings joy and confirms the partners' commitment and love. By the same token, however, there are some whose life goals are such that they may refrain from sexual activity altogether. For example, some members of the clergy have elected celibacy, and adjusted well to it, because of their life commitment. Because information about this subject is so crucial, we will begin our study of human sexuality by examining the studies and theories of "pioneer" scientists in the field.

THE PIONEER SCIENTISTS

As one author said: "Sexual behavior is usually judged by one of four criteria: statistical, medical, legal or moral" (Katchadourian, 1974). Each of these can provide ways of looking at sexuality, whether the purpose is to better understand the behavior of others or to gain increased knowledge about one's own sexuality.

The research work and theories of the pioneer scientists in the area of sexuality have produced data, led to the development of sex therapy techniques, affected lawmakers, and reshaped moral views. As a consequence of their work, and that of later scientists, each of us has a greater understanding of the role sex plays in our development.

The first pioneer was **Sigmund Freud.** Freud, of course, theorized that the need for sexual expression was a prominent factor in human development and that children proceeded, step-by-step, through psychosexual stages. As explained in Chapter 1, he believed that during the first three, the *oral, anal,* and *phallic stages,* the young child gains erotic pleasures in sucking and chewing on objects, in eliminating and withholding bowel movements, and in touching the genitals. His theory suggests that these stages are followed at about age four or five with a *latency period* during which sexual energy is directed into other channels (e.g., studies, hobbies, and sports) for which the child receives approval. The early teenage years usher in the *genital stage.* During this, the final stage in psychosexual development, the individual seeks an appropriate partner with whom to share genital sex.

Sigmund Freud
Theorized that the need for sexual expression was prominent across the life span.

Exploring Your Attitudes and Values about Human Sexuality in Today's Society

Over the course of recorded history, substantial changes have occurred in Western society's attitudes toward sex and sexual expression. Specifically, attitudes have ranged from the liberalness of the Greek city-states in the 4th century B.C. to the conservatism in Anglo-societies of the 19th century Victorian era. In ancient Greece, sex, including homosexuality, was considered a pleasure to be appreciated. This contrasts with the Victorian period that defined sex as spiritual and sacred. It was to be enjoyed only by married men who had been taught to conserve strength by carefully rationing the discharge of semen.

Excepting "the roaring 20s," which freed women to enjoy sex though they themselves were not thought to have erotic needs, pre-1960s American society maintained a conservative stance toward sex and human sexual expression. For instance, "good" people would not publicly discuss the topic of sex, particularly in "mixed company."

Outward signs of the then prevalent conservativeness included these facts: Literary masterpieces like D. H. Lawrence's *Lady Chatterly's Lover* could not be printed legally in the United States, bookstore owners were arrested during the 1950s for selling certain works by Henry Miller (author of *Sexus, Tropic of Cancer,* and *Tropic of Capricorn*), and the 1945 film, *Outlaw,* caused a stir because Jane Russell's cleavage appeared on the silver screen.

Societal attitudes changed drastically during the 1960s, leading some to speak of a "sexual revolution." Outward signs of change ranged from television programming showing married couples sharing a double bed to the growing popularity of Playboy magazine and Hugh Hefner's "Playboy Philosophy." The decades of the 1970s and 1980s brought Dr. David Reuben's book (and movie) *Everything You Wanted To Know About Sex But Were Afraid To Ask,* and media therapists like Dr. Ruth Westheimer dealing with human sexuality in TV broadcasts, printed material, and board games. On the college campus, the post-1960s changes in attitudes were accompanied by a growing percentage of single students who engaged in heavy petting and sexual intercourse, and a decreasing percentage who believe that premarital intercourse was immoral (Robinson & Jedlicka, 1982).

Alfred C. Kinsey
A pioneer scientist who interviewed over 11,000 people about their sexual behavior.

Although many claim Freud's work is dated and not scientifically sound, when Freud introduced these ideas, his thinking was revolutionary. The data Freud used to construct his theory were gathered primarily from patients whom he was treating and, therefore, his views may have been distorted. In contrast to Freud, **Alfred C. Kinsey** and his colleagues interviewed over 11,000 men and women (who were not patients) about their sexual behavior. The team's pioneering work was published in *Sexual Behavior in the Human Male* (1948) and in *Sexual Behavior in the Human Female* (1953). Notice how the Kinsey group justified study of what were then relatively taboo topics:

> For some time now there has been an increasing awareness among many people of the desirability of obtaining data about sex which would represent an accumulation of scientific fact completely divorced from questions of moral value and social custom. Practicing physicians find thousands of their patients in need of such objective data. Psychiatrists and analysts find that a majority

Why how did such drastic changes take place? Many factors were involved and historians will undoubtedly spend years in the process of sorting through them. Suffice to say that beyond the increased personal privacy provided by the automobile and urbanization, major contributing factors included: 1) the women's movement, which helped raise people's consciousness about gender-related discrimination and supported women who sought to free themselves from the "sexual double standard," and 2) scientific advances in developing reliable means to prevent pregnancy and to treat the sexually transmitted diseases that had been prevalent in the middle of the century.

Issue 1: How might your life be different if societal attitudes today were as conservative as they were when your grandparents or great-grandparents grew up? How might your life be different if attitudes were more liberal than they are today?

Issue 2: There are many ongoing debates in our society related to human sexuality that may well affect you personally in the near future. Battles, are being waged, for example, between: 1) those who favor legalized abortion early in a pregnancy and those who oppose it except, perhaps, in unusual circumstances (e.g., after rape or when a woman's life is endangered), 2) those who believe that freedom of speech guarantees the right to produce and distribute adult, x-rated material (books, films, and magazines) and those who oppose the availability of such material, judging it pornographic and lacking in redeeming social value, and, 3) those who favor incorporating sexual education into the public school curriculum and those who oppose such instruction outside the home.

Contact and gather information from advocacy organizations fostering one of these causes and critically evaluate their positions.

Issue 3: Argue the pros and cons to the individual of engaging in premarital, extramarital, or group sex. Do you think the pros and cons differ for men and women; for young, middle-aged, or older people? ▲

of their patients need help in resolving sexual conflicts that have arisen in their lives. An increasing number of persons would like to bring an educated intelligence into the consideration of such matters as sexual adjustments in marriage, the sexual guidance of children, the premarital sexual adjustments of youth, sex education, sexual activities which are in conflict with the mores, and problems confronting persons who are interested in the social control of behavior through religion, custom, and the forces of law. Before it is possible to think scientifically on any of these matters, more needs to be known about the actual behavior of people, and about the interrelationships of that behavior with the biologic and social aspects of their histories (Kinsey, Pomeroy, & Martin, 1948, p. 3).

Kinsey and his colleagues provided this needed information, and, although no survey matching theirs in thoroughness and quality has appeared since, others (Grosskopf, 1983; Hite, 1976; Hunt, 1974) have continued the task of monitoring sexual practices in contemporary society.

Alfred Kinsey, pictured here, led a team that collected a vast amount of data on the sexual behavior of Americans in the 1940s and 1950s. The researchers' goal was to obtain scientific information on a subject that had, to a large degree, been shrouded in secrecy.

The results yielded by the Kinsey team's interviews are undoubtedly dated, yet they are still of interest to scholars. The real importance of the studies was the impact they had on society. Kinsey and his coworkers opened the field to science in a new way. In general, readers in 1948 were surprised by the range of sexual activity that people acknowledged having been involved in. From the statistics, lawmakers and judges got a clearer idea of what contemporary community standards were, and so were better able to apply them to problems that arose.

While Kinsey and his coworkers informed us about the frequency and variety of sexual behavior, the pioneer research of Masters and Johnson taught us about physiological responses during sexual activity. In the late 1950s and early 1960s, Masters and Johnson scientifically studied the sexual response cycle, charting physiological changes during it. They found that when a person experiences sexual stimulation, a variety of muscular, vascular, neurological, and hormonal changes unfold. The total person, not just a small facet of the person, is involved.

Because of the work of Masters and Johnson and other pioneer researchers, a scientific approach to the topic of human sexuality has developed, and our understanding of this aspect of human life has been advanced.

THE HUMAN REPRODUCTIVE SYSTEM

Although the differences between the male and female genitals (reproductive organs or genitalia) are self-evident, the great similarities between them are not and, as a result, most people never recognize or learn about them. Both similarities and differences will be examined here.

Early Development of the Sex Organs

A fetus has the potential to develop the sex organs of either gender until about six weeks after conception. At this point a three-step differentiation process begins, the course of which depends on the directions carried by the sperm that fertilized the egg:

1. the external male or female genitals develop,
2. appropriate changes occur in the internal reproductive structures and,
3. the gonads (or sex glands) grow into either testes or ovaries.

Figure 9.1 shows the differentiation and development of the external genitalia of both males and females. Notice how the male and female organs develop from exactly the same tissue. Specifically, for example, the genital tubercle becomes either a penis or clitoris and the labioscrotal swellings either the scrotum or the labia majora. Thus the external genitalia of both males and females come from exactly the same structure (or are "homologous," in biological terminology). People sometimes wonder whether their own sexual feelings are at all like those of the opposite sex. While this question obviously

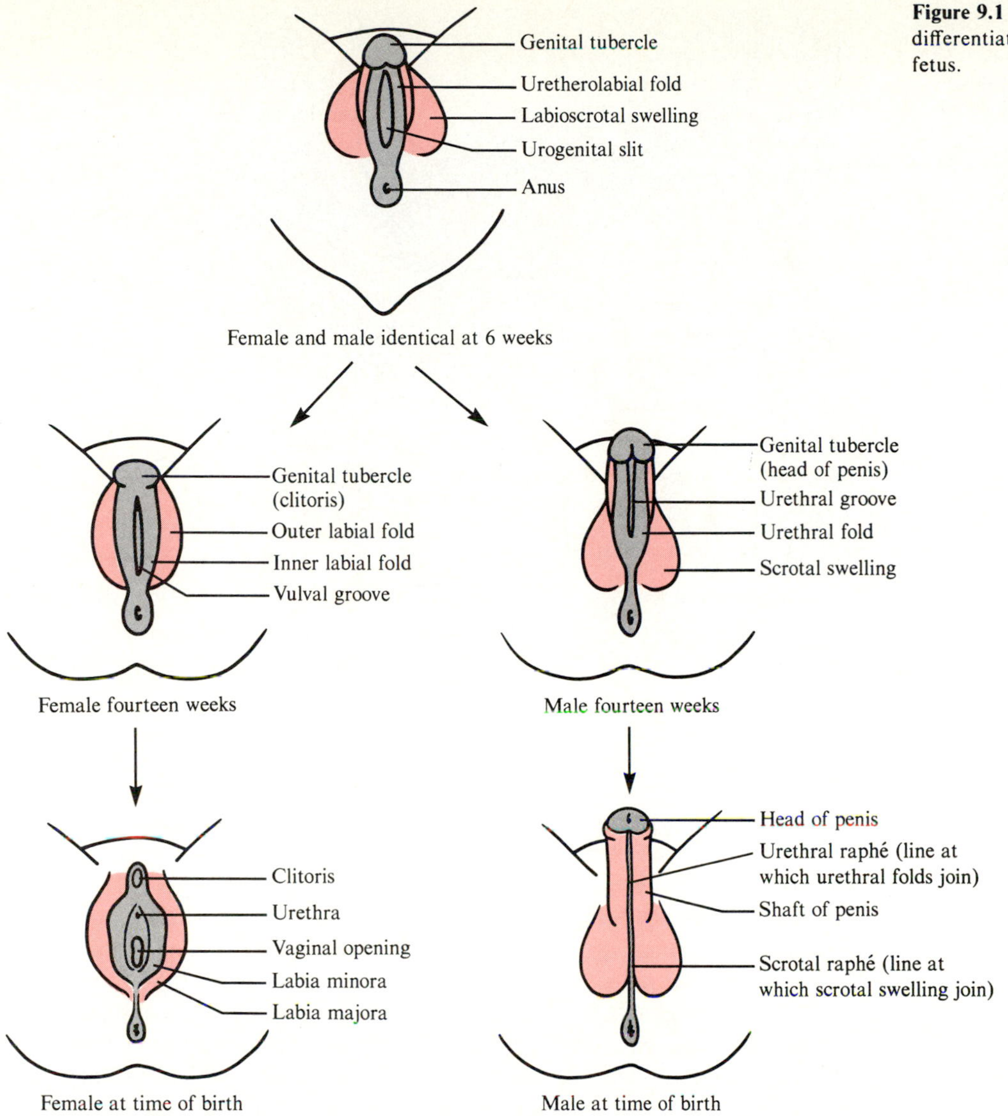

Figure 9.1 External genital differentiation in the human fetus.

Genital tubercle
Uretherolabial fold
Labioscrotal swelling
Urogenital slit
Anus

Female and male identical at 6 weeks

Genital tubercle (clitoris)
Outer labial fold
Inner labial fold
Vulval groove

Female fourteen weeks

Genital tubercle (head of penis)
Urethral groove
Urethral fold
Scrotal swelling

Male fourteen weeks

Clitoris
Urethra
Vaginal opening
Labia minora
Labia majora

Female at time of birth

Head of penis
Urethral raphé (line at which urethral folds join)
Shaft of penis
Scrotal raphé (line at which scrotal swelling join)

Male at time of birth

cannot be answered, it is worth considering that the sexual organs of both men and women develop from the same embryonic tissue.

Although the genitalia have the same beginnings, certain parts of the fetus' reproductive system develop only if the baby is female (i.e., the Müllerian structure grows into the uterus, fallopian tubes, and the upper part of the vagina) while others develop only if the baby is male (i.e., the Wolffian structure develops into the vas deferens, seminal vesicles, and the ejaculatory ducts).

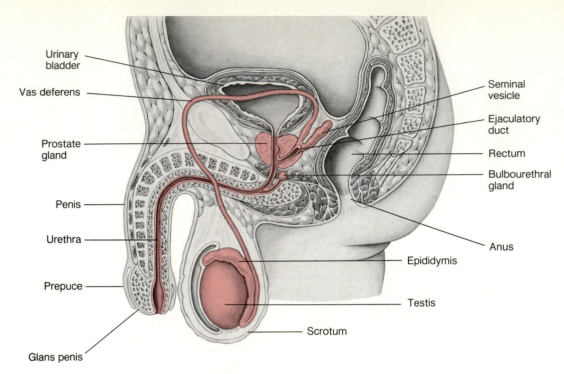

Figure 9.2 Male reproductive organs.

Urinary bladder

Vas deferens

Prostate gland

Penis

Urethra

Prepuce

Glans penis

Seminal vesicle

Ejaculatory duct

Rectum

Bulbourethral gland

Anus

Epididymis

Testis

Scrotum

The Male Genitals

Figure 9.2 is a diagrammatic illustration of the male pelvic region. The penis shown has not been circumcised; that is, the foreskin that covers the glans penis (head of the penis) was not surgically removed. Although the American Academy of Pediatrics in a 1975 report found no medical reasons for routine circumcision, estimates are that 85–90 percent of boys born today in the United States experience circumcision soon after birth (Mullen et al, 1986). One team (Stein, Marx, Taggart, & Bass, 1982) found that parents' decisions about this five-minute operation are not based on the physician's advice but rather on the father's circumcision status, the parents' beliefs about medical benefits, and religious customs. Further, these researchers and others (Williamson & Williamson, 1988) reported that a substantial number of the pediatricians, obstetricians, family physicians, and general practitioners lack important medical information about the circumcision procedure and about psychological factors parents take into account in making their decisions.

The shaft of the penis is made of spongy tissue known as cavernous bodies. The urethra, a canal running the length of the penis, transports urine, semen, and Cowper's gland's secretion (a pH-changing, lubricating fluid secreted during sexual excitement) out of a man's body.

Most of the time the penis is flaccid and measures from 2.5″ to 4″ in length and about 3.5″ in circumference (McCary, 1978). Adolescent boys and, in fact, adult men often harbor concerns about the size of their penis and may sometimes be tempted to make inconspicuous mental comparisons in locker

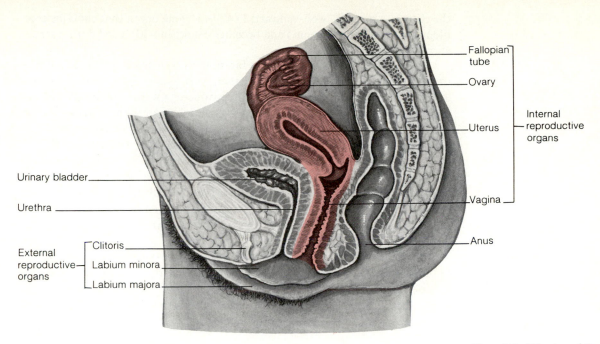

Figure 9.3 Side view of the organs of the female reproductive system.

rooms. Such comparisons tend to be inaccurate, of course, since two different visual perspectives are involved (looking straight down versus across the room). Further, penis size differences decrease with erection (Jamison & Gebhard, 1988); that is, when sufficient stimulation causes blood to fill the spongy cavernous bodies of the penis and it becomes erect or "hard." In fact, there is less variation in the dimensions of erect penises than in other parts of the male body (Cauthery, Stanway, & Stanway, 1983).

The scrotum, a skin pouch attached to the abdomen under the penis, contains egg-shaped testes, or testicles, and is capable of providing a temperature just under 98.6° F. The body maintains that temperature, a necessity in the production of sperm, by adjusting the scrotum. Specifically, in a cold environment muscles contract, pulling the testicles closer to the warmth of the body. Conversely, when the environment is too warm, the muscles relax allowing the scrotum to grow larger and the testes to drop further from the warmth of the abdomen.

The Female Genitals

A side view of the organs of the female reproductive system is shown in Figure 9.3. There are four parts of the vulva, the visible, external portion of the female sex organs. These are the mons pubis, or "mound of Venus," the hair-covered, fatty tissue that lies over the pubic bone; the outer lips, or labia (labium, sing.) majora, hair-covered, fatty folds of skin that begin at the mons pubis and form the external limits of the vulva; the inner lips or labia minora, thin sensitive folds of skin that meet at the clitoris and form a hood to cover its shaft; and the clitoris, a neurally well-endowed 1/4" to 1" long organ that contains erectile tissue (corpora cavernous) and becomes engorged with blood during sexual stimulation.

Men are generally much more familiar with their genitals than women, some of whom have never examined their vulvas. Several sexual awareness and therapy programs have suggested the value to a woman in finding privacy and, with the aid of a mirror, taking a good look. As is the case with men, there is substantial variation in the appearance of women's genitals, with few looking exactly like those carefully arranged for centerfold photographs.

The vagina begins inside the inner lips and angles up toward the small of the back. In a relaxed state it is shaped like a flattened muscular tube about 3.5" long. Normally "closed," in the sense that its walls lie against each other, the vagina naturally adjusts to accommodate a penis and, at the time of giving birth, is obviously capable of great expansion in that it enables passage of a baby.

In a newborn girl the vaginal opening is partly covered by a thin pinkish tissue called the hymen. The hymen, or maidenhead, has no known physical function and is only found in human beings. A virgin woman may have no hymen because it ruptured, perhaps without her knowledge, during childhood sports activities, accidents, or experimentation.

The Sexual Response

Sex therapists and marriage counselors have championed the position that the brain is humankind's "biggest sex organ." The so very human feelings of love, caring, tenderness, and concern can play a key role in people's sexual reactions. Even with regard to the physical experience, as Katchadourian (1974) has commented: " . . . sexual response, like sexual stimulation, involves the whole body; sex is in no sense a private affair between the genitals."

Masters and Johnson (1966), distilling years of research during which they measured changes in subjects engaged in sexual activity, noted four phases that both men and women pass through during the sexual response cycle. These are: excitement, plateau, orgasm, and resolution. A visual representation of how the sex organs change during the stages of the cycle is presented in Figures 9.4 and 9.5. The first and fourth phases are generally longest in terms of time.

Individuals do not necessarily pass through all stages during a sexual experience. However, the completion of the four stages is often a natural process associated with sexual activity if a person is knowledgeable about the physical aspects of sexual stimulation, psychologically comfortable with his or her body, and secure in sexual expression. Of course, key ingredients in satisfying shared sexual activity also include trust, mutual caring and love, and practical matters, such as having ample time and a private setting in which the partners feel safe.

The **excitement phase** begins with sexual stimulation from sources such as a romantic or lustful thought, a tender touch, or a special person's voice or sight. During the excitement phase both sexes experience erotic urges, general

Excitement Phase
Involves the physiological changes and the associated pleasure that take place as the body prepares itself for sexual activity.

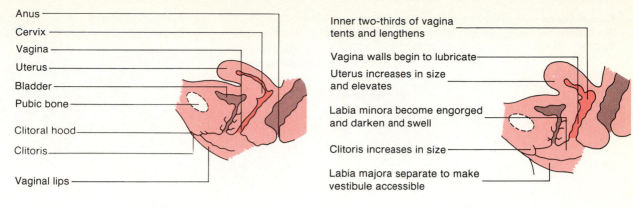

Unaroused State

Anus
Cervix
Vagina
Uterus
Bladder
Pubic bone
Clitoral hood
Clitoris
Vaginal lips

Excitement Phase

Inner two-thirds of vagina tents and lengthens
Vagina walls begin to lubricate
Uterus increases in size and elevates
Labia minora become engorged and darken and swell
Clitoris increases in size
Labia majora separate to make vestibule accessible

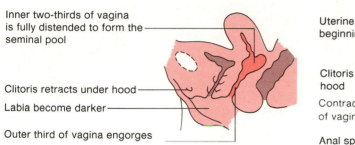

Plateau Phase

Inner two-thirds of vagina is fully distended to form the seminal pool
Clitoris retracts under hood
Labia become darker
Outer third of vagina engorges

Orgasm Phase

Uterine contractions occur beginning from the top
Clitoris is still retracted under hood
Contractions occur in outer third of vagina
Anal sphincter muscle contracts

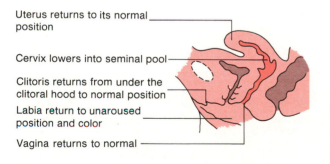

Resolution Phase

Uterus returns to its normal position
Cervix lowers into seminal pool
Clitoris returns from under the clitoral hood to normal position
Labia return to unaroused position and color
Vagina returns to normal

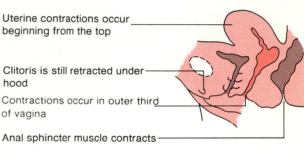

Breast Changes

Unaroused State

Excitement State
Breast size increases; nipples become erect; veins become more visible.

Plateau and Orgasm Phase
Breast size increases more; areola increases in size (making nipples appear less erect); skin color may become flushed from vasocongestion (called the sex flush).

Figure 9.4 Physical changes in the female during the sexual response cycle.

excitement and warmth, and, perhaps, depending on circumstances, mild fear or anxiety. Physical changes take place that ready the body for possible intercourse. Growing tension in the muscles, heavier breathing, and an increase in heart rate and blood pressure prepare the individual for the physical activity intercourse requires. Men attain an erection and their scrotums tighten. Women experience blood engorgement of the labia and clitoris, the development of vaginal lubrication, and the dilation and lengthening of the vagina. Finally, in women and in some men, the nipples become erect and a measles-like skin flush may develop.

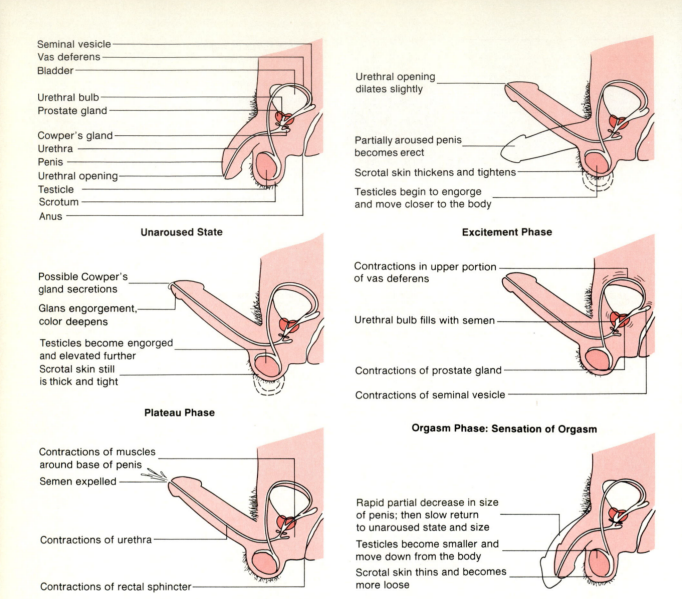

Seminal vesicle
Vas deferens
Bladder

Urethral bulb
Prostate gland

Cowper's gland
Urethra
Penis
Urethral opening
Testicle
Scrotum
Anus

Unaroused State

Urethral opening
dilates slightly

Partially aroused penis
becomes erect

Scrotal skin thickens and tightens

Testicles begin to engorge
and move closer to the body

Excitement Phase

Possible Cowper's
gland secretions

Glans engorgement,
color deepens

Testicles become engorged
and elevated further
Scrotal skin still
is thick and tight

Plateau Phase

Contractions in upper portion
of vas deferens

Urethral bulb fills with semen

Contractions of prostate gland

Contractions of seminal vesicle

Orgasm Phase: Sensation of Orgasm

Contractions of muscles
around base of penis
Semen expelled

Contractions of urethra

Contractions of rectal sphincter

Orgasm Phase: Ejaculation

Rapid partial decrease in size
of penis; then slow return
to unaroused state and size
Testicles become smaller and
move down from the body
Scrotal skin thins and becomes
more loose

Resolution

Figure 9.5 Physical changes in the male during the sexual response cycle.

Plateau Phase
Involves the heightening of sexual tensions, and the associated pleasure, as the body prepares itself for an orgasm.

As sexual activity continues, the individual reaches the **plateau phase,** marked by increased muscular tension observable in a strained face and often tightened buttocks. Blood pressure rises, the heart beat quickens, and vaso-congestion (accumulation of the blood) in the genitals peaks. As a result of vasocongestion, the penis stiffens, achieving its maximum size, and the outer third the vagina narrows, enhancing both partners' pleasure. The clitoris, still engorged, decreases in length and retracts under its hood. When excite-ment progresses to the point where orgasm is soon to follow, women's inner lips redden to a scarlet burgundy color from contained blood and men's testes are drawn up in the scrotum, readying them for the ejaculation. Moments before orgasm a man experiences the "point of no return," a feeling of "orgasmic inevitability" as his body readies the semen for ejaculation.

During the **orgasmic phase** breathing, heart rate, blood pressure, and skin flush peak. However, this phase is most obviously marked by a set of rhythmic, involuntary contractions at about .8 second intervals. These occur at the base of the penis, ejaculating semen, and in the uterus and outer third of the vagina. As the orgasm relieves the built-up psychological and physiological tension, the strongest, most intensely pleasurable sensations are obviously experienced in the genitals. However, muscles throughout the body react.

After orgasm, a man enters a refractory period, varying in length from minutes to hours, during which he cannot ejaculate again. In contrast, some women experience what has been called "multiple orgasms"; that is, if stimulation continues after their first orgasm, they soon experience another or several more orgasms in a series.

Following orgasm the **resolution phase** returns the body to its pre-excitement state, with the heart and respiration rates and blood pressure returning to normal. Many people excrete post-orgasm perspiration during this phase. While it generally occurs over a woman's entire body, in men it is often localized in the hands and the feet.

If orgasm is not reached and a man or woman passes to the resolution phase directly from a lengthy plateau phase, some psychological and pelvic discomfort may be felt as the blood slowly dissipates. Men who experience this may speak of having "blue balls."

Orgasmic Phase
Involves the sudden release of the built-up sexual tension and the associated heightened peak of sexual pleasure.

Resolution Phase
Involves the return of the body to the pre-excitement state and the feelings of contentment and relaxation associated with this.

FORMS OF SEXUAL EXPRESSION

The sexual behavior of lower species is guided by instinct and sexual hormones alone. While current research has shown that hormonal levels in the human body play a part in sexual feelings, we have freed ourselves from total domination by biological factors and have gone many steps beyond. Specifically, we have shaped nature's gift into much more than simply a vehicle for reproduction. For instance, we have learned to use sexual expression as a means of sharing love, of providing and receiving pleasure, and of cementing the complex of ties that bind people together in fulfilling relationships.

The many means by which people express themselves sexually range from unconscious sexual release (nocturnal orgasms) and masturbation to petting in its endless forms, sexual intercourse, and homosexual contact.

Nocturnal Orgasms

In some cases, if a person experiences a buildup of sexual tension, the body discharges the tension during sexual dreams. In boys, the first nocturnal orgasm often occurs in early adolescence, between 12 and 16. Nearly all men have sexual dreams, and so do most women. Seventy percent of the female subjects studied by the Kinsey team (1953) reported experiencing erotic dreams, and about half felt they had experienced a dream-produced orgasm.

Although some men and women feel guilty about having sexual dreams, particularly if the partner in the dream is not the person he or she is "supposed" to be (such as a fiancé or spouse), these dreams are normal, beyond the control of the sleeper, and appear to serve necessary biological and psychological functions.

Masturbation

Masturbation is the behavior of sexually arousing oneself. For many people, it is the first form of sexual activity (Atwood & Gagnon, 1987). Young children openly fondle their genitals until their parents teach them the behavior is inappropriate or should be only done in privacy. Masturbation is practiced widely among teenagers and is common among adults: it has been estimated that more than 90 percent of men and 60 percent of women have masturbated (Allgeier & Allgeier, 1984). A project involving married women reported that 61 percent enjoyed masturbation and 93 percent felt that this activity was not wrong (Grosskopf, 1983).

One study of undergraduates found that more than 80 percent of the men and 50 percent of the women engaged in sexual fantasies during masturbation (Loren & Weeks, 1986). Some fantasies involved activities far beyond those the person might ever engage in. A substantial number of individuals are concerned about their private sexual fantasies (Loren & Weeks, 1986) and about masturbation and its effects. Gagnon (1977) found that a group of college students were concerned that masturbating impaired study habits, meant being immature and immoral, or adversely affected one's health or later sexual competence.

In considering the issue of masturbation, personal values must be taken into account. A person who believes masturbation is morally wrong, perhaps for religious reasons, may find the practice induces great guilt over having departed from firmly held values. While that individual must come to terms with his values and guilt, he should also know that one's frequency of masturbation is not a problem as long as: The person is comfortable with his rate and the practice does not interfere with his carrying out his other responsibilities; the individual recognizes that masturbation is not harmful from a physical standpoint. In fact, many scientists believe it is a normal part of sexual development. Kinsey et al. (1953) found that women who had masturbated to orgasm were more likely than those who had not done so to experience climax during intercourse in their first year of marriage. Further, since masturbation is the form of stimulation most likely to produce orgasms in women, sex therapy practitioners often recommend it to women experiencing difficulty in achieving climaxes (e.g., Heiman, LoPiccolo, & LoPiccolo, 1976).

Studying Sexual Dreams

Study of sexual dreams can inform you in at least three ways, according to experts (Natterson & Gordon, 1977). Interpreting such dreams teaches you about your attitudes, thoughts, and feelings regarding sexual issues, interpersonal relations, and world outlook.

For instance, consider a dream Ellen reported:

"My fiancé Bill and I were at an expensive resort hotel restaurant. The settings included real silver and linen napkins. During dinner Bill kept kissing me and saying how much he loved me.

He was loud and people were looking at us. That didn't bother him. He tried to seduce me even though he knew I felt awful because I had failed my English midterm. After dessert I decided to give in to his wishes, but he had no money so I had to pay for the room."

In interpreting the dream Ellen thought about:

Sexual issues: Was she wishing for or opposed to engaging in sexual activity when feeling low about her academic performance? When she woke, how did the dream leave her feeling?

Interpersonal issues: Did Bill then or does he usually take advantage of her love for him? Was Bill trying to take care of her and lift her spirits with his romantic words and actions?

World outlook: Was this an example of how she feels men relate to women? Does she feel that people (like those in the restaurant) too often "listen into" other people's business?

Do you wish to experiment with studying one of your sexual dreams? If so, read on. Research indicates that people have several periods of dreaming every night. When you awaken and think that you did not have any dreams during the night, you probably did but failed to remember them. You can help yourself recall your dreams by asking yourself before you go to bed to try to remember your dreams and by placing a piece of paper near your bed so that you can jot down recollections during the night or first thing in the morning.

When you have a sexual dream you want to study, write down as much about it as you can remember. Next, conduct the following analysis of your dream (Natterson & Gordon, 1977):

a. Without censoring yourself, free associate and determine what thoughts and feelings come to mind when you think about the dream.
b. Determine the setting and role players. What role did you and others play? What was the significance, if any, of the location?
c. Did the dream relate to current events in your life, past happenings, or concerns about the future?
d. Consider the dream's content at face value and then search for symbolism.
e. Identify sexual content in the dream. Was there overt sexual behavior or symbolic sexual content in the dream? Were there symbols of sexual activity or of parts of the body (A railroad train through a tunnel, a hand going into a glove, and so forth)? Were sexual wishes or fantasies played out in the dream?
f. Consider the feeling the dream created. Did it bring happiness, discomfort, or other feelings?

With these issues in mind, ask what you learned from the dream about yourself and sexual issues, interpersonal issues, and world outlook.   ▲

Petting

Petting includes all forms of sexually oriented physical contact between two people *except* intercourse.

Young teenagers' first heterosexual experiences are usually petting. They typically begin with hand-holding, followed by putting their arms around or embracing each other. In time and with opportunity, brief kisses, prolonged kissing and hugging, and light petting while clothed typically follow.

Petting may lead to orgasm or may serve as foreplay before intercourse. While its form varies across cultural and socioeconomic groups, today, more than in earlier decades, nearly all people engage in premarital petting.

Table 9.1 shows the kind of petting (and sexual intercourse activity) in which college students reported engaging. Note that self-report surveys like this one have certain obvious limitations (i.e., subjects' ability to read and follow directions, subjects' memory, and subjects' honesty). One would expect these weaknesses to be exacerbated in sex research. Even on an anonymous questionnaire about sexual behavior, certain subjects exaggerate their experiences to stress worldliness while others understate them.

Sexual Intercourse

Sexual intercourse, depending on the status of the parties involved, can be described as either premarital, marital, extramarital, or postmarital. Individuals and societies assess the morality of these activities differently, with marital intercourse, or coitus between married individuals, being the only type that seems to be approved by all.

There is evidence that men and women react differently to their first experience of intercourse. When asked about their reactions immediately after their first experience, adolescent men most often described themselves as "excited," "satisfied," "thrilled," or "happy." The emotions most often reported by adolescent women, in contrast, were "afraid," "guilty," "worried," or "embarrassed" (DeLamater, 1987). A possible explanation of these differences is society's persistent "double standard," which tolerates or encourages men to have casual sex while at the same time discourages women and teaches them to connect sex more closely with marital love. Other explanations include a woman's fear of pregnancy and the fact that some women have intercourse to please persistent and demanding partners rather than because they desire it.

Although many people who engage in premarital intercourse believe that the experience strengthens their relationship, research findings in this area are mixed. One study showed that although college students may have felt having sexual intercourse further cemented their relationship, an actual count demonstrated that the experience did not actually increase the likelihood that couples would remain together (Peplau, Rubin, & Hill, 1977). Although the woman might feel more in love with the man after the experience, the man might not have the same reaction.

Married couples today report a greater frequency of intercourse than did couples in years past. The increase is due to several factors, one of which is probably the changing attitudes society has toward sexual behavior. A second

TABLE 9.1 *Sexual Behavior Among College Students*

Have You Ever Engaged In the Following Behavior with a Member of the Opposite Sex?	Percentage of Males Saying Yes	Percentage of Females Saying Yes
1. One minute of continuous kissing on the lips?	86.4	89.2
2. Manual manipulation of clothed female breasts?	82.7	71.1
3. Manual manipulation of bare female breasts?	75.5	66.3
4. Manual manipulation of clothed female genitals?	76.4	67.5
5. Kissing nipples of female breast?	65.5	59.0
6. Manual manipulation of bare female genitals?	64.4	60.2
7. Manual manipulation of clothed male genitals?	57.3	51.8
8. Mutual manipulation of genitals?	55.5	50.6
9. Manual manipulation of bare male genitals?	50.0	51.8
10. Manual manipulation of female genitals until there were massive secretions?	49.1	50.6
11. Sexual intercourse, face to face?	43.6	37.3
12. Manual manipulation of male genitals to ejaculation?	37.3	41.0
13. Oral contact with female genitals?	31.8	42.2
14. Oral contact with male genitals?	30.9	42.2
15. Mutual manual manipulation of genitals to mutual orgasm?	30.9	26.5
16. Oral manipulation of male genitals?	30.0	38.6
17. Oral manipulation of female genitals?	30.0	41.0
18. Mutual oral-genital manipulation?	20.9	28.9
19. Sexual intercourse, entry from the rear?	14.5	22.9
20. Oral manipulation of male genitals to ejaculation?	22.7	26.5
21. Mutual oral manipulation of genitals to mutual orgasm?	13.6	12.0

Source: From J. P. Curran, "Convergence Toward a Single Sexual Standard?" in *Social Behavior and Personality,* 3(2), 189–195. Copyright © Society for Personality Research. Reprinted by permission.

factor affecting the sexual behavior of couples is the increased effectiveness of contraceptives. A final factor is certainly the increased interest in sex on the part of women, a dramatic change from the days when intercourse was regarded as a wife's "duty."

Over the years of marriage, and as a husband and wife age, couples generally have intercourse less frequently. However, if they remain sexually active, they can extend their ability to function sexually well into their 80s or even 90s. Sexuality among older people—once considered nonexistent or, at best, inappropriate—is finally being given attention, not only in research studies but in books, television shows, and other media.

Extramarital intercourse, sometimes called adultery, has long been part of the human experience. (It is the one sexual prohibition in the Ten Commandments.) Because of its traditionally immoral status, people surveyed may hesitate to acknowledge having engaged in it. Nonetheless, estimates are that more than 50 percent of men (Allgeier & Allgeier, 1984) and perhaps 40 percent of all women have extramarital sex at some point in their lives (Grosskopf, 1983). The reasons people offer to explain extramarital affairs range from curiosity to sexual frustration at home. Some people state that their lover is more romantic and more accepting than their spouse, and, in the case of married men and single women, a safe person with whom to share grievances and vulnerabilities (Richardson, 1986). Others speak of emotional dissatisfaction or of revenge and of angry feelings they harbor toward their spouse. Another factor contributing to extramarital sex may be the so-called mid-life crisis. Some middle-aged married people find the need to reassert their youth by finding a younger lover.

Each year, because of divorce and widowhood, over a millon Americans become "single again." As the formerly married cope with their changed life circumstances, certain needs for companionship and sexual expression may emerge. Research is being conducted to identify how people adjust to these changes and, in time, come to meet their needs. (Schwebel, Fine, Moreland, & Prindle, 1988; Vess, Moreland, & Schwebel, 1986).

Homosexuality

Homosexuality is a sexual orientation in which a man's or woman's sexual interests are in people of the same sex. The cause or causes of homosexuality have not been determined (Luria, Friedman, & Rose, 1987). Although some have proposed biological theories (e.g., a genetic factor, hormonal differences), others have argued that psychological factors are key (childhood differences in the parenting received, friendship patterns at the onset of adolescence).

Once seen as indicative of serious psychological maladjustment, homosexuality is no longer categorized by the American Psychiatric Association as a mental disorder. Instead, it is regarded as problematic only if it disturbs or causes conflict in a person, and that person wants to change his or her sexual orientation. While the mental health professions have modified their stance toward homosexuality, American society has only slowly begun to accept the health professionals' view of homosexuality as a way of life, rather than as a mental illness. Weinberg and Williams (1976) found that 40 percent of their respondents thought homosexuals were mentally ill, 50 percent saw them as perverted, and 70 percent as sexually abnormal. In controversial areas such as this, public attitudes often change slowly. And many people will always oppose homosexuality on the basis of moral or religious beliefs.

It is commonplace to think of "homosexuality," like "virginity" and "pregnancy." It either describes a person or it does not. The findings of Kinsey's team (1948) suggested this is not the case. The researchers concluded that sexual orientation was a continuum, with exclusively heterosexual individuals falling at one extreme and exclusively homosexual people falling at the other. Those toward the middle have had both types of sexual or fantasy experiences. McCary (1978) reviewed available research and concluded that one third of the women and one half of the men in our society have at one point felt sexually attracted to a person of their own gender. The percentage of people exclusively homosexual in the United States has been estimated at about 2½ percent (Gagnon, 1977). While this statistic represents a significant number, the estimate is probably low. Because of societal attitudes, many people undoubtedly refrain from disclosing their homosexual orientation to pollsters.

In recent decades, some stereotypes about homosexuality have been disproved or questioned. For example, many homosexuals do not adopt dress, speech, or social behavior that heterosexuals identify as "gay;" rather they function in their jobs, schools, and communities without others being aware of their orientation. Bell and Weinberg (1978) concluded that their 1500 subjects were not easily identifiable as homosexuals, had satisfactory work records, had both homosexual and heterosexual friends, and had more close friends than their heterosexual counterparts. Many had experiences with the opposite sex, and a sizable minority had been married. A willingness to disclose their homosexual orientation was suggested by the fact that about 50 percent of the respondents' siblings, 20 percent of their neighbors, and 25 percent of their employers knew about their homosexuality.

Bell and Weinberg found support for the idea that some male homosexuals have had many partners, but other male subjects reported more limited numbers. The females interviewed generally had fewer partners than the males. This may be a reflection of the heterosexual world, in which women tend to report greater interest in developing long-term relationships, or may be due to sociobiological factors (Gallup, 1986).

Bell and Weinberg found their sample of subjects with homosexual orientations sufficiently diverse that they divided them into categories, based on their sexual lives and self-views. The types they found to be most well adjusted were the "close-coupled" (people strongly committed to a partner and tending not to regret their homosexuality) and the "functionals" (people not in a relationship who were sexually active and had a group of friends). While some researchers (Gonsiorek, 1982; Reiss, 1980) have reported no significant differences in the adjustment of homosexuals and heterosexuals, Bell and Weinberg found homosexuals as a group to be generally not as well adjusted. Whichever is the case, homosexuals face much the same stresses in life as heterosexuals and, in addition, must cope with the anxieties associated with following a life-style of which most of their society disapproves (Larsen, Reed, & Hoffman, 1980). Despite this and the sanctions they face from society, many homosexual individuals are psychologically healthy and lead lives they find rich and satisfying. Some homosexuals seek treatment designed to change their sexual orientation. A range of approaches have been used, with limited success. Marmor (1980) reports that those most likely to benefit from treatment have these characteristics: They are strongly motivated, young, have had previous heterosexual experiences, have more recently become homosexual, and look and act in ways traditionally consistent with their gender.

The majority of homosexuals who enter therapy, however, do so for the same reasons as heterosexuals and are not interested in altering their sexual orientation. They do so in order to deal with stress, anxiety, sexual dysfunctions, depression, or difficulty in establishing a long-term relationship. Besides or instead of seeing therapists, they may draw support from members of or counselors affiliated with organizations formed to assist homosexual women (lesbians) and homosexual men (gay men).

SEXUALITY ACROSS THE LIFE SPAN

At the turn of the century, humans were thought to be sexual beings only during their young adult and middle-aged years. Then Freud called attention to the fact that infants and children are sexual beings too. Now, researchers are reporting that people continue sexual activity into their 80s and 90s. Without a doubt, human beings are sexual beings across the life span. In this section we will look at our sexuality as it changes over the years.

As we saw in Chapter 7, newborns have an innate propensity to enjoy physical contact. It is, after all, in the interest of our species that the newborn baby be comforted by being held securely at the mother's breast, or cuddled by a protecting father. Those who have cared for babies—whether younger siblings or the new arrival down the street—know from direct experience how they seek and appreciate being touched, cuddled, squeezed, and doted upon. Early on most master the art of gaining the attention and affection they *need*. Use of the term "need" was intentional. Many years ago Spitz (1945) first discovered that infants deprived of social contact may become listless, apathetic, and generally unresponsive, eventually suffering retarded emotional and intellectual development. If infants are deprived of physical handling over a lengthy period of time, they may grow ill and even die.

At the time of birth the potential to grow psychologically and physically into a healthy sexual adult is present. For example, Harry Harlow, who is well known for his work with primates, speaks of sex as a "heterosexual affectional system" with three parts. These three, which can be applied to human beings, are mechanical, hormonal, and romantic. While the mechanical (the inborn set of reflexes necessary for sexual behavior and orgasm) and the hormonal subsystems take care of themselves, the romantic one must be learned. Harlow proposes the affectional interactions that the infant and then the child have with the mother, father, peers, and others are the vehicle through which he or she eventually learns how to love an adult partner.

Developmental psychologists explain that childhood is a period of orderly, step-by-step growth. Development takes place in many realms. Of specific interest here is the chain of events that lead a child to become ready to eventually function sexually as an adult. Physically, the body must mature in certain obvious ways. Psychologically, individuals must develop the social ability to attract others, good communication skills to promote a relationship, a sense of comfort with themselves, and a mastery of basic knowledge about sexuality.

Piaget has observed that humans have a propensity to explore and to learn about themselves and their world.

We can easily observe and measure many of the physical changes unfolding in children. Obviously, identifying and measuring psychological changes are more difficult tasks. Though we cannot precisely map out how children gain the social ability to attract a partner or how they learn to love, we know such growth occurs throughout childhood. Development does generally progress from the general to the specific and from the simple to the complex. For example, a newborn first experiences an emotion that can be described as a general state of excitement. In time he or she perhaps differentiates that feeling into two: feeling comfortable (fed and dry) and feeling uncomfortable (hungry or wet). During the course of childhood, the repertoire of emotions—at first very simple—grows to the point where a person experiences the complexity of adult love.

Piaget, as we saw earlier, pointed out that children are not "miniature adults" and that their thinking and behavior cannot be correctly understood by simply assessing them in the way adults' would be (Piaget, 1952). We can apply Piaget's findings to the area of sexuality. For example, infants who touch their genitals are not doing so with the same motivation as would be attributed to adults. And when preschoolers "play doctor," they are not in their terms doing something "naughty"; they are merely exploring each others' bodies and trying to gain a more realistic picture of them and how they differ. This experiential learning is a natural part of children's preparing themselves to become knowledgeable, competent adults.

Children build their repertoire of sexual knowledge in a step-by-step fashion. By interviewing children at different ages, one researcher was able to identify six levels of understanding that young people pass through en route to developing a "scientific grasp" of how humans reproduce (Bernstein, 1976).

TABLE 9.2	*A Seven Year Old's View of Modesty*

Ethan, a normally quiet child, began misbehaving in his second grade class a few months into the school year. At first the teacher took no action because Ethan's tantrums were so out of character. Eventually, however, she consulted with the school counselor who referred Ethan's parents to a clinical psychologist specializing in the treatment of children.

In gathering information the psychologist discovered that the onset of Ethan's problems was timed closely with the arrival in Ethan's home of a baby brother. As the psychologist, the parents, and Ethan were discussing the baby—seemingly out of nowhere—Ethan popped the BIG question for the first time ever.

"Where do babies come from, mother?" he probed.

"Well," the mother hesitantly began, "Mothers and fathers are very much in love with each other. Sometimes they get undressed . . . "

Before the mother could explain further Ethan interrupted: "Do you mean to get the baby you had to let Daddy see your butt! Geez! I can't believe it!"

She found that level 1 children (about three to four years old) and level 2 children (about age four or somewhat older) were concrete, the former explaining that babies "were gotten" at the hospital while the latter had advanced to believing babies "were built" at the hospital. At level 3 (between four or older to seven years old), youngsters knew some accurate details about human bodies and the roles of the mother and father in reproduction, but their ideas were not yet well organized. Level 4 children (about seven to ten years old) showed familiarity with the terms "sperm" and "egg" and some understanding of what causes what. At level 5, youngsters (about 11 or 12 years old) realized that the sperm joined the egg, but the role of each was not finally understood until level 6 (about age 12 or older).

Piaget has explained that humans have a propensity to explore and to learn about themselves and their world. That is why toddlers and young children will talk about sex, explore their bodies, and be interested in their friends' bodies. What parents do not say and what they do say and how they say it, and, perhaps most important, the models they provide, are the keys that guide their children's developing attitudes.

Sorenson (1973) surveyed individuals aged 13 to 19, and found that over half the boys expressed a desire to be able to discuss sex with their parents, although they also believed that their parents did not want to instruct them in this topic or even discuss it in any but a general way. Not unexpectedly, then, Sorenson found that about 70 percent of these teenagers stated they did not talk freely with their parents about sex. However, other research (Goldman & Goldman, 1982; Obstfeld & Meyers, 1984) has indicated that parents believe sex education should at least partly be taught in the home and that mothers, in particular, are a major source of sex information for their children. Table 9.2 provides an example of a child about to learn more about human sexuality from his mother.

Regardless of the adequacy or inadequacy of the sex instruction children receive from their parents, puberty confronts individuals with new challenges in the area of sexuality. In males, at puberty, large amounts of the sex hormone

androgen are manufactured, awakening interest in sex that may, in some adolescents, reach high levels. Puberty also brings a more intense interest in sex among adolescent females, but in most, this interest tends to be focused on being liked by a male and vice versa. Masturbation is common in the early teens, though more frequent among males. In the adolescent years, parental prohibitions against sexual activity and sexual intercourse often have practical as well as moral bases, especially because of the danger of unwanted pregnancy at this age and of sexually transmitted diseases.

During their late teens and early 20s people are often finishing an education, beginning a career, and making decisions of great consequence to their sexual development. In learning to achieve intimacy in an adult-to-adult relationship, individuals frequently choose and commit themselves to a partner. Perhaps helped by that partner, they grow more accepting of their body, at least partially conquering self-consciousness and embarrassment so these feelings do not interfere with sexual expression. This time of life is generally one of great sexual activity. During their 20s, for instance, couples have the highest rate of sexual intercourse.

The 30s bring many changes in a man's outlook on life and in the goals he holds. Sexual interest is still high, but fewer experiences of sexual intercourse per week are needed to satisfy him. Moreover, he is less likely to spend as much time fantasizing and thinking about sex, perhaps doing so most often when a situation dictates opportunity. In his 40s he experiences further change.

Orgasms become a less important part of the total sexual experience as his interests shift "from the intense genitally located sensations of youth to the more sensuous but diffused and generalized experience characteristic of middle and later life" (Kaplan, 1974, p. 107).

American women generally achieve their greatest sexual responsiveness during their 30s and 40s. Reasons for this may be that: (1) some women have finally altered negative attitudes about sex they learned while growing up, (2) they feel more secure with sexuality in the context of marriage, (3) through experience, their inhibitions have been reduced and they feel more comfortable in expressing their sexual preferences, (4) their partners have gained greater sexual endurance, and (5) childbirth has resulted in certain physiological changes that make sexual excitement more intense. However, because of sex-role training, and developing signs of aging, the 30s and 40s may present challenges to a woman's sense of sexuality. And menopause, occurring in a woman's late 40s or early 50s, is sometimes accompanied by unexpected changes—anything from a loss of interest in sex to an increased desire for it.

For a man, the beginning of the 50s is generally marked by a reduced frequency of sexual intercourse, but at this point in his life he may be satisfied with this reduced frequency. Women of this age also experience some physiological changes, in addition to the possible onset of menopause. But if two partners are well attuned, intercourse can be as satisfying and enriching as ever.

The 60s and 70s, and the decades beyond, bring further age-related changes to the human body. People who grow frustrated by and anxious about bodily changes may avoid sexual expression altogether. But those who are physically healthy and have a positive self-concept generally continue to seek sexual opportunities in these years.

At any age, sexual activity appears to be possible, and indeed enjoyable. Pfeiffer, Verwoerdt, and Wang (1968) studied over 250 women and men who ranged from 60 to 94 years of age (averaging 70.9). They found that 40–65 percent of those in the 60–71 group and 10–25 percent of those over 78 years of age continued to be sexually active. In their study, as is often the case, a major factor ending the practice of sexual intercourse was the loss of one's spouse. Adams and Turner (1985) sampled over 100 men and women aged 60–85, assessing their current practices and feelings about sexual activities and what they recalled feeling and experiencing when they were 20–30 years old. The researchers found most of the subjects were sexually active. They also discovered that a small percentage of the men and a substantial minority of the women were gaining more pleasure or satisfaction with sex at this point than when they were younger.

Further systematic research is needed to study people's sexual beliefs and practices, particularly in examining the middle years that have been virtually overlooked to this point. In sum, however, it is clear that males' and females' sexual patterns do not proceed in parallel fashion throughout the life span. Specifically, as Kinsey first noted and Masters and Johnson later confirmed, men's capacity peaks in their late teens and then levels off or declines slightly over the next decades, while women do not peak until their 30s or 40s,

Although we live in what many have called a youth-oriented society, older people who have positive self-concepts are often able to preserve and strengthen the romantic aspects of their relationship.

slowly declining in responsiveness after that. Although biological factors and the impact of our society have teamed up to cause these differences in the two genders, human beings have the capability to deal with this challenge and, over the course of their relationships, to continue to enjoy and share the warmth and pleasure offered by sexual expression.

SEXUAL DYSFUNCTIONS

Many people speak of the naturalness of sex, stressing that it is like other human bodily processes, eating, drinking, breathing, and so on. Of course there is a difference in that these latter processes must be done regularly for the survival of the individual, whereas someone can abstain from sexual inter-course for extended periods—or for a lifetime—without causing physical harm. This is true because the species', and not the individual's, survival is dependent on reproduction. Ironically, it is perhaps because of the reproductive conse-quences of sexual behavior that societies long ago began placing certain con-straints on individuals' sexual expression. These constraints have led many people to believe that their instinctive sexual feelings are not natural at all, but unnatural and wrong. Many societies' teachings concerning sexuality have been restrictive to the individual and therefore have tended to cause guilt about both engaging in the activity and enjoying it.

The holding of restrictive attitudes about sexual activity is one major cause of sexual dysfunction. Such attitudes typically developed during the childhood and adolescent years. In some cases they are not relaxed, even after marriage and may confuse or distress a person, and cause that person and the partner much unhappiness.

Another frequent cause of difficulties is performance anxiety, the belief that one should "perform" to certain standards during sexual expression. An individual striving to perform is liable to monitor what happens, spectator-like, and such "watching" and evaluating interferes with the natural reactions that would otherwise occur automatically. In other words, if a man worries about and regularly assesses the quality of his developing erection, he may well cause himself and his partner problems. Sexual dysfunction is also sometimes related to negative feelings a person harbors toward a partner. For instance, a man who has long withheld anger toward his lover may unwittingly strike back in a passive-aggressive way, depriving her of pleasure by ejaculating only moments after intercourse begins.

Finally, the cause of sexual difficulties can also be medical in nature, resulting from some disease, from the taking of certain drugs, or occasionally from a physical problem with the sexual organs. Whatever the cause, sexual dysfunctions prevent natural bodily processes from unfolding and can precipitate stress or a personal crisis in a number of ways. For example, an affected person may worry constantly about the problem, or difficulty with sexual expression may threaten the stability of his or her own marriage.

The kinds of sexual dysfunctions that patients report in treatment centers typically involve an inhibition in their desire for or enjoyment of sex or in their bodies' sexual reactions unfolding in a natural way. The types of problems that arise have been categorized in the DSM-III-R and are described below. For diagnostic purposes, the DSM-III-R partitions the sexual response into four phases, **appetitive, excitement, orgasm,** and **resolution,** and defines a sexual dysfunction as a significant problem in one or more phases that is not caused by medication or a physical disorder. For example, individuals are diagnosed as having a sexual dysfunction that occurs in the appetitive phase if, in the absence of organic causes, they have neither fantasies about nor desire for sexual activity.

Appetitive Phase
Involves the desire to engage in sexual activities and having fantasies about it.

Excitement Phase
Involves the physiological changes and the associated pleasure that take place as the body prepares itself for sexual activity.

Orgasm Phase
Involves the sudden release of the built-up sexual tension and the associated heightened peak of sexual pleasure.

Resolution Phase
Involves the return of the body to the pre-excitement state and the feelings of contentment and relaxation associated with this.

Sexual Desire Disorders

Obviously, there is no prescription for the "right" amount of sexual activity people should have. Partners who have similar desires are fortunate. Sex drive becomes an issue for couples only when one person desires more or less frequent sexual activity than the other.

Most couples whose desires are unequal, but not greatly so, can compromise and find a mutually satisfying frequency. More severe problems arise when one partner has almost no erotic interest. This situation, termed **hypoactive sexual desire disorder,** is common among those seeking treatment for sexual dysfunction. While a few such people report a lifelong lack of interest in sex, more frequently the person's history was normal until the present loss occurred.

The underlying causes of inhibited sexual desire are many. The problem may be attributable to any medical condition impairing hormone production, or to certain drugs that are known to inhibit desire, such as alcohol, narcotics, or sedatives. However, the cause is frequently depression, viewing oneself or one's partner negatively (e.g., disliking oneself because of being unemployed), a recent divorce, or other stress factors that the person has not found ways of handling effectively. Finally, poor communication or "game-playing" in a relationship can numb sexual appetite, particularly if sex has become a mechanism used by one partner to reward, punish, or gain control over the other. Inhibited sexual desire stemming from psychological causes is often treatable through the provision of information about sex, sex therapy, psychotherapy, or some combination of these.

Sexual Arousal Disorders

The problem of **male erectile disorder** refers to a man's inability to achieve or maintain an erection sufficient for intercourse. A substantial number of men experience this at some time in their lives, usually when they are under stress, intoxicated, or harboring anger toward or feeling guilty about being with a partner. Such transient dysfunction is not considered a problem, but persistent difficulties are. Physical causes of impotence, as it is sometimes called by lay people, include excessive consumption of alcohol and certain other drugs, physical exhaustion, circulatory and neurological disorders, and age-related changes in the body. Much of the time the problem is psychological, however. Strict traditional training, guilt about sexual experiences with prostitutes or with men, worry about the ability to please a partner, or fear of erectile difficulties can all contribute to this problem.

If erections are not being achieved at any time, a diagnostician may assume physical causes. But usually erections are gained in certain circumstances, such as during sleep, masturbation, or with one partner but not another. Here psychological causes are assumed, and sexual therapy, psychotherapy, or a combination is recommended.

Sex therapy programs focus on convincing the man that he does not need to "learn how" to have erections but that they will come naturally when allowed. His fear of failure, or "performance anxiety," is combated, as well as anxieties his partner may have developed about the situation. When sex therapy is used, generally intercourse is prohibited for several days. Instead the couple goes through a step-by-step procedure of experiencing other types of sexual pleasures, with the man gradually gaining confidence in his ability to achieve erection. It is interesting that in our achievement-oriented society, men, who

traditionally bear the burden of achieving, should apply such economically oriented words as "performance," "success," and "failure" to an area of activity that is biologically designed to provide simple pleasure.

Orgasm Disorders

This most prevalent sexual problem in women refers to the inability to achieve orgasm. It can be a lifelong problem, if orgasm has never been experienced, or a situational one wherein orgasm can be reached during one type of sexual activity but not another. (Most often women complain of inability to achieve orgasm during intercourse.) The problem was often referred to in the past as "frigidity," a term with extremely negative connotations which, in popular usage, covered lack of interest in sex as well. Scientists and practitioners now use noncondemning descriptive terms like **inhibited female orgasm** to describe the problem in women or call it "a preorgasmic state" (Barbach, 1976), because these labels better convey the notion that the problem is not indicative of sexual failure and often can be remedied.

Inhibited Female Orgasm
A sexual dysfunction in which a woman is not able to achieve an orgasm at all or during certain kinds of stimulation.

Some women may feel under pressure about orgasms, because of a partner's overanxiousness that they should achieve them or because of books and magazines they have read. Research has suggested that a substantial portion of women at one time have "faked" an orgasm to satisfy their partner (Butler, 1976). The reasons they reported were to bolster a partner's ego, to prove one was "a real woman," to "end an act of sex," and so on. Men, too, sometimes "fake" an orgasm. Generally, psychologists believe that such deception—even when carried out with the best of intentions—is ultimately harmful to the man and woman and to the relationship.

Further, people may certainly enjoy sex without orgasm. Many report experiencing great satisfaction during intercourse because of excitement, closeness, and warmth, even if they do not reach a climax. Orgasms tend to come when a person is knowledgeable about sexual stimulation, comfortable with her body, and secure about expressing herself sexually. A woman who has not yet experienced an orgasm during intercourse should not assume that she never will.

Although orgasmic dysfunction may be related to physical causes, it is nearly always due to psychological factors. Training that has inculcated guilty attitudes toward sexuality can adversely affect a woman's responsiveness. Conflicts with a partner can do the same. If neither of these factors is operating, it may be that the woman is receiving insufficient sexual stimulation. Greater assertiveness, or open discussions with her partner, may help. Other alternatives are psychotherapy and sex therapy training, which can usually alleviate this condition.

The condition of reaching an orgasm "too soon," or **premature ejaculation,** is the one most prevalent in males seeking treatment for sexual dysfunction. Unlike other sexual problems, premature ejaculation has not been linked to conflicts about sex or to psychological disorders (Kaplan, 1974). Physical causes of premature ejaculation are rare. There is no consensus about psychological causes, but several have been suggested. Explanations include early experiences that rewarded speed (adolescents' sexual encounters in the family living room while the parents were out shopping), an unhealthy attitude toward women, lack of self-confidence, and a man's not having learned to identify preorgasmic sensations and how to bring orgasm under voluntary control. Premature ejaculation can be treated successfully with techniques taught by sex therapists (reported in Kaplan, 1974).

Those experiencing **inhibited male orgasm** condition become sexually excited, attain an erection but, after adequate stimulation, find their ejaculatory response persistently inhibited in certain sexual encounters. Most frequently, the individual can achieve orgasm during masturbation but not during intercourse. Psychological causes include guilt about sexual activity, fear of causing pregnancy, and the harboring of anger or mixed feelings toward a partner. Physical injuries are sometimes responsible. Sex therapy or psychotherapy treatment can often alleviate this problem.

Sexual Pain Disorders

Dyspareunia is a condition in which sexual intercourse is painful; it is much more prevalent in women than in men. Generally, dyspareunia is caused by a physical condition of the sexual organs that can be corrected through medical intervention. Women may also experience pain as a result of an allergic reaction to contraceptive substances or because they are not sufficiently aroused during intercourse. If medical causes are discounted, psychological and interpersonal issues need exploration. These include anxiety or tension about sex, a man's lack of knowledge about his partners preferences, insufficient foreplay, or lovemaking in an atmosphere that is not conducive to sexual expression. The problem can often be helped by open discussions between the partners, sex therapy, or other measures.

Premature Ejaculation
A sexual dysfunction in which a man habitually achieves orgasm sooner than desired.

Inhibited Male Orgasm
A sexual dysfunction in which a man attains an erection and becomes excited, but persistently experiences difficulty in ejaculating, at least under some circumstances.

Dyspareunia
A sexual dysfunction, usually occurring in women, in which sexual intercourse is painful.

Vaginismus is a relatively rare condition that causes painful, powerful, involuntary muscle spasms in the outer third of the vagina, making intercourse difficult or impossible. While physical abnormalities can cause vaginismus, it is more likely to stem from guilty or fearful attitudes toward sex, anticipated pain, or a difficult past experience (such as rape or having been "caught" by parents in a past sexual experience). Finally, research has shown that vaginismus may be found in a woman whose partners have erectile dysfunction. Apparently, the frustrations of a history of unsatisfactory sex teaches some women to "protect" themselves in this manner. Vaginismus can be successfully treated by trained sex therapists.

An Overview of Treatment Approaches

As certainly would be expected, the problems described can at times cause great distress in the lives of those afflicted. It makes sense too that the longer a problem continues without change, the more impact it will have on the person's life and that of his or her partner. For example, after a period of time a husband who is troubled because of premature ejaculation may discover that his wife has a decreasing desire for sex. If, instead of dealing with their problems, he turns to drinking, he may next encounter erectile difficulties. And so their lives are further complicated. Sexual and relationship issues can also become intertwined after one partner experiences surgery or a life-threatening illness. If couples delay or avoid discussing their fears or post-problem capabilities and desires, other relationship difficulties can develop and deprive the individuals of opportunities for shared satisfaction in sexual expression (Andersen & Jochimsen, 1985; Vess, Moreland, & Schwebel, 1985a, 1985b). Single people who engage in premarital sex can also encounter certain kinds of problems. Specifically, fear of "failing" in the bedroom may cause them to shy away from dating because it might lead to sex. Missing out on a social life can lower self-esteem and produce loneliness.

In the very few years that scientists and clinicians have focused on developing treatments, great strides have been made. Specifically, effective therapies have been developed and the public has come to accept open discussion of the problems and their treatment.

Approximately 10 percent of sexual difficulties are due to organic problems (Burch, 1984). To rule out the possibility of a medical problem, all treatment should begin with a thorough physical examination. When such problems are ruled out, psychological therapy can proceed, following one of the four major treatment approaches (Sarason & Sarason 1984):

1. Masters and Johnson's well-known approach involves a carefully planned behavioral program that emphasizes transmitting information, lowering anxiety levels, and prescribing a series of sexual exercises (Sarason & Sarason, 1984).

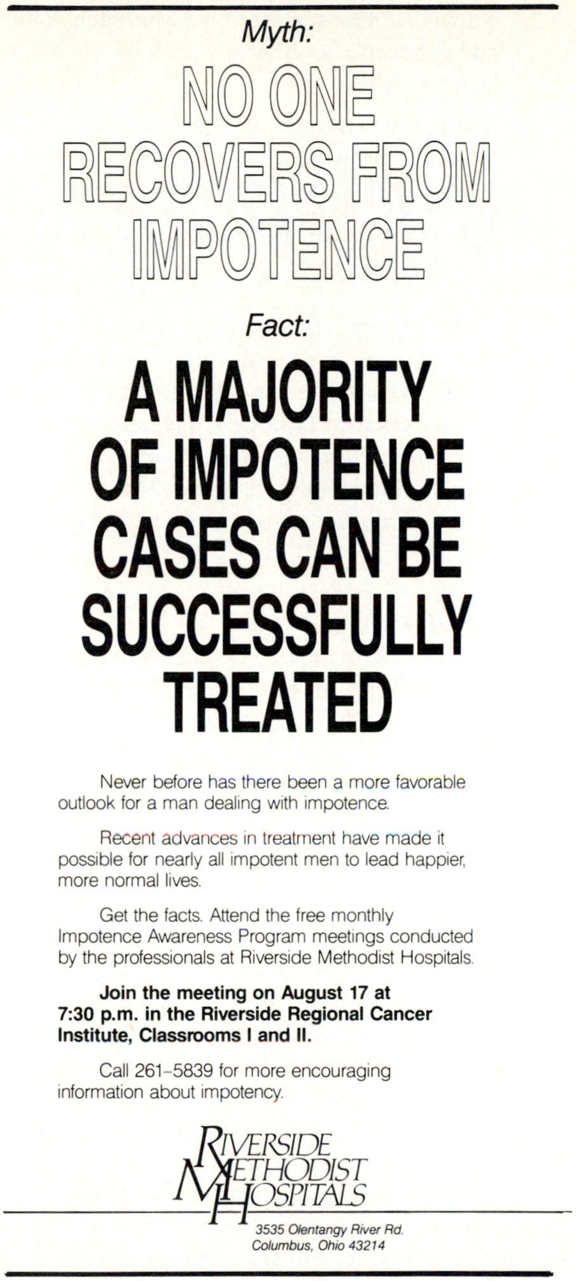

Figure 9.6 Advertisements, such as this one, are indicative of changed public attitudes toward open discussion of sexual dysfunction.
Courtesy Riverside Methodist Hospitals, Columbus, Ohio.

2. Kaplan's "new sex therapy" approach combines features of Masters and Johnson's sex therapy with psychodynamic theory (Sarason & Sarason, 1984).

3. The psychodynamic approach focuses therapy on psychological blocks to sexual enjoyment and assumes that sexual dysfunction is symptomatic of underlying unconscious conflicts.

4. Behavior therapy uses a variety of conditioning techniques, relaxation, and modeling.

Although progress has been made in developing these therapeutic approaches and some evaluative studies have been done, research results are not yet at a point where one can say method A works best for problem B in people who have personality type C. A person wanting treatment should determine the services offered in his or her area and investigate the qualifications and backgrounds of available therapists. It should also be remembered that if help is not found through one approach or therapist, another can be tried.

BIRTH CONTROL

Most of the time that people engage in sexual activity they do it mainly for love and pleasure and not to reproduce. If no birth control measures are taken, there is an 80 percent chance that a sexually active woman will become pregnant over the course of one year (Stewart et al., 1979). Many people believe it is morally wrong to interfere with this natural outcome, feeling that selective abstinence is the only means by which spouses should limit the size of their family. Other people, with different religious beliefs, accept the idea of other forms of birth control.

The most common methods of avoiding conception, along with their main advantages and disadvantages, are described here. The first is the *rhythm method*. This birth control technique is by and large ineffective. The method calls for careful record-keeping by the woman to determine at what point she is in her menstrual cycle. By charting the length of several cycles she may be able to predict when she will ovulate and use this fact to identify relatively safe times for intercourse. Some physical alterations can also be monitored. For instance, due to hormonal changes, a woman's temperature varies slightly over the cycle and this fact may also be used by couples who are seeking or trying to avoid conception. The problems with the method are that "safe" days are not always safe, and that spontaneity can be hampered.

In *coitus interruptus,* or the withdrawal method, the man withdraws his penis before orgasm. This method is also unreliable. Even if the man's withdrawal is well-timed, leakage and accidental pregnancy can still occur. A further complaint about withdrawal is that it takes the naturalness out of sexual expression and may frustrate both partners.

Prophylactics, or condoms, are devices that fit over the penis. If very carefully used and of good quality, they are highly effective. Moreover, well-made latex prophylactics provide important protection against sexually transmitted disease. Some men complain that condoms detract from spontaneity and blunt their sensations.

Spermicidal *foams, jellies,* and *creams,* if used by the woman in exactly the directed manner, can form a mechanical barrier to conception. These materials are also not as effective as other contraceptive techniques.

A *diaphragm* is a cap inserted by the woman over her cervix which, when coated with spermicidal cream or jelly, prevents conception. The diaphragm is an effective birth control device if carefully fitted by a physician and used properly, but it can cause difficulties for those with certain allergies.

Birth control pills are among the best known of contraceptive devices: The term "the pill" has become a household word. Different kinds of birth control pills are available for women, with the most widely used one containing two synthetic hormones, estrogen and progestin. A prescription is needed for birth control pills, and before pills are prescribed a woman should be given a thorough checkup and a medical history should be taken. If the woman or any of her blood relatives have experienced diseases or conditions associated with the pill—such as blood clots, diabetes, or severe headaches—use may not be recommended.

Birth control pills are highly effective, and many people appreciate their convenience and the fact that their use does not interfere with spontaneity. On the other hand, much attention has been given to the question of the pill's safety and to immediate side effects that may occur, ranging from fatigue and change in sexual desire to severe headaches and high blood pressure. Although the final answers are not yet in, there has been a decrease in the number of prescriptions filled in recent years.

The *vaginal contraceptive sponge,* a synthetic substance two inches in diameter and impregnated with spermicide, is worn over the cervix. Sponges have come on the market relatively recently. Each sponge is inserted only once, though it may be used as many times as desired over a 24-hour period.

The *intrauterine device* (IUD) is a small plastic or metal contraceptive worn in the uterus for an extended period of time. The mechanism by which IUDs work is not known. These devices are highly effective, and although they must be inserted by a physician, normally no action is needed until the next medical appointment, about six to twelve months later. A major complaint about IUDs is that they cause heavier menstruation and, in some, more frequent cramps. IUDs have also been associated with increased risk of pelvic infections (sometimes resulting in infertility) and with a greater likelihood of tubal pregnancy, a dangerous condition in which the fertilized egg is implanted in the fallopian tube instead of in the uterus. Fear of lawsuits has led most manufacturers in the United States to withdraw their IUDs from the market. For illustrations of these methods and their effectiveness rates, see Figure 9.7 and Table 9.3.

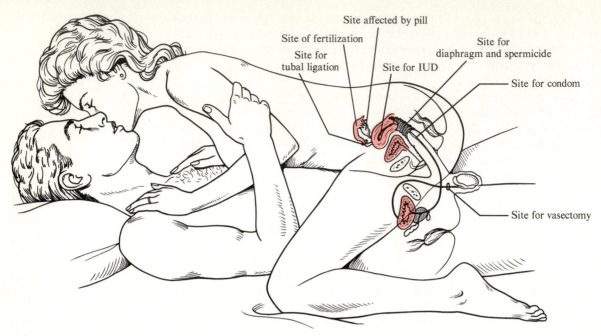

Site of fertilization

Site affected by pill

Site for tubal ligation

Site for IUD

Site for diaphragm and spermicide

Site for condom

Site for vasectomy

Figure 9.7 This drawing shows the site at which various birth control devices operate.

An individual who elects to use birth control must consider how comfortable he or she is with a method; its effectiveness, its cost, its availability, the protection it gives against sexually transmitted disease, its safety, and which person would be using it (a partner's dependability may be an important issue). A problem among young adolescents is that many do not engage in or are incapable of the thinking necessary to recognize the consequences of unprotected sexual activity (Pestrak & Martin, 1985). That partly explains why only 10 to 50 percent (estimates vary) of sexually active female teenagers use regular contraception (Wagner, 1980). Research further shows that teenagers who receive information from their parents or teachers tend to be more responsible and conservative in their sexual behavior (Wagner, 1980; Zelnik & Kim, 1982).

Some people who feel certain they do not want to conceive additional children take steps to ensure birth control that is permanent or usually permanent. In males, the surgical technique of *vasectomy* produces sterility; it can sometimes be reversed. Biologically the process does not affect hormone production or sexual functioning, but some men have an adverse psychological reaction and may, for example, feel some loss of sexual desire. Women may decide on *tubal ligation,* a surgical procedure that cannot be dependably reversed. As with vasectomy, there is no change in hormone production or the ability to function as a partner. Women are less likely to have psychological difficulties following this procedure; some experience increased sexual desire because the fear of pregnancy has been removed. Among married couples who do not plan on more children, 38.2 percent and 23 percent reported using female and male sterilization, respectively (Willis, 1985).

TABLE 9.3 *Effectiveness Rates of Birth Control Methods*

Prescription	Nonprescription	Permanent
The Pill 98%	Vaginal Contraceptive Sponge 90%	Abstinence 100%
Intrauterine Devices 95%	Condoms 90%	Tubal Ligation (women) 99%
Diaphragm 81%	Contraceptive Foam 82%	Vasectomy (men) 99%
	Rhythm Method 76%	

The percentages given above indicate the success rate achieved by couples over the course of a year, assuming a typical amount of care is given. If consistent and special care is taken, a higher success rate can be achieved.

In conclusion, the risk of having sexual intercourse without use of birth control is pregnancy and, depending on the values held by the partners, the prospect of either having a baby or arranging for and coping with an abortion. The outcome can be highly stressful, and is often psychologically damaging to loved ones as well. Individuals must make their own choices about whether to engage in a sexual activity and whether to use birth control. As in other areas of life they will weigh moral, psychological, and practical issues in reaching a personal decision.

SEXUALLY TRANSMITTED DISEASES

The term "venereal"—based on *venus,* the Latin word meaning "love"—quite accurately suggests that those afflicted with a venereal disease or "VD" obtained it through sexual contact. Today venereal diseases are generally referred to as sexually transmitted diseases. The organisms causing these diseases cannot live long outside the human body and therefore are not generally caught from a secondary source. Because such diseases are transmitted sexually, infected individuals usually undergo psychological stress along with the physical pain and discomfort. Further, embarrassment may prevent sufferers from seeking the prompt medical treatment they need, and from immediately informing recent partners about the problem so they can seek treatment.

Some three decades ago it was thought that sexually transmitted diseases (STDs) in the United States were under control. The prevalence had dropped sharply as a result of penicillin and other antibiotics and, if infections were treated promptly, the STDs could do no irreversible damage. However, circumstances have changed. At this point in the development of medicine, there are STDs that cause irremediable damage and that are life-threatening.

As the media have correctly reported, STDs afflict great numbers of people, particularly among the younger population. In fact, it had been said that after the common cold, gonorrhea was the second-ranking communicable disease in the United States (Stewart et al., 1979). Since then, chlamydia has passed gonorrhea in the number of cases, annually. Many factors account for the breadth of the STD problem, such as greater sexual freedom, many people's lack of initial awareness that they have a disease, unwillingness to inform others, and new, penicillin-resistant strains of some diseases.

Sexually transmitted diseases can and do attack people of all ages and socioeconomic backgrounds. They can be contracted during homosexual as well as heterosexual activities. As public health officials have pointed out, the people least likely to be infected are those who have no sexual relations or who have relations exclusively with one person.

Following are brief discussions of the most common sexually transmitted diseases. *Gonorrhea,* commonly called "clap," infects over one million Americans annually and new strains, treatable but resistant to the standard penicillin treatment, have developed (Brooks & Donegan, 1985). Once gonorrhea is contracted, medical intervention is necessary to rid the body of the disease. Early treatment is highly effective but if the disease is left untreated for a few weeks, the gonorrhea bacteria enter the blood, cause fever, and can threaten permanent damage to the joints. A problem with this disease is that most women and some infected men may note no symptoms. Therefore, it is suggested that those at risk ask to be tested for gonorrhea during regular medical examinations.

Syphilis, a disease some think was introduced to this continent by Christopher Columbus and his crew, eventually killed the man credited with discovering America. In 1943, penicillin was identified as an effective cure for syphilis, which today no longer poses the life-threatening consequences for the population as a whole that it once did.

Exposure to syphilis results in contraction of the disease 50 percent of the time (Taub, 1976). During the first two years following infection the disease is most easily spread but also is most easily cured. Because symptoms come in phases that disappear without treatment, people are tempted to ignore or discount them. However, without medication, the unchecked disease enters a latency period lasting for months or years. Eventually, sometimes decades later, permanent damage is done: a person may be crippled or disfigured and may die from the disease.

Genital herpes represents a serious health problem, infecting perhaps a half million or more people annually. This virus-caused acute disease produces small, usually painful fluid-filled blisters on the skin that may first tingle. Genital herpes can also produce fever and other infection-related symptoms, special problems during pregnancy, and an increased risk of cervical cancer.

While pain-relieving medications are available, no effective cure has yet been found for the disease, and it is highly contagious when in an active stage. Because genital herpes is incurable, many who contract it naturally experience it as a crisis, going through stages of shock, disbelief, anger, and perhaps, self-imposed isolation and hopelessness. In many cities, self-help groups of herpes victims aid one another in successfully coping with the crisis. The focus is on dealing with negative feelings, on informing partners about the disease, and on identifying when it is and is not contagious.

Chlamydia is the most common STD in the United States. The Centers for Disease Control in Atlanta estimated that in 1986 chlamydia, a bacterial disease transmitted during intercourse, caused more new cases than AIDS, syphilis, herpes, and gonorrhea together. Sometimes called the "silent disease," chlamydia bacteria can live unnoticed in the genital tracts of men and women for years, doing harm without causing noticeable symptoms. In fact, 70 percent of women with the infection have no early symptoms. If left untreated, it can cause sterility in both sexes and, in women, additional serious problems such as pelvic inflammatory disease (PID). Chlamydia can be successfully treated with antibiotics, and regular testing for chlamydia is suggested for those at risk.

Acquired Immune Deficiency Syndrome or *AIDS* is a relatively newly identified STD caused by the Human Immune Deficiency Virus (HIV) which was isolated in laboratories in Paris and Washington, D.C. in 1984. HIV causes AIDS by attacking a certain type of white blood cells (helper T-cells), thereby disabling the body's own immune system and making it less able to fight (in its usual efficient way) threats to the individual's health (Douglas & Pinsky, 1987). HIV also attacks other cells, including those in the central nervous system (Khouri, 1988).

Symptoms of AIDS include unexplained low fever for more than 10 days, prolonged weakness, swollen glands, soaking night sweats, unexplained weight loss and, in time, psychological disorders caused by damage to the nervous system. People with AIDS are susceptible to opportunistic diseases, ones that a healthy person's immune system would easily control. These disorders, such as Kaposi's sarcoma (a cancer) and Pneumocystis carinii (pneumonia produced by a protozoan), cause death in many AIDS patients.

Of the people infected by HIV, only a small percentage have AIDS. Most are asymptomatic, meaning the virus has not made them ill, or suffer from the AIDS-Related Complex (ARC), a milder form of infection that is typically not fatal. HIV-infected individuals who are asymptomatic or who have ARC may develop AIDS at a later date.

Blood testing can be done to determine whether an individual has been infected by the virus. A negative result indicates that no HIV antibodies were found in the blood. However, that result must be interpreted with caution as it typically takes 14 weeks after the individual is infected before the antibodies can be found in the blood. In some cases it may take as long as six months. A positive result suggests that the antibodies are present, that the person has been infected, and that he or she must recognize that he could infect others. Two different tests are conducted to establish a positive result.

TABLE 9.4   *Transmission of HIV*

Given that no cure for AIDS has been discovered, the need for information about how to avoid being infected by HIV—the virus which causes AIDS—is that much greater.

HIV infection is spread by sexual contact, needle sharing, or, less commonly, through transfusion of infected blood or its components. The risk of acquiring the infection is increased by having multiple sexual partners, either homosexual or heterosexual, and sharing of needles among those using illicit drugs. HIV may be transmitted from infected mother to infant before, during, or shortly after birth (probably through breast milk).

AIDS is difficult to catch, even among people at highest risk for the disease. The risk of transmitting AIDS from daily contact at work, school, or at home apparently is nonexistent. In virtually all cases, direct sexual contact or the sharing of IV drug needles has led to the illness.

Source: "Coping with AIDS," The National Institute of Mental Health, 1986.

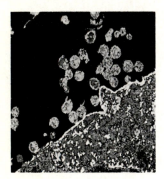

The HIV—which can cause AIDS—attacking white blood cells.

AIDS has potentially devastating psychological consequences for its victims (National Institute of Mental Health, U.S. Dept. of Health and Human Services, 1986):

70% of all people with AIDS die within 2 years of diagnosis.

90% of all adults with AIDS are in the prime of life—between the ages of 20 and 49—when people are not commonly prepared to deal psychologically with imminent death.

Few other diseases produce as many losses; loss of physical strength, mental acuity, self-sufficiency, social roles, income and savings, housing, and the emotional support of loved ones. Often, self-esteem also fades in the wake of such catastrophic losses (p. 1).

A motivated scientific community is searching for antiviral drugs to cure AIDS and medication to restore the damaged parts of the immune system of those infected. At this writing, however, there was no effective treatment program available.

In contrast to other STDs, which are curable or, at least, controllable, AIDS is a terminal illness. Sexually active individuals ought to take the responsibility of protecting themselves by being aware of how the virus is transmitted (see Table 9.4) and by following the recommendations developed by the National Institute of Mental Health, U. S. Department of Health and Human Services (1986) (see Table 9.5).

The latest information on steps people can take to protect themselves from AIDS is probably available at campus health facilities and through a variety of community outlets. Common sense, along with the latest information, can provide lifesaving protection. For instance, if one does not plan to abstain, it pays to be assertive in asking potential partners about their past activities and to reduce one's risk by engaging in safer sexual activity. If one decides to make a spontaneous decision, it is important that at the moment of decision about sexual activity a person be able to apply his or her judgment

TABLE 9.5   *Recommendations for the General Public for the Prevention of AIDS*

▶ Don't have sex with multiple partners or with persons who have had multiple partners (including prostitutes). The more partners you have, the greater your risk of contracting AIDS.

▶ Obviously, avoiding sex with persons with AIDS, members of the risk groups,* or persons who have had a positive result on the HIV antibody test would eliminate the risk of sexually transmitted infection by the virus. However, if you do have sex with a person you think is infected, protect yourself by taking appropriate precautions to prevent contact with the person's body fluids. ("Body fluids" include blood, semen, urine, feces, saliva, and women's genital secretions.)
　　—Use latex condoms, which may reduce the possibility of transmitting the virus.
　　—Avoid practices that may injure body tissues (for example, anal intercourse).
　　—Avoid oral-genital contact.
　　—Avoid open-mouthed, intimate kissing.

▶ Don't use intravenous drugs. If you do, don't share needles or syringes.

*Persons at increased risk of HIV infection include: homosexual and bisexual men; present or past intravenous drug users; persons with clinical or laboratory evidence of infection, such as signs or symptoms compatible with AIDS or AIDS-related illnesses; persons born in countries where heterosexual transmission is thought to play a major role in the spread of HIV (for example, Haiti and Central African countries); male or female prostitutes and their sex partners; sex partners of infected persons or persons at increased risk; persons with hemophilia who have received clotting factor products. . . .
Source: "Coping with AIDS," The National Institute of Mental Health, 1986.

and knowledge without being handicapped by the effects of alcohol or recreational drugs. However, the majority of sexually active students sampled at a southern California university were not taking care of themselves in these ways. Although knowledgeable about AIDS and safer sexual practices, less than one-fifth reported using condoms on a regular basis (Baldwin & Baldwin, 1988).

RAPE

Without doubt, one of the most stressful sexual situations is that of a violent assault or rape. The vast majority of rapes involve a man's assault on a woman, although homosexual rapes occur, and there have been instances of women being charged with raping men. Law enforcement agencies report that the incidence of rape is increasing. Between 1977 and 1986 the official count in the United States increased by 42.4 percent (U. S. Bureau of Census, 1987). The official count each year is undoubtedly low because rape is one of the most underreported crimes (U.S. Dept. of Justice, Uniform Crime Reports, 8/82).

Although the most frequent victim is between 15 and 24 years of age (Nadelson & Notman, 1985), people of all ages are raped. Further, not all rapes occur on dark streets or after forced entry to the victim's home; they are often committed by assailants known to the victim. The most usual rapist is a male in his early 20s, generally of below-average intellectual ability, and raised by psychologically weak parents in a deprived neighborhood. Although it is commonplace to view rape as a crime of lust, most psychologists regard it more as an act of hostility and violence in which the often-intoxicated perpetrator makes a futile attempt to demonstrate his overpowering masculinity.

Rape

The following is a personal account of one woman's experiences. Her report brings to light the meaning of rape in terms much different than statistics. You can sense the fear, anger, and other emotions that developed and endured in her as she weathered the episode. You can see why rape is an act of violence, although it happens to involve sexual activity. You can see why many women need long-term support to overcome a rape and its aftermath.

I was awakened at 7 A.M. by a creak. When I opened my eyes, I saw at the end of my bed a man wielding MY butcher knife and wearing MY pantyhose over his face.

Fear and instinct made me scream as loud as I could. Although my bedroom window was open, no one heard me. The man jumped on me, held the knife to my neck and put a pillow over my face.

It hadn't occurred to me yet what he wanted. I was hoping he'd just take our money, T.V.'s and stereos, but no such luck. "Shut up and cooperate or else this knife will be inside you," he threatened.

Again instinct took over as I did the only thing I knew: I prayed, "Lord, please get me through this alive and help me keep calm." From then on my fear lessened and common sense took over.

Still holding the pillow over my face and wearing my pantyhose, he lifted my night gown and removed my panties. He began kissing my breasts and fondling me. Since he was having difficulty achieving an erection, he made me perform oral sex. Once erect, he entered me and ejaculated quickly. It seemed like forever, but so far only 10 minutes had elapsed.

He sat and talked to me like we were old friends and allowed me to smoke a cigarette. Instead of revealing I was afraid of him, I answered his questions about the scars on my stomach. I knew the more I talked to him, the more information I would get and the more relaxed he became, the better my chance for escape. Because he was shaking more than I most of the time, I figured he was inexperienced.

After a few minutes of small talk, he was ready to try it again. When he couldn't get an erection, he again made me perform orally and subjected me to cunnilingus. When oral sex didn't work, he said he wanted me to enjoy it as much as he. I suggested I would enjoy it more if he took my pantyhose off his face.

This suggestion so irritated him that he held the knife to my neck again. HIS ANGER AROUSED HIM, and making sure the pillow was over my face, he entered me again.

Whenever I got the chance I looked for identifying birthmarks and clothes. I noted two moles on his groin, brown bikini underwear, white corduroy pants with stains on the knees, and beat up brown deck shoes. The two moles proved most conclusive when I later had to identify him to the police.

Finally, he made me go in the downstairs bathroom and shut the door. I kept waiting for him to lock me in or tie me up, but all he did was leave.

Source: "The Reality Behind the Headline of Rape," edited by Jeanne Marlowe from the victim's journal and personal interview. *Columbus Single Scene,* March 1986. Reprinted with permission.

When I finally opened the door and came out, I looked around the house to make sure he wasn't hiding, and locked the door and window where he'd broken in. I called a male friend but was hurt that he didn't want to come over. He wanted to stay out of the situation but finally agreed to come for a few minutes.

After trying to talk me into calling the police, he left. I didn't want to call because I thought there was no evidence and I had heard the police make the woman feel at fault for being raped.

Alone and afraid, knowing no one else to call, I decided to report a breaking and entering. When the policeman arrived, however, I broke down and told him I had been raped. He immediately called for more police and detectives.

Six more police and three detectives gathered the evidence I thought wasn't there: fingerprints, beer cans, and cigarette butts he'd dropped outside my window.

I was taken to a rape center. Then I was told to go to the police station.

I didn't get home until 2:30 P.M., when I took a shower and tried to get rid of the smell of my rapist and his beer. I continued to smell him for four days, and even now I can't stand to smell beer.

Supposedly safe at home, I became more frightened than I had been during the assault. My roommate and I walked around carrying knives. Every man who walked or drove by our apartment seemed to fit the rapist's description.

My roommate and I knew we couldn't sleep unless we got help. She called a male friend who agreed to spend the night. I figured once the rapist was behind bars my life would go on as usual. Wrong! First of all, I couldn't tell my parents and that really bothered me. We are very close, but I was (and still am) afraid they could not handle knowing the truth. Second, I had nightmares every night and could not sleep. Third, feelings of guilt, bitterness, and depression accompanied my continuing fear. Fourth, I dreaded having to endure a trial.

Although the prosecutor and the police were very helpful, even commending me for keeping my head and acquiring evidence, I'm fearful about recounting my experience to a jury and facing cross examination.

After reading this description consider the following activities:

1. Learn more about how to help a rape victim. Check your campus library to see what material they have on this topic.
2. Make inquiries about what services are available to rape victims in your community. Try to determine whether the services available are adequate, and whether enough resources are invested in rape-prevention programs. ▲

"Acquaintance rape" or "date rape" occurs when an acquaintance forcibly imposes himself on a woman. To begin the process of assessing this problem, Koss (1983) administered a survey to a representative sample of over 2,000 women at a midwestern state university. She found that 13 percent of the respondents had been physically threatened or forced, at one point in their lives, to engage in intercourse against their wills. Somewhat more than half (57 percent) of this 13 percent saw themselves as rape victims (acknowledged victims) while the others did not define themselves as such (unacknowledged victims). Among the unacknowledged victims, 76 percent had been assaulted by a man they had been seeing romantically. In another study of over 6,000 students at 33 campuses, Koss (1987) found similar results. Date rape can produce as much trauma as a rape committed by a stranger.

It is not easy for a person to come to terms with being a victim of any crime. This is especially true in the case of rape. The woman experiences a variety of painful emotions: She may feel violated, angry, fearful, and "used." Added to this she may have reactions of embarrassment, guilt, self-doubt, and concern about whether others will somehow blame her for the incident. The latter thought leads some victims to keep the rape secret. This decision deprives them of the opportunity to express their feelings to others, which is generally the healthiest course of action, and leaves them alone to bear the burden of resolving intense and sometimes confused emotions.

When a woman does reveal that she has been raped, others in her life can help by offering abundant comfort and support. Unfortunately, these are not always the reactions she receives. She may subtly be blamed for the incident, made to feel guilty, or regarded as having been tainted by the rape. Some people still hold the sexual stereotype that a woman who was raped somehow "brought on" the incident herself. If a rape victim encounters this reaction from those she counted on and feels she is not getting needed support, she can seek both immediate and longer-term assistance from a rape crisis, mental health, or college counseling center.

The distress that a woman experiences immediately after a rape may block from her mind thoughts of the physical repercussions of her experience. However, as soon as possible she should arrange for a dependable, supportive person to go with her to a hospital in order to establish that there are no internal injuries. She also will need to take tests to determine that the rape did not cause pregnancy or the acquisition of sexually transmitted diseases. Finally, if she can identify the assailant, she may wish to consider the possibility of legal prosecution.

CHANGING SEXUAL MORES: WHERE ARE WE NOW?

Our society has clearly come a long way from the days when a woman's leg was euphemistically referred to as a "limb," when couples were ignorant of sexual matters before their honeymoon night, and when women's sexuality was seen as nonexistent or, if existent, as immoral or depraved. The sexual revolution has generated a view among most people that sexual enjoyment between loving partners is natural, desirable, and a factor that helps cement the relationship.

Some have pointed out that the so-called changes have been more in attitude than in behavior, that people are much less sexually experimental than the media and some popular books would have us believe. There is still a wide range of sexual values, and these differ among different religious, racial, socioeconomic, and regional groups. The multitude of values and attitudes surrounding the subject has brought some young people to a state of confusion and difficulty in working out a personal code of sexual ethics. In fact, some people undergo a situational life crisis that they cannot easily resolve with the conflicting values and beliefs presented by parents, peers, and society in general. The new sexual freedom has brought other costs as well. Some people engage in sex because they feel it is "expected" of them. Men and women, having been fed a diet of high expectations about sex, become distressed when experience does not match fantasy, or worry about their "performance." And now sexual activity involves new health risks.

However, it is still probably true that a sexually repressive upbringing does the most harm in limiting later sexual enjoyment and creating various sexual dysfunctions. When children engage in sexual exploration, as all do, parents who make them feel strongly ashamed and guilty are setting the stage for later conflicted feelings about sexuality. Adults who have repressed or suppressed their sexual desires for many years, or have repeatedly experienced anxiety or other negative emotions in conjunction with sexual feelings, may have difficulty enjoying sex even with someone whom they deeply love and trust. In this area most would say that the sexual revolution has been beneficial: Parents' growing belief that sexuality is healthy and natural has reduced the number of people who grow up burdened with intense internal conflicts concerning sex.

Those who grow up feeling comfortable with their own sexuality, and those who have achieved greater comfort through therapy or counseling, find sex to be an avenue not only for pleasure but for self-expression and intimacy. In the context of a mutual commitment free from anxiety, exploitation, and destructive game-playing, partners can enjoy discovering each other's preferences and creatively expressing their sexuality. Of course, a sexual experience cannot be divorced from its context, so the general state of a relationship will affect its sexual aspects. One relationship in which this is strongly true is marriage, a topic that will be discussed in the next chapter.

Human Sexuality: Attitudes and Knowledge

1. Where did your attitudes and knowledge about sexuality come from? In the space below, rate the sources in order of importance (numbering 1–7 in each column).

	Attitudes	*Knowledge*
Parents		
Friends		
Church		
School		
Reading material		
Siblings or cousins		
Other (list)		

2. List two important changes in attitudes toward sexuality you would like to see take place in:

   Your male friends

   Your female friends

   Your dating partners

   Yourself

   Other adults

   Society ▲

SUMMARY

1. Coming to terms with one's sexuality is an important part of adjustment to adulthood.

2. The work of pioneer scientists like Kinsey and Masters and Johnson provided society with statistical, medical, and scientific data about sexual behavior. Kinsey and his coworkers reported on the frequency with which men and women engaged in certain activities. Masters and Johnson's major contribution was in describing the physiological changes that take place in the human body during sexual activities.

3. Although the differences between the male and female reproductive organs are self-evident, the great similarities between them are not.

4. Masters and Johnson noted four phases that both men and women pass through during the sexual response cycle: excitement, plateau, orgasm, and resolution.

5. There are many forms of sexual expression. Nocturnal orgasm is experienced by most men and some women; masturbation is commonplace for adults of both sexes. Petting is also widely practiced. Sexual intercourse can be described as premarital, marital, extramarital, or postmarital. Married couples today report a greater frequency of intercourse than did couples in years past.

6. Homosexuality is no longer regarded as a mental disorder by psychologists. However, social stigmas still cause many people to conceal their homosexual orientation. Research has shown that homosexuality is not an "all-or-nothing" sexual orientation; a sizable proportion of Americans reported having experienced some attraction toward a person of the same sex.

7. People are sexual beings across the entire life span, beginning in infancy with the child's desire to be touched and stroked. Children later explore their own and others' bodies and show curiosity about sexual matters. Puberty brings dramatic physical changes and an increased interest in sex; sexual activity is greatest during young adulthood. Men and women's degrees of sexual interest vary with age, but well-attuned partners can adjust to the differences and lead a sexually active life well into the seventies and beyond.

8. Two causes of sexual dysfunction are performance anxiety and the holding of restrictive attitudes about sexual activity. Dysfunctions fall into one of the following categories: sexual desire disorders, sexual arousal disorders, orgasm disorders, or sexual pain disorders. Because of progress in developing sex therapy treatment programs, as well as the effectiveness of psychotherapy in some cases, these difficulties can often be treated successfully.

9. An increasing number of people in our society use birth control methods. Most common are the rhythm method, withdrawal, prophylactics, spermicidal preparations, the diaphragm, birth control pills, and the intrauterine device. Some people take surgical actions— vasectomy or tubal ligation—that cannot always be reversed.

10. Sexually transmitted diseases (STD) afflict great numbers of people yearly. Early symptoms are often slight, so diagnosis by a qualified health professional is crucial if the disease is to be treated before it causes physical damage to the infected person. Gonorrhea and syphilis can be cured if treated sufficiently early, but herpes cannot and may therefore cause enduring stress in those who become infected. The bacteria causing chlamydia, the most common STD, can do harm without causing noticeable symptoms.

11. Acquired Immune Deficiency Syndrome or AIDS is a relatively newly identified STD. Most people who develop AIDS are in the prime of their lives and most die within two years after the disease is diagnosed.

12. Although it is commonplace to view rape as a crime of lust, most psychologists regard it as an act of hostility and violence. A woman who has been raped can best come to grips with her emotions by seeking support from friends and others (including a rape crisis center or mental health facility, if necessary), and by discarding any belief that she might have contributed to the crime.

13. The sexual revolution has brought benefits but costs as well. Overall there appears to be an increase in sexual enjoyment, though many have experienced confusion and value conflicts.

SUGGESTED READINGS

Barbach, L. (1976). *For yourself.* Garden City, New York: Doubleday. An excellent discussion of female orgasm, masturbation, and sexuality at various points in a woman's life span.

The Boston Women's Health Book Collective. (1984). *The new our bodies, ourselves.* New York: Simon & Schuster. An easy-to-read feminist reference book covering topics ranging from anatomy and the physiology of reproduction to health care, childbearing, nutrition, birth control, and rape and self-defense.

Craft, M and Craft A. (1982). *Sex and the mentally handicapped.* (rev. ed.) Boston: Routledge & Kegan Paul. The volume provides a positive, thoughtful exploration of an important, often neglected topic. Myths are identified and suggestions made for developing programs for the mentally retarded in love, health, and sex education.

Diamant, Louis. (1987). *Male and female homosexuality.* New York: Hemisphere Publishing Co. This volume examines homosexuality from the psychoanalytic, behavioral, humanistic, and psychobiological perspectives and presents a theory of normal homosexuality.

Hatcher, R., Guest, F., Josephs, N., Stewart, G., Stewart, F., & Kowai, D. (1982). *It's your choice*. New York: Irvington Publishers. After explaining the woman's cycle of fertility, this volume provides detailed information about each birth control method, and its advantages and disadvantages.

Ladas, A. K., Whipple, B., Perry, J. (1982). *The G spot and other recent discoveries about human sexuality*. New York: Holt, Rinehart & Winston. This paperback discusses some controversial ideas about the human sexual response.

Masters, W., Johnson, V., Kolodny, R. (1982, 1986). *Masters and Johnson on sex and human loving*. Boston: Little, Brown. These well-known researchers share information and practical advice that might assist readers in enriching their personal relationships.

Offit, A. (1981). *Night thoughts: reflections of a sex therapist*. New York: Congdon and Lattes. A psychiatrist discusses her views about human sexuality and the type of problems she has helped people deal with in the therapy office.

Westheimer, R. (1983). *Dr. Ruth's guide to good sex*. New York: Warner. Dr. Ruth, in her unique fashion, covers a wide range of issues in human sexuality.

Zilbergeld, B. (1978). *Male sexuality: A guide to sexual fulfillment*. Boston: Little, Brown. This excellent book deals with male sexuality, exploring it from both the physical and psychological perspective.

Marriage, Family, and Alternative Life-Styles

- Stages in the life of a family, beginning with the pre-family courtship stage and continuing through the retirement years

- The persistence of the family as a dominant social institution, various roles enacted by family members, and how these roles are changing

- Factors that are predictors of marital success, and the variety of marriage types—ranging from conflict-filled to "vital"—that couples may regard as satisfying

- The similarity of parents' goals in child-rearing, contrasted with the diversity of the styles they employ

- Nontraditional family forms and life-styles that are becoming more common, such as the single-parent family, the stepfamily, cohabitation, and the decision to remain single

- The kinds of conflict families encounter, ranging from everyday arguments to divorce

As Chris stared at her textbook, she daydreamed about the next night's dinner back home. She had accomplished a lot since that day in September when she first left for college. She was proud of having demonstrated she could do the work, live independently, and stick to her budget. Chris felt like a different person and wondered how her family would react to the change.

At 4:00 P.M. the next day, Chris arrived in her hometown, where she was met by her mother and sister, Jean. After an exchange of kisses, they began a nonstop conversation that continued through dinner preparations. Chris's father and 10-year-old brother Billy came home at about 5:30 and greeted Chris with the traditional "family bear-hug."

During dinner Chris's family showed great interest in her college life. Clearly, they were delighted to have her back again, even if only for a few days. She was somewhat disappointed that her parents kidded her about boyfriends at college with "Have you found a replacement for Rick?" and seemed less attentive when she discussed her studies. Still, Chris felt a special closeness that she sensed the others were experiencing too. Even Billy, who tended to be restless, stayed at the table and contributed to the conversation.

The next morning Chris knew she was back home when Billy asked her to wash the breakfast dishes for him. It was his job, it had been for years, but he said he had promised to meet some friends. Chris agreed to do the dishes, feeling amusement rather than the resentment she had in the past. "Some things never change," she thought.

Later Chris found that other things had not changed: First she and Jean got into an all-out fight. Less than a year apart, they had always competed, though their competition had shifted from battles over dolls and toys to conflicts over who was going to use the car. Second, after supper, when Chris told her parents she was going out with Rick and would be home by 2:00 A.M., her mother frowned. "That's too late. You'll have to be back earlier."

This woman is saying goodbye to her mother before boarding the bus that will carry her to New York and summer school. This sophomore—like Chris and a good many other college students—will experience a mix of emotions as the bus pulls away: relief, excitement, and a touch of "home sickness."

"You know Mom, I've been without a curfew at school for the past two months. You're treating me like a kid." Then Chris appealed to her father for support, but he stood by his wife. Chris was irritated by the restriction but offered to be back by midnight. Chris' reaction to this interchange surprised her. In high school she had sometimes accepted and sometimes rebelled against her parents' curfew, but always felt they had the right to impose it. Now she wondered about their authority. That evening, however, she *chose* not to upset them and came home on time.

On the way back to campus Chris thought about what had happened during her visit. After reviewing the events, she drew several conclusions:

1. Her family was special to her partly because all the members had played and would continue to play a unique role in her life, and she in theirs.

2. Because she and her family had a common history and were committed to each other for life, there was usually "instant meaning" in shared time and "instant interest" in what each person had to say.

3. When she went home there was a tendency for her and the others to fall into old patterns of relating to each other. This included both healthy and unhealthy patterns.

Going Home Again

Do parts of what Chris encountered sound familiar? After being away for a few months or more, most of us find part of the experience of going home enjoyable, predictable, and satisfying. However, another part of the experience is often discomforting because home never seems the same as it used to be. The universality of this paradox was well captured by Thomas Wolfe when he observed, "You can't go home again." Implied in his statement is the fact that what you experience when you revisit is different from what you recall. "Home" has changed, and so have you.

1. If you have been away from your family for an extended time period, how were things different when you returned? (If you have not been away, imagine what it would be like.)
2. Have your relationships with your parents changed since you began college? If so, how?
3. Have your relationships with your siblings changed since you began college? If so, how?
4. Look ahead ten years. List three ways in which you think you and your parents will relate to one another differently.
5. Look ahead twenty years. List three ways in which you think you and your parents will relate to one another differently. List three ways in which you think you and your siblings will relate to one another differently. ▲

4. It would be possible to make changes in the unhealthy patterns. Chris resolved to stop competing with Jean and decided to work at developing adult-to-adult relationships with her parents.

As this vignette illustrates, Chris is in the midst of an important developmental transition: that is, growing from dependence on her parents into independent adulthood. Meeting this challenge means giving up the role of full-time child-member of her **family of origin** (the family in which she was raised) in favor of the responsibilities of adulthood, probably (though not necessarily) including finding a mate with whom to build a **family of procreation** (a family in which she will have the role of mother). Chris' parents and siblings are adjusting to the changed family as well.

This chapter deals with the family, how it changes, the purposes it serves, and how people adjust to life as a family member. To understand family life, we must examine it with a life-span developmental perspective. If we took a snapshot look at the family at one point in time, we would fare no better than scientists trying to learn about the caterpillar by studying a photo of a butterfly. Specifically, we would miss noting how families and their members cope with the challenges they meet as the years pass, and how they grow from these encounters.

Family of Origin
The family in which one is reared.

Family of Procreation
The family in which one is a parent.

Marriage, Family, and Alternative Life-styles

449

SIX STAGES IN FAMILY LIFE

Six stages in family life have been identified by Lewis (1979): courtship, the early marriage stage, the early parenthood stage, the adolescent children stage, the empty nest stage, and the postretirement stage. Here we trace the stages, beginning with the courting period of the future spouses, emphasizing the challenges faced at each transition point and the resulting developmental tasks that must be addressed.

Courtship Stage

The first stage of the family is courtship. During it, even before the two people involved know they are destined to become a family, they are developing ways of relating to each other that will provide a foundation for later closeness. The developmental tasks of this stage include building a mutually satisfying relationship; creating "rules" about how the two will operate as a couple (for example, who takes responsibility for planning shared time); fostering a healthy level of independence from both sets of parents; and once marriage is thought to be a possibility, making a decision about whether the person is an appropriate choice for a mate.

Problems in the relationship will develop if the tasks of this stage are not adequately accomplished. For example, Scott surprised Wendy with an engagement ring for Christmas. After six months of dating, she was not ready for it, nor was she expecting it. However, flattered and proud, she accepted the ring, and they set a wedding date. As June and their wedding neared, Wendy began having doubts about Scott and his bossiness. She was particularly displeased when he limited her participation in planning the honeymoon, claiming that with their budget and his greater knowledge of travel, he should make the decisions. But she was afraid of the embarrassment delaying the wedding would cause and she hoped to "remold" Scott after they were married. Because the pair did not do the work of the courtship stage well, they experienced difficulties early in their marriage.

Early Marriage Stage

At this time spouses come to view their "family of procreation" as the primary base in their lives. When someone asks them, "How's the family?" they are more likely to talk about their spouse than parents and siblings. Living together full time, in the same quarters, and with a lifelong commitment, calls for certain adjustments. A key task is continuing to develop "rules" that the two will use to guide their interactions. The rules specify how power is to be shared, how decisions will be made, what personal feelings are acceptable to discuss, ways of showing closeness and obtaining privacy in the home, how the two will budget and use money, what their social life and relations with the extended family will be like, and so on. Jointly acceptable rules allow them to function smoothly as a couple and, at the same time, enable each spouse to meet personal needs. Most of the rule-building is done informally and without

full awareness, as the two interact, divide responsibilities, and evolve patterns regarding their use of time. However, sometimes explicit discussion is needed to clarify matters.

Soon after their honeymoon, Jim and Ellen had to face the "what-to-do-on-Sunday" problem, as they called it, and had to figure out a solution that met both their needs. Specifically, Jim's family of origin had always gotten up early on Sunday, attended church together, and held a weekly family brunch that began at 1:00 P.M. sharp. In contrast, Ellen's family slept late on Sundays, and as people woke, they fixed their own breakfasts and read the paper. After a thorough discussion, they agreed to test an every-third-week system: One Sunday they would spend alone doing whatever each felt like, the next with Jim's family, and the third with Ellen's. After a two-month test period, they agreed the arrangement was working well and, in fact, used it for years.

Early Parenthood Stage

The arrival of an infant can provide a couple with great satisfaction, an opportunity for personal growth, and a chance to extend their love to a third person, the new member of their family. It also adds new responsibilities. The spouses must cope with fatigue, the loss of leisure time, and a reduction in the amount of money available for "extras" (particularly if one mate leaves a paying job to carry child-care responsibilities). The family of three must adjust to these realities and plan a new allocation of financial resources. At this stage spouses often overlook their one-to-one relationship: They begin ignoring each other more, or take their love for granted. However, the relationship can continue to thrive if they invest energy in keeping it fresh. As additional children are born, issues of time, money, and parent-children and children-children relationships require continual discussion and effort.

Adolescent Children Stage

As the years pass, children reach their teens and their parents become older and usually more comfortable financially. At this point, a challenge for the children is to begin the process of becoming independent. Such a transformation is demanding to all parties. Adolescents have much to learn, as do their parents who must adopt new ways of relating to their offspring. Some parents have difficulty coping with the fact that their children now possess adult bodies and perhaps an interest in "adult" activities, like sex, drinking, and experimentation with drugs, experiences that can have dangerous outcomes. At this stage, growth is best fostered if parents acknowledge that the nature of their relationship to their children must change, and begin responding to them differently, offering them the adult responsibilities they can handle. In most families adolescents gain parental respect if they demonstrate sound judgment in carrying out delegated responsibilities and in exercising the greater freedoms that are allowed.

Often parents are more hesitant than teenagers in initiating this transfer of responsibilities. The example at the beginning of the chapter shows parents' resistance to the relinquishing of decision-making authority. Chris handled the curfew situation effectively in that she realized her own freedom but also felt a responsibility not to upset her parents. Conflicts that arise over such transfers of authority and responsibility are best handled if parents and adolescents examine the rationale behind the demands being made and strive to be more understanding of one another.

Empty Nest Stage

As children move out of their parents' home to establish their own, family relationships must again be redefined. In establishing their own residences and in beginning their own families grown children can most effectively assume their new role if they guard against dependency and relate to their parents as sources of mature, adult-to-adult support.

The empty nest stage presents a developmental challenge to the parents. With children no longer in their home, they must adjust to changed circumstances. The work needed to maintain the household is lessened, and this gives them free time to use in other ways. Although they will probably have fewer financial obligations, they may be commanding the highest salaries they have ever earned.

Some women and men experience difficulty with the empty nest. It may cause them to worry about how much of their lives has passed or about how to fill hours that had formerly been spent with their children. However, many wives and husbands view the empty nest stage favorably. They enjoy a less structured life-style and appreciate the fact that they have more time to spend with each other and to pursue work and hobbies.

The Smiths returned home after their youngest daughter's wedding, happy about how well it had gone, but a little afraid of entering what now loomed as a very empty house. They went right to the kitchen and made two overstuffed pastrami sandwiches. Mrs. Smith joked, "We were so busy talking that we never got near the buffet at the reception. I wonder if we can get a refund from the caterer." Instead of finding themselves lonely, they sat up half the night talking about plans for their "new life." The Smiths, like many couples (Campbell, 1981), would have little difficulty in finding new life-satisfactions now that they had successfully completed the child-rearing phase of their lives.

Postretirement Stage

This stage can be one of great fulfillment because, with neither partner working, couples have much time to share. However, during this period some couples face health problems, economic stress, fear of becoming dependent on their children, and worry about having enough ways to fill their time.

The challenges of this stage include accepting and adapting to the reality of growing older. Moreover, differences in the partners' ages and in the problems brought on by aging may force changes in their accustomed relationship. If a husband loses some capabilities first, the wife may need to assume them. For example, if his eyesight fails, she will have to do all the driving. Finally, when one partner dies, the other faces the challenge of living alone or making other suitable housing arrangements.

Besides this method of dividing the stages in family life, social scientists have proposed a number of other methods. For instance, McGoldrick and Carter's (1982) sequence begins with a stage in which the unattached young adult is "between families" and working toward separating from the parents and establishing a career. Duvall's (1977) begins with the married couple and has eight stages.

ADJUSTMENT TO FAMILY LIFE

If you were asked to describe your family, you would probably discuss its members first and next say something about the atmosphere in the home. After that, however, you might find the task difficult. Why? Because the task requires describing the family as an entity of its own, a unit that has particular challenges it must meet.

Understanding the personalities of its members only gives a partial picture. To complete it, we need to know what happens between and among the people, their joint hopes and aspirations, and so forth. In a sense, families obey a law of physics: "The total is equal to more than the sum of the parts." The family grows out of all aspects of its members and becomes something larger; to describe and understand its wholeness, certain theoretical concepts are needed.

To build an understanding of that complex social institution called the family, social scientists from many disciplines have used a variety of theoretical perspectives. Drawing from several of these, we will discuss concepts, models, and data that have proved helpful to people in understanding the experiences they had with their families of origin—experiences that often reappear later, in some form, in their families of procreation.

Basic Tasks of the Family

A great multitude of different societies are now, or once were, in existence. Each and every one of them has had to confront and independently solve the problem of enabling human beings to live and work together productively and harmoniously. The family has played a key role in solving this problem. In 1949, Murdock published a classic statement arguing that the **nuclear family** (husband, wife, and children) is a universal social grouping among human beings. He wrote:

Nuclear Family
A term used to describe a family unit consisting of only parents and their children.

> Either as the sole prevailing form of the family or as the basic unit from which more complex familial forms are compounded it exists as a distinct and strongly functional group in every known society. No exception, at least, has come to light in the 250 representative cultures surveyed for the present study (1949, p.2).

Since then some social scientists have challenged Murdock's position, citing a few possible exceptions. Still, nearly all human beings have chosen to organize themselves in the institution of the family—making this unit society's workhorse—because no institution has been invented that can do as well in meeting the diverse needs of individuals and at the same time those of society. Duvall's description of eight basic tasks the American family performs illustrates the range of needs this institution meets:

1. Providing shelter, food, clothing, health care, etc., for its members.
2. Meeting family costs and allocating such resources as time, space, facilities, etc., according to each member's needs.
3. Determining who does what in the support, management, and care of the home and its members.
4. Assuring each member's socialization through the internalization of increasingly mature roles in the family and beyond.
5. Establishing ways of interacting, communicating, expressing affection, sexuality, etc., within limits acceptable to society.

6. Bearing (or adopting) and rearing children; incorporating and releasing family members appropriately.
7. Relating to school, church, community life; establishing policies for including in-laws, relatives, guests, friends, mass media, etc.
8. Maintaining morale and motivation, rewarding achievement, meeting personal and family crises, setting attainable goals, and developing family loyalties and values (Duvall, 1977).

The family that is effective in completing these tasks serves both its members and society. Families benefit society through the economic contribution members make to the work force and by bearing children and preparing them to become competent, law-abiding citizens. Families benefit their members by providing a setting in which the whole range of human needs can be met (see Maslow's hierarchy, Chapter 2).

What enables families to provide these benefits? Nye et al. (1976) reviewed what social scientists had written about the family and identified eight roles, or areas of duties, that families have to perform in order to achieve these benefits. The roles are: provider, housekeeper, child care, child socialization, sexual, recreational, therapeutic, and kinship. Nye and his colleagues then developed and administered an instrument to assess husbands' and wives' thoughts and behaviors with regard to these roles. Their findings, the most important of which are discussed below, are based on data provided by 210 couples in which both spouses responded. Note the differences in what the respondents felt ought to be and what actually happened in practice—that is, the differences between expectation and enactment. For example, a couple might think a certain duty ought to be divided equally between husband and wife, but the husband might "enact" more than his share.

Child-Care Role This role "refers to the physical and psychological maintenance of the child. Activities such as keeping the child clean, fed, and warm, as well as protected from physical dangers and frightening experiences, . . . fall within the . . . role" (Nye et al., 1976, p. 34).

Respondents were asked, "Who should take care of the physical needs of your children?" While about half of the mothers and one quarter of the fathers felt the wives should carry more responsibility, 62 percent of the fathers and 44 percent of the mothers felt there should be equal responsibility. However, when asked who enacted the role, the majority agreed it was the mother.

Child-Socialization Role This role "is limited to the social and psychological development of the child. It refers to those processes and activities within the family which contribute to developing the child into a competent, social and moral person" (Nye et al., 1976, p. 33). Important tasks include teaching self-care skills (like eating and dressing), social skills, the difference between right and wrong, and a sense of responsibility. The main objectives here are to teach a youngster to function well in the society so he or she can develop into a productive citizen. Therefore, discipline and helping a child adapt to and succeed in the school setting are important components of this role.

Most respondents felt the socialization role should be shared by the parents, although there was variation from task to task. For instance, while about 90 percent of the mothers and an equal number of the fathers thought both parents should teach children right from wrong, half the men and about 75 percent of the women saw the job of training youngsters to eat and dress properly as more the mother's task. In terms of role enactment, although the mothers tended to do somewhat more, the chores were divided between the spouses in a fairly egalitarian way. Older siblings and grandparents also contributed.

Kinship Role   This involves maintaining contact with family members outside of the household, assisting them, and participating with them in rituals and ceremonies (weddings, communions, funerals, etc.). This role is important because contact with kin provides family members with a sense of identity and a base for emotional support.

About 75 percent of the respondents in the sample felt an obligation to the extended family and indicated that they would disapprove of people who did not perform kin-related duties. Of all the roles, this was viewed as most gender-related, with females being seen as having the most responsibility. Women were also the ones who usually enacted the role, with 84 percent of women making most of the contacts with their own relatives and about half doing the same with their husbands.'

Sexual Role   Most people in our society no longer think of sex as a duty, or something that "has to be done," but it is one of the reasons people marry and can be seen as a role because a partner more or less expects the other to provide sexual satisfaction.

Nye's team found that 45 percent of the husbands and 26 percent of the wives felt there should be equal responsibility for initiating sexual activity. However, 44 percent of the men and about 50 percent of the women felt this should be the husband's role, and a goodly percent of the wives felt no responsibility in this area. When asked who usually initiated sexual activity, about four-fifths of the respondents named the husband. The subjects further reported that when only one was in the mood, the husband, more frequently than the wife, consented to engage in sexual activities.

Therapeutic Role   This involves assisting a family member in dealing with a problem. Possible behaviors include being sympathetic, listening to a description of the difficulty, offering help, and being reassuring and affectionate. Over 70 percent reported having shared personal problems with their spouses. Surprisingly, only 60 percent of the male and female respondents felt it was one's duty to aid a spouse in dealing with a personal problem.

Nye and his colleagues also learned that the wife was more likely than the husband to discuss problems with members of the extended family and with people outside the family. One explanation for this relates to the way the therapeutic role is performed. While 75 percent of the men assessed their wives as competent in the therapeutic role, only about 50 percent of the wives felt their husbands were. Accordingly, some women probably look to others because they feel their spouse is not helpful enough. A second possible explanation relates to the kind of help offered. While equal numbers (about 55 percent) gave reassurance and affection, only 28 percent of the husbands, compared to 42 percent of the wives, offered sympathy. Thus, some women who discuss their problems with others may be seeking sympathy.

Recreational Role   This involves organizing and getting family recreation started. The respondents believed that this was a necessary role, but, as long as it was attended to, felt it was unimportant whether the man or woman took responsibility. Further, they saw the duty more as a parental than a marital one, identifying it as meeting an obligation to the children, not to the spouse. While the husbands believed they discharged more of the duties in this area, their spouses tended to report that work was done jointly. It is interesting that over 75 percent of both husbands and wives desired more family recreation.

Provider Role   In our great-grandparents' days, the man always "brought home the bacon." For a range of reasons, this task has become increasingly a shared burden. In 1960, for example, 25.5 percent of wives with employed husbands also worked for pay. By 1975, 45 percent and 37 percent of mothers with husbands present and children under 18 and under 6 years of age, respectively, worked outside the home. During 1987 the figures were 64 percent and 57 percent respectively (U.S. Census Bureau, 1987). Further, children often contribute by assuming a paper route, baby-sitting, or doing other jobs.

Another aspect of family finances that is changing is the management of money. In today's families, both the man and woman are often involved in handling their assets. And since many families face the reality of not having as much money as they would like, this area is one of possible conflict between a parent and working child. Maria, who was about to become a college freshman, had banked $1,000 in her college fund from her summer mother's-helper job. On the last day of work, Maria's employers surprised her with a $100 bonus. Maria was delighted, and on her way home bought a portable cassette recorder and a number of tapes. She wanted the recorder for enjoyment and thought she could use it to tape lectures and play restful music while she studied. Her parents were angry. "How could you waste that money?" her father asked. "How are you going to keep to a budget at school if you splurge like that?" After some discussion, Maria and her parents came to see each other's positions and resolved the issue.

Housekeeper Role   People who live in the White House, a space shuttle circling the earth, a suburban home, an urban apartment, or a college dorm all have the common needs of ensuring that food is available, living quarters are in order, and clean clothes are in the closets.

Once exclusively a woman's domain, housekeeping has come to be regarded as a family matter. Only about 30 percent of the men and 40 percent of the women thought that housekeeping duties should belong to the wife. The figures were even smaller (20 and 33 percent) when the wife worked outside the home. Further, tasks such as do-it-yourself home maintenance, minor automobile care, snow removal, lawn mowing, and livestock care were stereotypically seen as men's. In terms of the role's enactment, the vast majority agreed that the wife performed more of the work. This was particularly true when she was not employed outside the home.

Parents against children and siblings against each other are the battle lines that are frequently drawn in the home when it comes to assigning and completing household chores. The mother assigns tasks. Everybody objects. The father reminds his son about his messy room. The son answers, "I'll do it later." In trying to find the heart of the disagreements, one sees they have a variety of causes. Some stem from people forgetting their chores, some from people not liking their assignments, and some from less superficial causes, as when family members use chores to express conflicts over deeper family problems.

For example, Jesse believes his father favors his sister, Janice. He argues that Janice should take over his current responsibility of emptying the kitchen trash because she has charge of kitchen jobs. Jesse's parents answer that his jobs and Janice's take the same amount of time. Jesse feels that his take more physical work and are more tiring because he has to lift and carry. The interchange may continue on this level, but it is not resolvable at this level because the parents are not in touch with Jesse's real desire: to see signs that his father loves him as much as Janice.

Sex Roles and Family Work

The research findings described by Nye's team bring to mind the issue of the **sex roles** that men and women may assume and how these roles guide the division of labor in the home. Spiegel (1960) argued that societies develop sex roles to provide an "economy of effort and [to] relieve us from the burden of decision making: The person is spared the necessity of coming to decisions about most of the acts he performs because he knows his parts so well . . . He enacts them automatically, and all goes well" (p. 364). If a traditional couple approaches a door, traditional sex roles dictate who will open it; they need not decide.

Men and women who accept traditional sex roles expect the husband to be the "breadwinner" and the wife to be the homemaker and primary caretaker of the child. Further, both believe that his career is more important than any occupational interest she might have. According to Spiegel's theory, couples who follow this prescription benefit by having fewer decisions to make. However, in exchange they are less free to behave and use their time as they may wish.

Traditional sex roles have been influential in Western societies since industrialization split the family's workplace from its home, according to Scanzoni and Szinovacz (1980). However, as we are all very aware, views about following the dictates of sex roles have been changing. Many people, particularly women and the better-educated, are stating a preference for women to have equal (or at least greater) opportunity in work settings and for men to have equal (or at least greater) opportunity in the home.

Some people have put this value into practice with pleasing results. Others have encountered obstacles. For example, some spouses have struggled with questions about whether the wives' increased attention to a career will have detrimental effects on their children's development and on their family life. Others have coped with husbands' feelings of inadequacy as breadwinners (Staines, Pottick, & Fudge, 1986) and problems in marital harmony after wives take paid jobs and husbands increase their involvement with the children (Crouter, Perry-Jenkins, Houston, & McHale, 1987).

Sex Roles
The attitudes and behaviors typically associated with femininity and masculinity by a society.

Cooperating with domestic chores can increase the amount of shared time a couple has at its disposal and can promote psychological intimacy in their marriage.

When couples share roles with their spouses in new ways, some other values and behaviors do not necessarily change. Researchers have consistently found that women, whether employed outside the home or not, spend considerably more hours on household chores than men (Bianchi & Spain, 1986). If women are employed full time, they may have some relief in performing the traditionally female chores from their husbands, but assistance often comes from children or from paid help. In this regard Sexton (1979) speaks of the "Superwoman." The college women whom she studied reported that the educated men they knew wanted a wife "capable of cooking, cleaning, raising children, and entertaining his clients—all while simultaneously pursuing a full-time career of her own that would interfere with none of the above . . ." (p. 23).

Family Stages and Work Roles

Now, with an understanding of the stages of family development and of the roles a family must perform, we can gain insight into the kinds of demands spouses face at different stages of their family's life cycle. As Figure 10.1 indicates, families must continually adjust in order to meet their changing needs. For example, the arrival of the child-bearing stage and children means that the family must perform two new roles, child care and child socialization, and must supply more in the provider role. However, with the new time demands children bring, the family's kinship connection may slacken or increase, if grandparents or others visit more frequently or provide child care.

Figure 10.1 Developmental
role analysis of the nuclear
family system.

Stage of the Family Life Cycle	Stage-Critical Family Developmental Tasks	Roles[b]							
		P	H	T	R	S	K	CC	CS
Married Couple	Establishing a mutually satisfying marriage Adjusting to pregnancy and the promise of parenthood Fitting into the kin network								
Childbearing	Having, adjusting to, and encouraging the development of infants Establishing a satisfying home for both parents and infant(s)								
Preschool-age	Adapting to the critical needs and interests of preschool children in stimulating, growth-promoting ways Coping with energy depletion and lack of privacy as parents								
School-age	Fitting into community of school-age families in constructive ways Encouraging children's educational achievement								
Teenage	Balancing freedom with responsibility as teenagers mature and emancipate themselves Establishing postparental interests and careers								
Launching Center	Releasing young adults into work, military service, college, marriage, etc., with appropriate rituals and assistance Maintaining a supportive home base								
Middle-aged parents	Rebuilding marriage relationship Maintaining kin ties with older and younger generations								
Aging Family Members	Coping with bereavement and living alone Closing family home or adapting it to aging Adjusting to retirement								

[a]Adapted from works of Nye (1976), Duvall (1977), Vess, Moreland & Schwebel (1985-86).
[b]P = Provider; H = Housekeeper; T = Therapeutic; R = Recreation; S = Sexual; K = Kinship; CC = Child Care; CS = Child Socialization.
Width of band indicates relative importance of the role within a given stage.

ADJUSTMENT TO MARRIAGE

People speak of the family life cycle. The child begins life in a family of origin, and must adjust to it. In time, the individual develops to the point where he or she is capable of marrying and forming a family of procreation. As we turn to the next subject, marriage, we focus attention first on a poem, *My Prayer,* by Rose Pastor Stokes, which makes an important comment on the subject:

> Some pray to marry the man they love,
> My prayer will somewhat vary:
> I humbly pray to Heaven above
> That I love the man I marry.

This verse raises a provocative thought: The amount of love between two people at the beginning of their life together is less important to a marriage's success than the amount of love they have been able to build one, five, ten, or fifty years later.

While most of us have ideas about what a successful marriage is, researchers have sought to measure success in a reliable and valid way. One reason they seek this know-how is that it could give mental health professionals a sound, scientific knowledge base from which to evaluate couples' problems and offer advice. The early investigators tended to focus on only one dimension of marital success, such as happiness. On the basis of their work, and that of later researchers, it now appears that if the success of a marriage is to be evaluated, several aspects of it must be examined. Bernard suggested considering:

> (a) how well a marriage meets the needs and expectations of society; (b) its permanence or endurance; (c) the degree of unity and/or agreement or consensus developed between the members; (d) the degree to which it facilitates personality development; and (e) the degree of marital satisfaction or happiness it achieves (1964, p. 371).

From examining the five factors, it is clear that marriage, like the family, serves both society and the needs of the two people engaged in it. To Bernard's list we can add: the degree to which husband and wife have learned to deal effectively with the conflicts that are inevitable when two people live together (Schwebel, Schwebel, Schwebel, Schwebel, & Schwebel, 1989).

Some researchers, in seeking to develop a definition of a successful marriage based on empirical data, start with a list of characteristics. Stinnett and Walters (1977, p. 62) propose the following:

1. Both partners are happy with the relationship.
2. There is mutual fulfillment of basic emotional needs.
3. Each partner enriches the life of the other.
4. The marriage environment enhances the personality of each partner and is conducive to each moving toward his or her full potential as a person.

5. There is mutual emotional support; neither spouse threatens the ego of the other; they are comfortable with [each other].
6. There is mutual understanding and acceptance of each other as persons.
7. The relationship reflects a mutual (a) care and concern for the welfare and happiness of each other, (b) respect, and (c) voluntary sense of responsibility for meeting many of the partner's needs.

Using such a list, a researcher could design a draft of a marital adjustment questionnaire, administer it to several samples, refine it to the point where its reliability and validity are within acceptable limits, and then employ the final version of the instrument in future research to identify those with highly successful and unsuccessful marriages (Grover, Russell, Schumm, & Paff-Bergen, 1985; Lauer & Lauer, 1985).

Premarital Predictors of Marital Success

Many authors have written about factors that predict success in marriage. In our discussion, we draw from Stinnett and Walters and from the research of Grover, Paff-Bergen, Russell, and Schumm (1984) and Lauer and Lauer (1985).

Happiness of Parents' Marriage   Because children learn much about relating to others by observing their parents, men and women whose parents were happily married are more likely to be so themselves. Although young adults cannot change the quality of their parents' marriage, they can work toward acquiring any learnings they missed.

Happiness in Childhood   Those who were happy as children tend to be satisfied in marriage. While childhood experiences cannot be changed, those who had unhappy childhoods and remain unhappy as young adults can seek assistance from a counselor or therapist; this should also aid them in their marriage. Of course, many people emerge from unhappy childhoods as happier adults with an improved chance of marital success.

Length of Acquaintance   Research findings suggest that men and women who knew each other for a year or more before marrying have a greater likelihood of marital success than those who knew each other for less than that time. Obviously, the longer period of acquaintance allows people to get to know each other more fully, and to be surer of their decision to marry.

Age at Marriage   People who enter marriage at a young age are at a disadvantage for many reasons. Besides practical issues, such as lower earning potential and greater difficulty in furthering the spouses' education, there can be problems relating to the couple's readiness. Are both people sufficiently mature emotionally to be aware of their needs, their goals, and what they want in a mate? Research indicates that those marrying in their teens have more adjustment difficulties and a higher divorce rate than those marrying in their twenties. The **median** age for a woman at her first marriage increased from 21.1 to 23.3 from 1975 to 1985 (U. S. Census Bureau, 1987).

Parental Approval   The support of parents and their approval of a person's choice of mate are associated with more successful marriages. This is particularly true for younger couples and in instances where newlyweds live geographically close to their parents and are likely to interact with them regularly.

Reason for Marriage   Those who marry for love and for other positive reasons are more likely to be satisfied than those who do so because of loneliness, pregnancy, or a desire to "escape from their parents."

Postmarital Predictors of Marital Success

Relationship Factors   The heart of marriage lies in the nature of the relationship between husband and wife. Stinnett and Walters have noted: "Mutual respect, understanding, and expressions of appreciation and affection are important factors in contributing to a positive marital relationship and to happiness" (1977, p. 70). Obviously, how each partner feels about and acts toward the other is crucial. If one partner dominates, is extremely jealous, or feels more intelligent than the other (or superior in other ways), problems are more likely. Satisfactory marital adjustment is more probable if the partners regard and treat each other as equals. And, Sternberg's (1984) research suggests, couples are more satisfied if they love each other in roughly equal degrees.

Relationships with In-laws   Good relationships with in-laws enhance a marriage because, for one thing, the extended family can offer a wealth of support to a couple over the years. A small number of couples begin their married life by living with in-laws. While this can aid them financially, it can also deprive them of privacy and the opportunity to establish "their own family."

Common Interests   Marriages are more likely to be successful if spouses share interests in some activities. These provide a vehicle for being together and growing together.

Communication   It has almost become a cliché to speak of "communication problems." Yet, couples who are satisfied with their marriages tend to speak to each other more frequently, and be more effective in using nonverbal communication methods.

Compatibility of Role Expectations   Before marriage, both husband and wife have ideas as to how their spouse will act and relate to them. While women are somewhat more accepting of deviations from their expectation, people are happiest if their spouse behaves as they had expected.

Personality Characteristics   Stinnett and Walters (1977) report the following characteristics found in people with successful marriages:

> (1) emotional maturity and stability; (2) self-control; (3) ability to demonstrate affection; (4) willingness to take on responsibility; (5) ability to overcome feelings of anger; (6) considerateness; (7) tendency to be conventional; (8) favorable self-perceptions; (9) optimism.

Income and Occupation   Since financial matters are frequently a source of family friction, it is not surprising that a relatively high income and job stability are related to marital success. Couples with larger incomes tend to stay married longer, perhaps because they do not encounter conflict about how limited resources are to be spent. It is also important to note, however, that if a spouse becomes so involved in earning income that there is little or no family time, problems can develop.

   These factors give some idea of what can make a marriage go wrong—or go right. Of course, these factors can serve only as a guide. If spouses work at developing a relationship and have the necessary knowledge, willingness, and resourcefulness, they can overcome many obstacles and build a quality marriage (L'Abate, Ganahl, & Hansen, 1986; Lewis, Beavers, Gossett, & Phillips, 1976).

What Makes a Good Marriage?

Imagine that a debate on "what makes a good marriage" was held recently on your campus. Further, suppose that the contributions of five of the speakers were:

The bank account test: Mr. Silver argued that nobody should be allowed to marry unless they have $5000 in the bank. He stated that this would reduce the size of welfare rolls and prevent the birth of unwanted children that parents cannot support.

The parent arrangement plan: Miss Bosswell contended that young adults typically choose mates in response to the demands of their hormones. She argued that parents could make better choices for their offspring and proposed to cut the divorce rate by having parents arrange marriages.

The renewal plan: Former Judge Sanders stated that marriage is a contract and that we could do better if couples first signed a legally-binding document asserting that they had agreed to a temporary "test" marriage. After living together for at least a year, if both consented, they could then sign a permanent agreement.

The gay marriage proposal: Senator Stone argued that a person should be entitled to marry whomever he or she pleases. The Senator suggested that homosexual marriages would reduce stress and the cost of health services in America, thereby benefiting tax-paying citizens.

The gene idea: Dr. Buckler maintained that only people who pass a medical exam should be allowed to marry and have children; those who fail would have to agree to be sterilized before being granted a marriage license. This, the doctor explained, would reduce the incidence of costly societal problems like low intelligence, mental illness, and the genetic propensity for early death because of physical disorders.

---

1. Develop arguments to support or rebut the proposals of each speaker.
2. Interview several couples, asking them how they view marriage, what makes for a good marriage, and how their relationship has changed over time.
3. If you did not interview your parents or grandparents, try to imagine how they would have answered the questions posed in Question #2?
4. Imagine asking, "What makes a good marriage" to a young recently married couple, to an older recently married couple, to a middle-age couple with children, to a middle-age couple without children, to a stepfamily couple, and to a couple who has had a golden anniversary (50 years). What differences would you expect in their answers? ▲

Common Myths about Marriage and the Family

Since we are not taught in school how to be good spouses and good parents, one may wonder how people learn to perform these roles. The first, and probably most influential, learning comes from observing one's parents. This learning is informal, and from it, young adults tend to adopt their parents' styles of interacting with the opposite sex, making some of the same mistakes and having some of the same successes as their parents.

Another product of this informal learning is that people come to believe certain myths about marriage and the family. Goldenberg and Goldenberg (1980) and Glick and Kessler (1980) have identified many widely held myths (see Table 10.1). The healthier perspectives presented in the second column of the table, if truly integrated into spouses' beliefs, can improve their relationships and increase the probability of a successful marriage.

Types of Marriages

Another myth is that enduring marriages—ones presumably satisfying to those involved—are all similar in terms of how the spouses relate to each other. Cuber and Haroff (1980), after interviewing over 200 men and women wedded for 10 years or more, demonstrated that this was not the case. These investigators asked respondents why their relationships had lasted, inquiring specifically about current and past marriage-related thoughts, feelings, and behaviors. When the data were analyzed, the researchers were able to distinguish five distinct styles of marriage. They wrote that the couples practicing each of them "were remarkably similar in the ways in which they lived together, found sexual expression, reared children, and made their way in the outside world" (p. 204). These five types are discussed here.

Conflict-Habituated Marriage   This type of marriage is marked by a generally controlled state of tension and conflict that characterizes the couple's relationship. While spouses quarrel and nag in private and, intermittently, in front of the children, they generally conceal their difficulties from all but a few close relatives and friends. Because friction is always possible, the time that couples spend together is clouded by an atmosphere of tension. The following report made by a husband of 25 years illustrates how much energy goes into the ongoing battling, and how central never-ending conflict is to this type of marriage.

> You know, it's funny; we have fought from the time we were in high school together. As I look back at it, I can't remember specific quarrels; it's more like a running guerrilla fight with intermediate periods, sometimes quite long, of pretty good fun and some damn good sex. . . . It's hard to know what it is we fight about most of the time. You name it and we'll fight about it. It's sometimes something I've said that she remembers differently, sometimes a decision . . . [sometimes] politics, and religion, and morals . . . You know, outside of the welfare of the kids . . . we don't really agree about anything . . .
>
> Of course we don't settle any of the issues. It's sort of a matter of principle not to. Because somebody would have to give in then and lose face for the next encounter . . .
>
> When I tell you in this way, I feel a little foolish about it. I wouldn't tolerate such a condition in any other relationship in my life—and yet here I do and always have . . .
>
> A number of times there has been a crisis . . . and then I guess we really showed that we do care about each other. But as soon as the crisis is over, it's business as usual (Cuber & Haroff, 1980, pp. 205–206).

TABLE 10.1 *Common Myths about Marriage and the Family*

1. Marriage and families should be totally happy; each member should expect nearly all of their life satisfactions to come from the family unit.
2. Good marriages simply happen spontaneously, and require no effort.
3. "Togetherness" through close physical proximity or joint activities leads to satisfactory family life and individual gratification.
4. Marital partners should be totally honest with each other at all times.
5. In happy marriages there are no disagreements; when family members fight, it means they hate each other.
6. Marital partners should see eye to eye on every issue and work toward an identical outlook.
7. Marital partners should be unselfish and not think of their individual needs.
8. In a marital argument, one partner is right and the other wrong. Each spouse should try to "win" the argument by scoring more "points" in the argument.
9. Whenever something goes wrong in family life, it is important to determine who is at fault.
10. Rehashing the past is helpful when things are not going well at present.
11. A good sexual relationship inevitably leads to a good marriage.
12. In a satisfactory marriage, the sexual aspect will more or less take care of itself.
13. Marital partners understand each others' nonverbal communications and therefore need not check things out with each other verbally.
14. Positive feedback is not as necessary in marriage as negative feedback.
15. Any spouse can (and often should) be reformed and remodeled into the shape desired by the partner.
16. In a stable marriage, things do not change much over the years.
17. Everyone knows what a husband should be like and what a wife should be like.
18. If a marriage is not working properly, having children will rescue it.
19. If marriage does not work out, divorce and marriage to another spouse will cure the situation.
20. No matter how bad a marriage, it should be kept together for the sake of the children.

Source: Based on information in I. Glick & D. Kessler, *Marital and Family Therapy.* New York: Grune & Stratton, 1974, pp. 30–36 and a table from I. Goldenberg & H. Goldenberg, *Family Therapy: An Overview.* Monterey, Calif.: Brooks/Cole, 1980, pp. 66–67.

TABLE 10.1 Continued   *A Healthier, More Realistic View*

1. A romantic myth; overlooks the fact that many of life's satisfactions are commonly found outside the family setting.

2. Another romantic myth; good marriages require daily effort by both partners, with constant negotiation, communication, and mutual problem solving.

3. Varies greatly from one family to another; cannot be considered an ideal pattern for all families.

4. While openness and frankness are usually desirable, they may also be damaging if used in the service of hostile, destructive feelings.

5. Differences between family members are inevitable and often lead to arguments; if these clarify feelings and are not personal attacks, they may be constructive and preferable to covering up differences by always appearing to agree.

6. Differences in background, experiences, and personality make this impossible to achieve; actually different outlooks, if used constructively, may provide the family with more options in carrying out responsibilities.

7. Extremes of selflessness (or self-absorption) are undesirable; people need satisfactions as individuals, not merely as appendages to others (for example, when mother "lives" only to serve the family).

8. Marriages generally suffer when competition rather than cooperation characterizes a couple's interactions and their problem-solving.

9. Rather than blaming a single individual, family members should accept a fair share of the responsibility for the problem and for finding remedies.

10. Endless recriminations about past errors "invite" countercharges and generally escalate problems, rather than reduce them.

11. A good sexual relationship is an important component of a satisfactory marriage, but having one does not preclude interpersonal difficulties in other areas.

12. Not necessarily; a good sexual relationship may take effort. Sexual difficulties may develop in any couple because of stresses inside or outside of the marriage.

13. All couples benefit from effective use of verbal communication. Discussions are especially needed in troubled families, where misperceptions and misinterpretations of each other's meanings and intent are common.

14. Positive feedback (attention, compliments) increases the likelihood that desired behavior will recur. Further, it has advantages over each partner focusing on what is wrong with the other's behavior.

15. A poor premise in marriage, and one likely to lead to frustration, anger, and disillusionment. Instead, efforts should be directed toward partners being more accepting of and sensitive to each other's needs.

16. All living systems change, grow, and develop over time.

17. Untrue, especially in modern society, where new roles are being explored.

18. Not likely and, in fact, children usually become the victims of marital disharmony.

19. Possibly true, but if insight has not been gained, similar choices may be made in the new marriage and the same nongratifying patterns repeated.

20. Children may thrive better with relatively satisfied divorced parents than with those together in an unhappy marriage. In marriages where partners stay together as "martyrs" for the children's sake, children may bear the brunt of the resentment partners feel for each other.

Devitalized Marriage   As the name suggests, the couple's relationship has changed over the years from one of deep love, full sharing, and mutual interest to one of less sharing in terms of sexual intimacy and time spent together pursuing hobbies and other activities. After the shift, except for a mutual interest in the children and shared attention to the family's financial picture, there is little between the spouses but lifeless interactions. They do not argue, they do not plan and engage in joyful activities; they simply keep "plugging away."

Because this type of marriage is common, couples often compare themselves with others and conclude, "This is how it is—especially in the middle and later years." The following report provides a sense of this:

> Judging by the way it was when we were first married—say the first five years or so—things are pretty matter-of-fact now—even dull. They're dull between us, I mean. The children are a lot of fun, keep us pretty busy, and there are lots of outside things—you know, like Little League and the P.T.A. . . . But I mean where Bob and I are concerned—if you followed us around, you'd wonder why we ever got *married*. We take each other for granted. We laugh at the same things sometimes, but we don't really laugh together—the way we used to. . . .
>
>   Now, I don't say this to complain, not in the least. There's a cycle to life. There are things you do in high school. And different things you do in college. Then you're a young adult. And then you're middle-aged (Cuber & Haroff, 1980, p. 207).

The Passive-Congenial Marriage   This type of relationship is characterized by the fact that each person's creative energies and emotional involvements are directed toward outside activities or toward the children. Simply stated, there is little in each other that the spouses care deeply about. People in such a marriage are generally comfortable, feel that they have enough in common to maintain the relationship, and usually have little conflict, although each person may carry stored anger about one thing or another.

Couples generally drift into this type of relationship, although some may build it intentionally because it does provide much personal freedom and allows individuals to direct their energy to their career or children. However they arrive at this arrangement, the spouses still maintain feelings of love and appreciation, although not the usually associated sense of obligation to deal with each other's personal problems. The passive-congenial style is exemplified in this description:

> I don't know why everyone seems to make so much about men and women and marriage. . . . It's convenient, orderly, and solves a lot of problems. But there are other things in life. I spent nearly ten years preparing for the practice of my profession. The biggest thing to me is the practice of that profession, to be of assistance to my patients and their families. I spend twelve hours a day at it. And I'll bet if you talked with my wife, you wouldn't get any of that "trapped housewife" stuff from her either. . . . She finds a lot of useful and necessary work to do. . . . (Cuber & Haroff, 1980, p. 210).

Vital Marriage   In this type of marriage, the partners experience great satisfaction from whatever they share, be it children, a hobby, or a career. Without the involvement of the spouse, much of the satisfaction from an activity is lost. The fact that those with a vital relationship put primary emphasis on their shared marriage is illustrated by this husband's comments:

> I cheerfully, and that's putting it mildly, passed up two good promotions because one of them would have required some traveling and the other would have taken evening and weekend time—and that's when Pat and I live. The hours with her (after twenty-two years of marriage) are what I live for. You should meet her. . . . (Cuber & Haroff, 1980, p. 211).

While partners in a vital marriage do not smother each other, they do try to spend a lot of time together. Even so, each mate maintains his or her own identity, and though they do experience difficulties in areas that are important in their lives, they avoid petty arguments. Further, in contrast to those in conflict-habituated relationships, vital-marriage couples resolve their differences and try to avoid future battles.

Total Marriage   This type of relationship is like the vital one, only more—or even all—aspects of life are shared fully and are fulfilling. One of Cuber's and Haroff's respondents stated that his wife was his "friend, mistress, and partner."

Couples with this type of marriage generally had serious problems in the past and settled them at the time they arose in a way that strengthened their relationship. As a result, when occasional tensions arise in their current, day-to-day life, they handle them well. A couple comments on their total relationship:

> **He says:** [In business], her femininity, easy charm, and wit are invaluable assets to me. . . . I gladly acknowledge that . . . she's indispensable to me. [Further, we] enjoy each other's company—deeply. You know, the best part of a vacation is not *what* we do, but that we do it together. We plan it and reminisce about it and weave it into our work and other play all the time.

> **She says:** Bert exaggerates my help. It's not so much that I only want to help him; it's more that I want to do those things . . . together, even though we may not be in each other's presence at the time (Cuber & Haroff, 1980, p. 213).

Parents' Child-Rearing Goals

Couples have much work to accomplish in order to prepare themselves for the arrival of children. Some of their tasks are obvious, such as acquiring clothes, preparing a nursery, and planning new time and household chore schedules. Other tasks are not so readily apparent. For example, the new mother and father have the opportunity to plan how they will approach the task of parenting.

One of the authors of this book begins classes for expectant parents and parents of young children by asking them to imagine, in the best of all possible worlds, what characteristics they would like their offspring to have as children and as adults. Then each participant prepares a list and shares it with the group. Although class members are never in total agreement, there is nearly always surprising similarities between lists. Mothers and fathers alike cite the terms healthy, happy, loving, bright, able, honest, and successful. The comparability of such lists drives home an obvious but often overlooked fact: Parents fairly well agree on what is best for their children. In discussions, parents express a desire that their offspring enjoy childhood and adolescence and that they draw from these years all they have to offer. As adults they want them to become effective, genuinely satisfied people who are capable of making meaningful contributions to society.

Styles of Parenting

Although there tends to be substantial agreement among couples in desired qualities, there are great differences in the approaches they take to achieve them. The new and expectant parents then address the next question, how to interact with their children so as to maximize the chances that their parenting goals can be achieved. Many class members are surprised by this idea of thinking out the direct relationship between their actions today and their child's later abilities. However, once the idea is brought to their attention, nearly all the participants grow excited about the possibilities.

One useful way class members think about how they want to approach their parenting responsibilities is by considering the parenting style categories developed by Wood, Bishop, and Cohen (1978). These writers explain that patterns of parent-child interactions in a particular family fall into one of four types, depending on the style of parenting a mother or father adopts:

1. *The potter,* who molds the child into the kind of person he or she feels society requires;

2. *The gardener,* who creates the conditions necessary for the child's growth, providing nutrients and eliminating hampering forces;

3. *The maestro,* who conducts development but, like a great leader, leaves flexibility for the child; and

4. *The consultant,* who transfers more authority for growth to the child but is readily available to provide requested advice.

Although these styles of interaction differ greatly, it is important to recognize that one style is not necessarily better than another. Still, the actual orientation practiced in the family in which an individual is raised will teach that person certain ways of viewing family life and parent-children relationships, and can instill a broad variety of attitudes and behaviors.

Desirable Qualities for Your Children

Do you have children or plan to have children some time in the future? If so, please answer the questions below. If you do not expect to have children, answer with qualities you think the next generation of children ought to have.

1. List the qualities you would like to see in your children at age five.
2. List the qualities you would like to see in your children at age eighteen.
3. Compare your answers to Question 1 with those of two male and two female classmates or friends. What differences and similarities do you find?
4. Find a classmate or friend who you feel is different from you in some way (such as age, nationality, values, or personality), and compare your answers to Question 2.   ▲

NEW FAMILY FORMS

Some 30 or 35 years ago, the typical American family consisted of a working father, a mother who was a housewife, and children, all of whom lived under one roof. That stereotype was shown in the situation-comedy television programs of the 1950s and 1960s, such as *Father Knows Best* and *Leave It to Beaver,* as well as in later offerings such as *Happy Days* (set, by no coincidence, in the 50s). By comparison to your parents' and grandparents' times, a relatively small percentage of America's families have this structure. The Select Committee on Children, Adolescents and Families of the United States House of Representatives (1985) reported that 44 percent of American women are employed outside of the home, that 22 percent of children live in a single parent home, and that more than half of all U.S. children are being reared in families in which both parents, or the single parent household head, work(s). Bureau of Labor Statistics indicated that in 1985 half of mothers of children under two were working outside of the home.

Adapting to changing social and economic conditions, millions of Americans over the past few decades have chosen, or have found themselves in, living arrangements other than that of the typical American family of the 50s. Specifically, people have organized themselves in a variety of family forms:

1. Nuclear family: husband and wife and often, but not always, children

2. Single-parent family: household led by one adult, usually as a result of divorce, out of wedlock birth, or death of one parent

3. Blended family: husband, wife, and children from previous marriage(s) plus, perhaps, children from the current marriage

4. Cohabitation family: a more or less permanent relationship between two unmarried adults, most frequently of the opposite sex, sometimes including children.

Television's response to the change in American family life has in part been nostalgic, with programs such as *The Waltons* and *Little House on the Prairie,* which recall times when the nuclear and extended family was an important force in shaping people's lives, and in part realistic, with programs such as *Kate and Allie, Cosby, Family Ties,* and *thirtysomething,* which reflect the diversity of today's life-styles. The shift in family forms has prompted many popular writers and social critics to predict the decline of the American family, claiming it has outlived its usefulness. But most evidence does not point in this direction. Over 90 percent of American adults marry at some point in their lives (Norton & Moorman, 1987), and all but 5.8 percent of the white, 4.2 percent of the black, and 3.5 percent of the Spanish-surnamed wives expect to have one child or more (U. S. Census Bureau, 1979). The family will certainly continue to play an important role in our society, perhaps with newly developed forms existing side by side with older ones.

In a sense, the new forms of families are the product of complex forces that have affected prevailing attitudes, and fostered greater acceptance of divorce, single adults, and women working outside of the home. Although arrangements may not be as standard as they once were, it still seems clear that, at one point in their adult lives, most humans seek to live in a family unit with others to whom they have a commitment. At other points, however, people may decide to try the alternative of staying single: building a support network consisting primarily of friends rather than family members.

FAMILY CONFLICTS

Conflict between and among family members is inevitable. Adults and children cannot share limited physical space, financial and other resources, and the work of maintaining a household without having differences. Even in the most loving of homes, tensions are generated by envy and by differences in opinions and goals. And, of course, the happiest of couples battle at one point or at another over money, in-laws, sex, and child-rearing. Most difficulties, such as the "garden-variety" family argument discussed next, are minor in nature and of little consequence to family members. Other problems, however, such as abuse and divorce that are discussed later, have a more substantial impact.

Typical Family Arguments

Vuchinich (1985) videotaped dinner conversations in 52 typical families to learn more about their verbal conflict. He found that arguments occurred during these meals for a wide range of reasons. Sometimes they began because people were playful or "clearing the air." But sometimes disagreements grew from deep anger.

Arguments typically started with an attack. One person directed a criticism, challenge, or insult to another who ignored it, counterattacked, or tried to redirect energy toward rational consideration. Once verbal combat began, however, comments were bantered back and forth until one of four methods were used to end the episode:

▶ **Withdrawal** One individual halts the chain of aggression, usually by ceasing to talk or by physically leaving the room. By withdrawing the individual may be communicating that he is upset or that the other person went beyond the level of acceptability in attacking. Although not widely found in the 200 arguments that Vuchinich studied, repeated use of withdrawal may lead family members to conclude that they cannot communicate effectively.

▶ **Submission** One party "gives in." This method ended about 25 percent of the arguments videotaped. A person may initiate submission or it may occur when a third party intervenes, as when a parent demands that children stop arguing or offers knowledge that settles a dispute (It is Marv's turn to wash the dishes and Johnny's day to clear the table). If one party consistently submits to another, the submissive person may act out his feelings in more hidden, less desirable ways. For instance, a child who continues to lose arguments about being quizzed on her spelling words may "get revenge" by scoring poorly on spelling tests.

▶ **Compromise** One family member offers a concession and the other participant accepts it. Each may give a little and a feeling of solidarity is achieved. Less than a tenth of the studied disputes ended in this fashion.

▶ **Standoff** Participants "agree to disagree" and conclude the argument without resolution or submission. Many standoffs are facilitated with assistance from a third family member who interrupts with a new topic or a joke. While there is no "winner" and no "loser" with this method, frustration can develop if standoffs are used repeatedly. Standoffs, which emerged in about two-thirds of the arguments studied, are illustrated in the following example of a disagreement over sharing a candy bar. The conflict ended abruptly when the son, who had initially complained, changed the topic:

> "*Son:* I mean she just sat there and ate it all.
> *Mother:* (to daughter) That's bad. Don't ever do things like that. You're supposed to offer . . .
> *Daughter:* (interrupting): There wasn't enough to go around.
> *Mother:* Well, you shouldn't EAT it . . . .
> *Daughter:* Uh-uh, it woulda melted . . . .
> *Son:* Jim brought bubble gum and nobody would sit with him.
> *Daughter:* Jim?
> *Son:* Yeah (Vuchinich, 1985, pages 42–43).

Jack is smiling, Evan is not. Did Jack grab part of his younger brother's new gift? Is Evan jealous? Did Jack tease Evan? Sibling arguments and sibling rivalry are a part of life that call upon our personal adjustment resources.

People can learn to prevent family arguments and they can learn to end them effectively by using techniques developed from research and theory in family relations (L'Abate, Ganahl, & Hansen, 1986; Lewis, Beavers, Gossett, & Phillips, 1976). Specifically, certain types of problems can be minimized if work responsibilities and decision-making responsibilities are divided equitably between the spouses and among family members. It is also important that each spouse supports the other's autonomy. Parents can minimize episodes of misbehavior if they clearly convey their expectations to the children and if they consistently use appropriate discipline techniques (Schwebel, Fine, Moreland, & Prindle, 1988).

Effective communication helps family members manage unavoidable conflict. If people speak directly and clearly to each other and listen in a kind and active fashion, they will be better able to cope by finding mutually-satisfying answers to many difficulties.

Conflicts between Teenagers and Parents

Families are likely to encounter some unique problems at each point in the life cycle. For instance, in the Teenage Stage (see Figure 10.1) the children face the developmental task of working toward separating themselves psychologically and physically from their parents and becoming independent people. These young adults may willingly accept this challenge or may shy away from it. Similarly, parents may help or hinder their youngsters' movements toward independence. Whatever the pattern in a particular home, this period has great potential for causing strain.

A hallmark of a young person's developing maturity is the ability to look at his or her parents in an objective, nonjudgmental manner—that is, to be able to look at them as real people, each having certain strengths and weaknesses. Reaching such a point represents much progress from earlier views of one's parents. Specifically, young children generally think their parents are totally knowledgeable individuals who can solve any problem they confront, thus investing in them more power, ability, and goodness than is humanly possible to possess. Adolescents sometimes think the opposite of their parents, blaming them for many problems encountered, resenting them for restricting their freedom, and being angry at them for assigning chores. Eventually, however, by the late teens or early twenties, most people have built more accurate pictures of their mothers and fathers. They see them as they really are: special but real, with strengths and weaknesses. Mark Twain described the transition he experienced: "When I was 14 my father knew nothing, but when I was 21 I was amazed at how much the old man had learned in those seven years."

Older teenagers and young adults who are not happy about their relationship with one or both parents sometimes feel defeated. They may find that their worries about these relationships are causing discomfort or interfering with their day-to-day functioning. Often such individuals find that talking about the matter with a friend or with a counselor can be helpful.

For example, Art, a 21-year-old college junior, made an appointment at the University Counseling Center because he had trouble concentrating on his studies. At his first session he told the counselor:

> My father died when I was fourteen. Before then everything seemed perfect. School was good, I had friends, I was happy. But the death changed things. I felt different. Mom was different. She worked hard, day and night, it seemed. And anytime I did something wrong she cried a lot, as if I'd done it on purpose. Another thing was that after Dad died, Mom always expected me to keep her company. She didn't come right out and say that. But she never went out, and whenever I wanted to, she always found something wrong with my plans. She seemed to think I should just stay home, practice the piano, and study. I didn't go out much when I was in high school because it was easier not to. Sometimes I got angry and lashed out at her for that. With all those wasted weekends, I've never learned to relate well to women. I'm afraid to start a conversation with a woman I find attractive. I've tried several times lately, but I never can get that first word out. Maybe I'm afraid of rejection.

Art needed help from the counselor in coping with his feelings about his mother—feelings that were making it difficult for him to develop other relationships. During the sessions with the counselor, Art came to see his mother more fully as a human being and to accept her failings. At the same time he recognized that he must now take charge of his own life, learn to live in the present rather than the past, and work toward goals that he believed would make him a happy adult.

Conflicts Involving Abuse and Chemical Dependancy

In recent years both the public and the scientific community have taken a greater note of certain kinds of situational conflicts that can occur in families. Examples include: physical, emotional, and sexual abuse in the home, and difficulties stemming from a family member's psychological disorder or chemical dependency.

The fact that we, as a society, have many incidents of abuse in our homes has been attributed to factors ranging from social mobility, and the resultant lack of support from the extended family, to the mass media, which has exploited themes of violence and sexuality (Levine, 1986). In a family where one member might lose control, it is often difficult to settle arguments with rational discussion and straight-forward verbal arguments. Professional help can be valuable.

Families also may face substantial problems if one member has a psychiatric disorder or a chemical dependency. In such cases the troubled individual needs professional assistance and the family would likely benefit from information like that in Seixas and Youcha's (1985) book, *Children of Alcoholism,* or in Schwebel's (1989) book *Saying No is Not Enough: Raising Children Who Make Wise Decisions about Drugs*. For instance, if one parent is an alcoholic, the entire family will be affected. Professionals can teach the spouse and children how to manage conflict and stress by taking steps like these (Molineux, 1985):

1. Recognize that the alcoholic is dependent and that all family members have been affected by his problem

2. Discuss their feelings about the alcoholic and their family life

3. Learn about alcoholism and how it creates certain behavioral patterns in family members

4. Shift their energies to fulfilling activities and away from trying to help the alcoholic control his drinking

Adult children of alcoholics, estimated to be 20 million or more in the United States (Wanck, 1985), can consider whether they have traits that stem from being raised by an alcoholic parent. These include: procrastination, tendencies to lie and to overreact to changes, harsh self-expectations, problems in having fun and in taking the self seriously, feelings of isolation, and an overbearing need for approval.

Divorce

Unmanaged family conflict ultimately may lead to divorce. In the United States the yearly divorce rate has increased approximately 700 percent since the turn of the century (The Select Committee, 1985). Between 1960 and 1979 the figure rose from 2.2 divorces per 1000 couples per year to 5.4 per 1000. However, during the first half of the 1980s, the divorce rate seemed to level off (Norton et al., 1987). In 1985 there were 1,187,000 divorces granted (U. S. Census Bureau, 1987).

Perspectives on Divorce

The increase in the divorce rate is related to a complex variety of social factors, including greater rights for women; birth control advances, coupled with a decrease in family size; changes in public attitudes; and liberalized divorce laws in many states. These new laws permit dissolution of marriage, or no-fault divorce, which means that one spouse need not charge the other with cruelty or adultery but can gain a legal separation on the grounds of irreconcilable differences.

People seek divorces for many different reasons, such as personality clashes, physical or mental cruelty, neglect, infidelity, sexual incompatibility, or problems with gambling, money, alcohol, or drugs. Whatever the reasons they cite, couples arrive at the decision to divorce in widely differing ways. Wallerstein and Kelly (1980) noted that while some people seek divorce as a rational solution to an unfulfilling, growth-stunting relationship, others choose it for less thoughtful reasons. Divorce may be a stress-related response to events such as a death in the family, an accident to a child, or the diagnosis of a serious illness. The decision may be an impulsive response designed to punish a mate for an extramarital affair. Or it may be a step that was strongly encouraged by others to help the individual escape from a destructive situation or become more self-actualized.

While we tend to think about "divorce" as an event, it is actually a process—one that generally begins long before the court decree is issued and continues long afterwards, as all involved adjust to their new living conditions. Bohannan (1975) has described six aspects of the divorce process that couples and their children must cope with. These are: emotional divorce, characterized by friction and conflict in the home; legal divorce, involving hiring attorneys and following prescribed court procedures; economic divorce, requiring property settlement and perhaps the arrangement of monthly payments; co-parental divorce, pertaining to the assignment of a custodial parent and specification of visitation rights for the noncustodial parent; community divorce, requiring adjustment to the disapproval of some people and the building of new friendships as a single adult; and psychic divorce, which means viewing oneself as "single again" and achieving a psychological separation from the ex-spouse.

You may recall that on the Holmes and Rahe Social Readjustment Rating Scale (Chapter 3) the top three stressors involved the loss of a spouse. With that knowledge, one understands why Campbell (1981), in his book, "The Sense of Well-Being in America," states:

> Divorce and the events leading up to it are a damaging experience for the two people involved, sometimes for one more than the other but typically for both. It is no surprise then to discover in the national surveys that separated and divorced people have on the average the most depressed feelings of well-being of any of the major life-cycle groups. They are much more likely than married people to describe their lives as 'not too happy,' and they are less likely to report positive experiences and much more likely to report negative ones, especially feeling lonely and depressed. These people with failed or failing marriages are also much less willing than married people to call themselves 'very satisfied' with life in general and with specific domains of life (p. 198).

Succinctly, the divorce process is stressful and can produce symptoms in ex-spouses like: depression, lowered self-esteem, increased levels of anxiety, sleep difficulties, and poor work performance. Further, the stress can produce eating problems and increased consumption of tobacco and alcohol.

Children whose parents divorce are comparably effected. Guidubaldi, Cleminshaw, Perry, and Mcloughlin (1983) conducted a national study that showed that children from intact families outperformed those whose parents divorced on 14 of 16 classroom behavior measures; on communication, daily living, and social scales; on school attendance; on peer popularity; on IQ, academic achievement and spelling scores; and on grades in reading and mathematics. Further, children from intact families were less likely to be retained (held back) and, as measured by a psychological locus of control scales, felt more in control of their lives. These differences held when socioeconomic factors were taken into account.

Of course, children and adults vary in how well they cope with a divorce. Research suggests that people generally adjust more easily if parents minimize post-divorce conflict (at least in the presence of their children), if both stay involved with the children, and if they can come to agree on child-rearing strategies (Hetherington, Cox, & Cox, 1978; Schwebel, Fine, Moreland, & Prindle, 1988; Wallerstein & Kelly, 1980). Children fare better if they have effective social-cognitive skills, feel they have a measure of control over their lives, and live with the parent with the same gender (Kurdek & Berg, 1983; Guidubaldi et al., 1983; Warshak & Santrock, 1983). Adults fare better if they have a support group and sufficient meaningful involvement with the children (Kurdek et al., 1983; Stewart, Schwebel, & Fine, 1986).

Obviously, children's reaction to and understanding of their parents' divorce vary with age. Very young children may feel abandoned by the noncustodial parent and may even reason, "If Dad left, maybe Mom will too someday." While older children have a better understanding of the event, they may also

Figure 10.2 After their parent's divorce, elementary school children, when asked to draw "their home," often make pictures like this, showing both parent's residences.

have irrational thoughts, such as feeling guilty about having "caused it." Wallerstein and Kelly (1980) have reported in detail how children at certain stages adjust to their parents' divorce. Overall they found that 25 percent successfully adapted to the changed home situation; 50 percent muddled through, coping as best they could; and 25 percent never recovered, or else looked back longingly at the pre-divorce family.

By the time a decision is made to divorce, most spouses have generated a good deal of ill feeling toward each other. Their situation is often exacerbated by the fact that each must retain a lawyer and enter into an adversarial process. Those involved in divorce law reform have proposed **divorce mediation** as an approach which, along with no-fault divorce, will help reduce stress.

Divorce Mediation
A carefully structured process through which spouses are guided with the objective of their cooperatively reaching decisions about divorce-related matters.

Divorce mediation is a carefully structured problem-solving process through which a couple is guided in the hope that they can cooperatively reach decisions about divorce-related matters (Haynes, 1981; Schwebel, Schwebel, & Schwebel, 1985). If they can do so, less anger will build, both should be more satisfied than if they had to accept a judge's ruling, and parents and children will be in a better position to make necessary adjustments to their changed circumstances.

A successfully mediated divorce settlement may lead to the development of a plan for joint custody of the child(ren). Joint custody, which does not mean that children must live with each parent 50 percent of the time, has the advantage of structuring a cooperative relationship between the divorced parents that is typically to their benefit and will help the children to feel less of a sense of loss. Luepnitz (1986) studied 43 families to compare the impact of joint (legally shared responsibilities for the child or children), maternal, and paternal custody. In her sample, families with joint custody enjoyed the continued involvement of both parents in their children's lives and experienced no relitigation. In contrast, in half the single custody families, one parent was no longer seeing the children and, in more than half the cases, the parents returned to court. Luepnitz concluded that "joint custody at its best is superior to single parent custody at *its* best," but expressed concern that in situations where the ex-husband was abusive, a mother with joint custody would have less legal protection than if she were the sole custodian.

STEPFAMILIES

One problem parents face in the forming of stepfamilies is a lack of clear guidelines to assist them in the process of building a happy stepfamily home. It takes planning, and probably some trial-and-error learning, to develop effective family rules, mechanisms for discipline, and ways of relating to stepkin. Moreover, children need time to cope with the loss of the previous family, to develop love for the stepparents and stepsiblings, and to handle issues of loyalty and trust. Stepfamilies often begin their life together expecting "instant intimacy" and are frequently disappointed and unhappy when this does not occur. Expectations about responsibilities for child-rearing are sometimes unmet as well. Giles-Sims (1984) found that half the parents she interviewed expected the stepparents and biological parents to share these duties. This actually happened in less than a third of the families.

Early researchers who studied stepfamilies often focused on the deficits in these units as contrasted to intact families (Ganong & Coleman, 1986). However, effective stepfamilies do not differ that greatly from effective intact families and most material discussed elsewhere in this chapter applies to stepfamilies. For instance, research suggests that children from stepfamilies have self-image, social relationships, and cognitive development similar to those of age-mates from intact homes (Santrock, Warshak, Lindberg, & Meadows, 1982).

With the decline of the nuclear family and the rising divorce rate, a family form that became increasingly common in the 1970s—when this picture was taken—is the stepparent family. Here, children from the spouses' first marriages are present at their parents' second wedding ceremony.

One major difference between these family types is the adjustment stepparents and children must make. Problems often develop when people form new "step-relationships" and, as Sauer and Fine (1988) found, college students have more positive perceptions of their relationship with their biological parents than that with their stepparents. Studies of elementary school children have further suggested that stepparent-stepdaughter relationships tend to be most problematic (Clingempeel & Segal, 1986) and that boys tend to adjust more effectively to stepfathers than girls (Santrock & Sitterle, 1987).

ALTERNATIVE COMMITMENTS AND BEING SINGLE

Cohabitation

In some cultures cohabitation is a standard part of the courtship process. Young Peruvian Indians, for example, choose a partner to live with and, after an average of 15 months, about 80 percent marry (Price, 1965). Cohabitation has also been practiced in the United States over the years, but not as openly and to the extent it is today. Henslin (1980) estimates that about a third of American college students will cohabit at some point during their years at school. He further explains that those who do are quite similar to those who do not in terms of their background and their emotional and intellectual functioning. The main difference found between these two groups is that people who live together are less religiously committed and less influenced by their parents in making life decisions.

People choose to cohabit for a range of reasons. While some do so because of ideological beliefs, such as opposition to marriage, most do so for a variety of personal reasons. Examples include: (1) they care about each other deeply but are not ready to marry, (2) they want to test their relationship, (3) cohabitation prevents loneliness, (4) by not marrying they get a regular check (from social security or parents), (5) one or both persons are trying to upset parents, in order to strike back for grievances of the past.

The life-styles of cohabiting couples are as varied as their reasons for selecting this mode of living. These couples, like spouses, have work to divide and choices to make, so therefore, they must generate a set of rules to guide their day-to-day shared lives. Once people begin living together they, like the newly married, experience a dramatic change in the time spent together and must adjust to shared living quarters. Privacy and quiet time for oneself, among other issues, must be negotiated. With regard to the division of labor, research suggests that women tend to do the traditionally female chores, while men generally handle the traditionally male chores (Stafford, Backman, & Dibona, 1977).

Although cohabitants face many of the same problems as newlyweds, they also encounter unique ones that are a by-product of the nature of their relationship (Cunningham, Braiker, & Kelley, 1982). For instance, some feel a need to keep their living arrangements secret from their parents, which may produce guilt, fear, and disappointment about not being able to share an important part of their lives. The two may disagree about whether or when the arrangement is to lead to marriage. Finally, finances can be a problem. In marriage, the husband's and wife's incomes are generally pooled and property is jointly owned. Cohabiting couples must work out a system of who buys what, knowing that they have a limited commitment to each other.

Prenuptial Agreements: A Benefit or a Jinx?

Not many years ago experts advised against premarital agreements. Antenuptials, as these are also called, prepare couples for the worst and could jinx a marriage, some superstitiously thought. In recent times, however, courts have increasingly come to recognize and enforce them.

Premarital contracts can cover any aspect of the relationship but typically focus on the financial arrangements at its termination: How assets will be divided and whether alimony will be paid. Specifications can also be made about children born as a result of the relationship, recognizing that the courts ultimately will make the determination based on what they believe is in the best interests of the child(ren).

Melvin Belli and A. Wilkinson (1987) believe that prenuptial agreements should be written in simple English, based on full and fair disclosure of all relevant information by both parties, and independently reviewed by two lawyers, one attorney representing each party.

With a classmate or friend discuss the following:

1. In what ways can a premarital agreement help a marriage? What does it offer newlyweds? In what ways can an agreement harm a marriage?
2. Would you ever use a premarital agreement? Would you consider using an agreement in some situations and not in others?
3. Write a premarital agreement for one of these couples:
   a. a 21-year-old woman who will work as a waitress while her 21-year-old husband attends medical school
   b. a 24-year-old dietician and a 45-year-old man who owns a business and pays alimony and child support to his first wife
   c. a 33-year-old woman and a 31-year-old man who will live together unmarried until they decide to have children ▲

Cohabitating couples also face less obvious problems. For example, Abernathy (1981) found undergraduate men and women viewed cohabitation differently: Whereas males saw it as part of the dating process, females thought of it as being distinctively different. Such divergent perspectives can create substantial difficulties in areas such as expectations for the future and the level of commitment to the relationship. Legal problems provide another example. Legal entanglements, which can range from child custody to property division and inheritance (in the case of death), can be particularly complex if one or both individuals were formerly married and have children (Bernstein 1977).

During the mid 1970s, with about two million individuals living together (Glick & Spanier, 1980), it was clear that society had come to accept cohabitation in new ways. In the 1976 landmark *Marvin* v. *Marvin* case, or Palimony Suit as it came to be known, the law recognized and responded to the changed community standards. Before that decision, the law took a "hands-off" approach. In the Marvin case, Michelle Triola Marvin, who had lived seven years with actor Lee Marvin, argued that he had promised to share earnings and support her if she gave up her career to become a homemaker. The California Supreme Court ruled that this agreement between the parties was enforceable. The Court's decision set a precedent: Future courts would consider protecting nonmarried partners who could demonstrate that injustices would develop unless the court intervened.

Research into the effects of having cohabited on a couple's marriage are unclear. While Jacques and Chason (1979) found that cohabitation did not improve or harm a couple's chances for success in marriage, White (1987), studying Canadian couples, found cohabitation had a positive effect on the length of marriage. While Watson and DeMeo (1987), also studying Canadian couples, found that cohabitation had no long-term effect on marital adjustment, DeMaris and Leslie (1984) reported lower satisfaction in couples who had lived together, even after the researchers statistically controlled for church attendance and other sociocultural differences between cohabitators and noncohabitators. More research is needed to clarify the ways in which cohabitation later affects a couple's married relationship.

The "Single" Alternative

There are over 50 million single adults over age 18 in the United States (Cargan & Melko, 1982; Simenauer & Carroll, 1982). Although some people find that a stereotype comes to mind when they hear the term "single," in fact, there is great variation among members of this group, both statistically and psychologically. For example, some people in this category have never been married, others are divorced or widowed; some are young, others are old; some have many interactions with the opposite sex, others do not; some prefer to stay single, others plan to be a part of a couple when they find the appropriate person. The label "single" bridges these differences, describing one aspect of a person's status: the fact that he or she is not married.

The percentage of single people in our population is increasing. In 1986, 39.5 percent of women and 34.5 percent of men who were 18 or older had never been married, were widowed, or divorced. However, there is still a strong tendency to marry at least once during one's life. Among people aged 55 to 64 years, only 3.9 percent of women and 5.9 percent of men had never been married (U. S. Bureau of Census, 1988).

Society's Attitudes toward Singles

Only a decade or two ago, society tended to place a stigma on those who remained single. Marriage was seen as the positive, desirable choice that mature adults elected; those who were unmarried were seen as antisocial or as "losers." Even today some of that thinking persists. For example, single men are often stereotyped as barhopping individuals who have endless sexual adventures, while older single women are sometimes stereotyped as "old maids" who could not "land a man" or free themselves from mother's apron strings.

Your Thoughts about Single People

1. Jot down descriptive terms that immediately come to your mind when you think of the "typical" person who fits the descriptions below. Are your reactions positive, negative, or both?
   a. Single man, 25 years old
   b. Single woman, 25 years old
   c. Single woman, 55 years old
   d. Single man, 55 years old
2. Look up the words "bachelor," "spinster," and "old maid" in a dictionary. Do the sets of definitions given for each word surprise you? What do the definitions tell you about society's notions, either now or in the past, about single people? About differing attitudes toward unmarried men and unmarried women?
3. Can you imagine yourself choosing to be single over the next twenty years? Why or why not?
4. Do you think it is easier for a person your age of the opposite sex to choose to be single for the next twenty years? Why or why not?
5. Find six advertisements in magazines or six commercials on television aimed at selling products to single people. How are the actors or models portrayed? ▲

In order to learn how stereotypes and attitudes toward single people have varied with the times, Cargan and Melko (1982) surveyed the *Readers' Guide to Periodical Literature* since 1900. Over time, they found an increase in the number of articles printed and some significant changes in the nature of the stories. Six-decade-old pieces like "There is No Place in Heaven for Old Maids" and "The Necessary Melancholy of Bachelors" have been replaced with articles such as, "How to Travel Alone and Like It," "Should a Single Person Buy a House," and "Sex as Athletics in the Singles Complex." Most dramatically, the magazine writers of the 1970s and 1980s no longer needed to justify the rationale for staying single into one's 30s. To gain further insight into changes, look at Table 10.2, which illustrates the frequency of appearance of certain topics about singles during the first half of this century and during the third quarter.

While our society is beginning to recognize that being single may be a healthy, acceptable choice for some people, single individuals still face discrimination. In one study of major companies, the managers surveyed reported that marital status was not a factor in promotion; however, only 2 percent of these same companies' executives were single. Further, more than 60 percent

TABLE 10.2	Magazine Articles on Singles[1] Per Year On These Topics			
Topic		1900–1950	1951–1975	Increase (Decrease)
Getting married (how to find a spouse)		4.5	34	656%
Happiness (state of being single)		3.5	8	129%
Explanation (compensations for being single)		6.5	12	85%
Difficulties (dilemmas of being single)		4.5	3	33%
Old maids vs. swinging bachelors (the double standard)		9.5	1	89%
Living (housing, work, money)		2.5	17	580%
Love and friendship (with the opposite sex)		3.5	4	14%
Sex (whether and how)		0	8	NA
Outside perceptions (coping with singles)		1.5	2	33%
Total of all articles on these topics only		31.5	55	75%
Total of all articles on all topics aimed at issues of the never married		32	216	575%

[1]Based on Tables 3.1 and 3.2, p. 227, Cargan & Melko, 1982

From L. Cargan and M. Melko, *Singles: Myths and Realities.* Copyright © 1982 Sage Publications, Newbury Park, California. Reprinted by permission of the authors.

of those surveyed endorsed the notion that singles tended to make "snap judgments" (Jacoby, 1974). While employers often believe that single workers are less committed to their jobs, actually many are more willing to invest time and energy in their work than their married counterparts. Discrimination also takes place in areas other than employment. Single people may encounter difficulty in obtaining loans and credit (particularly women) and in finding housing (particularly men). Societal attitudes and possible discrimination can create adjustment problems for the unmarried.

Choosing a "Single" Life-Style

Given society's attitudes and the pressure that many young people feel from parents, relatives, and perhaps friends to marry and remarry, why do men and women stay single? Some, of course, have not yet found appropriate partners, perhaps because they have not been assertive enough in their search. Others actively choose this life-style. Reasons for this choice were voiced by a sample of single people, from 20–55 years of age, who took Simenauer and Carroll's (1982) instrument and identified the following advantages of being single: personal freedom, privacy, opportunities to make a variety of friends and to mold an ideal social life, being financially responsible for and only accountable to oneself, following one's own time schedule, making the home into one's ideal environment, both in terms of decorating and keeping it clean. The respondents also listed disadvantages including loneliness, which was by and far the most frequently mentioned concern, fear of being physically harmed (a problem primarily mentioned by women), economic insecurity, worries about becoming self-absorbed, having insufficient personal contact and sexual activity, coping with social prejudices, and dealing with the "dating grind." In considering these advantages and disadvantages, remember that each item is important to some people in evaluating their single life-style while being unimportant to others.

Campbell (1975, 1981), in considering the well-being of singles, looks within certain categories and draws attention to differences related to age, gender, and past marital history. He stated: "Women can get along better without men than men can get along without women, [for] single women of all ages are happier and more satisfied with their lives than single men" (Campbell, 1975, p. 38).

In a major study of the ways in which Americans view their mental health (Veroff, Douvan, & Kulka, 1981), the researchers found "an increasing dependence of men on the institution of marriage," largely because many men experience "warmth and expressiveness" only vicariously, through their wives. When asked about how they coped with problems and periods of unhappiness, men spoke of receiving emotional support only from their wives, whereas wives were more likely to turn to sources of informal support outside the marriage. Indeed, considerable research suggests that marriage is more crucial to the health and well-being of men than of women.

People under 30 who have not married "are consistently less positive in their feelings of well-being than the rest of their age group" (Campbell, 1981, p. 184). While they experience many positive feelings they have a balancing number of negative ones such as being restless, depressed, and bored, and the supposedly "carefree bachelors" are no more positive than single women. Another striking finding is that twice as many married compared to unmarried women in this age group report themselves as being "very happy."

The 4 percent of the population who are over 30 and never married face a society not well-designed for their needs (Campbell, 1981). Neither men nor women in this category report feeling that they have had a fair share of happiness but, again, women seem to manage matters better. Ironically, being in this category is associated with being discontented and that outlook, in turn, could hamper a person's ability to do what might make him or her happy: working at the task of finding a mate.

Of course, divorced and separated people who have responsibility for children face additional issues. While Campbell (1981) found divorced men felt less constrained, burdened, and tied down than married men, divorced women were far more likely to feel these things than married women. The differences in the feelings of strain are associated with the fact that after divorce, women typically assume great responsibilities. Specifically, mothers, whose income level (and ability to hire help) generally suffers after divorce, are most often awarded child custody and must cope with trying to make "ends meet" with a reduced income.

Social Support for Single People

"The greatest need single people feel in their departure from traditional family structure is for substitute networks of human relationships that provide the basic satisfactions of intimacy, sharing and continuity" (Stein, 1976, p. 109). Without a spouse, and perhaps without children, single individuals rely more heavily on friends, parents, siblings, cousins, and so forth to provide this support. The qualities they look for in people who might fill this role, according to Stein (1976), are:

> being caring and supportive; being willing to grow close; having a sense of give and take; being accepting yet providing straightforward reactions; being honest; and being open to the sharing of feelings and activities. (In contrast to those who are married) . . . singles can more easily have close friends of both sexes.

While some single individuals may effectively find people who can ably substitute for a spouse in providing support, Campbell (1981) found most are not fully successful in this search.

One fear people harbor is whether they can depend on keeping a close friend over the long run. Single people often worry that a good friend will someday marry and let the friendship decline. Without a permanent commitment to another, a single person may fear being alone in the future. One way people deal with this fear, build a network of friends, find support in coping with personal issues, and impact on political matters related to singleness and divorce, is by joining organizations such as Parents without Partners and groups involved with singles' issues. For example, the 1989 Buckeye Single Council Directory lists over 75 organizations that serve central Ohio's single individuals.

Most single people face a greater challenge than do their married counterparts in establishing a satisfying and relatively permanent support network. But those who are fairly assertive in befriending others can generally meet their needs for companionship, recreation, and support.

SUMMARY

1. Families should be looked at developmentally, because they are ever-changing entities with their own life cycles. Families begin when couples court, then pass through the early marriage stage, the early parenthood stage, the adolescent children stage, the empty nest stage, and the postretirement stage. Children are reared and leave their parents to establish their own families, repeating the cycle.

2. Nearly all societies have used the family as an institution to help people live and work together productively. Roles performed by family members include: child care, child socialization, maintenance of kinship ties, participation in sexual activity, provision of therapeutic support, recreation, and financial provision for and maintenance of the household. Traditional sex roles have changed greatly as more women enter the work force and more men participate in child care and housekeeping chores.

3. Successful marriages are characterized by satisfied mates who are united in building their partnership and in allowing each person freedom to grow. Some factors that affect marital success are: age at marriage, length of acquaintance, communication skills, and mutual respect.

4. One widely held myth is that enduring marriages are similar. In fact, researchers have discovered a number of distinctive styles of interaction that couples use. These range from constant conflict between spouses to a style in which the marriage is vital and full of love and mutual support. There are many other myths about marriage and the family.

5. Parents have many hopes in common, including that their children will be happy and healthy and will grow into satisfied adults who contribute to society. Parents differ in how they approach the child-rearing task. Parenting models range from the "potter," who molds the child into a certain kind of person, to the "consultant," who gives much freedom to the child but is readily available for advice. Children raised by parents using one style approach the world differently than those raised by parents using another style.

6. Many writers have spoken about the decline of the American family, citing the divorce rate and the increase in cohabitation, but the family has not died. It has adapted to changing social conditions and taken new forms. Today, along with the traditional family, there are single-parent families and blended families.

7. Conflict between and among people sharing a home is inevitable. Family members develop various ways to deal with the ordinary conflicts that develop during the course of their day-to-day lives. Sometimes, more severe conflicts emerge, perhaps because of a family member's problem with drinking and drugs. Outside help is often valuable to a family under such circumstances.

8. The divorce rate has climbed 700% since the turn of the century and millions of people are affected by divorce each year. Divorce poses adjustment problems for both spouses and their children.

9. Cohabitation has increased as attitudes toward divorce and premarital sex have changed. Cohabiting couples face many of the same issues as married couples and often must deal with special problems because of their unconventional status.

10. Partly as a result of the increased divorce rate, the number of single adult Americans has reached over 50 million. Some single people must contend with others' stereotyped attitudes and prejudice in the job, housing, and loan markets. Single people generally rely more heavily on friends to meet their needs for social support and recreation. While an unmarried status may carry with it some problems, many single people enjoy their life-style and have little difficulty developing a satisfying social network.

SUGGESTED READINGS

Andrew, J. (1978). *Divorce and the American family*. New York: Franklin Watts. A discussion of topics ranging from the history of divorce to alternative life-styles and the family's future.

Gordon, T. (1975). PET: *Parent effectiveness training*. New York: New American Library. A step-by-step presentation of a philosophy and basic skills that the author believes will enable parents to raise children who are responsible and happy.

Hewlett, S., Stinnett, N., & DeFrain, J. (1985). *Secrets of strong families*. Boston: Little, Brown & Co. A look at the qualities successful families have in common and the skills they use to solve problems that most families face.

Howell, M. (1975). *Helping ourselves*. Boston: Beacon Press. A thought-provoking discussion of how families could thrive by building a network of trusted people.

Knight, B. (1980). *Enjoying single parenthood*. Toronto: Van Nostrand Reinhold. A guide to meeting and overcoming the adjustment challenges of single parenthood.

Rossi, A., Kagan, J., & Hareven, T. (1978). *The family*. New York: W. W. Norton. A scholarly, interdisciplinary, and cross-cultural exploration of issues relating to the family.

Schwebel, A., Schwebel, B., Schwebel, C., Schwebel, M., & Schwebel, R. (1989). *A guide to a happier family: Overcoming the anger, frustration, and boredom that destroy family life*. Los Angeles: J. P. Tarcher. This book explains that conflict inevitably develops in marriage and family life and presents methods people can use to confront these inevitable problems and build a more satisfying home life.

Schwebel, R. (1989). *Saying no is not enough*. New York: Newmarket Press. This book explains how to teach children from the earliest ages how to make wise decisions about drugs.

Weiss, R. (1975). *Marital separation*. New York: Basic Books. A discussion of the range of issues that an individual encounters while in an ailing marriage, while going through separation and divorce, and when starting over again. Includes many comments made by people who themselves have gone through divorce.

Work and Career Development

- The contributions that work can make to a personal sense of autonomy, identity, and adult integrity

- The growth and exploratory stages of occupational choice experienced in youth, followed by a realistic choice stage in which one identifies interests, explores the environment, and seeks to match the two

- People's reactions when a career choice is difficult, such as indecision and delay, or acceptance of parents' wishes

- Stages in a person's working life, ranging from the first job with its entry-level blues to career consolidation

- The work-related problems of the physically, psychologically, and socially handicapped, and of women and minorities

- Coping strategies people use to deal with work-related crises including the challenges posed by job dissatisfaction, unemployment, **under**employment, and workaholism

Daniel Levinson, in his study of "The Seasons of a Man's Life," found **that** a great many of his college-aged subjects were inspired by a **certain** vision of themselves in adult life. Levinson called this vision **the Dream** (Levinson et al., 1978). The Dream was the private fantasy or **aspiration** that led a young biologist, for example, to imagine himself as a distinguished investigator, a Nobel laureate, or a figure of historical importance in his field or it was the vision of hard work and community life that inspired the business executive-to-be.

We often speak of remaining true to dreams, and indeed Levinson found that a person's dream has important consequences for the future. It creates "a soil in which joyful hopes can flower," as well as illusory beliefs that must be confronted at later stages in the life span.

Some dreams take the form of the "myth of the hero." A person may see himself or herself as engaged in a noble quest, as a great painter or poet, a powerful figure in government, a prize-winning scientist or athlete. Other dreams are a mixture of the inspiring and the mundane: a person may imagine becoming an excellent craftsman, a self-sufficient farmer, a parent in a certain kind of family (Levinson et al., 1978, p. 91). The Dream is something a person can almost articulate: It is more than a fantasy and less than a considered plan. In young adulthood, dreams become increasingly rational and realistic. People seek admission to appropriate training institutions and develop the skills, talents, and concrete plans that might enable them to reach their goals.

With some people, dreams can have a negative impact if their implications and degree of realism are not assessed. A person who has a strong emotional investment in a dream should ask the following questions:

1. What exactly would it mean if I did succeed in achieving my dream? What events would have had to occur for me to reach this point? What would I be and what would I have done?

2. Assuming the dream is attained, what might be the negative aspects of realizing it?

3. Do my answers to questions 1 and 2 raise any questions about my choice of occupation?

4. If I don't achieve my dream, what are my alternatives?

For most people, realizing their dream involves entering an occupation. The vision of adult life presumes a life-style that is organized around (and supported by) some form of work. In this chapter we will be concerned not with the Dream (which is intensely personal) but with the practical means people have for realizing their dream, on the job and in an occupation.

WORK AND ITS IMPLICATIONS

Work is an activity that adults undertake to ensure the survival of themselves, their families, and their communities. Dividing up tasks to ensure common survival seems to be among the oldest of human responsibilities. In early human history, when one group undertook the specialized work of gathering vegetables or raising children, while another set out for the hunt, a new and effective social form began to evolve. And only when some people assumed the special work of gathering and sharing knowledge did the perpetuation of more advanced cultures become possible. At the level of the individual, too, work is essential to survival. People work "for a living"—that is, for food, shelter, health care, and so on. If they cannot support themselves, they depend, directly or indirectly, on others who work to support them.

Definitions of Work

The term "work" is applied to many different activities, with different meanings. To some people work means paid employment, what one does for a salary, fee, or hourly wage. When asked "Do you work?" a woman who accepts this definition may say "I stopped working when my son was born, and I plan to go back to work next year." However, child care and homemaking are responsible and demanding activities. Thus many people would expand the definition of work to include these tasks, as well as other valued activities that are not paid for in the usual sense (Parker, 1983).

While realizing that people have different ideas, we define **work** as any activity by which a person actively contributes to the productivity or well-being of society. Under this definition, the homemaker works and so do the hospital volunteer, the unpublished writer or undiscovered painter, and the

Work
Any activity by which a person actively contributes to the productivity or well-being of society.

student in pursuit of a degree. Working is what we do when we produce something, invest in something, take care of someone, or prepare ourselves to do any of these things. Work may also be seen as the opposite of consumption. It is what we put into, as opposed to what we take out of, the system.

Work and Its Meaning

Hayes and Nutman (1981) state that work is important in our society because it fulfills many essential needs. First of all it provides a source of income. But this is not the sole need it fulfills and there is evidence that people would and do continue to work when there is no financial need. In addition to income work fulfills our need to be active. Think of the boredom that comes with the inactivity associated with illness, disability, or unemployment and the pleasure of once again returning to activity.

Work structures time. It differentiates weekends and holidays from working days and provides a timetable for progressing through a career (Hayes & Nutman, 1981). Work is also a source of creativity and mastery. It permits us to explore, to try new ideas and procedures, and to master and control parts of our environment. Furthermore, work provides us with a sense of identity. We are known as teacher, computer operator, or physician. Our identity is no longer primarily determined by our family. We are no longer known as Smythe-James from Northumberland. Our job provides us with our status and with our "way of life," and, finally, gives us a sense of purpose. We have a role to fill and a contribution to make.

Work and Adjustment

The hard necessity of work has long been recognized. To "live by the sweat of the brow" is the fate given humankind in the first book of the Old Testament. The relationship of work to emotional well-being is a much more recent concern.

One woman who was interviewed by Studs Terkel explained that work was necessary because one needed the feeling of "creating something new" (Terkel, 1972, p. 552). Although she was economically free from the necessity to work, this woman found that in idleness she lacked a reason or justification for living. She concluded: "Human beings must work to create some coherence. You can only do it through work and love" (p. 555). Her conclusions echo Freud's famous remark that to be a healthy adult is to have the capacity to love and to work. This is a common viewpoint. Most contemporary concepts of mental health refer to the ability of healthy individuals to devote themselves to something larger than themselves. And that something is usually work, including the work of caring for the next generation.

Most people have great difficulty imagining themselves without any form of work. In fact, work takes up a major portion of time in adulthood, an average of six to ten hours a day.

It is interesting that a group of blue-collar workers interviewed by Rubin (1979), when asked to fantasize about what they would do if they had a million dollars, did not exclude work—they imagined a form of work that might be more gratifying. Typical is the response of a 29-year-old postal clerk:

> Like I said, my job is tedious. I'd actually be glad to quit it. I don't mean I'd quit work; nobody should ever do that. I might buy a goat farm and raise goats and pigs—just something where I could do something a person could care about . . . (Rubin, 1979, p. 162).

Peterson (1986), studying work commitment of college women, asked them what they would do if paid employment was unnecessary for them. Eighty-seven percent said they would become involved with clubs, hobbies, volunteer efforts, and personal development. Interestingly, only a relatively small number of women reported a desire to concentrate exclusively on home and family or on personal development.

Autonomy and Adult Status

To one chronically unemployed woman, working means "you don't have to depend on nobody for nothin'" (Kaplan & Tausky, 1972). The sentiment is widely shared. Being able to perform some sort of work is basic to our sense of autonomy; it means that we have arrived at that potentially most independent stage of our lives—adulthood.

Many figures of speech point to the association between work, autonomy, and the achievement of adult status. It is working that enables us to "support ourselves," to be "on our own." It is with work that we stop being cared for by others and begin, in many cases, to care for other people ourselves. Holding a paid job is not always necessary to achieve this status. The unpaid home-maker or the retired grandfather who helps with the carpentry and baby-sitting may have feelings of autonomy that come with working for a larger good, that of the family. On the other hand, not being able to work (because of extended illness, for example) threatens a person with loss of adult autonomy and status.

Kaplan and Tausky (1972) interviewed 275 chronically unemployed men and women in a large New England city. The subjects led lives characterized by "extreme deprivation." Most had no more than an eighth-grade education and, employing the standards of the U. S. Department of Labor, all were classified as "disadvantaged." The researchers sought to ascertain the meaning of work for this group by asking the question, "What is the most important thing about having a job?" Not surprisingly, most respondents emphasized work's economic function. However, a great number (84 percent) also said that they would work even if by some chance they had enough money to live comfortably without working. Table 11.1 gives the reasons why work was important to this economically deprived group.

TABLE 11.1	*The Most Important Points about Holding a Job, Reported by a Group of Unemployed Men and Women*	
The Most Important Thing About Having a Job Is:		**Percent**
To make a living and help support myself and family		52.4%
Having the security of a steady job and a steady income		9.5%
Being able to stay off welfare		1.8%
Learning to develop good working habits, e.g., getting to work on time and following directions		4.0%
Being able to pass the time and keep busy		3.3%
It keeps you out of trouble.		2.2%
It gives me a chance to use my abilities and accomplish something.		4.0%
It is a chance to learn new things and have new experiences.		3.3%
It gives me self-respect.		2.9%
To like my work and have an interesting job		10.9%
It's good for your health.		1.5%
I don't know.		2.9%
Not ascertained		1.5%
	Total	100.0%

From H. R. Kaplan and C. Tausky. "Work and the Welfare Cadillac: The Function of and Commitment to Work Among the Hard-Core Unemployed" in *Social Problems*, 1972, 19: 469–483. Copyright © Society for the Study of Social Problems.

It is significant that in some authoritarian systems an attempt is made to increase childlike feelings of dependency and compliance by depriving people of chances to work at their usual professions. Bruno Bettelheim, a psychologist and former prisoner in a Nazi concentration camp, notes that no prisoners were allowed to work in their civilian capacities, even if their skills were vitally necessary (Bettelheim, 1943). For example, although there were many physicians in camp, surgery was performed on inmates by a former printer. Bettelheim attributes his own ability to maintain his psychological balance to the fact that he could continue to do meaningful work despite appalling conditions. As a psychologist, he could not be stopped from analyzing his own behavior and that of others. Bettelheim's experience and that of other prisoners suggests that being able to work, even in confinement, enables a person to maintain a sense of adult integrity.

This observation is supported by British physician Leonard Crome in his report of the experience of one survivor, Jonny, of nine years in Nazi prisons and concentration camps. Jonny attributed his survival and good mental condition both to active work and a close working relationship with other prisoners to protect themselves (Crome, 1989).

Identity

Another psychological reward provided by work is personal identity—a sense of who one is. Abraham Maslow, the humanist psychologist, wrote convincingly and at length about the degree to which the healthy person identifies with his or her work. When Maslow asked such a person, "Who are you?" the answer was almost always the name of some vocation: "I am a lawyer;" "I am a mother;" "I am an artist." and, psychologists have found, if the person were asked to suppose that he or she had a different job, the reaction was bewilderment and surprise. "If I weren't an artist, I wouldn't be me" (Maslow, 1967; Betz, 1984).

Maslow's respondents were, in his words, exceptionally "vocation-loving." Not all people identify so strongly with their work. But most of us derive at least some of our identity from the work we do or plan to do. We often respond to remarks such as "Tell me about yourself" by mentioning an occupational role. For example, if approached at a social gathering, we do not offer evidence of heritage or birthplace (we don't say, for example, I'm a Bassett-Smythe from Northumberland). Instead we report being a lawyer, a secretary, a student, or a computer programmer at IBM. This is common social shorthand; our style of life, where we live, what types of friends we have, how we raise our children, what aspirations we have for them, may all be assumed by others once they learn what we do for a living.

And yet the relationship of work to personal identity remains somewhat controversial. Some people are unwilling to identify themselves with an occupation (still less with a company or job title). Such an individual insists, "I am more than my role. I am myself." In other words, he or she sees identification with work as a threat to individuality. A strong statement of this position can be found in one young woman's refusal to answer a questionnaire sent by her high school in preparation for a ten-year reunion. She wrote, "Neither I nor my husband can be learned about by our jobs, colleges attended, or honors won. We are individuals seeking a lifestyle, with other individuals. . . ."

The importance of work to identity is something that each person arrives at individually. Psychologists have shown that many people do in fact derive a large part of their identity from work. The research of Maslow, as well as others, suggests that those who do are fortunate in that the major portion of their time is spent in an activity that is personally gratifying. On the other hand, work situations sometimes do not encourage individuals to identify with the job they must do, and we are wise to recognize the identity potential inherent in many of life's other activities. There is no one "right" view on the relationship of work to personal identity. Further, there is no view that is guaranteed to see us through all stages of our lives. The extent to which a person derives identity from his or her career can change in response to other life developments. Becoming a parent, for example, often means that the work from which one has derived identity is temporarily put aside in the interest of new work, child care. Entering retirement may mean that a person derives more identity from community activities, hobbies, or a general life-style.

CHOOSING A CAREER

Frankl (1973) has observed that a person's opportunity for fulfillment is not tied to any particular occupation. According to Frankl, we are not in a position of having to choose the "right occupation" or else be miserable for the rest of our lives: many forms of work give us the chance to bring to bear "our uniqueness and singularity." As for happiness, it is how we see our work and how we perform it that becomes important. In other words, people give meaning to work, not the reverse.

Nevertheless, each of us is, at some point in life, faced with the necessity of making choices. Even if we feel that there are several occupations in which we might find fulfillment, we still have the problem of making the best choice or the right choice. Sometimes the choice is between jobs and sometimes it is between schools, training programs, or entry-level jobs. Holland (1985) theorizes that career choice represents an expansion of personality and an attempt to translate personal styles of behavior into one's work life.

We reach the point of choice as part of a career development process that begins in early childhood and concludes after we have left the work force. Super (1957) describes two stages of occupational choice that are important during childhood and adolescence, the *growth stage* and the *exploratory stage*.

The growth stage, which begins at birth and continues until approximately age 14, is the time when play, school, and peer and adult interactions contribute to the development of the self-concept or image we have of ourselves. As development continues, other realities further shape the self-concept. We begin to learn about those activities that interest us and match our abilities, and then we identify some that seem acceptable as potential occupations. For example, a young boy who imagines himself as a great baseball player may discover an inability to hit a baseball very far. Or the young girl who wins a school science prize learns that there are several adult occupations in which she can utilize those abilities and interests.

During the ages of 14 to 18, the preparation for career choice becomes more purposeful and the youngster enters the exploratory stage. Summer or part-time jobs are used to test future occupations. In addition, courses are taken, and family, friends, and teachers are questioned about their occupations. Important decisions are also made such as whether to attend college after high school or enter the work force.

Between the ages of 18 and 21 steps must be taken to implement the decisions made. Applications for admission to college or other appropriate training and apprenticeship programs must be completed.

The Background of Your Occupational Choice

1. When you were a small child, what did you typically say you wanted to grow up to be?
2. What interest and capabilities became apparent during your elementary school years? For example, what was:
   a. your favorite toy or play material?
   b. your best school subject?
   c. a hobby or something you collected?
   d. a subject you liked to read about?
   e. an award you received?
3. Did you visit any workplaces that impressed you as a child (for example, your mother's or father's office, your grandfather's store, a local factory, a newspaper office, a farm, a hospital)? If so, note your impressions.
4. Did your teachers express any opinions about your future occupation? (For example, did a teacher say, "Your science fair project is so clever, I'll just bet you're going to be a scientist"?) If so, describe the feelings you had when you heard this prediction.
5. When you were in the fifth or sixth grade, did you have a hero or heroine whom you read about or watched on television or in the movies? If so, describe the person.
6. In this same period, were there any adults in your immediate environment whom you greatly admired? If so, describe them.
7. Did you have a best friend in those years? If so, recall any understandings the two of you had about your respective futures? ▲

The Decision Process

Carney and Wells (1987), like Super, believe that in order to decide on a career young people must have an understanding of themselves as well as information about the world of work. A career decision does not come full blown into a person's consciousness but is a process that takes time. They described the following stages of career decision making: awareness, self-assessment, exploration, integration, commitment, implementation, and reevaluation.

The *awareness* stage is experienced by people searching for a career as a discomfort with the status quo, as a pressure for change. The individual feels an excitement and a desire to move ahead, yet at the same time is insecure, wary of the future, and fearful of making a wrong choice. A way of handling this stage productively is to attempt to define the problem and try to determine that which is blocking a decision.

Understanding the problem and the blocks to a decision involve examining our beliefs, attitudes, and values, and the sources of our fears and anxieties. Accomplishing this often reduces our anxiety and allows us to look at various career alternatives realistically, without feeling overwhelmed. The process of learning about ourselves, about our beliefs, attitudes, personality, and abilities is part of the *self-assessment* stage of career decision making.

The next stage is *exploration*. Exploration involves close examination of our own characteristics as well as collecting information about the world of work. A part of the exploration is done realistically through part-time and summer jobs, courses, and extracurricular activities. Other parts of the exploration are done through fantasy as we imagine ourselves playing the role of school teacher, nursery owner, or corporate president. We try to match what we know about ourselves with the jobs likely to be available to us and determine how the match feels. We reject alternatives that do not feel right and keep those that do. As our experiences and explorations continue, we will reduce our alternatives.

Exploration usually results in *integration*. Integration can best be described as the coming together or coalescing of what we have learned about ourselves and what we have learned about career opportunities by gathering information about the work world and attending to our dreams, plans, and fantasies. Integration is the result of gathering information, holding on to our dreams and ideals while still being realistic, accepting external limitations, and managing our feelings.

The *commitment* stage is reached at the point the person decides to pursue one of the alternatives. This stage, like the others, is not reached easily or without anxiety. Sometimes people make a commitment hesitantly. They may be unhappy postponing their choice further or may be at the end of their schooling and feel they have no option but to decide. Or, they may choose, believing they will never find out about the job unless they try it. Carney and Wells (1987) maintain that "the outcomes of a commitment made and pursued to the best of our abilities are generally very positive in terms of growth and learning, even if the commitment is later changed or abandoned" (p. 77).

Once the commitment has been made it must be *implemented* through courses of action and behavior. The result of the commitment stage may mean beginning an education process or training program to enter the decided-upon occupation or it may mean beginning the search for an entry-level job. The implementation process may be blocked by the nature of the market place, insufficient funds, or poor grades. Many people with a dream and a goal can overcome the blocks, even if it means a delay or alteration in plans. For some, however, the blocks may be insurmountable and their dreams must be altered to fit reality.

Once the individual is in the job and has mastered its requirements, he may find that the career is not as fulfilling as he expected. Even if a person's first choice was a good one, circumstances change and situations cease to be as satisfying as they once were. Also, over time he may find new goals or discover that alternatives he had rejected at earlier times now seem attainable or desirable. In these cases the person may *reevaluate* his original decision and the entire decision process may start again from the beginning, from the awareness stage.

Carney and Wells (1987) conclude "the most important thing to remember about decision making is the inescapable nature of change. Everything changes . . . We can never be sure that any decision will be the right one at any time beyond the moment we make it. Our decisions and our world must grow and change with us" (p. 23).

Career choices made in young adulthood are reversible and reworkable. People continue to modify their career goals throughout their working lives and, as a result, many shift careers. One pioneer study on career change after age 35 found that it was not unusual for people who had decided on their careers early in life, and who had pursued them with marked success, to seek new careers as a result of changes within themselves or the work environment (Hiestand, 1971). Recent research suggests that career reassessment and change are so common that they can be considered part of a predictable transition of mid-life. The term "multiple career" has been applied to describe the working life of people who have made major shifts in jobs.

In sum, the vocational decisions people make in late adolescence and young adulthood are not necessarily more final than choices they make at other points in the life span. Theorists Super and Hall (1978) say that adolescence does offer special vocational challenges. However, "it is also true that exploration is a continuing process, engaged in not only as each new life stage is . . . entered, but also as new situations and occupations are entered during the course of the working career" (p. 336).

People can remain in their career and still bring about enriching changes in their work experience. An interesting example is John Coleman who, as president of Haverford College, gave himself a unique sabbatical. At age 51 he began a series of wandering adventures across the country. His life-style seemed more appropriate to a John Steinbeck than to a staid college president. Coleman, however, would return periodically to chair a board meeting at the university (Best, 1980).

One hears about other successful people who change jobs in midcareer. People often retire from the military at about age 40 and start lucrative businesses or become successful executives. And successful executives have left powerful positions and high paying jobs to set up chicken farms. We are likely entering a period in history when life-scheduling flexibility will become more common.

First Steps

During the high school or college years, most people seek career counseling. Some see vocational counselors or psychologists, usually those connected with a school or training institution, and most seek advice from teachers, older relatives, or friends. Such consultation is part of the exploratory process. Its chief value to a person is that he learns more about himself and obtains facts about the economic environment. The person who seeks professional assistance will find that the counselor does not offer direct advice on what occupation to pursue. Instead, she encourages exploration of the person's own thoughts, attitudes, and abilities. This is the first step in career decision making.

Identifying Interests

High school and college students can identify interests that have been important to their self-concept and development. Some interests are indicated by the extracurricular activities listed beside a student's name in the yearbook, or are reflected in a high school subject concentration or college major. During the years of schooling, people examine their interests and attempt to relate them to specific careers. If a woman has been interested in politics, for example, she considers a political science major. Ideally, she works with a counselor to discover *what exactly it is* about politics that interests her. Is it holding office—running, winning, and demonstrating political leadership? Is her interest really in the management of events, people, and resources? (If so, she might be better satisfied in a related field, such as corporate business.) Is her interest in government policy and legislation (which suggests law); in current events (which suggests journalism or political group activism); or in the subject matter of political science itself (which suggests teaching or research)? Asking questions like these helps a person relate identified interests to career goals even when he or she does not yet have all the answers.

As an additional tool, some counselors administer tests that profile a student's interest in quantitative terms. Among these are the Kuder Occupational Scale and the Strong Interest Inventory. The latter test compares the interests

STRONG INTEREST INVENTORY OF THE
STRONG VOCATIONAL INTEREST BLANKS

PROFILE REPORT FOR: DATE TESTED:

ID: DATE SCORED:
AGE: SEX:

SPECIAL SCALES: ACADEMIC COMFORT
INTROVERSION-EXTROVERSION

TOTAL RESPONSES: INFREQUENT RESPONSES:

GOT

R	
I	
A	
S	
E	
C	

OCCUPATIONAL SCALES

STANDARD SCORES F M

	VERY DISSIMILAR	DISSIMILAR	MODERATELY DISSIMILAR	MID-RANGE	MODERATELY SIMILAR	SIMILAR	VERY SIMILAR

REALISTIC

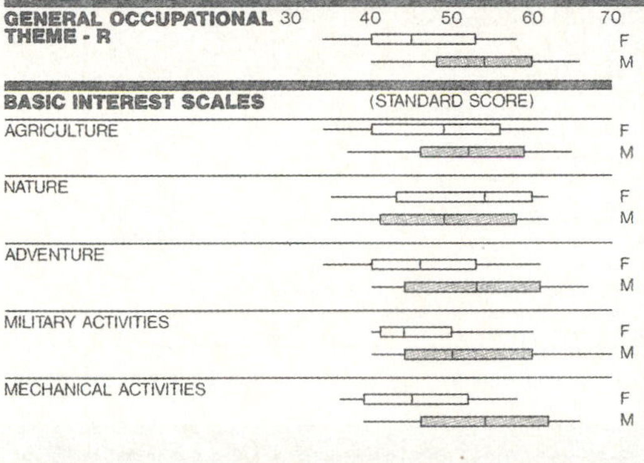

GENERAL OCCUPATIONAL THEME - R   30 40 50 60 70   F   M

BASIC INTEREST SCALES (STANDARD SCORE)

AGRICULTURE   F   M
NATURE   F   M
ADVENTURE   F   M
MILITARY ACTIVITIES   F   M
MECHANICAL ACTIVITIES   F   M

Standard scores scale: 15 25 30   40 45 55

F	M	Occupation	Score
[CRS]	RC	Marine Corps enlisted personnel	(CRS)
RC	RC	Navy enlisted personnel	
RC	RC	Army officer	
RI	RIC	Navy officer	
R	R	Air Force officer	
[C]		Air Force enlisted personnel	(C)
R	R	Police officer	
R	R	Bus driver	
R	R	Horticultural worker	
RC	R	Farmer	
R	RCS	Vocational agriculture teacher	
RI	R	Forester	
[IR]	RI	Veterinarian	(IR)
RIS	[SR]	Athletic trainer	(SR)
RS	R	Emergency medical technician	
RI	RI	Radiologic technologist	
RI	R	Carpenter	
RI	R	Electrician	
RIA	[ARI]	Architect	(ARI)
RI	RI	Engineer	

INVESTIGATIVE

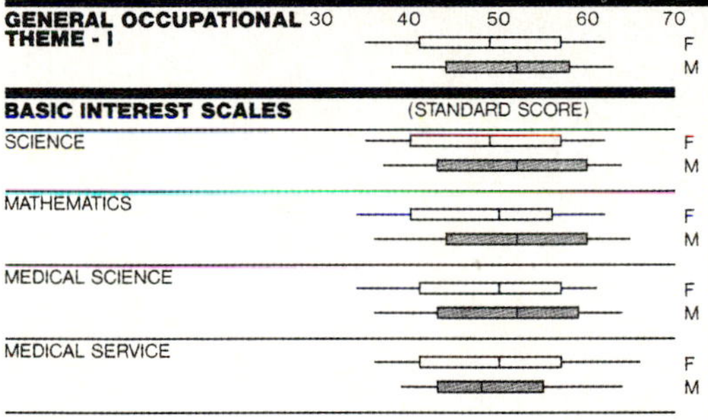

GENERAL OCCUPATIONAL THEME - I   30 40 50 60 70   F   M

BASIC INTEREST SCALES (STANDARD SCORE)

SCIENCE   F   M
MATHEMATICS   F   M
MEDICAL SCIENCE   F   M
MEDICAL SERVICE   F   M

Standard scores scale: 15 25 30   40 45 55

F	M	Occupation	Score
IRC	IRC	Computer programmer	
IRC	IRC	Systems analyst	
IRC	IR	Medical technologist	
IR	IR	R & D manager	
IR	IR	Geologist	
IR	[I]	Biologist	(I)
IR	IR	Chemist	
IR	IR	Physicist	
IR	[RI]	Veterinarian	(RI)
IRS	IR	Science teacher	
IRS	IRS	Physical therapist	
IR	IRS	Respiratory therapist	
IC	IR	Medical technician	
IC	IE	Pharmacist	
ISR	[CSE]	Dietitian	(CSE)
[SI]	ISR	Nurse, RN	(SI)
IR	I	Chiropractor	
IR	IR	Optometrist	
IR	IR	Dentist	
I	IA	Physician	
[IR]	I	Biologist	(IR)
I	I	Mathematician	
IR	I	Geographer	
I	I	College professor	
IA	IA	Psychologist	
IA	IA	Sociologist	

ARTISTIC

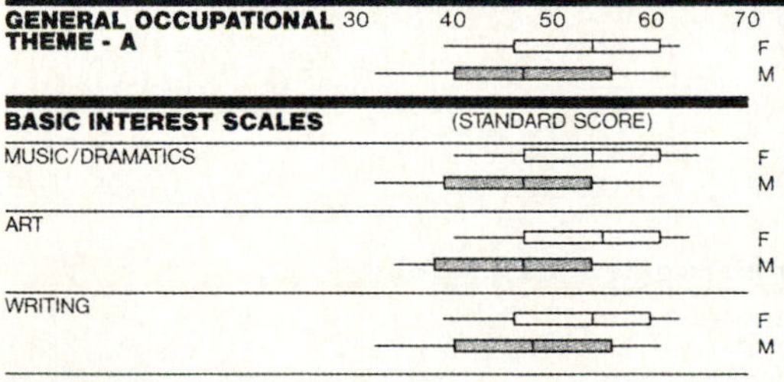

GENERAL OCCUPATIONAL THEME - A   30 40 50 60 70   F   M

BASIC INTEREST SCALES (STANDARD SCORE)

MUSIC/DRAMATICS   F   M
ART   F   M
WRITING   F   M

Standard scores scale: 15 25 30   40 45 55

F	M	Occupation	Score
AI	AI	Medical illustrator	
A	A	Art teacher	
A	A	Artist, fine	
A	A	Artist, commercial	
AE	A	Interior decorator	
[RIA]	ARI	Architect	(RIA)
A	A	Photographer	
A	A	Musician	
AR	[EA]	Chef	(EA)
[E]	AE	Beautician	(E)
AE	A	Flight attendant	
A	A	Advertising executive	
A	A	Broadcaster	
A	A	Public relations director	
A	A	Lawyer	
A	AS	Public administrator	
A	A	Reporter	
A	A	Librarian	
AS	AS	English teacher	
[SA]	AS	Foreign language teacher	(SA)

CONSULTING PSYCHOLOGISTS PRESS, INC.
577 COLLEGE AVENUE
PALO ALTO, CA 94306

Figure 11.1a Strong interest inventory of the Strong Vocational Interest Blanks.

PROFILE REPORT FOR: **DATE TESTED:**

ID: **DATE SCORED:**

AGE: **SEX:**

OCCUPATIONAL SCALES

	STANDARD SCORES		VERY DISSIMILAR	DISSIMILAR	MODERATELY DISSIMILAR	MID-RANGE	MODERATELY SIMILAR	SIMILAR	VERY SIMILAR
	F	M							

SOCIAL

			15 25 30			40 45 55			

GENERAL OCCUPATIONAL THEME - S 30 40 50 60 70 F / M

F	M		
SA	(AS)	Foreign language teacher	(AS)
SA	SA	Minister	
SA	SA	Social worker	
S	S	Guidance counselor	
S	S	Social science teacher	
S	S	Elementary teacher	
S	S	Special education teacher	
SRI	SAR	Occupational therapist	
SIA	SAI	Speech pathologist	
SI	(ISR)	Nurse, RN	(ISR)
SCI	N/A	Dental hygienist	N/A
SC	SC	Nurse, LPN	
(RIS)	SR	Athletic trainer	(RIS)
SR	SR	Physical education teacher	
SRE	SE	Recreation leader	
SE	SE	YWCA/YMCA director	
SEC	SCE	School administrator	
SCE	N/A	Home economics teacher	N/A

BASIC INTEREST SCALES (STANDARD SCORE)

TEACHING — F / M
SOCIAL SERVICE — F / M
ATHLETICS — F / M
DOMESTIC ARTS — F / M
RELIGIOUS ACTIVITIES — F / M

ENTERPRISING

			15 25 30			40 45 55			

GENERAL OCCUPATIONAL THEME - E 30 40 50 60 70 F / M

F	M		
E	ES	Personnel director	
ES	E	Elected public official	
ES	ES	Life insurance agent	
EC	E	Chamber of Commerce executive	
EC	EC	Store manager	
N/A	ECR	Agribusiness manager	N/A
EC	EC	Purchasing agent	
EC	E	Restaurant manager	
(AR)	EA	Chef	(AR)
EC	E	Travel agent	
ECS	E	Funeral director	
(CSE)	ESC	Nursing home administrator	(CSE)
EC	ER	Optician	
E	E	Realtor	
E	(AE)	Beautician	(AE)
E	E	Florist	
EC	E	Buyer	
EI	EI	Marketing executive	
EIC	ECI	Investments manager	

BASIC INTEREST SCALES (STANDARD SCORE)

PUBLIC SPEAKING — F / M
LAW/POLITICS — F / M
MERCHANDISING — F / M
SALES — F / M
BUSINESS MANAGEMENT — F / M

CONVENTIONAL

			15 25 30			40 45 55			

GENERAL OCCUPATIONAL THEME - C 30 40 50 60 70 F / M

F	M		
C	C	Accountant	
C	C	Banker	
CE	CE	IRS agent	
CES	CES	Credit manager	
CES	CES	Business education teacher	
(CS)	CES	Food service manager	(CS)
(ISR)	CSE	Dietitian	(ISR)
CSE	(ESC)	Nursing home administrator	(ESC)
CSE	CSE	Executive housekeeper	
CS	(CES)	Food service manager	(CES)
CS	N/A	Dental assistant	N/A
C	N/A	Secretary	N/A
C	(R)	Air Force enlisted personnel	(R)
CRS	(RC)	Marine Corps enlisted personnel	(RC)
CRS	CR	Army enlisted personnel	
CIR	CIR	Mathematics teacher	

BASIC INTEREST SCALES (STANDARD SCORE)

OFFICE PRACTICES — F / M

CONSULTING PSYCHOLOGISTS PRESS, INC.
577 COLLEGE AVENUE
PALO ALTO, CA 94306

ADMINISTRATIVE INDEXES (RESPONSE %)

OCCUPATIONS	%	%	%
SCHOOL SUBJECTS	%	%	%
ACTIVITIES	%	%	%
LEISURE ACTIVITIES	%	%	%
TYPES OF PEOPLE	%	%	%
PREFERENCES	%	%	%
CHARACTERISTICS	%	%	%
ALL PARTS	%	%	%

Figure 11.1b Strong interest inventory of the Strong Vocational Interest Blank (continued).

of the test-taker to the interests of successful people in a variety of professions. These tests do not usually reveal new and unsuspected interests, and are not designed to reveal abilities. Their chief value is in helping the counselor and student see the connections between interest patterns and broad career categories. Figures 11.1a and b give you an idea of the kind of information you can obtain by taking this test.

Taking a formal or informal inventory of one's interests is an important part of the career decision-making process because it allows counselors to compare results of tested interests with occupational directions under consideration. When tested interests do not match the proposed career choice(s), it may suggest uncertainty and a lack of identity in the young person. Very often counseling results in a closer alignment between tested interests and expressed career interests, which enhances the likelihood of a more stable and appropriate choice of occupation (Slaney, 1984). But it is important to note that interests are not a reliable guide to *all* possibilities. A person can only be interested in what he or she has been exposed to. For some young people, college represents a first introduction to disciplines such as philosophy or fine arts criticism, and it is not unusual to hear statements about "a whole new world opening."

Also, some kinds of endeavors only begin to appeal to us when we reach intellectual maturity (which happens, developmental psychologists suggest, in late adolescence). For example, a science writer who interviewed famous biologists found that science, as a calling, came during adolescence, at about age 16 or 17 (Judson, 1978). Presumably, this is because it is only then that a person begins to understand the abstract reasoning processes that underlie scientific discovery. For a variety of reasons, then, the young person cannot base an occupational choice wholly on interests that have been developed in earlier periods.

Testing Self-Perceptions

As people identify their interests and opportunities, they naturally ask themselves, "What kind of a person am I?" and "What kind of role can a person like me play?" In other words, they attempt to translate the self-concept into occupational terms (Super, 1953). This is basic to occupational choice, for in our society the kind of person you are is seen as determining the kinds of work you would do well at and enjoy.

People enter the exploratory stage of occupational choice with a lifelong history of self-perceptions. For example, in interviews with college students about their vocational futures, professors often hear comments such as:

"I need to be able to talk with others every so often. I'm a people person."
"I'm creative. I have to use my creativity."
"I hate being the center of attention."
"I need work where I look at both sides of a question."
"I don't like a boss looking over my shoulder."
"I couldn't sit at a desk all day."

An important step in the career decision-making process is to reexamine these perceptions. In some cases they are inaccurate or outdated. For example, inexperience in the world of work or overgeneralization from a particular experience may cause a person to hold a belief that has not yet been tested. The woman who stated she "needs to talk every so often" might have been generalizing from the fact that she has a sociable disposition and loves to talk to people or from a boring part-time job she once had, where the chief gratification was in talking with coworkers. In fact, she might well be able to work in a more isolated setting evaluating electrocardiograms or doing fashion layouts. An important step for her is to ask herself whether her self-concept about the work situation has a valid basis.

Some people's self-concepts are accurate but not sufficiently defined. Consider the person who feels he has to look at both sides of the question. This statement has become part of his self-concept, but before he uses it to select an occupation, he must know whether in fact he refers to a logical skill, a sense of fairness, an argumentative personality, or merely an inability to make up his mind.

Especially important is the evaluation of all the statements that people habitually make about their limitations. These are the "cannot do" statements: "I could never work in an office" or "I can't do a thing with figures." Sometimes, of course, they are accurate. But just as often they act as blinders. By believing them, people deny themselves opportunities, perhaps on the evidence of some childhood failure, real or imagined.

In this way, many people restrict their career choices in adolescence and adulthood. A typical example is Rita, a homemaker who always claimed to be poor with numbers and lacking "a business mind." She described herself as a person whose main talent was helping others. And in this she was accurate: she had enjoyed a brief career as a kindergarten teacher, and since marrying, had helped her husband with his home contracting business. When her husband was temporarily disabled, Rita had to assume some management responsibilities. To her surprise, her ability to get the most out of people made her quite successful in his small business where the main problem was in retaining unskilled and unmotivated help. And she learned to keep the company books. In short, she discovered that she was a skilled businesswoman. An untested assumption about herself and her limitations had prevented her from recognizing her broad career options earlier in life.

The tendency to make choices based on a limited self-concept is regularly observed, even in the most intelligent and confident people. For example, an American corporation that seeks to promote its best scientists to a high management position may find that the scientist often resists, saying, "I'm purely a technical expert. I couldn't be 'political' or profit-oriented." Whereas some scientists stay in technical positions because of their limited self-view and some because they love their work, others accept the opportunity to manage as a challenge, eventually overcoming their self-doubts, and finding they are well able to exercise corporate leadership.

During young adulthood it makes sense to reexamine the limitations we have set for ourselves and discard those that rest on childhood fictions. As our examples suggest, this is by no means the last chance to do this: life circumstances and the need for personal growth encourage people to reexamine their self-limitations at many points in the life span.

Are there sex differences in self-concept and to what extent do self-concepts predict life goals? Zuckerman (1985), after studying college students, concluded that men and women did not differ on important dimensions of self-concept such as self-esteem and interpersonal self-confidence. However, these global dimensions did not predict educational goals and life priorities as did more specific self-concept dimensions including perceived math and science ability, leadership, and public speaking. For example, women's self-confidence in math and science ability is associated with higher educational goals (Zuckerman, 1985).

Many people limit their career possibilities by coming to believe incorrect assumptions they draw about themselves. They may also impose limits on themselves by believing career myths.

A *career myth* can be defined as an irrational attitude about the career development process. Dorn and Welch (1985) described 13 career myths.*

1. Quitters never win, or once a career decision has been made, it can never be changed.
2. There is a proper work role for men and women.
3. The sole purpose of going to college is to obtain skills and find a job.
4. There is a specific person, expert enough about career development and career selection that he can tell individuals what career to select.
5. There is one perfect job for each individual.
6. The passage of time alone will contribute to a career decision.
7. By working harder, planning earlier, and moving quickly the process of career selection can be speeded up.
8. Work is the most important aspect of life.
9. Vocational planning is an exact science.
10. Anyone can do anything they want with enough hard work, regardless of their circumstances or abilities.
11. Happiness depends on vocational success.
12. People's intrinsic worth can be measured by the careers they have selected.
13. People can succeed because their interest is high even though their ability is low.

Defining Values

As we have seen, many of the statements people make about their career needs are based on experiences. For example, a man who feels he could never work for a large corporation may have had an experience that explains his attitude. Perhaps as a child he suffered personally from frequent relocations resulting from his father's changing corporate role. But it is just as likely that his at-

*From F. Dorn and N. Welch. "Assessing Career Mythology: A Profile of High School Students" in *The School Counselor*, 33 (2), 136–142, 1985. Copyright © 1985 American School Counselor Association.

Your Self-Limiting Statements: Justified or Not?

1. At the moment are you feeling:
   a. especially self-confident?
   b. lacking in confidence?
   c. about as confident as usual?
2. After having made this determination, list the things you feel you are "not good at." (For example: "I am not good at office work.")
3. List the environments that you could "never work in." (For example: "I could never work at a desk all day"; "I could never work for a large corporation.")
4. For each response you have made to Questions 2 and 3, describe the *experience* that accounts for your attitude. (For example, reexperience a failure in office work or some similar task; reexperience a difficulty you had in working for a large organization.)
5. Now, reevaluate: Do your experiences seem to justify the limitations you have found in yourself?
6. Develop counterarguments. Identify those strengths you have that might enable you to succeed in the things listed in Question 2. Figure out under what conditions you might be able to work in the environments listed in Question 3. ▲

titude reflects values. He may place a high value on altruism and assume that there is little opportunity for service to others in a corporate setting. In this case, he is introducing values and value assumptions into the career decision-making process. That is, he is attempting to express what things are important to him and what things are less important.

Some vocational counselors begin an interview with questions about values. These questions may touch upon broad, ideological values (one's ideas about altruism, military service, and the morality of different occupations) and also address values that may be more directly related to a given job (for example, the relative importance of a chance to earn a high salary or work with congenial people).

In the area of values, as in other areas, career decision making requires a careful statement and an examination of one's views. Even the values a person holds most strongly may not have been explicitly examined and related to career choice. For example, David, a politically active premed student, had always had an altruistic personality. However, he said: "When I told an instructor that I plan to work with people in some sort of helpful way as a profession, he said, 'Why?' and I was completely taken aback. I had never really asked the question why it was good to help others" (Goethals & Klos, 1976, p. 168). David found that his altruism was deeply instilled but never examined in detail.

In such a situation, self-questioning can lead to consideration of the gratifications that resulted from helping behaviors in the past, a weighing of the different types of gratifications experienced, and a choice of career based on increased self-knowledge.

Although values are more difficult to test and measure than achievements or interests, several tests have been developed to help students take inventory of their work-related values. The values that are measured differ from test to test. However, one researcher suggests that an "armchair list" of values would include clusters such as money-income, power-authority, stability-security, adventure-excitement-change, independence-autonomy, knowledge-new ideas, prestige-fame-recognition, and the like (Katz, 1966, p. 4). These values are not independent of one another, and they do not describe all the rewards that one can find in the workplace (the opportunity to work with congenial people is not on the researcher's list). The chief purpose of inventories that examine values is to help individuals look more closely at the things they care about and their order of importance. Using inventory results, a guidance counselor can help identify a group of occupations that seem to afford the best opportunities for satisfying the values expressed (Cochran, 1983).

Exploring the Economic Environment

Self-exploration is an important part of occupational decision making at every point in the life span. But it is only part of the process. At some point people turn their attention to prospective employers. Usually, they begin to consider the real economic environment that surrounds them. Typically they ask: What kinds of opportunities are available? What kinds of qualifications and training are necessary for a given occupation? And what kinds of rewards will be forthcoming?

These are difficult questions. The person who graduates from high school or college today is faced with an uncertain economic environment of tremendous complexity. The number of occupations that exist has grown dramatically over the last decade, with the greatest increases being in those white-collar categories most attractive to college-bound students. Many of these occupations are responses to technological or bureaucratic developments about which the high school or college graduate needs to be knowledgeable. It is often assumed that the career niches created by the new technology are available only to high-level engineers, computer specialists, and the like. In fact, many of the occupations that have grown most rapidly (such as paramedical specialties) require only apprenticeship or junior college training, and may thus be considered at an earlier time in a person's education.

No one individual can expect to be knowledgeable about all the existing occupational categories. Even vocational counselors must regularly consult directories, handbooks, and indexes. This points up an important fact about the strategy of career decision making: the effective person is the one who knows how to find and use information about occupations of interest and about the

economic environment in general. Knowing one's abilities, interests, and values suggest that one was "meant to be" an English teacher, for example, does not necessarily lead to good career adjustment. One needs to know about opportunities for English teachers (now and in the future), about training that is required, about advancement potential, and about alternative uses for that training. The individual who is relying on personal experience with a series of English teachers, or on advice from parents, has not yet done ample research.

A next step is to survey the environment, acquiring information that enables one to test his or her current ideas about careers and to gain a deeper understanding. One way to begin is to consult a general reference, such as the *Occupational Outlook Handbook.* This handbook, published by the U. S. Department of Labor, is available in most libraries. Following are the basic occupational categories listed in the table of contents, along with some examples.

> Administrative and managerial occupations (includes accountants, city managers, buyers, health services administrators, etc.)
> Engineers, surveyors, and architects
> Natural scientists and mathematicians (includes statisticians, chemists, oceanographers, foresters, etc.)
> Social scientists, social workers, religious workers, and lawyers (includes market research analysts, psychologists, recreation workers, pastors, etc.)
> Teachers, librarians, and counselors
> Health diagnosing and treating practitioners (includes physicians, veterinarians, etc.)
> Registered nurses, pharmacists, dieticians, therapists, and physician assistants
> Health technologists and technicians (includes dental hygienists, medical record technicians, etc.)

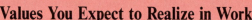
Values You Expect to Realize in Work

1. Below are some values that may be realized in work (Katz, 1966). List them in order of their approximate importance to you at this stage in your life span.

   money-income   knowledge-new ideas
   power-authority   altruistic service
   stability-security   prestige-fame-recognition
   adventure-excitement-change   intrinsic activity interest
   independence-autonomy

2. Define the two values you placed at the top of your list, giving examples of occupations that might allow you to realize these values.

3. What is there about you (for example, what experiences or parental training have you had) that might explain your having put these two values at the head of your list?

4. Next, experience a different perspective. Choose a value that you placed near the bottom of your list, and specify circumstances under which it might become important to you. For example, if stability-security is not now highly valued, are there circumstances in which it might become so?

▲

Writers, artists, and entertainers (includes reporters, interior designers, signers, etc.)

Technologists and technicians, except health (includes air traffic controllers, legal assistants, programmers, etc.)

Marketing and sales occupations (includes travel agents, models, insurance agents, etc.)

Administrative support occupations, including clerical (includes airline reservation agents, bank tellers, secretaries, etc.)

Service occupations (includes police officers, chefs, medical assistants, hotel housekeepers, barbers, etc.)

Agricultural and forestry occupations

Mechanics and repairers (includes appliance repairers, computer service technicians, etc.)

Construction and extractive occupations (includes bricklayers, insulation workers, carpenters, etc.)

Production occupations (includes bookbinders, furniture upholsterers, jewelers, welders, etc.)

Transportation and material moving occupations (includes intercity bus drivers, merchant marine officers, etc.)

Helpers, handlers, equipment cleaners, and laborers

Military occupations

For each occupation, the handbook gives the nature of the work, places of employment, training and other qualifications, employment outlook, requirements for advancement (if applicable), earning and working conditions, and—most important—sources of additional information. Another government source that is often helpful is the *Dictionary of Occupational Titles*. This dictionary is published in two volumes, with supplements. It offers descriptions of about 20,000 jobs. In addition, it provides a system for matching personality traits with different forms of work. Together the Handbook (see page 512) and the Dictionary (see above) can help expand a person's conception of the careers that are available.

There are also computer systems that present information and can guide an individual in making career decisions. An example is the System of Interactive Guidance and Information (SIGI). Through this system a student can interact with a computer in a way that allows him or her to examine personal values and obtain useful information (for example, about job trends and how they will affect different occupational choices). The interaction helps the student explore educational and occupational options, arrive at a tentative career decision, and modify the decision as new insights and information are gained (Katz, 1979).

Of course, general references and computer interactions do not give a detailed inside view of an occupation. Once a person has identified the occupation in which he or she is most interested, it is important to check more specialized sources. These range from biographies of well-known people in the field to self-help books on job preparation and advancement. A book, for example, on how to be a fashion designer or free-lance photographer, will give practical information on aspects of the job not usually known to the public. Books on running one's own business describe financial and legal tactics; topical books on corporate life tell what it is like to advance (or not advance) in a large organization. In addition to books, pamphlets on specific fields can often be located in the library, and current magazine articles are listed in the periodical guides. Finally, a true "inside" view of an occupation may be gained from materials published for those already working in the field. In this category are magazines and newspapers published by trade and professional organizations, and professional materials dealing with ethics, standards, licensing, and testing. For example, a person who wanted to know more about civil service opportunities in a large city might read through recent issues of the *Civil Service News*.

In addition to printed resources, most people utilize personal contacts to find out about an occupation. Often one knows someone in the field, especially when an occupation is traditional in a community. If not—or if the person feels a need to go beyond the authorities immediately at hand—interviews can be set up through a local professional organization or through the academic department related to the occupational area. For example, an anthropology professor might be able to set up an interview with an archeologist or linguist. In general, established workers can share a great deal about the actual *experience* of being in an occupation, at different levels of career development.

Lastly, besides having preparatory value, part-time work or courses involving field work are other ways students can have contact with workers in the desired field.

Exploration of the environment, no matter how thorough, does not result in a final "answer" or decision. First of all, much of the critical information about an occupation will not be learned until a person is on the job. Second, many economic events that vitally affect job holders in a field are not anticipated by economists and planners. And finally, even as you read this chapter, technological advances are in the process of creating new jobs that will be available in the future. Because technological change is so rapid, and affects job options so greatly, people must continually examine the environment to discover new niches that appear in the economic machinery. As one self-help writer points out, "If you're young, let's face it, the best job you're going to find in the next 40 years isn't yet institutionalized. It might exist in some people's heads or on the planning boards within university think tanks or in management consulting files" (Irish, 1973, p. xxi).

Problems of Choosing a Career

Between 1973 and 1983 high schools across the country have significantly increased their involvement with students in helping them choose careers. For example, there was a 16 percent increase in the proportion of 11th graders who reported receiving "some" or "a lot" of help with career planning from their schools. This translates into half a million more students. There was also an increase in the population of 8th and 11th graders who reported having talked several times to a teacher about goals, interest, and abilities related to different kinds of jobs. Significantly more 11th graders in 1983 than 1973 reported that they took a course that studied several different types of jobs (Prediger & Sawyer, 1986).

Moratorium: Indecision and Delay

In our society people are expected to commit themselves to a career, however tentatively, during their early twenties. A whole series of decisions force the issue: the young adult must choose a training course or a college, then a major, then perhaps field work or a graduate school—all in preparation for some type of vocation.

Yet there are many people who go through the college years without forming any occupational commitments. Some are actively struggling to make a commitment; others either are unconcerned or have worked out some satisfactory justification for avoiding the commitment (Orlofsky, Marcia, & Lesser, 1973). The inability to choose may lead to endless schooling, with the person sometimes referred to as a "professional student." Or it may lead to "dropping out." In either case, such people seem to need more time to explore themselves and their environment than is conventionally allotted. They are assumed to be in the middle of an identity crisis, and are said to be "trying to find themselves."

The period of indecision is usually a time of considerable anxiety, not only for the young adult but for the person's parents and teachers. It is assumed that something has gone wrong. Many psychologists take a different view, at least when considering the lives of some people. In these individuals, they observe, there is a healthy interval, or **moratorium** period, between childhood and full adult status. During this period people do what is necessary to establish a clearer identity and explore their potential. They cast about for a compelling idea to which they might devote their lives. Often they assume a series of transitory identities, and may literally wander from place to place (Erikson, 1976).

Erik Erikson has written at length and rather romantically about the youthful moratorium. In his own life it involved being an artist of sorts, constantly engaging in hiking, and reading and quoting from philosophy books carried in his knapsack. The moratorium drew to an end when a friend introduced Erikson to a teaching job and to the circle of Anna Freud. (The "compelling idea" to which Erikson became drawn was psychoanalysis.) As a youth, Erikson was not aware he was passing through a moratorium. But in retrospect—and in his study of others' lives—he identified this period as a necessary prelude to later creativity. Though seemingly conflicted and unable to progress, the person in a moratorium is unknowingly preparing to play some special role.

Not all psychologists agree with Erikson about the developmental importance or desirability of the moratorium. Nevertheless, there is a growing recognition that going from place to place, interrupting formal education temporarily, or simply keeping one's options open past the expected point is a desirable strategy for some young people. The period of confusion is thought to result in stronger eventual commitments and in personal growth. In studies of college students, for example, highest scores on various measures of ego identity were earned by those students who had lived through a moratorium. These students had experienced a crisis, involving confusion and an active search among alternatives, followed by a commitment to an occupation or a personal investment in an ideology (Podd, 1972). Most emerged from the moratorium stage with mature moral values and career decisions based on their own needs.

We can see that the moratorium tends to be interpreted positively, at least after the fact. However, the effect of a moratorium depends on individual circumstances. One important factor is the support that people receive for their behavior from people significant to them and from institutions. Erikson notes that the aimless wanderers of his own generation depended on some small stipend from home. Today, too, the student who "drops out" to look about him is usually in a better position if he can count on parental support, financial or otherwise.

Steve, for example, decided to delay his entry into college, knowing, as he put it, "I can always go back." His parents were professionals who had both worked their way through college. Given what they went through they expected a full-speed-ahead program for their son. But Steve, who had always been an academic achiever, did not know what he wanted to study. Because he took his studies very seriously, and was unable to conceive of himself picking and choosing among courses in an exploratory way, Steve did not want to enter college until his academic goals were definite. His parents were dismayed by his decision, but were quick to agree that Steve could "always go back." They utilized their many contacts to help Steve find a job. For about eight months Steve worked as a bookkeeper in a small firm. The work was not dehumanizing or boring, as he had feared, and he liked the "people" part of it. But it was not challenging to him either. He quit the job and took four months off to read and think about where his real interests lay. He then entered college with the goal of becoming a sociologist. Working for a year turned out to be a useful strategy for Steve because it allowed him to "see what work is really like" while keeping his options open.

For others, this kind of moratorium is not so easily managed. Financial constraints, the absence of parental support, and the practical difficulties of resuming one's coursework make actions like Steve's less feasible. The same factors can create problems with the less obvious types of moratorium—indecisive selection of courses or endless schooling at the graduate level. Much depends on support from parents and institutions and on the likelihood of being able to make a commitment under favorable conditions in the future. As Ginzberg said, "The principal challenge that young people face during their teens is to develop a strategy that will keep their options open, at least to the extent of assuring their admission to college or getting a job with a preferred employer" (1972, p. 171). While some students want to "eat their cake and have it, too"—maintain their freedom of choice while also maintaining the freedom to enter any career they wish—such an attitude is not always realistic.

Conflicts with Parents

In choosing an occupation, a person is dealing not only with interests, abilities, and economic forecasts; he or she is also dealing with parental expectations. Parents are influential in their children's choice of career. Young people tend to depend on their parents for guidance on issues of major concern.

A study of Stanford University students indicated that 70 percent of freshmen said their parents were a moderate to major influence on their career choices. Splete and Freeman-George (1985) listed family influence factors that affect one's career decision making and career development directly and indirectly. They are geographic location, genetic inheritance, family background, socioeconomic status, family composition, parenting style, and parental work-related attitudes.

The Educational Testing Service concluded from their research that parents and friends do the most to stimulate and moderate young people's occupational plans (Otto & Call, 1985). However, conflicts between parental expectations and the young persons's choice are common and to be expected. And when college students are asked to discuss the problems of career commitment, conflict with parents is a recurring theme. Some students speak of heated disagreements over an academic major. (Should one study fine art or something "practical" like art education?) Others seem to be embroiled in a conflict over who (they or their parents) will influence important decisions for the rest of their lives.

There are several reasons why occupational choice so often becomes a focus of parent-child conflict. First (and usually obvious to both parties) is that it raises the issue of identification. How closely does the person identify with the parents' occupations, social goals, or values? In choosing an occupation and life-style, one is in effect choosing to be similar to or different from one's parents. The issue is believed to be more pronounced in relation to the same-sex parent. For example, a son's identification with his father has been found to be especially significant in the development of career-related interests (Crites, 1962). Deviation from the parental pattern, unless supported by the parent, may be felt as a rejection.

It is easy to see why this is so. The successful businessman may wish to see his life justified and its value reinforced by a child who follows in his footsteps and his firm. If his child chooses to be a philosopher or an itinerant craftsman, if the child expresses displeasure at the prospect of sitting at a desk or making a sale, the parent may get the message that his own life was "not good enough," and a conflict may ensue.

In another scenario, conflict arises when parents expect their child to do what they were *not* able to do; for example, attain a higher economic level or occupational status. Ironically, if the child succeeds, the parents may feel ambivalent. They are pleased about the success, but fearful about eventual rejection and neglect by the "achieving offspring." If the child does not comply (for example, discontinues college or chooses a less prestigious field), the parents may be painfully disappointed, as they are, to some degree, with their own lives.

Finally, an explosive issue for most young adults is independence, or autonomy. As we have seen, working is essential to the achievement of adult status. Qualifying oneself for some form of work may rightly be seen as a realistic step toward independence. The problem is that many occupations require advanced education, and this in turn may require continued parental support. Parents may contribute tuition (wholly or in part), health insurance, a place to live, a part-time job in the family business, or financial resources in the event of an emergency. When so much must still be provided, development of autonomy becomes problematic. Young adults in this situation may have difficulty making a career choice that conflicts with parental expectations. If relationships with their parents become strained, they may make occupational choices that stem from a generalized desire to assert independence. For example, they may decide to take a job or join the Navy so as to be able to leave home, not because these choices are most likely to result in job satisfaction, but to achieve independence.

There is not one successful way of coping with parent-child conflict over career choice. However, psychologists agree that accepting without question the goals of parents or other significant adults is not an effective strategy—at least not in the long run. This reaction, sometimes called **foreclosure,** is associated with a low level of ego development. The state of being "one's own person" has not yet arrived. In accepting the goals of significant others, the individual has for a time passed up the opportunity to independently work out an occupational identity.

Foreclosure
A career choice in young adulthood that involves unquestioning acceptance of goals that parents have set for the person.

Personal Adjustment through the Life Span

One goal of vocational counseling is to help people understand the basis of their occupational choices and to reexamine those that are derived wholly from parents or others. The reexamination requires considerable insight. For example, foreclosure sounds like a grim process, accompanied by overt parental pressure, but it sometimes takes place quietly in the absence of parental directives. Sometimes people identify so closely with their parents' goals that they accept an occupational identity without realizing, perhaps for many years, how little thought they actually gave to it. This experience is described by a clergyman, who at the age of 39, asked himself, "What was the nature of the choice I made to become a minister?" He writes:

> In answer, it is clear to me now that [the choice] was based upon immature reasons not then realized or pointed out. The choice was then immediately acted upon and reacted to by people in such a way that continued liberty in the choice was taken away. It is not that the choice would have been reversed, but the choice would have been strengthened properly had it remained an open decision . . . (Whitlock, 1968).

As this experience suggests, the danger is not in choosing a vocation that is highly regarded by parents and others, but in acting in such a way that other options are prematurely foreclosed.

A strategy seemingly quite different from foreclosure is complete rejection of parental values. This involves outright violation of parents' expectations about schooling, jobs, and life-style. Examples might be the politician's son who becomes a farmer and free-lance poet, or the young woman of traditional background who forgoes marriage to pursue a career in physical chemistry. Complete rejection of a parent's work-related values may be a ploy in the larger struggle for autonomy. Or it may represent a profound and permanent commitment. As with other choices, this one is effective when it addresses the individual's real needs, and not when it is merely a reaction to others' opinions.

In most cases people choose neither foreclosure nor complete rejection of parental goals. They work out a compromise. They recognize some of their parents' values, and while fulfilling some of their expectations, shape their lives in ways that reflect their unique experience. One example of a compromise is a decision made by Anne, the daughter of a professional flutist and piano teacher. In her early college years, Anne was committed to studying music; she was a talented cellist who held first chair in the college orchestra. Her father, however, had long resented the low salary, long hours, and innumerable private lessons that went with being a professional musician. He had determined that Anne would enter a profession with more security and status: medicine.

Anne complied by taking premed courses and entering a Midwestern medical school. She did well enough, but disliked and felt alienated by many of her clinical duties. In her third year she became sufficiently depressed to request a leave of absence. After a year of counseling, she reentered medical school, resigned to becoming a physician, but with a new interest in psychiatry. It was not the kind of medicine her parents had envisioned for her, and they were nervous about what all that therapy and involvement with emotionally ill patients would do to their daughter. But Anne's choice turned out to be a fortunate one. Today she is a psychiatrist who appreciates many of the emotional and financial rewards that her medical degree has brought her. And she derives much pleasure from participating in a chamber orchestra. She is not sure that her father was wrong; nor is she sure that her father was right. In fact, she says that she is not sure about anything "except maybe Mozart."

Sometimes people become bound to parental goals and unable to compromise. Dan was a high school student during the years when the U.S. space program had caught everyone's imagination. His parents had a very high opinion of his potential; they encouraged him to go into some kind of engineering associated with space technology. Dan enrolled in advanced placement courses. At the same time he was encouraged to be popular and active in sports and school activities. In the autumn of his senior year, however, Dan suffered a psychological collapse. His parents reported that he was ill with mononucleosis because they did not want to jeopardize his acceptance at school or his popularity.

After Dan graduated with hard-won honors, he entered a competitive technical institute, as planned. But he could not keep up with the course work and suffered a second collapse. Although he could have made up the work, he was advised to transfer to the state university, which had a liberal arts orientation; the counselor pointed out that he could leave his options open for a few years. But Dan's parents blamed the school and the psychologists and urged Dan not to give up his idea of working in the space program. The situation was too difficult for Dan, who realized his limitations in technical areas. After much thought, he discounted his parents' wishes and pursued a long-held dream of air travel. He became a flight attendant. For years he enjoyed this work.

Gradually Dan discovered the strength of his need to hold a job that would contribute to social improvement. He then left the airline and went to work for an environmental interest group. After a time, his outgoing personality and quick grasp of scientific concepts earned him a promotion to a public relations post. Being a spokesman and attending conventions was highly gratifying and also gave him the travel he always liked. Although Dan was unable to effect a compromise with his parent's ideas while in school, he later discovered what was for him a meaningful compromise. Fortunately, many people who do not resolve such conflicts in their early adulthood years find a later opportunity to do so.

THE FIRST JOB

In entering the world of work, a person is often conscious of becoming part of the "adult" world. The initiation is the first job. By this we mean the first work commitment that one undertakes to support oneself fully and, usually, to create a sense of personal definition. Generally, this is the job assumed after graduation or with the understanding that schooling is, for the time being, complete.

A person's first job has the potential to greatly satisfy or to greatly disappoint. Some people who join a large organization, for example, feel swallowed up by the company and must strive to maintain feelings of autonomy and self-regard.

Many people take full- and part-time jobs during school years (or during a moratorium period). These jobs introduce people to the demands of the workplace: for example, they may give them some understanding of how to maintain good on-the-job relations or what qualities are usually associated with advancement in an organization. But the part-time, getting-through-school job is usually not as important to a person's identity or career development as the "first job." The part-time typist working his way through school seldom thinks of himself as a typist. When he is graduated from college and hired as a management trainee for AT&T, he may well identify with both his job and its assumed future.

The first job represents a transition from the student to the working person. It is often a source of satisfaction and pride, and equally often it is experienced as a first bout with adult reality. This stage of career development has also been termed, *finding a niche*. Young professionals search for jobs that will give them challenge, variety, and an organization with which they can identify. They are usually willing to forgo benefits to achieve this. If things do not work out they will go elsewhere or challenge their bosses for freedom from bureaucratic constraints (Raelin, 1985).

According to Kenneth Keniston (1970), who has studied young adulthood, the challenge of this period is to cope with social realities without losing one's selfhood. This may mean fitting into a large organization without becoming a mere "cog," or taking orders from others (including those less competent than oneself) without behaving in a child-like or rebellious manner. The goal, writes Keniston, is to engage oneself fully, while preserving a sense of oneself as "intact, whole, and distinct from society" (p. 642).

Job Satisfaction

Job satisfaction may be defined as a feeling of pleasure resulting from one's job or work experience. The feeling of pleasure results from the comparison of how much the person wants or expects from the job and how much they actually receive. To the extent that the rewards of the job, including money, promotion, satisfying coworkers and meaningful work, meet or exceed expectations, the employee is satisfied with his or her job. Steers (1984) describes five dimensions of a job about which people have expectations and desires:

the work itself—the extent to which tasks are meaningful and provide a learning experience and a sense of responsibility.

pay—the amount and equity of the pay.

promotion opportunity—the availability of opportunities for advancement.

supervision—the technical and managerial abilities of supervisors and the extent to which supervisors demonstrate consideration for and interest in employees.

coworkers—the extent to which coworkers are friendly, technically competent, and supportive.

While other dimensions of job satisfaction have been identified, these five are used most often in discussions and measurement of job satisfaction.

Relating to Supervisors

As most individuals are growing up they become accustomed to and accepting of the supervision of and directions from parents, teachers, and other authorities. But the work situation may seem different. Whereas the parent had a certain traditional right and the teacher was, in most cases, undeniably more learned than the student about a given subject area, in the world of work, supervisors may not be viewed as "superiors." They may derive their authority from "questionable advantages" such as years of experience, age, seniority, sex, convention, or friendly connections. The young adult may view these "advantages" negatively. For example, new workers may experience seniority as getting in the way of innovation. (A supervisor may say, "This is the way it has always been done," or "This, unfortunately, is what the client expects.") Difficulty in accepting supervision is often experienced on the first job.

New employees often feel they are receiving either too much or too little supervision. Louis felt he suffered from too much supervision on his first job. His boss seemed to hang over his shoulder telling him what to do every step of the way. There was only one way to do it and that was the boss's way. Louis felt that his own ability and creativity were being undermined. Sonia, on the other hand, thought she was suffering from too little supervision. Her boss gave her little direction and no feedback on her work. She felt her job was poorly defined and did not understand where she belonged in the organization. Her great fear was that she would soon lose her job because she was unwittingly doing the wrong tasks.

Personal Adjustment through the Life Span

For some people, difficulties with supervisors are temporary. They are directly related to being at the entry level in an organization and disappear as the person masters the work environment. Other people suffer throughout their working lives from an inability to resolve differences with supervisors. Hal, for example, is a middle-aged manager who has worked for numerous firms only to find himself "abused" and "mistreated" by all the powers that be. He continually fantasizes about the relief he will feel when he is able to work for himself, as a tax consultant or insurance broker. However, he does not realistically expect ever to have the means to do this. Right now, Hal is dissatisfied with his work environment but can do no more than look for a new employer. His work adjustment continues to be poor.

Employees such as Hal may gain insight into their problem if they recognize that relationships with supervisors are often mirror relationships they have had with parents and other significant adults. Employees, especially new employees, seek from supervisors many of the emotional services they have long sought from parents. They seek the supervisor's help in mastering new tasks and procedures; they need his or her approval; they count on the supervisor to give the security of knowing that they have done an adequate job (and will not be fired—which can be related to childhood fear of abandonment). The psychoanalytic conclusion is that those who experienced difficulty in obtaining emotional support from a parent may be ineffective in obtaining support from the supervisor on the job.

Hal, for example, is spurned by his supervisor because he tries too hard, expects too much, and is petulant, sulky, and demanding. In short, Hal relates to the supervisor as if the person were his father; like his father, the supervisor is exasperated by Hal's needs. In job after job, Hal reenacts being the neglected middle child, in an office without a title on the door.

In Hal's case, the actual personality of the supervisor is relatively unimportant. In other situations, the supervisor may contribute to the problem. For example, many young adults encounter a strict, authoritarian supervisor who resembles a parent. The old struggle for autonomy is reenacted on the job, with the result that a person may become unable to meet even the most reasonable demands of the supervisor. Of course the situation also offers an opportunity. The young adult who is motivated to succeed on the job may come to terms with the supervisor, winning from this person the respect and autonomy that was not won from the parent.

When a supervisor is very different from parents and others one has encountered, the opportunity for personal growth is also great. But the opportunity for conflict is there too. Tom, for example, was never able to gain his mother's approval. Her praise was always sparse, just enough to get him to work harder. When he encountered a demonstrative supervisor whose style was to heap praise on a good performer, Tom became depressed and anxious. He did not believe he was as good as his supervisor thought, and continually worried about when she would "discover" his inadequacies. As his anxieties increased, his performance deteriorated, and he started making loud comments to coworkers about the inevitability of his being fired. It happened that during this same period, Tom suffered numerous misunderstandings with a woman he was seeing. This problem caused him to enter therapy. With the support of his therapist, Tom came to see that he was being confronted with opportunities to create new kinds of relationships, both in his work and in his social life. His work adjustment improved, and he was able to see his relationship with the supervisor and the woman as opportunities for personal growth.

Many such examples can be found among a sample of young adults who enter the adult world of work at about the same time that they leave parental supervision. As Tom's experience suggests, an important step is to recognize the nature of the problem. Is it really a particular supervisor, or is it a more general problem in relating to authorities? Here counseling can be very helpful. But there are many other ways of gaining "reality feedback" on exactly what has gone wrong. The troubled employee can compare his or her relationship with the supervisor to that of others in the department. Is the supervisor generally held in high esteem, or is the environment one of large turnover and much grumbling? If the supervisor does not seem at fault, the employee must ask hard questions about past personal experiences (for example, whether there has been a pattern of difficult relationships with authorities) and decide what changes in behavior are indicated.

Coping with Entry-Level Blues

A common complaint about the first job is that it does not make use of one's potential. Perhaps there is too much routine or paperwork, or too many unnecessary procedures. Perhaps the job does not match the previously held image of oneself at work. One person lands a job with the Attorney General's office only to find that she is researching small points on cases for senior staff members. Another person envisions himself as an editor signing prominent authors, only to find that the first step is being a book salesperson on the road. Virtually every occupational field provides examples. Unless the entry-level job is structured so as to give the trainee a view of the top (as some experimental training programs are), work may at first be disappointing.

One entry-level problem is due to unrealistic expectations that are built into the hiring process. A study of AT&T managerial trainees attributed the "extreme favorability of expectations" to the fact that new employees had received most of their information about the job from company recruiters (Bray, Campbell, & Grant, 1974). In addition to creating a very positive impression of the company, the interviewers naturally emphasized their own high standards in hiring, making the successful candidate feel especially self-confident and optimistic. This appears to be a typical effect of the interviewing process. Many young people are told about the enormous demands of a position, only to discover that "almost anyone could do this job."

One way of coping with first-job disappointment is to wait and work for advancement. People who adopt this strategy see their problem as a temporary one. They employ their usual coping mechanisms and gradually gain ground. Another strategy is to change jobs. In fact, there are more frequent changes during the first years of work than later. Whether the individual leaves or remains with the organization, the problem usually resolves itself. The trainee achieves more of his or her potential as new responsibilities are granted. At the same time, the person becomes able to view chances for advancement more realistically.

The AT&T trainees who entered with "unblushing optimism" quickly changed their expectations without becoming negative about their work. Initially, each trainee thought that a vice presidency might be waiting around the corner. But after a few years the typical manager aspired to reaching the fourth or fifth level, rather than the vice-presidential sixth or seventh. The ease with which the subjects modified their work perceptions was striking (Bray et al., 1974, p. 178). And it appeared to be associated with continued cognitive growth, better adjustment, and greater independence. For many, a few years on the job brings not only advancement toward goals but more realistic definitions of goals.

CAREER CONSOLIDATION

The first job is significant, not only as a possible step to a higher-level job, but as an opportunity for exploration. It is during the first few jobs, usually in the late twenties or early thirties, that a person either strengthens or modifies an original occupational choice. Psychologists have different labels for career development during this period. Super refers to "stabilization" (1963), Vaillant to "career consolidation" (1977), Levinson to "forming an occupation and becoming one's own man" (1978), and Raelin (1983) to "digging in." We have used the term **career consolidation** to refer to the career development that enables the young adult to form a more concrete career identity.

A mutual acceptance between the employee and the organization may also develop (Schein, 1978) at this time. Schein describes this as a psychological contract in which each confirms the acceptance of the other. The employee signals a desire to remain in the company and to begin to play a significant role in it by taking on extra assignments, working overtime, accepting more responsibility, and being willing to accept delays and undesirable tasks. The organization on the other hand, provides salary increases, new and more important assignments, a promotion, and lets the employee in on the inner workings of the company. Though the psychological contract is implicit, according to Schein, it is real in that both the employee and the boss have strong expectations of each other. However, the expectations make them both vulnerable to disappointment. The contract is so important that if it is not established, the young adult should be ready to change organizations or perhaps redefine goals.

Career Consolidation
The career development that enables a person to form a more concrete career identity.

Forming a Relationship with a Mentor

One significant development that may occur during this period is the formation of a relationship with a mentor. The mentor is a person of greater experience in the world that the young adult is entering. He or she serves as a guide, counselor, or sponsor and is sometimes jokingly referred to as one's "guru." Generally the mentor is eight to fifteen years older. The young adult experiences the mentor as something between a parent and an intimate friend; sometimes the person resembles an admired older sibling (Levinson et al., 1978).

An important function of the mentor is to support the young person's vocational Dream—by sharing it, believing in it, and creating a space in which it can be pursued (Levinson et al., 1978). In some of these functions, the mentor resembles the loving spouse. However, the mentor is a transitional figure. He or she begins as a greatly admired and expert advisor but becomes, within a few years, nearly a peer. The young adult moves to a more mutual relationship with the mentor figure, and in so doing is conscious of becoming a real adult. When the relationship ends (as it inevitably does), the younger person usually has internalized some of the mentor's most positive qualities. The mentor has contributed to the individual's process of "becoming one's own person." Levinson sees this process as a major development of young adulthood. Other observers accord it less importance, but agree that it may be significant in individual occupational choices made during the early working years.

In recent years women have become mentors to younger women coming into the organization. Cross-gender mentoring is rare (Kram, 1985), probably because there are complexities with sexual attraction and increasing intimacy. Anxiety about the boundaries of the cross-gender mentoring relationship often cause both parties to withdraw and to avoid the frequent contact necessary for coaching and counseling discussions.

There is clear evidence that both individuals benefit from a mentoring relationship. For the senior person it provides a new, creative, and fulfilling job activity. For the junior member it provides both psychosocial and career support (Kram, 1985).

Job Stability

As people advance in their first few jobs, they begin to define their place in the world. An individual is likely to say that he or she is "in the printing business," "in agriculture," or "in academic life." A new period begins as the person builds a life around the initial job choices (Levinson et al., 1978). At this period, people are attracted to stability, commitment, and reputation. And most are married and beginning to form families, surrounded by new responsibilities, dependents, possessions, and worldly concerns.

The period between the early thirties and mid-forties is marked by the achievement of either stability or the acceptance of an unstable job pattern (Super, 1963). When stability is achieved, the person spends much time accumulating skills and experience, becoming a specialist with a reputation.

During these years a person is most likely to be described as "career-oriented." These are the years in which people are aware of succeeding or not succeeding, and are also the years during which they attempt to define for the future their social position and probable standard of living.

People who achieve their goals emerge from this period with a strong vocational self-concept. They may feel satisfied about being expert in a craft, a senior member of a firm, or respected in a profession. They begin to speak with their own voice and may be conscious of having authority over others. At the same time they begin to set their goals, some personal and some vocational. This is commonly a time for reflection. Career consolidation provides a secure position from which the middle-aged person can initiate further development and change.

SPECIAL NEEDS AND CONCERNS

Handicapped and Disabled Workers

People who are disabled or handicapped have the same needs for fulfillment through work as the rest of the community. The philosophy of vocational training is to help the disabled fulfill their needs through active participation in work. Disability in this context is defined broadly to include the physically, mentally, socially, and economically handicapped, including those living in poverty. Taken together, members of this group have been called the "employment handicapped."

The United States Government has played a major role in bringing handicapped workers to employment through a series of Vocational Rehabilitation Act amendments. Among the procedures developed as a result of the Act are sheltered workshops, direct job creation, employment subsidies, and antidiscrimination regulations. Sheltered workshops provide transitional employment designed to enable impaired workers to pass successfully into the workplace with the able bodied. Work activity centers are also available for long-term and permanent employment for the more severely handicapped.

The antidiscrimination provisions have had the most impact in integrating the handicapped into the employment mainstream. All businesses that receive money from the government must take appropriate action in the employment and advancement of qualified handicapped people. In addition, the companies must design internal procedures and facilities to insure that handicapped employees receive the same benefits and opportunities as other workers. It is estimated that these regulations affect the lives and careers of 35 million handicapped people (Haveman, Halberstadt, & Burkhauser, 1984).

Affirmative Action

Title VII of the Civil Rights Act of 1964 as amended in 1972 prohibits discrimination based on race, color, religion, national origin, or sex (Miner & Miner, 1979). The Equal Employment Opportunity Commission was created to enforce and interpret the law. The law (Title VII), and the Commission's and the courts' interpretation of the law, have changed the hiring practices of businesses and have provided job opportunities to minorities and women that were not available before. The interpretation of the law is that companies must develop and implement affirmative action plans to include the same percentages of minority and female employees in their companies as exist in the labor force in their community.

Affirmative action remains controversial in our society. Proponents of the law maintain that without it there would be insufficient job opportunities for women and minorities. Some proponents, including major corporations, believe that affirmative action has benefited business and has become part of corporate culture (BNA, 1986). Opponents say that the law has fostered programs of racial and sexual preferences that discriminate against white males and promote the hiring of less qualified people (BNA, 1986). Even as the controversy continues, it is clear that the law has resulted in an increased representation of minority group members and women and provided them with new opportunities for career development.

Career Pattern Issues for Women

Traditionally, the literature on career development has focused on men. We have long read about someone "becoming one's own man" after years in a vocation; the expression "becoming one's own woman" is a new one. Career planning can be more complicated for women than for men, and psychologists are only now beginning to investigate the process by which women achieve a strong work identity. Peterson's (1986) study of college women showed that a large number of their subjects intended to be employed in an area related to their major field following graduation and that 69 percent of them planned a lifelong career. However, research suggests that society creates and perpetuates sex-role differences that lead to divergent vocational aspirations and achievements on the part of men and women (Rosenzweig & Porter, 1981).

While the 1980s has been a time of improvement in career opportunities for women there is still a great need for legal and social changes before women will have the same career opportunities as men. It is generally believed that sex segregation of occupations contributes to the persistent salary differential between men and women (Terborg, 1985), and some believe the changes in our society will not alter the status of women in the near future (Cianni & Weitz, 1986). Workshops on career development for women have been designed to remedy the biases that affect careers. For example, one research team devised a training program to reduce sexism in the career planning of women (O'Neil, Ohlde, & Barke, 1979). They found that women who had participated in the workshops spent more time thinking about their careers and reported more scientific and enterprising career choices than did a similar group who did not attend the workshop.

In recent years, researchers and people active in the women's movement have tried to help women identify and overcome obstacles to successful career planning. Some obstacles are external, such as overt discrimination in the job market or subtle influences that college advisers may unwittingly apply when discussing career goals with female students. Other obstacles are internal factors, such as a woman's fear of success or the inability to assert herself in competitive situations.

Examination of womens' career patterns is certain to become important in the 1990s. Changes in our culture have increased the number of women in the labor force who were not there before. Nearly 42 percent of the labor force of 102 million are women. More than half of all women between the ages of 20 and 65 are employed outside the home. Approximately 13 million married women who work have children under the age of 18, and the number of working mothers with very young children is at an all time high. Also, single women with children and women who are heads of families make up a significant proportion of the work force (Voydanoff, 1987). In the past many have had to settle for a noncareer job. Compared with similarly qualified men, women have experienced greater problems in getting the job they want (Gurin, 1981) and were less able than men to translate their potential into work-related achievement (Card et al., 1980).

One constraint women may face is an **interrupted career pattern** (Super, 1957). This means that a woman works three or four years after completing her education, marries, has children, and leaves the work force for up to 10 years. After her last child enters school, she reenters the work force on a regular or part-time basis. Then she will remain in the work force for 20 to 30 years (Lemkau, 1980). For such women, career development is marked by shifts between home and the workplace; the husband's career, being more permanent usually takes precedence.

Women who follow the interrupted career pattern often view their time at home as a compromise. For example, Trish, a young nurse, explained that what she really wanted was to be a full-time worker whose child was cared for by a caretaker. Her husband was opposed to this so she decided, after negotiating a compromise with him, to take five to ten years off from her career. She said, "While my husband and I haven't reached perfect agreement on how to share chores, he has agreed to help more with child care and housekeeping so I can have time for private duty work."

Other women follow a **double-track career pattern,** which involves simultaneous commitment to work and family (Super, 1957). Though these women may proceed through the career consolidation period in the manner of their male counterparts, their experience is usually different.

Gail Sheehy, a journalist and mother who observed many double-track women, concluded flatly that a woman with a small child and a commitment to work can seldom be faithful to her career in the same way a man can (Sheehy,

Interrupted Career Pattern
A pattern in which a woman begins a career, interrupts it to take care of young children, and later resumes her career.

Double-track Career Pattern
A pattern in which a woman makes a simultaneous commitment to work and family.

1976, p. 157). The working mother is aware of "competing priorities." Often she speaks of a "difficult balancing act." And it *is* difficult: she does not, like her husband, have a wife to stay home with sick children, get the car fixed, fight with the painters, reconcile the bank statements, and so on (p. 157). If a woman can remain devoted to both her careers (and many women can), it is because she has achieved the balancing act with skill, self-confidence, and probably some adjustments from her husband.

The problem for many women is that the multiple demands must be faced relatively early in marriage and career, before the woman has "become her own person" vocationally. Sheehy notes that the woman in her twenties is not necessarily practiced or confident enough in any area to integrate her competing priorities. In her thirties, she may be. There is some evidence from personal histories that the difficulties of managing a career and family life are less formidable if a woman can face them after she has achieved some of her career goals (and perhaps can afford household help). However, this may require postponement of childbearing into the thirties. Thus, dual commitment to career and family usually results in a different career pattern than men's, or at least a career *experienced* differently by women.

Today's men and women who are involved in dual career marriages are, to a large extent, pioneers in the beginnings of new social and economic phenomena. Gupta and Jenkins (1985) defined a dual career couple as "two partners, each of whom feel an emotional commitment to the other partner and to his or her own work role" [p. 143]. They report that dual career couples have a great deal of stress, but nevertheless can achieve what is meaningful to them by using compromise, concern, consideration, and cooperation. However, coping with the stress and achieving work goals is not an easy task, as Staines, Pottick, and Fudge (1986) found, in their study of single career and dual career marriages.

Child care is an issue that still must be addressed by our society. Obviously it is of great significance in the lives and careers of working parents (Laver, 1985). Implementing an effective national program will reduce the stress in dual career marriages.

As our new career culture develops in the 1990s and into the 21st century, a new equilibrium is likely to develop in the role of men and women and in how they balance their careers and family life. The evolution of this new culture will be exciting, but often frustrating and stressful for those raising and supporting families in those years.

CAREER CRISES

Job Dissatisfaction

Practically everyone, at one time or another, experiences difficulty in getting through a day at work. A task may be boring, stressful, or simply ill-suited to one's abilities. Or a job may be difficult to handle in the face of other life crises. Even in the most successful careers, some jobs are, for a time, unsatisfying, and the individual is aware of the need to cope. The reaction to an unreasonable deadline or supervisor may be to talk it out, treat oneself to a meal in a good restaurant, or engage in physical exercise. However, some people use self-destructive mechanisms, such as drinking.

A person who is dissatisfied with his or her work generally relies on the coping strategies described in Chapter 4. Although sometimes a person has the option of simply leaving the job, if one has to stay in a position that is fundamentally unsatisfying or inconsistent with one's self-image, one uses defense mechanisms in order to live with the unresolvable conflict. As in other life contexts, the mature defenses are associated with successful adjustment. For example, the pattern of forbearance, which results from the defense mechanism of suppressing one's impulses, is a common way of dealing with job dissatisfaction. The person resists the impulse to quit in a huff. She may decide to stick it out for reasons that she can articulate. She is able to work because she looks forward to satisfaction at some later time (when a new opportunity opens up in the firm, for example, or when her boss retires).

Another strategy is based on the defense mechanism of compensation. The person seeks satisfaction in areas unrelated to work. Although work roles are important to many people's sense of identity, personal, social, and family roles also provide fulfillment. A person dissatisfied with his work as a factory foreman may compensate by emphasizing his role as a union representative, or as father of a family. A person who feels unable to accomplish anything "socially useful" as a salesperson, bureaucrat, or truck driver may compensate by undertaking volunteer work in the community. A parent in an unsatisfying job may derive pleasure from guiding children toward more attractive occupations. In these instances the person feels, for whatever reason, that it is impossible to change the working situation, and so compensates by enriching life after hours. Compensation is an especially well-regarded means of coping with job dissatisfaction.

Finally, a highly regarded defense is that attitude that enables some people to take pride in the performance of their work, no matter what it is. Martin Luther King, Jr., used to tell high school students that if they had to sweep streets, they should "sweep streets like Shakespeare wrote poetry." The assumption was that one way to live with an unsatisfying job is to take a certain attitude toward it and perform it with excellence.

This is perhaps a form of rationalization—the discovery of a silver lining in a rain cloud. The literary-minded individual who is sweeping streets may be denying some personal needs, perhaps deeply felt ones. Yet taking the attitude that what one does is worth doing well, and worth doing because one can do it well, seems to facilitate adjustment. This attitude is undeniably associated with self-esteem. In interviews with successful people, we find frequent reference to an early resolution to do well whatever one must do. And we find the same attitude in individuals who adjust to jobs that under other life circumstances might have seemed unappealing to them.

Studs Terkel's book *Working* contains the impressive story of Dolores, a waitress who went to work because she had three children, no support, and numerous debts (1972). Dolores found it tiresome to simply ask people for their orders, so she rephrased her questions in playful ways, with the result that she felt like Mata Hari on the stage. She found that her feet and body hurt at the end of the day, and she sometimes doubted that she could go on. But she was determined to take pride in her work.

> I want my hands to be right when I serve," she said, "I pick up a glass, I want it to be just right. I get to be almost Oriental in the serving. I like it to look nice all the way. To be a waitress, it's an art. I feel like a ballerina too. I tell everyone, I'm a waitress, and I'm proud." When a customer says to her, "You're great, how come you're just a waitress?" this woman answers, "Why don't you think you deserve to be served by me? (p. 391).

Taking the attitude that whatever one does can be done well seems to help people adjust to jobs that do not have high social status, are physically demanding, or are unsatisfying. It also helps young people who are temporarily "trapped" in jobs that seem unbearable. Doing the job well not only leads to increased self-esteem; it also leads, in some cases, to recognition and advancement.

Consequences of Unemployment

Unemployment deprives people of necessary income, and promotes feelings of despair, social isolation, and uselessness. Further, unemployed people may feel a detachment from reality. One man who was laid off from a textile factory described his day as: waking up, reading the paper, looking at what was on T.V., and going to bed (Hayes & Nutman 1981). A woman, who had returned to work after raising her family and then was laid off, said she felt trapped by the four walls of her house.

Prolonged unemployment poses a serious threat. The threat is not only to the individual worker's health and to the quality of life, but to his family's and community's (Liem & Rayman, 1982). When unemployment rises one percentage point, suicide increases 4.1 percent, homicides 5.7 percent, deaths from stress-related disorders 1.9 percent, and 4.3 percent more men and 2.3 percent more women are admitted to mental hospitals (Brenner, 1976). For husbands, being without work is related to psychiatric symptoms, and the symptoms worsen as the unemployment period lengthens. Their wives show increases in depression, anxiety, and phobic reactions, as well as an increased sensitivity about their interpersonal relations (Liem & Rayman, 1982). And rising unemployment in communities affected by major lay-offs of workers has been associated with significant increases in marital difficulties, parent-child conflict, and child abuse (Pines, 1982).

Individuals who can fulfill their work-related needs in other ways may have less difficulty adjusting to unemployment. For example, if loss of a job does not mean loss of vocation, and a person's identity remains intact, then unemployment may be more manageable. The financially well off and those given large severance payments (such as "golden parachutes") are better able to handle unemployment because it does not necessarily mean major changes in life-style.

If unemployment continues for a long time the individuals' attitude may change as part of his adjustment process. This is how the attitude change might take place. Being unemployed is inconsistent with the person's self-image. To resolve the inconsistency, he emphasizes the positive aspects of unemployment in an attempt to convince himself that the job loss will be beneficial in the long run. This process is illustrated in Alfano's (1973) findings that individuals' attitudes toward work become less favorable after six months of unemployment and continue to drop thereafter.

Unemployment with its psychological and economic consequences, is potentially so devastating that many researchers are calling for a national commitment to full employment. Yankelovich, et al., (1985) want the following social principles adopted: (1) no person capable of working and desirous of doing so should be left totally unemployed, (2) paid work is socially good. A coherent principle of social justice should be applied to prevent some from having excess work, while others are deprived of it, (3) everyone should have some degree of access to a paid working life.

Underemployment

It is commonplace to say that *underemployment* exists whenever we see a person with a Ph.D. driving a taxi or waiting tables in a diner. A worker is defined as underemployed if his or her education is considerably greater than the average education for that occupation (Burris, 1983). While there is little empirical research on underemployment, social scientists as far back as 1970 reported a drift of better educated people into middle and lower level jobs. Young people are among those most likely to be underemployed.

Research shows that underemployed graduates tend to see themselves as victims of fate and feel powerless (Burris, 1983). Those who define themselves as victims protect their self-concept: they do not believe they cause their underemployment. Organizations do not benefit from hiring underemployed people. Those working at a level lower than their education merits are generally unproductive, dissatisfied with their jobs, and have high rates of turnover and absenteeism.

Workaholism

People who are classified as workaholics work long hours, spend little time with their families, and attend primarily to their jobs. To them work is all-consuming and all-encompassing. The word "workaholism" combines "work" and "alcoholism." Workaholics, like alcoholics, may deny the problem, although it affects their life and those of family members. Machlowitz (1980), a leading writer and speaker on this subject, prepared a self-administered questionnaire (presented, in part, below) of use in diagnosing workaholism:

1. Do you get up early no matter what time you go to bed?
2. If you eat lunch alone, do you read or work while you eat?
3. Do you make daily lists of things to do?
4. Do you find it difficult to do nothing?
5. Are you energetic and competitive?
6. Do you work on weekends and holidays?
7. Can you work anytime and anywhere?
8. Do you find vacations hard to take?
9. Do you dread retirement?

Those who say yes to many or most of these questions might benefit from examining their life-style to consider whether it is compatible with their values and whether it is giving them fulfillment. Although workaholics are productive and often receive benefits for their efforts, those who work with them or live with them may have difficulties unless they learn how to cope with the workaholic's habits and life-style.

Mid-Career Crisis

Hall (1986) defines midcareer as the period in one's occupation that comes after one feels that he has mastered the job and established himself, and before one has begun disengaging from his work life. Whereas, in early career opportunities seemed wide open and the major issue was choosing among alternatives, in mid-career the task is to find an outlet for one's abilities and interests to keep from going stale. If an individual does not take positive steps he may begin to feel dissatisfied with his career and his purpose in it. He may begin to feel that there are fewer opportunities for advancement and personal growth. The question the individual (and the employer) face is whether changes can be made in the work structure that will make it challenging once again.

Many events that break the routine, such as job redesign, continued training and development, and mentoring, are ways of reducing and ending "mid-career doldrums." Some organizations offer mid-career counseling to help employees deal with this problem.

Age and Work Behavior

Rosen & Jerdee (1976) conducted a survey of top level management and found that for highly demanding and challenging jobs older workers were regarded as less skilled than younger workers. Older workers were perceived as being relatively inflexible and resistant to change, having less potential for development, and performing less well in tasks requiring high levels of creativity, productivity, and motivation.

Attitudes like these may explain why 78 percent of workers over age 45 experience discrimination seeking a job and 45 percent experience age discrimination in seeking a promotion. However, consider this: Findings indicate that when tasks make certain sensory demands on the capacity of the older person and the task situation is novel, age differences in performance are maximized. When these demands are absent or if the task is familiar, age differences in performance are negligible. Further, the number of absences from work declines with age, although the duration of absences increases.

Retirement is the last stage in career development. With the anticipated decline in the number of teenagers and young adults, pressure may develop to keep people working to an older age. Most Americans over age 65 say they would like to continue working, although a majority prefer part-time work. And the data indicate that they would be healthy enough to continue working. In 1980, 60 percent of the over-65 population reported their health was either good or excellent. This is an increase from 49 percent in 1972 (Laver, 1985).

Experiencing Failure

Nearly everyone encounters occasional failures on the job. Some people, however, conceive of themselves as career failures, experiencing what is sometimes called **psychological failure.** This is not simply (or necessarily) poor performance; it is a personal sense of failure, stemming from repeated inability to meet challenges and assert autonomy in one's work life. According to Argyris (1957), working people try to minimize their feelings of failure in predictable ways:

Psychological Failure
In the area of work, a person's general sense of being unable to meet challenges and assert autonomy.

1. They withdraw emotionally from the work situation by lowering their work standards and becoming apathetic and uninterested.

2. They place increased value on material rewards and depreciate the value of human, or nonmaterial, rewards. (For example, a man who is a teacher begins to refer to his work as a means of supporting himself and is apathetic about the progress of his students or about pedagogical advances in his field.)

3. They defend their self-concept with defense mechanisms. These include not only the mature defense mechanisms already mentioned, but immature defenses as well. For example, projection (blaming others for work-related failure) is common.

4. They fight the organization, or attempt in some way to force change in the work environment.

5. They try to gain promotion to a position with greater prospects of success.

6. They leave the organization (or perhaps make some larger change, such as pursuing a new occupation).

All of these strategies represent ways of adjusting and make sense from the individual's standpoint. That is, they offer protection from feelings of failure. Each of the strategies has its own costs and benefits to the individual. Some, however, are more likely than others to produce favorable outcomes. For example, strategies such as challenging or leaving the organization are more likely to result in personal growth than withdrawing or depreciating the value of human rewards.

Experiencing Success

In work, as in other areas, the word "success" is variously defined. To some it means earning a certain title or salary, to others, a certain sense of self. No matter what vocational goals people set for themselves, they are likely to feel a sense of satisfaction upon attaining them. This we define as **psychological success**—what a person experiences when he sets a goal that is challenging and intimately related to the self-concept, and then attains this goal (Argyris, 1964).

A path that leads one to psychological success as one's career develops has been diagrammed by Hall and Schneider (1973), who were most interested in the careers of people in organizations (in this case, the priesthood). Their portrayal of career development is shown in Figure 11.2.

As that figure suggests, a person makes an initial commitment to enter the world of work and sets career work goals. Goal attainment leads to psychological success, work satisfaction, and an enhanced self-image. These positive experiences motivate the individual to increase his or her career commitment. However, since the initial set of goals has been achieved, the person is now ready to choose new career goals, which generally will be more difficult to achieve than the earlier ones. The process repeats itself. The individual sets higher-level goals, achieves them and advances in the organizational hierarchy.

At the end of each cycle people who have achieved previous career goals are challenged to find new ones and must risk self-esteem in the process. If, at some point, they experience the new challenges as a crisis, they may be helped by the advice of self-help writers who suggest: "Remember that you

Psychological Success
In the area of work, a person's sense of satisfaction upon having attained important challenging goals that he or she established.

Personal Adjustment through the Life Span

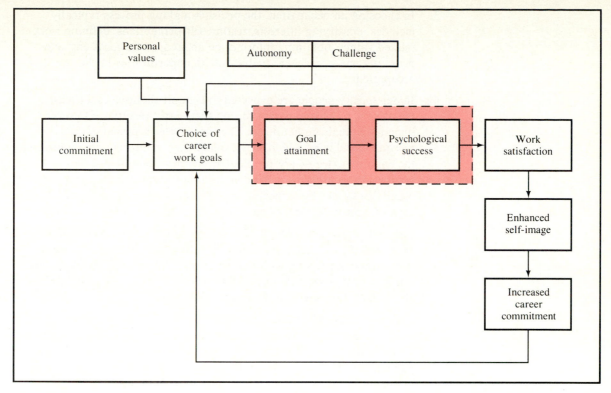

Figure 11.2 Career development in organizations: The path to psychological success.

achieved your previous goals and grew from the process." Then remind yourself, "I am ready to take on new challenges." This type of goal-setting/goal-achievement cycle, as we will see in the next chapter, is faced in other areas as one encounters the challenges of adulthood in mid-life and later years.

SUMMARY

1. Adults work to earn a living for themselves and their families. Work is defined as any activity by which a person actively contributes to the productivity of society. For most people, being able to work is basic to a sense of autonomy, represents achievement of adult status, and contributes to a sense of identity.

2. Most people become aware of a need to choose a career direction in adolescence or young adulthood. However, choosing an occupation is a lifelong process. It begins in the fantasies of early childhood and continues, in some cases, in mid-life, when career reassessment and change often take place.

3. In choosing an occupation, the decision-making process typically includes identifying interests, testing self-perceptions, defining work-related values, obtaining information about specific vocations, and matching one's personal attributes with opportunities in the world of occupations.

4. In our society people are expected to commit themselves, at least tentatively, to an occupation during their early twenties. However, some individuals do not do so. They may enter a period of *moratorium* during which they explore their interests and options. At the opposite extreme are people who commit themselves to an occupation seemingly too early in life; they *foreclose* their options, usually to satisfy the expectations of parents. Often the initial career commitment will be reevaluated at a later stage in life.

5. The first career-oriented job that an individual undertakes is often experienced as a challenge. Common difficulties include relating to supervisors and coping with the frustrations of an entry-level position. The ability to accept the temporary situation and modify perceptions about the future seems to facilitate adjustment.

6. *Career consolidation* occurs as a person strengthens and modifies his or her career choice, usually in the late twenties or early thirties. Formation of a relationship with a mentor is sometimes an important development in this period. In the early thirties and mid-forties, the person either achieves career stability or develops an unstable job pattern.

7. Antidiscrimination and affirmative action policies have helped open opportunities for jobs, and the associated benefits, to many people.

8. An unprecedented number of women work outside the home today. Some follow career patterns seemingly similar to those identified for men. Many women, however, hold "noncareer" jobs or fluctuate between these jobs and homemaking. Increasingly common is the *interrupted career pattern,* in which a woman works at a career job, remains at home when her children are small, and then resumes her career later. Also increasingly common is the *double-track career pattern,* which involves simultaneous commitment to career and family. Traditionally, career development research focused primarily on men. Much more of such research is needed on women.

9. A person who experiences job dissatisfaction relies on coping and defense mechanisms that have been utilized in other life contexts, such as talking it out or compensating. Among other stressful work-related experiences are job loss and a sense of *psychological failure.*

10. When people experience *psychological success* in a career (for example, by attaining self-defined goals), they are usually motivated to set new, higher-level goals. Success can sometimes be felt as a crises, because of the new challenges posed.

SUGGESTED READINGS

Alter, J. (1982). *A part-time career for a full-time you.* Boston: Houghton Mifflin. A useful book geared toward students and homemakers, listing many fulfilling part-time occupations.

Bloch, D. (1987). *How to have a winning job interview.* Lincolnwood, Ill.: VGM Career Horizons. This handbook guides the reader, step-by-step, through the process of getting an interview, preparing for it, and conducting oneself in a successful manner.

Bolles, R.N. (1988). *What color is your parachute?* Berkeley, CA: Ten Speed Press. A popular book for the job-hunter that contains extensive advice about job possibilities. Updated annually.

Carney, C. G., Wells, C. F., & Streufert, D. (1981). *Career planning: Skills to build your future.* New York: Van Nostrand Reinhold. A guide to acquiring skills and attitudes that facilitate career choice and enhance career development.

Depp, C. B. (1986). *Managing the new careerists.* San Francisco: Jossey-Bass. Not everyone wants to climb the corporate ladder. There are five distinct career orientations among today's employees. Each orientation can be of value to the organization.

Korman, A., & Korman, R. (1980). *Career success and personal failure.* Englewood Cliffs, NJ: Prentice-Hall. An interesting analysis of the conflicts between career advancement and the quality of family life.

Leibowitz, Z. B., Farren, C., & Kaye, B. L., (1986). *Designing career development systems.* San Francisco: Jossey-Bass. This book synthesizes the contributions from career planning, personal training, and organizational development to offer a model for designing strong organizational career development systems.

Morgan, M. (1980). *Managing career development.* New York: Van Nostrand Reinhold. An excellent overview of basic career issues within a life span framework.

Schuman, N. & Lewis, W. (1987). *Revising your résumé.* NY: Wiley. An outstanding résumé, which contains much more than a person's educational and work history, can make the difference in obtaining a desired job. This book tells the reader how to prepare one.

Stark, S. (1983). *Returning to work: A planning book for women.* NY: McGraw Hill. A comprehensive discussion of the unique career problems women face and ideas for addressing them successfully.

White, J. (1987). *The American almanac of jobs and salaries.* New York: Avon. A guide that gives an idea of what jobs are available and conservative estimates of annual earnings in different lines of work. Updated regularly.

Challenges and Rewards of Adulthood

- ▶ A theory of adult development

- ▶ How some adults become more limited with age but others draw strength from past crises, establish a firmer identity, expand their perceptions of individuals and society, and may transcend the self

- ▶ The widely publicized "mid-life crisis," with its changed time perceptions and questioning of one's career and marriage

- ▶ The adjustment demands posed by changes in the family constellation

- ▶ Common reactions to a sharpened awareness of the aging process, to physiological and social changes that affect sexuality, and to the new life-style of retirement

- ▶ How some people overcome the problems of the elderly years, primarily health-related and financial, by drawing on mature defense mechanisms and a well-developed sense of personal integrity

As a young man, Mr. S. was confined to prison for eight months. There he had an experience that nearly all people hope to have in the course of their adult lives: Mr. S. felt he had discovered his "real self." He learned to "value the inner success which alone maintains one's inward equilibrium and helps a man be true to himself."

The discovery was both a beginning and an end, for Mr. S. felt that his earlier, narrow self had ceased to exist. Once released from the confines of that self, he stepped into a "new and undiscovered world which is vaster and richer. . . ." The new self aspired to a higher, transcendental reality that included feelings of belonging to humanity rather than pursuing only an individual course.

Self-transcendence is not unusual. It is one of many growth trends that psychologists have discovered in adults who report themselves as most happy. We tend to think of adulthood as a place where we will one day arrive and stay, but developmental psychologists have shown that there is no such thing. Adulthood, like childhood, is an ever-enlarging world. But there is a difference: If we are fortunate, we bring to the adult world, our real, discovered selves that have been developing over many years. When Mr. S. stepped into the vaster, richer world, he did not step tentatively, like an adolescent who is constructing an identity; instead he stepped with confidence, describing his entry as a genuine conquest. The strength he drew upon was "a talent or capacity for change."

Mr. S.'s words have come to the attention of Gail Sheehy, a well-known writer on adult psychological development (1981). They have come to the attention of historians as well because Mr. S., when he became President Anwar Sadat of Egypt, was able to bring about major changes in world affairs. In

Self-Transcendence
A growth experience in which a person goes beyond narrow concerns about the self and feels a need to contribute to the larger society or develop spiritual aspects of the personality.

1977, he engaged in a political act of great daring and creativity and transcended the thinking that had ruled him and his countrymen for decades: He decided to go to Israel. His decision—symbolic of the creative decision making of the adult, which usually takes place on a less global scale—was explained by Sadat as follows:

> I drew, almost unconsciously, on the inner strength I had developed in Cell 54 of Cairo Central Prison—a strength, call it a talent or capacity for change. . . . My contemplation of life in that secluded place had taught me that he who cannot change the very fabric of his thought will never be able to change reality, and will never, therefore, make any progress (Sadat, 1978; quoted in Sheehy, 1981).

In this chapter, we will be concerned with the progress of adults, with their talent or capacity for change. We will consider the crises that tend to occur in middle and late adulthood and identify some factors that appear to help individuals respond successfully to these crises. Although much new information has come to light on the physiological aspects of aging, we will be concerned primarily with psychosocial developments, including, of course, the ways in which individuals respond to physiological changes.

A THEORY OF ADULT DEVELOPMENT

Era
People's lives can be divided into a sequence of eras, each with its own character and each shaped by the choices made as individuals seek to achieve their goals.

Life Structure
The pattern or style one follows during a given era in leading one's life.

Daniel Levinson (1986) believes that the course of human life has an underlying order that extends from birth through old age. This cycle of life can be divided into a sequence of eras. Each **era** has its own character and makes a distinctive contribution to the whole of life. There are many changes in our lives from one era to the next, and lesser but still important changes within each era. The eras of our lives partially overlap each other, and Levinson calls these overlaps *cross-era transitions*. Each such transition lasts about five years. The transition begins before a given era ends and continues until the next era is underway. Thus, the cycles of life alternate between eras and transitions.

During each era the individual must form a **life structure,** derived from the choices that are made to fulfill ones values and goals, and involving change and stress. The process of beginning, ending, or improving a marriage, leaving or staying in an occupation, striving to gain good grades or dropping out are all acts within the life structure. Eventually the life structure becomes stable, but after a time it is questioned. When the structure is challenged it is the beginning of a transition period, calling for reappraisal of existing structures and exploration of various possibilities for change. It is a time to decide on separations from existing situations and on new beginnings. Transitions are an important part of development, but are often painful.

The first era, called *preadulthood,* extends from birth to approximately age 22. This era brings the person from infancy to the beginning of adulthood. Around age 17, the first transition period begins. During this time, preadulthood draws to a close and early adulthood begins. The young adult begins to take leave of the preadult world and find a place in the adult world.

The second era, *early adulthood,* lasts from age 22 to 45. It is the era of greatest energy and greatest stress, with the 20s and 30s being peak years in the life cycle. Early adulthood is the time of pursuing aspirations, establishing a place in society, raising a family, and finding a position in the adult world. It is the time of rich satisfaction from love, sexuality, family life, creativity, and achievement of goals. But there are crushing stresses as well, from juggling parenthood while developing a career, to taking on financial obligations while earnings are low. It is a period of making important choices regarding marriage, family, career, and life-style at a time of little experience. Levinson says early adulthood is the time we are most buffeted by our own passions and ambitions from within and by demands of family and society from without.

The Mid-Life Transition from 40–45 brings about the termination of early adulthood and starts the next era of middle adulthood. If this transition is handled well, the person becomes more compassionate, more reflective, and less tyrannized by inner conflicts and external demands. A more genuine love of self and others emerge. If it is not handled well the person becomes stagnant and bogged down in trivia.

The third era, *middle adulthood,* lasts from age 40 to 65. During this era the biological capabilities are below those of early adulthood, but still sufficient for an energetic, valuable, and satisfying life. In fact, people in this age range are the leaders in politics, industry, science, and arts in every society. Those in this era of the life cycle also have the special responsibility for the development of the generation of young adults who will later take their place.

The last era, *late adulthood,* starts at age 60. The late adult transition that links middle and late adulthood occurs between 60 and 65. The following descriptions will give you a sense of what individuals experience at the points described by Levinson.

Jim Conner at age 18 is struggling to find direction in his life. He wants to continue his education, but does not want to be supported by his parents because that will make him too dependent on them. Although Jim wants to go to college, he is not quite sure what he wants to do when he gets there. Not a particularly good student, he does not like taking required courses that do not interest him. The courses that do interest him are not the kind that lead to a career. At times he thinks it would be best to get a job, move out of his home and marry the woman he has been dating for two years. But he knows that without a college degree he will not get a good job, and with marriage he will not gain the independence he wants so badly. Jim Conner is going through the Early Adult Transition.

Bradley Gordon is already in Early Adulthood. He has completed college, earned a degree in accounting, and landed an entry-level job in one of the big eight accounting firms. But Brad is not sure what type of accounting he wants to pursue or whether he should go to law school and combine the two fields. The firm is pressuring him to choose a specialty, but Brad is hoping to convince them to let him try out the different departments before he makes a choice. He is also thinking that while he explores various departments he will sign up for evening session law courses. Brad recently made an important personal decision. After dating Judith for four years, along with many other young women, he has decided to ask Judith to make a commitment to him. He is not ready to talk of marriage but is ready for an exclusive relationship with one woman. Brad is at a later stage in his development than Jim.

Floyd at age 31 is in Early Adulthood but is also experiencing what Levinson calls the Age Thirty Transition, a period of rethinking previous decisions and of considering changes in goals and life-styles. Floyd is feeling glum and out of sorts. Nothing seems right and life seems to be going nowhere. Floyd does not like his job, is unhappy in his marriage, and is frightened as he anticipates the birth of his child. When he thinks about his life to date, he begins to think "if only." If only he had made different decisions . . . If only he had been born wealthy or smarter or better looking . . . " Floyd finds the present life structure intolerable but seems unable to form a better one. It is a time of crisis.

When Floyd talked to his older brother, Martin, about his feelings, Martin understood. He said that some time ago he had similar feelings, but now at age 40 felt he was settling down. Martin described the discomfort he felt at work until he discovered a niche for himself. As a buyer in a department store, he found he was happiest and most successful running the furniture department. He was interested in the design and construction of furniture and enjoyed interacting with the manufacturers. Further, he liked teaching what he knew to his sales people and, under his guidance, they became better salespeople and earned larger commissions. Martin also described to Floyd his unhappiness with his marriage. After a good deal of soul searching and discussion with his wife, they decided to try and maintain the marriage. While the birth of their third child and the illness of his mother-in-law put additional pressure on them, Martin and his wife are developing ways to cope through marriage counseling. Martin is an example of someone in the culminating life structure of Early Adulthood.

Bill Smith is in his Mid-Life Transition, a time of questioning, a time to ask what have I done with my life? What do I really get from and give to my wife, children, friends, work, community and self? What is it I truly want from myself and others? "At this time a man yearns for a life in which his actual desires, values, and aspirations can be expressed" (Levinson 1981, p. 60). In the mid-life transition, those parts of the "self" that were neglected or overlooked come back to haunt the person. If Bill is typical, his questions of mid-life will be answered by age 45 and a new life structure will begin to take shape in middle adulthood.

Arthur Moreland made the decision to change his life's work during his Mid-Life Transition. As a successful stockbroker he put in long hours, leaving little time for his family and for his great passion, art. At age 45, with one child still in college, he decided to devote all his time to art. He was fortunate in having both the moral and financial support of his wife who moved with him into a small house with a barn. They converted the barn into a studio and he "got down" to his life's work. As the months passed, Arthur began to feel for the first time that he was living his life to its fullest. He described it as his "creative season."

Although Levinson did not study men after middle adulthood, he believes that the sequence of stable and transitional periods continues for the entire life cycle. As middle adulthood draws to a close, the late adult transition will prepare the individual to settle into the final stage of late adulthood.

Levinson points out that the human body, the personality, and the social environment operate jointly in building, maintaining, and modifying the life structure in every era. Therefore, in understanding the development of the individual through the life cycle it is necessary to examine both the characteristics of the person and the environment in which he or she exists.

Although Levinson's research has had a major impact on our thinking about adult development, there are some limitations to his research that prevent generalization to the total population. First, Levinson did not study women. Second, he studied only forty men from four occupational groups: executives, hourly workers, academic biologists, and novelists. These subjects are hardly representative of the entire population. However, what is unique about his research is how intensely they were studied. Rather than administering brief questionnaires to a large sample, Levinson conducted intensive biographical interviews with his much smaller group of subjects.

STRENGTHS OF ADULTHOOD

Consolidation of Identity

Consolidation of identity is a process, generally occurring in middle adulthood, in which a person builds a more solid self-concept. The consolidation of identity provides the person with an anchor; he or she has been strengthened by past decisions and accomplishments and these events will help the person in coping with new life crises. At this point the person recognizes that in deciding to become a parent, in deciding not to attend graduate school, and in selecting a job, he made choices that set him on a life path that significantly affected his identity. Although he may have later reevaluated these decisions, he knows he made a series of commitments that belong uniquely to him. And, in dealing with these choices, he has grown.

In contrast to those younger, it is easier for the middle-aged person to say, "I am the kind of person who can do this" or "I have never given in to this emotional state and I will not now." As adults grow older, they know more and more who they are. Their life experiences have included many choices and these have led to a more final self-definition (Erikson, 1959). To be sure, they question their identities, often with considerable distress, as we will see. Nevertheless, they gradually gain a more solid sense of personal capacities and limitations. They are less likely to be thrown by temporary setbacks, unfair criticism, and bad luck. Their accumulated experience allows them to make more reliable self-judgments, and to have more consistent effects on their environment (White, 1952/1975).

Consolidation of Identity
A process, generally occurring in middle adulthood, in which a person builds a more solid self-concept on the basis of past decisions and accomplishments.

The consolidation of identity that occurs in the adult years often brings an increased sense of peace. People still question their identities, often with considerable distress, but increasingly they believe that they can exert control over their future.

Increasingly, as people reach their fifties, they believe that they will not change: their personalities are set (Block, 1981). While some psychologists see a final identity as desirable, others believe that older people adjust best if they continually rework or reinvent their identities. Butler (1975), for example, finds that a continuing, lifelong concern with one's identity is a sign of good health. Nevertheless, Butler finds that the older person has "that firm root of sense of self," which makes it possible for him or her to deal with change without loss of identity.

Humanization of Relationships and Values

Freeing of Personal Relationships
A process, generally occurring in middle or later adulthood, in which a person becomes more tolerant and responds increasingly to others as individuals.

Another positive trend for middle-aged and older adults is the **freeing of personal relationships** (White, 1952/1975). Whereas children and young people tend to perceive others in terms of their own personal needs (needs for identification, superiority, dependence, and so on), the adult increasingly responds to others as individuals in their own right. Though moral judgments may still be made, the mature person becomes more tolerant. As a result, human relationships have a tendency to become "more friendly, less anxious, less defensive, less burdened by inappropriate past reactions" (White, 1952/1975, p. 345). Even old grudges against parents fall away; a man in his fifties finds

Personal Adjustment through the Life Span

Yourself as Survivor

Thomas Collins is a retirement counselor. He believes that the greatest error older people make is to lose sight of their own value (Collins, 1978). They fail to appreciate the many crises they have survived simply in reaching the age of 70 or 80. Collins notes that people in this age group have lived through:

World War I
The 1918 flu epidemic
The 1929 stock market crash
The Great Depression
The rise of Hitler, Mussolini, and Franco
The first imposition of income taxes
World War II
The H-bomb
The onset of freeways
The Korean War
The killer diseases of our times, heart attack and cancer (affecting oneself or others)
The Vietnam War
Increased air pollution and inflation

Every generation has a unique historical experience: the members of a generation who are about the same age and who have lived through certain events together are sometimes called cohorts. Because they have been affected, as age-mates, by certain events, they tend to experience life in similar ways, sharing attitudes and behaviors.

1. Collins notes that one cohort, now retired, experienced the Great Depression at about the time that they were making career plans or establishing careers. What effect might this have had on the way they later experienced life? How might it have strengthened them?

2. Look at Collins' list and decide if any of the events or trends listed have been important in shaping the life experiences of your own cohort. Consider both direct and indirect impact. (For example, were your parents affected by any of these events in ways that affected how they raised you?)

3. Make a list of social, political, economic, and other events and trends that have deeply affected people approximately your age. According to Collins, one way of appreciating the possible greatness in yourself is to appreciate what you have been able to survive. If any event you listed resulted in a crisis or ordeal, describe the coping mechanisms you used to survive it. ▲

that he can now refer affectionately to "Mom and Dad" (Gould, 1972). A woman's concern for her children's achievements may be replaced by a more relaxed concern for their personal happiness. And many old criticisms of the spouse are dropped in the interest of companionship (Gould, 1972). This growing ability to cope with personal relationships in a less costly way is sometimes called "mellowing."

Another growth trend is the **humanizing of values** (White, 1952/1975). The person uses his or her life experiences to revise, or humanize, values that were acquired, perhaps under duress, as a child. Fear of punishment no longer controls behavior; the adult is now in a position to question the received moral code without suffering the adolescent consequences. Soundness of judgment and empathy increase, and there is a growing ability to understand others. The young person who is confronted with a difficult choice in romantic commitment or business ethics tends to strike a panicky compromise between parental values and a perception of what peers will think or are doing in similar situations. Mature adults increasingly consult their own value system and are able to live with their choices, on their own terms. They are more tolerant of themselves when in error, and more accepting of others' mistakes.

Experience in Crisis Resolution

The older a person is, the more experience he or she is likely to have had with crisis resolution. This experience is important. Theorists in this area note that the person who resolves a crisis satisfactorily emerges with an improved capacity for adjustment. He or she now has a larger repertoire of problem-solving skills and will be less likely to revert to immature or unrealistic coping measures in the future (Caplan, 1964). People also tell us this from their personal experience. For example, a businessman will say that being in combat in World War II gave him the strength he later needed to assume leadership in a risky environment. An older woman will say with quiet dignity that, having accepted the death of her oldest son, she can "take anything." We see the strengthening effect of having "been through it" in many less extreme examples. For example, the second child is handled in a more relaxed manner than the first. Having had some experience dealing with the challenges of childbirth and parenthood, and of job loss, people find themselves prepared to cope with future crises of a similar nature.

Generativity and the Expansion of Caring

Another favorable development of later life is generativity (Erikson, 1963) or expansion of caring (White, 1952/1975). As we saw in Chapter 2, generativity is the growing capacity to love and care for others—not only for individuals but for the next generation and the society to which one belongs. Thus it includes the capacity to contribute, through one's work, to the well-being of those beyond one's immediate place and time. The career and family crises encountered in later adulthood are often struggles for generativity. Individuals must confront questions of whether or not their work is ultimately meaningful, their children foreseeably happy and productive. Perhaps the sense of contributing to future generations, through work and personal relationships, is a way of coping with the limits of one's one and only life span. Certainly it helps compensate for a personal future that is limited. It has been observed that middle-aged people who face death from terminal illness are helped most by thoughts of having completed some favorite project, of having seen a child through graduation, and so on (Pattison, 1977). In other words, it is generativity that enables the adult to cope with loss of health and life, as well as with reduction in some of life's alternatives.

Self-Transcendence and Spirituality

A number of writers have remarked on the transcendence of self that we encountered earlier in the example of Anwar Sadat. This **self-transcendence,** or "going beyond," seems to be part of the older person's adjustment to life. For example, Erikson notes that a person's full engagement in the life cycle is what ultimately gives him or her whatever chance there is to transcend the limitations of the self (Erikson, 1976, p. 23). Peck too finds that the "successful ager" is one who transcends narrow ego and bodily concerns (Peck, 1968). Instead of clinging to "a separate private identity," older people contribute to their culture in a way that "goes beyond the limits of their own skin and own lives." Kohlberg and Kramer, in more speculative research, suggest that a final stage in the individual's intellectual development involves looking at life from an "infinite perspective"—that is, achieving a state that a philosopher might describe as the union of mind with the whole of nature (Kohlberg & Kramer, 1973, p. 203).

Self-Transcendence A growth experience in which a person goes beyond narrow concerns about the self and feels a need to contribute to the larger society or develop spiritual aspects of the personality.

The capacity for being spiritual may increase with age. In some Asian and American Indian cultures, the individual is expected to become a pilgrim of sorts in the later part of the life span. Spiritual discipline in India, for example, traditionally begins after an individual has established a mature family and completed the expected work in the community. In Western cultures, spirituality as such has received little scientific attention. In art, however, spiritual serenity, as well as spiritual passion, are often associated with the aging individual. It is the older protagonist in a book, or in real life the older artist, who achieves a restoration of the sense of wonder, or a "triumph of the soul." Perhaps the most famous expression of this phenomenon is from the Irish poet Yeats, who wrote:

An aged man is but a paltry thing
a tattered coat upon a stick, unless
Soul clap its hands and sing, and louder sing
for every tatter in its mortal dress.

Transcendence of self, or spirituality—however an individual defines the experience—seems to be an important strategy by which older people define themselves against the sense of meaninglessness (or rage) they might otherwise feel concerning aging and the coming loss of self.

ADJUSTMENT CHALLENGES IN THE SECOND HALF OF LIFE

There are many ways of looking at the second half of life. Some of these ways lead us to think of a period of stability followed by inevitable and tragic decline. Other views encourage us to think of continuous growth, with some people even regarding death as a "final stage of growth." In the foregoing section we have emphasized the ways in which healthy adults continue to grow and are strengthened by the challenges they encounter.

But observations tell us that this is not the only reality. Many older people become more rigid and less realistic in their coping. Some, far from humanizing their values, become intransigent bigots. And there is a notable tendency for some older people, in the time of potential generativity, to become consistently more self-centered. In earlier life periods, to be sure, we saw that not everyone emerged with a favorable outcome after the age-appropriate crises. But the images of failure were not so striking, not so extreme. It would appear that both the opportunity and the danger increase as we grow older. Psychological growth may be a normal process and a lifelong possibility, but so is emotional disturbance.

There are vast differences in the way people meet the challenges of adulthood. In fact, people become more and more different from one another as they grow older (Neugarten, 1971). It is more difficult to generalize about the behavior of a group of 60-year-olds than it is, for example, about a group of 16-year-olds. Problems in adjustment, too, are more similar during the early years than later. For example, most 18-year-olds are struggling with the problem of attaining a vocational identity and establishing an intimate relationship with a person of the opposite sex. At 40, 50, or 60 only *some* individuals are coping with these problems. And those who are—those, in other words, who have not found at least some temporary resolution of the problem—experience life difficulties that distinguish them from their age-mates.

Age is apparently not the great leveler, not even in physical terms. For example, a researcher who directed one of the most significant longitudinal studies on aging found the variations among a group of 80- and 90-year-olds to be "just tremendous" (quoted in Schmeck, 1979). In addition to a unique genetic inheritance, each individual has a long and unique history of life crises and adjustments.

Recognition of Aging

A crisis that signals the onset of "middle age" and underlies many other changes in self-concept is the individual's recognition of the aging process that is taking place. Sometimes the event that triggers the crisis is serious: the 39-year-old executive is stopped on the jogging trail by a heart attack. (His physician calls it a "warning.") However, in many lives the first signs of aging are relatively trivial. Their chief significance is in making people feel that they are entering the stage of life formerly occupied by their parents. Slowly, unwillingly, and sometimes on the basis of the smallest physical clues, they begin to reorient themselves to being part of a different generation. Typical is the experience of a 41-year-old woman:

> It's odd how something can happen to you as a child, and you forget about it until years later. I had an aunt who some of the family used to make fun of behind her back. Fat, forty, and an old maid, or some such remarks. Even as a child, I recognized how mean they were.
>
> I used to spend a lot of time with her. I remember one evening in particular—I was about nine or ten—she was in her bedroom, and she called to me. I went in. She was standing looking into a mirror, and she had a tweezers in one hand. It looked to me like she was about to stab herself. I was honestly scared for a moment until she asked if I would help her pull gray hairs . . . She told me that she had heard from a friend's mother that if you pulled out gray hair as soon as they came in you stopped them from spreading or even growing. . . .
>
> I forgot all about that time until recently when I was looking into a bathroom mirror and I happened to notice a few gray hairs. I automatically reached for a tweezers. One by one I pulled them out. Almost thirty years later I was doing exactly the same thing as my aunt. It made me feel very strange. I realized that it was just a beginning—the start of the whole bit, rinses, touch-ups, trips to the beauty shop. Maybe I'm the kind who overdramatizes things, but it seemed to me at that moment, gray hairs initiated me into the forties. I was getting old (Davitz & Davitz, 1976, p. 143).

This sign of aging was slight and in no way interfered with this woman's ability to function. But it had a profound significance for her. Her immediate reaction to the issue of aging was to eradicate its symptoms—to tweeze and touch up.

Germaine Greer, the feminist and educator, described her sense of aging in an insightful article (Greer, 1986, p. 142).

> I can't pretend it's easy, aging, but it is interesting. You have to laugh at yourself when you realize that the dress you are thinking of as new has been hanging in the closet for ten years, and that you can't wear it, not because it shrank in the dry cleaning, but because you've become heavier. It hurts to realize that you can't let yourself fall off your bicycle or your horse these days because it takes so much longer to recover from your bruises. Old sprains and breaks are rheumatic and uselessly call attention to themselves. You begin to wish you had taken better care of yourself. You think twice before carrying out the trash, find easy ways to lift things, get sleepy after dinner, wonder if you are being foolish to plant slow-growing trees in the garden.—You care about yourself less and less. Your vanity and pride stop getting in your way. You begin to develop a sense of proportion. Your powers of concentration expand continually, as you stop squandering emotion on foolish things.—You can escape from the dominion of your own passions and enter into a calm wherein you can fix your eye upon a worthy objective and pursue it wholeheartedly. Old friends and loyalty come into their own.

In our culture any number of physical changes may initiate an aging crisis. If it is not gray hair, it may be a tendency to gain weight much more easily. Another troubling sign for some people is loss of skin elasticity, visible as wrinkles about the face and neck. Most middle-aged people also experience some reduction in sensory efficiency. For example, hearing gradually declines, especially among those who have noisy work environments. Eyesight, which was at its peak in adolescence, continues to deteriorate. By age 50 many people must use glasses to correct for farsightedness; the nearsighted may now need two pairs of glasses, one for distance and one for reading. Many middle-aged people lose teeth, acquire dentures, or suffer other dental insults that bring home the fact of aging.

Homeostatic mechanisms too become less efficient in ways that are noticed by the individual. The 50-year-old woman finds that she is "always cold." That is, she cannot easily adjust to temperature extremes. Perhaps her husband finds that he can no longer tolerate rich food or have more than two drinks if he wishes to avoid an upset stomach and sleep disturbances. The impairment of homeostatic functions also makes an impression in many less obvious ways. The aging individual is less able to use and store glucose, and suffers an increasing risk of diabetes. His or her blood vessels become less elastic, less able to contract and dilate as the situation demands, and the heart exhibits a lowered efficiency. The middle-aged person who is informed of such changes by a physician may experience an aging crisis. Not only is it necessary to confront the idea of having a cardiovascular or diabetic problem but in many cases the person must act on advice to "slow down," shape up, or make changes in life-style.

Finally, for women, menopause, the end of reproductive fertility, is unarguable evidence of aging. Menopause is generally experienced as irregular menstruation that finally ceases altogether at about the age of 50 (Greene, 1984). During this period of transition (sometimes called the "change of life"), many women experience hormonal instability that may manifest itself in dizziness, irritability, headaches, sweating, or palpitations. These symptoms seldom interfere substantially with daily functioning (and when they do, they can often be controlled by an estrogen supplement). However, menopause is experienced as a change in biological or reproductive status; like all changes, it must be dealt with.

In the past it was assumed that women always reacted to menopause with irritability and depression. Today these responses are less typical. Research suggests that some women do not attach much psychological importance to menopause (Neugarten, 1967). They, indeed, report benefits, such as improved sexual relations, higher spirits, and freedom from "aches and pains" (Neugarten et al., 1963). Margaret Mead coined the term "post menopausal zest" (quoted in Sheehy, 1976), perhaps to explain the energy that enabled her, at age 72, to travel to New Guinea and maintain a heavy schedule of field trips and lectures.

The way that men and women resolve the aging crisis varies. Some choose to deny or obliterate the signs of age. For example, they dye their hair or have cosmetic surgery to remove facial wrinkles. They may rebel, ignoring the recommendations of their physicians regarding work load, exercise, and diet. Others surrender. They "let themselves go" and relinquish all stake in appearances. Still others appear to accept aging with positive feelings. For example, they allow their hair to gray, perhaps feeling they look more distinguished or striking. At the same time they make subtle changes in dress, makeup, and deportment—all designed to take advantage of "dignity" and other prerogatives of the older person. (It is common to describe this person as one who "grows old gracefully.") Finally, there are people who attempt to compensate for the effects of age through health regimens. It has been shown that many of the physical losses we associate with later life are not inevitable or even normal, but are the result of sedentary life-styles, cigarette smoking, and other behaviors that can be changed. People who understand this cope with increased weight, for example, by modifying their diet and working out at the local gym. Health regimens encompassing diet and exercise are an important means of coping with aging in our culture.

America, which has always been a youth-oriented culture, is gradually coming to focus on the groups born in the 1930s and 40s. As one 50-year-old said, "America is making much of us—suddenly 50 is chic and sexy." The country is saying "Wow" to Joan Collins, Jane Fonda, and Linda Evans. Twenty years ago, the idea that a rock star could be over 30 was ludicrous. But Mick Jaggar or Tina Turner, both over 40, still attract crowds and sell records. In fact, America is even beginning to develop a more positive attitude to the over-65 group. The major reason for this change in attitude is that our population is aging. For the first time in history, there are more Americans over 65 than teenagers, and the fastest growing segment of the population is 85 and older (USA Today, 1984, p. 16). These changes in the population are leading to a new definition of old.

The question "How old is old?" is now answered in a new way, "It depends." Age, which has always been the final absolute, is now actually relative. A person of 45 is considered an older worker by the Department of Labor, but a 65-year-old retiree may feel it is the time to begin living. To a teenager, 15 years is an entire lifetime. A man of 65 can still look forward to 14.5 more years of life, and a woman to 19.1. What is "old" depends on the age of the person you ask. Aaron Lipman, a sociologist at the University of Miami (USA Today, 1984) pointed out that most people do not define themselves as old. Instead old is someone 15 years older than oneself. To a 10-year-old, 25 is old; to a 70-year-old, 85 is old. The old one is always someone else, and there is always someone older than you.

In the years to come we can expect social changes to meet the needs of the increased number of older people. By the year 2000, 20 percent of the population will be 55 or older. These individuals will demand and receive a share of the nation's comforts and resources. It has begun already with leisure cities, smaller living quarters that are more convenient to maintain, food packaged for one, and the tremendous growth of travel tours for the elderly.

The increase in the older population will also impact on what society defines as valuable, desirable, and beautiful. Only recently has it become "acceptable" to think of an older woman in her 40s and a younger man in his early 30s dating and marrying. Mary Cantwell (1986), looks forward to the day when a woman of 50 will no longer be "over the hill" but on top of it. She awaits the day when the nicest thing you can say to a woman is that she looks her age. What is wrong she asks, "with looking like you remember Clark Gable, have borne a few children, suffered a few sunburns, shed more than a few tears and known more than a few sleepless nights." If age and beauty are relative and the population is getting older, we can look forward to times ahead when the beauty of older people will be more fully appreciated.

No matter what their initial responses, people who deal successfully with the crisis of aging must eventually come to terms with the reality of biological decline. One way they can do so is by relinquishing their psychological investment in their physical powers and youthful attractiveness. They can calmly invert their hierarchy of values, putting wisdom and experience before the physical qualities they emphasized in their youth (Peck, 1968). This is a realistic strategy. The middle-aged person finds that nonphysical attributes, especially judgment and specialized knowledge, are highly rewarded in our complex technological culture. People tend to arrive at the top at about the time they begin to feel winded from the climb. But by then they have a better idea of the diversity of heights there are to scale—not only vocationally but psychologically, interpersonally, and spiritually.

THE MID-LIFE CRISIS

"Mid-life crisis" is no more than a convenient label to describe what people experience when they believe that they are passing into the second half of life. This may have little to do with their actual point in the life span or their biological condition. History is full of examples of people who held inaccurate perceptions of their life spans. Freud is a famous example of someone who expected to die in his 40s, but who after that age went on to publish work that would earn him great fame. Other people regard themselves as being in the mid-life passage but may in fact be entering the final period of their lives. A recent book on "starting in the middle" was authored by a woman who met death before her volume was published.

Recent findings suggest that people change psychologically as they approach the second half of life. For many people, these psychological changes are experienced as a **mid-life crisis,** or crisis of meaning. The crisis marks the transition, or passage, to the period of "middle age." Gail Sheehy described the mid-life passage in dramatic terms:

Mid-Life Crisis
A psychological crisis in middle or later adulthood in which a person confronts the fact of aging and questions the meaning of his or her life, usually having doubts about marriage, career, and the way future years are to be spent.

Mid-Life Macho

The term "macho" is Mexican-Spanish and means a virile, strong man—a he-man. The related word, "machismo," is used in Hispanic cultures to describe things that are very manly and also to refer to male domination. In commenting on machismo, Wrenn (1986) wrote:

> Machismo, celebrating as it does the marvelous difference between the sexes, is still important for men, however they may try to disparage it. But the forms it takes mellows with age. For me, machismo now means driving more slowly, as if to prove that my libido is not attached to the accelerator. I . . . do not think . . . gold neck chains make you . . . macho at all; they make the wearer look like an off-duty exotic dancer. But donning an apron to wash the dishes seems highly macho, for the dishwasher does not care what kind of image his apron projects. So does having the guts to say "Sorry" if you bump into someone. From the perspective of middle age, the litmus test of machismo is what you overcome, not merely accomplish. . . .

1. What is your reaction to these comments? How do you think people you know who are 20 years older would react?
2. Do the men in your peer group practice machismo? If so, what reactions do they get from other men? From women?
3. Ask a person from a Hispanic background (or someone familiar with Hispanic cultures) about the derivation of the term "machismo," and how it is used in Hispanic countries. ▲

Without warning, in the middle of my thirties, *I had a breakdown of nerve*. It never occurred to me that while winging along in my happiest and most productive stage, all of a sudden simply staying aloft would require a massive exertion of will (Sheehy, 1976, p. 2).

A psychiatrist touched on the same themes when he wrote that in mid-life "the usual bounce out of bed and arrogant knowing were all at once gone: I was left with an unanswerable question in place of knowledge" (Mandell, 1977, p. 35). At that point in his life he was forced to concede, "There's a blackness over my shoulder that I'll have to face, and I don't have the strength" (p. 35). In these very personal experiences, we hear the cry of a person caught in a crisis over the meaning of life itself. The mid-life crisis has been so widely discussed recently that perhaps people today do not approach it "without warning" as Sheehy did. But they do not approach it with the answers either.

Jacques (1965) related the mid-life crisis to creativity. He distinguished between two forms of the creative process, "hot-from-the-fire creativity, which occurs in the 20s and 30s and "sculptured" creativity, which appears after the late 30s. The former is characterized by sudden and spontaneous production of a superior object or a piece of work. In the latter, while the inspiration may be just as intense, there is a long time and a big effort between the first taste of inspiration and the final and finished creative product (Hamilton, 1981). According to the psychoanalyst James W. Hamilton (1981), the creative person in the throes of mid-life must deal with his new awareness of individual mortality and the presence of destructive impulses in his own being. For creative expression to emerge in the middle of life, these themes must be faced and dealt with. If not, Jacques maintains, a creative career may simply come to an end, either by the drying up of creative work, or in the death of the person.

The concept of a mid-life crisis is partly a cultural phenomenon as well. This is not to say that it is unique to our culture: Dante, Shakespeare, and the English Romantic poets wrote sensitively about the middle-age confrontation with questions of fate and meaning. However, certain trends in our culture have probably made the sense of crisis more common. For instance, women who have raised families are more often encouraged (because of new social attitudes or financial need) to begin or return to careers. Mid-life career changes, for both women and men, have become more ordinary events and, today it makes sense for 40-year-old people to question the life they have lived so far—since they have so many options and, because of medical advances, probably many more years ahead of them. In sum, the mid-life crisis is not a state of mind that arises in isolation from society; it is encouraged by trends and attitudes in our culture.

There is disagreement among scholars as to the age the mid-life crisis usually occurs. Bee and Mitchell (1984) state that all the major theories of adulthood mark the period around age 40 as the major transition point called the mid-life crisis. However, it is doubtful that the crisis is experienced by all or even most adults at that age. Newman (1982) said that the crisis occurs at the close of the middle third of the life span, around age 50. At whatever age it occurs, the crisis is "real" and, if it is resolved in a favorable way, individuals are able to successfully assume senior or more responsible positions in their work or community, as well as experience an increase in and more enjoyable leisure. The resolution of the crisis may also bring the anticipation or the acceptance of the possibility of illness, widowhood, or the redirecting of energies into new areas. Those who cannot adapt to changes in their physical capacities and cannot construct a new conceptualization of self may encounter difficulties. They may feel a loss of purpose, grow frustrated and stagnate, and experience a sense of "life passing them by."

Study of the mid-life transition (primarily conducted by middle-aged psychologists and other social scientists) is only now taking the form of longitudinal research. Several areas of concern that have been identified are discussed in the following paragraphs.

Lengthen Your Life by Changing Your Time Perceptions

Gay Gaer Luce is a psychologist who works with groups of middle-aged and older adults, helping them to experience a new sense of vitality and well-being. Luce finds that her group members (like others in our busy world) would like to be able to experience *hours* yet have them occur in just a few minutes (Luce, 1979, pp. 31–35). She offers exercises that enable a person to experience expanded time. In one exercise, members of the group set an egg timer for three minutes and sink back into a state of profound relaxation for which the exercise has prepared them. The instructor guides them further, through breathing techniques and bodily and mental images ("Imagine you are floating on your back in warm, shallow water like a heavy barge . . ."). Most participants experience expanded time. For example, one woman remarked, "I know I couldn't have gone through all that in three minutes. An hour maybe. It felt like a week."

Luce suggests other exercises that rely simply on time awareness, and that can be done individually.

1. Place a clock on the table and allow perhaps 45 minutes for relaxation, or for some other activity that you value. Tell yourself, "This 45 minutes will have to give me two hours." Does time expand?

2. Be a clock-watcher for one whole morning, noting what you do with each four-minute time span. Ask yourself, "How much of the time did I feel alive and good? When did time move 'fast,' and when did it seem 'slow'? Which were the four-minute periods that were most meaningful?"

3. Why do you suppose these exercises in time awareness and expansion are of interest to middle-aged and older adults? What special use might they have to people at your stage of the life span?

In older people, quality rather than quantity of time becomes important. There is an increased awareness of the sensations of life—colors, shapes, and textures (Butler, 1971)—such as one also sees in younger people who face death within a short time. Older people, having less time in their future, adjust by more intensely experiencing the time they have. And they generally sleep fewer hours. ▲

Changed Perceptions of Time

Middle-aged people develop a new awareness of time. In a classic study, Neugarten, one of the first researchers to examine middle age, noted: "Life is restructured in terms of time left to live rather than time since birth. Not only the reversal in directionality but the awareness that time is finite is a particularly conspicuous feature of middle age . . ." (1967). In interviews with middle-aged people Neugarten found that the recognition of there being only so much time left was a frequent theme.

Some researchers have related the new experience of time to proximity to death (see Chapter 13). But it has more immediate manifestations. Fried, for example, points out that people in the mid-life transition experience a diffusion of time, which means that "time is out of joint" for them (Fried, 1967). They worry about changed perceptions of time, both the future and the present.

They say, "I don't understand how this last year could go so fast when every day in it was absolutely endless" (p. 86). Boredom, a foreshortening of the future, and a feeling that one is growing older faster than others (particularly one's children) are characteristic. Like adolescents, people in the mid-life transition feel that nothing ever happens, but simultaneously regard each moment as unbearably important.

People cope with this problem in several ways. Some decide to do things that have long been postponed. "If not now, never," says the middle-aged person who takes up the violin, or travels to South America, or makes some larger change in career or marriage. Such people act upon long-held goals because, by their own reckoning, their time is running short. More often, people somehow bring a new order to their perception of time. As they approach later adulthood they learn to value each day without questioning it.

Career Reexamination

Psychologists characterize the 30s as the years of career consolidation, the years of "settling down" (Levinson et al., 1978). It is during these years that people establish themselves both in their occupations and as family members. At about age 40, give or take as many as 10 years, people take a kind of emotional vacation from their career and begin to explore the world within. Typically they look at their career and ask themselves, "Is this all there is?" Success now seems either less possible or less desirable. The early vocational dream is either out of date or out of reach. The person wonders, "What have I done with my life?" and "Is there time to change?" And, no matter what career they choose, some think they would have preferred another one (see Table 12.1).

The questioning is not necessarily a sign of dissatisfaction with work. People who are in their happiest, most productive stage are as likely to reexamine their careers as those who have met obvious disappointments.

Perhaps the most difficult adjustment is required of the person who has not, by mid-life, become established in the way originally intended. This person is forced to admit, "I haven't gotten what I wanted." He or she must acknowledge not having become a novelist, let alone a great novelist, or realize that it will never be possible to break into modeling, gain tenure at a prestigious university, or rise to company president. This realization is often followed by a period of depression, and a consideration of alternatives. In some cases the person is able to make a fortunate change—in occupation, location, company, and so on. In other cases the mid-life suspicion that it may be too late seems well-founded. Financial responsibilities, an inhospitable job market, and other realities may make career changes exceedingly difficult.

The person who is trapped in an unfulfilling job may suffer a general decline from which no escape seems possible (Levinson et al., 1978). For example, some people become alcoholics or estranged (or divorced) from their families (or spouse) as a result of work-related frustration. As noted in Chapter 11, a more favorable adjustment is made by those who invest themselves more fully in nonwork activities. The disillusioned worker may decide to "live for the weekends," feeling that his or her most important work is managing church

TABLE 12.1	*Percentages of People Who Would Choose Similar Jobs Again*

Occupation	Percent
Professional and White Collar	
Urban university professors	93
Mathematicians	91
Physicists	89
Biologists	89
Chemists	86
Firm lawyers	85
School superintendents	85
Lawyers	83
Journalists (Washington correspondents)	82
Church university professors	77
Solo lawyers	75
White-collar workers (nonprofessional)	43
Skilled Trades and Blue Collar	
Skilled printers	52
Paper workers	42
Skilled auto workers	41
Skilled steelworkers	41
Textile workers	31
Blue-collar workers	24
Unskilled steelworkers	21
Unskilled auto workers	16

Source: Adapted from R. L. Kahn, "The Work Module—A Tonic for Lunchpail Lassitude" in *Psychology Today,* 1973, 6(9), 39, and L. Davidoff, *Introduction to Psychology,* New York: McGraw-Hill, 1980, p. 463.

functions and renovating the house. Or that person may derive primary satisfaction from the progress that children are making in their careers. A long-term study of AT&T managers found that while successful men tended to emphasize occupational themes in interviews, less successful men showed greater involvement in marital and parental roles, as well as church or other "humanist" activities (Bray, Campbell, & Grant, 1974).

As noted earlier, people who are relatively or very successful in their careers also experience mid-life doubts about the meaning of their work. A person may find that he or she has achieved career goals without having found the anticipated fulfillment. A common feeling is: "I want to be the kind of person I was when I wanted to be what I am now." The problem is that he or she has become a different kind of person. Accordingly, it is necessary to set new goals. For example, the person who dreamed of leading the life of an account executive for a large advertising firm decides in her late 30s that she really wants to raise a family and manage a country house. She aspires to a new kind of fulfillment, or may find that her success in terms of the earlier dream is still gratifying but no longer enough.

Other people come to feel that their career success has been achieved at a great and unanticipated sacrifice. For example, a career-minded man may find that somehow he has neglected to spend time on personal relationships, has failed to take vacations that were necessary for his health, and has not developed interests that might have furthered his personal growth and enhanced eventual retirement. Typical is a noted dentist who complained that he had worked hard solely to ensure that his family was affluent ("I was from a poor family, so I wanted to give to them everything I never had"). At mid-life, he found that his children neither knew him well nor respected his values, and that his wife had developed a drinking problem during the years he had been emotionally absent. This person faced a mid-life crisis when he realized "I got what I wanted, but it wasn't worth it."

Finally, some successful people find that they have become too successful, too established. They enjoy the rewards and prerogatives, but some of the challenge has gone out of the work. A city manager in the Midwest describes this situation:

> It was not that I did not still enjoy my job, because I did. It was because I had gotten used to it. I had at least a general idea of the outcome of most of the events that would happen. I could at times even predict the behavior of my masters on the city council, and anticipate the demands of the unions. I could even guess what the hot subject would be at the Annual International City Management Association Convention. This familiarity with the job produced a warm and comfortable feeling that saved me from thinking too hard about what was going on or wondering if there wasn't a better way of doing it (Donaldson, 1979, p. 3).

This man decided to risk a career change because he wished to recapture the exhilaration and wonder he had experienced during the earlier period of career growth. He left his position to assume the presidency of a zoo in a different city—whereupon he was able to look at everything "with new eyes."

For a variety of reasons, then, relatively successful and well-adjusted people reexamine their work experience and contemplate a career change in mid-life. The nature of the career changes that actually emerge in mid-life has received much attention in recent years. We can tentatively conclude that most people use the mid-life period of uncertainty to strike a new balance; they begin to express parts of the personality that have been submerged during the early years of career consolidation and advancement.

For example, many psychologists have recognized the trend toward generativity—expanded interest in other people or larger entities—in career-minded men and women. In mid-life, there is a tendency to relinquish an earlier specialized role and take a greater part in the management and growth of the larger enterprise. There is new willingness to become a mentor, to teach as well as compete. And there is a desire to balance career with outside interests of an obviously generative character. Typical is a physician who emerged from the mid-life transition with a new interest in people. He writes:

My professional work still means much, but does not dominate as it used to. Our farm, our children's lives and ideas capture my mind more than the mechanisms of medicine. Working with [new students admitted] to medical school gives a special reward (Vaillant, 1977, p. 233).

Similar attitudes were found among women executives profiled by Henning (1978). All of the successful women had placed vocational concerns above their interest in emotional relationships until age 35 or so. The self-questioning during the mid-life crisis led them to recognize and more greatly enjoy what one woman called "another real part of me." The managerial women, like their male counterparts, became more open, more social, and more interested in family life. (Half subsequently married widowers or divorced men with children.)

Thus, in many careers, the mid-life crisis results in a turn toward generativity. But this is not the only possibility. Gould points out that the mid-life crisis prompts people to express *whatever it is* that has been discovered as a weakness, that represents a "dark" or unexpressed side (Gould, 1978). For the person who has been able to express generativity, this may be the more aggressive or achievement-oriented part of the personality. For example, a woman may find that after 20 years of child care and part-time teaching she needs to express her executive abilities in a business environment.

As Gould points out, the direction of change varies with the individual's history. "One minister may become an activist, while an activist minister may become more of a scholar. . . . One mathematician who's always been a loner may change to an institutional setting, while another who has worked for IBM all his life may move out so that he can finally do what he wants" (p. 243). The changes are part of the individual's attempt to grow or become more authentic. When change is made—when the individual learns to accept and enjoy "another real part of me"—the outcome is favorable. The personality becomes more fully integrated.

Older Workers and Preparing for Retirement   More and more people are choosing to continue working past the age they can begin collecting retirement benefits. Eighty percent of people over age 55 are physically and mentally able to continue in the work force. As a consequence of improved diet, more exercise, better education, and change in life-styles, these people are in better physical condition and more experienced than their counterparts were 10 to 20 years ago (Kieffer, 1984). However, older workers face prejudice and other difficulties. For example, they are often considered a liability by their bosses and an outmoded relic by younger coworkers, partly because companies have instituted early retirement programs to eliminate the older workers. Employees have complained that if your hair is gray the employer thinks your brain is not capable of thinking anymore, and that your hands and legs can no longer produce or carry you (Worne, 1984).

Research, however, has indicated that older workers can continue to perform productively and that in most jobs older employees perform as well as or better than younger employees. Studies of work loss due to illness show that workers age 65 and over have attendance records equal to or better than most other age groups of workers. For example, the National Center for Health Statistics found that in 1981 workers age 65 and over had 4.2 work loss days per year compared to 4.1 days for workers 17–24 and 5.7 for workers age 45 to 64 (Coberly & Newquist, 1984). Older workers are also safer. The Bureau of Labor Statistics found that workers over age 55 account for under 10 percent of all workplace injuries even though they make up 14 percent of the labor force. It is true, however, that once an older worker is injured, it is usually a more serious injury and the worker is apt to be out of work for a longer time (Coberly & Newquist, 1984).

Some employers believe older workers are less adaptable than younger ones and have difficulty learning new tasks and new technologies. Research however, shows that intellectual performance required to learn new tasks is less affected by age than previously believed. In fact, people who continue to use their intellectual abilities maintain their learning capacity as they age.

Surveys indicate that older persons are interested in working. A 1981 Harris poll found that 80 percent of those age 55 to 64 who were still working preferred to continue to work in either full- or part-time jobs after normal retirement age. Older persons also need jobs as much as many younger people. One out of every seven persons age 65 or older live in poverty. Many believe they will be healthier and have a better mental outlook if they keep busy (Kiefer, 1984). Moreover, among senior workers there is a precious and untapped wealth of knowledge and experience that will benefit society.

In the near future we will need older workers to fill jobs since, over the next several decades, the stream of younger entrants into the labor force will slow considerably. The talents, skills, and experience of older workers will become more valuable and become an important factor in our country's productivity. Former Secretary of Labor Raymond J. Donovan stated that today's emphasis on early retirement could become tomorrow's scramble to hire and retain older workers.

At some point, however, most people face retirement. A number of studies suggest that the retirement event itself is not so stressful as the uncertain period that precedes it. Corporations that retire large numbers of older people have observed that retirement anxieties adversely affect an employee's job performance years before the person retires. Fears of being idle, lonely, and possibly ill may result in increasing agitation as the person nears the retirement date. Research on marital satisfaction also suggests that the preretirement period is more difficult for couples than the period that follows (Rollins & Feldman, 1970).

For these reasons, social scientists tend to view retirement not as a single crisis, but as a process that begins with the individual's realization that he or she will one day retire (Atchley, 1972). Corporations that give retirement counseling to prevent "retirement shock" prefer to begin at age 55 or before— that is, at least eight to ten years before the average time of retirement. Topics addressed in the preretirement programs include money management, health and housing needs, and options such as hobbies, travel, and postretirement jobs.

Individuals who do not have access to preretirement counseling programs must anticipate their own needs in these areas. They may find help in the growing number of books, newspaper columns, and television talk shows on the subject of later life options. In these popular presentations, emphasis is usually placed on the development of hobbies or secondary career interests during mid-life. As Sheehy put it, "A man retired at 65 doesn't suddenly pick up a camera and revive himself with a second career as a photographer" (1976, p. 497). Enjoyable postretirement activities will, in most cases, have been taken up in mid-life or earlier. Anticipation is the recommended coping mechanism.

Marriage Reevaluation

To some people the mid-life crisis brings a reevaluation of the marital relationship. Because time and sexual abilities are no longer perceived as continuing indefinitely, infidelity may seem more attractive. Because children are nearly grown, divorce may seem more possible. Restlessness, emotional confusion, and physical change combine to produce what is often called a "second adolescence," with all the longing for romance that characterized the first.

One source of marital conflict is mid-life growth and development itself. A relationship that worked well in young adulthood works less smoothly because one partner (or both) has developed in unexpected directions. For example, women in mid-life tend to outgrow the assumption that they must rely on a male protector (Gould, 1978). A marital relationship structured primarily around the husband's protective role would naturally be threatened by the wife's new attitude. Another frequently cited example is that of the husband who outgrows his wife, in a sense, by developing business interests and social contacts she cannot share because she is occupied with her parenting and homemaking responsibilities. In such cases, the couple is confronted with an opportunity for growth and change—but also, of course, with the risk of estrangement.

In other cases a marriage is simply overwhelmed by the mid-life crisis of one or both of the partners. Perhaps the marriage has been unsatisfactory all along; perhaps the rift is merely a casualty of mid-life confusion. The person undergoing the crisis sometimes finds it difficult to separate disillusionment with the partner from the more general disillusionment that has set in. For example, the psychiatrist quoted earlier placed the breakdown of his marriage within a much larger context:

> [The crisis] began a while back. There was no energy. My older son had taken violent leave of the family circle to take his own turf. A tenuously supported, mutually held delusional system that backed my marriage contract . . . first grew depleted with long and desperate use and then disappeared. The cosmic feeling of specialness which came from doing scientific research and rescuing patients became the boredom of everyday work. There wasn't any saving greatness (Mandell, 1977, p. 34).

In such cases, marital estrangement or divorce is part of the mid-life crisis of meaning—or part of the resolution of the crisis. It is usually difficult to tell which, considering the complexity of factors involved.

Marriage is a developmental task, the success of which depends on the psychological readiness of the two people involved and their ability to adjust to the challenges they face over the years.

Often it takes years for a couple to become aware of, to talk about, and to act on a serious underlying deficiency in their marriage. Typically the partners are unhappy for some time but do not directly confront their problem. They may not have achieved the necessary perspective, or may have long been distracted by small children, career advancement, and financial pressures (Schwebel, Schwebel, Schwebel, Schwebel, & Schwebel, 1989). The mid-life crisis of meaning often brings an end to the silent standoff: It brings a confrontation. In some cases this results in improved communication or a commitment to marital therapy. The couple works to catch up developmentally. For example, a man may face his need to separate more fully from one of his parents and enlist his wife's support in doing so. In other cases the mid-life crisis is followed by separation or divorce. One or both individuals may accept the challenge to begin anew in the task of forming a successful, mature relationship.

CHANGES IN THE FAMILY

Among the life events that demand a high degree of personal readjustment are changes in the family (Holmes & Rahe, 1967). During middle age many changes may occur within a relatively few years. They may include the departure of children from the home; the death or serious illness of a spouse; or the death of a close family member, usually a parent. Events such as these represent a significant loss in the family structure from which the middle-aged person has derived comfort and identity.

Departure of Children

When the last child has left the home, the middle-aged parent enters what psychologists call the post-parental or "empty nest" stage of marriage (see Chapter 10). Typically the parent is ambivalent about this development—pleased that the children have made the necessary steps toward independent schooling, career, or marriage, but struggling to accept the end of the active parental role. Some parents find that being without child-related responsibilities gives them a surprising amount of free time—time to pursue new interests, to resume important career or educational goals, or simply to have fun.

Although the majority of parents show an increase in life satisfaction after the last child has left the home (Campbell, 1981), some fathers and mothers react with depression to the departure of their children. This type of reaction, sometimes called the "empty nest syndrome," occurs in fewer than 20 percent of parents.

During the post-parental years both sexes may reveal the potential that was blunted while they were concerned with procreation, providing, and parenthood (Norman, 1980). For instance, the husband who used to support the wife both physically and emotionally now often becomes more dependent on her; he tends to defer to her wishes and her requirements, acting toward her as he does toward other sources of security and authority in his life. The wife, on the other hand, may become more aggressive and less affiliative in later life. In short, each person becomes something of what the other used to be and through these changes, ushers in the normal androgyny of late life.

A favorable outcome of the post-parental crisis seems to depend on the individual's ability to anticipate post-parental needs. For the person who is primarily committed to being a parent during early adulthood, the best preparation is to develop interests, activities, and attitudes that will provide satisfaction during the long post-parental period that is now part of our life span. This need not necessarily involve relinquishing the child-caring role in later years. Many older people find meaningful work in day-care centers, in foster care, or in child-care responsibilities for grandchildren whose parents work outside the home.

The Aging Parent

A new area of concern for middle-aged people is their aging parents. At about the same time that they are "launching" their own children into the world, they may be called upon to assume some responsibility for parents who are trying to adjust to declining health, declining income, and so forth. Should a parent die during this period, the developmental consequences are significant. The mid-life confrontation with aging, for example, takes on a new meaning. And there are practical problems that must be resolved. For example, the middle-aged person must often assist the widowed parent, emotionally or financially. Sometimes the relationship with the surviving parent must be reworked under new and painful circumstances. And the middle-aged person may have to participate in health-related decisions, including, in some cases, the difficult decision of whether to provide home care or institutional care for the parent.

ADJUSTMENT CHALLENGES AND PROBLEMS OF THE ELDERLY YEARS

Retirement

Retirement from the job is an important milestone in late adulthood. For some people it represents a dramatic change in life-style. The office, the shop, the road, the plant is no longer the setting in which a person plays out the main part of his or her days. The 8:05 bus, the 12:00 to 1:00 lunch hour, the work brought home in the evenings, no longer force a structuring of the person's time.

For the man or woman who has held a full-time job, perhaps for as long as fifty years, retirement is obviously an event of great personal significance. It is also an event of social significance. Traditionally, many have viewed retirement as the transition from productive maturity to nonproductive old age (Maddox, 1966)—or, as we say today, from work to leisure. However, in Erikson's terms, retirement marks a transition from the struggle for generativity to the struggle for integrity. The retired person has reached the stage at which it is appropriate to review his or her life's work, and derive from it meaning and satisfaction—or despair.

In the past, society viewed retirement as a crisis of power loss: retired individuals lose their job, some of their influence, and much of their income. Today, however, there is a growing tendency to see retirement primarily as an opportunity for personal growth. Perhaps this is because our culture now places greater value on leisure roles in all age groups. Perhaps, also, this is because improved health care and increased longevity have enabled retired people to develop new and valued work roles, as consultants, community service workers, and the like.

There is considerable evidence that life transitions during the older years, like retirement, are well handled by the majority of people (McCallum, 1981). To illustrate, 68 percent of retirees adapted well to their new condition. Men who had no difficulty with this adjustment rated leisure, sports, hobbies, absence of a timetable, and freedom and independence as the best things about retirement. Women who adjusted well reported enjoying increased opportunities for seeing family and friends, staying in bed, and freedom and independence. McCallum (1981) concluded that "retirement for leisure is an attractive life option" (p. 235) for today's older citizens.

Postretirement Adjustment

The morale of retired individuals is naturally affected by their perceptions of how the retirement has come about, including their control over its timing. Adjustment appears to be easiest if retirement is voluntary—if, for example, the individual is not "forced to retire" because of health or a boss's decision but rather elects to retire because of personal preferences.

Today more people look forward to and willingly retire, and many elect to do so before the age of 65. At the same time, the mandatory retirement age has been raised to 70 years in some work settings, extending the time a "retirement resister" can remain on the job. This means that fewer older people are forced into retirement by institutional rulings.

Adjustment in the postretirement period is also affected by what the individual retires *to*. Here the evidence is strikingly clear: adjustment is best when the person has enough money. Atchley finds that only a minute proportion of those with moderate incomes miss their jobs (Atchley, 1972). The major cause of maladjustment in this period is economic deprivation. Another key problem for the retired is keeping occupied. Whereas some people welcome the freedom of retirement, others miss the externally imposed work schedule, the opportunity to exercise leadership in their customary work role, and social

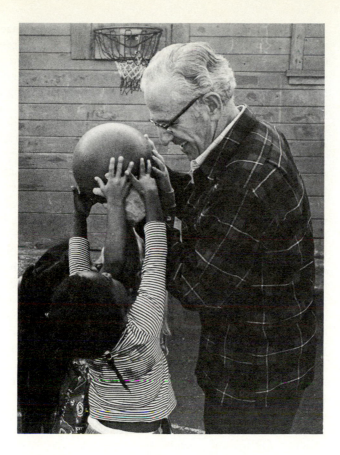

contacts with colleagues and younger people. Within a short time, however, most retired people create their own schedules and reorganize their social life around family and friends.

The variety of ways in which individuals adjust to the loss of a job and use their newly free time is a topic of increasing interest to social planners. Several possible adjustment approaches have been identified (summarized in Atchley, 1976). Some people adjust to retirement by finding a work substitute different from their former career. They engage in activities—either hobbies or second careers—designed to provide whatever satisfactions they once found in their jobs. Other retired people opt for continuity. They continue to play the roles of the past, only gradually reducing overall activity. Examples are the retired schoolteacher who tutors and teaches Sunday school or the retired business executive who continues to subscribe to *The Wall Street Journal* and starts selling real estate. Finally, some people disengage themselves from work and work roles. In retirement these people pursue nonwork activities that are meaningful to them, such as reading, talking with friends, and working in the garden. They feel that their work is done, and there is no need to replace it.

In sum, retirement, in and of itself, does not appear to be significantly associated with psychological difficulties. Most of the researchers who have examined adjustment in the postretirement period have found that the major sources of difficulty stem from loss of income and from conditions that have little to do with retirement per se—for example, declining health or the illness or death of one's spouse.

Widowhood

Although the anticipation of widowhood is a mid-life crisis, most people do not experience the bereavement until after the age of 65. Only about 17 percent of all women and 4 percent of all men are widowed before they are 65 (Schick, 1986). When the death occurs, it is potentially the most stressful of all life events. In addition to working through depression, grief, and anger, the bereaved person must deal with practical problems, such as managing financial affairs, developing new sources of support, and perhaps moving to a new residence. When the crisis of widowhood occurs in middle age, it is often experienced as the last event in a sequence of family dissolutions. It may also cause the individual to become aware of approaching entrance into a period of "old age." When widowhood occurs in the 70s or 80s, it is part of a larger problem of isolation, loneliness, and bereavement overload.

Unlike retirement, widowhood often comes more suddenly, and is almost always unwanted. Shortly after a death the longing for the dead spouse becomes an overwhelming emotion. In time, the reality of the absence and the finality and permanence of widowhood become accepted. The longing then gives way to a generalized loneliness, with the need for a support system of children, family, and friends. The depression that accompanies loneliness is transient for most widows and a resilience in them comes to promote adjustment (Belsky, 1984).

Health and Emotional Problems

The percentage of people 65 or older has more than doubled since 1900 (see Figure 12.1). High on the list of concerns of most older people is health. Among the larger population, too, failing health and the development of a terminal illness are the occurrences chiefly dreaded in old age. We picture old age and infirmity together—and a fair number of us say we hope we die before our time (Kastenbaum, 1971).

In reality the physical health of most old people is better than is generally believed (Butler, 1975). Whereas we tend to picture the aged as bedridden or institutionalized, 95 percent live in the community. Of the population over 65, 81 percent are fully ambulatory and able to come and go independently.

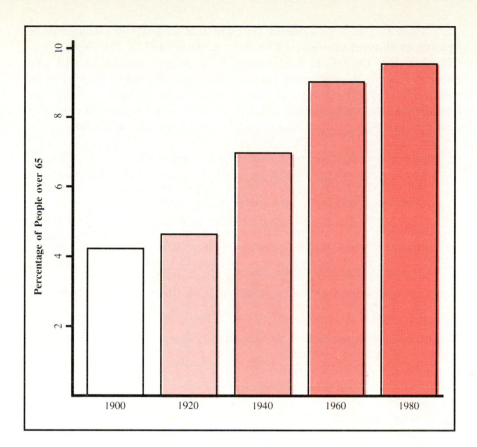

Figure 12.1 People over 65: 1900–1980.

Source: United States Bureau of the Census, Statistical Abstracts, *1980.*

As a group, older people are less often afflicted with acute conditions (such as influenza and colds) and more often afflicted with chronic illnesses and disabilities such as cardiovascular troubles, diabetes, arthritis, and hearing loss. Among the most common chronic conditions to which old people must adjust are arthritis and rheumatism; heart conditions and high blood pressure are also prevalent in the elderly population. Cancer, one of the illnesses most dreaded in our culture, tends to decrease in incidence after the sixties.

We still know rather little about the ways people adjust to a chronic illness. We are only now beginning to examine the relationship between personal adjustment and the onset of such an illness. And we have only begun to investigate the differing abilities of individuals to tolerate pain. One person, for example, may be overwhelmed by a cancer whereas another experiences the same condition as a speck on the horizon of consciousness (Luce, 1979). The best generalization we can make is that the integrity of the personality that has developed so far, and the presence of life goals, help a person adjust to chronic illness or chronic pain.

There is, too, some evidence that denial is an adaptive mechanism in illnesses of all types (Patterson, Freeman, & Butler, 1971). The older person will often deny the serious implications of his or her condition, or will joke about the condition—employing the mature defense of humor. In order to be effective, such denial must be combined with realistic attempts to master the situation. An example of adaptive response is that of a 68-year-old man who developed a benign prostatic condition that interfered with urination.

> He was at an engineers' survey camp where he was teaching. The local doctor placed an indwelling urethral catheter attached to a bottle to catch the urine so that he could drive himself home and avoid the need for someone to bring his car home for him. He was proud of having used his engineering skill to repair the catheter system with plastic tape when it broke during the trip. *When he got home, he promptly obtained the necessary surgery.* His delight at mastery over a frightening illness was expressed in his humorous retelling of the experiences during his trip home "tied to a bottle." He further mastered his experience by explaining his surgery in engineering terms for his friends— "They did a cotton cover job just south of the naval base almost to the penal colony" (Patterson, Freeman, & Butler, 1971, p. 63, italics added).

This and other examples show successful adaptation by people who deny the serious implications of their illnesses but who are nevertheless able to cope with pain, disease, and treatment at a practical level. The cognitive coping mechanisms described in Chapter 4 are also of value to people trying to adjust to chronic pain or that related to surgery or treatment (Butler, Damarin, Beaulieu, Schwebel, & Thorn, 1989).

Like physical illness, emotional illness becomes more prevalent with age (Kety, 1980). Research suggests that between 15 and 25 percent of the 28 million Americans over age 65 suffer from significant mental health problems (Rybal, 1988). Several disorders of particular concern are depression, alcohol abuse, and misuse of prescription drugs. Of all emotional illnesses, depression is the most common in old age (Rybal, 1988). It is a particular problem because, while the rate of successful suicides is 11 in 100,000 in the entire population, it is 17.7 among the over age 65 group (APA Monitor, 1987). Further, elderly men over the age of 75 display the highest suicide rate of any age group. We also know that beyond these statistics, a large number of deaths are "silent suicides" in which self-inflicted death is disguised by starvation or by not complying with a prescribed treatment program.

Psychotherapy

There are as many as several million elderly who need professional mental health services, but few are getting it. Elderly persons who make up almost 12 percent of the population represent only 6 percent of persons served by community health centers and 2 percent of those served by private therapists (Rybal, 1988). However, it is predicted that as America's population ages, more resources will be invested in mental health programs for the elderly, including therapy outreach services.

Before Your Time

"Suppose a person could preexperience himself as old while he was still chronologically young," writes Robert Kastenbaum. "What an opportunity this would be to develop strategies and resources for actual old age" (Kastenbaum, 1971).

With this opportunity in mind, Kastenbaum and his colleagues placed young and middle-aged subjects in experimental situations that closely resembled situations in which older people typically find themselves. When a difficult task was introduced into this experiment, most young people behaved in ways that we usually associate with the elderly.

1. Recall a situation you were in, or a task you undertook, when you felt yourself to be slower than almost everyone else in your environment. In this situation did you fumble and become anxious? Settle on one routine and stick to it? Withdraw altogether? Have you since developed strategies that are more effective?

2. Recall a group situation in which you and your advice were consistently disregarded. Did you react with impotent rage? With physical symptoms (such as a headache or pounding heart)? With brooding or mourning for times past? Have you since developed strategies that are more effective?

3. Recall a situation in which you were replaced in a job (formal or informal, paid or unpaid) just when you felt you had finally mastered your responsibilities. Did you react by trying to "hang on"? By talking incessantly about the way *you* used to do things? By complaining or engaging in other attention-getting maneuvers? Have you since developed strategies that are more effective?

4. What life experiences have helped you prepare for your elderly years? To what extent have they helped you understand the predicament of the older person?

Fred Kramer's case illustrates therapy outreach. When Fred lost his wife at age 75, he went into an extended depression. He refused to see friends or family members, sat around in his uncleaned apartment day after day, and watched a television screen that was often blank. He would cry uncontrollably and began to fear he was going insane. Although his minister suggested a therapist who saw groups of older patients, he refused to go. He believed that the minister's recommendation was another sign that he was crazy.

The minister persisted, however, and he and the therapist visited Mr. Kramer on several occasions, eventually persuading him to join the therapy group. At first Fred felt embarrassed and uncomfortable at hearing other patients talking about private matters during the session. Yet, after a few weeks, he adjusted and found himself telling the group things he had hardly been able to admit to himself.

Old age will always be a time of increased illness, intermittent grief, and feelings of helplessness and dependency. Therapy can help those who are having difficulty in facing these obstacles to use their accumulated wisdom and flexibility to cope and to develop a renewed zest for life while accepting the coming end.

Besides the more traditional therapies, many senior citizens now benefit from new approaches. For instance, reminiscence is a healthy, normal activity for older persons (Butler, 1984). Many senior-citizen centers have capitalized on older peoples' tendency to engage in this behavior and have established reminiscence programs under the guidance of therapists. Older people are interviewed on videotape and encouraged to write autobiographies. By reviewing the events of their lives they can often resolve old conflicts and gain a coherent view of themselves. In the future, other new and effective treatment procedures will be developed especially for the elderly.

Alzheimer's Disease

Tania Faye, a successful clothing designer for 40 years, had worked for some of the most famous fashion houses in Europe and New York. For the past 20 years she had been designing under her own label and was celebrated for her attention to detail of design and construction. She had a list of clients and knew their dress size, body dimensions, and taste preferences to the last detail. However, shortly after her 60th birthday, she began to experience difficulty in differentiating among her customers and for the first time delivered incorrect garments.

Shortly thereafter she began to forget to fill orders, and would leave garments half completed and forget about them. She tried writing detailed notes but would misplace them. Within two years she was unable to concentrate sufficiently to continue her business and was forced to retire. Tania's memory became worse after that. She could not remember where she lived, whether she had eaten, and where her own clothes were. She became frightened and felt terrorized and helpless. A once proud and independent person, she could no longer sleep nights, was irritable, and lashed out violently against friends, family, and trusted associates.

Tania is suffering from a form of senile dementia known as Alzheimer's disease. **Dementia** becomes increasingly prevalent with advanced age. It is estimated that 1.5 million people now suffer from severe dementia, including about 25 percent of persons over age 75 (U.S. Congress, 1987). About 50 to 60 percent of senile dementia is Alzheimer's (Terry & Katzman, 1983).

Alzheimer's disease has an irreversible progressive course that ends in complete mental and physical disability. It is the fourth leading cause of death in the United States.

There is no known prevention, no definitive treatment, and no cure. The disease had been thought to be caused by hardening of the arteries until the 1960s, when autopsies showed this was not the case. Since then, researchers have been looking for other explanations for the origin of the disease and the brain lesions that accompany it. At this time there are several hypotheses as to its cause, including a slow acting virus, a genetic defect, and an immunological breakdown. While there are improved techniques for diagnosing Alzheimer's, there has been little advance in treatment. We need more research focused on this disease.

Dementia
A disorder in which there is brain deterioration and associated losses in intellectual capabilities and emotional functioning.

Poverty

The National Council on Aging, as a result of intense and sympathetic study, concluded that "less money in old age is as certain as death and taxes" (Tives, 1971). In retirement the older person's income drops by as much as 60 to 80 percent. At the same time, medical expenses, property taxes, and the cost of virtually everything else rises. This presents a severe challenge to adjustment. Another government body, the White House Conference on Aging, stated what we all know to be true: "There is no substitute for income if people are to be free to exercise their choice in the style of lives" (1971, p. 37).

Poverty among older people has increased during the last 10 years and Social Security (Old Age Survivors and Disability Insurance) will not be able to solve the problem. Most recipients' payments are low. Moreover, the income that a person can earn is limited if he or she intends to collect the maximum Social Security payment. Of course, contrary to public understanding, Social Security was not designed to support the elderly person but to supplement his or her income. The payments are not, nor were they meant to be, sufficient to support older people in the life-styles to which they had become accustomed in earlier life.

For many people, then, the elderly years bring economic deprivation and adjustment to a very different life-style. Today, the economic situation of the older person is receiving considerable attention. Many studies document the problem and propose solutions. But they tell us little about how older people, including as many as one half of all unmarried older individuals receiving Social Security, cope with poverty. As one gerontologist admits, "We know very little about how people adjust to loss of income" (Atchley, 1976, p. 21).

Ageism

Ageism is a term used to describe the negative attitudes and stereotypes about aging and old people. Like racism and sexism, ageism is responsible for much of the social avoidance, segregation, discriminatory practices and belief that elderly individuals are a drain on society (Gatz & Pearson, 1988). "Unlike Japanese culture, in which aging is seen as positive, in our culture it is seen as negative or at best, ambivalent" (Kimmel, 1988; p. 175). Kimmel cites a number of studies to show that older people are perceived as having more negative characteristics than younger people. However, this may change as the average age of the population grows older and more attention is paid to older people in an attempt to sell them products and gain their vote.

Aging and Sexuality

Some of the physical changes people notice in middle age affect their perceptions of their sexuality. For example, excess weight makes many people feel less attractive sexually. If we are to accept the premises of television and magazine advertising, wrinkles and gray hair have the same effect. As people age, they become uncertain of how they appear to others. A typical dilemma is that of the man in his 50s who does not know how to interpret the behavior of a very young woman. Is it a sign of romantic interest (because he is distinguished-looking and at the height of his vocational power)? Or is it a simple demonstration of affection toward a "safe" and kindly older man?

Middle age offers a variety of challenges to sexual adjustment. For example, cardiac problems, a hysterectomy, or the chronic fatigue that comes from holding a demanding job may result in a temporary interruption of sexual activity—and sometimes in permanent change. Boredom that threatens the monogamous relationship is also a problem for some middle-aged couples. (Twenty years of sexual activity with the same partner may appear dull when contrasted with the life-style of their teenage children who are dating a variety of people.) Dissatisfaction with one's career or depression over death of a parent may also cause temporary loss of sexual interest. For a variety of reasons, then, middle age is a period in which many people encounter sexual problems.

On the other hand, middle age offers new opportunities for sexual expression. Privacy now that children are older, and absence of worry about pregnancy after menopause, are among the new benefits middle-age couples experience. Changes in the man's sexual response pattern, as well as the increased experience of both partners, may make sexual activity ultimately more satisfying.

Sexuality in later life is a complex subject. However, one generalization emerges from gerontological and sex research: The older person is physiologically capable of full sexual activity, assuming that he or she is in reasonably good health and has established patterns for sexual expression earlier in life. The appearance of a person is a poor index to sexual skill (Comfort, 1976).

Youth or youthful attractiveness are not necessary elements in sexual enjoyment. More important are experience and the quality of the relationship with one's partner. And these tend to improve over time. For example, among a sample of married women, a higher rate of orgasm was reported for the mid-30s to mid-50s group than for younger groups (Hunt, 1974). Middle-aged husbands in the same study reported little decline in the quality of marital sex since young adulthood. Fully 94 percent described marital sex during the past year as either very or mostly pleasurable. These results led the researchers to conclude that middle-aged husbands and wives "are now enjoying sex almost as much as the hot-blooded young" (Hunt & Hunt, 1975).

In later adulthood the individual does confront changes in sexuality. For example, most men find that their sexual abilities gradually diminish during this time. By 60, the far boundary of middle age, most men surveyed in one study reported they had experienced a decline in sexual interests or activity (Pfeiffer, Verwoerdt, & Davis, 1972). For some individuals the gradual changes that had taken place were unsettling. "It bothers me that I do not have the sexual powers that I took for granted before," admits one middle-aged man. "I've tried to persuade myself that at my age it is to be expected, but it is difficult" (Vaillant, 1977, p. 234).

Women, too, must adjust to physiological changes that affect sexual expression. Occasionally women find that after menopause intercourse becomes irritating or painful, and physical responsiveness has been shown to be slightly diminished. However, subjective feelings of pleasure and satisfaction remain the same or increase with age (DeLora & Warren, 1977). In general, women do not experience age-related anxieties over sexual performance. While women show a significant decline in sexual activity with increasing age, this is in most cases due to divorce, death of a spouse, or illness or disinterest of the spouse (Pfeiffer, Verwoerdt, & Davis, 1972).

There is ample reason for older people to have romantic and sexual interests and needs. They are living longer, staying healthier, and are more likely to be alone. The increase in divorce and widowhood among older people, have led to a greater number of older people looking for companionship and intimacy. And, the adage that love springs eternal is as true for the over-55 generation as for the adolescent. In fact, a research project showed that the feelings of love are the same regardless of age and include "all the physiological and psychological somersaulting such as a heightened sense of reality, perspiring hands, inability to concentrate and heart palpitations" (Bulcroft & O'Conner-Roden, 1986, p. 68). A 72-year-old widow told these researchers "you know you're in love when the one you love is away and you feel empty." The same study showed that older men, just like younger ones, equated romance with sexuality. One 75-year-old said "You can talk about a candlelight dinner and sitting in front of the fireplace but I still think the most romantic thing I've ever done is to go to bed with her."

Sexual relationships tend to develop rapidly among older people. Although sexuality includes intercourse, the stronger emphasis is on hugging, kissing, and touching. The physical closeness helps fulfill their intimacy needs, and contributes to their self-esteem. For most older couples the relationship is not so much one of passion as it is of closeness and caring. One man said, "passion is nice . . . it's the frosting on the cake, but it's the friendship, the way we spend our time that counts."

Successful sexual adjustment in later adulthood involves growth rather than nostalgia for the past: taking advantage of physiological changes and increased closeness with one's partner, rather than attempting to duplicate the sexuality of earlier years. In other words, later adulthood has its own sexual satisfactions. According to one writer, the only real change for the worse is that if the older person goes without sexual activity for any length of time, he or she may find it difficult to resume a sexual relationship (Comfort, 1976).

Aging and Memory

"Researchers on aging are spending less time looking at what we lose as we get older and more at what we keep or gain" (Meer, 1986, p. 60). Findings indicate that most mental skills remain intact as long as the person is mentally and physically active. Although, with age people slow down in all their activities, speed is not essential for most things we do. And, in most cases experience can compensate for speed.

It is commonplace to assume that memory deteriorates greatly with increasing age. Research has shown, however, that memory does not decline as much as is often thought. People who have difficulty remembering at 65 were usually forgetful at 35. Meer (1986) divides memory into three categories: *primary, secondary,* and *tertiary.* Primary, or immediate, memory does not decline at all and tertiary, or long-term, memory decreases very little or not at all. If you play Trivial Pursuit with 70 year olds you will discover the wealth of memories they have to draw upon. Secondary memory, however, or the short-term memory of lists of items for example, becomes less reliable with age. For instance, Arenberg (in Meer, 1986) showed that older people have a difficult time remembering a list of items if they are given another task to do in between. As a result, the 70-year-old housewife may forget what she came to the supermarket to purchase if, on the way to the store, she stopped to chat with a neighbor.

Aging and Intellectual Functioning

Vocabulary, comprehension, and reading speed, which are measured in most intelligence tests, do not decline with age. However, during the aging process some functions of intelligence do decline. Among these are reasoning ability, comprehension of complex relationships, drawing sound inferences, problem solving, concept formation, and abstraction. As a result of the decline, older adults, on the average, display less of these abilities than do younger adults (Horn, 1982). Taken as a whole, these functions are usually grouped together and labeled fluid intelligence. Evidence suggests that the loss in fluid intelligence is the result of the decline of short-term memory, the ability to pay close attention for a long period of time, and the ability to allocate attention to different things.

There is also a group of functions known as crystallized intelligence, which improve with age. These functions, which utilize a person's breadth of knowledge, experience, and sophistication, include comprehension of communication, good judgment, understanding connections, detecting relations among stimuli, and thinking reasonably. Because the increase in crystallized intelligence is approximately equal to the decrease in fluid intelligence over the same age period (Horn, 1982), an intelligence test that equally measures fluid and crystallized intelligence would show no change over age. Going beyond the testing situation, older people's intelligence in the workplace may increase because, evidence suggests, social and professional competence and the ability to deal effectively with one's environment increase with age (Perlmutter, in Meer, 1986).

ADJUSTING TO THE ENVIRONMENT

In many ways, and in many situations, the older person is at a disadvantage in the environment. His or her speed of response is slower than that of a younger person, especially in unfamiliar situations (Birren, 1974). Hearing and vision are less efficient, and in some situations, the person's apparent frailty makes him or her a target for crime. Older individuals must often work out a changed relationship to their environment. They become more cautious, less willing to take risks (Okun & DiVesta, 1976). They rely more on the protection afforded by taxicabs and policemen, for example. The kinds of adjustments that older people must make to their environment are beyond the imagination of most younger people. Here is an older woman's account of her adjustment to an urban environment:

> If you are old and you live in New York, your neighborhood has a special geography. On the West Side, for example, you learn that there are fewer stairs to climb from the subway at 96th Street than at 93rd Street. You learn where the police boxes are, and you worry as you walk down Columbus Avenue because all the stores have taken their pay phones out as a precaution against hold-ups. You know that it is hard to catch the bus at 99th and Columbus because the double parkers there cause the bus to stop way out in the middle of the avenue. You also learn which buildings kids usually play in front of, and you cross the street to avoid being knocked down. . . .
>
> Your day has a special schedule. You're most likely to get robbed after school gets out and kids know which days the checks are delivered, so you go early to the bank. Token takers and bus drivers are likely to get mad if you try to get onto public transportation with your half-fare card a minute before 10 or a minute after 4, so you time your trips carefully. To be sure of getting to talk to someone at the Medicaid office you have to be down at 34th Street and Ninth Avenue by 7:30, but you must dress warmly as the line on the sidewalk is long. Most of all you try to be home before dark, because you're an easy target for muggers (Cowan, 1971).

The elderly person is one who has survived many environments and continues to survive. Robert Butler, a noted gerontologist and psychiatrist, suggests that experiencing firsthand an older person's struggle to survive can help us to survive as well (Butler, 1975).

ELDERLY ABUSE

According to estimates from Senate and House Committees on aging, the number of cases of abused, neglected, and exploited elderly ranges from 600,000 to 1 million, or 4 percent of the elderly population (Eastman, 1984). The abuser is usually a son or daughter, and many of the abusers were themselves abused as children. Research has identified stress, poverty, alcoholism, and marital fights as being among the conditions that most often provoke abuse of the elderly.

Victims generally do not complain. Most are women, physically disabled and dependent. And they fear placement in an institution or further punishment if they attempt to seek help.

THE POTENTIAL FOR PSYCHOLOGICAL GROWTH

As we saw in earlier chapters, the biological pattern of human life is invariable. Human beings begin life with rapid growth, progress to the onset of reproductive ability, and then to a period of stationary growth that stretches for decades. During this period, individuals more or less stand their ground biologically. After that, they experience gradual and then perhaps more rapid biological decline.

We can make no similar generalizations about psychological development. There does not appear to be a necessary parallel between psychological adjustment and biological trends. That is, a person's ability to cope with difficulties—to remain healthy, happy, and sane—does not necessarily decline with age. As we saw earlier in this chapter, a number of developments can potentially contribute to improved psychological adjustment in the second half of life. In many people these growth trends counteract physical and other losses. And in some people they more than compensate for the losses, turning the later years of life into a period of renewal, enrichment, and enhanced self-knowledge.

SUMMARY

1. Daniel Levinson proposed a theory of development that extends from birth through old age. He suggests the life cycle is divided into *eras*, each with its own character.

2. Psychologists have identified strengths gained during the aging process that may contribute to improved adjustment in later life. Among these are greater experience in crisis resolution, consolidation of identity, and the humanization of relationships and values.

3. Middle-aged people often experience an age-awareness crisis, becoming aware of loss of youthful appearance or physical vigor. Many must also cope with changes in sexuality, and the most successful adjustments are made by those who accept the changes and make the most of them.

4. At approximately the midpoint of life, many people experience a mid-life crisis, or crisis of meaning. They realize that there is limited time left, question the value of their earlier choices and commitments, and may become depressed. They experience time differently, and may have doubts about and reevaluate their career and marriage.

5. The middle-aged person may have to adjust to the departure of children from the home and the end of an active parental role. He or she may also be called on to give emotional support to an aging parent or cope with the death of a close family member.

6. There are vast differences in the ways that people meet the challenges of adulthood. Indeed, the differences among people seem to be greatest in older age groups.

7. The ability and willingness to care for the younger generation and the capacity for being spiritual are favorable outcomes associated with the later years.

8. Retirement represents a major adjustment demand. Some psychologists view retirement as a process that begins with the individual's acknowledgement of it as an approaching fact of life. Preparation seems to reduce the stressfulness of the event. Postretirement adjustment is best if the person retires voluntarily, is in good health, and has at least a moderate income. The major cause of maladjustment during retirement is economic deprivation.

9. Most elderly people must cope with health-related problems, including sensory losses and chronic illnesses such as arthritis. Favorable outcomes at earlier life stages—the integrity of the personality and the presence of life goals—seem to help a person adjust to chronic illness. Denial is a common adaptive mechanism at this stage, with best results seen when the person denies the seriousness of a condition but obtains necessary treatment. Emotional illness, especially depression, becomes more common in later years.

10. A large number of elderly people live in poverty, as defined by the U. S. government, and most older people must adjust to a more limited income. Besides economic changes, they often must make other alterations in daily living in order to adjust to their environment.

11. The basic biological life pattern is invariable. However, the potential for psychological growth does not necessarily decline with age, and many people lead enriched lives during their elderly years.

SUGGESTED READINGS

Atchley, R. (1987). *Aging: Continuity and change*. Belmont, CA.: Wadsworth. What are the thoughts and experiences of the elderly and how can this knowledge help you deal more effectively with them as people.

Block, M., Davidson, J., Grambs, J. (1981). *Women over forty*. New York: Springer. Older women are here to stay and there will be more of them each succeeding decade. Examines approaches to gerontology specific to women.

Comfort, A. (1976). *A good age*. New York: Simon & Schuster. Organized in dictionary format the book, written by the well-known gerontologist and expert on the joys of living, is a vigorous assault on the idea that old age discounts a person's value.

Grollman, E. A., & Grollman, S. H. (1978). *Caring for your aged parents*. Boston: Beacon Press. An examination of the intergenerational stresses created by the increased dependency of aging parents and associated role reversals.

Halpern, H. (1979). *Cutting loose*. New York: Bantam. A self-help approach for improving patterns of parent-child interaction.

Lovejoy, H. (1978). *Second chance. Blueprints for life change*. A how-to guide for negotiating career and life-style changes in midstream.

Mayer, N. (1978). *The male mid-life crisis: Fresh starts after 40*. New York: Signet. An optimistic book that conveys to the reader the new beginnings that men can develop after age 40.

Neuhaus, R. & Neuhaus, R. (1982). *Successful aging*. New York: Wiley. Successful aging can be a reality. Case histories introduce readers to elderly persons to learn about their attitudes, trials, and successes.

Oberleder, M. (1982). *Avoid the aging trap*. Washington, DC: Acropolis Books Ltd. Explores the myths of aging. Old age need not be a problem. It can be a joyful and enriching experience.

Westoff, L. A. (1980). *Breaking out of the middle-age trap*. New York: Signet. A highly resourceful book, with many case studies, exploring the options available to women during the mid-life crisis.

Death, Dying, and Bereavement

- The lifting of taboos on discussions of death, and the realization that openness can make adjustment to death easier

- The adult ego strength of integrity, which involves affirmation of the life one has lived and promotes acceptance of approaching death

- How age affects the reaction to a personal encounter with death—with, for example, the young child not understanding death's finality and the adult often worrying about interruption of productivity

- The emotional stages through which many dying people proceed—optimally reaching a state of acceptance—and the subsequent bereavement experiences of others

- How grief, mourning, and bereavement are managed by individuals at different points in the life span

- New developments and perspectives: education regarding death, more positive environments for the dying, and the striking experiences of some who "returned" from clinical death

Robert Kastenbaum is a **thanatologist,** one of a growing number of scientists who study the experiences of death and dying. Kastenbaum likes to begin his lectures with an exercise in "self-exploration" (Kastenbaum, 1975, p. 20). The participants are asked to visualize the people who are closest to them. Then they are told: "One of these people will die before the others." They are asked to extinguish the faces of their loved ones, one by one, in the imagined sequence of death. And they are asked, "Whose face survives?"

If you work through this experiment, you will probably find (as most of Kastenbaum's subjects do) that the first person to "die" is the oldest person who is visualized. The survivor is usually the youngest. That is the easy part of the experiment. Usually, Kastenbaum's next questions are: "Where does your own face, your own life and fate, belong in this sequence? Would you have been the first to perish? The last? Which of these people do you implicitly expect to survive? Who will survive you?" Kastenbaum reminds people that there are other perspectives: "Think of yourself as the youngest and most 'survivable' face within the mind's eye of an aged relative; and then as the oldest and most 'perishable' face in the mind's eye of a younger person."

Most people find it difficult, if not impossible, to imagine their own death. The thought of it creates fear in some people. Until recently, it was rare to find college professors who would have asked their students to do so. The subject was avoided and so, for that matter, were dying people. Many writers, observing this attitude, spoke of a taboo, comparing the silence on death to the silence once held about sexuality. The fear of death has been found to relate to cemetery visits. People with high death anxiety generally avoided going to cemeteries to visit the gravesites of family or friends (Thorson, Horack, & Kara, 1987).

Thanatologist
A scientist who studies the experiences of death and dying.

The shock of unexpected loss is especially difficult to manage, especially when it defies the biological timetable of the life cycle. Americans— and people around the world— found the Space Shuttle catastrophe distressing.

Today there is a new openness about death—and, indeed, a new interest. A groundbreaking questionnaire on "You and Death" in *Psychology Today* (Shneidman, 1971) drew a record number of responses. Many of the respondents expressed gratitude for the opportunity to explore a meaningful subject. More recent self-help literature shows a tendency to see death as a part of life; books appear with titles such as *Necessary Losses* (Viorst, 1986) and *The Right to Die* (Humphry and Wickett, 1987). Terminal patients and their families are interviewed on television talk shows. Celebrities give candid details about how their malignancies affect their lives. Widows form self-help groups and write books about their bereavement experiences.

All these signs of a new openness do not change the fact that death remains very difficult for most of us—both as a theoretical and as an actual experience. This is especially so when death defies the biological timetable of the life cycle. Therefore, it is not surprising that when death results from a sudden or unexpected accident or trauma, the process of bereavement and grief is far different than when death occurs as a result of illness and/or old age. Natural disasters and man-made catastrophes such as earthquakes, terrorist attacks, plane crashes, and industrial fallout all underlie the precarious nature of life. The families of the astronauts aboard the space shuttle Challenger and the Russian workers at the nuclear power plant at Chernobyl were suddenly confronted with an unthinkable fatality and a massive psychological assault that overwhelmed their coping capacities. The shock of unexpected loss is especially difficult to digest.

Bereavements are the most painful of life's crises. And the thought of our own death, whether we conceive it to be painful or peaceful, threatens us with an almost unimaginable loss—the loss of consciousness, of everything we have known. Talking about death may not make it any easier to experience the death of a loved one. But there is some evidence that it makes later adjustment to death easier. For example, children who have heard death discussed in concrete terms can better adjust to the loss of a parent. Bereaved people who are able to speak of their loss are able to complete the process of mourning sooner and show signs of a quicker recovery (Kalish, 1981). Also, some recent research provides strong evidence that the availability of social support from family and friends, following loss experiences, is life-enhancing and contributes to longevity (Berardo, 1985).

The objective of this chapter is to increase our ability to deal with the experience of death—our own and the deaths of others.

DEATH AND THE OLDER PERSON

As Kastenbaum's exercise suggests, we hold in common certain expectations about the lives and deaths of others. Realistically, we know that death can come at any stage in the life span; yet because of well-known statistics, we normally associate death with the elderly years. A person who is born today could expect to encounter death approximately 75 years from now. For this reason, we will begin our discussion of death with the later years of life, and the final struggle for integrity.

"Integrity versus Despair"

According to Erikson, old age is the time of life at which a person fully confronts having one and only one life span; and must either accept or reject what has occurred during it (1963). Time is now too short to find alternate roads to integrity, which is the favorable outcome at this stage. The person who achieves integrity accepts his or her life as something that had to be. This aids in the acceptance of death—which also has to be. The basic virtue that emerges at this stage is wisdom, which Erikson describes as the detached yet active concern with life itself in the face of death itself (1976).

Erikson wrote his famous description of integrity when he was middle-aged. He confessed that he lacked a clear definition. Nevertheless, on at least one occasion he came close to illustrating integrity through example. He spoke of several older people whose faces captured the undefinable quality:

> The first [was] an old Jewish woman from Mt. Carmel in the state of Israel. Visiting California, she had impressed us all with the new sense of dignity and identity which her work had given her: the work of tending her grandchildren, freeborn Jews in their own State.
>
> The second was a grand old woman of the Pueblo community of San Ildefonso in the American Southwest. In perfecting her black pottery she has given new life to one of the oldest arts.
>
> The third was an old skier in the Sierras who as a youth had come from his native Finland to the then lonely country around Lake Tahoe, to range the snowbound trails between the early power stations (Coles, 1970, pp. 115–116).

What Erikson saw in these older people was depth and finality, beauty and simplicity, and faith and serenity. These appear to be qualities that are encompassed by integrity, which Erikson first described in his book published the following year.

Erikson finds that when a person achieves integrity, he or she is able to confront death without fear and loathing. The person begins to befriend death, without in any way inviting it (Erikson, 1949). But when a person fails to achieve integrity, the fear of death looms large. Despair, remorse, bitterness—a thousand little disgusts with daily life—intrude upon the personality (Erikson, 1963). The person may become demanding, depressed, or excessively concerned with bodily ills, and unable to experience a sense of joy in living.

Attitudes toward Death

It appears that many older people do have the integrity—or whatever quality is needed—to accept death. Attitudinal studies have generally shown that older people, who expect to die within a relatively short time, are not more anxious about death than those in other age groups. In fact, older people may be less anxious. One study found that people became accustomed to the idea of death in their elderly years. So special is this orientation that it forms a common bond between older people, often breaking through social barriers that had been present in earlier years (Bengston, Cuellar, & Ragan, 1977).

Once people reach middle age, it appears that increased age is associated with a *decrease* in death fears (so far as these can be measured). In fact, in a classic study Munnichs found that the most common orientation towa death among those 70 or older was acquiescence and acceptance (Munnichs, 1966). The final period of life was characterized as an "anticipated farewell." Likewise, a later study indicates that people who have achieved a purpose in life have relatively little fear of death (Durlak, 1973). These attitudinal studies tend to support Erikson's belief that a positive orientation toward death results from successful developmental outcomes of earlier crises.

DEATH ENCOUNTERS OVER THE LIFE SPAN

A **death encounter** is our confrontation with the imminence of our own death, perhaps a narrow escape from an accident or serious illness. The meaning of a death encounter, and the way it is experienced, depend on a person's maturational level, their previous level of adaptation, and the array of coping skills and supports available to them (Weisman, 1984). Next we discuss the effects of such a crisis at different stages of life.

Death Encounter
A person's confrontation with the imminence of his or her own death.

Childhood Encounters

Young children are usually curious about death. Even as toddlers they may show understanding and awe in the presence of death phenomena (such as a dead bird or squirrel). However, young children do not understand finality in any context. Death seems temporary and reversible (Schaefer, 1986). In examining children's conceptions of death, investigators found that while understanding the universality of death, young children cannot understand its irrevocable quality because their level of cognitive development has not yet advanced enough to grasp this concept (White, Elson, & Prawat, 1978). Therefore, many young children view death as a form of sleep or an act of disappearance. However, by about the age of nine or ten, most children have advanced to the point at which they can acknowledge the finality of death. They comprehend that death is universal as well as inevitable (Kastenbaum, 1977).

In past centuries, when infectious diseases were most virulent, childhood was a period of heightened vulnerability to death. Today the death of a child is an unusual life crisis. Carl Jung (1954) once called such a death "a period placed before the end of the sentence" (p. 7). When death is expected (for example, from certain forms of leukemia), adults involved are tormented by the question of whether or not the affected child should be told. In the past, it was assumed that since children could not intellectually understand death, they could not understand the seriousness of their condition. However, studies have shown that children as young as six can understand the fatal diagnosis, and can express their anxieties verbally (Waechter, 1971, 1974). When asked to tell stories, children with a terminal illness give evidence of higher death anxieties than other children who, for one reason or another, are chronically hospitalized (Spinetta, Rigler, & Karon, 1973).

Death: Reaching Out to the Past

It is difficult for us to understand the suffering endured by ordinary people in earlier periods of history when death came easily to people of all ages. James Lynch (1977, p. 13) suggests one way of identifying with the suffering: Read and respond to the tombstones in an old cemetery. He gave these examples:

Here rests Sarah Ann, age 6, 1820, may she rest in peace
John, age 6 months, 1810
My beloved wife, Martha Reynolds, age 24, 1826
Our son, Mark, age 14, 1841, God's will be done
My beloved husband, John, age 39, 1850

Locate an old cemetery in your area; pause a while and read the tombstones. Consider:

1. How many people buried there died before reaching your age?
2. At what points in the life span were people most likely to succumb to death?
3. From the inscriptions, what can you discover about prevailing attitudes toward death? Do you find much difference between old inscriptions and the newer ones?   ▲

How children respond to the crisis of serious illness depends on their developmental level and perception or interpretation of the event. According to Spinetta's summary of the research literature, preschool children are most concerned with separation from parents. As they undergo pain and hospitalization, they mainly want to be told that mother will be there when they awaken. Children between the ages of six and ten are most anxious about operations, mutilations, and intrusions on the body. They become interested in and knowledgeable about hospital procedures. Older children, who are better able to understand the implications of illness, are usually concerned with permanent loss of body functions (Spinetta, et al., 1973).

The child with a life-threatening illness seems to know that the illness is no ordinary one—even when adults contrive to conceal this. For example, adults have noted that children facing death have a compelling sense of time—feeling that they must not waste the life that remains to them (Bluebond-Langner, 1977). Whether or not they are told, they seem to understand why they get extra presents this year for their birthday or Christmas. Most children welcome concrete information about their disease and its relationship to death. They want, for example, to discuss the not-so-mysterious disappearance of other children from the hospital wards where they have shared so much.

Children seem to prefer frank discussion (appropriate to their age level) to the evasions adults sometimes offer. For example, when the child asks what happened to a friend, he or she can be asked in return, "What do you think happened?" When the child admits that it is unlikely that the friend has gone home or to another hospital, the adult can say, "She was very sick, much sicker than you, and she died" (Bluebond-Langner, 1977, p. 55).

Most children with cancer are eventually released from the hospital and returned to their homes, schools, and communities. Reentering the environment outside the hospital may be difficult. Some people in the community may stigmatize the child and exclude him or her from their activities. This may alienate the child who has had cancer and enforce a feeling of being very different from others (Blumberg, Flaherty, & Lewis, 1980). A child who continues to receive cancer therapy may suffer from side effects that alter his or her physical appearance or make it difficult to participate in sports and other activities important to children.

When a child has been in remission for a long time, the decision to terminate treatment may be made. Usually this decision is extremely stressful for parents (Blumberg, Flaherty, & Lewis, 1980). As for the long-term psychological consequences of having survived childhood cancer, very little is known. However, one study found that survivors of childhood cancer are at greater psychological risk than are children who recover from other diseases that are chronic but are not life-threatening (Koocher & O'Malley, 1981). About half of a sample studied had some psychiatric symptoms that impaired functioning, though in most cases the symptoms were mild. A favorable outcome seems to be associated with having experienced the cancer in infancy or early childhood, and having had a prolonged and uninterrupted remission.

Adolescent Encounters

Daniel Levinson has written: "Some preoccupation with death—fearing it, being drawn to it, seeking to transcend it—is not uncommon in all [life] transitions, since the process of [transition] involves the imagery of death and rebirth" (Levinson et al., 1978, p. 51). Adolescence is certainly a period of transition, termination (of childhood), and initiation (of adulthood). And there is a predictable upsurge in the individual's concern with death.

In practically all cultures adolescents indulge in risk-taking behaviors (Berman, 1987; Kastenbaum & Aisenberg, 1972). Through violent sports, drunken driving, and drug experiences they test their immortality (or "flirt with death"). Not surprisingly, the most common causes of death at this stage of life are "accidents"—the young person's unwise interaction with his or her environment. Also common are suicides and suicide attempts.

In adolescence the suicide rate rises significantly, particularly among girls (who, through social training, have been discouraged from engaging in the more minor risk-taking behaviors). Data from the National Institute of Health has shown a dramatic increase in suicide among children and adolescents over the last 25 years (Shneidman, 1985). In 1960, there were 1239 teenage suicides reported. By 1970, the number had nearly tripled to 3128. By 1980, almost doubling again, it had reached 5239.

Like all epidemics, suicide among teenagers spreads by contagion, evidenced by a clustering of suicidal deaths (Coleman, 1987; Pfeffer, 1986). Indeed, after every publicized case of suicide, the suicide rate in general rises temporarily, and most sharply among teenagers. "Copycat suicide" is the term coined to describe suicide when viewed as an imitative phenomenon, involving suggestion and modeling.

It is estimated that suicide attempts outnumber suicides by 50 to 1 (Spencer, 1979). Among those who attempt or actually succeed in committing suicide, the reasons for the action differ. In some cases the suicide seems to be part of a developmental crisis—failure to make expected changes, an inability to move from childhood to adulthood. Death becomes a way of escaping a very stressful life crisis. In other cases, the suicide reflects a hopelessness associated with an earlier loss, such as the death or disappearance of a parent. Researchers reporting on suicide among children found that children who do not learn verbal expressiveness tended to act out in self-destructive ways (Fish & Waldhard-Letzel, 1981). While the explanations vary widely, the statistics are clear: suicides rise in adolescence and roughly continue to rise over the life span. This pattern is shown in Figure 13.1.

Adolescent suicide frequently becomes a permanent solution to a temporary problem. Too frequently, for many teenagers, suicide is romanticized by some writers and poets as an expression of superior sensitivity. It is difficult for adolescents to believe their problems are time-limited and that life is infinitely precious despite the pain and anguish it may bring. In an attempt to stem the tide of teenage suicide, several investigators (Polly, 1986) have developed workshops for college, high school, and junior high school students so

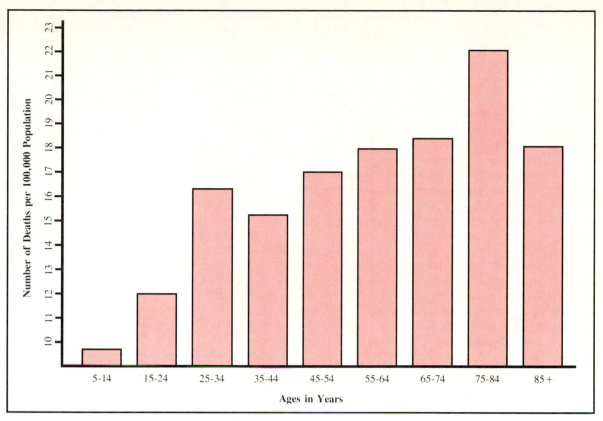

Figure 13.1 The suicide rate, by age bracket, over the life span.

Source: Adapted from National Center for Health Statistics, Vital Statistics of the United States, *Vol. 2, 1960–1980. Washington, D.C.: U.S. Government Printing Office, 1981, p. 141.*

that they can better understand the causes, symptoms, and treatment for suicidal feelings. These outreach programs, coordinated by schools, police departments, and community mental health facilities stress prevention, attempt to identify children and adolescents who are at risk, and provide therapeutic assistance when necessary.

Another crisis that confronts some individuals during their adolescence is serious illness. Normally at this period in their lives people begin to construct life programs (Hankoff, 1975). To have a life-threatening illness at this stage in the life span is to be suddenly bereft of the plan that they had developed to make their lives meaningful. It is to confront the oblivion that most adolescents deeply fear. Like their healthy friends, but with more urgency, adolescents who are seriously ill search for identities. They ask themselves "Am I really a decent human being?" "Will I die before I know who I am?" (Pattison, 1977b).

A life-threatening illness makes even temporary achievement of identity difficult. The hospitalized adolescent may feel reduced to a childlike state of dependency at the very moment when he or she would normally be separating from parents. In many cases the adolescent is unable to rely on friends. It is often observed that adolescents, who are themselves undergoing momentous physical and identity changes, are unusually threatened by the approaching death of a peer. One way the sick adolescent may respond is by denying the need for others—flinging aside unopened gifts and letters (Whitlock, 1978). However, some cope effectively, often due in part to the support they receive from family members and others.

Adult Encounters

In young adulthood people typically begin to consider the place of their own lives in the cycle of generations. If married, they may begin to think about children. Most couples (about 90 percent in our society) have at least one child. During pregnancy and childbirth, death-related thoughts are common. The mother fears for the safety of the fetus, and perhaps for her own safety. When the child is born, the couple may name him or her after a deceased relative. They may think ahead to the child's future and wonder if they will be there to share it. But the couple's thoughts will be primarily positive and based on the assumption of their continued good health.

Whether people are single or married, the occurrence of a life-threatening illness at this time harshly affects them. It undermines their sense of physical invulnerability (Blumberg, Flaherty, & Lewis, 1980). And it makes it difficult to form new relationships or maintain the newly established marriage and family life. For example, a young adult may temporarily relinquish his wage-earning role in a marriage or may have to appeal to parents for financial or child-care assistance. Having to monitor physical health and being unable to manage everyday matters unassisted represent serious blows to the pride and independence of the young adult (Blumberg, Flaherty, & Lewis, 1980). As with serious illnesses in any stage in the life span, the maturity of the coping mechanisms that have been developing will affect adjustment.

A death encounter later, during mid-life, is experienced somewhat differently. As we saw in Chapter 12, perspective changes during these years—sometimes suddenly. Adults of forty or so become aware of their distance from the young. They begin to think of life in terms of time remaining. The important question is no longer "How old am I?" but "How many years do I have left?"

Certain life events tend to bring on the death-related crisis. Signs of aging (everything from shortness of breath to hearing loss to menopause) give undeniable evidence of personal mortality. The death of a close friend usually first occurs in middle age; so does the death or decline of a parent. At this stage, we are confronted with the process of adult orphanhood: anticipating the death of a parent, mourning the parent, and internalizing the reality of the parent's death (Angel, 1987). Finally, the generation cycle is such that children reach adolescence just as middle-aged parents feel they are becoming less physically attractive and perhaps are experiencing some decline in sexual powers. For a variety of reasons, mid-life forces people to confront mortality.

In many lives a crisis is precipitated by experiencing the death of another. Gail Sheehy, for example, suffered "a breakdown of nerve" as the result of seeing a young boy's face blown off by a bullet in Ireland (Sheehy, 1976). She responded by telling herself: "Take stock: half your life has been spent." And she made major adjustments. "I broke off with the man who had been sharing my life for 4 years, fired my secretary, lost my housekeeper, and found myself alone with my daughter . . . marking time" (p. 5). For Sheehy, an outgrowth of this experience, and the experiences of others whom she interviewed, was her conclusion that the mid-life encounter with death and change is a predictable crisis of adult life.

Others draw similar observations. One psychoanalyst goes so far as to suggest that the awareness of the inevitability of one's own death is the central theme of mid-life (Jaques, 1964). It underlies many of the crises that middle-aged people experience about creativity, work, and family life. According to Jaques, a resolution of the mid-life crisis brings new serenity as well as greater creative powers. Jaques speaks of "constructive resignation"; Levinson of the "tragic sense of life" (Levinson et al., 1978). These phrases refer to people's efforts to come to terms with suffering and confusion—with the unhappiness they have brought about themselves and the unhappiness they have observed elsewhere. A successful outcome of this confrontation gives strength and serenity to old age.

People who face actual death in middle age are of course in a different position from people who encounter their mortality in symbolic terms. The middle-aged adult, like the younger person experiencing a death encounter, must cope with fears of nothingness and greater dependency on others. Several studies have revealed that middle-aged people have the highest fear of death compared to other age groups over the life span. The thought of death creates a considerable amount of anxiety in Type A individuals (Tramill & Kleinhammer-Tramill, 1984). As you may recall, people with a Type A personality experience high levels of competitive achievement striving, time urgency, and aggressiveness.

There is also a strong tendency to see death as an interruption of life's activities and responsibilities (Viorst, 1986). The adult who has a life-threatening illness worries about the emotional effects of his or her death on family members. There may also be worry about unfinished work. Death threatens the productivity of middle-aged adults (Whitlock, 1978), but in productivity—or what can be regarded as generativity—lies their solace. Many terminally ill adults express the desire to live to complete a project or see the birth of a first grandchild. They recognize that what they have generated in life continues to bring pleasure, if only on a day-to-day basis. In general, middle-aged adults are better able than younger people to confront death with mature coping mechanisms (Pattison, 1977b).

On the other hand, as we grow older and are confronted by overwhelming stresses and loss experiences, the risk of suicide increases (Butler, 1975). This is particularly true following the death of a spouse in the later years, where the "broken heart phenomenon" exemplifies the increased mortality risk in the survivor spouse (Lynch, 1977; Berardo, 1985). Frequently, grief is intense, the will to live is diminished, the natural immunity of the body is suppressed, and there may be a strong desire to be reunited with the lost spouse. However, the maintenance of caring relationships with significant others may help to diminish the grief experience and prevent premature death (Helsing, Szklo, & Comstock, 1981).

DYING

The psychosocial experiences that culminate in death have been the subject of much study in recent years. **Elisabeth Kübler-Ross** was one of the first clinicians to attempt to look at dying as an orderly, developmental process. As a psychiatrist, she worked with people in the last stages of terminal illnesses, usually cancer. She also worked with health professionals who were responsible for helping fatally ill patients through their final adjustment. For example, Kübler-Ross held seminars for hospital staff members at which patients were given a rare opportunity to speak openly about the process of dying.

From her interviews with dying patients, Kübler-Ross constructed a stage theory of the dying process (Kübler-Ross, 1969). She found that a person who becomes aware that he or she is going to die may well be expected to pass through five stages. These stages constitute, in a sense, gradual progress toward final acceptance.

Elisabeth Kübler-Ross
Dr. Kübler-Ross described dying as an orderly process involving five stages: denial, anger, bargaining, depression, and acceptance.

Personal Adjustment through the Life Span

The first stage is *denial*; the person will not (or cannot) acknowledge the reality of his or her own impending death. The person believes the diagnosis is incorrect, and ignores its implications. Common behaviors are refusal to talk about the matter and statements such as "I feel wonderful," or "Not me." In the second stage, *anger,* the dying person asks, "Why me?" He or she lashes out, blaming others (or God) for the intolerable condition. Anger is vented on relatives and hospital staff; relationships become very difficult. In the third stage, *bargaining,* the dying person attempts to "make a deal with fate." In return for "being good," he or she requests an extension of life, or at least a few days free of pain. When this fails, *depression* sets in. As conditions worsen—as hospitalization, surgery, or other special care is needed—the person realizes it is no longer possible to "smile it off." Anger disappears, bravery is compromised, and he or she is overcome with a sense of great loss.

Finally the dying person finds *acceptance,* an almost emotionless and very weary state of resignation. He says, for example, "I am ready now, and not even afraid anymore." This is the "final rest before the long journey" (Kübler-Ross, 1969, p. 100). In each of these stages the dying person dares to hope. Even the most accepting and realistic leave the possibility open for some cure—the discovery of a new drug, or a last-minute success in a research project (Kübler-Ross, 1969, p. 123).

Kübler-Ross notes that people do not invariably progress from one stage to the next. For example, a person who has relied on denial as a primary means of coping with life's difficulties may well die in a state of denial. A person can become "fixed" at an early stage of dying much as people become fixed at an early psychosocial stage of the life span. Another observation is that some people alternate between one stage and another—showing, say, denial and anger patterns during a single interview.

Kübler-Ross has done much to bring attention to the needs of dying patients and their families. (Ten years after its publication, her *On Death and Dying* still appeared occasionally on bestseller lists.) However, some clinicians criticize her stage theory on the grounds that there is little hard evidence of its universality. We do not necessarily "die according to the pattern" (Kastenbaum, 1975). The kind of death an individual experiences varies with developmental level, family situation, and many other factors. Schneidman (1973) observed alternation between acceptance and denial, rather than a sequential movement through the five stages. Different people die in different ways and may go through a wide range of reactions during the process, from hope to relief (Kalish, 1981).

An important factor is the nature of the disease process. Pattison points to possible differences between a person's experience of an acute disease, with death known and expected in a short time, and the experience of a serious disease with certain death at some unknown time in the future (Pattison, 1977b). When death can be foreseen, dying people and their families can ready themselves to cope within a relatively well-defined time frame. However, when the time of death is very uncertain—or when death itself is uncertain and the patient must continually wait for new results and diagnoses—the adjustment process is different. In such cases the patient and family undergo prolonged emotional stress. They usually cope with the uncertainties of death by focusing on what is certain—that is, by shifting attention from the death event to the ordinary events of daily living.

One group of researchers conducted a longitudinal study of 54 cancer patients and their families, investigating the ways people adjusted to the disease and the methods that had more favorable outcomes (Vess, Moreland, Schwebel, & Kraut, 1988). The findings pointed to the importance of clear communication throughout the adjustment process. At first, when the diagnosis is made, health professionals may have to continually repeat information about the illness and its treatment. Family members often use the defense mechanism of denial, so it takes time and the repetition of information before they can understand and assimilate what has happened to them.

Throughout the adjustment process, clear communication between the spouses allows them to cope together with their feelings and to make plans for the changes that will be needed in their family life. However, frank discussion may not come easily. Often, one spouse will "protect" the other, as a woman with cancer explained: "I have lots of fears. I don't confide in anyone because the only person I feel I can confide in is my husband, and he's taking this so hard that I don't want to add to his burden. So I hold it inside . . ." (Vess, et al., 1988, p. 43). Therapists working with families like this can support them in sharing important thoughts, feelings, and worries.

Communication can also help couples deal with irrational feelings of guilt. One mother, when she thought of her children, felt this way: "I don't want my illness to hold up their lives. What I've felt all along is this guilt that I'm disrupting their lives. It's stupid because there's nothing I can do about it. But I feel like they depend on me psychologically as a supportive person. I think that's a role a mother should play" (Vess et al., 1988, p. 47).

Finally, open and effective communication enables the spouses and their families to better manage the household work load when one parent is ill or hospitalized, and, after a death (Vess et al., 1985a, 1985b).

Many writers have observed that people die the way they live; perhaps this means that they adjust to the terminal stage of life with some of the same coping mechanisms that they used to meet earlier crises. Since the last stages of the dying process are often associated with great pain and heavy medication, however, this principle may not apply to every person's behavior during the final period of life.

BEREAVEMENT

Bereavement
The emotional experience undergone by a person in reaction to the death of an individual who was significant in his or her life.

Actual death comes only once to each of us, but we confront the deaths of others at many points in our life span. When a person who is significant to us dies, we experience a **bereavement** crisis. We grieve and mourn. Of all the life crises (excepting coping with one's own death), bereavement is thought to be the most painful. The author Robert Anderson expresses this very poignantly in his book, *I Never Sang for My Father:* "Death ends a life, but it does not end a relationship which struggles on in the survivor's mind toward some resolution it may never find" (Anderson, 1968).

Research tends to support this view. In a study of the 61 life events considered to be most upsetting, psychiatrists found that three of the first four were bereavements: death of a child, death of a spouse, and death of some other close family member (Paykel & Dienelt, 1971). Holmes and Rahe (1967) also found bereavements to be among the most stressful life events. These researchers, who scaled life event changes according to the magnitude of the adjustment they require, found death of a spouse to be the first item. Death of another family member and death of a close friend were items four and ten, respectively. Holmes and Rahe further found that experiencing serious life event changes like these often led to major health changes (see Chapter 3).

We can conclude that the stress of bereavement makes a person unusually vulnerable to illnesses and other disorders. In fact, numerous studies have shown that widows and widowers of any age—from twenty to eighty—suffer a higher rate of serious illness, hospitalizations, accidents, physical complaints, and psychological distress than others in their age group (Parkes, 1972; Glick, Weiss, & Parks, 1974; Parks, 1986). Widows and widowers also face an increased mortality risk. From the evidence, one thanatologist concludes that "bereavement is a serious state, amounting almost to a life-threatening illness" (Shneidman, 1977, p. 79).

Grief and Mourning

When adults are bereaved of a loved one, they experience severe emotional and psychological strain. Usually there is an initial numbness ("I can't believe it"); only gradually does this give way to awareness and pain (Lifton & Olson, 1974). **Grief** is a normal, healthy reaction when one has experienced a loss. Dealing with grief can be viewed as a time-limited process, with a beginning, a middle, and an end, or more realistically, with multiple endings (Cochran & Claspell, 1987). However, there is no shortcut through the process of incorporating the loss into one's life (Savine & Kamin, 1987). Despite occasional sadness and painful memories, completed grief enables the mourner to face and enjoy life again.

Grief
The feeling of loss a person experiences upon the death of another individual significant to him or her.

Grief over an unexpected death, particularly the death of a child or young adult, may be accompanied by shock and despair. In all cases, the bereaved are confronted with the psychological task of accepting the loss and continuing to live (Lifton & Olson, 1974, p. 33). Usually a period of mourning provides an outlet for the grief, by making it clear that death has actually occurred, that plans must be made, and that changes in life patterns must begin. When grief is prolonged and continues unabated, despite the passage of time and support from family and friends, professional help may be necessary. Here grief therapy or bereavement counseling or other forms of intervention can be particularly helpful in assisting individuals to arrive at some acceptance of their loss.

Acute Grief

As the news photographs of disaster victims make clear, human beings in a
state of acute grief are very similar in appearance. It appears, too, that most
bereaved people show certain physical and psychological symptoms in the
period immediately following the death of another. The symptoms were identified in a classic study by Lindemann (1944). They include "sensations of
[bodily] distress occurring in waves lasting from twenty minutes to an hour
at a time; a feeling of tightness in the throat, choking with shortness of breath,
need for sighing and an empty feeling in the abdomen, lack of muscular power,
and an intense subjective distress described as tension or mental pain" (p. 141).
Lindemann found that the waves of discomfort were brought on by mention
of the dead person, or by visits and other acts of sympathy. During this stage
of the grief period the person feels unable to make the slightest effort, and
may be unable to eat.

Also common are feelings of unreality. Bereaved people may see others
vaguely, at a distance; they are preoccupied with the image of the dead person.
At the emotional level, they may be overcome with guilt and hostility. They
accuse themselves of things said and unsaid, and find reasons to blame themselves for events leading up to the death. Feelings of hostility and irritability
are directed at God, fate, and those who attempt to give comfort. Some researchers have found that irrational hostile feelings may be directed at the
deceased as well—for example, for having abandoned the family (Bowlby,
1960). In this disorganized state, bereaved people typically say they do not
know what to do next. They lose their ordinary patterns of conduct, and may
become dependent on others.

Some of these symptoms are quite similar to those experienced by people who have psychiatric disorders (the feelings of unreality, for example, and the loss of patterns of conduct). In fact, many grief-stricken people fear that they are "going insane." Yet Lindemann found the symptoms of acute grief to be the normal and necessary part of "grief work" that survivors must accomplish if they are gradually to adjust to the loss.

It is generally agreed that the person who shows no reaction at the time of loss will experience a delayed reaction. For example, the unresolved grief will appear in an inappropriate form when the person experiences a later loss. Or it may be manifested in physical or emotional illness, especially depression. For this reason, psychologists and clergy who help with bereavement crises try to provide supportive situations in which bereaved people can express grief— including its hostile elements. Families are encouraged to confront the actuality of death, for example, by holding a conventional funeral and viewing the body. Psychologists believe that involvement in a process of this sort results in fewer adjustment problems and a more positive memory of the deceased.

In the months that follow the death and burial, some of the symptoms of acute grief disappear. But the grief work continues. For example, during the first month, widows and widowers reported such symptoms as excessive crying, a depressed mood, inability to sleep (and reliance on sleeping pills), poor concentration, lack of appetite, or weight loss, and loss of interest in friends and activities (Clayton, Halikes, & Maurice, 1971). These symptoms too disappear over time as the mourning period comes to an end. Depending upon the loss experience and the relationship with the deceased, the grief process can be completed in six months to a year in some cases, while for others it may probably take closer to two to three years.

Anticipatory Grief

In many cases (including those studied by Lindemann), bereavement comes unexpectedly. A loved one dies suddenly as a result of a heart attack or is killed in an accident or disaster. In other cases, a serious illness precedes the death, and those involved anticipate the loss that is inevitable. They experience **anticipatory grief.** Just as dying patients reach the stage of acceptance and rest, so too may their family come to terms with the death. Some of the grief work is thus accomplished in advance of death. A similar grief reaction is sometimes initiated by people whose loved ones are sent to dangerous situations—for example, to the battlefront.

Anticipatory Grief
Grief experienced over the expected death of a loved one.

Anticipatory grief can be adaptive if it gives the bereaved a final sense of having shared in a loved one's acceptance of death. Also it may protect the person against a highly acute reaction to sudden news of death (Lindemann, 1944). However, if the death does not occur, the grief work that has been performed may complicate the living relationship. For example, wives of prisoners of war whose husbands returned after having been given up for dead sometimes found it difficult to reestablish intimacy with their spouses, perhaps because they had performed the grief work too well.

Mourning and Adjustment

The Mourning Period

Mourning
The process of incorporating the loss of a person into one's life.

Grief and mourning are closely related. But if we wished to distinguish between the two, we might say that grief is the feeling of loss we experience as a result of a death and **mourning** is the process of incorporating that loss into our lives (Keleman, 1974).

In our society the outward signs of mourning are minimal. After a funeral or some other memorial rite, there are usually several weeks during which the bereaved are expected to need comfort and receive visitors. After that, the bereaved seem eager to demonstrate that they are "taking it well" and getting on with life. Nevertheless, there is usually a period of a year or so during which bereaved people function at a reduced level. For example, a widow may avoid parties or other optional social events, and she may put off making decisions about her job or life-style. During this period she engages in a life review process that focuses on the deceased and her relationship to him. Much of her behavior continues to be directed toward the deceased, as she makes arrangements to dispose of his effects and conclude his affairs. As these tasks become less pressing, life settles into a new and quiet pattern. In many cases, the person must begin to cope with loneliness.

As the mourning period draws to a close, the bereaved person mentally reorganizes her behavior toward the lost loved one. She makes inward decisions about the ways in which she will remember and speak of him from now on. When people mention his name she is now able to say, without thinking, "It's all right." She also may begin to have thoughts about dating again. Especially for younger people, this sometimes involves a period of indiscriminate dating during which the person seems unable to form a new relationship. The older person, who generally has fewer social opportunities, may experience a comparable period of "running around"—traveling, househunting, and choosing and rejecting friends haphazardly, perhaps on the basis of shared widowhood.

Many people eventually succeed in being able to love again. This happens despite the fact that bereaved people, at the beginning of their grief, can foresee no end to mourning and no restoration to normal life. It is often said that time (or being able to find a close companion) heals all wounds. Whether or not this is true is a matter for speculation. Kastenbaum, for one, finds it questionable that a person ever completely works through the death of a loved one, although many people do "get on with life" and "cover their wounds" (Kastenbaum, 1977, p. 41).

Finally, we should note that grief and mourning occur in crises other than bereavement. For example, the end of an important relationship sometimes leads to grief reactions. After a divorce, both partners usually mourn the loss of the relationship. When an adult child defects from family or family values (by forsaking religion, for example), a parent may mourn the estrange-

Bereavement

1. Make a record of the bereavements you have suffered. For each, give the relationship (grandmother, uncle, classmate, etc.) and your age when the death occurred.
2. Did any of the bereavements you have recorded greatly affect events or other relationships in your life? If so, how?
3. What, if anything, did you inherit from the bereaved? Include physical inheritances, such as possessions or money, as well as values, customs, career orientations, and so forth.
4. Has the death of a public figure ever affected you deeply? If so, how, and in what ways? ▲

ment with all the symptoms of grief. Mourning may also occur after an abortion, a miscarriage, or the surrender of a child for adoption. A person who is forced to leave his or her country, or leave an important position, will in some way mourn the loss. So may a person who loses an important physical ability, such as sight, hearing, or muscular coordination. Virtually every loss we experience is accompanied by mourning. In order to grow we must lose something, by changing, letting go, and moving on. Losses are a part of life and, according to a recent best seller *Necessary Losses* (Viorst, 1986), are necessary for our development throughout the life cycle. Mahler (1972) also speaks of a "life-long mourning process," by which she means development itself. Indeed, every new advance we make in our lives, insofar as it involves the loss of something once valued, involves a mourning for what is left behind.

Bereavement over the Life Span

The most stressful of life events, the death of a spouse, occurs most often in late adulthood. The death of one's own child (fortunately now rare) is also a bereavement crisis of adulthood. But there are earlier crises. An extremely upsetting experience in early childhood can be the loss of a beloved pet. By adolescence individuals may have experienced the death of a grandparent— perhaps one who lived in a distant city, or perhaps one with whom they have been close. Finally, most people survive their parents and lose close friends and perhaps siblings.

How people respond depends not only on the kind of loss sustained, but the point at which it occurs. That is, a person's responses to bereavement are greatly affected by his or her developmental level.

In Childhood

In general, young children have no genuine understanding of the permanence of death. If one parent dies, what matters to the child is the parent's failure to reappear in the usual manner. "I know father's dead," said one highly intelligent boy, "but what I can't understand is why he doesn't come home for supper" (Freud, 1917). When parents die, children suffer from separation anxiety and from the recurring fear they will be abandoned by the other parent. Since they do not understand why the parent died, they frequently conclude that it was because of them: they did something wrong. This can lead the child to feel guilt and omnipotence, and to fear close relationships. It can also lead to physical problems. Some children "punish" themselves by becoming sick or adopting symptoms associated with the deceased. Similar reactions occur when a sibling dies in childhood. Siblings of ill or dying children often suffer emotional stress that can affect their entire lives (Donnelly, 1986).

Adult explanations of the death may lead to adjustment problems. For example, adults sometimes say that God took father "because he was a good man," or that he died in his sleep "which we should all hope to do." Children, in their confusion, may fix on the explanation in a literal way, becoming afraid of sleeping or afraid of losing some equally good person. The child may come to equate being good with dying, and consequently, act up and avoid being good. In too many cases the child is offered little information and discouraged from asking questions.

The best strategy, it appears, is to discuss the physical reality of death before a loss occurs. Furman, who has written extensively on the effects of childhood bereavement, found that children are better able to adjust to a loss if they already have a realistic concept of death in its concrete manifestations (Furman, 1974, p. 13). Religious and philosophical concepts of death, though important to adults, tend to confuse and frighten the young child—who, after all, has little capacity for abstract thought. Even older children are best able to grasp abstract beliefs when they can add them to a concrete understanding of death. The important thing, then, is for adults to answer questions in realistic terms, distinguishing between real and imaginary death causes: for example, Grandfather died because his heart was too worn out to function well (instead of Grandfather died because he was a good man). Follow-up questions can be answered in the same spirit.

Children's pain can come to an end only if they are permitted to undergo a mourning process. When grief becomes a prohibited emotion, it simply postpones or prolongs the mourning process. Several studies have suggested that children are much more able to adjust to painful realities than we think (Rutter, 1987). Kübler-Ross (1975) noted that children are frequently better able to deal with death and dying than are adults. She also found that terminally ill children develop a more mature understanding of the permanence of death.

The mourning process is seen as a necessary mechanism of adaptation and mastery in normal growth and development (Altschul, 1988). Therefore, most psychologists feel that children should be involved in death and bereavement crises in a way appropriate to their developmental level. Death educators believe that it is beneficial to allow the child to participate in the loss of a family member in ways illustrated by the description of the experience of a five-year-old whose mother became seriously ill and died:

> He was an active participant in visits to the hospital in the final two months and he asked questions throughout the periods of his mother's hospitalization. He was included in the conversations when he chose to be included, his questions were answered when he asked them, and he indicated little curiosity about death. Since I openly shared my own tears and feelings of grief, and since [he] attended the memorial service, he was able to express some of his feelings through his participation in these experiences. Hence, [he] seemed to have internalized the actuality of his mother's death without undue psychological damage (Whitlock, 1978, p. 189).

This child was able to wholeheartedly accept another mother-figure in his life within a reasonable period of time.

The ways in which grief and mourning are handled are important to the child's future adjustment. Even more important is the quality of the relationships that remain open. Although it seems clear that the bereaved child is at risk, in the most favorable circumstances children do not experience later difficulties as a result of early loss. Put another way, if we help children engage in a mourning process compatible with their capacity and developmental level, we can help them to avoid later difficulties (Altschul, 1988). The same can be said about helping children deal with divorce, desertion, and prolonged separation, which may be experienced as losses similar to a death by children at certain levels of development (Schwebel, Fine, Moreland, & Pringle, 1988).

In Adolescence

In adolescence, people have come to understand the abstract and impersonal nature of death. They know rationally that angry thoughts do not cause another's death, that death comes equally to the good and the bad, and so forth. The more primitive notions of childhood do not disappear, of course. They can be reactivated in periods of crisis, at any later point in the life span. Still, most adolescents understand the concept of death as well as adults ever do.

They also come to experience bereavement as adults do. In childhood, reactions to the death of a parent usually appear sluggish and muted by adult standards. (It is generally many years before children can acknowledge the deep pain suffered.) Even in early adolescence, grief reactions do not appear in full force. Toward the end of the adolescent period, however, the bereavement responses more and more approximate those of the adult (Hankoff, 1975). Indeed, it may be that one of the accomplishments of adolescence is the ability to react to a traumatic loss at the time it occurs—that is, to develop an appropriate crisis reaction rather than submerge one's feelings.

The loss of a parent during adolescence creates obstacles to the achievement of identity. Bereaved adolescents lose the opportunity to work through rebellious feelings toward the parent, and are deprived of the opportunity of

The Vietnam Veteran's Memorial in Washington, D.C. offers solace to thousands of Americans who suffered losses in Southeast Asia.

ever proving themselves to that parent. As the surviving parent turns to them for emotional support, they find it difficult to assert their independence. Finally, the death may result in changes in career, marriage, or educational plans—in short, in any number of factors that affect the developing identity. Of course, some adolescents gain maturity from the responsibilities they assume upon a parent's death, and they may gain increased closeness with the surviving parent. The critical event may act as "an affirmation of the adolescent's identity in challenging and thereby underscoring his strengths and coping abilities" (Hankoff, 1975, p. 383).

In Adulthood

The person who loses a parent in young adulthood is deprived of the opportunity of knowing that parent as an adult equal—something that may have been consciously desired. Another common effect of bereavement in these years is to reinforce the person's sense of mortality. In middle age, death of a parent often precipitates the mid-life crisis; the person comes to see himself as "next on the list," no longer magically protected from death. The death may also involve the assumption of new responsibilities toward the surviving parent. This sometimes leads to a reversal of earlier relationships, and considerable stress.

Today, the person who is in ill health and fears that death may be near is often helped by new attitudes on the part of health professionals and the public in general. But perhaps the greatest help is a person's own sense of integrity, developed through many successful resolutions of life crises, and a sense of generativity—an expansion of caring for other individuals, for the next generation, and for society.

Also stressful are the deaths of friends and relatives belonging to one's own generation. Of course, these deaths occur with increasing frequency as the person enters late middle age. The threat of marital bereavement also increases during this period.

In old age, bereavement is a repeated crisis. Older people may suffer from "bereavement overload"; they are unable to recover fully from one loss before experiencing another (Kastenbaum, 1977). They lose loved ones and friends, and perhaps observe the deaths of age-mates in a retirement community or nursing home. Such events are traumatic, but older people may gradually become resigned to death because "so many are gone." They may also be grateful for their own situation and resolve to enjoy each day as it comes.

NEW WAYS OF CONFRONTING DEATH

Death is a subject that people are increasingly willing to discuss and study. The new openness has led to new ways of adjusting to death and dying. For example, health professionals have developed better understanding of their seriously ill patients (and of themselves) by conducting the kinds of seminars first championed by Kübler-Ross. Elementary school teachers are better able to help children deal with the death of a classmate because of a growing recognition that overt mourning activities can make a death more understandable and less frightening. For example, in the past it was customary to remove the dead child's belongings, magically, without a word; today, teachers are advised to discuss the disposal of the belongings with the class, and to consult them about sending a sympathy card or planting a memorial tree (Keith & Ellis, 1978). Most important, people who are seriously ill are not so often made to deny their condition and their feelings as before. The dying person today is less isolated and that is beneficial to everyone.

Hospice Care for the Dying

Another reflection of the new willingness to confront death is the dramatic growth of the *hospice movement* and of organizations that specialize in the care of dying people and their families. The **hospice approach** involves a team effort that provides medical, psychological, social, and spiritual support for both the patient and the family (Butterfield-Picard & Mague, 1982). The goals of a hospice organization are to provide services that enhance the patient's quality of life, to assist the family and the patient in the bereavement process, and to help manage the costs of caring for the terminally ill (Davidson, 1988).

Hospice Approach
A team effort to deliver varied support services to a dying person and his family.

A hospice program can be provided by a hospital, a free-standing community facility, or a home care organization. It can be operated by paid staff, by volunteers, or by both. In the early stage of the serious illness, the hospice organization may provide psychological counseling and other services that enable the dying person to remain at home. When the time becomes appropriate, the person is admitted to the hospice and helped to die with dignity.

The philosophy of the hospice staff is to "extend the quality of life, when we can't extend the quantity of life" (Wald, 1979). Medication is administered with an understanding of the patient's physical and emotional needs. (The nurse knows that one person may need sedation, while another needs someone to hold his hand.) Family members are welcome nearly all the time. Children—both visitors and the children of staff members—are constantly visible. In short, the patient lives, until he or she dies, as part of a community. So great is the involvement of the hospice in the family unit—and vice versa—that a person often returns to the hospice even after a loved one's death, and may work through his or her grief as a volunteer.

Cancer Care, a national organization, has as its goal to conquer cancer "another way"—by keeping the seriously ill person (and the person's family) at home, at work, and in the community. To this end, counselors create "care-at-home plans," utilizing nurses or homemakers where necessary. They help families solve practical problems together—not only problems involving illness and treatment, but problems concerning finances and the future education of children. Perhaps most important, counselors help family members cope with the guilt, anger, and strained relationships that accompany a devastating illness.

Bereavement counseling is a natural and effective intervention, after a death has occurred in a hospice program. It appears to reduce the incidence of serious illness suffered by widows and widowers in the first two years after the spouse's death (Cancer Care, 1978; Kalish, 1981). National organizations like Compassionate Friends also provide support groups for bereaved family members. The goal of these programs is to ensure family survival during the period of extreme stress, as well as afterward.

In sum, the hospice movement represents a new approach to the care and counseling of the dying. As Davidson (1988) explained, until the 1950s, we, as a society, took care of the sick and dying at home. After that, people with acute diseases were more commonly treated in hospitals while those with chronic illness were cared for in nursing homes. As a consequence, most Americans and Canadians were spending their last days in these facilities. The hospice movement is developing an alternative: final care provided in a setting and from people especially trained for providing this service. The hospice approach is becoming increasingly familiar to us, in a large part because it fills an important need.

Educational Programs

The new openness about death is perhaps best reflected in the growth of educational awareness programs dealing with death. According to the National Education Association, death is a recent arrival in school curricula—and there is a virtual proliferation of courses (Maeroff, 1978). Some courses are begun in response to the death of a student. In other words, they are crisis intervention measures. Other courses evolve because educators, parents, or students feel that the mastery of death anxiety is an appropriate goal of the educational process.

In the new courses related to death, students read novels and essays about death, visit cemeteries and funeral homes, and speak with elderly people who must confront death within a relatively short time. What is learned from these activities varies. One Midwestern school system that conducts field trips to cemeteries and funeral homes finds that both students and teachers emerge better able to verbalize their feelings. Similar effects are noted at the college level. Students not only learn to express their feelings about death; they learn to reflect upon the way they are living now. And often they emerge better able to cope with the future. In sum, for many students a college course on death seems to result in personal growth (Shneidman, 1977).

The Right to Die

A recent phenomenon that has generated quite a bit of controversy is the right-to-die movement. Supporters of this movement believe in the right of the elderly, terminally ill to control the time, place, and manner of their own deaths. There are right-to-die societies throughout the world who have published manuals detailing methods of suicide. Instead of employing the term suicide, these manuals utilize such terms as "accelerated death," death by design, death with dignity or self-deliverance (Humphry & Wickett, 1987). In *Last Rights,* an eloquent and moving plea for the right-to-die, Manya Mannes writes, "Now it is not dust to dust, but human to vegetable." Opponents of the right-to-die movement consider the movement an affront to the preservation of life and have labeled it a "death cult" that supports genocide. However, right-to-die organizations, like the Hemlock Society, suggest an alternative: legalized euthanasia, wherein the medical profession would permit terminally ill patients to die peacefully.

What Can I Do?

Nearly everyone feels helpless in the presence of a dying person, and yet, we probably have the ability within us to offer assistance. Sister Cotter, a nurse and a participant in a symposium on catastrophic illness, suggests how we might approach the task (Cancer Care, 1970): "Look back at moments when we wondered how we could bear tomorrow." When we want to support the dying person, says Sister Cotter, "we can identify and talk about the same things that helped us when we personally suffered deeply and reached out to find someone who could help."

In order to understand what you might be able to do to help a dying person:

1. Recall a time when you thought you could not bear tomorrow. Who helped most?
2. How did that person help? By acting on your behalf? By giving advice? By listening? By simply "being there"? In other ways?
3. Sister Cotter has said that what helps most is the "caring person." In your view, what does the caring person do?
4. Think of the last person you were with who was undergoing great emotional or physical stress. What actions did you take, and what other actions might you have taken?
5. When you visit a dying person, are you really helpless? Why, or why not?

Catastrophic Illness in the Seventies: Critical Issues and Complex Divisions in Cancer Care Symposium Proceedings, 1970. Cancer Care and the National Cancer Foundation, New York. ▲

Euthanasia

In its use today, the term "euthanasia" refers to the process through which a terminally-ill person can be helped to experience a dignified death. There has been some reluctance to use the word, however, because of its association with Nazi doctors (Lifton, 1987). In recent years, the medical profession, bolstered by court rulings and a sympathetic public, has been instrumental in making euthanasia a reality, and in assisting terminally ill patients who ask for final relief from unbearable pain and prolonged suffering. The toughest question facing euthanasia supporters is: What is euthanasia: mercy killing, murder, or a compassionate, humane means of ending a life?

The Netherlands has become a leader in voluntary euthanasia. Euthanasia is carried out only if there is no hope of recovery and if there is unbearable suffering that foils all pain-killing efforts. The patient and family are consulted at each step, but the patient controls his choices. Generally, euthanasia is accomplished through an injection of barbiturates to induce sleep.

Living Wills

Many states have enacted "living will" legislation to support a patient's right to refuse life-sustaining medical treatment in terminal cases. Living wills are documents prepared while an individual is still capable of specifying whether he or she would want to be kept alive by life-support systems. Generally, such a document helps to relieve any conflicts or burdens on loved ones. A typical living will might read as follows:

> I direct that life-sustaining procedures should be withheld or withdrawn if I have an illness or disease or injury . . . such that there is no responsible expectation of recovering or regaining a meaningful quality of life.

THE NEAR-DEATH EXPERIENCE

Within the last decade or two, physicians and psychologists have begun to study the reports of people who have survived clinical death; for example, people who have been resuscitated after cardiac or respiratory failure. One physician who has collected descriptions of "afterlife" or near-death experiences is Raymond Moody (1975, 1977). Although Moody's investigation is admittedly sympathetic, rather than strictly scientific, his work has enabled researchers to generalize about the near-death experience. Typically it includes the following elements:

> . . . ineffability [a feeling of overwhelming sacredness]; hearing doctors or spectators pronouncing one dead; feelings of peace and quiet; a loud ringing or buzzing noise; a dark tunnel through which one may feel oneself moving; out of body experiences; meeting others, including guides, spirits, dead relatives, and friends; a being of light; a panoramic review of one's life; a border or limit beyond which there is no return; visions of great knowledge; cities of light; a realm of bewildered spirits; supernatural rescues from real physical death by some spirit; a return or coming back with changed attitudes and beliefs (Moody, summarized in Siegel, 1980).

Numerous investigators have remarked upon the strikingly similar content of different near-death reports. Some propose that these experiences, so real to the person that has them, are also genuine in the sense of describing some objective reality. In other words, they suggest that there may be an actual life after death that is accompanied by out-of-body sensations and that is approached through a passage resembling a tunnel (Kastenbaum, 1979). In *Otherworld Journeys,* a recent book on near-death experiences, Zaleski (1987) reported that survivors generally recall a sensation of leaving their bodies and hovering above them, and of struggling from a darkness into the light.

Other investigators have pointed out striking resemblances between the afterlife vision and certain hallucinatory experiences—for example, drug-induced hallucinations and religious or mystical experiences (Siegel, 1980).

These writers suggest that the afterlife vision can best be understood as a dissociative hallucinatory activity of the brain that takes place under unusual conditions involving the excitation of the central nervous system. They note, for example, that drugs, a state of shock, or the stresses of dying may release stored perceptions that are normally suppressed by the brain in favor of incoming information, and this might account for vivid panoramic memories.

These investigators also point out that sensory deprivation, as well as the experience of dying, can result in a stimulation of the central nervous system that mimics the effect of light in the retina, and produces bright light and tunnel vision. In fact, some researchers feel that the deathbed itself is a "unique setting for the production of hallucinatory phenomena" (Siegel, 1980). The person (possibly hospitalized) is isolated from the usual perceptions, afraid, overwhelmed by memories and inner fantasies, and perhaps actively engaged in forms of mental concentration to provide disengagement from the physical reality of pain.

Scientific investigation of life after death is relatively new. Data on near-death experiences did not begin to appear in medical and psychological journals in significant quantity until the 1970s. This research has of course generated a great deal of controversy (Gibbs, 1985). It has also, for some of the dying who believe in an afterlife, strengthened this conviction and probably made the last moments of life more peaceful—less fearful and more anticipatory. The subjective experience of concluding one's life span is still as mysterious as the subjective experience of beginning it. Perhaps in these areas, science and speculation will never join hands. But the events will continue to fascinate many—as do, indeed, all the other highly significant points in the life span.

SUMMARY

1. In recent years there has been a new willingness to discuss death, dying, and bereavement. Being able to talk about death seems to make adjustment to death easier.

2. Most people can expect to die in their elderly years. According to Erikson, a favorable outcome in old age is integrity: the person accepts his or her life and the fact of death. Negative outcomes include despair and bitterness. Increased age appears to bring a decrease in death fears.

3. At every stage in the life span, people may experience *death encounters* (confrontations with the imminence of their death). Young children understand death differently than adults; they do not see it as irreversible. A small child with a life-threatening illness fears separation from parents; older children are more concerned with operations and intrusions on the body. Adolescents are often concerned with their life plans and the dependency induced by the illness. Adults see death as an interruption of life's activities and responsibilities.

4. Adolescents become concerned about their own death and may test their immortality through risk-taking activities. The suicide rate rises dramatically in adolescence and continues to rise afterwards.

5. Death anxiety seems to peak in middle age.

6. Dying is an experience about which we know relatively little. Kübler-Ross has described a stage theory of dying, in which the person progresses from denial to anger to bargaining to depression to acceptance and resignation. All people do not pass through the stages Kübler-Ross described; there are many individual variations.

7. A *bereavement* crisis is generally thought to be the most painful of all life's crises, except one's own death. A bereaved person usually experiences many painful symptoms, such as guilt, difficulty in daily functioning, and a sense of unreality. These reactions are normal; indeed, if grief is not expressed or experienced, it will often manifest itself later, for example, in the form of a physical illness. When death is expected, a person may engage in *anticipatory grief.*

8. The experience of *bereavement* depends on the developmental level of the bereaved person. The young child does not understand that death is irreversible and sometimes believes that he or she has caused a person's death. For adolescents, bereavement may involve a threat to identity development. In adulthood, bereavements become increasingly frequent and force people to confront their own mortality.

9. New ways of adjusting to death have become important in recent years. Among these are education about death and hospice care for the dying. The right to die, euthanasia, and living wills have emerged as controversial issues.

10. Scientists have begun to investigate near-death experiences reported by people who "returned" from a state of clinical death. While no conclusions can be drawn from existing evidence, researchers have been impressed by the similarity of reports and their comparability with certain hallucinatory experiences.

SUGGESTED READINGS

Becker E. (1972). *The denial of death.* New York: Free Press. An excellent integration of psychological and theological insights into the human need to avoid the burdens of death.

Goodman, L. M. (1980). *Death and the creative life.* New York: Springer. A compendium of interviews with world-renowned artists and scientists revealing some unique attitudes toward death.

Gunther, J. (1973). *Death be not proud.* New York: Random House. A moving and insightful book written about an adolescent dying of cancer.

Kavanaugh, R. E. (1972). *Facing death.* New York: Penguin Books. A discussion of ways to come to grips with the realization that death is inevitable, with many insightful thoughts that are applicable to the healthy as well as the terminally ill.

Krementz, J. (1981). *How it feels when a parent dies.* New York: Alfred A. Knopf. An exploration of grief as a necessary and appropriate reaction, with explanations of the feelings of both children and adults.

Lerner, G. (1985). *Death of one's own.* Wisconsin: University of Wisconsin Press. A moving document of the author's husband's death and how she coped with the moral questions of the patient's right to know, to choose, and to die.

Mack, J. E. and Hickler, H. (1981). *Vivienne: The life and suicide of an adolescent girl.* Boston: Little, Brown. A thought-provoking book, dealing with the death of a fourteen-year-old girl, that chronicles the last months of her life through her diary and letters to a favorite teacher.

Maguire, D. C. (1984). *Death by choice.* New York: Image Books. An examination of the major issues in the "right-to-die" controversy.

Rollin, B. (1985). *Last wish.* New York: Warner Books. A controversial true story of a mother's decision to choose suicide, and the involvement of her daughter.

Sabom, M. B. (1982). *Recollections of death: A medical investigation.* New York: Harper & Row. A fascinating empirical investigation of the near death experience by an author who was initially skeptical about the phenomenon.

References

Abel, T. M., & Metraux, R. (1974). *Culture and psychotherapy.* New Haven, CT: College & University Press.

Abernathy, T. (1981). Adolescent cohabitation: A form of courtship or marriage? *Adolescence, 16*(64), 791–797.

Adams, B. (1979). Mate selection in the United States: A theoretical summarization. In W. Burr, R. Hill, F. I. Nye, & I. Reiss (Eds.), *Contemporary theories about the family* (Vol. 1). New York: Free Press.

Adams, C. G., & Turner, B. F. (1985). Reported change in sexuality from young adulthood to old age. *Journal of Sex Research, 21*(2), 126–141.

(1986). *Affirmative action today: A legal and practical analysis.* Washington, DC: The Bureau of National Affairs.

Aguilera, D. C., & Messick, J. M. (1982). *Crisis intervention: Theory and practice* (4th ed.). St. Louis: Mosby.

Ainsworth, M. D. (1967). *Infancy in Uganda.* Baltimore: Johns Hopkins Press.

Ainsworth, M. D., & Bell, S. M. (1970). Attachment and separation: Illustrated by the behavior of one-year-olds in a strange situation. *Child development, 41,* 49–67.

Alexander, F. (1946). The principle of flexibility. In F. Alexander & T. M. French (Eds.), *Psychoanalytic therapy.* New York: Ronald Press.

Alexander, L. (1950). *Psychosomatic medicine: Its principles and applications.* New York: W. W. Norton.

Alfano, D. (1973). Unemployment duration and attitudes toward work. *Journal of Vocational Behavior, 3,* 83–96.

Allgeier, E., & Allgeier, A. (1984). *Sexual interactions.* Lexington, MA: D.C. Heath.

Alloy, L., & Abramson, L. (1980). The cognitive component of human helplessness and depression: A critical analysis. In J. Garber & M. Seligman (Eds.), *Human helplessness* (pp. 59–70). New York: Academic Press.

Altmaier, E. M., & Happ, D. A. (1985). Coping skills training's immunization effects against learned helplessness. *Journal of Social and Clinical Psychology, 3*(2), 181–189.

Altmaier, E. M., Leary, M. R., Halpern, S., & Sellers, J. E. (1985). Effects of stress inoculation and participant modeling on confidence and anxiety: Testing predictions of self-efficacy theory. *Journal of Social & Clinical Psychology, 3*(4), 500–505.

Altman, I., & Taylor, D. (1973). *Social penetration.* New York: Holt, Rinehart & Winston.

Altschul, S. (Ed.). (1988). *Childhood bereavement and its aftermath.* New York: International Universities Press.

Altus, W. D. (1966). Birth order and its sequelae. *Science, 151,* 44–49.

American Cancer Society. 1978. (1977). *Cancer facts and figures.* New York: American Cancer Society.

American Psychiatric Association. (1980). *Diagnostic and statistical manual of mental disorders* (3rd ed.). Washington, DC.

American Psychiatric Association. (1987). *Diagnostic and statistical manual of mental disorders* (3rd ed. rev.). Washington, DC: American Psychiatric Association.

Andersen, B., & Jochimsen, P. (1985). Sexual functioning among breast cancer, gynecologic cancer and healthy women. *Journal of Consulting and Clinical Psychology, 53*(1), 25–32.

Anderson, R. (1968). *I never sang for my father.* New York: Random House.

Angel, M. (1987). *The orphaned adult: Confronting the death of a parent.* New York: Human Sciences Press.

Anthony, E. J., & Cohler, B. J. (Eds.). (1987). *The invulnerable child.* New York: Guilford Press.

Anthony, J., & Koupernik, C. (Eds.). (1974). *The child in his family: Children at psychiatric risk.* New York: Wiley.

Antonov, A. (1947). Children born during the siege of Leningrad in 1942. *Journal of Pediatrics, 30,* 250–259.

Antonucci, T., & Akiyama, H. (1987). An examination of sex differences in social support among older men and women. *Sex Roles, 17*(11/12), 737–749.

Apgar, V. (1953). A proposal of a new method of evaluation of the newborn infant. *Anesthesia and Analgesia: Current Research, 32,* 260–267.

Applebaum, E. (1979). Measuring musical abilities of autistic children. *Journal of Autism and Developmental Disorders, 9,* 279–285.

Argyris, C. (1957). *Personality and organization.* New York: Harper & Row.

Argyris, C. (1964). *Integrating the individual and the organization.* New York: Wiley.

Aristotle. (1957). *Poetics.* Trans. by T. Twining. In *Aristotle's politics and poetics.* Trans. by B. Jowell & T. Twining. New York: Viking Press.

Arkowitz, H., Hinton, R., Perl, J., & Himadi, W. (1978). Treatment strategies for dating anxiety in college men based on real-life practice. *The Counseling Psychologist, 4,* 41–46.

Ash, P. (1949). The reliability of psychiatric diagnosis. *Journal of Abnormal and Social Psychology, 44,* 272–276.

Aspects of anxiety (2nd ed.). (1968). Philadelphia: J. B. Lippincott.

Atchley, R. C. (1972). *Social gerontology.* Belmont, CA: Wadsworth.

Atchley, R. C. (1976). *The sociology of retirement.* Cambridge, MA: Schenkman.

Atkins, S. (1985). Acting out in children: A review of the literature. *Child and Adolescent Social Work, 2*(4), 247–257.

Atwood, J., & Gagnon, J. (1987). Masturbatory behavior in college youth. *Journal of Sex Education and Therapy, 13*(2), 32–35.

Avison, W., & Speechly, K. (1987). The discharged psychiatric patient. *American Journal of Psychiatry, 144*(1), 10–18.

Ayllon, T., & Azrin, N. (1968). *The token economy: A motivational system for therapy and rehabilitation.* New York: Appleton-Century-Crofts.

Azrin, N., & Besalel, V. (1979). *A parent's guide to bedwetting control.* New York: Pocket Books.

Badalamenti, A. F. (1984). Successful psychotherapy. *Journal of Contemporary Psychotherapy, 14,* 120–130.

Baker, D. (1984, August). The neurological basis of the talents of dyslexics. *Perspectives on Dyslexia.* Baltimore: Orton Dyslexia Society, 1.

Bakshian A., Jr. (1986). America's gray wave of the future. *Nation's Business,* 4.

Baldwin, B. A. (1979). Training in crisis intervention for students in the mental health professions. *Professional Psychology,* 161–167.

Baldwin, J., & Baldwin, J. (1988). AIDS information and sexual behavior on a university campus. *Journal of Sex Education and Therapy, 14*(2), 24–28.

Bandura, A. (1969). *Principles of behavior modification.* New York: Holt, Rinehart & Winston.

Bandura, A. (1974). Behavior therapy and the models of man. *American Psychologist, 29,* 859–869.

Bandura, A. (1977). *Social learning theory.* Englewood Cliffs, NJ: Prentice-Hall.

Bandura, A. (1986). *Social foundations of thought and action: A social cognitive theory.* Englewood Cliffs, NJ: Prentice-Hall.

Bandura, A., Ross, D., & Ross, S. (1961). Transmission of aggression through imitation of aggressive models. *Journal of Abnormal and Social Psychology, 63,* 575–582.

Bandura, A., Ross, D., & Ross, S. (1963). Imitation of film-mediated aggressive models. *Journal of Abnormal and Social Psychology, 66,* 3–11.

Barbach, L. (1976). *For yourself: The fulfillment of female sexuality.* New York: New American Library.

Bard, M. (1970). The price of survival for cancer victims. In A.L. Strauss (Ed.), *Where medicine fails.* Chicago: Aldine.

Barnes, G. (1984). *Alcohol use among secondary school students in New York State.* Buffalo: New York State Research Institute on Alcoholism.

Barocas, H., & Barocas, C. (1980). Separation-individuation conflicts in children of holocaust survivors. *Journal of Contemporary Psychotherapy, 11*(1), 16–25.

Baron, R., & Byrne, D. (1981). *Social psychology: Understanding human interaction.* Boston: Allyn & Bacon.

Barrera, M., & Ainlay, S. (1983). The structure of social support: A conceptual and empirical analysis. *Journal of Community Psychology, 11,* 133–143.

Barrett, K. (1980, May 15). Prisoner of fear. *Family Circle,* 16–17, 132, 134.

Bart, P. (1970). Mother Portnoy's complaint. *Trans-action. 8,* 69-74.

Batchelor, I. (1954). Alcoholism and attempted suicide. *Journal of Mental Science, 100,* 451–461.

Beardslee, W., Bemporad, J., Keller, M., & Klerman, G. (1983). Children of parents with major affective disorder: A review. *American Journal of Psychiatry, 140,* 825–832.

Beardslee, W. R., & Podorefsky, M. A. (1988). Resilient adolescents whose parents have serious affective and other psychiatric disorders: Importance of self-understanding and relationships. *American Journal of Psychiatry, 145*(1), 63–69.

Bebbington, P. E. (1985). Three cognitive theories of depression. *Psychological Medicine, 15*(4), 759–769.

Beck, A., Sethi, B. S., & Thothil, R. (1963). Childhood bereavement and adult depression. *Archives of General Psychiatry, 9,* 295–302.

Beck, A. T. (1976). *Cognitive therapy and the emotional disorders.* New York: International Universities Press.

Beck, A. T., & Emery, G. (1985). *Anxiety disorders and phobias.* New York: Basic Books.

Beck, A. T., Rush, A. J., Shaw, B. F., & Emery, G. (1979). *Cognitive therapy of depression.* New York: Guilford Press.

Beck, S., Collins, L., Overholser, J., & Terry, K. (1985). A cross-sectional assessment of the relationships of social competence measures to peer friendship and likability in elementary-age children. *Psychology Monographs, 111*(1), 41–63.

Beck, S., Neeper, R., Baskin, C., & Forehand, R. An examination of children's perceptions of themselves and others as a function of popularity level. *Journal of Social and Clinical Psychology, 1,* 259–271.

Becker, E. (1973). *The denial of death.* New York: Free Press.

Bee, H. L., & Mitchell, S. K. (1984). *The developing person: A life span approach.* Cambridge: Harper & Row.

Beitchman, J. (1985). Childhood schizophrenia. *Psychiatric Clinics of North America, 8*(4), 793–813.

Bell, A. P., & Weinberg, M. S. (1978). *Homosexualities: A study of diversity among men and women.* New York: Simon & Schuster.

Bell, R. (1981). *Worlds of friendship.* Beverly Hills: Sage Publishing.

Belli, M., & Wilkinson, A. (1987). *Everybody's guide to the law.* New York: Perennial Library.

Belsky, J. (1984). *The psychology of aging.* Monterey, CA: Brooks/Cole.

Belsky, J., Garduque, L., & Hrncir, E. (1984). Assessing performance, competence and executive capacity in infant play: Relations to home environment and security of attachment. *Developmental Psychology, 20,* 406–417.

Bem, D. J. (1972). Self-perception theory. In L. Berkowitz (Ed.), *Advances in experimental social psychology* (Vol. 6). New York: Academic Press.

Bem, S. (1974). The measurement of psychological androgyny. *Journal of Consulting and Clinical Psychology, 42,* 155–162.

Bem, S. L. (1976). On the utility of alternative procedures for assessing psychological androgyny. *Journal of Consulting and Clinical Psychology, 42*(2), 155–162.

Bengston, V. L., Cuellar, J. B., & Ragan, P. K. (1977). Stratum contrasts and similarities in attitudes toward death. *Journal of Gerontology, 32*(1), 76–88.

Bennett, W. (1987). The role of the family in the nurture and protection of the young. *American Psychologist, 42*(3), 246–250.

Berardo, F. (1985). Social networks and life preservation. *Death Studies, 9,* 37–50.

Bergin, A. E. (1971). The evaluation of therapeutic outcomes. In A. E. Bergin & S. L. Garfield (Eds.), *Handbook of psychotherapy and behavior change.* New York: John Wiley & Sons.

Berman, A. (1987). Adolescent suicide: Clinical consultation. *Clinical Psychologist, 40*(4), 87–91.

Berman, E. M., & Lief, H. I., (1975). Marital therapy from a psychiatric perspective: An overview. *American Journal of Psychiatry, 132*(6), 583–592.

Bernard, J. (1964). The adjustment of married mates. In H. Christensen (Ed.), *Handbook of marriage and the family.* Chicago: Rand McNally.

Berne, E. (1964). *Games people play.* New York: Grove Press.

Bernstein, A. (1976). How children learn about sex and birth. *Psychology Today, 66,* 31–36.

Bernstein, B. (1977). Legal problems of cohabitation. *Family Coordinator, 26*(4), 361–366.

Berrueta-Clement, J., Schweinhart, L., Barnett, W., Epstein, A., & Weikart, D. (1984). *Changed lives.* Ypsilanti, MI: High/Scope Press.

Berscheid, E. (1985). Interpersonal attraction. In G. Lindzey & E. Aronson (Eds.), *The handbook of social psychology* (Vol. 2). New York: Random House.

Berscheid, E., & Walster, E. (1974). A little bit about love. In T. Huston (Ed.), *Foundations of interpersonal attraction.* New York: Academic Press.

Berscheid, E., & Walster, E. (1978). *Interpersonal attraction* (2nd ed.). Reading, MA: Addison-Wesley.

Best, F. (1980). *Flexible life scheduling.* New York: Praeger.

Bettelheim, B. (1943). Individual and mass behavior in extreme situations. *Journal of Abnormal and Social Psychology, 38,* 417–452.

Bettelheim, B. (1976). *The uses of enchantment.* New York: Alfred A. Knopf.

Betz, E. (1984). Two tests of Maslow's theory of need fulfillment. *Journal of Vocational Behavior, 24,* 204–220.

Bianchi, S., & Spain, D. (1986). *American women in transition.* New York: Russell Sage Foundation.

Binder, U. (1977). Behavior modification: Operant approaches to therapy. In U. Binder, A. Binder, &

B. Rimland (Eds.), *Modern therapies*. Englewood Cliffs, NJ: Prentice-Hall.

Biorch, G. (1971). In synposis of the general discussion. In L. Levi (Ed.), *Society, stress and disease: Vol. 1, The psychosocial environment and psychosomatic disease*. London: Oxford University Press.

Birren, J. E. (1974). Transitions in gerontology: Psychophysiology and speed of response. *American Psychologist, 29,* 808–815.

Birren, J. E., Cunningham, W. R., & Yamamoto, K. (1983). Psychology of adult development and aging. *Annual Review Psychology, 34,* 543–575.

Blanck, R., & Blanck, G. (1968). *Marriage and personal development*. New York: Columbia University Press.

Block, J. (1981). The mental health of the aging. *The Gerontologist, 22,* 227–228.

Block, J. (1984). *Sex-role identity and ego-development*. San Francisco: Jossey-Bass.

Bloom, B. (1988). *Health psychology: A psychosocial perspective*. Englewood Cliffs, NJ: Prentice-Hall.

Bluebond-Langner, M. (1977). Meanings of death to children. In H. Feifel (Ed.), *New meanings of death*. New York: McGraw-Hill.

Blumberg, B., Flaherty, M., & Lewis, J. (Eds.). (1980). *Coping with cancer: A resource for the health professional*. Bethesda, MD: National Cancer Institute.

Blythe, R. (1979, July). Living to be old. *Harper's,* July 1979 (pp. 35–54). Excerpted from *The view in winter: Reflections on old age*. New York: Harcourt Brace Jovanovich.

Bohannan, P. (1975). The six stations of divorce. In R. E. Albrecht & W. Bock (Eds.), *Encounter: Love, marriage and family*. Boston: Holbrook Press.

Bolton, E. (1980). An occupational analysis of the mentor relationship in the career development of women. *Adult Education, 30*(4), 195–207.

Bord, R. (1971). Rejection of the mentally ill: Continuities and further

developments. *Social Problems, 18,* 496–509.

Borys, S., & Perlman, D. (1985). Gender differences in loneliness. *Personality and Social Psychology Bulletin, 11*(1), 63–74.

Bossert, S. (1979). *Tasks and social relationships in classrooms*. Cambridge, U.K.: Cambridge University Press.

Boston Women's Health Book Collective. (1979). *Our bodies, ourselves* (3rd ed.). New York: Simon & Schuster.

Bottari, M. A., & Rappaport, H. (1983). The relationship of patient and therapist-reported experiences of the initial session to outcome: An initial investigation. *Psychotherapy: Theory, Research and Practice, 20,* 355–358.

Bottoms, S., Kuhnert, B., Kuhnert, P., & Reese, A. (1982). Maternal passive smoking and fetal serum thiocyanate level. *American Journal of Obstetrics and Gynecology, 144,* 787–791.

Bowde, C. L. (1985). Current treatment of depression. *Hospital and Community Psychiatry, 36,* 1192–1200.

Bowlby, J. (1960). Grief and mourning in infancy and early childhood. *Psychoanalytic Study of the Child, 15,* 9–32.

Bowlby, J. (1969). The nature of the child's tie to his mother. *International Journal of Psychoanalysis, 39,* 350–373.

Bowlby, J. (1982). *Attachment and loss* (2nd ed.). New York: Basic Books.

Bowlby, J. (1988). Developmental psychiatry comes of age. *American Journal of Psychiatry, 145*(1), 1–10.

Bradley, R. (1982). Using birth order and sibling dynamics in career counseling. *Personnel and Guidance Journal, 61,* 25–31.

Bray, D. W., Campbell, R. J., & Grant, D. L. (1974). *Formative years in business: A long-term AT&T study of managerial lives*. New York: John Wiley & Sons.

Breckenridge, J. S., Zeiss, A. M., & Thompson, L. W. (1987). The life satisfaction course and intervention for the elderly. In R. F. Muñoz (Ed.), *Depression prevention:*

Research directions. Washington, DC: Hemisphere Pub. Corp.

Brenner, C. (1974). *An elementary textbook of psychoanalysis* (rev. ed.). Garden City, NY: Anchor Press.

Brenner, M. H. (1976). *Estimating the social costs of national economic policy: Implications for mental and physical health and criminal violence*. Report for the Joint Economic Committee of Congress. Washington, DC: U.S. Government Printing Office.

Brenner, M. H. (1985). Economic change and suicide rate: A population model including loss, separation, illness, and alcohol consumption. In M. R. Zales (Ed.), *Stress in health and disease*. New York: Brunner/Mazel.

Bretherton, I. (1985). Representing the social world in symbolic play: Reality and fantasy. In I. Bretherton (Ed.), *Symbolic play*. (pp.1–39). New York: Academic Press.

Brett, J. (1982). Job transfer and well-being. *Journal of Applied Psychology, 67*(4), 450–463.

Brien, J., Loomis, C., Tranmer, J., & McGrath, M. (1983). Disposition of ethanol in human maternal venous blood and amniotic fluid. *American Journal of Obstetrics and Gynecology, 146,* 181–186.

Brody, J. E. (1979, May 16). Personal health: The masks of childhood depression are varied and often misleading. *The New York Times, III,* 12.

Brody, J. E. (1980, May 21). The evidence builds against marijuana. *The New York Times.*

Brody, J. E. (1981, October 28). Guide through maze of psychotherapies. *The New York Times.*

Bromley, D. B. (1974). *The psychology of human aging* (2nd ed.). Middlesex, England: Penguin.

Brooks, G., & Donegan, E. (1985). *Gonococcal infection*. London, England: Eugene Arnold.

Brown, B. (1981). A life-span approach to friendship: Age-related dimensions of an ageless relationship. In H. Lopata & D. Maines (Eds.), *Research on the* interweave of social roles (Vol. 2): Friendship. Greenwich, CT: JAI Press.

Brown, F. (1961). Depression and childhood bereavement. *Journal of Mental Science, 107,* 754–777.

Brown, G. W., Craig, T. K., & Harris, T. O. (1985). Depression: Distress or disease? Some epidemiological considerations. *British Journal of Psychiatry, 147,* 612–622.

Brown, J. M., O'Keefe, J., Sanders, S. H., & Baker, B. (1986). Developmental changes in children's cognition to stressful and painful situations. *Journal of Pediatric Psychology, 11*(3), 343–357.

Brown, S. L. (1973). Family experience and change. In R. Friedman (Ed.), *Family roots of school learning and behavior disorders.* Springfield, IL: Charles C. Thomas.

Buhler, C. (1959). *Der Menschliche Lebenslauf als psychologisches Problem [The human course of life as a psychological problem]* (2nd ed.). Göttingen, Germany: Hogrefe. (Original work published 1933)

Bulcroft, K., & O'Connor-Raden, M. (1986). Never too late. *Psychology Today* (20), 66–69.

Burch, G. K. W. (1984). Structured assessment of sexual dysfunction. In P. A. Keller & L. G. Ritt (Eds.), *Innovations in clinical practice: A source book.* Sarasota, FL: Professional Resource Exchange.

Bureau of National Affairs. (1986). *Affirmative action today: A legal and practical analysis.* Washington, DC.

Burgess, R., & Huston, T. (1979). *Social exchange in developing relationships.* New York: Academic Press.

Burhenne, D. P., Kaschak, E., & Schwebel, A. I. (1973). The effect of altering the administration procedure on four WAIS subtests. *Educational and Psychological Measurement, 33,* 663–668.

Burr, W. R. (1970). Satisfaction with various aspects of marriage over the life cycle: A random middle-class sample. *Journal of Marriage and the Family, 32,* 29–37.

Burris, B. H. (1983). *No room at the top: Unemployment and alienation in the corporation.* New York: Praeger.

Buss, D. (1985). Human mate selection. *American Scientist, 73*(1), 47–51.

Butler, C. A. (1976). New data about female sexual response. *Journal of Sex and Marital Therapy, 2,* 40–46.

Butler, R. (1975). *Why survive: Being old in America.* New York: Harper & Row.

Butler, R., Damarin, F., Beaulieu, C., Schwebel, A., & Thorn, B. (1989). Assessing cognitive coping strategies for acute post-surgical pain. *Psychological Assessment: A Journal of Consulting and Clinical Psychology, 1*(1), 41–45.

Butler, R. N. (1971, December). The life review. *Psychology Today, 89,* 49–51.

Butler, R. N. (1975). *Why survive? Being old in America.* New York: Harper & Row.

Butler, R. N. (1984). Senile dementia: reversible and irreversible. 198*Counseling Psychology, 12*(2), 75–79.

Butterfield-Picard, H., & Mague, J. (1982). Hospice, the adjective, not the noun: The future of a national priority. *American Psychologist, 37*(11), 1254–1259.

Cabral, R. J., Best, J., & Paton, A. (1975). *American Journal of Psychiatry, 132,* 1052–1054.

Caldwell, E. (1959). *Creating better social climate in the classroom through sociometric techniques.* San Francisco: Fearon.

Campbell, A. (1975). The American way of mating: Marriage si, children only maybe. *Psychology Today, 8*(12), 37–42.

Campbell, A. (1981). *The sense of well-being in America.* New York: McGraw-Hill.

Cancer Care. (1970). *Catastrophic illness in the seventies: Critical issues and complex decisions.* New York: Cancer Care and National Cancer Foundation.

Cannon, W. B. (1967). *The wisdom of the body.* New York: W. W. Norton. (Original work published 1932)

Caplan, F. (1981). *The first twelve months of life.* New York: Bantam.

Caplan, F. (Ed.). (1973). *The first twelve months of life: Your baby's growth month by month.* New York: Grosset & Dunlap.

Caplan, G. (1964). *Principles of preventive psychiatry.* New York: Basic Books.

Caplan, G. (1974). *Support systems and community mental health.* New York: Behavior Publications.

Card, J. J., Steel, L., & Abeles, R. P. (1980). Sex differences in realization of individual potential for achievement. *Journal of Vocational Behavior, 17,* 1–21.

Cargan, L., & Melko, M. (1982). *Singles: Myths and realities.* Beverly Hills, CA: Sage Publications.

Carnegie, D. (1981). *How to win friends and influence people* (rev. ed.). New York: Simon & Schuster. (Original work published 1936)

Carney, R., & Wells, J. (1987). Career decision-making in late adolescence. *Journal of Vocational Behavior, 31,* 217–221.

Carter, E. A., & McGoldrick, M. (1980). *The family life cycle: A framework for family therapy.* New York: Gardner Press.

Carver, C., & Scheier, M. (1978). Self-focusing effects of dispositional self-consciousness, mirror presence, and audience presence. *Journal of Personality and Social Psychology, 36*(3), 324–332.

Cash, T., & Derlega, V. (1978). The matching hypothesis: Physical attractiveness among same-sex friends. *Personality and Social Psychology Bulletin, 4,* 240–243.

Cauthery, P., Stanway, A., & Stanway, P. (1983). *Loving sex: A lifetime guide.* New York: Stein & Day.

Cavan, R. S. (1971). Unemployment: Crisis of the common man. In J. P. Wiseman (Ed.), *People as partners: Individuals and family relationships in today's world.* San Francisco: Canfield Press.

Cheek, J., & Busch, C. (1981). The influence of shyness on loneliness in a new situation. *Personality and Social Psychology Bulletin, 7*(4), 572–577.

Chess, S., & Thomas, A. (1982). Infant bonding: Mystique and reality. *American Journal of Orthopsychiatry, 52,* 213–222.

Chess, S., & Thomas, A. (1987). *Know your child.* New York: Basic Books.

Childress, A. R., McLellan, A. T. & O'Brien, C. P. (1985). Behavioral therapies for substance abuse. *The International Journal of Addictions, 20,* 947–969.

Cianni, M., & Weitz, A. (1986). The technological society: implications for women in the workplace. *Journal of Counseling and Development, 64,* 63–66.

Cimbalo, R. S., Faling, V., & Mousaw, P. (1976). The course of love: A cross-sectional design. *Psychological Reports, 38,* 1292–1294.

Clark, M. (1980, June 23). The curse of hyperactivity. *Newsweek* pp. 59–62.

Clarke, A. (1952). An examination of the operation of residential propinquity as a factor in mate selection. *American Sociological Review, 17,* 17–22.

Clarke-Stewart, A., & Fein, G. (1983). Early childhood programs. In P. Mussen, M. Haith, & J. Campos (Eds.), *Handbook of child psychology: Vol. II. Infancy and developmental psychobiology,* pp. 917–1000. New York: Wiley.

Clausen, J. (1975). The social meaning of differential physical and sexual maturation. In S. Dragastin & G. Elder (Eds.), *Adolescence in the life cycle.* Washington, DC: Hemisphere.

Clayton, P. J., Halikes, J. A., & Maurice, W. L. (1971). The bereavement of the widowed. *Diseases of the Nervous System, 32*(9), 597–604.

Cline, V. B., Mejia, J., Coles, J., Klein, N., & Cline, A. (1984). *Journal of Clinical Psychology, 40,* 691–704.

Clingempeel, W., & Segal, S. (1986). Stepparent-stepchild relationships and the psychological adjustment of children in stepmother and stepfather families. *Child Development, 57,* 474–484.

Coates, D. (1987). Gender differences in the structure and support characteristics of black adolescents' social networks. *Sex Roles, 17*(11/12), 667–687.

Cobb, S. (1974). Physiologic changes in men whose jobs were abolished. *Journal of Psychosomatic Research, 18,* 245–258.

Coberly, L., & Newquist, J. (1984). Incentives for hiring older workers. Are employers interested? *Aging and Work, 6*(1), 37–47.

Cochran, L. (1983). Implicit versus explicit importance of career values in making decisions. *Journal of Counseling Psychology, 30*(2), 188–193.

Cochran, L., & Claspell, E. (1987). *The meaning of grief.* Westport, CT: Greenwood Press.

Cofer, C. N., & Appley, M. H. (1964). *Motivation: Theory and research.* New York: John Wiley & Sons.

Cohen, C. I., Teresi, J., & Holmes, D. (1985). Social networks, stress, and physical health: A longitudinal study of an inner-city elderly population. *Journal of Gerontology, 40*(4), 478–486.

Cohen, S., & McKay, G. (1985). Social support, stress, and the buffering hypothesis: A theoretical analysis. In A. Baum, J. Singer, & S. Taylor (Eds.), *Handbook of psychology and health, Vol. 4.* Hillsdale, NJ: Erlbaum.

Cohen, S., & Hoberman, H. (1983). Positive events and social supports as buffers of life change stress. *Journal of Applied Social Psychology, 13,* 99–121.

Cohen, S. L., & Sands, L. (1978). The effects of order of exercise presentation on assessment center performances: One standardization concern. *Personnel Psychology, 31,* 35–47.

Cole, P., & Kaslow, N. (1988). Interactional and cognitive strategies for affect regulation: A developmental perspective on childhood depression. In L. Alloy (Ed.), *Cognitive processes in depression.* New York: Guilford Press.

Coleman, L. (1987). *Suicide clusters.* Winchester, MA: Farber & Farber.

Coles, G. (1987). The learning mystique: A critical look at "learning disabilities." New York: Pantheon.

Coles, R. (1970). *Erik H. Erikson: The growth of his work.* Boston: Little, Brown.

Coles, R. (1977). *Eskimos, Chicanos, and Indians.* Boston: Little, Brown.

Collins, J. K. (1974). Adolescent dating intimacy: Norms and peer expectations. *Journal of Youth and Adolescence, 3*(4), 317–328.

Collins, T. (1978). *What you don't know can hurt you: Retirement Living Magazine's guide to planning for your successful retirement.* New York.

Comfort, A. (1976). *A good age.* New York: Simon & Schuster.

Cookerly, J. R. (1980). Does marital therapy do any lasting good? *Journal of Marital and Family Therapy,* 393–397.

Coping with cancer: A resource for the health professional. (1980). NIH Pub. No. 80–2080. Bethesda, MD: National Cancer Institute.

Costa, P. T., Jr., & McCrae, R. R. (1983). Contribution of personality research to an understanding of stress and aging. In H. I. McCubbin (Ed.), *Social stress and the family: Advances and developments in family stress theory and research* (pp. 157–173). New York: The Haworth Press.

Cowan, R. (1971, January 21). The new minority: Senior citizens as victims of geronticide. *The Village Voice.*

Coyne, J. C., & Lazarus, R. S. (1980). Cognitive style, stress perception, and coping. In L. Kutash, et al. (Eds.), *Handbook on stress and anxiety: Contemporary knowledge, theory, and treatment.* San Francisco: Jossey-Bass.

Crites, J. O. (1962). Parental identification in relation to vocational interest development. *Journal of Education Psychology, 53*(6), 262–270.

Crome, L. (1989). *Unbroken: Resistance and survival in the concentration camps.* NY: Schocken.

Crouter, A., Perry-Jenkins, M., Huston, T., & McHale, S. (1987). Processes underlying father involvement in dual-earner and single-earner families. *Developmental Psychology, 23*(3), 432–440.

Crozier, B. (1973). *De Gaulle* (pp. 672–73, 680–81, 683–84). New York: Scribner's.

Cuber, J., & Haroff, P. (1980). Five types of marriage. In J. Henslin (Ed.), *Marriage and family in a changing society.* New York: Free Press.

Cunningham, J., Braiker, H., & Kelley, H. (1982). Marital-status and sex differences in problems reported by married and cohabiting couples. *Psychology of Women Quarterly, 6*(4), 415–427.

Curran, J. P. (1984). The social psychology of sexual behavior. In K. Deaux & L. Wrightsman (Eds.), *Social psychology in the 1980's* (4th ed.). Belmont, CA: Brooks Cole.

Custer, R. F. (1987). The diagnosis and scope of pathological gambling. In T. Galski (Ed.), *The handbook of pathological gambling.* Springfield, IL: C. E. Thomas.

Cutrona, C. (1982). Transition to college: Loneliness and the process of social adjustment. In L. Peplau & D. Perlman (Eds.), *Loneliness: A sourcebook of current theory, research and therapy.* New York: Wiley-Interscience.

Davanloo, H. (1980). *Short-term dynamic psychotherapy.* New York: Jason Aronson.

Davidoff, L. (1980). *Introduction to psychology.* New York: McGraw-Hill.

Davidson, G. W. (1988). Hospice care for the dying. In H. Wass, F. Berardo, & R. Neimeyer (Eds.), *Dying: Facing the facts* (2nd ed.). New York: Hemisphere.

Davidson, L. M., & Baum, A. (1986). Chronic stress and posttraumatic stress disorders. *Journal of Consulting and Clinical Psychology, 54*(3), 303–308.

Davies, D. R., & Sparrow, P. R. (1985). Age and work behavior. In N. Charness (Ed.), *Aging and human performance* (pp. 293–331). Chichester: John Wiley & Sons.

Davis, K. (1985). Near and dear: Friendship and love compared. *Psychology Today, 19*(2), 22–30.

Davis, K., & Todd, M. (1981). Assessing friendships: Prototypes, paradigm cases and relationship description. In S. Duck & D. Perlman (Eds.), *Understanding personal relationships* (pp. 17–38). Beverly Hills, CA: Sage Publications.

Davitz, J., & Davitz, L. (1976). *Making it from 40 to 50.* New York: Random House.

De Casper, A., & Fifer, W. (1980). Of human bonding: Newborns prefer their mother's voices. *Science, 208,* 1174–1176.

De Meuse, K. P. (1985). The relationship between life events and indices of classroom performance. *Teaching of Psychology, 12*(3), 146–149.

Dean, A. (1985). *Depression in multidisciplinary perspectives.* New York: Brunner/Mazel.

DeLamater, J. (1987). Gender differences in sexual scenarios. In K. Kelley (Ed.), *Females, males, and sexuality.* Albany, NY: State University of New York Press.

DeLora, J. S., & Warren, C. (1977). *Understanding sexual interaction.* Boston: Houghton Mifflin.

DeMaris, A., & Leslie, G. (1984). Cohabitation with the future spouse: Its influence upon marital satisfaction and communication. *Journal of Marriage and the Family, 46,* 77–84.

Dendato, K. M., & Diener, D. (1986). Effectiveness of cognitive/relaxation therapy and study-skills training in reducing self-reported anxiety and improving the academic performance of test-anxious students. *Journal of Counseling Psychology, 33*(2), 131–135.

Diamond, G., & Bachman, J. (1986). High school seniors and the nuclear threat, 1975–1984: Political and mental health implications of concern and despair. In M. Schwebel (Ed.), *Mental health implications of life in the nuclear age.* Armonk, NY: M. E. Sharpe, Inc. (Also, *International Journal of Mental Health, 15*(1–3), 210–241.)

Dickens, W., & Perlman, D. (1981). Friendship over the life-cycle. In S. Duck & R. Gilmour (Eds.), *Personal relationships Vol. 2: Developing personal relationships* (pp. 91–122). New York: Academic Press.

Dodge, C. P., & Raundalen, M. (Eds.). (1987). *War, violence, and children in Uganda.* Oslo: Norwegian University Press.

Dohrenwend, B. S. (1973). Social status and stressful life events. *Journal of Personality and Social Psychology, 28,* 225–235.

Dollard, J., & Miller, N. E. (1950). *Personality and psychotherapy.* New York: McGraw-Hill.

Donaldson, W. V. (1979, November 1). Mid-career change: From city hall to city zoo. *Public Administration Times, 2*(21), 3.

Donnelly, K. (1986). *Recovering from the loss of a sibling.* New York: Aronson.

Dorn, F., & Welch, N. (1985). Assessing career mythology: A profile of high school students. *The School Counselor, 33*(2), 136–142.

Doty, L. (1987). *Communication and assertion skills for older persons.* Washington: Hemisphere.

Douglas, P., & Pinsky, L. (1987). *The essential AIDS fact book.* New York: Pocket Books.

Driscoll, R., Davis, K., & Liptez, M. (1972). Parental interference and romantic love: The Romeo and Juliet effect. *Journal of Personality and Social Psychology, 24,* 1–10.

Duck, S. (1977). *The study of acquaintance.* Westmead, England: Saxon House.

Duck, S. (1988). *Relating to others.* Chicago: Dorsey Press.

Duellea, G. (1979, April 26). Health survey finds poor habits prevail. *New York Times,* C1, C8.

Duke, P., Carlsmith, J., Jennings, D., Martin, J., Dornbusch, S., Gross, R., & Siegel-Gorelick, B. (1982). Educational correlates of early and late sexual maturation in adolescence. *The Journal of Pediatrics, 100*(4), 633–637.

Dunbar, F. (1955). *Mind and body: Psychosomatic medicine.* New York: Random House.

Durlak, J. A. (1973). Relationships between attitudes toward life and death among elderly women. *Developmental Psychology, 8*(1), 146.

Dusay, J. M. (1986). Transactional analysis. In I. L. Kutash & A. Wolf (Eds.), *Psychotherapist's casebook.* San Francisco: Jossey-Bass.

Duvall, E. (1977). *Marriage and family development* (5th ed.). New York: J. B. Lippincott.

Eastman, M., & Marziller, J. (1984). Theoretical and methodological difficulties in Bandura's self-efficacy theory. *Cognitive Theory and Research, 8*(3), 213–229.

Edelman, R. J. (1985). Dealing with embarrassing events: Socially anxious and non-socially anxious groups compared. *British Journal of Clinical Psychology, 24,* 281–288.

Ehrenberg, O., & Ehrenberg, M. (1977). *The psychotherapy maze.* New York: Holt, Rinehart & Winston.

Ellis, A. (1962). *Reason and emotion in psychotherapy.* New York: Lyle Stuart.

Ellis, A. (1984). Rational-emotive therapy. In R. J. Corsini (Ed.), *Current psychotherapies* (3rd ed.). Itasca, IL: Peacock.

Ellis, A., & Bernard, M. E. (1986). What is rational-emotive therapy (RET)? In A. Ellis & R. M. Grieger (Eds.), *Handbook of rational-emotive therapy.* New York: Springer.

Ellis, A., & Bernard, M. (Eds.). (1985). *Clinical applications of rational-emotive therapy.* New York: Plenum.

Ellis, A., & Dryden, W. (1987). *The practice of rational-emotive therapy.* New York: Springer.

Ellis, A., & Grieger, R. (Eds.). (1986). *Handbook of rational-emotive therapy.* New York: Springer.

Ellison, J., Blum, N., & Barsky, A. (1986). Repeat visits in the psychiatric emergency service: A critical review of the data. *Hospital and Community Psychiatry, 37*(1), 37–41.

Engel, G. L. (1962). *Psychological development in health and disease.* Philadelphia: W. B. Saunders.

Epstein, N. B., & Vlok, L. A. (1981). Research on the results of psychotherapy: A summary of evidence. *American Journal of Psychiatry, 138,* 1027–1035.

Epstein, S. (1967). Toward a unified theory of anxiety. In B. A. Maher (Ed.), *Progress in experimental personality research* (Vol. 4). New York: Academic Press.

Epstein, S. (1972). The nature of anxiety with emphasis upon its relationship to expectancy. In C. D. Spielberger (Ed.), *Anxiety: Current trends in theory and research* (Vol. 2). New York: Academic Press.

Erickson, E. (1982). *The life cycle completed.* New York: W. W. Norton.

Erikson, E. H. (1949). Ruth Benedict. In A. L. Kroeber (Ed.), *Ruth Fulton Benedict, a memorial* (pp. 14–17). New York: Viking Fund. Cited in R. Coles (1970). *Erik H. Erikson: The growth of his work.* Boston: Little, Brown.

Erikson, E. H. (1959). Identity and the life cycle. *Psychological Issues* (Vol. I, No. 1). New York: International Universities Press.

Erikson, E. H. (1963). *Childhood and society* (2nd ed.). New York: W. W. Norton.

Erikson, E. H. (1968). *Identity: Youth and crisis.* New York: W. W. Norton.

Erikson, E. H. (1976, Spring). Reflections on Dr. Borg's life cycle. *Daedalus, 105*(2), 1–28.

Etaugh, C. (1983). The influence of environmental factors on sex differences in children's play. In

M. Liss (Ed.), *Social and cognitive skills: Sex roles in children's play* (pp. 1–19). New York: Academic Press.

Ettedgui, E., & Bridges, M. (1985). Posttraumatic stress disorder. *Psychiatric Clinics of North America, 8*(1), 89–103.

Eysenck, H. J. (1987). Preface. In H. J. Eysenck & I. Martin (Eds.), *Theoretical foundations of behavior therapy.* **New York: Plenum.**

Facts on file (1988, January 22). Marijuana use at 13-year low. New York: Facts of File, 34–35.

Farina, G., Ghila, D., Boudreau, L., Allen, J., & Sherman, M. (1971). Mental illness and the impact of believing others know about it. *Journal of Abnormal Psychology, 77,* 1–5.

Feiring, C., & Lewis, M. (1987). The child's social network: Sex differences from three to six years. *Sex Roles, 17*(11/12), 621–636.

Fenigstein, A. (1984). Self-consciousness and the overperception of self as a target. *Journal of Personality and Social Psychology, 47*(4), 860–870.

Fenz, W. D., & Epstein, S. (1967). Gradient of physiological arousal in parachutists as a function of an approaching jump. *Psychosomatic Medicine, 29,* 33–51.

Festinger, L., Schachter, S., & Back, K. (1950). *Social pressures in informal groups: A study of a housing community.* New York: Harper.

Feuerstein, R. (1979). *The dynamic assessment of retarded performer.* Baltimore, MD: University Folk Press.

Feuerstein, R., Rand, Y., Hoffman, M. B., & Miller, R. (1980). *Instrumental enrichment.* Baltimore: University Park Press.

Finkel, S. I., & Cohen, G. (1982). Guest editorial: The mental health of the aging. *The Gerontologist, 22*(3), 227–228.

Fischer, J. (1981). Transitions in relationship style from adolescence to young adulthood. *Journal of Youth and Adolescence, 10,* 11–23.

Fish, W., & Waldhart-Letzel, E. (1981). Suicide and children. *Death Education, 5,* 215–222.

Fishbein, H. (1984). *The psychology of infancy and childhood.* Hillsdale, New Jersey: Erlbaum.

Fisher, J. D., Bell, A. P., & Baum, A. (1984). *Environmental psychology* (2nd ed.). New York: Holt, Rinehart & Winston.

Fleming, R., Baum, A., Gisriel, M., & Gatchel, R. J. (1982). Mediating influence of social support on stress at Three Mile Island. *Journal of Human Stress, 8,* 14–22.

Fraiberg, S. (1977). *Every child's birthright: In defense of mothering.* New York: Basic Books.

Framo, J. L. (1986). Couples group therapy with family-of-origin sessions. In I. L. Kutash & A. Wolf (Eds.), *Psychotherapist's casebook.* San Francisco: Jossey-Bass.

Frank, J. D. (1973). *Persuasion and healing* (rev. ed.). Baltimore, MD: The Johns Hopkins University Press.

Frank, R. (1931). The hormonal causes of premenstrual tension. *Archives of Neurological Psychiatry,* 99–106.

Frank, V. E. (1955). *The doctor and the soul: From psychotherapy to logotherapy* (2nd ed.). Trans. by R. & C. Winston. New York: Alfred A. Knopf.

Frankl, V. (1984). *Man's search for meaning* (3rd ed.). New York: Touchstone Books.

Freud, A. (1966). *The ego and the mechanisms of defense* (rev. ed.). Trans. by C. Maines. New York: International Universities Press. (Original work published 1936)

Freud, A. (1969). Adolescence as a developmental disturbance. In G. Caplan & S. LeBovici (Eds.), *Adolescence: Psycho-social perspective.* New York: Basic Books.

Freud, S. (1933). *Standard edition of the complete psychological works of Sigmund Freud* (Vol. 22), J. Strachey (Ed.). London: Hogarth Press.

Freud, S. (1936). *The problem of anxiety.* New York: W. W. Norton.

Freud, S. (1938). *The interpretation of dreams* (3rd English ed.). Trans. by A. A. Brill. In A. A. Brill (Ed.), *The basic writings of Sigmund Freud.* New York: Modern Library.

Freud, S. (1947). *Leonardo da Vinci: A study in psychosexuality.* New York: Random House. (Original work published 1910)

Freud, S. (1948). *Inhibitions, symptoms and anxiety.* London: Hogarth Press. (Original work published 1926)

Freud, S. (1949). *New introductory lectures on psychoanalysis.* New York: W. W. Norton. (Original work published 1933)

Freud, S. (1949). *An outline of psychoanalysis.* New York: W. W. Norton. (Original work published 1938)

Freud, S. (1959). Mourning and melancholia. In E. Jones (Ed.), *Collected papers of Sigmund Freud* (Vol. 4). New York: Basic Books. (Original work published 1917)

Freud, S. (1959). Psychoanalytic theory. In E. Jones (Ed.), *Collected papers of Sigmund Freud* (Vol. 5). New York: Basic Books.

Freud, S. (1960). *Jokes and their relation to the unconscious.* Trans. by J. Strachey. New York: W. W. Norton. (Original work published 1905)

Freud, S. (1964). Anxiety and instinctual life. In *New introductory lectures in psychoanalysis.* Trans. by J. Strachey. New York: W. W. Norton. (Original work published 1933)

Freud, S. (1967). *Beyond the pleasure principle.* New York: Bantam. (Original work published 1920)

Freud, S. (1969). *A general introduction to psychoanalysis.* New York: Simon & Schuster. (Original work published 1938)

Fried, B. (1967). *The middle-age crisis.* New York: Harper & Row.

Friedman, H. S., & Booth-Kewley, S. (1987). The "disease-prone personality": A meta-analytic view of the construct. *American Psychologist, 42*(6), 539–555.

Friedman, M., & Rosenman, R. H. (1974). *Type A behavior and your heart.* New York: Knopf.

Fromm, E. (1974). *The art of loving.* New York: Harper & Row. (Original work published 1956)

Fuller-von Bozzay, G. (1986). Biofeedback. In I. L. Kutash & A. Wolf (Eds.), *Psychotherapist's casebook.* San Francisco: Jossey-Bass.

Furman, E. (1974). *A child's parent dies.* New Haven, CT: Yale University Press.

Furstenberg, F. F., Jr. (1981). Remarriage and intergenerational relations. In J. G. March (Ed.), *Aging: Stability and change in the family* (pp. 115–141). New York: Academic Press.

Futterman, A. D., & Shapiro, D. (1986). A review of biofeedback for mental disorders. *Hospital and Community Psychiatry, 37,* 27–33.

Gadow, K. (1985). Relative efficacy of pharmacological, behavioral, and combination treatments for enhancing academic performance. *Clinical Psychology Review, 5,* 513–533.

Gagnon, J. (1977). *Human sexualities.* Glenview, IL: Scott, Foresman.

Gallup, G. (1986). Unique features of human sexuality in the context of evolution. In D. Byrne & K. Kelley (Eds.), *Alternative approaches to the study of sexual behavior.* Hillsdale, NJ: Lawrence Erlbaum Associates.

Gallwey, W. T. (1979). *The inner game of tennis.* New York: Random House.

Gandy, G. L. (1973). Birth order and vocational interest. *Developmental Psychology, 9*(3), 406–410.

Ganong, L., & Coleman, M. (1986). A comparison of clinical and empirical literature on children in stepfamilies. *Journal of Marriage and the Family, 48,* 309–318.

Garmezy, N. (1983). Stressors of childhood. In N. Garmezy & M. Rutter (Eds.), *Stress, coping, and development in children* (pp. 43–85). New York: McGraw-Hill.

Garmezy, N. (1985). Stress, resistant factors: The search for protective factors. In J. Stevenson (Ed.), *Recent research in developmental psychopathology.* Oxford: Pergamon Press.

Garmezy, N., & Rutter, M. (Eds.). (1988). *Stress, coping and development in children.* Baltimore, MD: Johns Hopkins University Press.

Garner, A. M., & Wenar, C. (1959). *The mother-child interaction in psychosomatic disorders.* Urbana, IL: University of Illinois Press.

Garner, D., Garfinkel, P., Schwartz, D., & Thompson, M. (1980). Cultural expectations of thinness in women. *Psychological Reports, 47,* 483–491.

Gatz, M., & Pearson, C. G. (1988). Ageism revised and the provision of psychological services. *American Psychologist, 43,* 184–188.

Gay, P. (1988). *Freud: A life for our time.* New York: W. W. Norton.

George, L., & Neufeld, R. (1985). Cognition and symptomatology in schizophrenia. *Schizophrenia Bulletin, 11*(2), 264–285.

Gibbs, J. C. (1985). Moody's vs. Siegel's interpretation of the near death experiences: An evaluation based on recent research. Anabiosis—*The Journal of Near Death, 5*(2), 67–81.

Giles-Sims, G. (1984). The stepparent role: Expectations, behavior, and sanctions. *Journal of Family Issues, 5,* 116–130.

Gillan, P., & Gillan, R. (1977). *Sex therapy today.* New York: Grove Press.

Ginzberg, E. (1972). Toward a theory of occupational choice: A restatement. *Vocational Guidance Quarterly, 20,* 169–176.

Ginzberg, E., Ginsburg, S. W., Axelrod, S., & Herma, J. L. (1951). *Occupational choice: An approach to general theory.* New York: Columbia University Press.

Glass, D. C. (1977). *Behavior patterns, stress and coronary disease.* Hillsdale, NJ: Erlbaum.

Glass, D. C., & Singer, J. E. (1972). *Urban stress: Experiments on noise and social stressors.* New York: Academic Press.

Glass, D. C., Singer, J. E., Leonard, H. S., Krantz, P., Cohen, S., & Cummings, H. (1973). Perceived control of aversive stimulation and the reduction of stress responses. *Journal of Personality, 41,* 577–595.

Glick, I., & Kessler, D. (1980). *Marital and family therapy.* New York: Grune & Stratton.

Glick, I. O., Weiss, R. S., & Parkes, C. M. (1974). *The first year of bereavement.* New York: John Wiley.

Glick, P., & Spanier, G. (1980). Married and unmarried cohabitation in the United States. *Journal of Marriage and the Family, 42*(1), 19–30.

Goethals, G. W., & Klos, D. S. (1976). *Experiencing youth: First person accounts.* Boston: Little, Brown.

Goffman, E. (1963). *Stigma: Notes on the management of spoiled identity.* Englewood Cliffs, NJ: Prentice-Hall.

Golan, N. (1980). Using situational crises to ease transitions in the life cycle. *American Journal of Orthopsychiatry, 50,* 542–550.

Golan, N. (1983). *Passing through transition: A guide for practitioners.* New York: Free Press.

Golan, N. (1986). *The perilous bridge: Helping clients through mid-life transition.* New York: Free Press.

Gold, S. R., Gold, R. G., Milner, J. S., & Robertson, K. R. (1986–87). Day dreaming and mental health. *Imagination in Cognition and Personality, 6,* 65–73.

Goldenberg, I. (1974). Reading groups and some aspects of teacher behavior. In F. Kaplan & S. Sarason (Eds.), *The Psycho-educational clinic papers and research studies.* Massachusetts Department of Mental Health Monograph, Vol. 4.

Goldenberg, I., & Goldenberg, H. (1980). *Family therapy: An overview.* Monterey, CA: Brooks/Cole.

Goldenson, R. (1984). *Longman's dictionary of psychology and psychiatry.* New York: Longman.

Goldin, V., & Winston, A. (1985). The impact of short-term dynamic psychotherapy on psychoanalytic psychotherapy. In A. Winston (Ed.), *Clinical and research issues in short-term dynamic psychotherapy.* Washington: American Psychiatric Press.

Goldman, R., & Goldman, J. (1982). *Children's sexual thinking.* London, England: Routledge & Kegan Paul.

Goldstein, A. P., & Krasner, L. (1987). *Modern applied psychology.* New York: Pergamon.

Goleman, D. (1980, August). Leaving home: Is there a right time to go? *Psychology Today,* 52–61.

Gonsiorek, J. (1982). Results of psychological testing on homosexual populations. In W. Paul, J. Weinrich, J. Gonsiorek, & M. Hotvedt (Eds.), *Homesexuality: Social, psychological and biological issues.* Beverly Hills, CA: Sage Publications.

Goodman, G. (1984). The child witness. *Journal of Social Issues, 40,* 1–175.

Goodwin, D. W. (1986). *Anxiety.* New York: Oxford University Press.

Goodwin, J. (1980). The etiology of combat-related posttraumatic stress disorders. In T. William (Ed.), *Post-traumatic stress disorders of the Vietnam veteran.* Cincinnati, OH: Disabled American Veterans.

Gottesman, I., & Shields, J. (1982). *Schizophrenia: The epigenetic puzzle.* New York: Cambridge University Press.

Gottlieb, B., & Pancer, S. M. (1987). Social networks and the transition to parenthood. In G. Michaels & W. Goldberg (Eds.), *The transition to parenthood* (pp. 235–269). New York: Cambridge University Press.

Gould, M., Wunsch-Hitzig, R., & Dohrenwend, B. (1981). Estimating the prevalence of childhood pathology: A critical review. *Journal of American Academy of Child Psychiatry, 20,* 462–476.

Gould, R. L. (1972). The phases of adult life: A study in developmental psychology. *American Journal of Psychiatry, 129*(5), 33–43.

Gould, R. L. (1978). *Transformations: Growth and change in adult life.* New York: Simon & Schuster.

Grasha, A., & Kirschenbaum, D. (1980). *Psychology of adjustment and competence.* Cambridge, MA: Winthrop.

Greenacre, P. (1957). The childhood of the artists: Libidinal phase development and giftedness. In P. Greenacre (Ed.), *Psychoanalytic study of the child* Vol. 12 (pp. 27–72). New York: International Universities Press.

Greenberg, J., Bruess, C., & Sands, D. (1986). *Sexuality: Insights and issues.* Dubuque, IA: Wm. C. Brown.

Greenberg, M., & Morris, N. (1974). Engrossment: The newborn's impact upon the father. *American Journal of Orthopsychiatry, 44,* 520–531.

Greene, J. (1984). *The social and psychological origins of the climacteric syndrome.* London, England: Gower Publishing.

Greenfeld, J. (1977, June 29). Noah: Six years later. *The New York Times.*

Greer, G. (1986). Health style. *Vogue,* 232.

Greist, J. H., Jefferson, J. W., & Marks, I. M. (1986). *Anxiety and its treatment.* Washington: American Psychiatric Press.

Griffith, M. S. (1977). The influences of race on the therapeutic relationship. *Psychiatry, 40,* 27–40.

Grosskopf, D. (1983). *Sex and the married woman.* New York: Simon & Schuster.

Grossman, F. K., Eichler, L., & Winickoff, S. (1980). *Pregnancy, birth, and parenthood.* San Francisco: Jossey-Bass.

Grover, K., Paff-Bergen, L., Russell, C., & Schumm, W. (1984). The Kansas City marital satisfaction scale: A further brief report. *Psychological Reports, 54,* 629–630.

Guidubaldi, J., Cleminshaw, H., Perry, J., & McLoughin, C. (1983). The impact of parental divorce on children: Report of the nationwide NASP study. *School Psychology Review, 12*(3), 300–323.

Gunderson, J., & Zanarini, M. (1987). Current overview of the borderline diagnosis. *Journal of Clinical Psychiatry, 48*(8, Suppl), 5–11.

Gurin, P. (1981). Labor market experiences and expectancies. *Sex Roles, 7,* 1079–1092.

Gustafson, J. P. (1986). *The complex secret of brief psychotherapies.* New York: W. W. Norton.

Gupta, N., & Jenkins, G. (1985). Dual career couples: Stress, stressors, strains, and strategies. In T. Beehr & R. Bhagat (Eds.), *Human stress and cognition in organizations* (pp. 141–175). New York: Wiley.

Haan, N., & Day, D. (1974). A longitudinal study of change and sameness in personality development: Adolescence to later adulthood. *International Journal of Aging and Human Development, 5*(1), 11–39.

Haemmerlie, F., & Montgomery, R. (1982). Self-perception theory and unobtrusively biased interactions: A treatment for heterosexual anxiety. *Journal of Counseling Psychology, 29,* 362–370.

Haley, J. (1963). *Strategies of psychotherapy.* New York: Grune & Stratton.

Haley, J. (1976). *Problem-solving therapy: New strategies for effective family therapy.* New York: Harper & Row.

Haley, J. (1987). *Problem-solving therapy* (2nd ed.). San Francisco: Jossey-Bass.

Hall, C. S. (1954). *A primer of Freudian psychology.* New York: New American Library.

Hall, C. S., & Lindzey, G. (1978). *Theories of personality.* New York: Wiley.

Hall, D. T. (1986). Breaking career routines: Midcareer choice and identity. In D. T. Hall and associates (Ed.), *Career development in organizations* (pp. 120–139). San Francisco: Jossey-Bass.

Hall, D. T., & Foster, L. W. (1977). A psychological success cycle and goal setting: Goals, performance, and attitudes. *Academy of Management Journal, 20*(2), 282–290.

Hall, D. T., & Schneider, B. (1973). *Organizational climates and careers: The work lives of priests.* New York: Seminar Press.

Hall, R. (1979, April 28 & May 5). An obscure hurt: The sexuality of Henry James. *The New Republic* (pp. 25–31).

Halpern, H. (1982). *How to break your addiction to a person.* New York: McGraw-Hill.

Hamberger, L. K., & Lohr, J. M. (1984). *Stress and stress management.* New York: Springer.

Hamilton, K. P. (1981). Midas and other mid-life crises. In W. H. Norman and T. J. Scaramella (Eds.). *Mid-life: Developmental and clinical issues* (pp. 3–19). New York: Brunner/Mazel.

Hankoff, L. D. (1975, Fall). Adolescence and the crisis of dying. *Adolescence, 10*(39), 373–389.

Hansen, G. (1985). Perceived threats and marital jealousy. *Social Psychology Quarterly, 48*(3), 262–268.

Haraway, M., & Moss, L. (1983). Sex differences: The evidence from biology. In M. Liss (Ed.), *Social and cognitive skills: Sex roles in children's play* (pp. 22–44). New York: Academic Press.

Harlow, H. F. (1958). The nature of love. *American Psychologist, 13,* 673–685.

Harlow, H. F. (1971). *Learning to love.* San Francisco: Albion.

Harlow, H. F., & Harlow, M. K. (1962). Social deprivation in monkeys. *Scientific American, 207,* 136–146.

Harlow, H. F., & Harlow, M. K. (1966). Learning to love. *American Scientist, 54,* 244–272.

Harlow, H. F., & Harlow, M. K. (1969). Effects of various mother-infant relationships on rhesus monkey behaviors. In B. M. Foss (Ed.), *Determinants of infant behavior* (Vol. 4). New York: Barnes & Noble.

Harris, L., et al. (1979). *The Playboy report on American men: A study of the values, attitudes, and goals of U.S. males 18–49 years old.* Analysis and interpretation by W. Simon & P. Y. Miller. Chicago: Playboy Press.

Harris, T. (1967). *I'm Okay—You're OK.* New York: Harper & Row.

Harshbarger, D. (1975). Death and public policy: A research inquiry. In N. Datan & L. Ginsberg (Eds.), *Lifespan developmental psychology: Normative life crises.* New York: Academic Press.

Hatfield, E., & Traupmann, J. (1981). Intimate relationships: A perspective from equity theory. In S. Duck & R. Gilmour (Eds.), *Personal relationships* (pp. 165–178). London: Academic Press.

Haverman, B., Halberstadt, G., & Burkhauser, M. (1984). Effects of handicap on obtaining employment. *Personnel Psychology, 37,* 301–306.

Hayes, J., & Nutman, P. (1981). *Understanding the unemployed: The psychological effects of unemployment.* London: Tavistock Publications.

Haynes, J. (1981). *Divorce mediation.* NY: Springer.

Heiman, J., LoPiccolo, L., & LoPiccolo, J. (1976). *Becoming orgasmic: A sexual growth program for women.* Englewood Cliffs, NJ: Prentice-Hall.

Helmreich, R. L., & Collins, B. E. (1967). Situational determinants of affiliative preference under stress. *Journal of Personality and Social Psychology, 6,* 79–85.

Helsing, K. J., Szklo, M., & Comstock, C. W. (1981). Factors associated with mortality after widowhood. *American Journal of Public Health, 17,* 802–809.

Henning, M. (1978). Career development for women executives. Doctoral Dissertation. Quoted in R. L. Gould, *Transformations: Growth and change in adult life.* New York: Simon & Schuster.

Henslin, J. (1980). Cohabitation: Its context and meaning. In J. Henslin (Ed.), *Marriage and family in a changing society.* New York: Free Press.

Hergenhahn, B. (1984). *An introduction to theories of personality.* Englewood Cliffs, NJ: Prentice Hall.

Herink, R. (Ed.). (1980). *The psychotherapy handbook.* New York: New American Library.

Hersen, M., Eisler, R., & Miller, P. (Eds.). (1988). *Progress in behavior modification* Vol. 22. Beverly Hills, CA: Sage Publications.

Hess, B. (1972). Friendship. In M. Riley, M. Johnson, & A. Foner (Eds.), *Aging and society* (Vol. 3). New York: Russel Sage Foundation.

Hessellund, H. (1977). Masturbation and sexual fantasies in married couples. In D. Byrne & L. Byrne (Eds.), *Exploring human sexuality.* New York: Thomas Y. Crowell.

Hetherington, E. M., Cox, M., & Cox, R. (1978, May). *Family interaction and the social, emotional, and cognitive development of children following divorce.* Paper presented at Symposium on the Family: Setting Priorities, Washington, DC.

Hiestand, D. L. (1971). *Changing careers after 35.* New York: Columbia University Press.

Hill, C., Rubin, Z., & Peplau, L. (1976). Breakups before marriage: The end of 103 affairs. *Journal of Social Issues, 32*(1), 147–168.

Hilton, T. L. (1962). Career decision making. *Journal of Counseling Psychology, 9,* 291–298.

Himle, D. P., Thyer, B. A., Papsdorf, J. D., & Caldwell, S. (1984). In vivo distraction-coping in the treatment of test anxiety: A 1–year follow-up study. *Journal of Clinical Psychology, 40,* 458–462.

Hiroto, D. S., & Seligman, M. E. P. (1975). Generality of learned helplessness in man. *Journal of Personality and Social Psychology, 31,* 311–327.

Hite, S. (1976). *The Hite report.* New York: Macmillan.

Hoelter, J., & Harper, L. (1987). Structural and interpersonal family influences on adolescent self-conception. *Journal of Marriage and the Family, 49,* 129–139.

Holahan, C. J., & Moos, R. H. (1985). Life stress and health: Personality, coping, and family support in stress resistance. *Journal of Personality and Social Psychology, 49*(3), 739–747.

Holahan, C. J., & Moos, R. H. (1986). Personality, coping, and family resources in stress resistance: A longitudinal analysis. *Journal of Personality and Social Psychology, 51*(2), 389–395.

Holden, C. (1986). Counting the homeless. *Science, 234,* 281–282.

Holland, J. (1985). *Making vocational choices: A theory of vocational personalities and work environments.* Englewood Cliffs, NJ: Prentice-Hall.

Hollon, S. D., & Beck, A. T. (1986). Cognitive and cognitive-behavioral psychotherapies. In S. L. Garfield & A. E. Bergin (Eds.), *Handbook of psychotherapy and behavior change* (3rd ed.). New York: Wiley.

Holmes, K. K. (1975, February). Average risk of gonorrheal infection after exposure. *Medical Aspects of Human Sexuality, 83.*

Holmes, T. H., & Masuda, M. (1972, April). Psychosomatic syndrome. *Psychology Today, 106,* 71–72.

Holmes, T. H., & Masuda, M. (1974). Life changes and illness susceptibility. In B. S. Dohrenwend & B. P. Dohrenwend (Eds.), *Stressful life events: Their nature and effects.* New York: John Wiley & Sons.

Holmes, T. H., & Rahe, R. H. (1967, April). The social readjustment rating scale. *Journal of Psychosomatic Research, 11*(2), 213–218.

Holroyd, K. A., & Lazarus, R. S. (1982). Stress, coping and somatic adaptation. In L. Goldberger & S. Breznitz (Eds.), *Handbook of stress: Theoretical and clinical aspects.* New York: Free Press.

Holt, J. (1978). *Never too late.* New York: Delacorte.

Hopkins, J., Marcus, M., & Campbell, S. B. (1984). Postpartum depression: A critical review. *Psychological Bulletin, 95*(3), 498–515.

Horn, J. L. (1982). The aging of human abilities. In B. Wolman (Ed.), *Handbook of developmental psychology* (pp. 847–870). Englewood Cliffs, NJ: Prentice-Hall.

Horney, K. (1937). *The neurotic personality of our time*. New York: W. W. Norton.

Horowitz, M. (1986). Stress-response syndromes: A review of post-traumatic and adjustment disorders. *Hospital and Community Psychiatry, 37*(3), 241–249.

Horwitz, A. (1984). The economy and social pathology. *Annual Review of Sociology, 10*, 95–119.

Humphry, D., & Wickett, A. (1987). *The right to die*. Englewood Cliffs, NJ: Prentice-Hall.

Hunt, B., & Hunt, M. (1975). *Prime time: A guide to the pleasures and opportunities of the new middle age*. New York: Stein & Day.

Hunt, M. (1974). *Sexual behavior in the 1970s*. New York: Playboy Press.

Hunt, M. (1982). *The universe within: A new science explores the human mind*. New York: Simon & Schuster.

Huston, T., & Levinger, G. (1978). Interpersonal attraction and relationships. *Annual Review of Psychology, 29*, 115–156.

Hyde, J., & Linn, M. (Eds.). (1986). *The psychology of gender*. Baltimore: The Johns Hopkins University Press.

Insel, T. (1985). Obsessive-compulsive disorder. *Psychiatric Clinics of North America, 8*(1), 105–117.

Irish, R. K. (1973). *Go hire yourself an employer*. New York: Doubleday.

Iscoe, I., & Harris, L. (1984). Social and community interventions. *Annual Review of Psychology, 35*, 333–360.

Jacobson, E. (1938). *Progressive relaxation*. Chicago: University of Chicago Press.

Jacobson, E. (1978). *You must relax* (5th ed.). New York: McGraw-Hill.

Jacoby, S. (1974, February 17). Forty-nine million singles can't be all right. *New York Times Magazine*.

Jacques, A. (1965). *Midlife crisis as an opportunity for creativity*. Presented at the American Psychological Association Annual Meeting. Washington, DC.

Jacques, J., & Chason, K. (1979). Cohabitation: Its impact on marital success. *Family Coordinator, 28*, 35–39.

Jahoda, M. (1958). *Current concepts of positive mental health*. New York: Basic Books.

James, M. (1973). *Born to love*. Reading, MA: Addison-Wesley.

James, M., & Savary, L. (1976). *The heart of friendship*. New York: Harper & Row.

Jamison, P. & Gebhard, P. (1988) Penis size increase between flaccid and erect states: An analysis of the Kinsey data. *Journal of Sexuality Research 24* (1), 177–183.

Jaques, E. (1964). Death and the mid-life crisis. *International Journal of Psychoanalysis, 46*, 502–514.

Joan, P. (1986). *Preventing teenage suicide*. New York: Human Sciences Press.

Johnson, J. H. (1986). *Life events as stressors in childhood and adolescence*. Newbury Park, CA: Sage Publications.

Johnson, J. J., & McCutcheon, S. M. (1980). *Assessing life stress in older children and adolescents: Preliminary findings with the life events checklist*. Washington, DC: Hemisphere.

Johnson, S. M., & Greenberg, L. S. (1985). *Journal of Consulting and Clinical Psychology, 53*, 175–184.

Johnson, W. (1974). The fateful process of Mr. A talking to Mr. B. In R. Cathcart & L. Samovar (Eds.), *Small group communication*. Dubuque, IA: W. C. Brown.

Jones, B. E. (Ed.). (1986). *Treating the homeless: Urban psychiatry's challenge*. Washington: American Psychiatric Press.

Jones, E., Rhodewalt, F., Berglas, S., & Skelton, J. (1981). Effects of strategic self-presentation on subsequent self-esteem. *Journal of Personality and Social Psychology, 41*(3), 407–421.

Jones, M. C. (1926). The development of early behavior patterns in young children. *Journal of Genetic Psychology, 33*, 537–585.

Jones, M. C. (1957). The later careers of boys who are early- or late-maturing. *Child Development, 28*, 113–128.

Jones, M. C., & Mussen, P. H. (1958). Self-conceptions, motivations, and interpersonal attitudes of early- and late-maturing girls. *Child Development, 29*, 441–501.

Jones, W., Hobbs, S., & Hockenbury, D. (1982). Loneliness and social skills deficits. *Journal of Personality and Social Psychology, 42*, 682–689.

Jong, E. (1974). *Fear of flying*. New York: Signet.

Jourard, S. M. (1971). *The transparent self* (2nd ed.). New York: Van Nostrand.

Jourard, S. M. (1974). *Healthy personality: An approach from the viewpoint of humanistic psychology*. New York: Macmillan.

Judson, H. (1978, November 27). Annals of Science, DNA-I. *The New Yorker*.

Jung, C. (1954). *Collected works* (Vol. 17). Princeton, NJ: Princeton University Press.

Kagan, J. (1972). Do infants think? *Scientific American*, pp. 74–82.

Kagan, J. (1984). *The nature of the child*. New York: Basic Books.

Kahnert, M., Pitt, D., & Taipale, I. (Eds.). (1983). *Children and war*. Geneva: Geneva International Peace Research Institute.

Kalish, R. A. (1981). *Death, grief and caring relationships*. Monterey, CA: Brooks/Cole.

Kalish, R. A. (1982). *Late adulthood: Perspectives on human development* (2nd ed.). Monterey: Brooks/Cole.

Kaplan, H. R., & Tausky, C. (1972). Work and the welfare Cadillac: The function of and commitment to work among the hard-core unemployed. *Social Problems, 19*, 469–483.

Kaplan, H. S. (1974). *The new sex therapy*. New York: Brunner/Mazel.

Kaplan, J. (1979). The naked self and other problems. In M. Patcher (Ed.), *Telling lives: The biographer's art*. New York: New Republic Books.

Kaplan, M. (1983). A woman's view of DSM-III. *American Psychologist, 38*, 793–798.

Kasl, S. V., & Cobb, S. (1970). Blood pressure changes in men undergoing job loss: A preliminary report. *Psychosomatic Medicine, 32*, 19–38.

Kaslow, N., & Wamboldt, F. (1985). Childhood depression: Current perspective and future directions. *Journal of Social and Clinical Psychology, 3*(4), 416–424.

Kassovic, J. (1980,.April). A study presented to the 1979 Meeting of the American Folklore Society in Los Angeles. Cited in C. Rubenstein, Gallows humor and religious fallout. *Psychology Today, 33*.

Kastenbaum, R. (1971, December). Getting there. *Psychology Today, 53*.

Kastenbaum, R. (1975). Is death a life crisis? On the confrontation with death in theory and practice. In N. Datan & L. Ginsberg (Eds.), *Life-span developmental psychology: Normative life crises*. New York: Academic Press.

Kastenbaum, R. (1977). Death and development throughout the lifespan. In H. Feifel (Ed.), *New meanings of death*. New York: McGraw-Hill.

Kastenbaum, R., & Aisenberg, R. (1972). *The psychology of death*. New York: Springer.

Kastenbaum, R. J. (1977). *Death, society and human experience*. St. Louis: Mosby.

Kastenbaum, R. J. (Ed.). (1979). *Between life and death*. New York: Springer.

Katchadourian, H. (1974). *Human sexuality: Sense and nonsense*. San Francisco: W. H. Freeman.

Katz, M. (1966, September). A model of guidance for career decision-making. *Vocational Guidance Quarterly*, 2–10.

Katz, M. R. (1979). Career decision-making: A computer based system of interactive guidance and information. In S. G. Wenrach (Ed.), *Career counseling* (pp. 207–230). New York: McGraw-Hill.

Kazdin, A. E., & Smith, G. M. (1979). Covert conditioning: A review and evaluation. *Advances in Behaviour Research and Therapy, 2*, 57–79.

Keith, C. R., & Ellis, D. (1978, March). Reactions of pupils and teachers to death in the classroom. *The School Counselor, 25*, 225–234.

Keleman, S. (1974). *Living your dying*. New York: Random House.

Kendall, P. C. (1984). Behavioral assessment and methodology. In C. M. Franks, G. T. Wilson, P. C. Kendall, & K. D. Brownell (Eds.), *Annual review of behavior therapy* (Vol. 10). New York: Guilford.

Keniston, K. (1970, Autumn). Youth: A "new" stage of life. *The American Scholar*, 631–654.

Kennedy, J. H. (1985). Age and types of stress: A comparison of college-age and elderly adults. *Psychological Reports, 57*, 302.

Kephart, W. M. (1970, Autumn). The "dysfunctional" theory of romantic love: A research report. *Journal of Comparative Family Studies*, 22–36.

Kety, S. (1980). Mental illness in the biological and adoptive relatives of schizophrenic adoptees. *American Journal of Psychiatry, 140*(6), 720–727.

Keyes, R. (1973). *We, the lonely people*. New York: Harper & Row.

Khouri, P. (1988). AIDS—The brain on fire: Cerebral manifestations of the HIV infection. *Carrier Foundation Newsletter, 130*(1).

Kieffer, C. (1984). Citizen empowerment: A developmental perspective. *Prevention in Human Services, 3*(2–3), 9–36.

Kiesler, C. (1982). Mental health and alternative care. *American Psychologist, 37*, 349–360.

Kimmel, D. C. (1988). Ageism, psychology and public policy. *American Psychologist, 43*, 175–178.

Kinsey, A. C., Pomeroy, W. B., & Martin, C. E. (1948). *Sexual behavior in the human male*. Philadelphia: Saunders.

Kinsey, A. C., Pomeroy, W. B., Martin, C. E., & Gebhard, P. D. (1953). *Sexual behavior in the human female*. Philadelphia: Saunders.

Kish, R. A. (1982). *Life adulthood: Perspectives on human development* (2nd ed.). Belmont, CA: Brooks/Cole Publishing Co.

Klaus, D., Hersen, M., & Bellack, A. (1977). Survey of dating habits of male and female college students: A necessary precursor to measurement and modification. *Journal of Clinical Psychology, 33*, 369–375.

Klerman, G. L. (1986). Drugs and psychotherapy. In S. L. Garfield & A. E. Bergin (Eds.), *Handbook of psychotherapy and behavior change* (3rd ed.). New York: Wiley.

Knitzer, J. (1984). Mental health services to children and adolescents: A national view of public policy. *American Psychologist, 39*, 905–911.

Koch, H. L. (1956). Some emotional attitudes of the young child in relation to characteristics of his siblings. *Child Development, 27*, 393–426.

Kohlberg, L. (1963). Moral development and identification. In *Child Psychology*. National Society for the Study of Education, 62nd Yearbook, Part I. Chicago: University of Chicago Press.

Kohlberg, L. (1968, September). The child as a moral philosopher. *Psychology Today*, 25–30.

Kohlberg, L. (1981). *Essays on moral development*. San Francisco: Harper & Row.

Kohlberg, L., & Kramer, R. (1973). Continuities and discontinuities in childhood and adult moral development revisited. In P. B. Baltes & K. W. Schaie (Eds.), *Life span developmental psychology: Personality and socialization*. New York: Academic Press.

Kolata, G. (1986). Manic-depression: Is it inherited? *Science*, 575–576.

Koocher, G. P., & O'Malley, J. E. (1981). *The Damocles syndrome: Psychosocial consequences of surviving childhood cancer*. New York: McGraw-Hill.

Koops, B. & Battaglia, F. C. (1987). The newborn infant. In C. H. Kempe, H. K. Silver, D. O'Brien, V. A. Fulginiti, and others (Eds.), *Current pediatric diagnosis & treatment*, (1987). Norwalk, CT: Appleton & Lange.

Korchin, S. T. (1976). *Modern clinical psychology: Principles of intervention in the clinic and community.* New York: Basic Books.

Korner, A. (1971). Individual differences at birth: Implications for early experiences and later development. *American Journal of Orthopsychiatry, 41,* 608–619.

Koss, M. (1983). The scope of rape: Implications for the clinical treatment of victims. *The Clinical Psychologist, 36,* 88–91.

Koss, M., Gidycz, C., & Wisniewski, N. (1987). The scope of rape: Incidence and prevalence of sexual aggression and victimization in a national sample of higher education students. *Journal of Consulting and Clinical Psychology, 55*(2), 162–170.

Kovacs, M., Rush, A. J., Beck, A. T., et al. (1981). Depressed outpatients treated with cognitive therapy or pharmacotherapy. *Archives of General Psychiatry, 38,* 33–39.

Kovel, J. (1976). *A complete guide to therapy: From psychoanalysis to behavior modification.* New York: Pantheon.

Kraemer, D. L., & Hastrup, J. L. (1986). Crying in natural settings: Global estimates, self-monitored frequencies, depression and sex differences in an undergraduate population. *Journal of American College Health, 34,* 24–32.

Kram, K. (1985). Improving the mentoring process. *Training and Developmental Journal, 39*(4), 40–43.

Kram, K. (1986). Mentoring in the workplace. In D. T. Hall and associates (Ed.), *Career development in organizations* (pp. 160–201). San Francisco: Jossey-Bass.

Kratcoski, P. C. (1982 November 22). Color the 21st century gray. *USA Today,* 70.

Kübler-Ross, E. (1969). *On death and dying.* New York: Macmillan.

Kübler-Ross, E. (1975). *Death: The final stage of growth.* Englewood Cliffs, NJ: Prentice-Hall.

Kübler-Ross, E. (Ed.). (1975). *Death: The final stage of growth.* Englewood Cliffs, NJ: Prentice-Hall.

Kunz, J. (Ed.). (1982). *Family medical guide.* New York: Random House.

Kurdek, L., & Berg, B. (1983). Correlates of children's adjustments to their parents' divorces. In L. Kurdek (Ed.), *Children and divorce.* San Francisco: Jossey-Bass.

L'Abate, L., Ganahl, G., & Hansen, J. C. (1986). *Methods of family therapy.* Englewood Cliffs, NJ: Prentice-Hall.

L'Abate, L., & McHenry, S. (1983). *Handbook of marital interventions.* Orlando, FL: Grune & Stratton.

Lader, M. (1975). The nature of clinical anxiety in modern society. In C. D. Spielberger & I. G. Sarason (Eds.), *Stress and anxiety* (Vol. 1). Washington: Hemisphere.

Lahey, B., Hammer, D., Crumrine, P., & Forehand, R. (1980). Birth order sex interactions in child behavior problems. *Developmental Psychology, 16*(6), 606–615.

Lamaze, B. (1972). *Painless childbirth: The Lamaze method.* New York: Pocket Books.

Lambert, M. J., Shapiro, D. A., & Bergin, A. E. (1986). In S. L. Garfield & A. E. Bergin (Eds.), *Handbook of psychotherapy and behavior change* (3rd ed.). New York: Wiley.

LaPanto, R., Mooney, W., & Zenhausen, R. (1965). The contribution of anxiety to the laboratory investigation of pain. *Psychonomic Science, 3,* 475.

Lapham, L. H. (1979, June). A juggernaut of words. *Harper's,* 8–16.

LaRoche, C. (1986). Prevention in high risk children of depressed parents. *Canadian Journal of Psychiatry, 31,* 161–165.

Larsen, K., Reed, M., & Hoffman, S. (1980). Attitudes of heterosexuals toward homosexuality: A Likert-type scale and construct validity. *Journal of Sex Research, 16*(3), 245–257.

Lasswell, T., & Lasswell, M. (1980). The meaning of love. In J. Kenslin (Ed.), *Marriage and family in a changing society.* New York: Free Press.

Lauer, G., & Lauer, R. (1986). *'Til death do us part: How couples stay together.* New York: Haworth Press.

Laver, H. (1985). The influx of women into the labor force. In D. Yankelovich, H. Zetterbergh, B. Stumpel, & M. Shanks (Eds.), *The world of work.* New York: Octogon.

Laver, H. (1985). The retirement dilemma: The trend toward early retirement and an overburdened working population. In D. Yankelovich, H. Zetterbergh, B. Stumpel, & M. Shanks (Eds.), *The world of work.* New York: Octogon.

Lawrence, D. H. (1979). *The letters of D. H. Lawrence: September 1901– May 1913* (Vol. 1). J. T. Boulton, Ed. New York: Cambridge University Press. Text quotation from letter (1910) cited in *Harper's,* March 1979, p. 92.

Lazar, I., & Darlington, R. (1982). Lasting effects of early education: A report from the Consortium for Longitudinal Studies Whole Issue. *Monograph of the Society for Research in Child Development, 47* (Nos. 2–3).

Lazarus, A. (1976). *Multimodal behavioral therapy.* New York: Springer.

Lazarus, A. (1985). *Casebook of multimodal therapy.* New York: Guilford Press.

Lazarus, A. A. (1981). *The practice of multimodal therapy, systematic, comprehensive & effective psychotherapy.* New York: McGraw-Hill.

Lazarus, A. A. (1981). *The practice of multimodal therapy.* New York: McGraw-Hill.

Lazarus, A. A. (1984). *In the mind's eye: The power of imagery for personal enrichment.* New York: Guilford Press.

Lazarus, A. A. (1986). Multimodal therapy. In J. Norcross (Ed.), *Handbook of eclectic psychotherapy.* New York: Brunner/ Mazel.

Lazarus, A. A. (1987). The multimodal approach with adult outpatients. In N. S. Jacobson (Ed.), *Psychotherapists in clinical practice.* New York: Guilford Press.

Lazarus, R. S. (1966). *Psychological stress and the coping process.* New York: McGraw-Hill.

Lazarus, R. S. (1971). The concepts of stress and disease. In L. Levi (Ed.), *Society, stress and disease* (Vol. 1: *The Psychosocial environment and psychosomatic disease*). London: Oxford University Press.

Lazarus, R. S. (1975). The healthy personality: A review of conceptualizations and research. In L. Levi (Ed.), *Society, stress and disease* (Vol. 2: *Childhood and adolescence*). London: Oxford University Press.

Lazarus, R. S. (1979, November). (interviewed by D. Goleman). Positive denial: The case for not facing reality. *Psychology Today, 13*(6), 44–57.

Lazarus, R. S., & Averill, J. R. (1972). Emotion and cognition: With special reference to anxiety. In C. D. Spielberger (Ed.), *Anxiety: Current trends in theory and research* (Vol. 2). New York: Academic Press.

Lazarus, R. S., & DeLongis, A. (1983). Psychological stress and coping in aging. *American Psychologist, 38,* 245–254.

Lazarus, R. S., & Folkman, S. (1984). *Stress, appraisal, and coping.* New York: Springer.

Leaf, P., Weissman, M., Myers, J., Tischler, G., & Holland, C. (1984). Social factors related to psychiatric disorder: The Yale epidemiological catchment area study. *Social Psychiatry, 19,* 53–61.

Leboyer, F. (1975). *Birth without violence.* New York: Alfred A. Knopf.

Lee, J. (1974, October). The styles of loving. *Psychology Today,* 43–51.

Leman, K. (1985). *The birth order book: Why you are the way you are.* Old Tappan, NJ: F. H. Revell.

Lemkau, J. P. (1980). Women and employment. In C. L. Heckerman (Ed.), *The evolving female.* New York: Human Sciences Press.

Leonard, W. E. (1927). *The locomotive god.* New York: Appleton-Century-Crofts.

Levi, L. (1981). *Preventing work stress.* Reading, MA: Addison-Wesley.

Levi, L. (1983). Stress and coronary heart disease—Causes, mechanisms, and prevention. In R. H. Rosenman (Ed.), *Psychosomatic risk factors and coronary heart disease: Indications for specific prevention therapy.* Berne: Hans Huber Publishers.

Levine, E. M. (1986). Sociocultural causes of family violence: A theoretical comment. *Journal of Family Violence, 1*(1), 3–12.

Levine, M., & Perkins, D. (1987). *Principles of community psychology.* New York: Oxford University Press.

Levinson, B. M. (1984). Human/companion animal therapy. *Journal of Contemporary Psychotherapy, 14,* 131–144.

Levinson, D. (1986). A conception of adult development. *American Psychologist,* 3–13.

Levinson, D., with Darrow, C., Klein, E., Levinson, M., & McKee, P. (1978). *The seasons of a man's life.* New York: Alfred A. Knopf.

Levinson, D. J. (1978). *The seasons of a man's life.* New York: Ballantine.

Levitt, E. E. (1967). *The psychology of anxiety.* Indianapolis: Bobbs-Merrill.

Lewinsohn, P. M. (1981). A behavioral approach to depression. In R. J. Friedman & M. Katz (Eds.), *The psychology of depression: contemporary theory and research.* Washington: U.S. Government Printing Office.

Lewinsohn, P. M. (1987). The coping-with-depression course. In R. F. Munoz (Ed.), *Depression prevention, research directions.* Washington: Hemisphere.

Lewis, J. (1979). *How's your family?* New York: Brunner/Mazel.

Lewis, J. M., Beavers, W. R., Gossett, J. T., & Phillips, V. A. (1976). *No single thread: Psychological health in family systems.* New York: Brunner/Mazel.

Lewis, O. (1959). *Five families: Mexican case studies in the culture of poverty.* New York: Basic Books.

Lewis, O. (1966). *La Vida: A Puerto Rican family in the culture of poverty, San Juan and New York.* New York: Random House.

Liang, J. (1982). Sex differences in life satisfaction among the elderly. *Journal of Gerontology, 37*(1), 100–108.

Lidz, T. (1976). *The person: His and her development throughout the life cycle* (rev. ed.). New York: Basic Books.

Lieberman, M., & Tobin, S. (1983). *Experiences of old age: Stress, coping and survival.* New York: Basic Books.

Liem, R., & Rayman, P. (1982). Health and social costs of unemployment. *American Psychologist, 37,* 116–123.

Lifton, R. J. (1987). *The Nazi doctors.* New York: Basic Books.

Lifton, R. J., & Olson, S. (1974). *Living and dying.* New York: Praeger.

Lindemann, E. (1944). Symptomatology and management of acute grief. *American Journal of Psychiatry, 101*(2), 141–148.

Lipman, A. (1984). Cited in U.S.A. Today, August 3, 1984.

Loftus, E. F. (1980, March). Alcohol, marijuana, and memory. *Psychology Today, 92,* 42–56.

Long, J. V. F., & Valliant, G. E. (1984). Natural history of male psychological health, XI, Escape from the underclass. *American Journal of Psychiatry, 141*(3), 341–346.

Lord, L., Goode, E., Gest, T., McAuliffe, K., Moure, L., Black, R., Linnon, N., and bureau reports. (1987, November 30). Coming to grips with alcoholism. *U.S. News & World Report,* 56–63.

Loren, R., & Weeks, G. (1986). Sexual fantasies of undergraduates and their perceptions of the sexual fantasies of the opposite sex. *Journal of Sex Education and Therapy, 12*(2), 31–36.

Lorenz, K. (1963). *On aggression.* Trans. by M. K. Wilson. New York: Harcourt, Brace & World.

Lowen, A. (1976). *Bioenergetics.* New York: Penguin Books.

Lubin, B., Larsen, R. M., Matarazzo, J. D., & Seever, M. F. (1986). Selected characteristics of psychologists and psychological assessment in five settings: 1959–1982. *Professional Psychology: Research and Practice, 17,* 155–157.

Lubin, B., & Rubio, C. T. (1985). Strain-producing aspects of life events. *Psychological Reports, 57,* 259–262.

Luce, G. G. (1979). *Your second life: Vitality and growth in middle and later years.* New York: Delacorte Press.

Luepnitz, D. (1986). A comparison of maternal, paternal, and joint custody: Understanding the varieties of post-divorce family life. *Journal of Divorce, 9*(3), 1–12.

Luft, J. (1974). *Group processes: An introduction to group dynamics* (2nd ed.) Palo Alto, CA: Mayfield Publishing.

Luft, J. (1984). *Group processes: An introduction to group dynamics* (3rd ed.). Palo Alto, CA: Mayfield Publishing.

Luria, Z., Friedman, S., & Rose, M. (1987). *Human sexuality.* New York: Wiley.

Lutz, D., & Snow, P. (1985). Understanding the role of depression in the alcoholic. *Clinical Psychology Review, 5,* 535–551.

Lynch, J. (1977). *The broken heart: The medical consequences of loneliness.* New York: Basic Books.

Lyons, R. D. (1977, September 16). 20 million people or more need mental care, U.S. Panel asserts. *The New York Times.*

Maas, H. (1984). *People and contexts: Social development for birth to old age.* Englewood Cliffs, NJ: Prentice-Hall.

Maccoby, E., & Jacklin, C. (1985). The psychology of sex differences. In M. Bloom (Ed.), *Life span development* (pp. 164–169). New York: Macmillan.

Maccoby, M. (1976). *The gamesman.* New York: Simon & Schuster.

Machlowitz, M. (1980). *Workaholics living with them, working with them.* Reading, MA: Addison-Wesley.

Macklin, E. (1972). Heterosexual cohabitation among unmarried college students. *Family Coordinator, 21,* 463–472.

Maddi, S., Hoover, M., & Kobasa, S. (1982). Alienation and exploratory behavior. *Journal of Personality and Social Behavior, 42*(5), 884–890.

Maddox, G. L. (1966). Retirement as a social event in the United States. In J. C. McKinney & F. T. de Vyver (Eds.), *Aging and social policy* (pp. 119–135). New York: Appleton-Century-Crofts.

Maeroff, G. I. (1978, March 6). Schools take up study of death. *The New York Times.*

Mahler, M., Pine, F., & Bergman, A. (1975). *The psychological birth of the human infant.* New York: Basic Books.

Mahler, M. S. (1972). On the first three subphases of the separation-individuation process. *International Journal of Psychoanalysis, 53,* 333–338.

Mahler, M. S., Pine, F., & Bergman, A. (1970). The mother's reaction to her toddler's drive for individuation. In J. E. Anthony & T. Benedek (Eds.), *Parenthood: Its psychology and psychopathology.* Boston: Little, Brown.

Mainprice, J. (1974). *Marital interaction and some illnesses of children.* London: Tavistock Institute.

Malone, T., & Malone, P. (1988). *The art of intimacy.* New York: Prentice-Hall.

Mandell, A. J. (1977). *The coming of age: A journey.* New York: Summit Books.

Manosevitz, M., Prentice, N. M., & Wilson, F. (1973). Individual and family correlates of imaginary companions in preschool children. *Developmental Psychology, 8,* 72–79.

Marcia, J. E. (1966). Development and validation of ego-identity status. *Journal of Personality and Social Psychology, 3,* 551–558.

Marks, I. M. (1986). *Fears, phobias, and rituals: An interdisciplinary perspective.* New York: Oxford University Press.

Marmor, J. (1980). Clinical aspects of homosexuality. In J. Marmor (Ed.), *Homosexual behavior.* New York: Basic Books.

Martin, B., & Burks, N. (1985). Family and nonfamily components of social support as buffers of stress for college women. *Journal of Applied Social Psychology, 15*(5), 448–465.

Marziali, E., Marmar, C., & Krupnick, J. (1981). Therapeutic alliance scales: Development and relationship to psychotherapy outcome. *American Journal of Psychiatry, 138,* 361–364.

Maslow, A. H. (1954/1970/1987). *Motivation and personality.* New York: Harper & Row.

Maslow, A. H. (1967). Neurosis as a failure of personal growth. *Humanitas, 3,* 153–170.

Maslow, A. H. (1967). A theory of metamotivation: The biological rooting of the value-life. *Journal of Humanistic Psychology, 7,* 93–127.

Maslow, A. H. (1968). *Toward a psychology of being* (2nd ed.). New York: Van Nostrand Reinhold.

Maslow, A. H. (1971). *The farther reaches of human nature.* New York: Viking.

Mason, S. T. (1984). *Catecholamines and behavior.* Cambridge: Cambridge University Press.

Masserman, J. H. (1964). *Behavior and neurosis.* Chicago: University of Chicago Press. (Original work published 1943)

Masserman, J. H., & Siever, P. W. (1944). Dominance, neurosis, and aggression: An experimental study. *Psychosomatic Medicine, 6,* 7–16.

Masters, W., & Johnson, V. (1966). *Human sexual response.* Boston: Little, Brown.

Masters, W., & Johnson, V. (1979). *Homosexuality in perspective.* Boston: Little, Brown.

Maurer, A. (1961). The child's knowledge of non-existence. *Journal of Existential Psychology, 2,* 193–212.

May, R. (1961). The emergence of existential psychology. In R. May (Ed.), *Existential psychology.* New York: Random House.

May, R. (1977). *The meaning of anxiety* (rev. ed.). New York: Ronald Press. (Original work published 1950)

Mays, D. T., & Franks, C. M. (1985). *Negative outcome in psychotherapy and what to do about it.* New York: Springer.

McCallum, S. (1981). An examination of the age-deficiency hypothesis: Aging and mental health. *Journal of Applied Gerontology, 9*(2), 71–78.

McCary, J. (1978). *Human sexuality* (3rd ed.). New York: Van Nostrand Reinhold.

McCaul, K. D., & Malott, J. M. (1984). Distraction and coping with pain. *Psychological Bulletin, 95,* 516–533.

McGhee, P., & Frueh, T. (1980). Television viewing and the learning of sex-role stereotypes. *Sex Roles, 6*(2), 179–188.

McGoldrick, M., & Carter, E. A. (1982). The family life cycle. In F. Walsh (Ed.), *Normal family processes* (pp. 167–195). New York: Guilford Press.

McGoldrick, M., & Gerson, R. (1985). *Genograms in family assessment.* New York: W. W. Norton.

McGrath, N., & McGrath, C. (1975, May 25). Why have a baby? *The New York Times Magazine.*

McGuigan, F. J. (1984). An overview of contemporary work in the field of stress and tension control. In F. J. McGuigan, W. E. Sime, & J. M. Wallace (Eds.), *Stress and tension control, 2.* New York: Plenum.

McLanahan, S. S., & Sorensen, A. B. (1984). Life events and psychological well-being: A reexamination of theoretical and methodological issues. *Social Science Research, 13,* 111–128.

McNally, R. (1987). Preparedness and phobias: A review. *Psychological Bulletin, 101*(2), 283–303.

McNeal, E. T., & Cimbolic, P. (1986). Antidepressants and biochemical theories of depression. *Psychological Bulletin, 99,* 361–374.

Meador, B., & Rogen, C. (1979). Person-centered therapy. In R. Corsini (Ed.), *Current psychotherapies* (2nd ed.). Itasca, IL: Peacock.

Mednick, S. A., & Witkin-Lanoil, G. H. (1977). Intervention in children at high risk for schizophrenia. In G. W. Albee & J. M. Joffe (Eds.), *Primary prevention of psychopathology* (Vol. 1: *The issues*). Hanover, NH: University Press of New England.

Meer, J. (1985). Loneliness. *Psychology Today, 19*(7), 28–33.

Meer, J. (1986). The reason of age. *Psychology Today, 20*(6), 60-64.

Meichenbaum, D. H. (1977). *Cognitive-behavior modification: An integrative approach.* New York: Plenum.

Meislin, R. J. (1977, November 27). Poll finds more liberal beliefs on marriage and sex roles, especially among the young. *The New York Times.*

Menninger, K. (1963). *The vital balance: The life process in mental health and illness.* New York: Viking Press.

Merloo, J. A. M. (1950). *Patterns of panic.* New York: International Universities Press.

Messer, S. B. (1986). Behavioral and psychoanalytic perspectives at therapeutic choice points. *American Psychologist, 41,* 1261–1272.

Messer, S. B., & Winokur, M. (1980). Some limits to the integration of psychoanalytic and behavior therapy. *American Psychologist, 35,* 818–827.

Milgram, S. (1970, March). The experience of living in cities. *Science, 167,* 1461–1468.

Miller, A. (1981). *Prisoners of childhood.* New York: Basic Books.

Miller, N. E. (1980). A perspective on the effects of stress and coping on disease and health. In S. Levine & H. Urin (Eds.), *Coping and health.* New York: Plenum.

Miner, M. G., & Miner, J. B. (1979). *Employee selection within the law.* Washington, DC: The Bureau of National Affairs.

Mischel, W. (1973). Toward a cognitive social learning conceptualization of personality. *Psychological Review, 80,* 252–283.

Mitchell, R., Billings, A., & Moos, R. (1983). Social support and well-being: Implications for primary prevention. *Journal of Primary Prevention, 3,* 77–98.

Mogul, K. M. (1982). Overview: The sex of the therapist. *American Journal of Psychiatry, 139,* 1–11.

Molineux, J. B. (1985). *Family therapy: A practical manual.* Springfield, IL: Charles C. Thomas.

Money, J., & Clopper, R. R., Jr. (1974). Psychosocial and psychosexual aspects of errors of pubertal onset and development. *Human Biology, 46,* 173–181.

Monroe, S., Bromet, E., Connell, M., & Steiner, S. (1986). Social support, life events, and depressive symptoms: A 1-year prospective study. *Journal of Consulting and Clinical Psychology, 54,* 124–131.

Moody, R. (1975). *Life after death.* New York: Bantam/Mockingbird.

Moody, R. (1977). *Reflections on life after life.* New York: Bantam/Mockingbird.

Moreland, J., & Schwebel, A. (1981). A gender role transcendent perspective on fathering. *Counseling Psychologist, 9*(4), 45–54.

Moreland, J., Schwebel, A., Beck, S., & Wells, R. (1982). Parents as therapists. *Behavior Modification, 6*(2), 250–276.

Morgan, H., Purgold, J., & Welbourne, J. (1983). Management and outcome in anorexia nervosa. *British Journal of Psychiatry, 143,* 282–287.

Morganthau, T., & Miller, M. (1988, November 28). Getting tough on cocaine. *Newsweek,* 76–79.

Mowbray, C. (1985). Homelessness in America: Myths and realities. *American Journal of Orthopsychiatry, 55,* 4–8.

Mullen, K., Gold, R., Belcastro, P., & McDermott, R. (1986). *Connections for health*. Dubuque, IA: Wm. C. Brown.

Munnichs, J. M. A. (1966). *Old age and finitude*. Basel, Switzerland and New York: Karger.

Munoz, R. F. (1987). *Depression prevention, research directions*. Washington: Hemisphere.

Murdock, G. (1949). *Social structure*. New York: Macmillan.

Murphy, G. E., Simons, A. D., Wetzel, R. D., & Lustman, P. J. (1984). Cognitive therapy and pharmacotherapy. *Archives of General Psychiatry, 41,* 33–41.

Murphy, L. B., & Moriarty, A. E. (1976). *Vulnerability, coping and growth: From infancy to adolescence*. New Haven: Yale University Press.

Murphy, P. A. (1986–87). Parental death in childhood and loneliness in young adults. *Omega, 17*(3), 219–228.

Murstein, B., & Brust, R. (1985). Humor and interpersonal attraction. *Journal of Personality Assessment, 49*(6), 637–640.

Mussen, P. H., & Jones, M. C. (1957). Self-conceptions, motivations, and interpersonal attitudes of late- and early-maturing boys. *Child Development, 28,* 243–256.

Myers, J., Weissman, M., Tischler, G., Holzer, C., Leaf, P., Orvaschel, H., Anthony, J., Boyd, J., Burke, J., Kramer, M., & Stoltzman, R. (1984). Six-month prevalence of psychiatric disorders in three communities. *Archives of General Psychiatry, 41,* 959–967.

Myers, R. A. (1986). Research on educational and vocational counseling. In S. L. Garfield & A. E. Bergin (Eds.), *Handbook of psychotherapy and behavior change* (3rd ed.). New York: Wiley.

Nadelson, C., & Notman, M. (1985). Rape. In Z. DeFries, R. Friedman, & R. Corn (Eds.), *Sexuality: New perspective*. Westport, CT: Greenwood Press.

Nadelson, C. C., & Polonsky, D.C. (1984). *Marriage and divorce: A contemporary perspective*. New York: Guilford Press.

Naeye, R. (1981). Influence of maternal cigarette smoking during pregnancy on fetal and childhood growth. *Obstetrics and Gynecology, 57,* 18–21.

Nahemow, L., & Lawton, M. (1975). Similarity and propinquity in friendship formation. *Journal of Personality and Social Psychology, 32*(2), 205–213.

Namir, S., & Weinstein, R. (1982). Children: Facilitating new directions. In L. Snowden (Ed.), *Reaching the underserved: Mental health needs of neglected populations*. Beverly Hills, CA: Sage.

Nathan, P., Titler, N., Lowenstein, L., Solomon, P., & Rossie, A. (1970). Behavioral analysis of chronic alcoholism. *Archives of General Psychiatry, 22,* 419–430.

National Center for Health Statistics. (1960–1968). *Vital statistics of the United States* (Vol. 2). Washington, DC: U.S. Government Printing Office.

National Center for Health Statistics. (1985, July). *Legislative authorities for the National Center for Health Statistics*. Hyattsville, MD: U.S. Dept. of Health and Human Services.

National Institute of Mental Health, U.S. Department of Health and Human Services. 1986. *Coping with AIDS*. Available from the Superintendent of Documents, Government Printing Office, Washington, DC 20402.

Natterson, J., & Gordon, B. (1977). *The sexual dream*. New York: Crown Publishers.

Neff, J., & Husaini, B. (1985). Lay images of mental illness: Social knowledge and tolerance of the mentally ill. *Journal of Community Psychology, 13,* 3–12.

Nelson, N., Enkin, M., Saigal, S., Bennett, K., Milner, R., & Sackett, D. (1980). A randomized clinical trial of the Leboyer approach to childbirth. *The New England Journal of Medicine, 302*(12), 655–660.

Neugarten, B. L. (1967). The awareness of middle age. In R. Owen (Ed.), *Middle age*. London: British Broadcasting Corporation.

Neugarten, B. L. (1971, December). Grow old along with me: The best is yet to be. *Psychology Today,* 45.

Neugarten, B. L., Moore, J. W., & Lowe, J. C. (1965). Age norms, age constraints, and adult socialization. *Americal Journal of Sociology, 70,* 710–717.

Neugarten, B. L., Wood, V., Kraines, R., & Loomis, B. (1963). Women's attitudes toward the menopause. *Vita Humana, 6,* 140–151.

(1986). *Affirmative action today: A legal and practical analysis*. Washington, DC: The Bureau of National Affairs.

(1986, May). Vogue's Health Style. *Vogue,* 232.

(1986 October). Where are the teenagers? *Nation's Business,* 24.

(1987). *New York Institute of Technology Catalog.*

(1988). *Baruch Undergraduate Bulletin.*

New York Times, November 23, 1980, p. 28.

Newman, B. M. (1982). Mid-life development. In B. Wolman (Ed.), *Handbook of developmental psychology* (pp. 617–634). Englewood Cliffs, NJ: Prentice-Hall.

Nietzel, M. E., & Bernstein, D. A. (1987). *Introduction to clinical psychology* (2nd ed.). Englewood Cliffs, NJ: Prentice-Hall.

Nisbett, R. E., & Schachter, S. (1966). Cognitive manipulation of pain. *Journal of Experimental Social Psychology, 2,* 227–236.

Nock, S. L. (1982). The life cycle approach to family analysis. In B. Wolman (Ed.), *Handbook of developmental psychology* (pp. 636–645). Englewood Cliffs, NJ: Prentice-Hall.

Nolen-Hoeksema, S. (1987). Sex differences in unipolar depression: Evidence and theory. *Psychological Bulletin, 101*(2), 259–282.

Norcross, J. C. (1986). *Handbook of eclectic psychotherapy.* New York: Brunner/Mazel.

Norman, J., & Harris, M. W. (1981). The private life of the American teenager. New York: Rawson, Wade.

Norman, W. (1980). Role change in older years. *Journal of Personality and Social Psychology, 40,* 501–510.

Norton, A., & Moorman, J. (1987). Current trends in marriage and divorce among American women. *Journal of Marriage and the Family, 49,* 3–14.

Nuechterlein, K. (1986). Childhood precursors of adult schizophrenia. *Journal of Child Psychiatry and Psychology, 27*(2), 133–144.

Nuernberger, P. (1981). *Freedom from stress.* Honesdale, PA: Himalayan International Institutes.

Nussel, F. H., Jr. (1982). The language of ageism. *The Gerontologist, 22*(3), 273–276.

Nye, F. I., with Bahr, H., Bahr, S., Carlson, J., Gecas, V., McLaughlin, S., & Slocum, W. (1976). *Role structure and analysis of the family.* Beverly Hills, CA: Sage Publications.

Nye, R. (1973). *Conflict among humans.* New York: Springer.

Nye, R. (1981). *Three psychologists: Perspectives from Freud, Skinner, and Rogers* (2nd ed.). Belmont, CA: **Brooks/Cole.**

Oates, J. C. (1969). *Them.* New York: Vanguard Press.

Obstfeld, L., & Meyers, A. (1984). Adolescent sex education: A preventive mental health measure. *JOSH, 54*(2), 68–70.

Oden, S., & Asher, S. (1977). Coaching children in social skills for friendship making. *Child Development, 48,* 495–506.

Oetting, E., & Beauvis, F. (1987). Peer cluster theory, socialization characteristics, and adolescent drug use: A path analysis. *Journal of Consulting Psychology, 34*(2), 205–213.

Okun, M. A., & DiVesta, F. J. (1976). Cautiousness in adulthood as a function of age and instructions. *Journal of Gerontology, 31*(3), 371–376.

Olson, G. (1981). The recognition of specific persons. In M. Lamb & L. Sherrod (Eds.), *Infant social cognitions.* Hillsdale, NJ: Lawrence Erlbaum Associates.

O'Neil, J. M., Ohlde, C., & Barke, C. (1979). Research on a career workshop to reduce sexism with women. Presented at the 87th annual meeting of the American Psychological Association, New York.

Orlofsky, J. L., Marcia, J. E., & Lesser, I. M. (1973). Ego identity status and the intimacy versus isolation crisis of young adulthood. *Journal of Personality and Social Psychology, 27,* 211–219.

Otto, L. B., & Call, V. R. (1985). Parental influence on young peoples' career development. *Journal of Career Development, Sept.,* 65–69.

Packard, V. (1972). *A nation of strangers.* New York: David McKay.

Palmore, E. B., & Maeda, D. (1985). *The honorable elders revisited.* Durham: Duke University Press.

Pargman, D. (1986). *Stress and motor performance: Understanding and coping.* Ithaca: Mouvement Publication.

Parke, R., Tinsley, B. J. (1987). Fathers as agents and recipients of support in the postnatal period. In C. F. Z. Boukydis (Ed.), *Research on support for parents and infants in the postnatal period.* Norwood, NJ: Ablex Publishing Co.

Parker, S. (1983). *Leisure and work.* London: Allen & Unwin.

Parks, C. M. (1972, 1986). *Bereavement: Studies of grief in adult life.* New York: International Universities Press.

Parks, M., Stan, C., & Eggert, L. (1983). Romantic involvement and social network involvement. *Social Psychology Quarterly, 46*(2), 116–131.

Parloff, M. G., London, P., & Wolfe, B. (1986). Individual psychotherapy and behavior change. *Annual Review of Psychology, 37,* 321–349.

Patterson, C. H. (1984). Empathy, warmth, and genuineness in psychotherapy: A review of reviews. *Psychotherapy, 21,* 431–438.

Patterson, R. D., Freeman, L. C., & Butler, R. N. (1971). Psychiatric aspects of adaptation, survival, and death. In S. Granich & R. D. Patterson (Eds.), *Human aging II: An eleven-year follow-up biomedical and behavioral study.* Rockville, MD: U.S. Department of Health, Education and Welfare.

Pattison, E. M. (1977a). Death throughout the life cycle. In E. M. Pattison (Ed.), *The experience of dying* (pp. 18–27). Englewood Cliffs, NJ: Prentice-Hall.

Pattison, E. M. (1977b). The dying experience: Retrospective analyses. In E. M. Pattison (Ed.), *The experience of dying* (pp. 303–315). Englewood Cliffs, NJ: Prentice-Hall.

Paul, G. L. (1966). The specific control of anxiety: "Hypnosis" and "conditioning." Paper presented at the American Psychological Symposium: Innovations in Therapeutic Interactions. Cited in R. H. Redd, A. L. Porterfield, & E. L. Anderson, *Behavioral modification: Behavioral approaches to human problems.* New York: Random House, 1979.

Pavlov, I. P. (1927). *Conditioned reflexes.* (G. V. Anrep, Ed. and trans.) London: Oxford University Press.

Paykel, E. S., & Dienelt, M. N. (1971). Suicide attempts following acute depression. *Journal of Nervous and Mental Disorders, 153*(4), 234–243.

Pearl, D., Bouthilet, L., & Lazar, J. (Eds.). (1982). *Television and behavior: Ten years of scientific progress and implications for the eighties* (Vols. 1 & 2). Washington, DC: U.S. Government Printing Office.

Peck, R. C. (1968). Psychological development in the second half of life. In B. L. Neugarten (Ed.), *Middle age and aging* (pp. 88–98). Chicago: University of Chicago Press.

Peplau, L., Rubin, Z., & Hill, C. (1977). Sexual intimacy in dating relationships. *Journal of Social Issues, 2*, 86–109.

Perlman, D., Gerson, A., & Spinner, B. (1978). Loneliness among senior citizens: An empirical report. *Essence, 2*(4), 239–248.

Perlman, D., & Peplau, L. (1984). Loneliness research: A survey of empirical findings. In L. Peplau & S. Goldston (Eds.), *Preventing the harmful consequences of severe and persistent loneliness* (pp. 13–46). Rockville, MD: National Institute of Mental Health.

Perls, F. (1973). *The gestalt approach and eyewitness to therapy*. Palo Alto: Science & Behavior Books.

Persson, G., & Nordlund, C. (1985). Agoraphobics and social phobics: Differences in background factors, syndrome profiles, and therapeutic response. *Acta Psychiatr. Scandinavia, 71*, 148–159.

Pestrak, V. A., & Martin, D. (1985). Cognitive development and aspects of adolescent sexuality. *Adolescence, XX*(80), 981–987.

Peterson, K. (1986). Work commitment of college females. *College Student Journal*.

Pettis, K., & Hughes, R. (1985, February). Sexual victimization of children. A current perspective. *Behavioral Disorders*, 136–144.

Peznecker, B. L., & McNeil, J. (1975). Relationship among health habits, social assets, psychologic well-being, life change, and alterations in health status. *Nursing Research, 24*(6), 442–449.

Pfeffer, C. R. (1986). *The suicidal child*. New York: Guilford Press.

Pfeiffer, E., Verwoerdt, A., & Davis, G. C. (1972). Sexual behavior in middle life. *American Journal of Psychiatry, 128*(10), 82–87.

Pfeiffer, E., Verwoerdt, A., & Wang, H. S. (1968). Sexual behavior in aged men and women. *Archives of General Psychiatry, 19*, 153–158.

Phares, E. J. (1988). *Clinical psychology: Concepts, methods, and profession* (3rd ed.). Chicago: Dryden.

Phillips, D., McCartney, K., & Scarr, S. (1987). Child-care quality and children's social development. *Developmental Psychology, 23*(4), 537–543.

Piaget, J. (1952/1966). *The origins of intelligence in children*. Trans. Margaret Cook. New York: International Universities Press.

Piaget, J. (1972). Intellectual evolution from adolescence to adulthood. *Human Development, 15*, 1–12.

Piaget, J., & Inhelder, B. (1969). *The psychology of the child*. New York: Basic Books.

Pines, M. (1979, January). Superkids. *Psychology Today*, 53–63.

Pines, M. (1982, April 6). Recession is linked to far-reaching psychological harm. *The New York Times*.

Plomin, R. (1986). *Development, genetics, and psychology*. Hillsdale, NJ: Erlbaum.

Podd, M. H. (1972). Ego identity status and morality: The relationship between two developmental constructs. *Developmental Psychology, 6*, 497–507.

Polansky, N. (1981). *Damaged parents: An anatomy of child neglect*. Chicago: University of Chicago Press.

Polly, J. (1986). *Preventing teenage suicide*. New York: Human Sciences Press.

Prasinos, S., & Tittler, B. (1984). The existential context of lovestyles: An empirical study. *Journal of Humanistic Psychology, 24*(1), 95–112.

Prediger, D. J., & Sawyer, R. L. (1986). Ten years of career development: A nationwide survey of high school students. *Journal of Counseling and Development, 65*, 45–49.

President's Commission on Mental Health, 1977. (1978). Report to the President. Washington, DC: U.S. Government Printing Office.

Previn, L. A. (1963). The need to predict and control under conditions of threat. *Journal of Personality, 31*, 570–587.

Price, R. (1965). Trial marriage in the Andes. *Ethnology, 4*, 310–322.

Pringle, M. L. K., & Fides, D. O. (1970). *The challenge of Thalidomide: A pilot study of the educational needs of children in Scotland affected by the drug*. London: Longman Group Ltd., in association with the National Bureau for Co-operation in Child Care.

Provence, S., & Lipton, R. C. (1962). *Infants in institutions*. New York: International Universities Press.

Putnam, F., Guroff, J., Silberman, E., Barban, L., & Post, R. (1986). The clinical phenomenology of multiple personality disorder: Review of 100 recent cases. *Journal of Clinical Psychiatry, 47*(6), 285–293.

Quindlen, A. (1977, November 28). Relationships: Independence vs. intimacy. *The New York Times*.

Quinn, S. (1982, January). The competence of babies. *Atlantic Monthly*, 54–62.

Rada, R. (1975, March). Alcohol and rape. *Medical Aspects of Human Sexuality*, 48–60.

Rada, R. (1977, January). Commonly asked questions about the rapist. *Medical Aspects of Human Sexuality*, 47–56.

Raelin, J. A. (1985). Work patterns in the professional life cycle. *Journal of Occupational Psychology, 58*, 177–187.

Rank, O. (1929). *The trauma of birth*. New York: Harcourt.

Rapoport, D. (1976). Pour une naissance sans violence: Résultats d'une première enquête. *Bulletin de Psychologie, 29*(322), 552–560. Summarized in D. Kliot & L. Silverstein, The Leboyer approach: A new concern for the psychological aspects of the childbirth experience. In B. Blum, et al. (Eds.), (1980). *Psychological aspects of pregnancy, birthing, and bonding* (pp. 283–284). New York: Human Sciences Press.

Rayner, E. (1986). *Human development*. London: Allen & Unwin.

Redd, W. H., Porterfield, A. L., & Anderson, B. L. (1979). *Behavioral modification: Behavioral approaches to human problems*. New York: Random House.

Reichard, S., Livson, F., & Peterson, P. G. (1962). *Aging and personality: A study of eighty-seven older men*. New York: John Wiley & Sons.

Reid, W. (1985). The antisocial personality: A review. *Hospital and Community Psychiatry, 36*(8), 831–837.

Reinhold, R. (1982, February 25). Student abuse of drugs reported to decline. *The New York Times*.

Reisman, J. M. (1981). Adult friendships. In S. Duck & R. Gilmour (Eds.), *Personal relationships Vol. 2: Developing personal relationships* (pp. 205–230). New York: Academic Press.

Reiss, B. F. (1980). Psychological tests in homosexuality. In J. Marmor (Ed.), *Homosexual behavior*. New York: Basic Books.

Reker, G. T., Peacock, E. J., & Wong, P. T. P. (1987). Meaning and purpose in life and well-being: A life-span perspective. *Journal of Gerontology, 42*(1), 44–49.

Revenson, T., & Johnson, J. (1984). Social and demographic correlates of loneliness in late life. *American Journal of Community Psychology, 12*(1), 71–85.

Richardson, L. (1986). *The new other woman*. New York: Free Press.

Riley, M. W., & Foner, A. E. (1968). *Aging and society* (Vol. 1: *An inventory of retirement findings*). New York: Russell Sage Foundation.

Roberto, K., & Scott, J. (1986). Friendships of older men and women: Exchange patterns and satisfaction. *Psychology and Aging, 1*(2), 103–109.

Roberts, R. E. (1987). Epidemiological issues in measuring preventive effects. In R. F. Munoz (Ed.), *Depression prevention, research directions*. Washington: Hemisphere.

Robinson, B. E., Rowland, B. H., & Coleman, M. (1986). *Latchkey kids*. Lexington, MA: Lexington Books.

Robinson, I. E., & Jedlicka, D. (1982). Change in sexual attitudes and behavior of college students from 1965 to 1980: A research note. *Journal of Marriage and the Family, 44*(1), 237–240.

Rogers, C. (1959). A theory of therapy, personality, and interpersonal relationships, as developed in the client-centered framework. In S. Koch (Ed.), *Psychology: A study of a science: Vol. 3*. New York: McGraw-Hill.

Rogers, C. M. (1961). *On becoming a person: A therapist's view of psychotherapy*. Boston: Houghton Mifflin.

Rogers, C. R. (1951). *Client-centered therapy*. Boston: Houghton Mifflin.

Rogers, C. R. (1959). A theory of therapy, personality, and interpersonal relationships, as developed in the client-centered framework. In S. Koch (Ed.), *Psychology: A study of a science* (Vol. 3). New York: McGraw-Hill.

Rogers, C. R. (1961). *On becoming a person: A therapist's view of psychology*. Boston: Houghton Mifflin.

Rogers, C. R. (1961). *On becoming a person*. Boston: Houghton Mifflin.

Rogers, C. R. (1986). Client-centered therapy. In I. L. Kutash & A. Wolf (Eds.), *Psychotherapist's casebook*. San Francisco: Jossey-Bass.

Rogers, D. (1982). *The adult years: An introduction to aging*. Englewood Cliffs, NJ: Prentice-Hall.

Rohsenow, D. (1983). Drinking habits and expectancies about alcohol's effects for self versus others. *Journal of Consulting and Clinical Psychology, 51*, 752–756.

Rollins, B. C., & Feldman, H. (1970). Marital satisfaction over the life cycle. *Journal of Marriage and the Family, 32*, 20–37.

Rose, S. (1985). Same- and cross-sex friendships and the psychology of homosociality. *Sex Roles, 12*(1,2), 63–74.

Rosecan, J., & Spitz, H. (1987). Cocaine reconceptualized: Historical overview. In H. Spitz & J. Rosecan (Eds.), *Cocaine abuse: New directions in treatment and research* (pp. 5–18). New York: Brunner/Mazel.

Rosen, B., & Jerdee, T. H. (1976). The nature of job-related age stereotypes. *Journal of Applied Psychology, 61*, 180–183.

Rosenblatt, J. (1981, May). Teenage drinking. *Editorial Research Reports* (Vol. 1, No. 18) (pp. 351–367). Washington, DC.

Rosenhan, D. (1973). On being sane in insane places. *Science, 179*, 250–257.

Rosenhan, D. L., & Seligman, M. E. P. (1984). *Abnormal psychology*. New York: W. W. Norton.

Rosenman, R. H., & Chesney, M. A. (1986). Type A behavior pattern: Its relationship to coronary heart disease and its modification by behavioral and pharmacological approaches. In M. R. Zales (Ed.), *Stress in health and disease*. New York: Brunner/Mazel.

Rosenzweig, M. R., & Porter, L. W. (1981). Counseling psychology: Career interventions, research and theory. In M. R. Rosenzweig & L. W. Porter (Eds.), *Annual Review of Psychology*. Palo Alto, CA: Annual Reviews.

Ross, C., & Huber, J. (1985). Hardship and depression. *Journal of Health and Social Behavior, 26*(4), 312–326.

Rotenberg, K. (1986). Same-sex patterns and sex differences in the trust-value basis of children's friendships. *Sex Roles, 15*(11,12), 613–626.

Rowe, C. J. (1983). *An outline of psychiatry* (8th ed.). Dubuque, IA: Wm. C. Brown Company.

Roy, A. (1986). Depression, attempted suicide, and suicide in patients with chronic schizophrenia. *Psychiatric Clinics of North America, 9*(1), 193–206.

Rubenstein, C., & Shaver, P. (1982). *In search of intimacy.* New York: Delacorte.

Rubin, L. B. (1976). *Worlds of pain: Life in the working-class family.* New York: Basic Books.

Rubin, Z. (1974). Liking and loving. In Z. Rubin (Ed.), *Doing unto others.* Englewood Cliffs, NJ: Prentice-Hall.

Rubin, Z. (1979, October). Seeking a cure for loneliness. *Psychology Today,* 82–90.

Rubin, Z., Hill, C., Peplau, L., & Dunkel-Schetter, C. (1980). Self-disclosure in dating couples: Sex roles and the ethic of openness. *Journal of Marriage and the Family, 42*(2), 305–317.

Rudin, G. (1986). Depression in the mentally ill: An overview. *American Journal of Psychiatry, 143*(6), 696–705.

Rusbult, C., Zembrodt, I., & Iwaniszek, J. (1986). The impact of gender and sex-role orientation on responses to dissatisfaction in close relationships. *Sex Roles, 15* (1,2), 1–20.

Russek, H. I., & Russek, L. G. (1981). Behavior patterns and emotional stress in the etiology of coronary heart disease: Sociological and occupational aspects. In D. Wheatly (Ed.), *Stress and the heart.* New York: Raven Press.

Russell, D., Peplau, L. A., & Ferguson, M. L. (1978). Developing a measure of loneliness. *Journal of Personality Assessment, 42*(3), 290–294.

Rutter, M. (1978). Early sources of security and competence. In J. Bruner & A. Garton (Eds.), *Human growth and development.* Oxford: Clarendon Press.

Rutter, M. (1984, March). Resilient children. *Psychology Today,* 56–65.

Rutter, M. (1987). Psychosocial resilience and protective mechanisms. *American Journal of Orthopsychiatry, 57*(3), 316–331.

Rybal, E. R. (1988). Mental health and aging. *American Psychologist, 42* (3), 189–194.

Sadat, Anwar. (1978). *In search of identity: An autobiography.* New York: Harper & Row.

Safier, G. (1964). A study in relationships between the life and death concepts in children. *Journal of Genetic Psychology, 105,* 283–294.

Sagan, L. (1988). *The health of nations: True causes of sickness and well-being.* New York: Basic Books.

Sager, C. J. (1986). Couples therapy and marriage contracts. In I. L. Kutash & A. Wolf (Eds.), *Psychotherapist's casebook.* San Francisco: Jossey-Bass.

Salovey, P., & Rodin, J. (1985). The heart of jealousy. *Psychology Today, 19*(9), 22–29.

Salovey, P., & Rodin, J. (1986). The differentiation of social-comparison jealousy and romantic jealousy. *Journal of Personality and Social Psychology, 50*(6), 1100–1112.

Sameroff, A. J. (1975). Early influences on development: Fact or fancy? *Merrill-Palmer Quarterly of Behavior Development, 21,* 267–294.

Santrock, J., & Sitterle, K. (1987). Parent-child relationships in stepmother families. In K. Pasley & M. Ihinger-Tallman (Eds.), *Remarriage and stepfamilies today: Theory and research.* New York: Guilford Press.

Santrock, J., Warshak, R., Lindberg, C., & Meadows, L. (1982). Children's and parents' observed social behavior in stepfather families. *Child Development, 53,* 472–480.

Sanua, V. (1987). Standing against an established ideology: Infantile autism, a case in point. *The Clinical Psychologist, 40*(4), 96–101.

Sarason, I. (1972). *Abnormal psychology: The problem of maladaptive behavior.* New York: Appleton-Century-Crofts.

Sarason, I., & Sarason, B. (1980). *Abnormal psychology.* Englewood Cliffs, NJ: Prentice-Hall.

Sarason, I., & Sarason, B. (1984). *Abnormal psychology.* Englewood Cliffs, NJ: Prentice-Hall.

Sarason, I. G., Johnson, J. H., & Siegel, J. M. (1978). Assessing the impact of life changes: Development of the Life Experience Survey. *Journal of Consulting and Clinical Psychology, 46,* 932–946.

Sauer, L., & Fine, M. (1988). Parent-child relationships in stepparent families. *Journal of Family Psychology, 1,* 434–451.

Savine, W., and Kamin, P. (1987). *About mourning.* New York: Human Sciences Press.

Scanzoni, J., & Szinovacz, M. (1980). *Family decision-making: A developmental sex role model.* Beverly Hills, CA: Sage Publications.

Scarf, M. (1981, January 29). Hers. *The New York Times.*

Schacter, S. (1964). The interaction of cognitive and physiological determinants of emotional states. In L. Berkowitz (Ed.), *Advances in experimental social psychology* (pp. 49–80). New York: Academic Press.

Schaefer, E. (1986). *How do we tell the children.* New York: Newmarket Press.

Scheff, T. (1975). *Labeling madness.* Englewood Cliffs, NJ: Prentice-Hall.

Schein, E. H. (1978). *Career dynamics: matching individual and organizational needs.* Reading, MA: Addison-Wesley.

Schick, F. (Ed.). (1986). *Statistical handbook on aging Americans.* Phoenix: Oryx Press.

Schill, T., Ramanaiah, N., & O'Laughlin, S. (1985). Relation of expression of hostility to coping with stress. *Psychological Reports, 56,* 193–194.

Schmeck, H. M., Jr. (1979, June 19). Researchers find surprises in process of aging. *The New York Times.*

Schmidt, H., & Fonda, C. (1956). The reliability of psychiatric diagnosis: A new look. *Journal of Abnormal and Social Psychology, 52,* 262–267.

Schmidt, N., & Sermat, V. (1983). Measuring loneliness in different relationships. *Journal of Personality and Social Psychology, 44*(5), 1038–1047.

Schnieder, D., Hastorf, A., & Ellsworth, D. (1979). *Person perception* (2nd ed.). Reading, MA: Addison-Wesley.

Schonfield, D. (1982). Who is stereotyping whom and why? *The Gerontologist, 22*(3), 267–272.

Schopler, E., & Dalldorf, J. (1980). Autism: Definition, diagnosis, and management. *Hospital Practice, 15*(6), 64–69, 72–73.

Schultz, D. (1976). *Growth psychology: Models of the healthy personality.* New York: Van Nostrand Reinhold.

Schultz, N., & Moore, D. (1984). Loneliness: Correlates, attributions, and coping among older adults. *Personality and Social Psychology Bulletin, 10*(1), 67–77.

Schur, M. (1972). *Freud: Living and dying.* New York: International Universities Press.

Schutz, W. (1986). Encounter groups. In I. L. Kutash & A. Wolf (Eds.), *Psychotherapist's casebook.* San Francisco: Jossey-Bass.

Schwartz, M. (1982). *TV and teens.* Reading, MA: Addison-Wesley.

Schwebel, A., & Cherlin, D. (1972). Effects of social and physical distance in teacher-pupil relationships. *Journal of Educational Psychology, 63,* 543–550.

Schwebel, A., Kaswan, J., Sills, G., & Hackel, A. (1976). University extension in urban neighborhoods: A new approach. *Journal of Higher Education, 17,* 205–215.

Schwebel, A., Schwebel, B., Schwebel, C., & Schwebel, M. (1979). *The student teacher's handbook.* New York: Barnes and Nobel.

Schwebel, A., Schwebel, B., Schwebel, C., Schwebel, M., & Schwebel, R. (1989). *A guide to a happier family: overcoming the anger, frustration, and boredom that destroys family life.* Los Angeles: J. P. Tarcher.

Schwebel, A. I., & Bernstein, A. J. (1970). The effects of impulsivity on the performance of lower-class children on four WISC subtests. *American Journal of Orthopsychiatry, 40,* 629–636.

Schwebel, A. I., Fine, M., Moreland, J. R., & Prindle, P. (1988). Clinical work with divorced and widowed fathers: The adjusting family model. In P. Bronstein & C. P. Cowan (Eds.), *Fatherhood today: Men's changing role in the family.* New York: Wiley.

Schwebel, A. I., Jones, D. A., Kaswan, J. W., & Napier, J. (1978, Spring). Developing a community concern index. *Journal of Community Development Society of America, 9*(1), 80–89.

Schwebel, A. I., Moreland, J., Steinkohl, R., Lentz, S., & Stewart, J. (1982). Research-based interventions with divorced families. *Personnel and Guidance Journal, 60,* 523–528.

Schwebel, M. (1986). The study of stress and coping in the nuclear age: A new specialty. In M. Schwebel (Ed.), *Mental health implications of life in the nuclear age.* Armonk, NY: M. E. Sharpe. (Also, *International Journal of Mental Health, 15*(1–3), 5–15.)

Schwebel, M., & Maher, C. M. (Eds.). (1986). *Facilitating cognitive development: International perspectives, programs and practices.* New York: Haworth Press.

Schwebel, M., & Schwebel, B. (1981). Children's reactions to the threat of nuclear plant accidents. *American Journal of Orthopsychiatry, 51*(2), 260–270.

Schwebel, R. (1989). *Saying no is not enough.* New York: Newmarket Press.

Schwebel, R. S., Schwebel, A. I., & Schwebel, M. (1985). The psychological/mediation intervention model. *Professional Psychology, 16,* 86–97.

Segal, E. (1977). *Love story.* New York: Avon.

Segal, M. (1974). Alphabet and attraction: An unobtrusive measure of the effect of propinquity in a field setting. *Journal of Personality and Social Psychology, 30,* 654–657.

Seixas, J., & Youcha, G. (1985). *Children of alcoholism: A survivor's manual.* New York: Crown Publishers.

Seligman, M. E. P. (1975). *Helplessness: On depression, development, and death.* San Francisco: W. H. Freeman.

Seligman, M., Peterson, C., Kaslow, N., Alloy, L., & Abramsom, I. (1984). Attributional style and depressive symptoms among children. *Journal of Abnormal Psychology, 93,* 235–238.

Selim, R., & the Editors of *The Futurist.* (Feb. 1979). World Future Society, 4916 St. Elmo Ave. Bethesda, MD 20814.

Selman, R., & Selman, A. (1979, October). Children's ideas about friendship: A new theory. *Psychology Today, 114,* 70–80.

Selye, H. (1976). *The stress of life* (2nd ed.). New York: McGraw-Hill. (Original work published 1956)

Selye, H. (1980). *The guide to stress research.* New York: Van Nostrand Reinhold.

Selye, H. (1980). The stress concept today. In I. L. Kutash, L. B. Schlesinger, & Associates (Eds.), *Handbook on stress and anxiety.* San Francisco: Jossey-Bass.

Selye, H. (1982). History and present status of the stress concept. In L. Goldberger & S. Breznitz (Eds.), *Handbook of stress.* New York: Free Press. (Original work published in 1936)

Serafica, F., & Rose, S. (1982). Parents' sex role attitudes and children's concept of femininity and masculinity. In I. Gross, J. Downing, & A. D'Heurle (Eds.), *Sex role attitudes and cultural change* (pp. 11–24). Boston: Reidel.

Sexton, L. (1979). *Between two worlds: Young women in crisis.* New York: William Morrow.

Shaffer, M. (1982). *Life after stress.* New York: Plenum.

Sheehy, G. (1976). *Passages: Predictable crises of adult life.* New York: E. P. Dutton.

Sheehy, G. (1981). *Pathfinders.* New York: William Morrow.

Shneidman, E. S. (1971, June). You and death. *Psychology Today,* 43.

Shneidman, E. S. (1973). *Deaths of man.* New York: Quadrangle, *New York Times.*

Shneidman, E. S. (1977). The college student and death. In H. Feifel (Ed.), *New meanings of death.* New York: McGraw-Hill.

Shneidman, E. S. (1985). *Definition of suicide.* New York: Wiley.

Siegel, O. (1982). Personality development in adolescence. In B. Wolman (Ed.), *Handbook of developmental psychology* (pp. 537–548). Englewood Cliffs, NJ: Prentice-Hall.

Siegel, R. K. (1980, October). The psychology of life after death. *American Psychologist, 35*(10), 911–931.

Sigall, H., & Landy, D. (1973). Radiating beauty: The effects of having a physically attractive partner on person perception. *Journal of Personality and Social Psychology, 28,* 218–224.

Simenauer, J., & Carroll, D. (1982). *Singles: The new Americans.* New York: Simon & Schuster.

Singer, J., & Singer, D. (1986). Family experiences and television viewing as predictors of children's imagination, restlessness, and aggression. *Journal of Social Issues, 42*(3), 107–124.

Singer, J. L. (1976, July). Fantasy: The foundation of serenity. *Psychology Today,* 32–37.

Sivy, M. (1985, October). The middle-aged shape of things to come. *Money,* 67–72.

Skinner, B. F. (1938). *The behavior of organisms.* New York: Appleton-Century-Crofts.

Skinner, B. F. (1948). *Walden two.* New York: Macmillan.

Skinner, B. F. (1953). *Science and human behavior.* New York: Macmillan.

Skinner, B. F. (1971). *Beyond freedom and dignity.* New York: Alfred A. Knopf.

Skinner, B. F. (1974). *About behaviorism.* New York: Alfred A. Knopf.

Skinner, D. (1980). Dual career family stress and coping: A literature review. *Family Relations, 29,* 473–480.

Slade, A. (1987). Quality of attachment and early symbolic play. *Developmental Psychology, 53*(1), 78–85.

Slade, P., & Russell, G. (1973). Awareness of body dimensions in anorexia nervosa: Cross-sectional and longitudinal studies. *Psychological Medicine, 3,* 188–199.

Slaney, R. B. (1984). Relation of career indecision to changes in expressed vocational interests. *Journal of Counseling Psychology, 31*(3), 349–355.

Sloan, I. (1980). *Living together: Unmarrieds and the law.* Dobbs Ferry, NY: Oceana Publications.

Smith, C. (1947). Effects of maternal undernutrition upon the newborn infant in Holland. *Journal of Pediatrics, 30,* 229–243.

Smith, M. L., Glass, G. V., & Miller, T. I. (1980). *The benefits of psychotherapy.* Baltimore, MD: Johns Hopkins University Press.

Snyder, E. (1973). Attitudes: A study of homogeny in marital selectivity. In M. Lasswell & T. Lasswell (Eds.), *Love, marriage, family.* Glenview, IL: Scott, Foresman.

Sobel, D. (1980, March 11). Problems of infants lead to new psychiatric focus. *The New York Times.*

Somerville, A. W., Allen, A. R., Noble, B. A., & Sedgwick, D. L. (1984). Effect of a stress management class: One year later. *Teaching of Psychology, 11,* 82–85.

Sontag, L. W. (1941). The significance of fetal environmental differences. *American Journal of Obstetrics and Gynecology, 42,* 996–1003.

Sorenson, R. (1973). *Adolescent sexuality in contemporary America.* New York: World.

Spence, K. W. (1960). *Behavior theory and learning.* Englewood Cliffs, NJ: Prentice-Hall.

Spencer, S. (1979, May). Childhood's end. *Harper's,* 16–19.

Spiegel, J. (1960). The resolution of role conflict within the family. In N. Bell & E. Vogel (Eds.), *A modern introduction to the family* (pp. 365–381). New York: Free Press.

Spielberger, C. D. (1966). Theory and research on anxiety. In C. D. Spielberger (Ed.), *Anxiety and behavior.* New York: Academic Press.

Spielberger, C. D. (1976). The nature and measurement of anxiety. In C. D. Spielberger & R. Diaz-Guerrero (Eds.), *Cross-cultural anxiety.* Washington: Hemisphere.

Spielberger, C. D., & Sarason, I. G. (1986). *Stress and anxiety* (Vol. 10). Washington: Hemisphere.

Spielberger, C. D., & Sarason, I. G. (1985). *Stress and anxiety, volume 10: A sourcebook of theory and research.* Washington: Hemisphere.

Spinetta, J. J., & Rigler, D. (1972). The child-abusing parent: A psychological review. *Psychological Bulletin, 77*(4), 296–304.

Spinetta, J. J., Rigler, D., & Karon, M. (1973). Anxiety in the dying child. *Pediatrics, 52,* 841–844.

Spitz, R. A. (1945). Hospitalism. In O. Fenichel (Ed.), *The psychoanalytic study of the child* (Vol. 1). New York: International Universities Press.

Spitz, R. A. (1945). Hospitalization: An inquiry into the genesis of psychiatric conditions in early childhood. In A. Freud, et al. (Eds.), *The psychoanalytic study of the child.* New York: International Universities Press.

Spitz, R. A. (1965). *The first year of life.* New York: International Universities Press.

Splete, H., & Freeman-George, A. (1985). Family influences on the career development of young adults. *Journal of Career Development,* (Vol. 12). 55–64.

Spock, B., & Rothenberg, M. (1985). *Baby and child care.* New York: Pocket Books.

Srole, L., Michael, S. T., Opler, M. K., & Rennie, T. A. C. (1962). *Mental health in the metropolis: The midtown Manhattan study.* New York: McGraw-Hill.

Sroufe, L. A. (1986). Appraisal: Bowlby's contribution to psychoanalytic theory and developmental psychology; attachment, separation, loss. *Journal of Child Psychology and Psychiatry and Allied Disciplines, 27*(6), 841–849.

Stafford, R., Backman, E., & Dibona, P. (1977). The division of labor among cohabiting and married couples. *Journal of Marriage and the Family, 34,* 43–59.

Staines, G., Pottick, K., & Fudge, D. (1986). Wives' employment status and husbands' attitudes toward work and life. *Journal of Applied Psychology, 71*(1), 118–128.

Staines, G. L., Pottick, K. J., & Fudge, D. (1986). Wives' employment and husbands' attitudes toward work and life. *Journal of Applied Psychology 71,* 118–128.

Stark, E. (1985, December). Stress, depression and herpes. *Psychology Today, 19,* 12.

Steele, C. M., Southwick, L., & Pagano, R. (1986). Drinking your troubles away: The role of activity in mediating alcohol's reduction of psychological stress. *Journal of Abnormal Psychology, 95*(2), 173–180.

Steers, R. M. (1984). *Organizational behavior.* Glenview, IL: Scott, Foresman.

Stein, D. M., & Lambert, M. J. (1984). Telephone counseling and crisis intervention. *American Journal of Community Psychology, 12,* 101–126.

Stein, M., Marx, M., Taggart, S., & Bass, R. (1982). Routine neonatal circumcision: The gap between contemporary policy and practice. *The Journal of Family Practice, 15*(1), 47–53.

Stein, M., & Schleifer, S. J. (1985). In M. R. Zales (Ed.), *Stress in health and disease.* New York: Brunner/Mazel.

Stein, P. (1976). *Single.* Englewood Cliffs, NJ: Prentice-Hall.

Stein, R. (1984). The Pentagon employee referral service. *Employee Assistance Programs Digest, 4*(5), 22–24.

Steinberg, L. (1985). Early temperamental antecedents of adult Type A behaviors. *Developmental Psychology, 21*(6), 1171–1180.

Steiner, C. (1981). *Healing alcoholism.* New York: Grove Press.

Sterling, S., Cowen, E. L., Weissberg, R. P., Lotyczewski, B. S., & Boike, M. (1985). Recent stressful life events and young children's school adjustment. *American Journal of Community Psychology, 13*(1), 87–98.

Sternberg, R. (1986). A triangular theory of love. *Psychological Review, 45*(2), 119–135.

Sternberg, R., & Grajek, S. (1984). The nature of love. *Journal of Personality and Social Psychology, 47*(2), 312–329.

Sternberg, R. cited in Goleman, D. (1984, November 20). Psychologists start to take the measure of love. *New York Times,* C1 & C12.

Sternberg, R. J. (1985). *Beyond IQ: A triarchic theory of human intelligence.* New York: Cambridge University Press.

Stewart, A. J., Sokol, M., Healy, J. M. Jr., & Vhester, N. L. (1986). Longitudinal studies of psychological consequences of life changes in children and adults. *Journal of Personality and Social Psychology, 50*(1), 143–151.

Stewart, F., Guest, F., Stewart, G., & Hatcher, R. (1979). *My body, my health: The concerned woman's guide to gynecology.* New York: Wiley.

Stewart, J., Schwebel, A. I., & Fine, M. (1986). The impact of custodial arrangement on the adjustment of recently divorced fathers. *Journal of Divorce, 9*(3), 55–65.

Stinnett, N., Collins, J., & Montgomery, J. E. (1970). Marital need satisfaction of older husbands and wives. *Journal of Marriage and the Family, 32,* 428–434.

Stinnett, N., & Walters, J. (1977). *Relationships in marriage and family.* New York: Macmillan.

Stokols, D. (1986). A congruence analysis of human stress. In C. D. Spielberger & I. G. Sarason (Eds.), *Stress and anxiety,* (Vol. 10). Washington: Hemisphere.

Strain, J. S. (1978). *Psychological interventions in medical practice.* New York: Appleton-Century-Crofts.

Strong, C. (1974). *Interest inventory of the Strong Vocational Interest Blank.* Stanford, CA: Stanford University Press.

Suiin, R. M. (1976, December). How to break the vicious cycle of stress. *Psychology Today,* 69–70.

Sullivan, H. S. (1953). *The interpersonal theory of psychiatry.* New York: W. W. Norton.

Sullivan, H. S. (1970). *The psychiatric interview.* New York: W. W. Norton. (Original work published 1954)

Sundberg, N. D., Tyler, L. E., & Taplin, J. R. (1973). *Clinical psychology: Expanding horizons.* New York: Appleton-Century-Crofts.

Super, D. E. (1953). A theory of vocational development. *American Psychologist, 8,* 185–190.

Super, D. E. (1957). *The psychology of careers.* New York: Harper & Row.

Super, D. E., & Hall, D. T. (1978). Career development: Exploration and planning. In N. R. Rosenzweig & L. W. Porter (Eds.), *Annual review of psychology.* Palo Alto, CA: Annual Reviews Inc.

Super, D. E., et al. (1957). *Vocational development: A framework for research.* New York: Teachers College, Columbia University.

Super, D. E., et al. (1963). *Career development: Self-concept theory.* New York: College Entrance Examination Board.

Sutherland, S., & Scherl, D. (1970, April). Patterns of response among victims of rape. *American Journal of Orthopsychiatry, 40,* 503–510.

Sutton-Smith, B., & Rosenberg, B. G. (1970). *The sibling.* New York: Holt, Rinehart & Winston.

Svein, K., & Sherlock, D. (1979). Dyscalculia and dyslexia. *Bulletin of the Orton Society, 29,* 269–276.

Szasz, T. (1961). *The myth of mental illness.* New York: Harper & Row.

Szulc, T. (1979, May 27). Homecoming for the pope. *The New York Times Magazine*, 14–22, 44–52.

Taber, J., & McCormick, R. (1987). The pathological gambler in treatment. In T. Galski (Ed.), *The handbook of pathological gambling* (pp. 137–168). Springfield, IL: Thomas.

Taub, W. (1976). Sex and infection: Venereal diseases. In B. J. Sadock, H. I. Kaplan, & A. M. Freedman (Eds.), *The sexual experience*. Baltimore, MD: Williams & Wilkins.

Teplin, L. (1984). Criminalizing mental disorder: The comparative arrest rate of mentally ill. *American Psychologist, 39*(7), 794–803.

Terborg, J. R. (1985). Working women and stress. In T. Beehr & R. Bhagat (Eds.). *Human stress and cognition in organizations* (pp. 245–286). New York: Wiley.

Terestman, N. (1980). Mood quality and intensity in nursery school children as predictors of behavior disorder. *American Journal of Orthopsychiatry, 50*(1), 125–138.

Terkel, S. (1972). *Working*. New York: Random House.

Terry, R. D., & Katzman, R. (1983). Senile dementia of the Alzheimer type. *Annals of Neurology, 14,* 497–506.

Tesch, S., & Martin, R. (1983). Friendship concepts of young adults in two age groups. *Journal of Psychology, 115,* 7–12.

The Select Committee. (1985, Summer). Findings of the select committee on children, adolescents and families: Excerpts from the 1983 report to the U.S. Congress. *International Journal of Family Therapy, 7*(2), 63–95.

Thibaut, J., & Kelley, H. (1959). *The social psychology of groups.* New York: Wiley.

Thoits, P. A. (1986). Social support as coping assistance. *Journal of Consulting and Clinical Psychology, 54*(4), 416–423.

Thomas, A., & Chess, S. (1977). *Temperament and development.* New York: Brunner/Mazel.

Thomas, A., & Chess, S. (1982). Temperament and follow-up to adulthood. In R. Porter & G. Collins (Eds.), *Temperamental differences in infants and young children* (pp. 168–175). London: Pitman.

Thomas, A., & Chess, S. (1984). Genesis and evolution of behavior disorders: From infancy to early adult life. *American Journal of Psychiatry, 141,* 1–10.

Thomas, A., Chess, S., Birch, H. G., Hertzig, M. E., & Korn, S. (1963). *Behavioral individuality in early childhood.* New York: New York University Press.

Thompson, S., & Kahn, J. (1988). *The group process: Extensions and applications of basic principles.* Oxford: Pergamon.

Thoresen, C. F. (1980). Reflections on chronic health, self-control, and human ethology. *Counseling Psychologist, 8*(4), 48–58.

Thorson, G., Horack, B., & Kara, G. (1987). A replication of Kalish's study of cemetery visits. *Death Studies, 11,* 117–182.

Timiras, P. S. (1972). *Developmental physiology and aging.* New York: Macmillan.

Tives, M. B. (1971). *Older Americans: Special handling required.* Washington, DC: National Council on Aging.

Tramill, J. L., & Kleinhammer-Tramill, P. J. (1984). The relationship between Type A behavior pattern, fear of death, and manifest anxiety. *Bulletin of the Psychonomic Society, 22*(1), 42–44.

Trief, P., Elliott, D., Stein, N., & Frederickson, B. (1987). Functional organic pain: A meaningful distinction? *Journal of Clinical Psychology, 43*(2), 219–226.

Troll, L. E. (1975). *Early and middle adulthood.* Monterey, CA: Brooks/Cole.

Trujillo, M. (1986). Short-term dynamic psychotherapy. In I. L. Kutash & A. Wolf (Eds.), *Psychotherapist's casebook.* San Francisco: Jossey-Bass.

Turner, R. (1983). Direct, indirect, and moderating effects of social support upon psychological distress and associated conditions. In H. Kaplan (Ed.), *Psychological stress: Trends in theory and research.* New York: Academic Press.

U.S. Bureau of Census. (1987). *Statistical Abstract of the United States: 1988* (108th ed.). Washington, DC.

U.S. Department of Health and Human Services. (1986). *Vital statistics of the United States 1982 Volume III-Marriage and divorce.* Hyattsville, MD: National Center for Health Statistics.

U.S. Department of Health and Human Services. (1987). *Vital statistics of the United States 1983 Volume III-Mortality.* Hyattsville, MD: National Center for Health Statistics.

U.S. Department of Justice Statistics Bulletin. (1985). *The crime of rape.* Washington: U.S. Department of Justice.

United States Bureau of the Census. (1979). *Pocket Data Book,* USA.

United States Congress, Office of Technology Assessment. (1987). *Losing a million minds: Confronting the tragedy of Alzheimer's disease and other dementias.* (Publication No. OTA-BA-323). Washington, DC: Government Printing Office.

United States Department of Health and Human Services. (1980). *Alcohol and health: 4th special report to the U.S. Congress.* Washington, DC: U.S. Government Printing Office.

Urbain, E., & Kendall, P. (1985). Review of social-cognitive problem-solving interventions with children. In M. Bloom (Ed.), *Life span development* (pp. 124–142). New York: Macmillan.

USA Today. August 3, 1984. p. 16.

Vaillant, G. E. (1977). *Adaptation to life*. Boston: Little, Brown.

Vaillant, G. E. (1986). Appendix. In G. E. Vaillant (Ed.), *Empirical studies of ego mechanisms of defense*. Washington: American Psychiatric Press.

Vaillant, G. E., & Vaillant, C. O. (1981). Natural history of male psychological health, X: Work as a predictor of positive mental health. *American Journal of Psychiatry, 138*(11), 1433–1440.

Vane, J., & Motta, R. W. (1984). Group intelligence tests. In G. Goldstein & M. Hersen (Eds.), *Handbook of psychological assessment*. New York: Pergamon.

Veroff, J., Douvan, E., & Kulka, R. (1981). *The inner American: Life works and mental health from 1957–1976*. New York: Basic Books.

Vess, J., Moreland, J., Schwebel, A., & Kraut, E. (1988). Psychosocial needs of cancer patients: Learning from patients and their spouses. *Journal of Psychosocial Oncology, 6*(1,2), 31–51.

Vess, J., Moreland, J. R., & Schwebel, A. I. (1985a). An empirical assessment of the effects of cancer on family role functioning. *Journal of Psychosocial Oncology, 3*(1), 1–16.

Vess, J., Moreland, J. R., & Schwebel, A. I. (1985b). A follow-up study of role functioning and the psychological environment of families of cancer patients. *Journal of Psychosocial Oncology, 3*(2), 1–14.

Vess, J., Moreland, J. R., & Schwebel, A. I. (1986). Understanding family role reallocation following a death: A theoretical perspective. *Omega, 16*(2), 115–128.

Vetter, H. (1985). Psychodynamic factors and drug addiction. *Journal of Drug Issues, 15*(4), 447–461.

Vinokur, A., & Selzer, M. L. (1975). Desirable versus undesirable life events: Their relationship to stress and mental distress. *Journal of Personality and Social Psychology, 32*(2), 329–337.

Viorst, J. (1986). *Necessary losses*. New York: Simon & Schuster.

Voydanoff, P. (1987). *Work and family life*. Newbury Park, CA: Sage.

Vuchinich, S. (1985, October). Arguments, family style. *Psychology Today, 19*(10), 40–46.

Wachtel, P. (1983). *The poverty of affluence*. New York: Free Press.

Wachtel, P. L. (1982). What can dynamic therapies contribute to behavior therapy? *Behavior Therapy, 13*, 594–609.

Waechter, E. H. (1971). Children's awareness of fatal illness. *American Journal of Nursing, 71*, 1168–1172.

Waechter, E. H. (1974). Death anxiety in children with fatal illness (Doctoral dissertation, Stanford University, 1968). University Microfilms, No. 72–26, 056. Cited in J. J. Spinetta, The dying child's awareness of death: A review. *Psychological Bulletin, 81*(4), 256–260.

Wagner, C. (1980). Sexuality of American adolescents. *Adolescence, XV*(59), 567–580.

Wald, M. L. (1979, April 22). Hospices give help for dying patients. *The New York Times*.

Wall Street Journal, May 27, 1971, p. 1.

Wallerstein, J., & Kelly, J. (1980). *Surviving the breakup*. New York: Basic Books.

Walster, E., Bersheid, E., & Walster, G. (1973). New directions in equity research. *Journal of Personality and Social Psychology, 25*, 151–176.

Wanck, B. (1985, September). Treatment of adult children of alcoholics. *Carrier Foundation Letter*, #109. Belle Meade, NJ.

Wanderer, Z., & Cabot, T. (1978). *Letting go*. New York: Warner Communications.

Waring, E. M., Carver, C., Moran, P., & Lefcoe, D. H. (1986). Family therapy and schizophrenia: Recent developments. *Canadian Journal of Psychiatry, 31*, 154–159.

Warshak, R., & Santrock, J. (1983). The impact of divorce in father-custody and mother-custody homes: The child's perspective. In L. Kurdek (Ed.), *Children and divorce*. San Francisco: Jossey-Bass.

Washton, A., & Gold, M. (1987). Recent trends in cocaine abuse as seen from the "800-Cocaine" hotline. In A. Washton & M. Gold (Eds.), *Cocaine: A clinician's handbook* (pp. 10–22). New York: Guilford Press.

Watson, R., & DeMeo, P. (1987). Premarital cohabitation vs. traditional courtship and subsequent marital adjustment: A replication and follow-up. *Family Relations, 36*, 193–197.

Weideger, P. (1976). *Menstruation and menopause: The physiology and psychology, the myth and the reality*. New York: Alfred A. Knopf.

Weinberg, M. S., & Williams, C. J. (1976). Male homosexuals: Their problems and adaptations. In M. S. Weinberg (Ed.), *Sex research: Studies from the Kinsey Institutes*. New York: Oxford University Press.

Weiner, H. (1985). The concept of stress in the light of studies on disasters, unemployment, and loss: A critical analysis. In M. A. Zales (Ed.), *Stress in health and disease*. New York: Brunner/Mazel.

Weisman, A. (1977). The psychiatrist and the inexorable. In H. Feifel (Ed.), *New meanings of death*. New York: McGraw-Hill.

Weisman, A. (1984). *The coping capacity*. New York: Human Sciences Press.

Weiss, E., & English, O. S. (1957). *Psychosomatic medicine* (3rd ed.). Philadelphia: W. B. Saunders Company.

Weiss, J. (1981). *Your second child*. New York: Summit Books.

Wenar, C. (1982, 1989). *Psychopathology from infancy through adolescence*. New York: Random House.

Wentworth-Rohr, I. (1984). *Symptom reduction through clinical biofeedback.* New York: Human Sciences Press.

Werman, D. S. (1985). Suppression as a defense. In H. P. Blum (Ed.), *Defense and resistance: Historical perspectives and current concepts.* New York: International Universities Press.

Werner, C., & Latane, B. (1974). Interaction motivates attraction: Rats are fond of fondling. *Journal of Personality and Social Psychology, 29,* 328–334.

Werner, E. E., & Smith, R. S. (1983). *Vulnerable but invincible: A longitudinal study of resilient children and youth.* New York: McGraw-Hill.

West, L. J. (1975). A clinical and theoretical overview of hallucinatory phenomena. In R. K. Siegel & L. J. West (Eds.), *Hallucinations: Behavior, experience, and theory.* New York: John Wiley & Sons.

White House Conference on Aging. (1971, November 28–December 2). *Toward a national policy on aging: Proceedings of the 1971 Conference on Aging* (Vol. 2). Conference findings and recommendations from sections and special concerns sessions.

White, E., Elson, B., & Prawat, R. (1978). Children's conception of death. *Child Development, 49,* 307–310.

White, G., Fishbein, S., & Rutstein, J. (1981). Passionate love and the misattribution of arousal. *Journal of Personality and Social Psychology, 41,* 56–62.

White, J. (1987). Premarital cohabitation and marital stability in Canada. *Journal of Marriage and the Family, 49,* 641–647.

White, K., Speisman, J., Jackson, D., Bartis, S., & Costos, D. (1986). Intimacy maturity and its correlates in young married couples. *Journal of Personality and Social Psychology, 50*(1), 152–162.

White, R. W. (1972). *The enterprise of living: Growth and organization of personality.* New York: Holt, Rinehart & Winston.

White, R. W. (1975). *Lives in progress: A study of the natural growth of personality* (3rd ed.). New York: Holt, Rinehart & Winston. (Original work published 1952)

Whitlock, E. E. (1978). *Understanding and coping with real-life crises.* Monterey, CA: Brooks/Cole.

Whitlock, G. E. (1968). *From call to service.* Philadelphia: Westminster Press.

Whitney, C. (1978, December 29). Schools in Soviet are thorough but leave many things unsaid. *The New York Times.*

Whybrow, P. C., Akiskal, H.S., & McKinney, W. T., Jr. (1984). *Mood disorders: Toward a new psychobiology.* New York: Plenum.

Williams, D. (1985). Gender, masculinity-femininity, and emotional intimacy in same-sex friendship. *Sex Roles, 12*(5/6), 587–600.

Williams, J. (1982, April 25). Young suicides: Tragic and on the increase. *The New York Times.*

Williams, J., & Solano, C. (1983). The social reality of feeling lonely: Friendship and reciprocation. *Personality and Social Psychology Bulletin, 9*(2), 237–242.

Williams, T., & Kornblum, W. (1985). *Growing up poor.* Lexington, MA: Lexington Books.

Williamson, M., & Williamson, P. (1988). Women's preferences for penile circumcision in sexual partners. *Journal of Sex Education and Therapy, 14*(2), 8–12.

Willis, J. (1985). *Comparing contraceptives.* FDA Consumer, HHS Publication No. (FDA) 85–1123. [US Gov Printing Office 1985–416–367, 20069].

Wilson, E. O. (1978). *On human nature.* Cambridge, MA: Harvard University Press.

Winberg, J., & de Château, P. (1982). Early social development. In W. Hartup (Ed.), *Review of child development research 6*(1–44). Chicago: University of Chicago Press.

Winokur, G. (1981). *Depression, the facts.* Oxford: Oxford University Press.

Witter, F., & King, T. (1980). Cigarettes and pregnancy. *Progress in Clinical and Biological Research, 36,* 83–92.

Wolberg, L. K. (1977). *The technique of psychotherapy* (3rd ed.). New York: Grune & Stratton.

Wolff, P. (1959). Observations on newborn infants. *Psychosomatic Medicine, 21,* 110–118.

Wolff, P. (1963). Observations on the early development of smiling. In B. M. Foss (Ed.), *Determinants of infant behavior* (Vol. 2). London: Methuen.

Wolff, T., Friedman, S. B., Hoffer, M. A., & Mason, J. W. (1964). Relationships between psychological defenses and mean urinary 17-OHCS excretion rates, Part 1. A predictive study of parents of fatally ill children. *Psychosomatic Medicine, 26,* 576–591.

Wolpe, J. (1982). *The practice of behavior therapy* (3rd ed.). New York: Pergamon Press.

Wood, S. J., Bishop, R. S., & Cohen, D. (1978). *Parenting.* New York: Hart.

Woods, R. T., & Britton, P. G. (1985). *Clinical psychology of the elderly.* Rockville, MD: Aspen.

Worne, R. L. (1984). Discrimination and the older worker. *Journal of Gerontology, 34,* 861–869.

Wren, C. (1986). Midlife macho. *The New York Times,* May 10.

Yahraes, H. (1978). *Causes, detection, and treatment of childhood depression.* Washington: U.S. Department of Health, Education and Welfare.

Yalom, I. D. (1985). *Theory and practice of group psychotherapy.* New York: Basic Books.

Yankelovich, D. (1978, May). The psychological contracts at work. *Psychology Today,* 46–50.

Yankelovich, D., Zetterbergh, H., Stumpel, B., & Shanks, M. (1985). *The world of work.* New York: Octogon.

Yerkes, R. M., & Dodson, J. E. (1908). The relation of strength of stimulus to rapidity of habit formation. *Journal of Comparative Neurology and Psychology, 18,* 459–482.

Z

Zaleski, C. (1987). *Otherworld journeys.* New York: Oxford University Press.

Zegman, M. A. (1983). Women, weight, and health. In V. Franks & E. D. Rothblum (Eds.), *The stereotyping of women.* New York: Springer.

Zelnik, M., & Kim, J. (1982, May/June). Sex education and its association with teenage sexual activity, pregnancy and contraceptive use. *Family Planning Perspectives, 3,* 117–126.

Zibergeld, B. (1982, February). Bespoke therapy. A review of the practice of multimodal therapy, by A. A. Lazarus. *Psychology Today, 16*(2), 85–86.

Zimbardo, P. (1977). *Shyness.* Reading, MA: Addison-Wesley.

Zimbardo, P. (1979). *Psychology and life.* Glenview, IL: Scott, Foresman.

Zimet, C. N. (1979). Developmental task and crisis groups: The application of group psychotherapy to maturation processes. *Psychotherapy: Theory, Research and Practice, 16*(1), 2–8.

Ziv, A. (1984). *Personality and sense of humor.* New York: Springer.

Zuckerman, D. M. (1985). Confidence and aspirations: Self-esteem and self-concepts as predictors of student's life goals. *Journal of Personality, 53*(4), 543–558.

Zuckerman, M. (1976). Sexual behavior of college students. In W. W. Oaks, G. A. Melchiode, & I. Ficher (Eds.), *Sex and the life cycle.* New York: Grune & Stratton.

Credits

Box pp. 508–509 From F. Dorn and N. Welch, "Assessing Career Mythology: A Profile of High School Students" in *The School Counselor*, 33:(2), 136–142, 1985. Copyright © 1985 American School Counselor Association. **Fig. 11.2** From D. T. Hall and B. Schneider, *Organizational Climates and Careers: The Work Lives of Priests.* Copyright © 1973 Academic Press, Inc., Orlando, FL. Reprinted by permission.

Chapter 12

Extract, p. 555 From Christopher S. Wren, "Midlife Macho" in *About Men, The New York Times,* 4 May 1986. Copyright © 1986 by the New York Times Company. Reprinted by permission. **Extract, p. 578** Excerpted from Rachel Cowan, "The New Minority: Senior Citizens as Victims" in *The Village Voice.* By permission of the author and *The Village Voice.*

PHOTO CREDITS

Part Openers

Part One: © Ulrike Welsh/Photo Researchers; **Part Two:** © Robert Kalman/The Image Works.

Chapter 1

Page 7: (top) © Laimute E. Druskis/Jeroboam; (bottom left and right) © Andrew Schwebel; **page 11:** The National Library of Medicine; **page 13:** © Jane Reed/Harvard University News Office; **page 16:** Courtesy Albert Bandura; **page 19:** UPI Photo; **page 29:** NASA; **pages 30, 31:** The Bettmann Archive; **page 35:** © Andrew Schwebel; **page 36:** The Institute of Rational-Emotive Therapy.

Chapter 2

Page 50: © Hazel Hankin/Stock, Boston; **page 56:** UPI Photo; **page 61:** © Jean-Claude Lejeune; **page 63:** © Howard Dratch/The Image Works; **page 67:** © Bob Daemmrich/The Image Works; **page 69:** © James Shaffer.

Chapter 3

Page 80: © Elizabeth Crews; **page 82:** © Peter Menzel; **page 83:** © Elizabeth Crews; **page 85:** Bernard Bisson/Sygma;

page 87: © Evan Johnson/Jeroboam; **page 91:** © Roger Lubin/Jeroboam; **page 95:** © Elizabeth Crews/Stock, Boston; **page 99:** (top left) © Peter Vandermark, (top right) © Mark Antman/The Image Works, (bottom) © Arthur Grace/Stock, Boston; **page 102:** © Bruce Forrester/Jeroboam; **page 107:** © Will McIntyre/Photo Researchers; **page 109:** © David Wells/The Image Works; **page 120:** © Howard Dratch/The Image Works; **page 123:** © Jean-Claude Lejeune.

Chapter 4

Page 134: © Dion Ogust/The Image Works; **page 139:** © Jean-Claude Lejeune; **page 145:** © Bruce Roberts/Rapho/Photo Researchers; **page 147:** © Alan Carey/The Image Works; **page 149:** © Miro Vintoniv/The Picture Cube; **page 153:** © Jean-Claude Lejeune; **page 160:** © Tom Wurl/Stock, Boston; **page 175:** © John Griffin/The Image Works.

Chapter 5

Page 182: © Elizabeth Crews; **page 184:** © Andrew Schwebel; **page 186:** © Bruce Kliewe/Jeroboam; **page 192:** © Elizabeth Crews; **page 194:** © E. R. Bernstein/Peter Arnold, Inc.; **page 197:** © Schiffmann/Gamma Liaison; **page 204:** Bettmann Newsphotos; **page 208:** both from *The Minds of Billy Milligan,* Daniel Keyes, Randomhouse, 1981; **page 211:** Bettmann Newsphotos.

Chapter 6

Pages 233, 237: © Alan Carey/The Image Works; **page 243:** © Mark Antman/The Image Works; **page 251:** © Evan Johnson/Jeroboam; **page 257:** © Van Bucher/Photo Researchers; **page 259:** © Eric A. Roth/The Picture Cube; **page 262:** © Annie Hunter; **page 263:** © Jane Scherr/Jeroboam; **page 270:** © Billy E. Barnes/Jeroboam; **page 272:** © Frank Keillor/Jeroboam.

Chapter 7

Page 289: © Michael Hayman/Photo Researchers; **page 294:** © Suzanne Arms/Jeroboam; **page 305:** © Laima E. Druskis/Jeroboam; **page 309:** (box) © The Houghton Library; **page 311:** © Janice Fullman/The Picture Cube; **page 314:** © Elizabeth Crews/Stock, Boston; **page 319:** © Elizabeth Crews;

page 326: © Peter Menzel; **page 332:** © Alan Carey/The Image Works.

Chapter 8

Page 338: © Joseph Nettis/Photo Researchers; **page 340:** © Rick Smolan/Stock, Boston; **page 353:** © Michael Hayman/Stock, Boston; **page 357:** © Steve Takatsuno/The Picture Cube; **page 359:** © Barbara Alper/Stock, Boston; **page 367:** © Peter Southwick/Stock, Boston; **page 371:** © John Running/Stock, Boston; **page 375:** © Arvind Garg/Photo Researchers; **page 383:** © Jean-Claude Lejeune; **page 391:** © Elizabeth Crews; **page 394:** © Nancy Bates/The Picture Cube.

Chapter 9

Page 404: Dellenback/The Kinsey Institute; **pages 419, 421:** © Peter Menzel; **page 423:** © Frank Siteman/Stock, Boston; **page 426:** UPI/Bettmann Newsphotos; **page 436:** Phototake.

Chapter 10

Page 448: © John Coletti/Stock, Boston; **page 451:** © Renee Lynn/Photo Researchers; **page 458:** © Elizabeth Crews; **page 460:** © W. Marc Bernsau/The Image Works; **page 465:** © George W. Gardner/The Image Works; **page 476:** © Peter Menzel; **page 483:** © Elizabeth Crews; **page 484:** © Jean-Claude Lejeune.

Chapter 11

Page 502: © Elizabeth Crews/The Image Works; **page 512:** © Hazel Hankin/Stock, Boston; **page 521:** © Frank Siteman/The Picture Cube; **page 530:** © Alan Carey/The Image Works.

Chapter 12

Page 546: © Frank Siteman/The Picture Cube; **pages 567, 573:** © Elizabeth Crews; **page 575:** © Mikki Ansin/The Picture Cube.

Chapter 13

Page 584: Bettmann Newsphotos; **page 586:** © James Shaffer; **page 589:** © Elizabeth Crews; **page 593:** © Frank Siteman/The Picture Cube; **page 598:** © Michael Hayman/Stock, Boston; **page 604:** UPI/Bettmann Newsphotos; **page 605:** © Abraham Menashe/Photo Researchers.

Name Index

Crouter, A., 459
Cuber, J., 467, 470, 471
Cuellar, J.B., 586
Cunningham, J., 484
Curran, J.R., 415 (Table 9.1)
Custer, R.F., 218
Cutrona, C., 366

Dalldorf, J., 190
Damarin, F., 570
Darlington, R., 243
Darrow, C., 99, 174, 494, 526, 558, 590, 593
Davidson, G.W., 606, 607
Davidson, L.M., 107
Davis, G.C., 575
Davis, K., 380, 386
Davitz, J., 551
Davitz, L., 551
Day, D., 358
Dean, A., 122
DeCasper, A., 352
de Chateau, P., 292, 293
DeLamater, J., 414
DeLongis, A., 111
DeLora, J.S., 575
DeMaris, A., 486
DeMeo, P., 486
De Meuse, K.P., 116
Dendato, K.M., 79
Diamond, G., 109
Dibona, P., 484
Dickens, W., 358
Dienelt, M.N., 597
Diener, D., 79
DiVesta, F.J., 578
Dodge, C.P., 109
Dodson, J.E., 86
Dohrenwend, B.S., 70, 190
Dollard, J., 134
Donaldson, W.V., 560
Donegan, E., 434
Donnelly, K., 602
Dorn, F., 508
Dornbusch, S., 323
Doty, L., 372
Douglas, P., 435
Douvan, E., 70, 145, 489
Driscoll, R., 386
Dryden, W., 265
Duck, S., 393
Duke, P., 323
Dunbar, F., 143

Dunkel-Schetter, C., 375
Durlak, J.A., 587
Dusay, J.M., 275
Duvall, E., 453, 455

Eastman, M., 578
Eggert, L., 385
Ehrenberg, M., 248, 250
Ehrenberg, O., 248, 250
Eichler, L., 290
Eisler, R., 188
Elliott, D., 206
Ellis, A., 35, 61, 265, 275
Ellis, D., 606
Ellison, J., 212
Ellsworth, D., 342
Elson, B., 587
Emery, G., 119, 120, 264, 275
Engel, G.L., 185
Enkin, M., 293
Epstein, A., 290
Epstein, N.B., 280
Epstein, S., 86, 92
Erikson, E.H., 24, 42, 50, 51 (Table 2.1), 51, 54, 94, 98, 146, 290, 302, 303, 304, 306, 320, 321, 356, 516, 545, 548, 549, 585, 586
Etaugh, C., 306
Ettedgui, E., 204
Eysenck, H.J., 264

Facts on File, 223
Farina, G., 189
Fein, G., 311
Feiring, C., 352
Feldman, H., 562
Fenigstein, A., 361
Fenz, W.D., 86
Ferguson, M.L., 369
Festinger, L., 340
Feuerstein, R., 243, 244
Fides, D.O., 66, 67
Fifer, W., 352
Fine, M., 416, 476, 480, 483, 603
Fischer, J., 384
Fish, W., 590
Fishbein, H., 315
Fishbein, S., 382

Fisher, J.D., 107
Flaherty, M., 589, 592
Fleming, R., 107
Folkman, S., 82, 100, 121, 134, 135, 153, 154, 176
Fonda, C., 189
Forehand, R., 315
Fraiberg, S., 96, 301
Framo, J.L., 271
Frank, J.D., 248
Frank, R., 185
Frankl, V., 27, 500
Franks, C.M., 281
Frederickson, B., 206
Freeman, L.C., 570
Freeman-George, A., 517
Freud, A., 157, 162, 163, 185, 320
Freud, S., 19–23, 89, 90, 94, 161, 167, 168, 255, 307, 401, 602
Fried, B., 557
Friedman, H.S., 143
Friedman, M., 102, 103, 105
Friedman, S., 416
Friedman, S.B., 154
Fromm, E., 24, 374
Fudge, D., 459, 530
Fuller-von Bozzay, G., 263
Furman, E., 602
Futterman, A.D., 264
Futurist, Editors of, The, 39, 40

Gadow, K., 193
Gagnon, J., 412, 417
Gallup, G., 417
Gallwey, W.T., 146
Ganahl, G., 269, 270, 465, 476
Ganong, L., 482
Garduque, L., 306
Garfinkel, P., 197
Garmezy, N., 74, 331
Garner, D., 197
Gatchel, R.J., 107
Gatz, M., 574
Gay, P., 50
Gebhard, P.D., 411, 412
Gecas, V., 455, 456, 457
George, L., 212
Gerson, A., 370
Gerson, R., 270
Gest, T., 220
Ghila, D., 189

Loren, R., 412
Lorenz, K., 106
Lotyczewski, B.S., 112
Lowe, J.C., 42
Lowen, A., 141
Lowenstein, L., 220
Lubin, B., 106, 245
Luce, G.G., 557, 568
Luepnitz, D., 482
Luft, J., 348
Luria, Z., 416
Lustman, P.J., 264
Lutz, D., 220
Lynch, J., 588, 594

Maas, H., 360
Machlowitz, M., 534
Maddi, S., 332
Maddox, G.L., 567
Maeroff, G.I., 607
Mague, J., 606
Maher, C.M., 243
Mahler, M.S., 72, 303, 304, 601
Mainprice, J., 268
Malone, P., 392
Malone, T., 392
Malott, J.M., 140
Mandell, A.J., 555, 563
Marcia, J.E., 515
Marcus, M., 123, 124
Marks, I.M., 81, 86, 98
Marmar, C., 280
Marmor, J., 417
Martin, B., 150
Martin, C.E., 403, 411, 412, 416
Martin, D., 432
Martin, J., 323
Martin, R., 358
Marx, M., 406
Marziali, E., 280
Maslow, A.H., 29, 54, 55, 56, 57,
    58 (Table 2.2), 62, 168, 303, 373,
    499
Mason, J.W., 154
Mason, S.T., 84
Masserman, J.H., 86
Masters, W., 404, 408
Masuda, M., 143
Maurice, W.L., 119, 599
May, R., 82, 86, 93, 257
Mays, D.T., 281
McAuliffe, K., 220

McCallum, S., 567, 568
McCartney, K., 310, 311
McCary, J., 406, 417
McCaul, K.D., 140
McCormick, R., 218
McCutcheon, S.M., 328
McGoldrick, M., 270, 453
McGrath, M., 292
McGuigan, F.J., 150
McHale, S., 459
McHenry, S., 272
McKay, G., 339
McKee, P., 99, 174, 494, 526, 558, 590,
    593
McKinney, W.T., Jr., 118
McLanahan, S.S., 135
McLaughlin, S., 455, 456, 457
McLellan, A.T., 262
McLoughlin, C., 480
McNally, R., 200
Meadows, L., 482
Mednick, S.A., 72
Meer, J., 366, 576, 577
Meichenbaum, D.H., 37, 61, 176
Melko, M., 486, 487, 488 (Table 10.2)
Menninger, K., 131, 132, 134, 137, 138,
    144, 145, 186
Messer, S.B., 265
Messick, J.M., 232, 252
Metraux, R., 49
Meyers, A., 420
Michael, S.T., 70
Miller, A., 73
Miller, M., 226
Miller, N.E., 134
Miller, P., 188
Miller, R., 243, 244
Miller, T.I., 280, 282
Milner, J.S., 147
Milner, R., 293
Miner, J.B., 528
Miner, M.G., 528
Mischel, W., 61
Mitchell, R., 339
Mitchell, S.K., 556
Mogul, K.M., 281
Molineux, J.B., 478
Monroe, S., 338
Montgomery, R., 380
Moody, R., 609
Mooney, W., 34
Moore, D., 370
Moore, J.W., 42
Moorman, J., 474
Moos, R.H., 107, 176, 339
Moran, P., 270

Moreland, J.R., 188, 416, 428, 476,
    480, 596, 603
Moreno, J.L., 350
Morgan, H., 196
Morganthau, T., 226
Moriarty, A.E., 73, 300
Morris, N., 293
Moss, L., 306
Motta, R.W., 243
Moure, L., 220
Mowbray, C., 70
Munnichs, J.M.A., 587
Munoz, R.F., 122
Murdock, G., 454
Murphy, G.E., 264
Murphy, L.B., 73, 300
Myers, J., 181, 227
Myers, R.A., 255

Nadelson, C., 437
Naeye, R., 292
Nahemow, L., 340
Namir, S., 288, 290
Napier, J., 116, 117 (Table 3.3)
Nathan, P., 220
National Center for Health Statistics,
    406, 591
National Institute of Mental Health,
    U.S. Department of Health and
    Human Services, 436 (Table 9.4),
    436, 437 (Table 9.5)
Natterson, J., 413
Neeper, R., 315
Neff, J., 182
Nelson, N., 293
Neufeld, R., 212
Neugarten, B.L., 42, 550, 552, 557
Newman, B.M., 556
Newquist, J., 562
Nietzel, M.E., 207, 259, 262
Nisbett, R.E., 34
Nolen-Hoeksema, S., 184
Norcross, J.C., 266
Nordlund, C., 201
Norman, W., 565
Norton, A., 474
Notman, M., 437
Nuechterlein, K., 212
Nuernberger, P., 143
Nutman, P., 496, 532
Nye, F.I., 455, 456, 457
Nye, R., 363

T

Taber, J., 218
Taggart, S., 406
Taipale, I., 109
Taplin, J.R., 237, 238
Taub, W., 434
Tausky, C., 497, 498 (Table 11.1)
Teplin, L., 189
Terborg, J.R., 528
Teresi, J., 116
Terestman, N., 312
Terkel, S., 496, 532
Terry, K., 315
Terry, R.D., 572
Tesch, S., 358
Thibaut, J., 376
Thoits, P.A., 149
Thomas, A., 74, 293, 296, 297, 298, 300
Thompson, L.W., 122
Thompson, M., 197
Thompson, S., 275
Thoresen, C.F., 104
Thorn, B., 570
Thorson, G., 583
Thyer, B.A., 140
Tillich, P., 27
Tischler, G., 181, 227
Titler, N., 220
Tittler, B., 390
Tives, M.B., 573
Tobin, S., 54
Tonsley, B.J., 293
Tramill, J.L., 594
Tranmer, J., 292
Traupmann, J., 376
Trief, P., 206
Trujillo, M., 266, 267
Turner, B.F., 422
Turner, R., 339
Tyler, L.E., 237, 238

U

U.S. Bureau of Census, 369, 437, 457, 464, 474, 479, 486
U.S. Congress, 572
U.S. Department of Justice, 289
Uniform Crime reports, 437
Urbain, E., 315
USA Today, 553

V

Vaillant, C.O., 321
Vaillant, G.E., 50, 74, 85, 157, 158 (Table 4.1), 162, 169, 172, 173, 321, 525, 561, 575
Vane, J., 243
Veroff, J., 70, 145, 489
Verwoerdt, A., 422, 575
Vess, J., 416, 428, 596
Vetter, H., 226
Vinokur, A., 110
Viorst, J., 584, 594, 601
Vlok, L.A., 280
Voydanoff, P., 529
Vuchinich, S., 474, 475

W

Wachtel, D., 265
Wachtel, P., 72
Waechter, E.H., 587
Wagner, C., 432
Wald, M.L., 606
Waldhard-Letzel, E., 590
Wallerstein, J., 213, 479, 480, 481
Walster, E., 376, 382
Walster, G., 376
Walters, J., 462, 464, 465
Wamboldt, F., 198
Wanck, B., 478
Wanderer, Z., 394
Wang, H.S., 422
Waring, E.M., 270
Warren, C., 575
Warshak, R., 480, 482
Washton, A., 226
Watson, R., 486
Weeks, G., 412
Weikart, D., 290
Weinberg, M.S., 416, 417
Weiner, H., 85, 142
Weinstein, R., 288, 290
Weisman, A., 587
Weiss, J., 307
Weiss, R.S., 597
Weissberg, R.P., 112
Weissman, M., 181, 227
Weitz, A., 528
Welbrone, J., 196

Welch, N., 508
Wells, J., 501, 503
Wells, R., 188
Wenar, C., 303
Wentworth-Rohr, I., 263
Werman, D.S., 171
Werner, C., 338
Werner, E.E., 74
Wetzel, R.D., 264
White, E., 587
White, G., 382
White, J., 486
White, K., 384
White, R.W., 297, 545, 546, 548
Whitlock, E.E., 149, 252
Whitlock, G.E., 519, 592, 594, 603
Whitney, C., 183
Whybrow, P.C., 118
Wickett, A., 584, 607
Wilkinson, A., 485
Williams, C.J., 416
Williams, D., 358
Williams, J., 366
Williams, T., 68
Williamson, M., 406
Williamson, P., 406
Willis, J., 432
Wilson, E.O., 301
Winberg, J., 292, 293
Winickoff, S., 290
Winokur, G., 122
Winokur, M., 265
Winston, A., 268
Witkin-Lanoil, G.H., 72
Witter, F., 292
Wolberg, L.K., 234, 248, 254
Wolfe, B., 280
Wolff, T., 154
Wolpe, J., 260, 261
Wood, S.J., 472
Wood, V., 552
Woods, R.T., 126
Worne, R.L., 561
Wrenn, C., 555
Wunsch-Hitzig, R., 190

Y

Yahraes, H., 214
Yalom, I.D., 273, 274
Yankelovich, D., 533
Yerkes, R.M., 86
Youcha, G., 478

Zaleski, C., 609
Zanarini, M., 216
Zegman, M.A., 139
Zeiss, A.M., 122
Zelnik, M., 432
Zembrodt, I., 393
Zenhausen, R., 34
Zetterbergh, H., 533
Zimbardo, P., 367, 368
Zimet, C.N., 251, 277
Ziv, A., 169
Zuckerman, M., 509

Subject Index

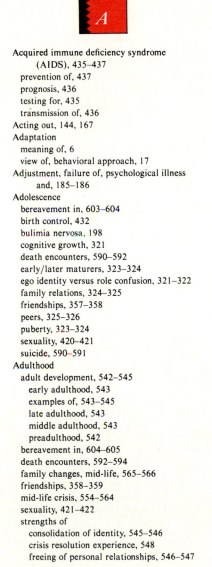

early parenthood stage, 451–452
empty nest stage, 452–453
postretirement stage, 453
tasks of family, 454–455
Family relations, adolescence, 324–325
Family therapy, process in, 268–270
Fantasy formation, use of, 164–165
Female genitals, 407–408
Fight or flight, 84, 101
Fixation, definition, 23
Fluid intelligence, 577
Forbearance, use of, 171–172
Foreclosure, 518
Formal operations, 321
Free association, psychoanalysis, 20, 255–256
Freeing of personal relationships, adulthood, 546–547
Friendships
adolescence, 357–358
adulthood, 358–359
associative friendships, 337
barriers to
communication problems, 362–363
individual differences, 363
problems in individuals, 361–362
psychological games, 363–365
value differences, 363
childhood, 353–355
stages of, 354–355
cognitive approach, 353–356
definition, 337
developing friendships, signs of, 344
factors in formation of
attraction, 341
impression formation, 341–343
proximity, 340
infancy, 349, 352
matching hypothesis, 341
psychoanalytic approach, 356–357
receptive friendships, 337
reciprocal friendships, 337
rules for winning friends, 337
support system, 338–339
Frigidity, female, 426
Fully functioning person, Rogers' theory, 59

Gambling, pathological, 218
Games
ending, techniques for, 365
psychological games, 363–365
Gender differences
friendships, 358
mate selection, 385
play, 306
self-concept, 509

General adaptation syndrome, 101
Generalization, anxiety, 90–92
Generativity, 54
adulthood, 548–549
mid-life crisis, 560–561
Genital herpes, 434–435
Genital stage, 23, 401
Gestalt therapy, process in, 258–259
Gonorrhea, 434
Grief, 597–598
acute grief, 598–599
anticipatory grief, 599
Group therapy, 272–277
benefits of, 273–274
choosing type of, 275
developmental task groups, 276–277
encounter groups, 276

Health problems
adolescence, 591–592
childhood, 588–589
elderly, 568–570
Heroin dependence, 220, 223
Hierarchy of needs, levels of, 55
High-risk environments, 71–73
children of wealthy, 72–73
latchkey kids, 72
parental inadequacies, 72
social deprivation, 71
Homelessness, 70–71
Homeostasis, 132–135
physiological basis, 132
psychological basis, 133–134
Homosexuality, 416–418
categories of life-styles, 417
stereotypes, 417
views of, 416
Hospice care, 606–607
Housekeeper role, in family, 458–459
Humanistic approach, 28–31
anxiety, 96
hierarchy of needs, 55
love, 373
meta-needs, 57, 58
psychological health, view of, 54–59
Rogers' theory, 30–31
self-actualization, 29
characteristics of, 55–57
Humanizing of values, adulthood, 548
Humor, use of, 168–169
Hypoactive inhibited sexual desire disorder, characteristics of, 425
Hypochondriasis, characteristics of, 206
Hysteria, 188

Id, 20
Identification, use of, 165
Identity, work and, 499–500
Identity crisis, 24
Illness, as coping mechanism, 143
Imaging, as coping mechanism, 155
Immunization, to stress, 175–176
Impression formation, friendships, 341–343
Impulse control disorder, pathological gambling, 218
Incongruence, 30
Individuation, infancy, 303
Industry versus inferiority, 320–321
Infancy
attachment, 300–301
differentiation, 303
early needs
oral, 302
tactile, 303
early practicing stage, 303–304
friendships, 349, 352
individuation, 303
prenatal environment, effects of, 290–292
recognition of mother, 352
reflexes of newborn, 294, 296
social skills, 352
temperamental differences, 296–297
categories of temperament, 298–299
difficult child, 297, 300
easy child, 297, 300
slow-to-warm-up child, 300
trust, 302–303
Inhibited female orgasm, characteristics of, 426–427
Inhibited male orgasm, characteristics of, 427
Initiative versus guilt, 306
Instrumental conditioning. *See* Operant conditioning
Intellectual functioning, elderly, 577
Intellectualization, use of, 156–157
Intelligence
crystallized intelligence, 577
fluid intelligence, 577
Intelligence testing
psychological assessment, 242–244
triarchic theory, 244
Wechsler Adult Intelligence Scale-Revised (WAIS-R), 244
Interaction (personal)
Johari's window, 348–349
self-disclosure, 347–348
sociometry, 350
transactional analysis, 345–347

Interests tests, 244
Interview, psychological assessment, 240–241
Intimacy, 382, 383–384
Intrauterine device (IUD), 431
Invulnerable children, 73–75, 331–333

Jealousy
    dealing with, 392
    romantic, 390–392
Job dissatisfaction, 531–532
    strategies for coping, 531–532
Johari's window, 348–349

Kinship role, in family, 456
Kuder Occupational Scale, 504

Latchkey kids, 72
Latency, 23, 401
Learned helplessness, depression, 121
Learning disabilities
    dyscalculia, 195
    dyslexia, 194–195
Life events
    Life Events Checklist, 328–330
    stress, 110–112
Life Experience Survey (LES), 111, 113–115
Life Satisfaction Course, 122
Life span approach, 38–43
    challenges of, 39, 42
    depression, 123–126
    life-cycle calendar, 40–41
    sexuality, 418–423
    stages of life span, 39
Living wills, 609
Loneliness
    causes
        shyness, 366–368
        social factors, 368–369
    coping with, 370–371
    definition, 369
    Loneliness Scale, 369
    situational versus chronic, 366
    as stressor, 106–107
    as widespread problem, 369–370
Love
    capacity to love, 376
    components of, 382
    dating, 375–381

feeling of, 382–383
forms of, 374
humanistic approach, 373
intimacy, 383–384
and liking, 380–381
mate selection, 384–386
need for love, 372–374
problems in
    addiction to lover, 395
    changes in love, 392–393
    end of relationship, 393–395
    jealousy, 390–392
psychoanalytic approach, 372–373
social learning approach, 374
Lovers, styles of
    lifelong-friends type, 390
    logical-sensible type, 388, 390
    possessive-intensely dependent type, 388
    romantic type, 387
    self-centered game-player type, 387
    totally lover-centered type, 388

Male erectile disorder, characteristics of, 425–426
Male genitals, 406–407
Manic-depressive disorder. *See* Bipolar disorder
Marijuana abuse, 223–224
Marital therapy
    collaborative therapy, 271
    concurrent therapy, 271
    conjoint therapy, 271
    process in, 271–272
Marriage
    aspects for evaluation of, 462
    definition of successful marriage, 462–463
    mid-life crisis and, 563–564
    myths about, 466–467, 468–469
    parenting, 471–472
    predictors for success
        postmarital, 464–465
        premarital, 463–464
    types of marriages
        conflict-habituated marriage, 467
        devitalized marriage, 470
        passive-congenial marriage, 470
        total marriage, 471
        vital marriage, 471
Masked depression, 125
Masturbation, 412
Matching hypothesis, friendships, 341
Mate selection, 384–386
    characteristics sought by mate, 385
    gender differences, 385
    homogamy, 384
Maturational crisis, 288

Media overload, as stressor, 106
Memory
    elderly, 576–577
    primary/secondary/tertiary, 576–577
Menopause, 552
Mentor relationship, 526
Mid-career crisis, 534–535
    solutions to, 535
Mid-life crisis, 554–564
    age of occurrence, 556
    career reexamination, 558
    creativity and, 556
    cultural aspects, 556
    definition, 554
    generativity, 560–561
    marriage reevaluation, 563–564
    midlife macho, 555
    time perception, 557–558
Minnesota Multiphasic Personality Inventory (MMPI), 241
Modeling, 15
    disinhibitory effect, 15
    observational learning effect, 15
    response facilitation effect, 15
Monsters/night terrors/punishment anxieties, 97
Mood disorders
    bipolar disorder, 214–215
    cyclothymia, 214–216
    depression, major, 213–214
    dysthymic disorder, 212–213
Moral anxiety, 89–90, 97–98
Moral development, childhood, 320
Moratorium, Erikson's theory, 516–517
Mourning, 600
Multimodal therapy, process in, 266
Multiple personality disorder, characteristics of, 207, 209

Narcissistic personality disorder, characteristics of, 217–218
Near-death experience, 609–610
Neo-Freudians, 24–25
Neurotic anxiety, 89
New York Longitudinal Study, 296–297
Nocturnal orgasms, 411–412
Nuclear family, 454, 473
Nuclear power plants, as stressor, 107–109

Object loss, depression, 119
Observational learning effect, modeling, 15
Obsessive-compulsive disorders, characteristics of, 202–203

eclectic therapy, 266
elderly, 570–572
evaluation of, 280–282
existential/humanist therapies, 258
family therapy, 268–270
gestalt therapy, 258–259
group therapy, 272–277
marital therapy, 271–272
multimodal therapy, 266
psychoanalysis, 255–256
psychological assessment, 239–245
purposes of, 236–239
rational emotive therapy, 265
situational supports, 232–236
therapeutic relationship, 246–251
therapist, choice of, 278–279
Psychotropic drugs, 277
Puberty, 323–324, 421
Punishment, 14

R

Rape
aftereffects, 440
date rape, 440
personal account, 438–439
rapist, profile of, 437
Rational emotive therapy, 35–36
process in, 265
Rationalization, use of, 166–167
Reaction formation, use of, 162–163
Reality anxiety, 89
Reality principle, 20
Receptive friendships, 337
Reciprocal determinism, 16–17
Reciprocal friendships, 337
Reconceptualizing the problem, as coping
mechanism, 152–153
Recreational role, in family, 457
Reflexes, newborn, 294, 296
Regression, use of, 163–164
Relaxation techniques
as coping mechanism, 150–151
progressive relaxation, 151
Reliability, psychological assessment, 240
Repression, 22
use of, 161–162
Reproductive system, 404–408
development of sex organs, 404–405
female genitals, 407–408
male genitals, 406–407

Resilient children, 331–333
Resistance, psychoanalysis, 256
Resolution, therapeutic relationship, 250
Resolution phase, sexual response, 411
Respondent conditioning. *See* Classical
conditioning
Response availability, anxiety and, 92–93
Response facilitation effect, modeling, 15
Retirement, 535, 561–563
adaptation to, 566–568
postretirement adjustment, 565–566
preretirement period, 562–563
Rhythm, as coping mechanism, 138
Right to die, 607
Rogers' theory, 30–31
fully functioning person, 59
incongruence, 30
positive regard, 30
self-concept, 31, 58
therapeutic relationship, 247–248
unconditional positive regard, 58–59
Role-playing, as coping mechanism, 155
Rooting reflex, 294
Rorschach ink blot test, 242

S

Schedule of Recent Events (SRE), 110
Schizophrenia, 209–212
characteristics of, 209–212
course/phases of, 211
types of, 211
School, 310–315
coping, indicators of, 312–315
social skills and, 315
Screaming, as coping mechanism, 142
Seasonal affective disorder (SAD), 215
Self-actualization, 29
Self-concept, 31
career choice and, 507–509
gender differences, 509
Rogers' theory, 58
Self-confidence, 62–63
Self-directed change, process of, 262
Self-disclosure, 347–348
Self-righting mechanisms, 132
Self-theory. *See* Rogers' theory
Self-transcendence, adulthood, 549
Separation anxiety, 94–97

Sex roles, 317–319
androgyny, 319
changing attitudes, 459–460
in family, 459–460
learning about, 317–318
stereotypes, 318–319
Sexual attitudes, development of, 441–442
Sexual dysfunctions
causes of, 424
dyspareunia, 427
hypoactive inhibited sexual desire disorder,
425
inhibited female orgasm, 426–427
inhibited male orgasm, 427
male erectile disorder, 425–426
premature ejaculation, 427
treatment approaches, 428–430
vaginismus, 428
Sexual feelings
childhood, 306–307
puberty, 323
Sexual intercourse, 414–416
Sexuality
elderly, 574–576
life span approach, 418–423
adolescents, 420–421
adulthood, 421–422
children, 419–420
elderly, 422
pioneer researchers, 401–404
reproductive system, 404–408
sexual dreams, 413
sexual expression
homosexuality, 416–418
masturbation, 412
nocturnal orgasms, 411–412
petting, 414
sexual intercourse, 414–416
sexual response, phases in, 408–411, 424
Sexually transmitted diseases
acquired immune deficiency syndrome
(AIDS), 435–437
chlamydia, 435
genital herpes, 434–435
gonorrhea, 434
incidence of, 434
syphilis, 434
Sexual role, in family, 456
Shaping, 14
Shopping, as coping mechanism, 147–148
Shyness
causes of, 368
definition, 367
and loneliness, 367